Brief Contents

Joining the Conversation

A Guide for Writers

THIRD EDITION

Mike Palmquist

Colorado State University

bedford/st.martin's
Macmillan Learning

Boston | New York

For Bedford/St. Martin's

Vice President, Editorial, Macmillan Learning Humanities: Edwin Hill
Editorial Director, English: Karen S. Henry
Senior Publisher for Composition, Business and Technical Writing, Developmental Writing: Leasa Burton
Executive Editor: Molly Parke
Senior Developmental Editor: Rachel Goldberg
Assistant Editor: Jennifer Prince
Senior Production Editor: Gregory Erb
Media Producer: Melissa Skepko-Masi
Senior Production Supervisor: Jennifer Wetzel
Executive Marketing Manager: Joy Fisher Williams
Copy Editor: Kathy Smith
Indexer: Jake Kawatski
Photo Editor: Martha Friedman
Photo Researcher: Sheri Blaney
Permissions Editor: Kalina Ingham
Senior Art Director: Anna Palchik
Text Design: Lisa Garbutt, Claire Seng-Niemoeller
Cover Design: John Callahan
Composition: Jouve
Printing and Binding: RR Donnelley

Printed in China

1   0   9   8

f   e   d   c

For information, write: Bedford/St. Martin's, 75 Arlington Street, Boston, MA 02116 (617-399-4000)

ISBN   978-1-319-04723-8

Acknowledgments

Text acknowledgments and copyrights appear at the back of the book on pages 715–716, which constitute an extension of the copyright page. Art acknowledgments and copyrights appear on the same page as the art selections they cover.

Preface for Instructors

When I joined the field of rhetoric and composition, I was surprised by its depth and complexity. As an undergraduate, I'd studied Plato's dialogues and had gained some insights into the rich history of rhetoric and how it could help me become a better writer. Still, it had not occurred to me — nor, it seems, to my professors — that writing was an area worthy of the same theoretical attention that they routinely gave to literary studies. As a graduate student at Carnegie Mellon, I encountered a group of faculty who thought quite differently. Listening to their conversations about an emerging body of theory and practice, I found myself drawn to the ideas of Richard Young, Dave Kaufer, and Chris Neuwirth, and under their guidance, designed a dissertation study that has continued to shape my thinking about the theory and teaching of writing. In the classes I studied, I was able to see the impact of engaging in written conversation about a shared topic. Students who reflected on and wrote about their own writing developed richer understandings of what it means to be a writer. As a faculty member at Colorado State University, I applied the insights I'd gained to my work as a writing instructor. Through my work as writing program administrator, they became a central part of *Joining the Conversation*.

Among the many changes in this new edition, an emphasis on understanding oneself as a writer is the most prominent. The framing discussions in Part One introduce students to the rich history and practices of writing studies. The student examples throughout Parts One, Three, and Four support the focus on writing as a discipline and can be used to emphasize metacognition and reflection on one's own writing processes. And, with these changes, you'll find deeper discussions of writing processes, genre, and design.

Joining the Conversation continues to strongly emphasize rhetorical situation and argument. And it continues to rely heavily on Kenneth Burke's notion of the parlor (although admittedly one that is both less confrontational and more collaborative than Burke's early vision) to help students build on their experiences with spoken conversation and grow as writers. It also maintains its commitment to recognizing how the composing process is necessarily shaped by technology, examining how computers, tablets, and smartphones allow us to access information, ideas, and arguments and how they inform our interactions with readers and peers.

v

New to the Third Edition

This edition of *Joining the Conversation* includes the following new features.

NEW CHAPTER 1, "UNDERSTANDING YOURSELF AS A WRITER"

A new introductory chapter establishes a stronger foundation for successful writing. Based on feedback from dozens of reviewers, this chapter emphasizes reflection and transfer as key skills that are developed further in Chapter 6, "Writing to Reflect." A scenario of student writers illustrates the centrality of inquiry and reflection skills, while model readings from composition studies give students further practice in summary, paraphrase, and note taking.

NEW READINGS TO CHALLENGE AND ENGAGE STUDENTS

With four selections in each assignment chapter, this edition offers more sophisticated academic readings to help students grow as readers. Professional documents such as infographics and progress reports offer a variety of genres, purposes, and tones.

Eighteen engaging new readings include

- a literacy narrative showing one writer's path from high school washout to award-winning novelist (Writing to Reflect)

- a profile on African American ballerina Misty Copeland (Writing to Inform)

- an interview with public policy experts evaluating the food stamps program (Writing to Evaluate)

The "Starting a Conversation" readings apparatus have been updated to reflect the new level of challenge in the readings.

"GENRE TALK," A FEATURE THAT LINKS THE BOOK AND LAUNCHPAD

Each assignment chapter includes "Genre Talk," focusing on the distinctive design features of particular genres and the range of writing conventions used to reflect, inform, evaluate, analyze, solve problems, and convince or persuade. Carefully annotated documents on issues students care about, such as child slavery in the cocoa

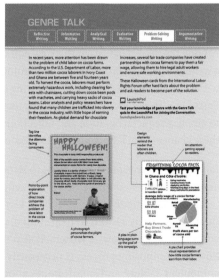

▲ **See page 365.**

industry or the costs of "fast fashion," highlight how purpose, audience, and context shape a document's design. Auto-graded activities in LaunchPad provide further practice in analyzing genre and design.

NEW TREATMENT OF FIELD RESEARCH

The new Chapter 14 is dedicated to in-depth coverage of field research methods. It offers practical advice on how to conduct observations, interviews, surveys, and correspondence; how to analyze the results; and how to assess the value of field research. Reflecting changes in the technological contexts that shape our use of sources, this edition offers an updated discussion of how to work with digital and print sources most effectively.

THREE NEW THOUGHT-PROVOKING STUDENT ESSAYS

Half the featured student writers in the third edition are new, and they focus on compelling topics, such as puppy mills, police officers' use of deadly force, and trigger warnings on college campuses. These student writers put a face on purpose-based writing, while "In Process" boxes trace their progress with glimpses of their notes, outlines, and other process documents.

EXPANDED PROJECT IDEAS FOR INNOVATIVE ASSIGNMENTS

The suggested project ideas at the end of each chapter have been updated and improved. With ideas for both essays and public genres, each set includes extended treatments of rhetorical situations, sources, and writing and design conventions. Among others, new project ideas include rhetorical analyses, literature reviews, and treatments of problems and solutions.

Key Features of *Joining the Conversation*

THE CONVERSATION METAPHOR THAT MAKES SENSE TO STUDENTS

Lucid and easy to understand, the conversation metaphor that underpins the book inspires students to become the best writers they can be. It guides students in considering purpose, readers, sources, context, and genre in everything they read and write. Understanding writer's roles, such as interpreter or problem solver, helps students keep the rhetorical situation at the forefront of their writing activities.

A VARIETY OF READINGS ACROSS GENRES AND MEDIA

Chapters 6 through 11 include a diverse selection of professional readings by authors such as Margo Jefferson, David Sedaris, Rivka Galchen, Brooke Gladstone, Anu Partanen, and Chris Colin. Readings not only serve as examples of admirable writing but also demonstrate successful design choices, whether traditional print essays or magazine articles, blog posts, or infographics. The layout of the readings has been carefully designed to give students a realistic sense of the original source. Each selection is accompanied by questions for critical reading that ask students to consider both the piece's writing situation and its genre.

OFFERING AMPLE STUDENT SUPPORT

The true measure of a textbook should be how well it works for student writers. *Joining the Conversation* supports students as they work through their own writing processes. **"Your Turn" boxes** offer specific, accessible strategies for finding a conversation to join, gathering information from sources, and preparing a draft, while **"Working Together" boxes** provide opportunities for collaboration. Throughout Chapters 6 through 11, **"In Process" boxes** highlight the featured student writers' processes, showing their brainstorming notes, outlines, survey questions, and peer-review materials.

AVAILABLE IN TWO VERSIONS—ONE WITH A BRIEF HANDBOOK

The guide and handbook version offers three chapters of lively examples and friendly advice on matters of style, grammar, punctuation, and mechanics. Written by professional editor and writer Barbara Wallraff, formerly a columnist at *The Atlantic* magazine, the brief handbook acts as both a quick reference tool and a foundation for in-depth revision and editing.

Acknowledgments

This project represents another long stretch of weekends and evenings that might otherwise have been spent with my family. For their patience and support, I offer my deepest thanks to my wife, Jessica, and our children, Ellen and Reid.

I offer my thanks as well to the colleagues who have inspired me as I worked on this book. David Kaufer and Chris Neuwirth helped me understand the power of the conversation metaphor and provided valuable advice as I entered the discipline. Richard Young not only inspired me but also provided me with the tools to think carefully and productively about the role of textbooks within the discipline. I owe much to the colleagues with whom I regularly discuss the teaching of writing: Will Hochman, Nick Carbone, Lynda Haas, Sue Doe, Lisa Langstraat, Tim Amidon, Janice Walker, Michael Pemberton, Michael Day, and Chuck Bazerman.

A project like this necessarily involves the contributions of a wide range of colleagues who worked on key resources for the book. I am grateful to Barbara Wallraff, for her work on the handbook included with some editions of this book; to Heather Landers, for her contributions to the materials on oral and multimedia presentations; to Sue Doe, for her work on the original instructor's guide for the book; to Madelyn Tucker Pawlowski, for updating and expanding the instructor's manual for this third edition; and to Beth Rice, for researching potential reading selections.

I am also indebted to the following reviewers who offered careful critiques of drafts of this book: Hillary AcMoody, California State University, East Bay; Kris Bigalk, Normandale Community College; Christopher Blood, California State University, East Bay; Jeremy Brandstad, North Shore Community College; Ron Brooks, Oklahoma State University; Mary Paniccia Carden, Edinboro University of Pennsylvania; Michael Catrillo, Northampton Community College; Teresa Cusumano, Northampton Community College; Eric House, University of Arizona; Brad Jacobson, University of Arizona; Shawn Jasinski, State University of New York at Albany; Elenore Long, Arizona State University; Catherine Olson, Lone Star College–Tomball; Cynthia Ostrom, University of Nebraska–Kearney; Emily Palese, University of Arizona; Madelyn Tucker Pawlowski, University of Arizona; Kathleen Pfeiffer, Oakland University; Penelope Piercy, Lone Star College–Tomball; Van Piercy, Lone Star College–Tomball; John Pietruszka, University of Massachusetts, Dartmouth; Penny Piva, Bristol Community College; Heather Rosewell, Northern Kentucky University; Rebecca Samberg, Housatonic Community College; Kirsten Schwartz, California State University, East Bay; Janice Walker, Georgia Southern University; Jennifer Williams, Chandler Gilbert Community College. Their feedback and thoughtful suggestions helped me understand how I could improve upon the second edition of *Joining the Conversation*, and I thank them for the time and care they took in their reviews.

Once again, I have been extraordinarily fortunate to find, in my colleagues at Bedford/St. Martin's, a group of editors and assistants who care deeply about producing the best possible textbooks. For her support, encouragement, and generous approach to editing, I thank my developmental editor, Rachel Goldberg. Her good ideas, clear feedback, and good humor sustained me as I worked on this edition. I am also grateful to assistant editor Jennifer Prince for her many contributions to this project, from finding additional readings and developing quiz questions to tracking down sources to responding quickly and well to the unexpected tasks that came up so often. I am indebted, as well, to Anna Palchik and Claire Seng-Niemoeller for the outstanding design of this book; to my production editor, Greg Erb, for his attention to detail in directing its complex production; and to Kathy Smith for her careful copyediting. I also offer my thanks to editor in chief Karen Henry for her leadership throughout the editions of this book, and to Molly Parke, Emily Rowin, and Jimmy Fleming for their work in helping instructors understand how *Joining the Conversation* might make a contribution in their classrooms. I offer particular thanks to Leasa Burton for her contributions to this project. From her ideas about the overall direction of the book to her feedback on the revision plan, Leasa's investment of time and effort into this book has been a continuing source of inspiration to me.

Many years ago, Rory Baruth introduced me to the editors at Bedford/St. Martin's. I am grateful not only for the introduction but also for the good advice he has offered since. Through Rory, I've been able to work with an outstanding group of colleagues at Bedford/St. Martin's. In many ways, they've been my best writing teachers and I've gained immeasurably from working with them.

Finally, I offer my thanks to the six student writers whose work is featured in this book and on the companion website: Caitlin Guariglia, James Hardjadinata, Dwight Haynes, Elisabeth Layne, Mackenzie Owens, and Ellen Page. I deeply appreciate their willingness to share their work and their insights about their writing processes with other student writers. I hope that their superb examples inspire the students who use this book to join and contribute to their own written conversations.

Mike Palmquist
Colorado State University

With Bedford/St. Martin's, You Get More

At Bedford/St. Martin's, providing support to teachers and their students who use our books and digital tools is our top priority. The Bedford/St. Martin's English Community is now our home for professional resources, including Bedford *Bits*, our popular blog with new ideas for the composition classroom. Join us to connect with our authors and your colleagues at **community.macmillan.com**, where you can download titles from our professional resource series, review projects in the pipeline, sign up for webinars, or start a discussion. In addition to this dynamic online community and book-specific instructor resources, we offer digital tools, custom solutions, and value packages to support both you and your students. We are committed to delivering the quality and value that you've come to expect from Bedford/St. Martin's, supported as always by the power of Macmillan Learning. To learn more about or to order any of the following products, contact your Bedford/St. Martin's sales representative or visit the website at **macmillanlearning.com**.

LaunchPad for *Joining the Conversation*: Where Students Learn

LaunchPad provides engaging content and new ways to get the most out of your book. Get an interactive e-Book combined with assessment tools in a fully custom-izable course space; then assign and mix our resources with yours.

- "Genre Talk" extends the book feature with additional real-world documents across genres. Annotations and a brief auto-graded quiz help students analyze how the rhetorical situation influences design choices.

- Reading comprehension quizzes for all selections in Part Two provide **easy assessment.**

- Diagnostics and Exercise Central provide opportunities to assess areas for improvement and assign additional exercises based on students' needs. Eight diagnostic quizzes — pre- and post-tests on sentence grammar, punctuation and mechanics, reading skills, and reading strategies — offer visual reports that show performance by topic, class, and student as well as comparison reports that track improvement over time. Use these reports to target additional practice by assigning quizzes from the Exercise Central question bank.

- Pre-built units — including readings, videos, quizzes, discussion groups, and more — are **easy to adapt and assign** by adding your own materials and mixing them with our high-quality multimedia content and ready-made assessment options, such as **LearningCurve** adaptive quizzing.

- LaunchPad also offers access to a **Gradebook** that provides a clear window on the performance of your whole class, individual students, and even results of individual assignments.

- Use LaunchPad on its own or **integrate it** with your school's learning management system so that your class is always on the same page.

LaunchPad for *Joining the Conversation* can be purchased on its own or packaged with the print book at a significant discount. An activation code is required. To order LaunchPad for *Joining the Conversation* with the print book, use these ISBNs:

- 978-1-319-11888-4 (*Joining the Conversation: A Guide and Handbook for Writers*)

- 978-1-319-11887-7 (*Joining the Conversation: A Guide for Writers*)

For more information, go to **launchpadworks.com**.

CHOOSE FROM ALTERNATIVE FORMATS OF *JOINING THE CONVERSATION*

Bedford/St. Martin's offers a range of affordable formats, allowing students to choose the one that works best for them.

- Paperback version with handbook To order *Joining the Conversation* with the handbook, use ISBN 978-1-319-05554-7.

- Paperback brief version To order the brief version of *Joining the Conversation*, use ISBN 978-1-319-04723-8.

- Popular e-Book formats For details of our e-Book partners, visit **macmillanlearning.com/ebooks**.

SELECT VALUE PACKAGES

Add value to your text by packaging one of the following resources with *Joining the Conversation*. To learn more about package options for any of the following products, contact your Bedford/St. Martin's sales representative or visit **macmillanlearning.com**.

LaunchPad Solo for Readers and Writers allows students to work on whatever they need help with the most. At home or in class, students learn at their own pace, with instruction tailored to their unique needs. *LaunchPad Solo for Readers and Writers* features:

- **Pre-built units that support a learning arc.** Each easy-to-assign unit is composed of a pre-test check, multimedia instruction and assessment, and a post-test that assesses what students have learned about critical reading, the writing process, using sources, grammar, style, and mechanics. Dedicated units also offer help for multilingual writers.

- **Diagnostics that help establish a baseline for instruction.** Assign diagnostics to identify areas of strength and areas for improvement on topics related to grammar and reading and to help students plan a course of study. Use visual reports to track performance by topic, class, and student as well as comparison reports to track improvement over time.

- **A video introduction to many topics.** Introductions offer an overview of the unit's topic, and many include a brief, accessible video to illustrate the concepts at hand.

- **Twenty-five reading selections with comprehension quizzes.** Assign a range of classic and contemporary essays, each of which includes a label indicating Lexile level to help you scaffold instruction in critical reading.

- **Adaptive quizzing for targeted learning.** Most units include LearningCurve, game-like adaptive quizzing that focuses on the areas in which each student needs the most help.

- **The ability to monitor student progress.** Use our Gradebook to see which students are on track and which need additional help with specific topics.

LaunchPad Solo for Readers and Writers can be packaged with *Joining the Conversation* at a significant discount. For more information, contact your sales representative or visit **macmillanlearning.com/readwrite**.

Writer's Help 2.0 is a powerful online writing resource that helps students find answers whether they are searching for writing advice on their own or as part of an assignment.

- **Smart search.** Built on research with more than 1,600 student writers, the smart search in Writer's Help provides reliable results even when students use novice terms, such as *flow* and *unstuck*.

- **Trusted content from our best-selling handbooks.** Choose *Writer's Help 2.0, Hacker Version*, or *Writer's Help 2.0, Lunsford Version*, to ensure that students have clear advice and examples for all their writing questions.

- **Diagnostics that help establish a baseline for instruction.** Assign diagnostics to identify areas of strength and areas for improvement on topics related to grammar and reading and to help students plan a course of study. Use visual reports to track performance by topic, class, and student as well as comparison reports to track improvement over time.

- **Adaptive exercises that engage students.** *Writer's Help 2.0* includes LearningCurve, game-like online quizzing that adapts to what students already know and helps them focus on what they need to learn.

Writer's Help 2.0 can be packaged with *Joining the Conversation* at a significant discount. For more information, contact your sales representative or visit **macmillanlearning.com/writershelp2**.

MACMILLAN LEARNING CURRICULUM SOLUTIONS

Curriculum Solutions brings together the quality of Bedford/St. Martin's content with Hayden-McNeil's expertise in publishing original custom print and digital products. Developed especially for writing courses, our ForeWords for English program contains a library of the most popular, requested content in easy-to-use modules to help you build the best possible text. Whether you are considering creating a custom version of *Joining the Conversation* or incorporating our content with your own, we can adapt and combine the resources that work best for your course or program. Some enrollment minimums apply. Contact your sales representative for more information.

INSTRUCTOR RESOURCES

You have a lot to do in your course. Bedford/St. Martin's wants to make it easy for you to find the support you need — and to get it quickly.

Teaching with Joining the Conversation is available as a PDF that can be downloaded from **macmillanlearning.com**. Visit the instructor resources tab for *Joining the Conversation*. In addition to chapter overviews and teaching tips, the instructor's manual includes sample syllabi, correlations to the Council of Writing Program Administrators' Outcomes Statement, and classroom activities.

Joining the Conversation Works with the Council of Writing Program Administrators' (WPA) Outcomes

In 2014 the Council of Writing Program Administrators updated its desired outcomes for first-year composition courses. As an inquiry-based rhetoric focusing on purpose and genre, *Joining the Conversation* helps instructors and students accomplish these teaching and learning goals. The following table provides detailed information on how *Joining the Conversation* supports each outcome.

WPA Outcomes	Relevant Features of *Joining the Conversation*
Rhetorical Knowledge	
Learn & use key rhetorical concepts through analyzing & composing a variety of texts.	Using the metaphor of a conversation, **Chapter 1** establishes the **rhetorical concepts of purpose, audience, context, and genre**. These rhetorical concepts become the bedrock of the rest of the book, as the **assignment chapters (Chapters 6–11)** offer texts for analysis and detailed instruction on how to compose texts across genres.
Gain experience reading and composing in several genres to understand how genre conventions shape and are shaped by readers' and writers' practices and purposes.	**Chapter 1** defines **genre** and offers multiple visual examples of print and digital genres. **Chapters 6–11** each feature four readings that span multiple genres. The **"Writer's Role"** box in these chapters identifies the **purpose, readers, sources, and context for each rhetorical situation** (e.g., p. 116). Each assignment chapter also includes a **"Genre Talk"** feature (e.g., p. 145), highlighting specific genre and design conventions. An auto-graded assessment in **LaunchPad** provides further practice for students.
Develop facility in responding to a variety of situations and contexts calling for purposeful shifts in voice, tone, level of formality, design, medium, and/or structure.	The **"Starting a Conversation" questions** that follow each reading in **Chapters 6–11** call attention to the authors' style, voice, language, organization, and design choices. Then, the **"Prepare a Draft"** section in each of these chapters gives drafting and design advice specific to the chapter's writing purpose, culminating in real essays by **featured student writers**. **Chapter 18** guides students in **drafting and designing** their own documents, with attention to appropriate conventions for academic writing. **Chapter 22** and the **handbook** (Part Six in some versions of this book) provide practical advice for **writing with style and using appropriate voice, tone, language, and formality.**
Understand and use a variety of technologies to address a range of audiences.	**Chapter 5** explains the technological tools that can aid in effective **peer review.** **Chapter 20** discusses **presenting your work**, with detailed instruction on the technologies that can help students create effective **oral, multimedia, and group presentations and portfolios.**
Match the capacities of different environments (e.g., print & electronic) to varying rhetorical situations.	With selections as varied as blog posts, infographics, photo essays, and editorials, the **readings in Chapters 6–11** and their **"Starting a Conversation"** questions show how different genres and media are suited to different rhetorical situations. **Chapter 19** addresses **choosing the right genre** and covers composing **articles, multimodal essays, and Web pages** to suit various purposes and audiences.
Use composing & reading for inquiry, learning, thinking, & communicating in various rhetorical contexts.	Beginning in **Chapter 1**, the metaphor of the **conversation** emphasizes writing as a tool for inquiry and the exchange of ideas. **Chapter 2** gives extensive coverage of **inquiry**, showing how students can "listen in" on interesting conversations around them as they search for a writing topic. **Chapter 3** provides advice and strategies for **critical reading, summarizing, and responding** to sources.

WPA Outcomes	Relevant Features of *Joining the Conversation*
Critical Thinking, Reading, & Composing	
Read a diverse range of texts, attending especially to relationships between assertion and evidence, to patterns of organization, to interplay between verbal and nonverbal elements, and to how these features function for different audiences and situations.	With **24 readings,** *Joining the Conversation* offers a wide range of print, digital, text, and multimodal selections across many genres. The **"Starting a Conversation"** questions that accompany each reading ask students to consider the visual elements, design, organization, and tone of the piece and how the authors' choices suit the **writing situation and audience**. **Chapter 11** models how writers **make claims and support them with evidence**. **Chapter 16** then guides students in **developing and supporting their own thesis statements**, while **Chapter 17** discusses **organizing patterns**.
Locate & evaluate primary & secondary research materials, including journal articles, essays, books, databases, & informal Internet sources.	**Chapter 4** covers **evaluating print and digital sources**, while **Chapter 12** discusses how to **manage source material. Chapter 13** discusses the range of research methods, with detailed instruction on using **electronic library catalogs, scholarly databases, and media search sites**, and demonstrates how **Boolean terms and search limits** can yield targeted results. **Chapter 14** discusses **field research** and collecting information sources via **interviews, observations, and surveys**.
Use strategies — such as interpretation, synthesis, response, critique, and design/redesign — to compose texts that integrate the writer's ideas with those from appropriate sources.	**Chapter 3** shows students how to summarize and respond to sources with **main-point summaries, key-point summaries, outline summaries, agree/disagree responses, reflective responses, and analytic responses**. Once students have learned how to research effectively, **Chapter 21** gives detailed information on **integrating source material into a draft** in purposeful ways. This chapter covers **quoting strategically, attributing sources correctly, and paraphrasing and summarizing**. **Chapters 23 and 24** help students **document sources in MLA and APA styles** correctly.
Processes	
Develop a writing project through multiple drafts.	Writing processes based on multiple drafts are demonstrated throughout **Chapters 6–11**, with examples from the **featured student writers**. Each of these chapters invites students to **reflect on their writing situation as they revise their drafts**. **Chapter 22** emphasizes the importance of **revising and editing** and offers specific advice for working with multiple drafts.
Develop flexible strategies for reading, drafting, reviewing, collaborating, revising, rewriting, rereading, and editing.	**Chapter 3** offers multiple strategies for **reading critically and actively**, while **Chapter 5** gives **guidelines for conducting peer review and writing collaboratively. Chapter 22** provides practical **checklists and strategies for revising and editing**.
Use composing processes and tools as a means to discover and reconsider ideas.	In **Chapter 2**, students learn to brainstorm, freewrite, blindwrite, loop, cluster, and map to **generate ideas** from the sources they encounter. The writing process sections in **Chapters 6–11** include occasions for **asking questions and reconsidering the writing situation and reviewing drafts**.
Experience the collaborative and social aspects of writing processes.	By framing **writing as a conversation**, *Joining the Conversation* underscores the social nature of the writing we do. **Chapter 5** focuses exclusively on **the benefits and processes of collaborative writing**, covering group brainstorming and role-playing. **"Working Together"** boxes in **Chapters 1–11** suggest group activities to help students work through assignments collaboratively.

(continued on next page)

WPA Outcomes	Relevant Features of *Joining the Conversation*
Processes (continued)	
Learn to give and act on productive feedback to works in progress.	**Chapter 5** also focuses on **peer review**, with **guidelines for giving and receiving feedback on written work**. Peer Review boxes in Chapters 6–11 walk students through the process of reviewing each other's drafts.
Adapt composing processes for a variety of technologies and modalities.	"**Tech Tips**" woven into the book offer suggestions for using technology at every stage, from **creating a writer's notebook** to **managing digital sources** to **composing multimodal documents** and **creating multimedia presentations**.
Reflect on the development of composing practices and how those practices influence their work.	The **conversation metaphor** at the heart of the book addresses how composing practices develop and change. Students are continually invited to **reflect on their writing situation** and reconsider **how their purpose, audience, and context influence their document**.
Knowledge of Conventions	
Develop knowledge of linguistic structures, including grammar, punctuation, and spelling, through practice in composing and revising.	**Chapter 22** calls attention to **spelling, grammar, and punctuation** during the revision process. The **handbook (Part Six)** offers clear instruction on **sentence structure, grammar, punctuation, and mechanics**. **LearningCurve** activities in LaunchPad provide extra help and **practice with common grammatical errors**.
Understand why genre conventions for structure, paragraphing, tone, and mechanics vary.	The focus on **genre** throughout the book gives continual attention to how genre conventions differ. These differences are illustrated in the **"Genre Talk"** feature in **Chapters 6–11**, and **readings from a variety of genres** model the differences in structure, tone, and style. **Handbook chapters** discuss why some genres may have differences in mechanics, tone, and sentence structure.
Gain experience negotiating variations in genre conventions.	**Chapters 18 and 19** explain **genre conventions for academic essays, articles, multimodal essays, and Web pages**. "**Project Ideas**" in Chapters 6–11 invite students to compose in different genres.
Learn common formats and/or design features for different kinds of texts.	**Chapters 18 and 19** discuss **genre conventions for academic essays, articles, multimodal essays, and Web pages** and provide visual examples.
Explore the concepts of intellectual property (such as fair use and copyright) that motivate documentation conventions.	**Chapter 15** defines **plagiarism and research ethics**, with detailed strategies for **avoiding plagiarism**.
Practice applying citation conventions systematically in their own work.	**Chapters 23 and 24** provide clear information on correct citation in **MLA and APA styles**. Dozens of source types and **full-page "Tutorials"** model correct citation.

Contents

xvii

READING TO WRITE   54

WORKING WITH SOURCES   80

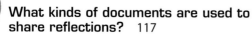
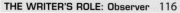

XX
CONTENTS

7 WRITING TO INFORM   172

8 WRITING TO ANALYZE   224

9 WRITING TO EVALUATE   284

10 WRITING TO SOLVE PROBLEMS 342

PART THREE: Conducting Research 453

19 WORKING WITH GENRES   586

20 PRESENTING YOUR WORK   609

PART FIVE: Documenting Sources 669

 23 USING MLA STYLE 671

24 USING APA STYLE 695

Joining the Conversation

A Guide for Writers

PART ONE

Joining a
Conversation

Understanding Yourself as a Writer

What do you think when you hear someone say, "I'm a writer"? Do you think novelist? Poet? Journalist? Blogger?

Or do you simply wonder what they mean?

Our understanding of what is involved in being a writer is complicated by characterizations of writers in the news media, movies, books, and television. It's not unusual, for example, to hear someone say, "But I'm not a real writer."

But of course they are. Almost everyone is. Writing is something most of us do on a daily basis. Whether we're posting to Twitter or Facebook, adding a caption to a photo on Instagram, or responding to a discussion forum in a class, we're writing.

The idea that we're all writers becomes clearer when you think of writing as a form of conversation. When we join this kind of conversation, we read what others have written. We think about the information, ideas, and arguments they've shared. We decide whether we want to respond. And we shape our contributions to the conversation, if we make them, to fit the writing situation in which we find ourselves.

That seems fairly straightforward, but as with most things it's the details that matter. This chapter explores those details by examining how writing is similar to engaging in conversation, considering key aspects of the situations in which writers find themselves, discussing the roles of genre and design in writing, calling attention to the composing processes you can use to engage in written conversations, and taking a look at the strategies you can use to make your writing successful.

Why Think of Writing as Conversation?

Writing is often referred to as a mysterious process. Some people even consider the ability to write well a rare and special gift. Well . . . perhaps. But only if you're talking about the ability to write a prize-winning novel or a poem that will be celebrated for generations. If, on the other hand, you're talking about conveying information, ideas, and arguments clearly and convincingly, the writing process is anything but mysterious.

In fact, once you realize that writing shares a surprising number of similarities with participating in a conversation, you'll find that writing is an activity you can approach with confidence. In this book, writing is treated as an activity similar to conversation. The documents you'll write are contributions that move a conversation forward. The designs you'll choose reflect your purposes and those of your readers. And the processes you'll use to write are similar to those used to participate in a discussion. By thinking of writing as conversation, you'll be able to use your already extensive understanding of how conversations work to become a confident, effective writer.

You Already Know How Conversations Work— Online and Off

Imagine yourself at a party. When you arrived, you said hello to friends and found something to eat or drink. Then you walked around, listening briefly to several conversations. Eventually, you joined a group that was talking about something you found interesting.

If you're like most people, you didn't jump right into the conversation. Instead, you listened for a few minutes and thought about what was being said. Perhaps you learned something new. Eventually, you added your voice to the conversation, other members of the group picked up on what you said, and the conversation moved along. The same thing happens when you join a new group online. Whether you join a discussion board or a Facebook group, more than likely you listen in (or read what's been posted) to learn about the group's interests before you make any posts.

You can use your understanding of how conversations work to become a better writer. You'll realize fairly quickly that good writing involves more than simply stating what you know. You'll see writing, instead, as a process of joining, reflecting on, and contributing to a conversation about a topic or an issue.

Because written conversations take place over much longer periods of time than spoken conversations do, you can use your conversational skills to far greater advantage. You can thoroughly consider your purposes and analyze your readers' needs, interests, and backgrounds. And you can explore the contexts — physical, social, and cultural — that will shape how your document is written and read.

Today, many of us are as likely to engage in conversations through writing as through speaking. Some of us prefer a text message to a phone call. Some of us spend more time using e-mail than talking with friends. Some of us spend entire evenings on Web discussion forums, sharing information or arguing about the best new games, music, or movies. Some of us post, read, and reply to blogs on a regular basis. And some of us spend more time keeping up with friends on Facebook, Twitter, or Tumblr than we do hanging out together.

Interestingly, if you ask people who spend significant amounts of time online whether they do much writing, they'll often say they don't. They don't think of creating text messages, e-mail messages, status updates, comments, notes, forum posts, or blog entries as writing. Yet it is. And the writing you've done in these settings can help prepare you for the writing you'll be asked to do in class or at a job.

Your Turn: Inventory Your Writing Life

We all have writing lives. In fact, you probably do much more writing than you think. Conduct an inventory of your writing activities and reflect on how your experiences might enhance the writing you'll do for class assignments. To get started, use the following prompts:

1. **Create a list of everything you do that involves typing.** Be sure to include typing on phones, tablets, and computers.

2. **List everything you do that involves hand-writing.** Include everything from grocery lists to notes taken in class to personal letters.

3. **Identify the purposes and audiences of each activity you've listed.** For each item, indicate why you do it or what you hope to accomplish by doing it (purpose). Then indicate who reads it (audience). In some cases,

such as shopping lists or class notes, your audience will most likely be yourself.

4. **Identify activities that involve locating information.** For each activity on your list, indicate whether you read sources (such as newspaper or magazine articles, websites, blogs, or books), search the Web, collect information through observation, or talk to others in the course of carrying out the activity.

5. **Review your list to identify writing activities that might prepare you for academic writing.** Look for activities that involve accomplishing a purpose; thinking about the needs, interests, and experiences of your readers; or collecting information. Consider how carrying out these activities might help you succeed at academic writing assignments.

Of course, there are differences between the writing you do online and the writing you do in an academic essay. Using abbreviations such as OMG or LOL in an essay might go over just about as well as writing "In summary, the available evidence suggests" in a text message. Despite these differences, you can build on your experiences as a writer in a wide range of settings. Just as you will adapt your tone or level of formality in a spoken conversation to the people involved in the conversation — for example, treating new acquaintances differently than you treat old friends — you're likely to adapt your writing to the situation in which you find yourself. Just as you'll tailor your comments to friends when you write on their Facebook pages, you can consider the interests and experiences of the people who will read your next academic essay. And just as you've learned to be critical — even suspicious — of what you read online, you can apply the same caution to your reading of the sources you encounter as you work on assignments.

Conversations Help You Share Information, Ideas, and Arguments

Much like a spoken conversation, a written conversation involves an exchange of information, ideas, and arguments among readers and writers. Instead of using spoken words, however, participants in a written conversation communicate through documents. And just as most people listen to what's being said before contributing to a spoken conversation, most writers begin the process of writing about a topic by reading.

After reflecting on what they've learned, writers will search for something new to offer to the conversation. Then they'll write their own document. In turn, that document will be read by other members of the conversation. If some of them are interested, concerned, or even offended by the writer's contribution, they might write their own documents in response. In this sense, a conversation among writers and readers becomes a circular process in which the information, ideas, and arguments shared through documents lead to the creation of new documents.

Consider the experiences of Gina Colville, a college student taking a first-year writing course at Front Range Community College north of Denver. Gina's instructor was teaching a *writing-about-writing* course, in which the content of the course focuses not on a particular theme or topic but on research and theory about writing. Gina's instructor had asked her to reflect on her experiences as a writer and to locate a few recent articles and blog posts that might speak to those experiences. To learn about writing research and theory, Gina started to listen in on written conversations about writing instruction, academic writing, professional writing, and writing on social media. She looked for information in her library's databases (see p. 481), searched the Web (see p. 484), and read articles and blog posts. Some of what she read was written by writing instructors. Other sources were written by journalists and professional writers. Still others were written by students themselves. Gina found herself drawn to discussions of different approaches to preparing future high school teachers to teach writing. She compared what she read with her own experiences as a student and reflected on how she was taught to write during high school. Eventually, she would write an evaluative essay that compared and made judgments about various instructional approaches.

As she learned more about how high school teachers are trained to teach writing, Gina decided to share her ideas about these approaches with friends and family, as well as with others who were interested in the topic. To get started, she posted on Tumblr and shared her posts on Facebook. Some of Gina's friends and classmates responded by posting comments on her Facebook page. Some "liked" her Tumblr posts and shared them with their friends. Eventually, a student reporter for her college newspaper commented on her ideas in an article about Colorado guidelines for teaching writing to high school students.

Writers learn about a topic through reading.

You can see conversational exchanges among readers and writers in a number of contexts. Articles in scholarly and professional journals almost always refer to previously published work. Similarly, letters to the editors of newspapers and magazines frequently make references to earlier letters or articles. You can even see this process in writing classes. As writers share their work with classmates and instructors, they receive feedback that often leads to important changes in their final drafts. In turn, as writers read the work of their classmates, they often refine their thinking about their own writing projects.

As you work on your own writing projects, keep in mind the circular nature of written conversations. Remember: just as when you join a group of friends who

After reading about a topic, writers share information with readers, who may respond in writing themselves.

are chatting at a party, you'll be entering a situation in which others have already contributed their observations and ideas. Your contribution should build on what has already been written. In turn, other members of the conversation will read what you've written and build on the ideas, information, and arguments you've shared with them.

Conversations Allow You to Adopt Roles

In spoken conversations, we often take on roles. A speaker might explain something to someone else, in a sense becoming a guide through the conversation. Another speaker might advance an argument, taking on the role of an advocate for a particular position. These roles shift and change as the conversation moves along. Depending on the flow of the conversation, a person who explained something at one point in the conversation might make an argument later on.

Your Turn: Find a Written Conversation

We're surrounded by written conversations. Some focus on politics, others on sports, and still others on issues in an academic discipline. You'll find contributions to conversations on the front page of newspapers, on websites such as CNN.com and Foxnews.com, in academic and professional journals, and in the blogs at Tumblr or Blogger .com. Spend some time locating a conversation about a topic that interests you. Use the following prompts to find the conversation:

1. **List a topic that interests you.** Because you'll be searching for sources, jot down a list of search terms, or keywords (see p. 474), that you can use to locate sources on the topic.

2. **Choose a newspaper or magazine or search for sources.** Browse a newspaper or magazine or search for sources on a Web search site (see p. 484), in a library database (see p. 481), or in a library catalog (see p. 477) using the keywords you jotted down about your topic.

3. **Identify sources that seem to address the topic.** Skim each source (see p. 58) to get a sense of how it addresses your topic.

4. **Decide whether the sources are engaged in the same conversation.** Ask whether the sources are addressing the same topic. If they are, list the ways in which they are "talking" to one another about the topic. Identify any agreements, disagreements, or differences in their approach to the topic.

5. **Reflect on the conversation.** Ask whether the sources you've identified tell you enough to understand the conversation. Consider whether you might need to locate more sources to give you a fuller picture of the conversation.

OBSERVERS (Chapter 6) focus on learning about and exploring the implications of a person, an event, an object, an idea, or an issue. They typically reflect on their subject and often trace their thinking about it.

I wonder what my life would be like if I majored in advertising.

REPORTERS (Chapter 7) present themselves as experts and offer detailed but neutral information. A reporter might also provide an overview of competing ideas about a topic, such as a guide to the positions of candidates for public office.

I'm focusing on the advertising dollars generated by sites like Facebook and Amazon.

INTERPRETERS (Chapter 8) analyze and explain the significance of ideas or events.

I have to wonder about the truthfulness of the ads aired during this year's Super Bowl. I think I'll check a few of them out.

EVALUATORS (Chapter 9) consider how well something meets a given set of criteria. Their judgments are usually balanced, and they offer evidence and reasoning to support their evaluation.

Who cares about the truth? I wonder which ads were most effective. Did sales actually go up as a result of the ads? Did people view the products more favorably?

PROBLEM SOLVERS (Chapter 10) identify and define a problem, discuss its impact, and offer solutions based on evidence and reasoning.

The problem I'm wrestling with is how smaller companies can benefit from events like the Super Bowl. How can they get their message out when the ads are so expensive?

ADVOCATES (Chapter 11) present evidence in favor of their side of an argument and, in many cases, offer evidence that undermines opposing views.

If anybody cares about the truth, it's me. And I'm sure I'm not alone. We need to do something about deceptive advertising. And I know just what that is.

A similar form of role-playing takes place in written conversation. The roles writers take on reflect their purpose, their understanding of their readers, and the types of documents they plan to write. To help them achieve their purpose, writers typically adopt one or more of the roles you'll learn about in later chapters of this book.

As in spoken conversations, the roles writers play are not mutually exclusive. In an introduction to an argumentative essay, you might find yourself adopting the role of reporter, helping your readers understand an issue so that they will be better positioned to understand the argument you'll advance later. Similarly, you might find yourself adopting the role of advocate in a problem-solving essay as you shift from explaining a potential solution to arguing that it should be put into effect. To understand how this fluid shifting of roles can take place — and make sense — reflect on your experiences in spoken conversations. Thinking of writing as a conversation will make it easier to understand how, and when, to shift roles.

Working Together: Explore Roles

Explore the roles you and your classmates take during a conversation. In a group of five, ask three people to talk about a topic that has recently been in the news or that has been the focus of attention on campus. As the conversation unfolds, the other two members of the group should listen and write down the different roles that are adopted during the conversation, noting when and why the roles were adopted. After five minutes of conversation, respond to the following prompts:

1. **What roles were adopted?** The two observers should share their list of roles. Ask whether the observers noticed the same roles. If there are differences, discuss them.

2. **When were different roles adopted?** Ask when each role was adopted. Which roles were adopted at the beginning of the conversation? Did the members of the conversation shift roles during the conversation? If so, when?

3. **Why were different roles adopted?** Explore the reasons for adopting each role. For example, ask whether people who knew more about the topic adopted different roles than did those who knew less. If you saw shifts in role, ask why those shifts occurred.

4. **Connect the activity to your work as a writer.** Consider how the idea of roles might play out in your own writing. As a group, discuss roles you've adopted in the past, and consider how you might use the idea of roles in your future writing.

What Should I Know about Writing Situations?

When people participate in a spoken conversation, they pay attention to a wide range of factors: why they've joined the conversation, who's involved in the conversation, and what's already been said. They also notice the mood of the people they're speaking with, their facial expressions and body language, and physical factors such as background noise. In short, they consider the situation as they listen and speak. Similarly, when writers engage in written conversation, they become part of a **writing situation** — the setting in which writers and readers communicate with one another. Writing situations — the phrase we'll use in this book to refer to rhetorical situations — are shaped by these and other important factors, including the sources you use and the type of document you decide to write.

Writing Situations Are Rhetorical Situations

A writing situation is another name for a **rhetorical situation**, a concept that has been studied for thousands of years. The ancient Greeks, particularly Plato, Socrates, and Aristotle, contributed in important ways to our understanding of rhetorical situations. So did rhetoricians in China, Japan, India, Africa, Rome, the Arab world, and other cultures. Viewing writing as a rhetorical act helps us understand how writers or speakers pursue their purposes; consider the needs and interests of their audiences; adapt to the conditions in which they address their audiences; and present, organize, or design their documents or speeches.

This book is based strongly on a *rhetorical approach* to writing. Throughout the book, you'll find yourself considering why writers pursue particular purposes and the roles they adopt; how readers' reactions are affected by their needs, interests, knowledge, and backgrounds; and how the contexts in which documents are written and read shape the experience of reading them. You'll also consider not only the opportunities you can take advantage of as you create your contribution to the conversation but also the limitations you'll face as you craft your document.

Writing Has a Purpose

As is the case with spoken conversations, writers join written conversations for particular **purposes**, which in turn affect the roles they adopt (see pp. 10–12). Writers hoping to persuade or convince their readers, for example, take on the role of advocate, while those hoping to inform readers take on the role of reporter. You can read more about the roles writers adopt in Chapters 6 through 11.

Writers often have more than one purpose for writing a document.

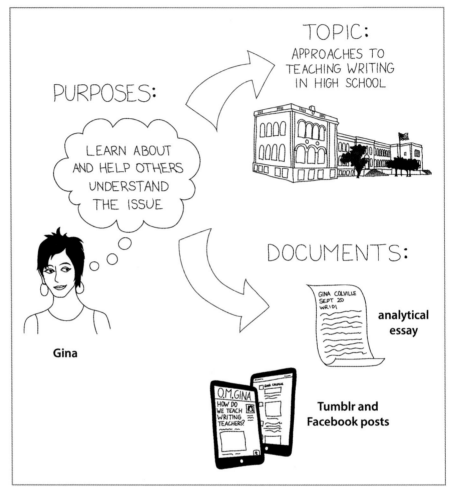

Writers often have more than one purpose for writing a document. Writers of academic essays, for instance, might complete their essays not only to earn a grade and pass the course but also to learn about a particular topic or improve their composition skills. Writers of newspaper and magazine articles may have been assigned their topics, but they often find themselves interested in their subjects and end up writing as much for themselves as for their readers.

Writers' purposes for joining a conversation are shaped by their **needs, interests,** and **backgrounds**. For example, a person who suffers from asthma might wonder whether plans to build a coal-powered electricity plant near his neighborhood will take health concerns into account. Another person interested in clean coal technologies might want to support proposed legislation on reducing power-plant emissions. Still others, such as those employed by the power industry, might be concerned about how proposed legislation on power-plant emissions might affect their employment.

Your purposes will affect what you choose to write about and how you compose a document. Gina Colville, the student who posted on Tumblr and Facebook about preparing future high school teachers to teach writing, wanted not only to learn about the issue but also to call attention to the training and support high school teachers need to do a good job in the classroom. As she wrote in her posts, her purposes affected her choice of what to write about, which information to use as supporting evidence for her points, and how to address the information, ideas, and arguments she encountered in her reading.

Readers Have Purposes, Needs, Interests, Knowledge, and Backgrounds

Just as writers have purposes, so do readers. Among other purposes, readers often want to learn about a subject, assess or evaluate ideas and arguments, or understand opposing perspectives. And like writers' purposes, readers' purposes are strongly influenced by their own needs, interests, knowledge, and backgrounds. Gina's interest in how high school teachers learn approaches to writing instruction, for example, was driven by the experiences she and her friends and family had had in high school. Her readers were probably drawn to her post by similar personal experiences — their memories of writing assignments, their knowledge of the challenges faced by high school teachers, or the perspective they have gained through reading a magazine article or hearing a news report about the issue.

As writers craft their contributions to a written conversation, they ask who their readers are likely to be. They reflect on their readers' values and beliefs, determine what their readers may already know about a subject, and take into account their readers' likely experiences — if any — with the subject. They consider what readers need to learn about a subject and what readers might be interested in knowing. They ask why potential readers would want to read their document — and what might cause readers to stop reading. In short, writers try to understand and connect with their readers.

Writers consider the needs, interests, and backgrounds of their readers.

FAMILIES

GRAD SCHOOLS OF EDUCATION

HIGH SCHOOL ENGLISH TEACHERS

Gina

Writing Builds on the Work of Others

One of the most important ways in which writing situations resemble spoken conversations is their reliance on taking turns. In spoken conversations — at least in those that are productive — people take turns sharing their ideas. To move the conversation forward, speakers build on what has been said, often referring to specific ideas or arguments and identifying the speakers who raised them. Comments such as "As Ellen said . . ." and "Reid made a good point earlier when he pointed out that . . ." are frequently made in spoken conversations or class discussions. They show respect for the contributions made by others and help speakers align themselves with or distance themselves from other members of the conversation.

Written conversations also build on earlier contributions. Writers refer to the work of other authors to support their arguments, to provide a context for their own contributions, or to differentiate their ideas from those advanced by other authors. For example, an opinion columnist might contrast her ideas with those offered by other members of the conversation by quoting another columnist. Later in the same column, she might include a statement made by yet another author to support her argument.

Writers also use sources to introduce new ideas, information, and arguments to a conversation. As she listened in on the conversation about how high school teachers are trained to teach writing, Gina Colville read a blog post by a graduate student in teacher education. The blogger was concerned about standardized testing in schools and how these high-stakes tests were affecting both students and teachers. The blogger posted national survey data showing the number of classroom hours devoted to preparing students for these kinds of tests. Other students and teachers around the country commented on the blog post, sharing anecdotal evidence about how standardized tests were affecting their classroom experiences. When writers use sources in this way, they provide citations to indicate where the information comes from and to help readers locate the sources in case they wish to review them.

Even when writers do not refer directly to other sources, the work of other writers may influence their thinking about a subject. As you write, be aware that what you've read, heard, seen, and experienced will shape your thinking about the subject — and the information, ideas, and arguments in your document.

Writing Takes Place in Context

Just as in spoken conversations, written conversations are affected by the contexts — or settings — in which they take place.

- **Physical context** affects how you read and write (on paper or on a computer screen) and how well you can concentrate (for example, consider the differences between trying to read in a noisy, crowded, jolting bus and in a quiet, well-lit room).

- **Social context** affects how easily writers and readers can understand one another. Readers familiar with topics such as violence in American high schools, for example, will not need to be educated about them — they will already know the key points. This reduces the amount of time and effort writers need to devote to providing background information.

- **Disciplinary context** refers to the shared writing practices, general agreements about appropriate types of documents, and shared assumptions about what is worth writing about that are common to a particular profession or academic discipline, such as history, accounting, construction management, or chemistry.

- **Cultural context** refers to a larger set of similarities and differences among readers. For instance, readers from the American Midwest might find it easier to understand the allusions and metaphors used in a document written by someone from Kansas than those in a document written by someone from Peru or Sri Lanka. Similarly, today's teenagers might find it easier to follow what's being said in a document written one month ago by a high school senior in Milwaukee than a document written in 1897 by a retired railroad engineer from Saskatchewan.

Physical, social, disciplinary, and cultural contexts affect the writing and reading of documents.

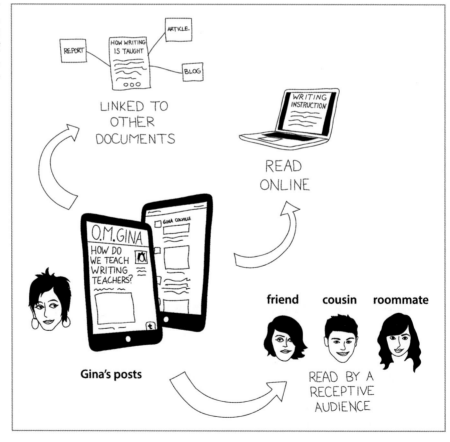

For students, one of the most important social and cultural contexts shaping their written work is academic life itself, that complex mix of instructors, fellow students, classes, tests, labs, and writing assignments that they negotiate on a daily basis. Academic culture — and U.S. and Canadian academic culture in particular — is the product of hundreds of years of arguments, decisions, revisions, and reinventions of a way of thinking and behaving. Academic culture affects far more than how you behave in class, although that's certainly an important element of it. It also shapes the writing you'll do during and after your time in college.

In nearly every instance, what you say and how you say it will reflect a combination of contexts. For example, the fact that Gina's posts were both written and read online allowed her to link directly to other digital documents, such as news articles, scholarly articles, Facebook posts, and blogs. At the same time, because her work would be read on a computer monitor, she was cautious about readers having to scroll through multiple screens. As a result, her posts tended to be brief. Because she was writing to an audience that knew her well (friends and family), she didn't need to provide a great deal of information about her background. And because so many of her friends and family had had similar experiences in high school, she did not feel that she had to explain her perspective as clearly as she might have were she writing to people with different backgrounds.

Writing Situations Are an Important Area of Scholarly Inquiry

It's also useful to understand that writing is the subject of intense scholarship. For more than a century, researchers and theorists have approached the study of writing from a wide range of perspectives: historical, cultural, psychological, social, anthropological, educational, and rhetorical, to name only a few. From teachers who focus on the creative side of writing to theorists who explore the political implications of writing in the world (and in the classroom) to cognitive scientists who try to understand the mental processes involved in writing, scholars have published research findings, theoretical insights, and innovative approaches to writing instruction. Fred Newton Scott, for example, who served as chair of the University of Michigan's Department of Rhetoric from 1903 to 1927, launched and edited for twenty years what has been called the first series of research publications on writing, *Contributions to Rhetorical Theory*.

Despite the early prominence of writing studies in rhetoric programs, writing research was for most of the 20th century a somewhat underemphasized part of academic scholarship in the United States. That began to change in the 1960s and

1970s as increasing numbers of students began to seek college degrees — and a growing number of faculty members began studying how best to teach them. By the early 1980s, English departments once again began offering doctorates in the study of writing and rhetoric. And by the late 1990s, doctoral programs were being offered by independent writing programs that had broken away from English departments.

The strong growth in scholarly work on writing and writing instruction over the past five decades has fueled significant changes in how writing is taught. More recently, transformative changes in information technology, in particular the World Wide Web, social media, and the tools we use to create and distribute texts and media, have influenced writing instruction. As scholars continue to grapple with what it means to write and to be a writer, the ways in which writing is taught have changed dramatically. Throughout this book, you'll find discussions of relevant research on writing and writing instruction, the role of technology in writing, and the implications of writing in today's society. The ability of individual writers to shape public discourse has never been greater.

Working Together: Analyze a Writing Situation

Work together with your classmates to analyze a writing situation. Generate a list of documents that members of the group have written recently. Then choose one and analyze its writing situation. To conduct your analysis, respond to the following prompts:

1. **What was written?** Describe the document in enough detail to allow other members of the class to understand its main point.

2. **What were the writer's purposes?** List the purpose or purposes that drove the writer's work on the document. Why did he or she write it? What did he or she hope to gain by writing it? How was the writer's purpose shaped by his or her needs, interests, values, beliefs, knowledge, and experience?

3. **Who were the intended readers?** Describe the people who might have been expected to read the document, and list their purpose or purposes for reading it. How would their reading of the document have been shaped by their needs, interests, values, beliefs, knowledge, and experience?

4. **What sources were used in the document?** Identify the sources of information, ideas, and arguments used in the document. Indicate how the sources were used (for example, to support a point or to differentiate the writer's ideas from those of another author).

5. **What contexts shaped the writing and reading of the document?** Identify the physical, social, disciplinary, and cultural contexts that shaped the writer's work on the document and the readers' understanding of it.

What Should I Know about Genre and Design?

As you craft your contribution to a written conversation, you can draw on two powerful tools to create an effective document: genre and design. Genre and design are closely related. In fact, typical design characteristics — for example, columns, headings, and photographs in a newspaper article — can help you distinguish one type of document from another.

Genres Are General Categories of Documents

Given the influx of technology and the ease of sharing ideas on the Web, writers have tremendous choice in the types of documents they create. General categories of documents are called *genres*. When you use the word *novel*, for example, you're referring to a general category of long fiction. If you say that you like to read novels, you aren't talking about reading a particular book; instead, you're expressing a preference for a type of writing that is distinct from poetry or biography, for instance.

Opinion columns, academic essays, scholarly articles, and personal Web pages are all genres. So are personal journals, thank-you letters, and entries on personal blogs. In fact, there are a wide variety of genres, and the number seems to grow larger every few years. Until the 1990s, for example, personal and company Web pages didn't exist. Nor did blogs. Nor, for that matter, did text messages, tweets, or Facebook posts. Yet all these have become important genres.

Although *genre* typically refers to general categories of documents, such as novels or Web pages, it can also be used to refer to more specific categories. For example, you might refer not simply to novels but also to romance novels, mystery novels, and historical novels. Or you might refer to different types of academic essays, such as reflective essays, argumentative essays, or analytical essays. The word *genre*, in this sense, can be used flexibly. Sometimes it's used in the largest possible sense, and sometimes it refers to highly specific categories of documents.

Design Is a Writing Tool

Document design is the use of visual elements — such as fonts, colors, page layout, and illustrations — to enhance the effectiveness of written documents. A well-designed chart, for example, can be far more effective at conveying complex information than even the most clearly written paragraph. Similarly, the emotional impact of a well-chosen illustration, such as a photograph of a starving child or a video clip of aid workers rushing to help victims of a natural disaster, can do far

Brochures provide information by using large, descriptive titles to draw attention to important information.

Including an eye-catching image makes this brochure even more persuasive than text alone might have.

The Lee College

Writing Center

"We are not here because students can't write; we are here because they do."

Feeling overwhelmed with a writing assignment?
The Lee College Writing Center can help!

Tutors assist students with all aspects of the writing process:

- Brainstorming
- Understanding the assignment
- Thesis development
- Organization
- Introductions/Conclusions
- Grammar

Live Chat Online Tutoring:

Make an appointment, submit your paper by email, and chat with a tutor via computer. Call the Writing Center for an appointment or for more information: **281.425.6534**.

Here are some things to remember about live or online sessions:

- Have your assignment instructions available.
- Students are allotted up to 45 minutes per tutoring session.
- If you arrive more than 10 minutes late, you may have to reschedule.
- We are happy to help with grammar issues; however, we cannot provide editing or be responsible for correcting every error.
- Students may print academic papers for free—up to ten pages.

LEE COLLEGE

How to Have the Best Appointment Ever!

The Writing Center staff can help you at any stage of the writing process: brainstorming, revising, or fine tuning the final version. **There are a few key things to bring to your appointment:**

Your questions: What is your primary concern about your writing? Please let us know specifically what you would like to address as well as any feedback you have from your instructor.

Your assignment: You could have the best paper in the world, but if it does not match the requirements of the assignment, the essay may be in danger of receiving a low grade. If you do not have a copy of the instructions, be sure to know what is required.

What you have so far: It helps greatly to print out what you have written so far. This provides us with something for the student to look at and discuss. Writing notes on a piece of paper allows you to remember revision ideas better and helps you learn the revision process for your next paper.

Every session can greatly help your writing, but you are the most important factor in

having a GREAT session. Don't be afraid if you didn't have time for printing out two copies, or even one copy, or if your computer broke, or if you sent yourself the wrong file; we can still talk about your writing process, brainstorm your ideas, or talk about writing strategies—**just be sure to come!** Remember that the writing tutors are here to coach you through the writing process—NOT to judge your writing.

Many times you may walk into the Writing Center and a tutor can see you immediately. However, if you have a specific time that you need to be seen, please call ahead or speak with the tutor at the front desk to make an appointment. Simply call and cancel if your plans change–so that another student may utilize that session time.

We also offer a variety of free handouts that you may take with you in order to be a more successful writer. If you have a quick question to be addressed, you may stop by and chat with one of the available tutors.

We look forward to having the best semester ever . . . with YOU!

The Lee College

Writing Center

Location: Bonner Hall 225
Phone: 281.425.6534

FALL/SPRING HOURS:

Monday & Tuesday
7:30am–7:30pm

Wednesday & Thursday
7:30am–6:00pm

Friday
9am–noon

SUMMER HOURS:

Monday-Thursday
9:00am-5:00pm

Friday
9am-noon

LEE COLLEGE

more than words alone to persuade a reader to take action. By understanding and applying the principles of document design, you can increase the likelihood that you'll achieve your purposes as a writer and address the needs and interests of your readers. Throughout this book, you'll find design treated as a central writing strategy, and you'll find numerous examples of the design characteristics of the genres discussed in each chapter. You'll also find an in-depth discussion of design in Chapters 18, 19, and 20.

Genre and Design Are Related

Think about a website you visited recently. Now picture an article in a print news-paper or magazine. The differences that come to mind reflect how genre and design are intertwined. You can tell genres apart by focusing on why they are written, how they are written, and what they look like. On the basis of design alone, it's usually quite easy to tell the difference between an academic essay and an article in a popular magazine. The style in which a document is written, its organization and use of sources, and its appearance work together to help you understand that a document is, for example, a scholarly journal article, a blog entry, a letter to the editor, or a brochure. As you read a document (and often without really think-ing about it), you may notice characteristic features of a genre, such as the use of boldface headlines or detailed footnotes. And once you've identified the genre, you can read the document more effectively. Understanding how a document is organized can make it easier to locate information. It can also make you a more astute reader. If you recognize a document as an advertisement, for example, you're less likely to be swayed by questionable reasoning.

The documents on pages 22 and 24–25 illustrate a wide range of genres that might be used to write about a topic. Each document addresses the topic of preparing future high school teachers to teach writing effectively. The documents range from a brochure and a PowerPoint presentation to a website and a journal article. As you look at each document, think about the purpose for which it was written, the read-ers it addresses, the genre conventions it follows, and the design it uses.

Genres and Design Help Writers Achieve Their Goals

Genres develop to help writers accomplish a general purpose. Academic essays help writers demonstrate their knowledge to an instructor, while informative articles in newspapers, magazines, and newsletters help writers share information and ideas with their readers. Opinion columns and letters to the editor, in contrast, are often used by writers to advance arguments.

A PowerPoint presentation uses color, fonts, bulleted lists, and images to convey information and ideas.

Websites provide information, links to other documents, and contact information.

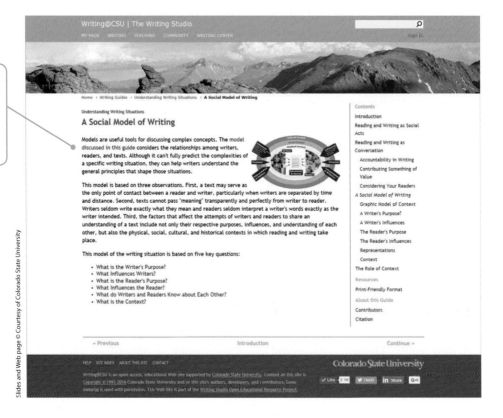

AMERICAN SECONDARY EDUCATION 41(1) FALL 2012

TEACHING WRITING IN THE SHADOW OF STANDARDIZED WRITING ASSESSMENT: AN EXPLORATORY STUDY

Authors

HUNTER BRIMI, ED.D., is an English teacher at Farragut High School in Knoxville, Tennessee.

> An article published in a scholarly journal is directed at readers who are familiar with research on a topic. It offers information about the author and an abstract to help readers determine quickly whether it will meet their needs.

Abstract

This exploratory study results from interviews with five high school English teachers regarding their writing instruction. The researcher sought to answer these questions: (1) How had the Tennessee Comprehensive Assessment Program's (TCAP) Writing Assessment affected their teaching as gauged by the teachers' statements regarding the assessment, emphasis on the writing process, and use of multiple writing genres? and (2) How did these teachers learn to teach writing, and did their training mitigate the influence of standardized testing? The teachers indicated that the TCAP Writing Assessment palpably affected their instruction. Additionally, the teachers revealed that they struggled to teach the writing process and showed reluctance to teach or assign multi-genre writing. This may result from their dearth of training to teach writing before entering the field.

"Most of us are English majors and not writing teachers. I think teachers need much more instruction on how to teach writing," said Layla Canton, a 20-year veteran English teacher. Ms. Canton's words illustrate the frustration that many English teachers feel concerning teaching composition. Teachers often enter the field inadequately prepared to teach this cardinal component of their subject matter due to preparation programs that do not always give abundant instruction on how to teach writing (Smith, 2003).

In a summary of "professional trends and issues," the commissioners of

Documents in a particular genre usually share a general purpose and tend to use similar writing conventions, such as level of formality or the type of evidence used to support a point. For example, newspaper obituaries are usually formal and serious, while e-mail messages are often informal and relaxed. Scholarly articles almost always refer to the source of evidence offered to support their points, while letters to the editor sometimes offer no evidence at all. In addition, documents in a particular genre often use similar design elements. Academic essays, for example, are usually written with wide margins and double-spaced lines, while magazine articles often use columns and make extensive use of color and illustrations.

In most cases, genres are shaped by the social, cultural, and disciplinary contexts from which they emerge. When writers and readers form a community — such as an academic discipline, a professional association, or a group that shares an interest in a particular topic or activity — they develop characteristic ways of communicating with one another. Over time, members of a community will come to agreement about the type of evidence that is generally accepted to support arguments, the style in which sources should be cited, and how documents should be designed and organized. As the needs of a community evolve, the genre will adapt as well. Articles in magazines for automobile or motorcycle enthusiasts, for example, differ in important ways from articles in magazines about contemporary music. In the same

Your Turn: Analyze a Genre

For this exercise, analyze the Lee College Writing Center brochure on page 22 and respond to the following prompts:

1. **Writing style.** Is the brochure written in a formal or an informal style? Somewhere in between? How would you describe the relationship that the authors of the brochure attempt to establish with readers?

2. **Evidence.** What types of evidence are used in the brochure? Why do you think the authors chose these types of evidence?

3. **Organization.** How is the brochure organized? Did you find it easy to follow? Difficult? Somewhere in between? Why?

4. **Citation style.** Are sources cited in the brochure? If so, how are the sources cited — in a works cited list, in footnotes, or in the text itself? Why do you think the author cites (or doesn't cite) sources in this way?

5. **Design.** Briefly identify the design elements used in the document, such as columns, photographs, and text formatting. (For more information on design elements, see Chapter 18.) How does the design of the document set up expectations about its content? To what extent does the design help or hinder your ability to read and understand the document?

way, scholarly articles written by sociologists, civil engineers, and chemists also use evidence or organization in distinct ways.

As the needs and interests of a community change, genre will change as well. Academic essays, for example, might begin to make greater use of color and illustrations. In other cases, a single genre might evolve into several distinct genres. For example, as the number of readers on the Web has exploded over the past two decades, websites have become far more specialized. In the mid-1990s, most websites looked alike. Today, characteristic differences can be seen among personal blogs, commercial websites, government websites, and entertainment websites.

Consider the role that genre and design might play in your writing process (see p. 570). Your choice of genre should reflect your writing situation, in particular your goals, your readers, and the context in which your document will be read. The design of your document should also align with your writing situation. You can think of these choices as part of your effort to share your ideas with your readers. The rhetorical concept of delivery — one of the five canons of classical rhetoric — has most often been associated with techniques for delivering a speech, but as writers have gained greater control over how they can design and share their documents, delivery has become an increasingly important consideration.

To learn more about genre and design, pay attention to the wide range of documents you encounter in your reading. Simply being aware that genres exist and that your design choices will be shaped by the genre you choose can help you contribute effectively to a written conversation.

What Should I Know about Writing Processes?

Ask most writing instructors what's involved in writing and they're likely to say something about the composing process. If they say more than a sentence or two, you'll almost certainly hear that the process varies from writer to writer and situation to situation. Writing, they'll tell you, is a series of decisions and activities that takes into account the distinctive demands writers face as they work on particular writing projects.

Writing Is Like Other Complex Activities

Writing is a lot like skiing. It's also a lot like teaching, coaching, managing a budget, and selling trucks.

It might seem absurd to compare writing to skiing or selling trucks, but there are surprising similarities among these and other complex activities. As a skier, your goals might vary each time you get off a lift at the top of a mountain. You might want to make it down the slope safely. You might want to win a race. Or perhaps you might want to work on a new skill, such as carving turns or landing jumps. To accomplish your goals, you can draw on your knowledge of snow conditions, weather, the training techniques used by expert skiers, and so on. You can use specific strategies, such as slowing down where trails merge or timing your run to avoid that group of skiers who seem to be enjoying life a bit too much. And you can draw on a set of processes, such as parallel turns, snowplowing, and hockey stops, to accomplish your goals — and stay upright.

The key factors in complex activities such as skiing — goals, knowledge, strategies, and processes — are similar to those involved in writing. In fact, what you've learned in other areas can often help you gain new knowledge and skills as a writer.

It Takes Time and Effort to Become a Good Writer

As a writer, you will benefit from understanding your writing situation and the kinds of composing processes and strategies you might use to accomplish your goals. You'll also benefit from practice. The more you write, and the more often you receive useful feedback on your writing, the better you'll become. Just as musicians benefit from practice and lessons, writers benefit from time spent writing, along with the guidance and feedback they receive from instructors and other writers.

Since the middle of the 19th century, a surprisingly large number of teachers have told their students, "Writers are born, not made." That notion emerged from a mixture of romantic theory (which swept Europe and the United States in the 18th and 19th centuries and continues to have a strong influence today) and faculty psychology (a psychological theory with 18th-century roots that held that people are born with or without innate "faculties" — or abilities). Some writing teachers went as far as to discourage any students they felt lacked the "gift" to write well from even attempting to improve their skills.

It is true that some people are born with a combination of cognitive abilities and emotional sensibilities that allows them to be truly exceptional writers, much as basketball players like Stephen Curry and LeBron James are born with a mix of exceptional physical abilities, spatial reasoning aptitudes, and emotional sensibilities that allows them to succeed as athletes. But the idea that the lack of these abilities will doom you to failure in a particular area — to the point that you might as well not even try to develop those abilities — is nonsense. You don't need to be a LeBron James to enjoy — and enjoy success at — basketball. You don't need to be a Mozart or a Beethoven to be a fine musician. You don't need to be a "gifted" writer to be a successful writer.

Success in writing does require time and effort, however. And all writers can benefit from good advice. Seeking guidance from more experienced writers — including writing teachers, writing center consultants, and colleagues or supervisors who understand what makes a successful document — will help you improve more quickly.

Writing Processes Vary from Project to Project

Most of the writing projects you'll work on over your lifetime will share some basic characteristics. For each, you will have a purpose, a set of readers, and a context within which your writing will take place. You also might have a deadline or expectations about length or the kinds of sources you might use to support your argument.

These similarities in writing projects contribute to similarities in the processes writers use as they work on a project.

As you start a project, remember two things. First, because general types of writing projects share similarities, you can build on what you've learned from past projects. Second, despite these similarities, it's rare to use every one of the typical writing

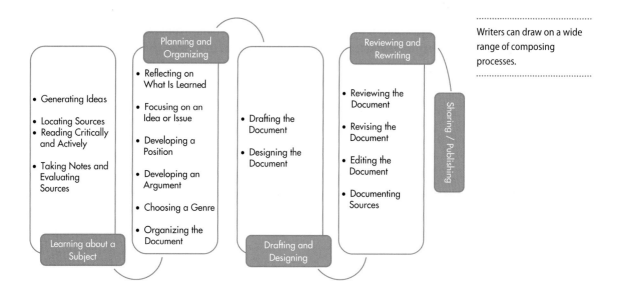

Writers can draw on a wide range of composing processes.

processes in a given writing project. You might already know a great deal about a topic, for instance, or design choices might be limited or nonexistent. Whatever the cause, you'll almost always find that some aspect of a writing project will distinguish it from the projects you've worked on in the past.

Writing Processes Are Recursive

Writing is anything but a step-by-step process. You'll repeat processes, rethink earlier decisions, and delete sentences that no longer work. If you don't like your first or second or third draft, you can revise it, rethink its organization, or learn more about your subject. At its heart, writing is a process of making judgments about whether you've done enough to accomplish your goals and deciding what to do if you haven't.

Cognitive scientists call this pattern of returning to and repeating processes *recursion*. By definition, recursive processes are somewhat messy. In fact, the composing process is seldom as orderly as depicted in the figure on page 29. The process of writing this book, for example, looked a bit more like the figure below, with each path between processes being repeated dozens of times.

Understanding that writing is recursive can help you avoid frustration. Knowing that learning more about an issue may lead you to rethink your position will prepare you to return again and again to the work of developing and refining your line of argument. Rather than viewing this work as unnecessary and repetitive, you'll understand it as a natural and effective process of improving your argument. In other words, just as you'll change your strategies and tactics to reflect what you learn about your opponent in a video game, you'll adapt to

Writing processes are recursive.

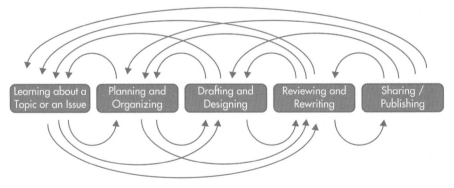

| Learning about a Topic or an Issue | Planning and Organizing | Drafting and Designing | Reviewing and Rewriting | Sharing / Publishing |

what you learn as you work on a writing project. Knowing that writing processes are recursive is a critical part of achieving success, particularly on a longer and more complex project.

Writing Processes Are Studied Intensely

The idea that writing is a process is far from new. In the late 19th century, rhetorician John Quackenbos, citing Benjamin Franklin, characterized writing as a three-part process that modern writing teachers would immediately recognize as generating ideas, planning, and drafting. This conception of writing as a process was widely shared by Quackenbos and other 19th-century rhetoricians, including Alexander Bain, Henry Day, John F. Genung, Adams Sherman Hill, and David Hill, and these ideas influenced writing instruction well into the 20th century. Yet, as scholars such as James Berlin, Sharon Crowley, David R. Russell, and Richard Young have argued, prior to the early 1980s most writing instruction in higher education involved a highly reductive notion of what aspects of writing could and could not be taught.

The ways in which writing was taught began to change only after three groups of scholars came into conflict — and eventually into a semblance of cooperative co-existence. In the 1960s (but with strong roots going back to the early 20th century), a group of writing scholars took an *expressivist* perspective on writing. Expressivists, including Peter Elbow, Ken Macrorie, and Donald Murray, argued that good writing resulted from a search for an authentic voice that expressed a genuine self. Writing, these scholars believed, could be learned — through experience and with feedback from teachers and other writers — but it couldn't be taught directly. To become a writer, you needed to write.

In the 1970s and 1980s, another group of writing scholars began studying the cognitive processes writers used as they wrote. *Cognitive rhetoricians* John R. Hayes and Linda Flower, for example, developed an influential model (which Hayes has continued to refine) of the composing process that focuses on planning (setting goals, generating ideas, and organizing ideas), drafting, and reviewing and revising — all of which interact with the writer's memory, the tools used during composing, and the writing situation. Other important models, all emerging from studies of writers as they composed, were developed by Carl Bereiter, Janet Emig, Ann Matsuhashi, Sondra Perl, and Marlene Scardamalia, among others. Eventually, recognizing their response to the important role played by social context in cognition, these scholars came to be referred to as *socio-cognitive rhetoricians*.

In the early to late 1980s, *social epistemic rhetoricians* argued that we needed to look at the various contexts in which writers worked. Scholars including David Bartholomae, James Berlin, Patricia Bizzell, Joseph Harris, and James Porter, among many others, argued from various historical and theoretical perspectives that the thinking of the individual — cognition — is linked deeply and inseparably to social interaction. Essentially, they argued, no one is an island; we are all connected to each other through language and those connections shape how we think and what we do.

Since these critical debates in the 1970s, 1980s, and 1990s, writing scholars have looked broadly at issues that extend fairly naturally from the ideas that writing is a form of expression that requires complex thinking processes and that these processes are shaped in important ways by social, political, cultural, historical, and technological forces. Applying a wide variety of theoretical lenses, ranging from feminism to cultural materialism to various forms of critical theory and critical pedagogy, writing scholars have approached the question of writing processes by exploring the cultural, historical, and political aspects of writing, by looking at the interactions between writing and technology, and by looking at the place of writing in a complex, multiracial, multiethnic, gender-inclusive world. Some of these scholars have argued for a "post-process" perspective on writing, contending that it is useful to look beyond the questions that preoccupied writing scholarship as it established itself as a distinct discipline and to begin to grapple with newer and potentially larger questions about what it means to write and to be a writer.

How Can I Prepare for a Successful Writing Project?

You can improve your chances of successfully completing a writing project by taking ownership of your writing project, creating a writer's notebook, and learning to manage your sources and your time.

Take Ownership

Successful writers have a strong personal investment in what they write. Sometimes this investment comes naturally. You might be interested in a topic, committed to achieving your purposes as a writer, intrigued by the demands of writing for a particular audience, or excited about the challenges of writing a new type of document, such as content for a website or a magazine article. At times, however, you need to create a sense of personal investment by looking for connections between your interests and your writing project. This can be a challenge, particularly when you've been assigned a project that normally wouldn't interest you.

The key to investing yourself in a project you wouldn't normally care about is to make it your own. Look for ways in which your project can help you pursue your personal, professional, and academic interests. Consider how it might help you meet new people or develop new skills. Or look for opportunities associated with the project, such as learning how to build arguments or design documents. Your goal is to find something that appeals to your interests and helps you grow as a writer.

To take ownership of a writing project, carry out the following activities:

- **Explore academic connections.** Is the writing project relevant to work you are doing in other classes or, more generally, in your major or minor? Look for ways that working on this project might help you develop useful academic skills or might expose you to information, ideas, or arguments that allow you to make progress as a student.

- **Consider personal connections.** Sometimes your personal interests — such as hobbies and other activities — can spark an interest in the writing project. Do any of your experiences relate to the project in some way? Will working on this project allow you to develop skills and abilities that might help you in your personal life?

- **Look for professional connections.** Does the writing project have any relevance to the job you currently have or one day hope to have? Will working on this project help you develop skills or expose you to information, ideas, or arguments that might be relevant to your professional goals?

Create a Writer's Notebook

A writer's notebook — where you can keep the sources you collect along the way and record your thoughts, observations, and progress — can help you keep track of what you find and think about as you work on your project. A writer's notebook can take many forms:

- a notebook
- a word-processing file or a folder on your computer
- a folder or binder
- a set of note cards

- notes taken on a smartphone or a tablet
- a tape recorder or voice recorder

Although it might seem like extra work now, creating a writer's notebook at the beginning of your project will save you time in the long run.

Manage Your Time

Time management should be a high priority as you begin your writing project. Without adequate time management, you might, for example, spend far too much time collecting information and far too little time working with it. As you begin to think about your writing project, consider creating a project timeline. A project timeline can help you identify important milestones in your project and determine when you need to meet them.

Your Turn: Create a Project Timeline

In your writer's notebook, create a project timeline like the one shown here. The steps in your process might be slightly different, but most writing projects involve these general stages. As you create your timeline, keep in mind any specific deadlines given in your assignment, such as the dates when you must hand in first drafts and revised drafts.

Project Timeline

Activity	Start date	Completion date
Analyze your assignment		
Generate ideas		
Collect and read potential sources		
Choose a focus		
Develop your ideas		
Write a first draft		
Review and revise your first draft		
Write and revise additional drafts		
Polish your final draft		
Edit for accuracy and correctness		
Finalize in-text citations and works cited list		

In Summary: Understanding Yourself as a Writer

* Think of writing as a form of conversation (p. 5).

* Understand the rhetorical nature of writing situations (p. 13).

* Learn about genre and design (p. 21).

* Understand composing processes (p. 27).

* Lay the foundation for a successful writing project by taking ownership of your project, creating a writer's notebook, and managing your time (p. 32).

 # Finding and Listening In on Conversations

▶▶ In the most general sense, getting started on a writing project involves "listening in" on conversations and choosing one that interests you. To begin this process, analyze your assignment and generate ideas about potential topics. Then spend time learning about the conversations that interest you most.

How Can I Analyze an Assignment?

Writers in academic and professional settings usually work in response to an assignment. You might be given general guidelines; you might be asked to choose a topic within a general subject area; or you might be given complete freedom. No matter how much freedom you have, however, your assignment will provide important clues about what your instructor and your other readers will expect.

A close reading of an assignment can reveal not only its basic requirements and goals but also useful information about your purpose, readers, sources, and context. Most important, a close reading can help you develop a successful response to the assignment.

Assess Your Writing Situation

What you write about depends on your writing situation — your purpose, readers, sources, and context. In many cases, your assignment will identify or suggest these elements for you. If it doesn't, take some time to think about the situation that will shape your work.

DETERMINE YOUR PURPOSE

Every writer has a purpose, or reason, for writing. In fact, most writers have multiple purposes (see pp. 13–15). In Chapters 6 through 11, you'll explore a range of goals that you might be asked to pursue: to reflect, to inform, to analyze, to evaluate, to solve problems, and to convince or persuade. You will also bring your personal goals to a writing project, such as learning something new, improving your writing skills, convincing others to adopt your point of view, gaining respect from others, getting a good grade, or earning a promotion.

DETERMINE WHO YOUR READERS ARE AND WHAT MOTIVATES THEM

Your assignment might identify your readers, or audience, for you. If you are working on a project for a class, one of your most important readers will be your instructor. Other readers might include your classmates, people who have a professional or personal interest in your topic, or if your project will be published, the readers of a particular newspaper, magazine, or website. If you are writing in a business or professional setting, your readers might include supervisors, customers, or other people associated with the organization. You can read more about readers on page 15.

The choice of topic is left to the writer, although some general guidelines are provided. The purpose is discussed here and in the requirements section.	**Essay Assignment** For this assignment, you'll identify and describe a problem that affects veterans as they return from active duty. Your purpose will be to inform members of your community about how the problem affects them, the consequences of not addressing the problem, and the costs of addressing it effectively. **Due Date:** October 1, at the beginning of class
The assignment specifies the readers and defines the role the instructor will play as a reader.	**Your Readers:** Your audience will be the members of your community. I will also be a reader, but my primary role will be to consider how well you've addressed the members of your community. **Essay Requirements:** Your essay should be between 750 and 1,000 words in length. Your essay should
The genre is identified as a standard academic essay.	• introduce the problem you are addressing • describe the potential effects of the problem
The repeated use of the words *problem* and *solution* indicates that the writer's purpose is to write a problem-solving essay.	• propose a solution to the problem • estimate the costs of putting the solution into effect • support your points with evidence (personal experience, information from sources)
Aside from the due date, requirements are listed in a separate section. Key requirements include length, content, and documentation system.	• clearly document your sources following MLA style Conclude your essay by doing more than simply summarizing what you've said so far. In general, try to leave your readers with something to think about after they've read your essay. Finally, revise to clarify and strengthen your argument, and edit to remove errors in spelling, grammar, and mechanics so that your writing is clear and readable.
The assignment requires students to turn in not only the final essay but also rough drafts, homework, and comments on classmates' drafts.	**Format:** Please submit your essay in a folder clearly labeled with your name and e-mail address. Your folder should contain the following: • the final draft of your essay, formatted with one-inch margins, double-spaced lines, and a readable (e.g., not italic or script) 12-point font • rough drafts of your essay • a list of additional sources you consulted as you created your essay • the homework you completed as you worked on your essay • the workshop comments you received from your classmates on drafts of your essay • your workshop comments on your classmates' essays

▲ Essay assignment

CONSIDER THE ROLE OF SOURCES

Most documents are influenced by the work of other writers (see pp. 16–17). As you analyze an assignment, determine whether you'll need to draw on information from other sources, such as magazine or journal articles, websites, or scholarly books. Ask whether you'll need to cite a minimum or a maximum number of sources and whether you're required to use a specific documentation system, such as the Modern Language Association (MLA) or the American Psychological Association (APA) styles.

Whether or not an assignment provides guidelines for sources, ask what you'll need to learn to complete your project, and then identify potential information resources. You can read more about finding and using sources in Part Three of this book.

IDENTIFY THE CONTEXT AND GENRE

Context refers to the physical, social, disciplinary, and cultural settings that shape the writing and reading of a document (see pp. 17–19). To identify the context for your writing project, ask whether your document will be read in print or online. Ask whether it will need to take the form of a particular genre (or type of document), such as a report, an opinion column, a blog post, or a multimedia presentation. Consider how social and cultural contexts — such as recent events and shared history — will shape the attitudes and understanding of your readers. Consider as well how the genre and context will influence your decisions as a writer.

Note Requirements, Limitations, and Opportunities

Your analysis should identify your assignment's requirements. You should also consider potential limitations and look for opportunities. Being aware of these factors will help you weigh the potential drawbacks of choosing a particular topic. In the face of a looming due date or a limited word count, for example, you might find that you need to narrow the scope of a topic significantly.

Requirements can include

- required length or word count
- due date
- number and type of sources you must use (digital, print, and field)
- suggested or required resources
- document organization (title page, introduction, body, conclusion, works cited list, and so on)
- documentation format (such as MLA, APA, *Chicago*, or CSE)
- intermediate reports or activities due before you turn in the final document (such as thesis statements, notes, outlines, and rough drafts)

Limitations might include lack of access to sources, insufficient time to work on a project, or limited access to software or hardware (such as printers or video cameras) that would help you produce a quality document.

Sometimes writers get so wrapped up in the requirements and limitations of an assignment that they overlook their opportunities. As you think about possible topics, ask whether you can take advantage of opportunities such as

- access to a specialized or particularly good library
- personal experience with and knowledge about a topic
- access to experts on a topic

Working Together: Analyze an Assignment

Work together with your classmates to analyze your assignment. Use the following prompts to guide your analysis:

1. **Determine whether a topic has been assigned.** If a topic has been assigned, look for indications of how you should address the topic. If you are allowed to choose your own topic, look for indications of what the instructor considers an appropriate topic.

2. **Examine the assignment for discussions of purpose.** What purposes might a writer pursue through this assignment? Identify your own purposes — personal, professional, academic — and those of your classmates for working on this assignment.

3. **Identify and describe potential readers.** Describe their likely needs, interests, backgrounds, and knowledge of the topic. Ask why readers would want to read your document.

4. **Determine the role of sources in your document.** Identify potential sources of information that will help you learn about your topic. Then determine whether you need to cite a

minimum number of sources or use a specific documentation system, such as MLA or APA.

5. **Identify the context in which the document will be written and read.** For example, will your document be read in print or online? How have historic or recent events shaped your readers' understanding of and attitudes toward your topic?

6. **Identify the genre, if any, defined by the assignment.** If the assignment leaves the choice of genre open, identify genres that are well suited to the assignment.

7. **Understand requirements and limitations.** Look for specific requirements and limitations, such as document length and due date, that will affect your ability to address a particular topic. Identify other requirements, such as number of sources, document structure, documentation system, and intermediate assignments or rough drafts.

8. **List potential opportunities.** Identify opportunities that might save time or enhance the quality of the document.

How Can I Find Interesting Conversations?

Writers aren't mindless robots who create documents without emotion or conviction — or at least they shouldn't be. One of the most important things you can do as a writer is to look for a conversation that will hold your interest as you work on your writing project.

Even if you are assigned a specific topic, you can almost always find an approach that will engage you and still accomplish the goals of the assignment. In fact, most successful writers have learned to deal with "boring" topics by creating personal or professional connections to them. Essentially, they try to convince themselves that they actually care about a topic — and in many cases, they end up developing a genuine interest. You can do this by generating ideas and asking questions about potential topics, taking care not to rule out any topics until you've given them a chance.

Generate Ideas

You can generate ideas about possible topics of conversation by using prewriting activities such as brainstorming, freewriting, blindwriting or dictating, looping, clustering, mapping, and using sentence starters. These activities are useful not only for deciding which topics interest you most but also for identifying a focus that is well suited to your writing situation.

BRAINSTORM

Brainstorming involves making a list of ideas as they occur to you. This list should not consist of complete sentences — in fact, brainstorming is most successful when you avoid censoring yourself. Don't worry about weeding out ideas. You'll have time for that later.

Brainstorming sessions usually respond to a specific question, such as "What interests me personally about this project?" or "Why would anyone care about _____?" For example, Henry Garcia, a student in the same writing course as Gina Colville (see p. 7), was planning to pursue a career in marketing. That semester, he had joined the staff of the college newspaper to gain some practical experience as a writer. He drew on his experiences as he brainstormed the following list in response to the question "What do I want to learn from a writing course?"

How to write a good argument   *How to connect with my readers*

How to use sources   *How to prep for my career*

How to have a good style   *Which courses to take next*

How to use good grammar   *Whether I like this career idea*

This brainstorming list helped Henry recognize that he might take a reflective approach to the assignment, contemplating his own plans for a career in light of what he might learn from articles and other sources that address his topic.

FREEWRITE

Freewriting involves writing full sentences quickly, without stopping and — most important — without editing what you write. You might want to start with one of the ideas you generated in your brainstorming activity, or you could begin your freewriting session with a prompt, such as "I am interested in _____ because . . ." Some writers set a timer and freewrite for five, ten, or fifteen minutes; others set a goal of a certain number of pages and keep writing until they meet that goal.

After brainstorming about what he wanted to learn from a writing course, Henry freewrote about how to connect with his readers' purposes and interests.

> *I'll have to find a way to explain it and make a career in marketing interesting. I don't have a lot of experiences to draw on, just some work with my high school newspaper and now at Front Range. But maybe those experiences writing for an audience can come in handy as I learn to develop a marketing campaign. In all those situations, I think you need to get in people's heads, figure out their interests and what drives them, get a sense of what they want and need.*

To freewrite, write as much as you can, don't pause to consider whether your sentences are "good" or "bad," and don't pay attention to details such as spelling and grammar. If all this work results in a single good idea, your freewriting session will be a success.

BLINDWRITE OR DICTATE

If you find it difficult to freewrite without editing, try blindwriting — freewriting on a computer with the monitor turned off. Or consider dictating. Many smartphones and tablets allow you to speak your thoughts aloud and convert them immediately to text. These forms of freewriting can take your focus away from generating text, largely because you can carry them out without looking at the screen.

LOOP

Looping is yet another form of freewriting. During a looping session, you write (or dictate) for a set amount of time (five minutes works well) and then read what you've written. As you read, identify one key idea in what you've written, and then repeat the process with this new idea as your starting point. If you're using a word-processing program, you can copy the sentence and paste it below your freewriting; if you are writing by hand, highlight or draw a circle around the sentence. Repeat the looping process as needed to refine your ideas.

Henry's looping session built on the last sentence of his freewriting exercise.

> I could think about how you need to get in people's heads, figure out their interests and what drives them, get a sense of what they want and need. I like that aspect of marketing, and of writing, too. It's a challenge for marketing professionals to make consumers pay attention to the product or service you are offering, just like it's a

challenge for reporters to grab the attention of their readers. People are bombarded by so much media and advertising these days that good marketing and good writing need to stand out to get noticed. That's what I really want to practice in this course.

CLUSTER

Clustering involves putting your ideas about a topic into graphic form. As you map out the relationships among your ideas, clustering can help you gain a different perspective on a topic. It can also help you generate new ideas.

Henry created the cluster on page 45 to explore the topic of connecting his writing class to a career in marketing.

To cluster ideas about a topic, place your main idea, or a general topic that interests you, at the center of a page. Jot down key ideas — such as subcategories, causes and effects, or reasons supporting an argument — around the main idea. Then create clusters of ideas that branch out from the key ideas. In these clusters, list groups of related ideas, evidence, effects, causes, consequences — in short, ideas that are related to your key ideas.

MAP

Mapping is similar to clustering in that it places related ideas about a topic in graphic form. Unlike clustering, however, mapping helps you define the relationships among your ideas. The practice is especially helpful if you are exploring a topic in terms of causes and effects, sequences of events, costs and benefits, or advantages and disadvantages. For example, you might create a map to predict what would happen if cigarette taxes were doubled. Or you might create a map to identify factors that led to an oil spill along the Oregon coast.

Henry used his word-processing program to create a map that explored the kinds of courses he might take to prepare for a career in marketing (see p. 46).

To map a topic, place your main idea at the top of a page. If you are looking at more than one aspect of a topic, such as costs and benefits, list as many relationships as you can think of. If you are looking at causes and effects, start with a single effect. Then explore the topic by identifying related causes and effects, costs and benefits, advantages and disadvantages, and so on. For example, if you are mapping a topic using causes and effects, treat each effect as a new cause by asking yourself, "If this happened, what would happen next?" Then use arrows to show the consequences. If you are mapping a topic using costs and benefits, show groups of costs and identify the relationships among them.

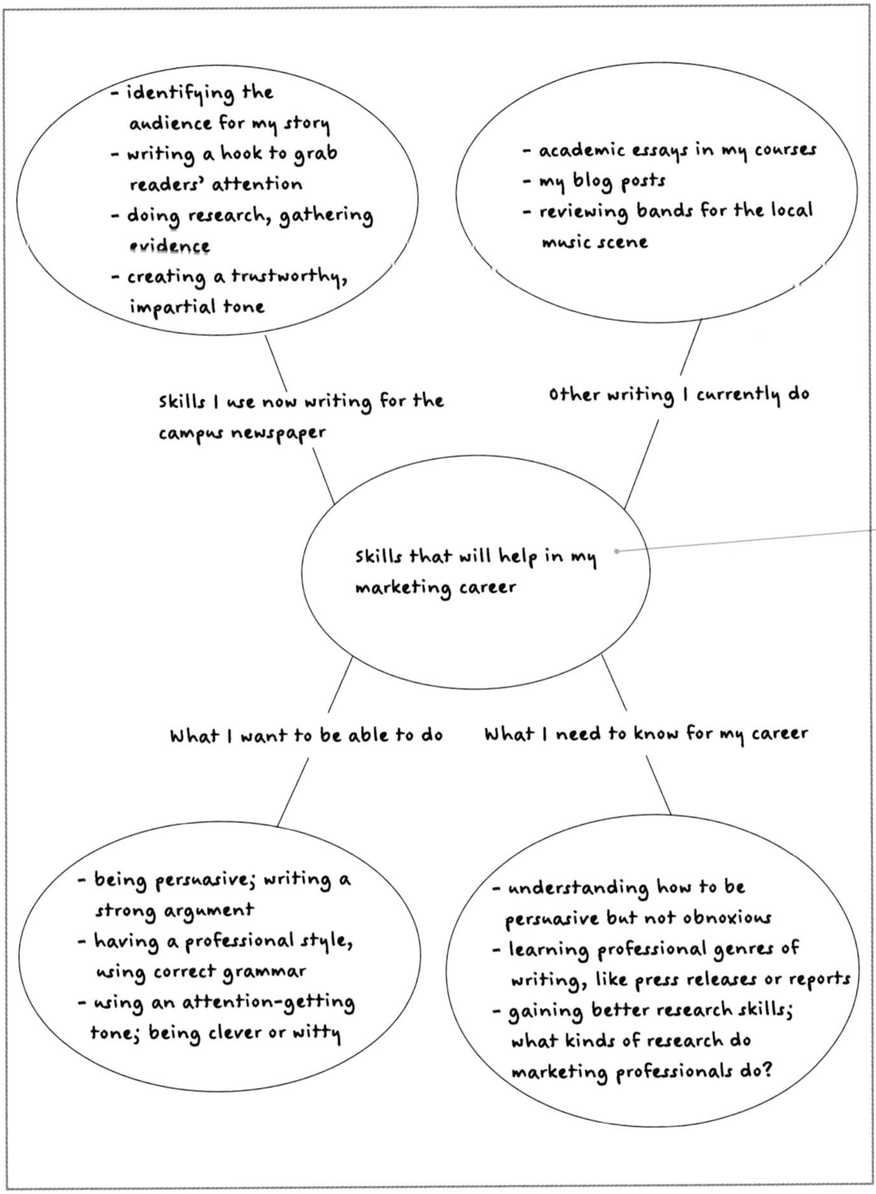
- identifying the audience for my story
- writing a hook to grab readers' attention
- doing research, gathering evidence
- creating a trustworthy, impartial tone
- academic essays in my courses
- my blog posts
- reviewing bands for the local music scene
Skills I use now writing for the campus newspaper
Other writing I currently do
Skills that will help in my marketing career
What I want to be able to do
What I need to know for my career
- being persuasive; writing a strong argument
- having a professional style, using correct grammar
- using an attention-getting tone; being clever or witty
- understanding how to be persuasive but not obnoxious
- learning professional genres of writing, like press releases or reports
- gaining better research skills; what kinds of research do marketing professionals do?

Henry has listed a central idea and four key areas.

▲ **A cluster of ideas about preparing for a career in marketing**

Henry listed a central idea and then mapped its advantages and disadvantages.

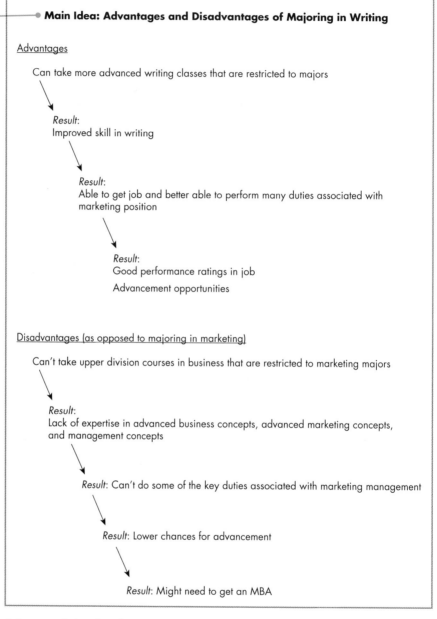

● **Main Idea: Advantages and Disadvantages of Majoring in Writing**

<u>Advantages</u>

Can take more advanced writing classes that are restricted to majors

> *Result*:
> Improved skill in writing

> > *Result*:
> > Able to get job and better able to perform many duties associated with marketing position

> > > *Result*:
> > > Good performance ratings in job
> > > Advancement opportunities

<u>Disadvantages (as opposed to majoring in marketing)</u>

Can't take upper division courses in business that are restricted to marketing majors

> *Result*:
> Lack of expertise in advanced business concepts, advanced marketing concepts, and management concepts

> > *Result*: Can't do some of the key duties associated with marketing management

> > > *Result*: Lower chances for advancement

> > > > *Result*: Might need to get an MBA

▲ **A map exploring the advantages and disadvantages of majoring in writing versus majoring in marketing**

USE SENTENCE STARTERS

Sentence starters help you generate ideas by "filling in the blanks" in each sentence. Here's a sentence starter a writer used to generate ideas about her writing assignment:

> **Sentence Starter:** Although we know that _____, we also know that _____.
>
> Although we know that the growing opposition to standardized testing in high schools should encourage more teachers to use writing assignments instead, we also know that most high school teachers typically teach so many students that it can be difficult to respond effectively to all of those assignments.

There are nearly as many sentence starters as there are ideas about how to structure a sentence. You can make up your own or you can try some of the following.

Exploring Interests

I would like to understand [how / why / whether] _____ happened.

I want to know more about _____, especially the aspects of _____.

I am interested in _____ because _____.

Explaining

There are three reasons this is [true / not true / relevant / important / essential]. First, _____. Second, _____. Third, _____.

We can [change / improve / fix] this by _____.

To accomplish _____, we must _____.

People do this because _____.

We were trying to _____, but we ended up _____.

Interpreting and Analyzing

This means that _____.

If we were starting over, we would _____.

It has always been the case that _____.

Understanding Causes and Effects

When I was _____, I decided _____. That decision has _____.

When I was _____, I believed _____. But now I believe _____.

The root cause of this problem is _____.

This happened because _____.

Predicting

When this happens, _____.

We would prefer that _____ is true, but we must recognize that _____.

Too often, we _____.

If we _____, then _____.

Stating Beliefs

I believe _____.

We have to _____.

I want to _____.

Exploring Possibilities

If this is [true / happening / important], then _____.

Sometimes, _____.

We could _____

How can we _____?

Evaluating

The most important aspect of _____ is _____.

This is better because _____.

Comparing and Contrasting

Like _____, _____.

Unlike _____, _____.

I know _____, but I don't know _____.

Ask Questions

When you have completed your brainstorming, freewriting, blindwriting or dictating, looping, clustering, mapping, or sentence starter activities, review what you've written. In all likelihood, these idea-generating techniques have provided you with a useful list of ideas for a topic. You can select the strongest candidate and generate additional ideas by asking questions. Writers often ask questions to

- define a topic
- evaluate a topic
- consider goals
- explore potential outcomes
- consider appropriate courses of action
- compare and contrast topics
- understand causes and effects
- solve problems

Each of the chapters in Part Two provides a series of questions that will help you narrow your focus and explore ideas for a particular kind of writing project. You can create your own exploratory questions by pairing question words — *what, why, when, where, who, how, would, could, should* — with words and phrases that focus on different aspects of a topic.

For example, Gina generated the following questions to explore and focus her topic on how to prepare high school teachers to teach writing:

> *What are the biggest challenges facing high school writing teachers?*
>
> *What kinds of support do teachers who use writing in their courses need?*
>
> *Which kind of feedback did I get on my writing assignments in high school? How useful was it?*
>
> *Should the state mandate particular types of writing assignments?*

As you ask questions, be aware of the role you are adopting as a writer. If you are writing an informative essay, for example, the words *what, when,* and *where* are appropriate. If you are conducting an analysis, you might use the words *why* and *how.* If you are interested in goals and outcomes, try the words *would* and *could.* If you want to determine an appropriate course of action, ask questions using the word *should.*

The questions you ask will probably change as you learn more about a topic, so it's best to think of them as flexible and open-ended. By continuing to ask questions that reflect your growing understanding of a topic, you can build a solid foundation for your own contribution to the conversation.

Your Turn: Find a Topic That Interests You

Generate ideas for possible writing topics by conducting at least three of the prewriting activities described on pages 41–49: brainstorming, freewriting, blindwriting or dictating, looping, clustering, mapping, using sentence starters, and asking questions. Then use your responses to the following prompts to decide which topic interests you most.

1. What are the three most important topics I have identified so far?

2. Of these topics, which one will best sustain my interest in this project?

3. Which one will best help me achieve my purposes as a writer?

4. Which one will best address my readers' needs, interests, and backgrounds?

5. Which one best fits the requirements of my assignment?

6. Which one is most appropriate for the type of document I plan to write?

7. Which one has the fewest limitations?

8. Which one allows me to best take advantage of opportunities?

9. Based on these answers, the topic I want to choose is _____.

How Can I "Listen In" on Written Conversations?

If you've chosen a topic that appeals to more than a few individuals, you can be sure it's the subject of several ongoing conversations. Listening in on these conversations can familiarize you with various aspects of the topic. Written conversations about the broad topic of federal regulation of new drugs, for example, might focus on issues such as childhood vaccination, prevention of birth defects, and the treatment of illnesses such as AIDS and Alzheimer's disease. Each of these issues, in turn, might be addressed by different groups of people, often for quite different purposes. Childhood vaccination, for instance, might draw the attention of parents worried about potential side effects, health officials concerned about epidemics, and researchers interested in the growth of drug-resistant diseases.

Listening in on these conversations allows you to determine which group you want to join. To make that decision, you don't have to engage in a full-blown research project. You simply have to invest enough time to determine whether you want to learn more. At this early stage in your writing project, you are essentially eavesdropping in order to find the conversation you want to join.

To learn more about each of the conversations you've identified and to figure out what — or whether — you might contribute to it, "listen in" by discussing your ideas with others, observing a situation firsthand, and finding and reviewing published sources.

Discuss the Topic with Others

Discussing your writing project can provide insights you might not find on your own. Identify resources by talking with an instructor, a supervisor, or a librarian. Learn what other people think about a topic by conducting interviews (see p. 499). Gather information and insights by corresponding with experts or with people who have been affected by a topic (see p. 511). Get a sense of how readers might respond to your ideas by posting on Facebook, Tumblr, or Twitter and seeing how your friends respond to your ideas.

Observe the Topic Firsthand

Observing something for yourself allows you to learn about a topic without filtering it through the interpretation of other writers. If you are considering a topic that focuses on a particular place, event, or activity, you might want to conduct one or more observations. If you're interested in a local issue, attend a community meeting and listen to what people have to say. If you're interested in the impact of parental involvement in youth sports, spend time at a youth soccer game. If you're interested in the effects of fast food on health, you might watch people place their orders at a fast-food restaurant. For more on planning and conducting observations, see page 503.

Read What Others Have Written

Even if you are familiar with a topic, you need to learn as much about it as you can before you begin to write. Reading what others have written about a topic will help you gather new information and ideas; it is also an important step in identifying conversations and determining which ones interest you.

- **Search online library catalogs** for sources using title, author, and subject words. Before you begin your search, generate a list of words and phrases that are related to the topic you want to explore.

- **Browse library shelves** to find sources related to those you've already located. Review the works cited lists, footnotes, endnotes, or in-text citations or particularly useful sources. Then find and review these cited sources.

- **Visit the periodicals room** to find the latest magazines, newspapers, and scholarly journals.

- **Search databases** just as you would search an online library catalog. To identify relevant databases, ask a reference librarian for assistance.

- **Search the Web** using the search terms you used for your catalog and database searches. Remember, though, that many Web-based sources will not have undergone the same scholarly review process applied to sources in library catalogs and databases.

- **Browse the Web** by following useful links from one site to another.

- **Use social media** since tweets, Facebook updates, or blog posts on your topic can lead to other relevant sources.

- **Visit online discussion groups**, such as e-mail lists, newsgroups, and Web discussion forums, to find everything from expert opinions to the musings of people who know little or nothing about a topic. If you read with a bit of skepticism, however, you can begin to learn about the issues surrounding a topic.

To learn more about using digital and print sources, see Chapters 12 and 13.

Review Your Sources

As you learn about a topic, you'll begin the process of focusing your attention on a specific issue — a point of disagreement, uncertainty, concern, or curiosity that is being discussed by a community of readers and writers. Look for patterns in the information, ideas, and arguments you encounter.

- **Notice central concepts.** When several sources refer to the same idea, you can assume that this information is central to the topic.

- **Find broad themes.** Sources that discuss the same general theme are most likely involved in the same conversation. By recognizing these broad themes, you can identify some of the key issues addressed in the conversations about your topic.

- **Look for disagreements.** Some sources will explicitly indicate that they disagree with the arguments, ideas, or information in other sources. If you look for explicit statements of disagreement, you can identify a group of sources that are engaged in conversation with one another.

- **Recognize recurring voices.** You might find that some authors write frequently about your topic or that some are cited frequently. These authors might have significant experience or expertise related to the topic, or they might represent particular perspectives on the topic.

You can learn more about searching for patterns for sources and other critical reading strategies in Chapter 3.

Your Turn: Choose a Conversation

Take the topic you selected at the end of the activity on page 49, and listen in on a few of the conversations taking place about it. You might discuss this topic with other people, conduct an observation, or read a few sources that address your topic. Identify the three most promising conversations you've found. To choose among the conversations, ask the following questions about each one:

1. Will joining this conversation help me accomplish my purpose?

2. Do my readers need to be exposed to this conversation?

3. Do my readers want to be exposed to this conversation?

4. How will my readers' backgrounds affect their reactions to this conversation?

As you review the conversations you've identified, ask what interests you most about each one. At a minimum, you'll want to choose a focus that interests you and is appropriate for your assignment. Ideally, this focus will also match up well with the purposes, needs, interests, and backgrounds of your readers.

In Summary: Finding and Listening In on Conversations

* Get started by analyzing your assignment and assessing your writing situation (p. 37).

* Generate ideas for finding conversations about interesting topics (p. 41).

* Ask questions about the conversations you've found (p. 48).

* Listen in on promising conversations by discussing your topic with others, observing the topic firsthand, and reading what others have written (p. 50).

* Review what you've learned to determine which conversation to join (p. 51).

03 Reading to Write

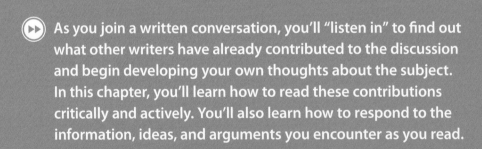

As you join a written conversation, you'll "listen in" to find out what other writers have already contributed to the discussion and begin developing your own thoughts about the subject. In this chapter, you'll learn how to read these contributions critically and actively. You'll also learn how to respond to the information, ideas, and arguments you encounter as you read.

How Can I Read Critically?

Reading critically means reading with an attitude. It also means reading with your writing situation in mind. Through critical reading, you can quickly recognize the questions — points of disagreement, uncertainty, concern, or curiosity — that are under discussion in a written conversation as well as think about how you'll respond to one of these questions.

Read with an Attitude

As you learn about and prepare to contribute to a written conversation, both your point of view and your attitude are likely to change. Initially, you might be curious, noting new information in sources and marking key passages that provide insights. Later, as you determine whether sources fit into the conversation or are reliable, you might adopt a more questioning attitude. Eventually, after you begin to draw conclusions about the conversation, you might become skeptical and more willing to challenge the arguments you read.

Growing familiarity with and understanding of an issue ———————➤

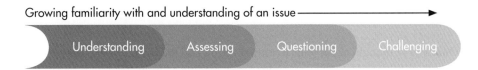

Understanding   Assessing   Questioning   Challenging

Regardless of where you are in your writing process, you should always adopt a critical attitude. Accept nothing at face value; ask questions; look for similarities and differences among the sources you read; examine the implications of what you read for your writing project; be on the alert for unusual information; and note relevant sources and information. Most important, be open to ideas and arguments, even if you don't agree with them. Give them a chance to affect how you think about the conversation you've decided to join.

Consider Writing Situations

Reading critically involves approaching each source with an awareness not only of your own writing situation but also of the writing situation that shaped the source. Remember that each document you read was written to accomplish a particular purpose and was intended for a particular group of readers. Realize that the physical, social, disciplinary, and cultural settings in which the document was produced affected how the writer presented information, ideas, and arguments. And be aware that the writing situation that helped produce the source might differ significantly from your own.

As you read, remember what you are trying to accomplish. Your purpose will affect your assessment of the information, ideas, and arguments you encounter. Moreover, your readers' purposes, needs, interests, and backgrounds will affect how you use what you've learned.

Finally, and perhaps most important, remember that you are working on your writing project to make a contribution, to shape your readers' thinking about your subject. Avoid being overly deferential to the authors who have written before you. You should respect their work, but don't assume that their conclusions about the subject are the last word. Be prepared to challenge their ideas and arguments. If you don't do this, there's little point in writing, for you'll simply repeat the ideas of others instead of advancing your own.

What Strategies Can I Use to Read Actively?

Once you've thought about your writing situation and the writing situations that shaped your sources, you're ready to start reading actively. Reading actively means interacting with sources and considering them in light of the conversation you've decided to join. When you read actively, you might do one or more of the following:

- skim the source to get a general sense of what it's about
- write questions in the margins
- jot down your reactions
- identify key information, ideas, and arguments
- note how you might use information, ideas, and arguments in your document
- visually link one part of the source to another
- identify important passages for later rereading

To read actively, focus on three strategies: skimming, marking and annotating, and examining sources closely.

Identify the type of document to remind yourself of typical purposes, forms of evidence, and conventions of a genre. This page is part of an article from the professional journal *Educational Leadership*.

Check the title (and table of contents, if one is provided) for cues about content.

Skim opening paragraphs to learn about the purpose and scope of the document.

Check headings and subheadings to learn about content and organization.

Look for pull quotes (quotations or passages called out into the margins or set in larger type) for a sense of the writer's main idea.

Read the first and last sentences of paragraphs to find key information.

Skim captions of photos and figures, which often highlight important arguments, ideas, and information.

Look for publication information, such as journal title and publication date.

G·U·I·D·I·N·G
the Budding Writer

How we comment on students' work can give students a larger vision for their own potential.

Peter Johnston

If teachers commit to **involving students in personally meaningful projects,** productive feedback will follow.

▲ **How to skim a print document**

Skim for an Overview

Before investing too much time in a source, skim it. Skimming — reading just enough to get the general idea of what a source is about — can tell you a great deal in a short amount of time and is an important first step in reading a source critically. To skim sources, glance at surface elements without delving too deeply into the content.

Quinn Jackson, a student working on an assignment in the same writing-about-writing course as Gina Colville (see p. 7) and Henry Garcia (see p. 41), used skimming to gain a quick overview of an article published in *Educational Leadership*. The article explored the impact of teacher comments on student writing. She also skimmed the journal's website to locate additional articles on the topic.

Guiding the Budding Writer

How we comment on students' work can give students a larger vision for their own potential.

Peter Johnston

Thomas Newkirk, a seasoned and successful writer, once took a draft of his writing to the Pulitzer Prize–winning author Donald Murray for feedback. After scanning the draft, Murray simply asked, "What's this about?" His question caused Newkirk to reflect on this piece of writing and better focus it by cutting the first three pages (Newkirk, 2012, p. 116).

Four-year-old Abby had a similar experience when she made a book in preschool and showed it to educator Matt Glover. Matt asked her what the book was about. Seeing that she didn't understand his question, he said, "Remember how *Owl Babies* was all about the owls and their mommy, and Tessa's book was all about a butterfly and a lady? What's your book about?" (Ray & Glover, 2008, p. 144).

In both these cases, feedback helped develop the authors' vision for themselves and their work. Both anecdotes shed light on the relationship between feedback and the development of authors of all ages. Let's consider the significance of the feedback for Abby. With two sentences, Matt helped her understand that books are *about* something, that a book is an important social contract. He accomplished this by drawing Abby's attention to a helpful resource for reflection — other authors' work. He made it clear that Abby is an author, just like Martin Waddell, who wrote *Owl Babies*, and Tessa, who wrote about the lady and the butterfly.

Matt's feedback positioned Abby to begin to think, as authors do, about other authors' work and what she might learn from them. In response to this feedback and the related classroom conversations, Abby began to have conversations with her peers about their writing. Thus Matt began the process of making Abby independent of her teachers' feedback. This is one thing effective feedback accomplishes; beyond improving one particular book, essay, or assignment, it has a larger vision. Matt's feedback looked to the future, inviting Abby to become the kind of person who makes books about something and who observes work by people similar to herself to learn new possibilities.

Four Truths about Feedback

These examples illustrate four important points about feedback that we often miss. First, giving feedback doesn't necessarily mean telling students what's good or bad. Actually, it doesn't necessarily mean *telling* them anything; notice how Donald Murray and Matt Glover began with questions.

Second, feedback should be inseparable from the larger classroom conversations. Matt's feedback to Abby didn't stand alone. Abby's preschool teacher had already fostered conversations that drew attention to the choices authors make and the logic of those choices. We might call this *public feedback*. In a 1st grade class, public feedback might include observations like,

> I notice Jamal made this word big and bold and in uppercase letters with an exclamation point. That means he wants me to read it very loudly. Remember how in *Roller Coaster*, Marla Frazee wrote the word WHOOSH in big uppercase letters, too?

Such public feedback is part of the same conversation that identifies students as authors. It draws the classroom community's attention to processes that inform authors' decisions. Adding, "That means he wants me to read it very loudly" reminds students that the teacher, now in the role of reader, is partly under the control of the writer, thus focusing young authors on strategic thinking in relation to readers.

Similarly, when reading *What Happened to Cass McBride?* to 8th graders, the teacher might say, "I wonder why Gail Giles chose to use so many flashbacks in the story." Such conversations about authors' mental processes have an additional benefit. They require imagining what's going on in another person's mind. The more students practice imagining authors' thinking, the more they are inclined to do so independently and to become better writers and readers. At the same time, as students imagine fellow authors' thoughts and feelings, their social imagination expands — which leads to better social behavior (Johnston, 2012).

Third, feedback is not merely cognitive in reach, nor merely corrective in function. Like the rest of classroom talk, feedback affects the ways students understand themselves and one another — how they perceive themselves as writers. When a teacher draws a student's attention to the compositional choices he or she made to construct a convincing argument, the teacher invites that student to construct a self-narrative that says, I did *x* (added a detail to my illustration of a key point), the consequence of which was *y* (I got my meaning across better). This kind of feedback positions students as people who can accomplish things by acting strategically.

Fourth, optimal feedback is responsive, meaning it's adjusted to what the individual writer is likely to need. To give Abby feedback, Matt had to know something about what young authors

> If teachers commit to involving students in personally meaningful projects, productive feedback will follow.

need to understand—and he had to recognize the signs of her understanding.

Teachers who want to provide feedback that strengthens each learner's writing skills, motivation, and independence should keep five principles in mind. Although I've used writing as the focus of my examples, the same principles hold for other areas of academic learning.

> Feedback sets in motion conversations that affect how students make sense of themselves.

Five Key Principles
1. Context matters.
Context affects feedback. When students are fully engaged, we can provide ample differentiated feedback to individuals because we don't have to worry about managing the behavior of other students. Students who are working on something personally and socially meaningful know when they need feedback and come looking for it (Ivey & Johnston, 2012), and they are more receptive to critical feedback. By contrast, a student reading an unengaging text or doing a math problem that's too difficult will likely disengage. Teachers' feedback will then be about behavior rather than academic learning, and any academic feedback will likely be given too quickly, leaving little thinking time and undermining the student's control. If teachers commit to involving students in personally meaningful projects, productive feedback will follow.

There are, of course, contexts in which feedback is unlikely to be heard. When we give a grade as part of our feedback, students routinely read only as far as the grade. In general, students value feedback less after the work is completed than when it's still in progress. If we give a writer more control over the feedback—such as by asking what aspect of the work he or she would like feedback on—the writer is more likely to tune in.

2. Teachers aren't the sole source.
Feedback comes from other students as much as from teachers—which is a good thing if we capitalize on it. When we teach students to teach as well as to learn about good writing, feedback becomes more immediately available and plentiful. This means that part of our students' language arts development should involve learning how to give feedback to others—how to respond to other learners. Fostering peer feedback expands the reach of our teaching.

With peer feedback, classroom talk becomes a reflective surface in which students can see their own work. They hear students talking with peers or with the teacher about writing and use those conversations to reflect on their own writing. Ideally, community conversations will respond to all students' efforts. Students will then have a forum in which they can request feedback from peers and teach others.

3. A focus on process empowers students.
Responsive feedback communities use three key practices. The first is listening. Until we understand where a person is coming from, it's hard to provide responsive feedback. The second is publicly noticing the significant decisions authors make and encouraging students to do the same. The third practice I call *causal process feedback*. This is feedback on how a student's choices affected the finished product. For example, "Look how you revised that—you added examples of the colonists' complaints against tyranny to your essay. Now I see what you mean" (Ray & Glover, 2008, p. 164). This feedback turns the student's attention to the writing process and makes the student's experience into a tool for future composing. Causal process feedback is at the heart of

building a sense of agency: It helps demystify the skill of writing.

We can turn students' attention to the process by asking something like, "How did you solve that problem with your lead paragraph?" The question invites students to articulate a causal connection between a set of behaviors and an outcome.

Feedback that emphasizes processes helps learners not only persist in the face of difficulty but also find more solutions to problems. Feedback that focuses on effort ("You really tried hard") has the same benefits (Kamins & Dweck, 1999). In my view, however, it's less useful for two reasons. First, you can't say it unless you know the student *did* try hard. Second, a comment focused only on effort misses the chance that other students will overhear — and benefit from — a teacher's comment about how a strategy one student used improved a piece of writing.

4. "Positive" doesn't mean praising.

Positive feedback motivates students and gives them the tools to improve. Teachers often confuse being positive with providing praise. They are not the same. The trouble with praise is that it has side effects (Dweck, 2007). If we praise a student who's fully engaged, we simply distract her and suggest that her real goal should be to please us. In Matt's feedback to Abby, he did not say, "I like the way you . . ." because that would place him in the authority role and suggest that the goal of Abby's efforts is to please him. Feedback like, "Good girl," is even less helpful because it carries no useful information — it merely lets the student know that she is being judged. Public praise is even more problematic: If we say "good" to one student and "excellent" to another, suddenly "good" damns with faint praise.

> Teachers often confuse being positive with providing praise. They are not the same.

Praise is not so good for creating independently driven writers, and sometimes it's downright destructive. Phrases that invite a symmetrical power relationship and a message of student contribution ("Thank you for helping us figure that out" or even "Thank you") are more useful.

Ordinarily, teachers don't need praise to make a student feel good about the book he has just made or the math problem she has solved. We can just point out what was accomplished and ask, "How did you do that?" Or, respond to each as one writer (or researcher or filmmaker) to another ("Your piece made me really want to do something about homelessness"). Or, we might ask, "How does it feel to have completed your first poem?"

The challenge in being positive comes when students attempt something that stretches them beyond what they can do and results in errors. These errors may nonetheless reflect useful strategic thinking. Being positive here requires not being distracted by the many things that did *not* go well, and instead focusing students' attention on what was partially successful. For example, "I see you figured out the first part of that word by using a word you already know. I wonder whether that would also work for the second part of the word." Drawing attention to the successful part not only consolidates a useful strategy, but also builds a foundation for further productive writing.

5. Feedback shifts how students see themselves.

Feedback sets in motion conversations that affect how students make sense of themselves. Thus, it's particularly important that feedback not contain judgmental comments or comments that cast students in terms of permanent traits. This includes comments like, "You're a good writer," "That's what good readers do," and even, "I'm proud of you." If we make these statements when students are successful, when they fail, they will fill in the other end of the conversation ("You're not good at this," "I'm disappointed in you") (Kamins & Dweck, 1999). Judgment-tinged feedback nudges students toward a world made up of people who are good artists or not good artists, smart or not.

By contrast, students who hear "You did a good job," which mildly turns attention to the process rather than the person, are more likely to try again the activity at which they were previously unsuccessful. Even better is something akin to "You found a way to solve the problem. Are there any other ways you can think of to solve it?"

What's the Point?

The primary goal of feedback is to improve the future possibilities for each individual learner and for the learning community. This means expanding, for every learner, the vision of what's possible, the strategic options for getting there, the necessary knowledge, and the learner's persistence. Teachers aren't merely teaching skills and correcting errors. We're teaching *people* who wish to competently participate in valued social practices — the practices that writers, mathematicians, artists, and others do every day.

References

Dweck, C. S. (2007). The perils and promises of praise. *Educational Leadership, 65*(2), 34–39.

Ivey, G., & Johnston, P. H. (2012). *Engagement with young adult literature: Processes and consequences.* Manuscript submitted for publication.

Johnston, P. H. (2012). *Opening minds: Using language to change lives.* Portland, ME: Stenhouse.

Kamins, M. L., & Dweck, C. S. (1999). Person versus process praise and criticism: Implications for contingent self-worth and coping. *Developmental Psychology, 35*(3), 835–847.

Newkirk, T. (2012). *The art of slow reading: Six time-honored practices for engagement.* Portsmouth, NH: Heinemann.

Ray, K. W., & Glover, M. (2008). *Already ready: Nurturing writers in preschool and kindergarten.* Portsmouth, NH: Heinemann.

Check the page title in the title bar of the browser for information about the purpose and content of the page.

Check the URL to learn about the purpose of a Web page — for instance, whether the page is part of a larger site. Extensions such as .com (for business), .edu (for education), .org (for nonprofit organizations), and .gov (for government) can provide clues about the site's purpose.

Check the navigation headers and menus to learn about the site's content and organization.

Check for information about the author to learn about the author's background, interests, and purposes for writing the document.

Check the title.

Check for links to other sites to learn more about the issue.

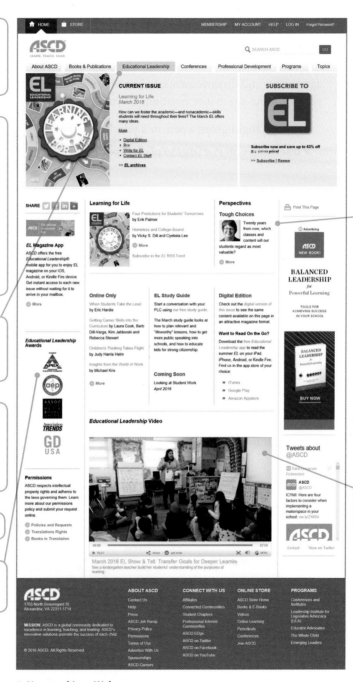

Skim captions of photos and figures, which often highlight important arguments, ideas, and information.

Read the first and last sentences of paragraphs to find key information.

Scan for boldface, colored, or italic text, which might be used to emphasize important information.

View media such as video files and scan for links to social media sites.

▲ **How to skim a Web page**

Mark and Annotate

Marking and annotating are simple yet powerful active-reading strategies. Mark a source to identify key information, ideas, and arguments. Annotate a source to note agreements and disagreements, to identify support for your argument, or to remind yourself about alternative positions on your issue. Common techniques include

- using a highlighter, a pen, or a pencil to identify key passages in a print source
- attaching notes or flags to printed pages

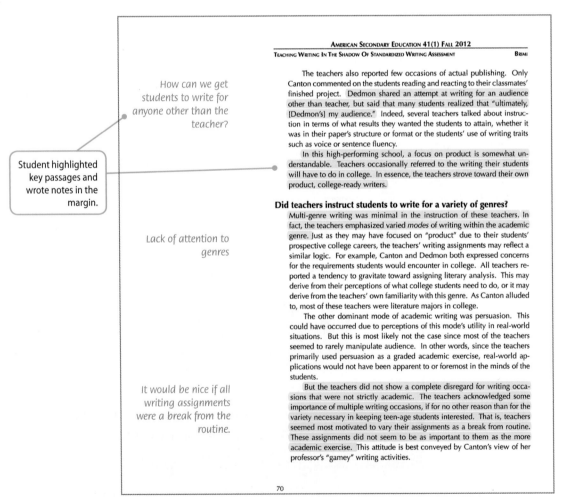

▲ Marking and annotating a source

- identifying important passages in digital texts using the highlighting tool in your word-processing program
- writing reactions and notes in the margins of print sources
- creating comments in digital texts

Notes provide a compact, easy-to-review record of the most important information, ideas, and arguments you've found in your sources. Notes can help you identify significant patterns in your sources, such as similarities and differences, repeated ideas and arguments, and frequently cited information. Notes can also help you keep track of your thoughts as you plan your document. Equally important, careful note taking helps you avoid plagiarism. For these reasons, note taking is one of the most useful skills you can draw on as you work on your writing project.

Notes can include direct quotations, paraphrases, and summaries, as well as your thoughts about your sources as a group and your plans for your document. You can read more about taking notes in Chapter 4. You can read about avoiding plagiarism in Chapter 15.

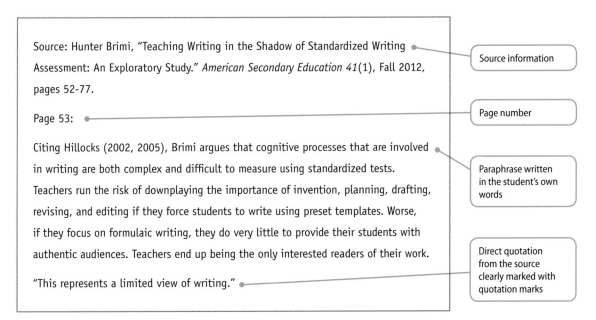

Source: Hunter Brimi, "Teaching Writing in the Shadow of Standardized Writing Assessment: An Exploratory Study." *American Secondary Education 41*(1), Fall 2012, pages 52-77.

— Source information

Page 53:

— Page number

Citing Hillocks (2002, 2005), Brimi argues that cognitive processes that are involved in writing are both complex and difficult to measure using standardized tests. Teachers run the risk of downplaying the importance of invention, planning, drafting, revising, and editing if they force students to write using preset templates. Worse, if they focus on formulaic writing, they do very little to provide their students with authentic audiences. Teachers end up being the only interested readers of their work.

— Paraphrase written in the student's own words

"This represents a limited view of writing."

— Direct quotation from the source clearly marked with quotation marks

▲ **Notes on a Source**

Pay Attention

Examine at least some sources closely for key information, ideas, and arguments. Noting various aspects of a written work during your active reading will help you better understand the source, its role in the conversation you've decided to join, and how you might use it in your own writing.

RECOGNIZE THE GENRE

Pay attention to the type of document — or genre — you are reading. For example, if a source is an opinion column rather than an objective summary of an argument, you're more likely to watch for a questionable use of logic or analysis. If you are reading an article in a company newsletter or an annual report, you'll recognize that one of the writer's most important concerns is to present the company in a positive light. If an article comes from a peer-reviewed scholarly journal, you'll know that it's been judged by experts in the field as well founded and worthy of publication.

Recognizing the type of document you are reading gives you a context for understanding and questioning the information, ideas, and arguments presented in a source.

CONSIDER ILLUSTRATIONS

A growing number of documents use illustrations — photographs and other images, charts, graphs, tables, animations, audio clips, and video clips — in addition to text. Illustrations can demonstrate or emphasize a point, help readers better understand a point, clarify or simplify the presentation of a complex concept, or increase the visual appeal of a document. Illustrations can also serve as a form of argument by presenting a surprising or even shocking set of statistics or setting an emotional tone. As you read, be aware of the types of illustrations and the effects they produce. The types of illustrations you are likely to encounter include the following:

- **Photographs and images.** Photographs and other images, such as drawings, paintings, and sketches, are frequently used to set a mood, emphasize a point, or demonstrate a point more fully than is possible with text alone.

- **Charts and graphs.** Charts and graphs provide a visual representation of information. They are typically used to present numerical information more succinctly than is possible with text alone or to present complex information in a compact and more accessible form.

- **Tables.** Tables provide categorical lists of information. Like charts and graphs, they are typically used to make a point more succinctly than is possible with text alone or to present complex information in a compact form. Tables are frequently used to illustrate contrasts among groups, relationships among variables (such as income, educational attainment, and voting preferences), or change over time (such as growth in population during the past century).

- **Digital illustrations.** Digital documents, such as PowerPoint presentations, Web pages, and word-processing documents intended for reading on computers, tablets, or phones, can include a wider range of illustrations than print documents can. Illustrations such as audio, video, and animations differ from photographs, images, charts, graphs, and tables in that they don't just appear on the page — they do things.

You can read more about the uses of illustrations in Chapter 18.

RECORD NEW INFORMATION AND CHALLENGING IDEAS

As you read, mark and annotate passages that contain information that is new to you. In your writer's notebook, record new information in the form of a list or as a series of brief descriptions of what you've learned and where you learned it.

You might be tempted to ignore material that's hard to understand, but if you do, you could miss critical information. When you encounter something difficult, mark it and make a brief annotation reminding yourself to check it out later. Sometimes you'll learn enough from your continued reading that the passage won't seem as challenging when you come back to it. Sometimes, however, you won't be able to figure out a passage on your own. In that case, turn to someone else for help — your instructor, a librarian, members of an online forum or a newsgroup — or try searching a database, library catalog, or the Web using key words or phrases you didn't understand.

IDENTIFY SIMILARITIES AND DIFFERENCES

You can learn a lot by looking for similarities and differences among the sources you read. For example, you might identify which authors take a similar approach to an issue, such as favoring increased government support for wind energy. You could then contrast this group with other groups of authors, such as those who believe that market forces should be the primary factor encouraging wind power and those who believe we should focus on other forms of energy. Similarly, you might note when information in one source agrees or disagrees with information in another. These notes can help you build your own argument or identify information that will allow you (and potentially your readers) to better understand the issue.

Understand the Writer's Argument

Written conversations typically include a range of positions on an issue. Determining where authors agree and disagree can help you understand the conversation as a whole. Similarly, identifying the reasons and evidence authors offer to support their positions can help you gain insights into the conversation.

IDENTIFY THE MAIN POINT

Most sources make a main point that you should pay attention to. An editorial in a local newspaper, for example, might urge voters to approve financing for a new school. An article might report a new advance in automobile emissions testing, or a Web page might emphasize the benefits of a new technique for treating a sports injury. Often the main point will be expressed in the form of a thesis statement. As you read critically, make sure you understand what the writer wants readers to accept, believe, or do as a result of reading the document.

FIND REASONS AND EVIDENCE THAT SUPPORT THE MAIN POINT

Once you've identified the main point, look for the reasons given to accept it. If an author is arguing, for instance, that English should be the only language used for official government business in the United States, that author might support his or her argument with the following reasons:

The use of multiple languages erodes patriotism.

The use of multiple languages keeps people apart—if they can't talk to one another, they won't learn to respect one another.

The use of multiple languages in government business costs taxpayers money because so many alternative forms need to be printed.

Working Together: Identify Information in a Source

Working with a group of classmates, identify the main point, reasons, and evidence in the article "Guiding the Budding Writer" (p. 58).

1. **List the main point at the top of your page.** Determine what the author is asking you to know, believe, or do.

2. **Briefly list each reason to accept the main point in the order in which it appears in**

the source. You might want to brainstorm lists individually based on your reading of the article and then share your ideas to create the group's list.

3. **Determine the most important evidence offered as proof for each reason.** Once you've agreed on the reasons, work together to identify the evidence used to support each reason.

Reasons can take a wide range of forms and are often presented in forms that appeal to emotions, logic, principles, values, or beliefs (see p. 436). As persuasive as these reasons might seem, they are only as good as the evidence offered to support them. In some cases, evidence is offered in the form of statements from experts on a subject or from people in positions of authority. In other cases, evidence might include personal experience. In still other cases, evidence might include firsthand observations, excerpts from an interview, or statistical data.

When you find empirical evidence used in a source, consider where the evidence comes from and how it is being used. If the information appears to be presented fairly, ask whether you might be able to use it to support your own ideas, and try to verify its accuracy by consulting additional sources.

Learn more about arguments on pages 420–444.

How Can I Read Like a Writer?

When you read like a writer, you prepare yourself to become an active member of the conversation you've decided to join. You learn where the conversation has been — and where it is at the moment. In short, reading like a writer helps you think critically about what you've read and prepares you to write your own document.

To engage more fully with the information, ideas, and arguments you encounter in your reading, go beyond simply knowing what others have written. By reading to understand, reading to respond, and reading to make connections — and putting your thoughts into words — you can begin to find your voice.

Read to Understand

Reading to understand involves gaining an overview of the most important information, ideas, and arguments in a source. When writers read to understand, they often create summaries — brief descriptions of the main idea, reasons, and supporting evidence in a source. Depending on the complexity of the source, summaries can range from a brief statement about the argument found in a source to a detailed description of the key points and evidence it provides.

Many writers believe that a summary should be objective. It would be more precise to say that a summary should be accurate and fair. That is, you should not misrepresent the information, ideas, or arguments in a source. Achieving accuracy and fairness, however, does not necessarily mean that your summary will be an objective presentation of the source. Instead, your summary will reflect your purpose, needs, and interests and — if you're writing for an audience — those of your readers. You'll focus on information, ideas, and arguments that are relevant to your writing situation. As a result, your summary is likely to differ from one written by another writer. Both summaries might be accurate and fair, but each one will reflect its writer's writing situation.

As you read to understand, highlight key points in the source, and note passages that include useful quotations or information you might use to add detail to your summary. If you are writing a summary for a class, it will typically take one of three forms: a main-point summary, a key-point summary, or an outline summary.

In doing research for her essay, Quinn Jackson found this article during her search for information about preparing teachers to teach writing. Published by *Teaching English in the Two-Year College*, an academic journal, the article focused on keeping the teaching of writing "fresh and new."

Living Composition

Nancy Sommers | A veteran writing teacher asks the question—What keeps teaching fresh and new?—and discovers, in the process of writing a teaching narrative, how her teaching voice and writing voice intertwine, both in the classroom and on the page.

It is 1965, career day at Woodrow Wilson Junior High. Girls assemble in the home economics room to learn about becoming nurses, homemakers, or teachers; boys assemble down the hallway in the woodworking room to learn about careers as doctors, lawyers, or engineers. My friends and I aren't surprised to be sitting in a room of stoves and sewing machines, where we've learned to bake biscuits and wind bobbins, cook Welsh rarebit and sew aprons. What surprises me now is that we never thought of storming the wood shop to demand a seat at the workbench. But feminism hadn't found its voice in our corner of Indiana; we were content then with the choices given.

At the end of career day, we are asked to choose one profession. Rather randomly, and without any particular passion for teachers or teaching, I announce that I will become a teacher, an idea that sticks in my head throughout college and graduate school, more as default than commitment. But teaching, especially teaching writing, wasn't an inevitable choice. In my family, reading was fine, in moderation, but too much reading could be dangerous. Various aunts who wore thick glasses or needed cataract surgery, for instance, were held up as object lessons from the *Merck Manual* of maladies, proof of the dangers of excessive reading under bed covers with a flashlight. And writing—even more fraught, warned my parents, nervous immigrants: if you write down what you believe, people will know your thoughts.

Despite all these warnings, I loved to read and write, studied American literature in college, and imagined teaching to be nothing more than bringing my love of Walt Whitman to my first classroom, eighth graders in Chicago. I imagined my students would love Whitman, too, if they could read poetry outdoors, luxuriating in the leaves of grass, marveling at the conjugation of the color green. I'm not sure whether my students learned to become better readers and writers that year, but I do know that I couldn't control them, either inside or outside the classroom. They laughed and hooted when I announced, meekly, at the start of class: "Let's be quiet now." They had no desire to be quiet or to celebrate leaves of grass, though they had plenty to say, their bodies electric, brimming with the rhythms of Chicago's South Side.

Looking back on the naïveté and youthful arrogance of that first year of teaching, I see that it's clear how much that year was a song of myself, more soliloquy than exchange of voices, more my performance than the students'. It would take a decade or more for me to understand that teaching requires both humility and leaps of faith, and most importantly, a willingness to listen to, and learn from, students.

Narratives often unfold in surprising ways and as improbable as it seems from that first unsuccessful performance, I became a teacher and have stayed a teacher for thirty-five years. After all these years, I have started to wonder what sustains a life of teaching writing over a long career. Semester after semester, how do I find those corners in myself that rhyme with my students — and subject matter — to keep it fresh and new? When mentoring new teachers, their passions palpable, enthusiasm unbridled, I ask them to reflect on what brought them to education and find myself asking, after all these years of teaching, what has kept me here?

It is easy to answer such questions with a simple — well, of course, the students! Teaching,

as Theodore Roethke remarked, "is one of the few professions that permits love." And I love my students in all their particularity — the infinite variety of subjects they choose to write about, their compelling cultural backstories, present on every page, and their specific questions that unhinge long-held assumptions about writing. I can't imagine more intimate and more important work than helping students develop as thinkers and writers. After class, I walk around, absorbed, as if in a trance, their questions and stories lodged in my brain.

Teaching writing is like that, absorbing and exhausting, in equal measures, and occupationally strange; we spend more time with students' papers than with the students themselves — devoting nights and weekends to their words, careful not to leave traces of mustard or spill coffee on their pages, and puzzling, in their absence, about how to respond to their ambitious, sweeping introductions — "Since the dawn of humankind."

I do not believe that I would return to the classroom, year after year, with the same passion for students or for teaching writing if I hadn't joined my students on the page, not simply as the critic in the margins of their drafts, but as a fellow writer. When I began college teaching, I wouldn't have dared to consider myself a writer, let alone someone who would pen anything other than required graduate seminar papers and a dissertation. It was my students, though, who in their struggles to become college writers gave me a subject to write about: it started with revision, and a passionate curiosity to understand why students' revised drafts were often weaker than their initial attempts. What was going on, I wondered — why do some students prosper as college writers, while others lag, and what does revising have to do with these differences? In my students' struggle to revise and in my difficulties responding to their drafts, I found subjects I loved writing about.

If my students gave me permission to write about them, and teaching gave me a subject, then CCCC gave me an audience. Most of my published essays were first delivered as talks in convention centers, or in Hyatt and Hilton hotels, where writing teachers mingle each year with other professional associations — Kiwanis and Elk, African violet growers and Bovine practitioners — also gathered for their national conventions. In my gathering, I found a generous audience of fellow teachers, a willing group of listeners who might, if I could make the research interesting, listen to my observations about students and their writing. What I learned from my fellow teachers is the power of an audience to shape ideas and be shaped by them.

My students often ask me, "How do you write?" as if I might, magically, pull back a swirling curtain and offer passage through writing's secret door. They want writing to become easier, more predictable, and seek a pass code to manage their unruly writing process. In answering, I like to defer to Saul Bellow, who when asked that question responded: "I wake up in the morning and check the alphabet to see if all the letters are still there. Then it is simply a matter of arrangement." And sometimes writing seems that simple, moving the letters around to see where they land, being surprised, like a child playing with primary-colored block letters, to find these twenty-six letters arranging into recognizable words. At other times it feels as though I'm working in the wrong mother tongue, with consonants that don't shape into words, an alphabet splayed on a page without form or meaning.

I don't know how I write, really, only that when I write, the world has a certain tilt — everything is more interesting and vivid; everything becomes relevant in a different way, as if I'm searching for clues on a great scavenger hunt, filtering life through an idea I'm trying to locate. Like teaching, writing has its own consuming trance. If, after three decades, I'm more surefooted about teaching writing and more passionate about it, I imagine it is because I teach not from a set of secret codes or passwords, but from my own work as a writer, waiting to be surprised by the alphabet's infinite possibilities; and from encouraging students to write as if they have an audience, a gathering, waiting to receive their words.

Perhaps my teaching narrative, when told retrospectively, seems inevitable, as narratives often do. But my narrative, more oscillating than sequential, has its threads of discontinuities and detours — of not being hired, six-months pregnant, because a department chair thought it unfair to students if I gave birth in the classroom; or of finding myself, in rural New Jersey, balancing motherhood with part-time teaching, a double life of diapering by day/teaching by night.

As my children grew up and I started writing, I led another kind of double life — teaching by day/writing by night or vice versa. The teacher in the classroom, dressed in a pin-stripe suit, exhorting her students not to split infinitives or dangle modifiers, sounded very different from the writer at home who composed sentences as she curried chicken, wiping cumin, cardamom, and cayenne off her fingers; or as she crafted essays to include all the living, breathing sources around her — found objects from home and work. The writer by night wanted to connect the dots, to figure out what she could make of these sources and her double life, teaching and writing, and to write as if everything were relevant.

It all sounds simple in retrospect, but writing is neither simple nor straightforward. I tell my students—writing is so uncomfortable and difficult at times, so always wear socks. And as I write, I wear my winter woolen socks, even in summer, to protect against the inevitable—an idea that seemed so interesting in its conception, but insubstantial in its execution; or a reviewer's big red question marks to say, "You were really seeking the wrong clues on that scavenger hunt of yours; try again." It takes many leaps of faith to write into, and not away from, the jumble of confused ideas in an early draft, and even more leaps to know how to do something different, better, in the next draft, hoping that on the other side, possibly, perhaps, a clearer vision will emerge.

Over the years as my teaching and writing narratives intertwined, I pulled up my socks and worked across drafts, seeking a voice that could push against the either/or categories of being personal *or* being academic. Voice is that elusive category we talk about with students—"find your voice," we urge, as if they left it somewhere, in a dresser drawer, perhaps, as if they could purchase it on Amazon. But there is no lost and found drawer for voice, no way to shop for it, or stumble upon it. It is something you have to write your way into, something that takes practice and play, attempt after attempt, as you arrange the alphabet into comfortable shapes and sounds, listening for your own idiosyncratic take on the world. I tell my students they can't park their voice at the college gates; they can't write as if they're wearing someone else's socks. I, too, had to learn that I couldn't write in the meek voice of a girl who winds bobbins, nor in the strident voice of a feminist who storms the woodworking shop. Part and parcel of who I am in the world is a teacher, and I want to write as I have come to teach: setting out on a quest, with leaps of faith

and good humor, attempting, as essayists do, to figure something out, and always, always imagining an audience on the other end.

What sustains a career in teaching writing, year after year, to keep it fresh and new? Looking back, I see that what brought me to teaching—a desire to convert students into people who love to read poetry and conjugate the color green—is quite different from what has kept me in the classroom. What has kept me here is the passionate belief that teaching writing is, as it has always been "since the dawn of humankind," both a literary and civic calling: helping students write clear declarative sentences repairs the world. To write "Be Specific" in the margins of students' papers is to encourage a habit of mind—an attentiveness to details and particulars, to words and their meanings—a way of being thoughtful, both on the page and in life. And to comment on their drafts "Develop this" or "Analyze more" is to encourage students to add to the world through writing, to make new ideas possible, by contributing their idiosyncratic voices to the ongoing conversation of humankind.

What keeps me in the classroom, exhilarated each September to return after summer's interlude, is that teaching, by now, *is* practiced and comfortable, familiar and recognizable, and not at all fresh and new. Perhaps these terms "fresh and new" are more suited to a double life, where something new, something fresh is always needed. Yes, each semester brings the excitement of new students, but after decades of teaching, you come to welcome being practiced and surefooted, with an anecdote always at hand, building on what you've done before, with a keener sense of *how* to help students write with clarity and precision. And you welcome the comfortable feeling that you and your students, collectively, have a hunch that the writing class matters—that if you do your part, and they theirs, they'll become stronger writers. You believe it because you've seen it happen, abundantly so. You've sat with students, bewildered when their ideas wouldn't arrange, and gently asked: "Tell me what are you trying to say?" You've found ways to coax the saying, ways to turn students into writers, a class into an audience for each other's work. And you know if you didn't quite get it right one semester, you'll tweak and adjust, revise it the next; teaching, like writing, is always a work-in-progress. You welcome the chance for your teaching voice and your writing voice to merge, giving you a sense of belonging, both in the classroom and on the page.

Sometimes I like to imagine a gathering of all my former students, a reunion of sorts, nothing gauzy or sentimental, no need for streamers or balloons, toasts or fancy speeches. I just want to ask: What did you make of our time together? Where have you taken your writing as you moved through college and into the wider world?

Writing is too small a word to describe what happened in our class. And if *writing* is too small a word, *teaching writing* is too small a phrase for something I hope extends beyond the classroom walls. I hope that they've taken the lessons of our class—about argument and audience, voice and style—to enter public debates, as thoughtful educated citizens. And I hope that they've found their own writing trances, their worlds tilting, absorbed and consumed by the pleasures of writing. Yet perhaps that's not what they took from our time together. What I know, though, is that our narratives are inevitably woven together—that during our time together, we've helped each other find something to say, and a reason to say it.

MAIN-POINT SUMMARIES

A main-point summary reports the most important information, idea, or argument presented in a source. You can use main-point summaries to keep track of the overall claim made in a source, to introduce your readers to a source, and to place the main point of that source into the context of an argument or a discussion of a subject. Quinn might have written the following main-point summary of Nancy Sommers's article:

> Main-point summaries are brief. They identify the source and its main point.

In her article "Living Composition," Nancy Sommers reflects on how her work as a writer and as a teacher of writing have combined to keep classroom teaching "fresh and new."

KEY-POINT SUMMARIES

Like a main-point summary, a key-point summary reports the most important information, idea, or argument presented in a source. However, it also includes the reasons (key points) and evidence the author uses to support his or her main point. Key-point summaries are useful when you want to keep track of a complex argument or understand an elaborate process.

> In her article "Living Composition," Nancy Sommers reflects on how her work as a writer and as a teacher of writing have combined to keep classroom teaching "fresh and new." Recounting how her varied experiences as a teacher, mother, and writer have shaped her understanding of writing, she notes the shift in her perspective over the many years since she was a novice teacher. "I see that it's clear how much that year was a song of myself, more soliloquy than exchange of voices, more my performance than the students'," she writes. "It would take a decade or more for me to understand that teaching requires both humility and leaps of faith, and most importantly, a willingness to listen to, and learn from, students" (33). Looking back on her students, she notes her hope that they've left her classrooms to become active writers, participating in public and professional discourse as well as in the kind of personal writing that she has enjoyed. No matter what her students have done, however, she points out that "our narratives are inevitably woven together — that during our time together, we've helped each other find something to say, and a reason to say it" (36).

The author, source, and main point are identified.

Quotations from the article are provided.

Key lessons learned over a lifetime of teaching are identified.

OUTLINE SUMMARIES

Sometimes called a plot summary, an outline summary reports the information, ideas, and arguments in a source in the same order used in the source. In a sense, an outline summary presents the overall "plot" of the source by reporting what was written in the order in which it was written. Outline summaries are useful when you need to keep track of the sequence of information, ideas, and arguments in a source.

> In her article "Living Composition," Nancy Sommers reflects on how her work as a writer and as a teacher of writing have combined to keep classroom teaching "fresh and new." Recalling her early life as a writer and reader, she points out that despite growing up in a family where reading was considered "fine, in moderation, but too much reading could be dangerous" (32), she would go on to study literature in college and eventually find herself teaching writing to eighth graders in Chicago. Noting her "naïveté and youthful arrogance" (33), she points out that in retrospect her first year of teaching "was a song of myself, more soliloquy than exchange of voices, more my performance than the students'" (33).
>
> Over the years, Sommers would grow as a teacher and writer, balancing writing, the teaching of writing, and family life. Along the way, she encountered the — at the time — normal challenges facing women pursuing a career, including not being hired

The author, source, and main point are identified.

The summary identifies each of the major points made in the article in the order in which they were made.

> The author's name is mentioned whenever information from the source is used.

for a teaching position because she was pregnant and dividing time between caring for her family, teaching her students, and pursuing her work as a writer and writing scholar. Yet Sommers also notes that it was through writing and the teaching of writing that she found a professional community, the Conference on College Composition and Communication, where she could share her ideas and benefit from a larger audience of writing scholars.

> Phrases such as "shares" and "She concludes" provide a sense of movement through the source.

Sommers shares the hopes she has for her students — that they have all become active writers, participating in public and professional discourse as well as in the kind of personal writing that she has enjoyed. She concludes, however, that no matter what her students have done as writers, "our narratives are inevitably woven together — that during our time together, we've helped each other find something to say, and a reason to say it" (36).

Read to Respond

Reading to respond allows you to begin forming your own contribution to a conversation. Your response will help you focus your reactions to the information, ideas, and arguments you've encountered in a source. To prepare to write a response to a source, note passages with which you agree or disagree, reflect on interesting information and ideas, and record your thoughts about the effectiveness of the argument advanced in the source.

AGREE / DISAGREE RESPONSES

If you want to explore an idea or argument in a source, try freewriting about why you agree or disagree with it. In your response, clearly define the idea or argument to which you are responding. Then explain whether you agree or disagree with the idea or argument — or whether you find yourself in partial agreement with it — and why.

Your Turn: Summarize a Source

Using the following guidelines, write an outline summary of the article "Guiding the Budding Writer" (p. 58):

1. **Record the author and title of the source.**

2. **Identify the main point and key points made by the writer.** Present the main point and key points in the order in which they appear in the source. For each point, briefly describe the evidence provided to back it up.

3. **Clearly credit the author for any information, ideas, and arguments you include in your summary:** use quotation marks for direct quotations, and identify the page from which you've drawn a paraphrase or quotation. (See Chapter 21 for guidelines on citing sources.)

REFLECTIVE RESPONSES

A reflective response allows you to consider the meaning or implications of what you read. You might focus on a key passage or idea from a source, explaining or elaborating on it. Or you might reflect on your own experiences, attitudes, or observations in relation to a piece of information, an idea, or an argument. You can also use a reflective response to consider how an idea or argument might be interpreted by other readers, how it might be applied in a new context, or how it might be misunderstood.

ANALYTIC RESPONSES

An analytic response focuses on the important elements of a source, such as its purpose, ideas, argument, organization, focus, evidence, and style. For example, you might ask whether the main point is stated clearly, or whether appropriate types of evidence are used to support an argument. You might also analyze the logic of an argument or map its organization. Or you might offer suggestions about how an author could have made the source more effective.

Even when writers choose a particular type of response, they often draw on the other types to flesh out their ideas. For example, you might consider why you disagree with an argument by analyzing how effectively the source presents the

Your Turn: Respond to a Source

Putting your response into words can help you sort out your reactions to the ideas, information, and arguments in a source. Use the following guidelines to write an informal response to Peter Johnston's article "Guiding the Budding Writer" (p. 58) or Nancy Sommers's article "Living Composition" (p. 70):

1. **Identify a focus for your response.** You might select important information, an intriguing idea, or the author's overall argument.

2. **Decide what type of response you are going to write:** agree / disagree, reflective, analytical, or some combination of the three types.

3. **Write an introduction that identifies the information, idea, argument, or source** to which you are responding, lays out your overall response (your main point), and identifies the source's author and title.

4. **Provide reasons to support your main point and evidence to support your reasons.**

5. **Clearly credit the sources of any information, ideas, or arguments you use to support your response:** use quotation marks for direct quotations, and identify the page or paragraph from which you've drawn a paraphrase or quotation. (See Chapter 21 for guidelines on documenting sources.)

argument. Or you might shift from agreeing with an idea to reflecting on its implications.

Read to Make Connections

You can learn a lot by looking for similarities and differences among the sources you read. Which authors approach the subject in a similar way? Can you identify different camps or approaches among the sources you have read? Do sources make use of the same information or evidence? Is the information or evidence across the sources consistent or is it contradictory? Making connections like these can help you build your own argument or identify information that will allow you (and your readers) to better understand a conversation.

As you read more and more about a subject, you'll start to notice common themes and shared ideas. Recognizing these connections among groups of authors can help you understand the scope of the conversation. For example, knowing that people involved in your conversation agree on the overall definition of a problem might lead you to focus your efforts on either challenging that definition with an alternative one or suggesting a possible solution. If you find yourself agreeing with

Working Together: Make Connections among Sources

Work together with a group of classmates to identify general approaches to the subject of how writing is taught. To prepare for the group activity, each member should read, mark, and annotate the articles and Web page in this chapter. During class, you should carry out the following activities:

1. Members of the group should take turns reporting what they've learned about one of the sources.

2. As each report is made, the other members of the group should take notes on the key ideas highlighted by the reporter.

3. When the reports have been completed, the group should create an overall list of the key ideas discussed in the individual reports.

4. Identify sources that seem to share similar approaches to the issue. Give each group of sources a name, and provide a brief description of the ideas its authors have in common.

5. Describe each group of sources in detail. Explain what makes the authors part of the same group (their similarities) and how each group differs from the others you've defined.

Once you've completed the activity, consider how you would respond to each group of authors. Ask whether you agree or disagree with their approaches, and describe the extent to which you agree or disagree. Consider whether you would want to join a group, whether you would want to refine a particular approach to better fit your understanding of the subject, or whether you would rather develop a new approach.

one group of authors, you might start to think of yourself as a member of that group — as someone who shares their approach to the subject. If you don't agree with any of the groups you've identified, perhaps you are ready to develop a new approach to the subject.

To make connections among authors, jot down notes in the margins of your sources or in your writer's notebook. Each time you read a new source, keep in mind what you've already read, and make note of similarities and differences among your sources. When you notice similar themes in some of your sources, review the sources you've already read to see whether they've addressed those themes.

Beyond a collection of notes and annotations, reading to make connections might also result in longer pieces of freewriting (see p. 42). In some cases, you might spend time creating a brief essay that defines each group, identifies which authors belong to each group, and reflects on the strengths, weaknesses, and appropriateness of the approach taken by each group.

In Summary: Reading to Write

* Read with a purpose (p. 55).

* Read actively (p. 56).

* Summarize useful ideas, information, and arguments (p. 74).

* Respond to what you read (p. 76).

* Explore connections among sources (p. 78).

04 Working with Sources

Taking notes does far more than simply help you keep track of information. It allows you to understand the issue that is driving the conversation. Similarly, evaluating sources will help you do more than weed out weak sources. It helps you identify key ideas and arguments, important information, and strong voices among the contributors to a conversation. Taking notes and evaluating sources will also help you form your own position on an issue. Working with sources, as a result, not only helps you better understand the issue, but also lays the groundwork for your contribution to the conversation.

How Can I Take Notes?

Notes — in the form of direct quotations, paraphrases, and summaries — provide you with a collection of important information, ideas, and arguments from your sources, as well as a record of your reactions to your sources. Taking notes early in your work allows you to keep track of what you've learned from your sources. Later, as you begin to plan and write your document, review your notes to determine whether to reread a source or set it aside because you have found other, more relevant sources.

The methods you use to take notes — such as using note cards, a paper notebook, a word-processing program, Web-based tools, or an app on a smartphone or tablet, for example — should reflect how you like to work with information. If you're uncertain about which method might suit you, talk to other writers, your instructor, or a librarian and then try a few of the most promising methods. Each method has its own advantages and disadvantages, and no single method is always right for every situation.

You should take notes when a source

- features an idea that surprises or interests you or that you think you might want to argue for or against
- provides a statement that enhances your understanding of the issue
- offers insights into how an authority or expert understands the issue
- conveys an understanding of someone else's firsthand experience with an issue or event

As you take notes, remember that they should help you accomplish your purposes as a writer and address your readers effectively. Make sure that you quote your sources accurately, paraphrase passages fairly and appropriately, and summarize clearly and fairly. In every case, provide enough source information so you can locate the original source when you need to check for accuracy or want to find additional information.

Quote Directly

A direct quotation is an exact copy of words found in a source. Taking notes that contain quotations can help you accurately keep track of the information, ideas, and arguments you encounter as you learn about a conversation.

When you use quotations in your notes, be sure to place quotation marks around any quoted passage. If you don't, you might later think that the passage is a paraphrase or a summary and then unintentionally plagiarize it when you draft your document (see Chapter 21). The solution to this problem is simple: ensure that you take notes carefully and accurately. Be sure to do the following:

- Enclose quoted passages in quotation marks.

- Identify the author and title of the source for every quotation.

- List the page number (or paragraph number, if you are using a source that does not have page numbers) where the quotation can be found.

- Proofread what you have written to make sure it matches the original source exactly — including wording, punctuation, and spelling.

Learn more about plagiarism in Chapter 15.

Quinn Jackson decided to quote from an article about teaching writing that appeared in the academic journal *Teaching English in the Two-Year College*. The article, written by Nancy Sommers, describes her growth as a teacher over the past three decades.

Source: Nancy Sommers, "Living Composition," p. 34

"If, after three decades, I'm more surefooted about teaching writing and more passionate about it, I imagine it is because I teach not from a set of secret codes or passwords, but from my own work as a writer, waiting to be surprised by the alphabet's infinite possibilities; and from encouraging students to write as if they have an audience, a gathering, waiting to receive their words."

▲ **A direct quotation**

See Chapter 21 to learn more about using direct quotations.

Paraphrase

When you restate a passage from a source in your own words, you are paraphrasing. Using paraphrases in your notes serves three purposes. First, restating a passage in your own words can help you remember it better than if you simply copy and paste a quotation. Second, because paraphrases are written in your own words, they're usually easier to understand later, when you're drafting. Third, paraphrasing as you take notes will help you save time during drafting, since good writers seldom rely exclusively on direct quotations.

Paraphrasing is a useful skill that takes practice. One of the most common problems writers have as they paraphrase is mirroring the source material too closely — that is, making such minor changes to the wording and sentence structure of a source that the paraphrase remains nearly identical to the original passage. Another common problem is distorting the meaning of the source.

Consider the differences among the original passage (shown in the note on p. 82) and the appropriate and inappropriate paraphrases shown next.

Appropriate Paraphrase

Sommers's growth as a teacher has little to do with some sort of privileged, insider knowledge and everything to do with her own work as a writer who loves language and her desire to help students understand that they write best when they write for an interested and receptive group of readers.

> Preserves the meaning of the original passage without replicating the sentence structure and wording.

Inappropriate Paraphrase

Sommers notes that, after roughly thirty years, she is more confident about teaching writing and more excited about it. It is not because she draws on a sort of secret sauce for teaching, but because of her experiences working as a writer. She is always ready to be surprised by the possibilities of language and wants to help students write as if they are addressing readers who care about the words they have to share.

> Does not differ sufficiently from the original; uses similar sentence structures and changes only some key words.

Inappropriate Paraphrase

Sommers writes that she continues to be passionate about teaching writing because she remains open to the infinite possibilities of language and its power to reach an audience.

> Distorts the meaning of the original passage.

When paraphrasing, focus on understanding the key ideas in the passage, and then restate them in your own words. Begin a paraphrase with the phrase "In other words." This strategy reminds you that it's important to do more than simply change a few words in the passage. You might want to set the original source aside while you paraphrase so that you won't be tempted to copy sentences directly from it.

In your note, identify the author and title of the source, and list the page number (or paragraph number, if you are using a source that does not have page numbers) where the paraphrased passage can be found. After you've completed your paraphrase, check it for accuracy and ensure that the wording and sentence structure differ from the original passage.

See Chapter 21 to learn more about using paraphrases.

Summarize

A summary is a concise statement of the information, ideas, and arguments in a source. You can write summaries to capture the overall argument and information in a source or to record a writer's main idea so that you can respond to it later. The following notes contain appropriate and inappropriate summaries of the journal article on page 25.

Appropriate Summary

In the article "Teaching Writing in the Shadow of Standardized Writing Assessment: An Exploratory Study," Hunter Brimi reports on a study in which five high school teachers considered the impact of a state-mandated standardized writing assessment on their efforts to teach writing. Brimi based his conclusions about the impact of the writing assessment on the teachers' comments about the assessment itself, the importance of teaching composing processes, and their willingness to assign multiple genres. Analysis of the interviews indicated that the standardized writing assessment affected their teaching and their willingness to assign genres that were not addressed in the state-mandated writing assessment. The interviews also suggested that the teacher's lack of preparation to teach writing might have affected their behaviors regarding the standardized writing assessment.

> The summary gives a broad overview of the article's argument and avoids close paraphrases of key points.

Problems can arise when a writer fails to summarize ideas and instead either creates a close paraphrase or writes a patchwork summary that is little more than a series of passages copied from the source.

Inappropriate Summary

An exploratory study involving interviews with five high school English teachers regarding their writing instruction showed that the Tennessee Comprehensive Assessment Program's (TCAP) Writing Assessment affected their teaching, particularly in terms of its impact on teaching the writing process and their use of multiple writing genres. The teachers indicated that the TCAP Writing Assessment measurably affected their teaching. Additionally, the teachers revealed that they struggled to teach the writing process and showed reluctance to teach or assign multi-genre writing. It is possible that this might be the result of their lack of training to teach writing before becoming teachers.

> The summary consists of a series of unattributed quotations and close paraphrases of the article's abstract.

In your note, identify the author, the title, and, if you are summarizing only part of a source, the pages or paragraphs where the information can be found. To avoid mirroring the language and sentence structure of the source, begin your summary with

"The author argues that" or "The author found that." As with paraphrases, you might want to put aside the original source so that you won't be tempted to copy sentences directly from it. After you've completed your summary, check it for accuracy and unintentional plagiarism.

See Chapter 21 to learn more about summarizing.

Use Notes to Improve Your Understanding of an Issue

Because taking notes requires thought and effort, the process of choosing quotations, creating paraphrases, and summarizing sources can help you gain a deeper understanding of an issue. Yet taking notes can do far more than simply help you remember and understand your sources. It can help you keep track of ideas that occur to you as you work with sources and gain insights into how they are related to each other. Taking notes, in a real sense, plays an important role in planning your contribution to the conversation you've decided to join.

RECORD YOUR REACTIONS AND IMPRESSIONS

You can use your notes to keep track of your reactions and impressions. If you've read a source before — perhaps while you first explored a topic — you might have jotted down brief notes in the margins or added comments using a word-processing program. Look for those now and use them as the basis for a more substantial reflection on the source. For example, you might have written, "This makes sense" in the margin. If so, take some time to create a note that explains why it makes sense and what the source adds to your understanding of the issue. Learn more about annotating sources during critical reading on pages 64–65.

If you are reading or viewing a source for the first time, use your notes to record your initial impressions, ask questions, and respond to claims made by the author. Identify weaknesses in the argument or gaps in the evidence. Then review your notes and expand them by reflecting in more detail.

COMPARE SOURCES

Reviewing your notes can help you identify relationships among information, ideas, and arguments. Paying attention to your sources as a group — not just to individual sources — helps you gain a more complete understanding of your issue. It also can be useful when you begin planning and organizing your document, since those connections can help you frame your argument. To compare sources, use the following techniques.

- **Look for similarities.** As you take notes, identify similarities among your sources. Later, this can help you define groups of authors that you can use to support your argument, point to as misguided for the same general reason, or use to illustrate a particular point.

The title of the source is listed at the top of the note.

The quotation is surrounded by quotation marks.

The writer jots down reactions to the quotations.

Page numbers follow quotations.

Notes on "Guiding the Budding Writer" by Peter Johnston

Quotes	Notes and Reactions
"Public feedback is part of the same conversation that identifies students as authors. It draws the classroom community's attention to processes that inform authors' decisions" (p. 65).	An interesting observation, since so many people (including a lot of teachers, I think) consider feedback on writing a quiet, private event. I can use this to push back against the idea that classroom writing is just between student and teacher.
"Feedback is not merely cognitive in reach, nor merely corrective in function. Like the rest of classroom talk, feedback affects the ways students understand themselves and one another—how they perceive themselves as writers" (p. 65).	A key observation here. I'd like to see if I can find another source to back this up.
"Teachers aren't merely teaching skills and correcting errors. We're teaching *people* who wish to competently participate in valued social practices—the practices that writers, mathematicians, artists, and others do every day" (p. 67).	This ties into the idea of why writing instruction is so important. It's not just about communication—and it's not just about correctness. It's about getting people ready to contribute to society.

- **Look for disagreements.** Taking note of disagreements among your sources can help you determine the sticking points in the conversation you've decided to join. In turn, understanding where your sources disagree can help you decide where to make your contribution to the conversation.

- **Look for common citations.** Any source that is being referenced frequently is likely to contain important information, ideas, or arguments. Take note of frequently cited sources and consult them later.

CLASSIFY SOURCES

As you take notes, use them to classify your sources. Among other purposes, you can keep track of sources that might be used to support particular points in your document, that represent various approaches to your issue, and that include important information or ideas. Strategies for classifying sources include tagging, labeling, grouping, listing, and visualizing.

- 🖋 TECH TIP: **Tagging and Labeling.** Tags are words or phrases that can be associated with digital notes. Labels, in turn, can be applied to print notes. You can use tags and labels to remind yourself about the purpose or content of a note or to help you remember something about the source. You might tag a note with one of the reasons you're planning to use in your document, for example, or you might label a note as useful for your introduction. Later, as you're working on your introduction or fleshing out that reason, you can quickly call up all of your relevant tagged notes. Similarly, you might label a note to remind yourself about the approach taken in the source to which it refers and later, as you draft, look for notes with that label. Apply as many tags as are relevant to each note.

- **Grouping.** Use groups to organize notes by the part of the document in which you plan to refer to the source, the approach advanced in the source, or the kind of evidence contained in the source. If you are working with print notes, put them in piles, envelopes, or folders. If you are working with digital notes, drag each note into a group (within, for example, a word-processing file) or into a folder (if you are saving each note as a distinct file).

- **Listing.** Listing is similar to grouping, but it does not require you to move your notes into a particular location. Instead, create notes that list your

Your Turn: Respond to Sources

As you take notes, you'll gain a deeper understanding of your sources, both individually and as a group. Use your knowledge of your sources to create a response that will help you plan and draft your project document. Use one or more of the following prompts as the basis for your response.

1. **What do you agree with in one or more of your sources?** Briefly summarize the idea or argument with which you agree and then explain why you agree.

2. **What do you disagree with in one or more of your sources?** Briefly summarize the idea or argument with which you disagree and then explain why you disagree.

3. **What do you see as the most important idea emerging from your research so far?** Briefly summarize the idea and then explain its importance.

4. **Why do you think one or more of the authors you've taken notes on so far approach the issue as they have?** Briefly describe their approach and then explain why they are taking it.

5. **What approach do you think should be taken on this issue?** Briefly describe the approach and then explain its importance.

sources. You might, for example, create a list of all the sources that contain information used to support your position and then make another list of sources that contain information that contradicts your position.

- **Visualizing.** You can use the same mapping and clustering techniques as you take notes that you use as you generate ideas and organize your document (pp. 41–48 and p. 538). For example, you can create notes that contain a sketch of the relationships among the sources you've read so far. Or you could draw clusters of sources that support or illustrate a particular approach to your issue and then write brief notes about what they have in common, how the clusters of sources differ from each other, and so on. Similarly, you can draw maps showing the relationships among important ideas in your sources and identify which sources are associated with each idea.

PLAN YOUR DOCUMENT

Planning notes include directions to yourself about how you might use a source in your project document, thoughts about how you might organize the document, or ideas you will want to remember later. You can use planning notes to keep track of how you want to use the information, ideas, and arguments you encounter. Consider jotting down notes — such as *How will this tie in?* or *Use in introduction?* — as you work with your sources.

How Can I Evaluate Sources?

At the beginning of a writing project, you'll usually make quick judgments about the sources you come across. Skimming an article, a book, or a website (see p. 58) might be enough to tell you that spending more time with the document would be wasted effort. As you learn more about your topic and issue, however, you should evaluate potential sources in light of your writing situation and your needs as a writer. Evaluation involves examining the relevance, evidence, author, publisher, timeliness, comprehensiveness, and genre of your sources.

Determine Relevance

Relevance is the extent to which a source provides information you can use in your writing project. Remember your purpose when you evaluate potential sources. Even if a source provides a great deal of information, it might not meet your needs. For example, a review of the latest iPhone might contain a great deal of accurate and up-to-date information — but it won't be of much use if you're writing about the use of tablets in college classrooms.

Your readers will expect information that meets their needs as well. If they want to read about inexpensive mobile technologies for college students, for instance, pass up sources that focus on the latest enterprise technologies.

Consider the Use of Evidence

Evidence is information offered to support a point. Statistics, facts, expert opinions, and firsthand accounts are among the many types of evidence you'll find. As a writer, you can evaluate not only the kinds of evidence in a source but also the quality, amount, and appropriateness of that evidence. Ask yourself the following questions:

- **Is enough evidence offered?** A lack of evidence might indicate fundamental flaws in the author's argument.

- **Is the right kind of evidence offered?** More evidence isn't always better evidence. Ask whether the evidence is appropriate for the reasons being offered and whether more than one type of evidence is being used. Many sources rely far too heavily on a single type of evidence, such as personal experience or quotations from experts.

- **Is the evidence used fairly?** Look for reasonable alternative interpretations, questionable or inappropriate use of evidence, and evidence that seems to contradict points made elsewhere in a source. If statistics are included, are they interpreted fairly or presented clearly? If a quotation is offered to support a point, is the quotation used appropriately?

- **Are sources identified?** Knowing the origins of evidence can make a significant difference in your evaluation of a source. For example, if a writer quotes a political poll but doesn't say which organization conducted the poll, you might reasonably question the reliability of the source.

Identify the Author

The significance of authorship is affected by context. For example, take two editorials that make similar arguments and offer similar evidence. Both are published in your local newspaper. One is written by a fourteen-year-old middle school student, the other by a U.S. senator. You would certainly favor the senator's editorial if the subject was U.S. foreign policy. If the subject was student perceptions about drug abuse prevention in schools, however, you might value the middle school student's opinion more highly.

Ask the following questions about the author of a source:

- **Is the author knowledgeable?** An author might be an acknowledged expert in a field, a reporter who has written extensively about an issue, or someone with firsthand experience. Then again, an author might have little or no experience with a subject beyond a desire to say something about it. How can you tell the difference? Look for a description of the author in the source. If none is provided, look for biographical information on the Web or in a reference such as *Who's Who*.

- **What are the author's biases?** We all have biases — a set of interests that shapes our perceptions. Try to learn about the author's affiliations so that you can determine the extent to which his or her biases affect the presentation of arguments, ideas, and information in a source. For instance, you might infer a bias if you know that an author writes frequently about gun control and works as a regional director for the National Handgun Manufacturers Association.

Learn about the Publisher

Publishers are the groups that produce and provide access to sources, including books, newspapers, journals, websites, sound and video files, and databases. Like authors, publishers have biases. Unlike authors, they often advertise them. Many publishers have a mission statement on their websites, while others provide information that can help you figure out their priorities. You might already be familiar with a publisher, particularly in the case of major newspapers or magazines, such as *The New York Times* (regarded as liberal) or *U.S. News and World Report* (regarded as conservative). If the publisher is a scholarly or professional journal, you can often figure out its biases by looking over the contents of several issues or by reading a few of its editorials.

Establish Timeliness

The importance of a source's date of publication varies according to your writing situation. For example, if you're writing a feature article on the use of superconducting materials in new mass-transportation projects, you probably won't want to spend a lot of time with articles published in 1968. However, if you're writing about the 1968 presidential contest between Hubert Humphrey and Richard Nixon, then sources published during that time period will take on greater importance.

Print sources usually list a publication date, but Web sources do not always indicate when they were created or last updated. Look for posts or articles with dates or copyright years. When in doubt, back up undated information found on the Web with a dated source.

Assess Comprehensiveness

Comprehensiveness is the extent to which a source provides a complete and balanced view of a subject. Like timeliness, the importance of comprehensiveness varies according to the demands of your writing situation. If you are working on a narrowly focused project, such as the role played by shifts in Pacific Ocean currents on snowfall patterns in Colorado last winter, comprehensiveness in a source might not be important — or even possible. However, if you are considering a broader issue, such as the potential effects of global climate change on agricultural production in North America, or if you are still learning as much as you can about your subject, give preference to sources that provide full treatment.

Consider Genre and Medium

Genre and medium can help you understand the roles authors take on as they develop their contributions to a written conversation. Understanding the typical characteristics of a genre, for example, can help you recognize whether an author is considering the needs, interests, and backgrounds of readers. Similarly, understanding how medium — print, digital, broadcast — shapes the manner in which authors typically share ideas with readers can help you make judgments about a particular source.

USE GENRE TO UNDERSTAND PURPOSES AND AUDIENCES

Sources in three general categories (scholarly publications, trade and professional publications, and popular publications) typically are written for distinctly different purposes, are directed toward readers who have strikingly different levels of expertise on a subject, and are evaluated with widely varying levels of review by experts on a subject. As you evaluate your sources, consider the characteristics of these three types of publications.

EVALUATE DIGITAL SOURCES

TECH TIP: Because anyone can create a website, start a blog, contribute to a wiki, or post a message to a social-networking site, e-mail list, Web discussion forum, message board, or comments list, approach these sources with more caution than you would reserve for print sources such as books and journal articles, which are typically published only after a lengthy editorial-review process.

Websites and blogs To assess the relevance and credibility of a website or a blog, consider its domain (.com, .edu, .gov, and so on) and look for information about the site (often available on the "About This Site" or "Site Information" page).

	Scholarly Publications	Trade and Professional Publications	Popular Publications
Purposes	Report original research, review original research, or analyze trends in recent research	Focus on new developments within a field, but are not usually as technically challenging as scholarly publications	Report or comment on events, individuals, groups, or activities
Writers	Have significant expertise in a given field	Usually have expertise on an issue, but can be freelancers hired by a company or professional organization	Know a great deal about a subject but would be more accurately characterized as generalists
Readers	Possess specialized knowledge about the subject	Members of a profession interested in developments in the field	General audience; most popular publications are written at a reading level appropriate for an eighth- to tenth-grade education
Sources	Extensive in-text citations and works cited lists or bibliographies	Sources are cited, but often less thoroughly than in scholarly publications	Seldom include citations, although newspaper articles, magazine articles, and blogs often identify sources in general terms
Review	Almost always reviewed by other experts in the same field	Sometimes peer-reviewed, but usually reviewed only by editorial staff	Not peer-reviewed and not always carefully reviewed by editorial staff
Genres	Journal articles, books, conference papers	Journal articles, newsletter articles, blogs, websites	Newspaper and magazine articles, blogs, websites, wikis, videos

Check the domain to learn about the site's purpose and publisher:

.biz, .com, .coop: business
.edu: higher education
.org: nonprofit organization

.mil: military
.gov: government
.net: network organization

Check the title bar and page headers or titles to learn about the site's purpose, relevance, and publisher.

Check the site's timeliness by looking for publication and "last modified" dates.

Search for information about the author or publisher.

Read the body text and review illustrations to evaluate relevance, evidence, and comprehensiveness.

Check page footers for information about the publisher and author. Look for "About" or "Contact" links.

▲ **How to evaluate a website**

NEA/National Education Association

Social-networking sites and discussion venues To assess the relevance and credibility of a message on one of these online venues, try to learn something about the author.

- On social-networking sites, you can usually link back to authors' personal pages.
- In e-mail lists, discussion forums, and message boards, check for a "signature" at the end of the message and try to locate a Frequently Asked Questions (FAQ) list.
- In comments lists following articles and blogs, look for signed comments and attempt to learn something about the author.

Wikis Wikis are websites that can be added to or edited by visitors to the site. Wikis such as Wikipedia (en.wikipedia.org) have grown in importance on the Web, and many Wikipedia pages are highly ranked by Web search sites. Wikis can be good resources as you start a writing project because they help you gain an initial under-standing of an issue. In some cases, people who are experts on an issue contribute to wikis and provide information and analyses. Wikis also may link to other resources that can help you learn about the issue. Unfortunately, it can be difficult to evaluate the credibility of wiki pages because their creators and editors are often not known and because changes to wiki pages can occur quickly. Some entries are edited so frequently that they become the subject of "edit wars," in which edits to a page are undone almost instantly by those who disagree with the edits. In some cases, the entry you found yesterday might bear little or no resemblance to the entry available today.

With this in mind, it is best to use wikis when you are beginning to learn about an issue. Avoid citing them as the "last word" on a topic because those last words might change before you submit your final draft.

EVALUATE FIELD SOURCES

Print and digital sources are not the only sources of information available to you. Sometimes, collecting information firsthand provides valuable insight into a conversation, showing you aspects of the situation that you might not find in published research. Field research methods (see chapter 14) include conducting observations of a scene or experience, interviewing or corresponding with experts or witnesses to an event, conducting surveys of people affected by a situation, and attending public events and performances.

If you are studying the impact of an event that occurred sometime in the past few decades, for instance, you might reach out to people who were involved with or affected by the event. Interviews with one or more of these individuals might help you gain an understanding of the event that you might not be able to gain through reading historical accounts. Additionally, you might be able to gain access to primary sources, such as letters or diaries, written by people who were affected by the event. You can also correspond with individuals who were involved with or affected by the event. E-mail messages, letters, and even text messages can be valuable for informative or analytical writing projects.

Finally, consider attending an event or visiting a particular location and jotting down your thoughts, feelings, and impressions. This approach can be extremely useful across a wide range of writing projects. Imagine yourself grappling with the topic of race relations in your hometown, for instance. Observing a Black Live Matter rally could help you understand race relations more fully than simply visiting their website, watching cable news shows, or reading articles about the movement. Similarly, if you are working on a writing project about immigration policy, you might decide to attend a naturalization ceremony. Observing the ceremony or talking with people at the ceremony might deepen your understanding of the issue and the audience you are addressing.

Ask the following questions as you evaluate information you might gain through field research methods.

- Are there experts or knowledgeable individuals whom you could interview or correspond with to get a deeper understanding of the conversation you are joining?

- Does the conversation you are joining involve a situation that affects a large group of people? Conducting a survey can help you collect data from many individuals in an efficient manner.

- Would your understanding of the conversation grow by observing a scene directly? Conducting an observation gives you a chance to experience a new facet of the conversation yourself.

Your Turn: Evaluate a Source

Select a source you have found as you've learned about a topic. In your writer's notebook, respond to the following questions:

1. Is the source relevant to your writing proejct?

2. Does the source present evidence and use it appropriately?

3. What can you learn about the author?

4. What can you learn about the publisher?

5. Is the source timely?

6. Is the source comprehensive enough?

7. What genre is the source?

In Summary: Working with Sources

✱ **Take notes carefully (p. 81).**
- Quote sources (p. 81).
- Paraphrase sources (p. 82).
- Summarize sources (p. 84).
- Look for larger patterns among your sources (p. 85).

✱ **Evaluate sources (p. 88).**
- Consider relevance (p. 88).
- Consider evidence (p. 89).
- Consider the author (p. 89).
- Consider the publisher (p. 90).
- Consider timeliness (p. 90).
- Consider comprehensiveness (p. 91).
- Consider genre and medium (p. 91).

Working Together

 With rare exceptions, writing is a social act. We write to inform, to entertain, to bring about change. We write to share ideas. We write to make a difference. Most important, we write *to someone* and *for a purpose*. To write more effective documents, writers frequently turn to other writers for feedback and advice. The skills required to give useful feedback and advice — and to use that feedback and advice effectively — are among the most important a writer can have. In fact, they're strongly related to the skills you use in conversation — listening carefully, treating others with respect, and deciding how to make a useful contribution. In this chapter, you'll learn how to benefit from working with other writers and how to do so effectively and efficiently.

How Can Collaborative Activities Improve My Writing?

Writers frequently solicit support from other writers as they work on individual projects. In some cases, they seek this support independently by asking for advice about their choice of a topic or by requesting feedback on a draft. In other cases, a writing instructor might direct students to work together to generate ideas, collect sources on a common topic, engage in peer review, and develop and refine arguments.

Work Together to Generate Ideas

Writers often collaborate to generate ideas. Common strategies for generating ideas with other writers include group brainstorming and role-playing activities.

GROUP BRAINSTORMING

Group brainstorming draws on the differing backgrounds and experiences of the members of a group to generate ideas for a writing project. For example, you might work with a group to create a list of ideas for an essay about new advances in communication technologies or social media, or you might collaborate to generate possible solutions to a problem with funding for a local school district.

To engage in group brainstorming, follow these guidelines:

- **Take notes.** Ask someone to record ideas.

- **Encourage everyone in the group to participate.** Consider taking turns. Establish a ground rule that no one should cut off other group members as they're speaking.

- **Be polite. Avoid criticisms and compliments.** Treat every idea, no matter how odd or useless it might seem, as worthy of consideration.

- **Build on one another's ideas.** Try to expand on ideas that have already been generated, and see where they take you.

- **Generate as many ideas as possible.** If you get stuck, try asking questions about ideas that have already been suggested.

- **Review the results.** Once you've stopped brainstorming, look over the list of ideas and identify the most promising ones.

ROLE-PLAYING

Role-playing activities are frequently used to generate and refine ideas. By asking the members of a group to take on roles, you can apply a variety of perspectives to a subject. For example, you might ask one person to play the role of a "doubting Thomas," someone who demands evidence from a writer for every assertion. Or you might ask someone to play the role of a "devil's advocate," who responds to a writer's arguments with counterarguments. (The term is drawn from the process by which the Roman Catholic Church confers sainthood, in which an advocate of the devil argues that the candidate is not worthy of sainthood.) Role-playing activities that are useful for generating and refining ideas include staging debates, conducting inquiries, and offering first-person explanations.

Staging a debate In a debate, speakers who represent different perspectives argue politely with one another about an issue. You might try one or more of the following role-playing activities:

- **Adopt the role of the authors of readings used in a class.** Each "author" presents his or her perspective on the issue.

- **Adopt the role of a political commentator or celebrity who has taken a strong stand on an issue.** One member of a group might adopt the role of Rachel Maddow, for example, while another might adopt the role of Rush Limbaugh, and still others might adopt the roles of Megyn Kelly, Joe Scarborough, or Bill O'Reilly. Each "commentator" or "celebrity" presents his or her perspective on the issue. To prepare for the debate, watch or listen to commentaries on a site such as YouTube.com to learn about the positions these commentators have taken in the past.

- **Adopt the role of an authority on an issue,** such as a scientific adviser to a local zoning commission, the manager of a small business, or the director of a nonprofit organization. To prepare for the debate, conduct research in your library's databases or on the Web about the person whose role you are adopting.

- **Adopt the role of someone affected by an issue or event.** For example, if you were generating ideas about a natural disaster, such as the effects of a flood in the Mississippi River valley, you might take on the roles of people who lost their homes and were forced to move, health care workers and police officers who stayed on duty, students who lost their schools, or small business owners who lost their livelihoods, all of whom could discuss the impact of this natural disaster on their lives. To prepare for the debate, you could conduct research on how the community was affected by the event.

Conducting an inquiry An inquiry is an attempt to understand a situation or an event. For example, a military tribunal might review soldiers' actions during a military operation, while a medical inquiry might focus on the causes of a problem that occurred during a medical procedure. To conduct an inquiry, try the following role-playing activities:

- **Defend a contemporary or historical figure.** The writer presents a case for this person, and the other group members ask questions about the person's actions or ideas.

- **Review a proposal.** The writer presents a proposal to address an issue or a problem. The other members of the group raise questions about the merits of the proposal and suggest alternatives.

Giving testimony First-person explanations offer insights into the causes of, effects of, or solutions to a particular issue or problem. Role-playing activities that involve giving testimony include the following:

- **Adopt the role of devil's advocate.** The writer offers an explanation, and one or more respondents offer reasonable objections. Each devil's advocate asks for clarification of the points made by the writer and suggests alternative explanations.

Working Together: Role-Play

Work together with your classmates to generate and refine ideas for your writing project. Choose one of the categories of role-playing activities — staging a debate, conducting an inquiry, or giving testimony — and assign roles to the members of your group. Then do the following:

1. Appoint a member of your group — ideally, someone who is not involved in the role-playing activity — to record the ideas.

2. Create a framework for the role-play. Decide who will speak first, how long that person will speak, and what sort of responses are appropriate.

3. As you conduct the role-play, be polite (within bounds, of course — some political commentators are far from polite to their opponents).

4. If you are responding to a writer's ideas, ask for evidence to support his or her arguments or explanations.

5. If you are adopting a role that requires you to disagree, don't overdo it. Be willing to accept a reasonable explanation or argument.

Once you've completed the activity, review the notes taken by your recorder, and assess what you've learned.

- **Adopt the role of a person affected by an issue.** The writer takes on the role of someone who has been affected by the issue. After the writer explains the effects, the other members of the group ask questions about the writer's experiences.

Work Together to Collect and Work with Information

You might be asked — by an instructor or by another writer — to work together to collect, critically read, evaluate, and take notes on information from sources. Common collaborative activities for collecting and working with information include the following:

- **Develop a search strategy for published sources.** Depending on the scope of a writing project, creating a plan for finding sources can be quite challenging. Working with other writers can improve the odds of developing an effective and appropriate plan. You can learn more about developing a search plan on page 459.

- **Assign responsibility for locating sources.** When a group is working on a shared topic, dividing up research responsibilities can be an efficient way to create a collection of sources. For example, one person might search for sources through a library catalog, another through full-text databases, and still another through searches on the Web. Each person can locate promising sources and make copies for other members of the group. See Chapters 12 through 15 for more information about locating sources.

Need a refresher on evaluating sources? See Chapter 4.

- **Assign responsibility for field research.** In writing projects that involve surveys, interviews, observation, or correspondence (see Chapter 14), each member of the group can carry out his or her assigned research task and share the results with the group.

- **Create shared annotated bibliographies.** Members of a group working on a shared topic can create citations and annotations (brief summaries) for each source they collect. You can learn more about creating annotated bibliographies on page 470.

- **Share evaluations of sources.** Writers working on a shared topic can discuss the merits of the sources they've collected and read. For more information on evaluating sources, see pages 88–95.

- **Share notes on sources.** Writers working on a shared topic can compile their notes on the sources they've read. You can learn more about taking notes on pages 81–88.

Work Together to Refine Your Argument

Writers usually express their main point through a thesis statement (see Chapter 16). A good thesis statement invites readers to learn something new, suggests that they change their attitudes or beliefs, or advocates taking action of some kind. In effect, your thesis statement serves as a brief summary of the overall argument you want to make to your readers.

To determine whether your thesis statement conveys your main point clearly and effectively, ask for feedback from other writers. You might ask friends or family members to read your thesis statement and tell you what they think it means, as Quinn Jackson did with an early draft of a thesis statement she developed for an argumentative essay about preparing teachers to teach writing. You might ask them to offer counterarguments or alternative perspectives on your issue or to engage in a role-playing activity in which they pretend to disagree with your perspective. Or you might ask for feedback during a peer-review session in class.

Regardless of where it comes from, listen carefully to the feedback you receive. Your thesis statement plays a central role in shaping the decisions you'll make about the reasons and evidence you'll offer to support your main point, and it can also affect the organization and design of your document.

I'm not sure how you'd define "future writing teachers." Do you mean only English language arts students or do you mean anyone— even a biology major—who will be using writing assignments when they teach?	Future writing teachers should receive much stronger preparation than they currently receive in the theory and practice of writing instruction.	*Do you have any ideas about what "much stronger preparation" would involve? Are you thinking about hands-on training? Theory? Actual writing that they do themselves?*

▲ **Feedback on a draft of Quinn Jackson's thesis statement**

As you develop a set of reasons to accept your main point, ask for feedback on them as well. You might create an outline of your argument (see p. 542) or write a rough draft (see Chapter 18). Friends, family, and classmates should be able to provide their reactions to the reasons you are offering. They can give you feedback on the appropriateness and effectiveness of the evidence you've selected to support your reasons and the order in which you present your reasons and evidence. And they can help you generate ideas for new and potentially more effective reasons and sources of evidence. Just as you can with a thesis statement, you can ask people to offer counterarguments or to adopt roles. And, of course, you can solicit feedback on your reasons and evidence from classmates during peer-review or idea-generation sessions.

Teacher education programs should provide strong theoretical grounding in writing instruction for all future teachers, help future teachers understand how to assign and respond to student writing, and require future teachers to take advanced writing courses.

    Reason 1. Because writing is used in all courses — not just language arts — all future teachers should receive instruction in writing theory and practice.

    Reason 2. It's important to understand how to teach writing — and even more important to understand why some instructional choices are better than others.

    Reason 3. Teachers who assign writing should be good writers themselves.

    Evidence: Brimi, Johnston, Sommers

> *Do you really think you can make all teachers good writers?*

> *How will faculty in the sciences react to the writing requirement? Won't they worry about adding more credits to the major?*

> *Good choice of articles. But are three enough to support your argument?*

▲ **Feedback on an informal outline**

Your argument — your main point, reasons, and evidence — is the heart of your contribution to the conversation you've decided to join. By working with other writers, you can gain valuable feedback on your argument, feedback that can help you refine it and make it more effective.

How Can I Use Peer Review to Improve My Writing?

When designed carefully and treated seriously, peer review can provide valuable information to writers about the effectiveness, clarity, and organization of their drafts. Few experienced writers, in fact, produce major documents without asking for feedback on their drafts. They've learned that it can help them enhance their composing processes, improve their documents, and increase the likelihood of successfully completing a major writing project.

Use Peer Review to Enhance Your Writing Process

Peer review benefits the reviewer as well as the writer. By helping another writer generate ideas, you can practice effective brainstorming strategies. By participating in a planning session, you can learn something new about planning your own documents. By reading and responding to documents written by other writers, you might pick up some new strategies for organizing an essay, crafting an introduction, incorporating illustrations, or using evidence effectively. Perhaps most important, learning how to analyze other people's work can help you assess your own writing more productively.

Use Peer Review to Improve Your Document

Peer review gives you the benefit of multiple perspectives. The feedback you receive from other writers can help you learn whether you have conveyed your main point clearly, whether you have offered sufficient evidence, whether you have organized your document effectively, and whether readers are likely to react favorably to the information, ideas, and arguments you have presented in a draft. Feedback from other writers can also help you identify passages in a draft that might benefit from additional revision, polishing, or editing.

To increase your chances of creating an effective document, you might ask for feedback on your overall argument, your reasoning about an issue, and your use of evidence. You might ask a friend or classmate, "What do you know about . . . ?" or "Do you think it would be effective if . . . ?" or "Does this seem convincing to you?" You might ask a reviewer to pretend to be part of the intended audience for your document, or you might ask for feedback on specific aspects of your document, such as its organization, style, or design.

Use Peer Review to Succeed on a Major Project

Working on collaborative projects has become common in many writing and writing-intensive courses. In engineering courses, for example, teams of students often carry out a complex project and produce presentations and written reports. Web design courses frequently require students to work on group projects. Similarly, first-year writing courses often include a collaborative writing project. Typically, these projects are far more ambitious than those assigned to individual students. It is only through the contributions of all the members of the group that they can be completed at all.

How Can I Conduct an Effective Peer Review?

As you engage in peer review, either as a writer or as a reviewer, consider what stage the project is in. Early in a writing project, a writer is likely to be most interested in feedback about the overall direction of the project. Big-picture concerns such as the purpose of the document, the general soundness of an argument, and how readers are likely to react to that argument will probably be more important than issues such as style and tone. Later, questions about the integration of evidence from sources, style and tone, and design will grow in importance, particularly in terms of how they help the writer pursue his or her purpose and goals. Consider, too, the contexts in which a peer review takes place and the technologies that might be used to carry out the review.

Consider Context

As you begin a peer review, consider the context in which it is taking place. If you are conducting a peer review in a classroom, you might have limited time to read and reflect on a document. Try to focus specifically on a few primary concerns — either those defined by your instructor, perhaps through a rubric or a set of key questions, or those defined by the writer, who might ask for help in particular areas. If you are conducting a peer review outside of class, you might have more time to consider a fuller range of issues related to the document. If so, think carefully about the kind of feedback that would help the writer, and then read the document — ideally more than once — with those concerns in mind.

Consider Technology

Peer review often calls to mind images of students hunched over desks in a classroom, marking paper drafts with pens or pencils before they offer feedback to one another. Increasingly, however, peer review takes place on computers, tablets, or even smartphones, both inside and outside the classroom. Most programs allow you to save comments and revise them before you return a draft to a writer. You'll find tools for highlighting text and suggesting text edits. You'll be able to link to related documents, websites, and databases. And you will be able to share your comments not only with the writer but also with other members of the class, including your instructor. Some instructors, in fact, ask to see the feedback writers give to one another as a means of ensuring greater attention to the peer-review process and also to get a sense of the kinds of writing issues members of the class are struggling to address.

Consider Your Needs as a Writer

Whenever you ask for feedback from other writers, keep the following guidelines in mind.

When you ask for feedback on a draft:

- **Be clear.** Tell your reviewers where you'd like them to focus. For example, let them know that you are struggling with the transition from one point to another or that you would appreciate feedback on your conclusion.

- **Be reasonable.** Your reviewers have more to do in life than review your draft. Don't expect — or ask — them to spend more time reviewing a draft than you spent writing it. For that matter, don't expect them to put more than half an hour into a review — if that.

- **Be prepared.** Provide a draft that is easy to review. If you are asking the reviewer to comment on a printed draft, format it with double-spaced lines and wide margins. If you are providing a digital draft, make sure the reviewer can access, read, and comment on your file easily.

When you receive feedback on a draft:

- **Be open to criticism.** Don't dismiss constructive criticism as a problem with the reviewer's comprehension. A reviewer might make poor suggestions for revision, but it's more likely that he or she is reacting to a problem in the draft. Even when the suggested revision is inappropriate, it might point to an area that needs attention.

- **Be willing to ask questions.** If you aren't sure what a reviewer's comments mean, ask for clarification.

- **Be willing to change.** If a reviewer offers a critique of your argument or ideas, consider addressing it in your document. You will make a stronger argument if you tell readers about alternative ways of looking at an issue — particularly when you can counter the alternatives effectively.

- **Be fair to yourself.** It's your draft. Don't feel obligated to incorporate every suggested change into your draft.

Consider Your Role as a Reviewer

When you provide feedback to another writer, consider the following guidelines.

To prepare for a peer-review session:

- **Understand the assignment.** Read the assignment sheet, if there is one, and ask the writer to describe the draft's purpose and audience.

Ineffective and effective feedback on Quinn Jackson's first draft

How would you feel if the only feedback you received on a 2500-word writing assignment was "nice job" or "needs work" or "good argument"? How would you feel if the only feedback you received was on grammar and style?

> Nice introduction!

> Are you being serious?

> Maybe include some evidence that teachers don't always provide substantive feedback. Did you find any studies about feedback?

Too many high school students receive little or no feedback on their work—even on assignments that require literally hours of work. Most shrug it off and say, "What can you expect? The teacher is incredibly busy" or "It makes sense. It was just an assignment for a science class." But a growing number are asking for more. They want to improve as writers. They want to be prepared for college or a job. They want to see some return on their investment of time and effort.

> Do you have any information on how many hours a week teachers typically work or on the number of students they usually teach?

These students need to be heard. High school principals need to reward teachers who design good assignments and provide strong feedback. College and university teacher education programs need to pay serious attention to writing theory, instruction, and practice. And teachers themselves need to recognize that it's never enough to read and grade an assignment. They need to see that feedback on writing is a critical part of the teaching process.

> Awkward sentence! You might want to buy a better handbook.

> Great job so far.

> I think you might want to introduce these ideas in a different order and then make changes to reflect that order later in the document.

- **Understand the writer's needs.** Ask the writer what type of response you should provide. If you are reviewing an early draft that will be revised before it's submitted for a grade, focus on larger writing concerns such as the overall argument, evidence, and organization. If the writer wants help with proofreading and editing, focus on accuracy, economy, consistency, biased language, style, spelling, grammar, and punctuation (see pp. 664–65).

- **Understand any peer-review guidelines.** If you are using a feedback form or a set of questions provided by your instructor, make sure you understand these guidelines. If you don't, ask the instructor or the writer for clarification.

- **Set aside sufficient time to review the draft.** Take your job seriously, and give the draft the time it deserves. You'll want the same courtesy when your draft is reviewed.

Before you make comments:

- **Be prepared.** Read the draft all the way through at least once before making any comments. This will help you understand its overall structure and argument.

- **Be organized.** Take a few minutes to identify the areas most in need of work. On a first draft, for instance, you might identify three main areas that need the writer's attention, such as thesis statement, organization, and effective use of sources.

As you make comments:

- **Be positive.** Identify the strengths of the draft. Be specific in your praise: "This quotation really drives home your point about teachers' frustrations with changing standards" is more helpful, for instance, than "Nice quotation" because the first comment allows the writer to see why a certain strategy is effective.

- **Be judicious.** Focus on the areas of the draft most in need of improvement. Avoid commenting on everything that might be improved. In most cases, a limited set of suggested changes — particularly those that focus on bigger-picture concerns such as purpose, audience, argument, and organization — will ripple through a document in ways that make many of the other changes you might have suggested irrelevant.

- **Be clear.** If you are addressing an overall issue such as structure or integration of evidence from sources, discuss it thoroughly enough that the writer will understand your concerns. If you are addressing a specific passage, indicate where it can be found.

- **Be specific.** Avoid general comments, such as "The writing isn't clear enough." This kind of statement doesn't give the writer direction for improving the draft. Instead, offer specific comments, such as "I found it difficult to understand your explanation of the issue in the second paragraph." Similarly, focus your questions. Instead of asking, "What are you trying to do here?" ask a question such as "It seems as though you are trying to build on what you stated in the previous paragraph. Can you show the connection more clearly?"

- **Be constructive.** Offer concrete suggestions about how the draft might be improved, rather than just criticizing what you didn't like. Being constructive can also mean encouraging the writer to continue doing what you see as effective.

- **Be reasonable.** Keep the writing assignment in mind as you make suggestions for improvement. Don't hold the draft to a higher standard than the instructor's.

- **Be kind.** Be polite. Don't put down the writer simply because you find a draft inadequate, confusing, or annoying.

- **Be responsible.** Review your comments before you give them to the writer.

Understanding how to conduct and use feedback from peer review not only will help you improve a particular document but also will enable you to become a better writer. As you consider the type of document you'll write to contribute to a written conversation, keep these principles in mind. Also keep in mind the distinctive characteristics of writing for particular purposes, such as writing to inform or writing to solve problems. Chapters 6 through 11 provide carefully designed peer-review activities that will help you get feedback on drafts for the kinds of writing projects featured in those chapters.

What Resources Can I Draw On as I Review and Collaborate?

Resources that support peer review and other forms of collaborative work include technological tools as well as your instructor, classmates, friends, and family.

Use Technological Tools

For many writers, the phrase "working together" implies face-to-face meetings, often during class. In fact, many collaborative activities can be carried out without the need to meet in person.

- If you are working with other writers to generate and refine ideas, use chat, instant messaging, or video tools to meet online.

- If you are collaborating with other writers to collect and work with sources for a shared topic, use discussion forums, wikis, cloud-based file sharing (such as Dropbox, iCloud, and OneDrive), and e-mail to distribute sources, source citations, source evaluations, and source notes.

- If your class is supported by a course management system such as Blackboard or Canvas, ask your instructor to create discussion forums, wikis, and file-sharing folders to support your group work. Take advantage of e-mail to share ideas, schedule meetings, and exchange files. You might also have access to electronic whiteboard programs that allow you to meet online and work on drafts of your document.

- If you are conducting a peer review, you can share your drafts by sending them as e-mail attachments, uploading them to the cloud, or posting them to a course management system. Reviewers can open the attachments in a word-processing program, comment on them using Comment and Track Changes tools, save the file with a new name, and return them to you.

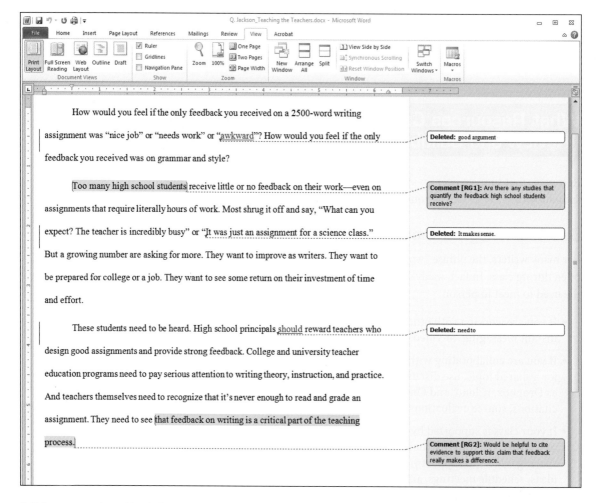

▲ Using comments and track changes

Consult Instructors, Classmates, Friends, and Family

The most important resources for peer review and collaboration are your instructor, your classmates, and your friends and family. Not only can family and friends provide honest feedback on the quality of your drafts, but they can also be resources for generating ideas about and planning a writing project. Simply discussing a writing project with sympathetic friends or family members can help you make progress on the project. They might remind you of something you'd forgotten about the topic; they might share new information with you; or they might respond in a way that sparks a new idea.

Similarly, classmates and instructors can help you fine-tune a draft by serving as a sounding board for your ideas and by responding to it. Instructors can also show you how to work with peer-review forms and can provide feedback on the quality of the comments you offer your classmates. Finally, and perhaps most important, instructors can help you understand your assignment — but only if you ask them for advice.

In Summary: Working Together

* **Understand how collaborative activities can improve your writing (p. 98).**

* **Use peer review to enhance your writing process, improve your document, and succeed on writing projects (p. 103).**

* **Take advantage of resources that help writers work together (p. 109).**

PART TWO

Contributing to a Conversation

06 Writing to Reflect

I write as an **observer** when I reflect on a topic.

What Is Writing to Reflect?

Writing to reflect is one of the most common activities writers undertake. At the beginning of almost every writing project, writers spend time exploring and deepening their understanding of their subject. In this sense, writing to reflect provides a foundation for documents that inform, analyze, evaluate, solve problems, and convey arguments.

Reflection can also be the primary purpose for writing a document. In journals and diaries, writers reflect on a subject for personal reasons, often with the expectation that no one else will read their words. In more public documents — such as memoirs, letters, opinion columns, and blogs — writers also use reflection to share their thoughts in ways that benefit others.

Reflective writing is carried out by writers who adopt the role of *observer*. These writers spend time learning about and considering a subject. Sometimes they explore the implications of putting a particular idea into practice. Sometimes they trace relationships among ideas and information. Sometimes they ask whether or how an author's words might help them better understand their own lives. Sometimes they ask whether their understanding of one situation can help them better understand another.

Readers of reflective documents usually share the writer's interest in a subject. They want to learn what another person thinks about the subject, and often they'll use what they've read as the basis for their own reflections. In general, readers of reflective documents expect writers to provide a personal treatment of a subject, and they are willing to accept — and are likely to welcome — an unusual perspective.

To gather details for their observations, writers of reflective documents use sources, including their personal experiences and expertise, reports of recent events, and cultural materials such as music, art, movies, plays, books, short stories, and poems. These sources can also provide the inspiration for a reflective document. For example, a writer might reflect on an experience, a book, a poem, or a song.

The Writer's Role: Observer

PURPOSE

- To share a writer's insights about a subject
- To connect with readers

READERS

- Want to learn about other people's ideas and experiences
- Expect a personal treatment of the subject
- Welcome an unusual perspective

SOURCES

- Personal experiences and observations are often the major sources for reflective writing.
- Published sources might provide additional information to support a reflection.
- Cultural productions, such as music, art, movies, plays, and literature, can inspire reflection.

CONTEXT

- Reflections often draw on readers' knowledge of social events and their awareness of cultural context.
- Design choices anticipate the physical context in which the document is likely to be read.

Writers of reflective documents often connect their observations to the social, cultural, and historical contexts they share with their readers. For example, they might refer to events or people who have recently received attention in the news media. In addition, they might refer to works of art, such as the *Mona Lisa*, or quotations from well-known works of literature, such as Hamlet's question "To be, or not to be?" Writers of reflective documents are also aware of the physical contexts in which their documents are likely to be read, and they design their documents to meet the needs of those contexts: for instance, a short essay for a writing class will typically feature double-spaced text with wide margins and few, if any, illustrations or adornments, while a blog entry might include animated graphics, audio and video clips, or links to related websites.

Whether writing for themselves or others, writers use reflective writing to connect ideas and information, often in new and intriguing ways. Through reflection, writers can create new ways of understanding the world in which we live.

What Kinds of Documents Are Used to Share Reflections?

As a writer, you can use the reflections of other writers in many ways. Among other purposes, they can help you gain firsthand impressions from people who have been affected by an event. They can allow you to learn more about a particular historical period. They can help you understand the motivations and experiences of key figures in a political, cultural, or social movement. And they can help you develop a fuller understanding of your own experiences as you prepare your own reflective document.

You can begin to understand the contributions made by reflective documents by learning about the purposes, readers, sources, and contexts that have influenced other writers. In the following sections, you'll find discussions and examples of memoirs, reflective essays, photo essays, and literacy essays.

Reflective Essays

Reflective essays convey a writer's observations and thoughts on a subject to the members of a written conversation. Like memoirs and literacy narratives, reflective essays draw on personal experience and are often written from a first-person

(*I, me, my*) point of view. However, writers of reflective essays generally move beyond themselves as the primary focus of their essays, typically by using personal experience as a foundation for exploring more abstract ideas. In doing so, they show the significance of their experiences in a broader context.

In academic settings, such as writing and writing-intensive classes, reflective essays are often written in response to the information, ideas, or arguments found in another document, such as an article, an opinion column, or a personal essay. (If writers refer to another source, they cite it in the body of the essay and in a works cited or references list using a documentation system such as MLA or APA; see Chapters 23 and 24.) Because instructors and classmates will review and comment on them, reflective essays written for college courses are usually designed with wide margins, readable fonts, and double-spaced lines. In some cases, writers use illustrations, such as photographs and drawings, to set a mood or illustrate a point.

In nonacademic essays, writers frequently assume the role of observers and interpreters. Occasionally, as in the following essay by David Sedaris, humor is used to share reflections. The subjects — and objects — of humor can be sobering, even as they make us laugh: human fallibility, the disparity between the "ideal" and the "real," the incongruities and ironies of everyday life. Sometimes they try to make sense of obviously absurd or comic situations; at other times, they reveal the subtle absurdity of day-to-day life. In both cases, they make connections and share insights with readers, almost always from an eccentric, original, and profoundly personal point of view. When they succeed, our own point of view may be altered — permanently.

 David Sedaris

Keeping Up

"Keeping Up" first appeared in *The New Yorker* and was later published in *When You Are Engulfed in Flames,* David Sedaris's 2008 book of essays. Here, Sedaris considers his experience of traveling with and living with his partner, Hugh. Yet the essay ultimately highlights Sedaris's own unusual behavior, even as it touches on foreign travel, language, and dysfunctional relationships — all filtered through the writer's comic sensibility. Sedaris is the author of several books, including *Dress Your Family in Corduroy and Denim* (2004). He also contributes regularly to Public Radio International's *This American Life.*

Keeping Up
by David Sedaris

My street in Paris is named for a surgeon who taught at the nearby medical school and discovered an abnormal skin condition, a contracture that causes the fingers to bend inward, eventually turning the hand into a full-time fist. It's short, this street, no more or less attractive than anything else in the area, yet vacationing Americans are drawn here, compelled for some reason to stand under my office window and scream at each other.

For some, the arguments are about language. A wife had made certain claims regarding her abilities. "I've been listening to tapes," she said, or, perhaps, "All those romance languages are pretty much alike, so what with my Spanish we should be fine." But then people use slang, or ask unexpected questions, and things begin to fall apart: "*You're* the one who claimed to speak French." I hear this all the time, and look out my window to see a couple standing toe to toe on the sidewalk.

"Yeah," the woman will say. "At least *I* try."

"Well, try *harder*, damn it. Nobody knows what the hell you're saying."

Geographical arguments are the second most common. People notice that they've been on my street before, maybe half an hour ago, when they only thought they were tired and hungry and needed a bathroom.

"For God's sake, Philip, would it kill you to just ask somebody?"

I lie on my couch thinking, *Why don't you ask? How come Philip has to do it?* But these things are often more complicated than they

seem. Maybe Philip was here twenty years ago and has been claiming to know his way around. Maybe he's one of those who refuse to hand over the map, or refuse to pull it out, lest he look like a tourist.

The desire to pass is loaded territory and can lead to the ugliest sort of argument there is. "You want to *be* French, Mary Frances, that's your problem, but instead you're just another American!" I went to the window for that one and saw a marriage disintegrate before my eyes. Poor Mary Frances in her beige beret. Back at the hotel it had probably seemed like a good idea, but now it was ruined and ridiculous, a cheap felt pancake sliding off the back of her head. She'd done the little scarf thing, too, not caring that it was summer. It could've been worse, I thought. She could have been wearing one of those striped boater's shirts, but, as it was, it was pretty bad, a costume, really.

Some vacationers raise the roof — they don't care who hears them — but Mary Frances spoke in a whisper. This, too, was seen as pretension and made her husband even angrier. "Americans," he repeated. "We don't live in France, we live in Virginia. Vienna, Virginia. Got it?"

I looked at this guy and knew for certain that if we'd met at a party he'd claim to live in Washington, D.C. Ask for a street address, and he'd look away mumbling, "Well, just outside D.C."

When fighting at home, an injured party can retreat to a separate part of the house, or step into the backyard to shoot at cans, but outside my window the options are limited to crying, sulking, or storming back to the hotel. "Oh, for Christ's sake," I hear. "Can we please just try to have a good time?" This is like ordering someone to find you attractive, and it doesn't work. I've tried it.

Most of Hugh's and my travel arguments have to do with pace. I'm a fast walker, but he has longer legs and likes to maintain a good twenty-foot lead. To the casual observer, he would appear to be running from me, darting around corners, intentionally trying to lose himself. When asked about my latest vacation, the answer is always the same. In Bangkok, in Ljubljana, in Budapest and Bonn: What did I see? Hugh's back, just briefly, as he disappeared into a crowd. I'm convinced that before we go anywhere he calls the board of tourism and asks what style and color of coat is most popular among the locals. If they say, for example, a navy windbreaker, he'll go with that. It's uncanny the way he blends in. When we're in an Asian city, I swear he actually makes himself shorter. I don't know how, but he does. There's a store in London that sells travel guides alongside novels that take place in this or that given country. The idea is that you'll read the guide for facts and read the novel for atmosphere—a nice thought, but the only book I'll ever need is *Where's Waldo?* All my energy goes into keeping track of Hugh, and as a result I don't get to enjoy anything.

The last time this happened we were in Australia, where I'd gone to attend a conference. Hugh had all the free time in the world, but mine was limited to four hours on a Saturday morning. There's a lot to do in Sydney, but first on my list was a visit to the Turanga Zoo, where I'd hoped to see a dingo. I never saw that Meryl Streep movie, and as a result the creature was a complete mystery to me. Were

> All my energy goes into keeping track of Hugh, and as a result I don't get to enjoy anything.

someone to say, "I left my window open and a dingo flew in," I would have believed it, and if he said, "Dingoes! Our pond is completely overrun with them," I would've believed that as well. Two-legged, four-legged, finned, or feathered: I simply had no idea, which was exciting, actually, a rarity in the age of twenty-four-hour nature channels. Hugh offered to draw me a picture, but, having come this far, I wanted to extend my ignorance just a little bit longer, to stand before the cage or tank and see this thing for myself. It would be a glorious occasion, and I didn't want to spoil it at the eleventh hour. I also didn't want to go alone, and this was where our problem started.

Hugh had spent most of his week swimming and had dark circles beneath his eyes, twin impressions left by his goggles. When in the ocean, he goes out for hours, passing the lifeguard buoys and moving into international waters. It looks as though he's trying to swim home, which is embarrassing when you're the one left on shore with your hosts. "He honestly does like it here," I say. "Really."

Had it been raining, he might have willingly joined me, but, as it was, Hugh had no interest in dingoes. It took a solid hour of whining to change his mind, but even then his heart wasn't in it. Anyone could see that. We took a ferry to the zoo, and while on board he stared longingly at the water and made little paddling motions with his hands. Every second wound him tighter, and when we landed I literally had to run to keep up with him. The koala bears were just a blur, as were the visitors that stood before them, posing for photos. "Can't we just . . . ," I wheezed, but Hugh was rounding the emus and couldn't hear me.

He has the most extraordinary sense of direction I've seen in a mammal. Even in Venice, where the streets were seemingly designed by ants, he left the train station, looked once at a map, and led us straight to our hotel. An hour after checking in he was giving directions to strangers, and by the time we left he was suggesting shortcuts to gondoliers. Maybe he smelled the dingoes. Maybe he'd seen their pen from the window of the plane, but, whatever his secret, he ran right to them. I caught up a minute later and bent from the waist to catch my breath. Then I covered my face, stood upright, and slowly parted my fingers, seeing first the fence and then, behind it, a shallow moat with water. I saw some trees — and a tail — and then I couldn't stand it anymore and dropped my hands.

"Why, they look just like dogs," I said. "Are you sure we're in the right place?"

Nobody answered, and I turned to find myself standing beside an embarrassed Japanese woman. "I'm sorry," I said. "I thought you were the person I brought halfway around the world. First-class."

A zoo is a good place to make a spectacle of yourself, as the people around you have creepier, more photogenic things to look at. A gorilla pleasures himself while eating a head of iceberg lettuce, and it's much more entertaining than the forty-something-year-old man who dashes around talking to himself. For me, that talk is always the same, a rehearsal of my farewell speech: ". . . because this time, buddy, it's over. I mean it." I imagine myself packing a suitcase, throwing stuff in without bothering to fold it. "If you find yourself missing me, you might want to get a dog, an old, fat one that can run to catch up and make that distant panting sound you've grown so accustomed to. Me, though, I'm finished."

I will walk out the door and never look back, never return his calls, never even open his letters. The pots and pans, all the things that we acquired together, he can have them, that's how unfeeling I will be. "Clean start," that's my motto, so what do I need with a shoe box full of photographs, or the tan-colored belt he gave me for my thirty-third birthday, back when we first met and he did not yet understand that a belt is something you get from your aunt, and not your boyfriend, I don't care who made it. After that, though, he got pretty good in the gift-giving department: a lifelike mechanical hog covered in real pigskin, a professional microscope offered at the height of my arachnology phase, and, best of all, a seventeenth-century painting of a Dutch peasant changing a dirty diaper. Those things I would keep — and why not? I'd also take the desk he gave me, and the fireplace mantle, and, just on principle, the drafting table, which he clearly bought for himself and tried to pass off as a Christmas present.

Now it seemed that I would be leaving in a van rather than on foot, but, still, I was going to do it, so help me. I pictured myself pulling away from the front of our building, and then I remembered that I don't drive. Hugh would have to do it for me, and well he should after everything he'd put me through. Another problem was where this van might go. An apartment, obviously, but how would I get it? It's all I can do to open my mouth at the post office, so how am I going to talk to a real estate agent? The language aspect has nothing to do with it, as I'm no more likely to house-hunt in New York than I am in Paris. When discussing sums over sixty dollars, I tend to sweat. Not just on my forehead, but all over. Five minutes at the bank, and my shirt is transparent. Ten minutes, and I'm stuck to my seat. I lost twelve pounds getting the last apartment, and all I had to do was sign my name. Hugh handled the rest of it.

On the bright side, I have money, though I'm not exactly sure how to get my hands on it. Bank statements arrive regularly, but I don't open anything that's not personally addressed or doesn't look like a free sample. Hugh takes care of all that, opening the icky mail and actually reading it. He knows when our insurance payments are due, when it's time to renew our visas, when the warranty on the washer is about to expire. "I don't think we need to extend this," he'll say, knowing that if the machine stops working he'll fix it himself, the way he fixes everything. But not me. If I lived alone and something broke, I'd just work around it: use a paint bucket instead of a toilet, buy an ice chest and turn the dead refrigerator into an armoire. Call a repairman? Never. Do it myself? That'll be the day.

I've been around for nearly half a century, yet still I'm afraid of everything and everyone. A child sits beside me on a plane and I make conversation, thinking how stupid I must sound. The downstairs neighbors invite me to a party and, after claiming that I have a previous engagement, I spend the entire evening confined to my bed, afraid to walk around because they might hear my footsteps. I do not know how to turn up the heat, send an e-mail, call the answering machine for my messages, or do anything even remotely creative with a chicken. Hugh takes care of all that, and when he's out of town I eat like a wild animal, the meat still pink, with hair or feathers clinging to it. So is it any wonder that he runs from me? No matter how angry I get, it always comes down to this: I'm going to leave and then what? Move in with my dad? Thirty minutes of pure rage, and when I finally spot him I realize that I've never been so happy to see anyone in my life.

"There you are," I say. And when he asks where I have been, I answer honestly and tell him I was lost.

Starting a Conversation: Respond to "Keeping Up"

In your writer's notebook, analyze how Sedaris's writing strategies contribute to his humorous reflection by responding to the following questions:

1. What roles does Sedaris take on in this piece? At what points in the reading would you describe him as an observer, an interpreter, or a problem solver?

2. How does Sedaris connect his observations of traveling couples early in the reading to his own relationship with Hugh later on? What kind of context does he set up for his own personal story?

3. "Keeping Up" originally appeared in *The New Yorker*, which generally has an educated and relatively affluent audience. What aspects of this essay reflect that readership and the assumptions Sedaris makes about them?

4. Although much of what Sedaris publishes is rightly considered humor, what other genres might you use to classify this reading? What elements of his writing make the "humor" label suitable?

5. **Reflection:** Toward the end of the essay, Sedaris muses, "It's all I can do to open my mouth at the post office, so how am I going to talk to a real estate agent?" How does his self-deprecating tone throughout the essay affect your view of him and his reflections?

Photo Essays

A photo essay combines text and photographs to create a dominant impression of a subject, often suggesting the author's main idea rather than stating it outright. As a visual document, a photo essay offers a powerful and refreshing opportunity to convey thoughts and emotions that might not easily be put into words and to present complex concepts in a way that readers can grasp almost intuitively.

Many reflective photo essays visually explore subjects that have spurred debate, seem misunderstood, or are relatively unknown to readers. Others are deeply personal, highlighting images and experiences intimately connected to the writer's life. Writers might rely on published images from historical and contemporary sources or present original photographs. In either case, the pictures serve a central role in the author's reflection because they contribute to the meaning of the document. Text and image play off each other to reinforce ideas and to clarify what the writer has to say. Readers are invited to draw their own conclusions from what they see, although the author typically uses the surrounding text to nudge them in a particular direction.

James Mollison
Where Children Sleep

The photos reprinted on pages 124–135 are from *Where Children Sleep* (2010), a collection of photographer James Mollison's portraits of children from around the world and the rooms in which they sleep. When he embarked on the project, Mollison says, "I soon realized that my own experience of having a 'bedroom' simply doesn't apply to so many kids." Along with each set of photographs, he includes biographical details about each child to provide context for the portraits. Born in Kenya, Mollison grew up in England and currently lives with his family in Venice. His work has been featured in many international publications.

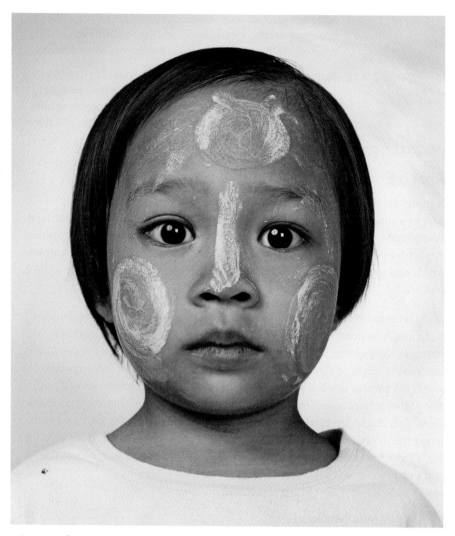

▲ Lay Lay is four years old. The cream she has on her face is made from the bark of the thanaka tree, used to condition and protect the skin. Lay Lay lives in Mae Sot, Thailand, close to the border with Burma. When her mother died, no other members of her family came to claim her, so she was placed in an orphanage. She shares this home with twenty-one other nursery-aged children. The orphanage consists of two rooms. During the day, one room is the classroom and the other is a dining room. At night, these rooms become bedrooms. The tables are pushed to one side and mats are rolled out for the children to sleep on. Each child has one drawer in which to keep their belongings. Lay Lay does not have many belongings — just a few clothes. All that is known of her background is that she is from an ethnic group of people called the Karen, one of the persecuted minority ethnic groups which make up about forty percent of the Burmese population. Lay Lay and her mother fled from the brutal Burmese military dictatorship and arrived in Thailand as refugees.

Where Children Sleep by © James Mollison, published in 2010

Where Children Sleep by © James Mollison, published in 2010

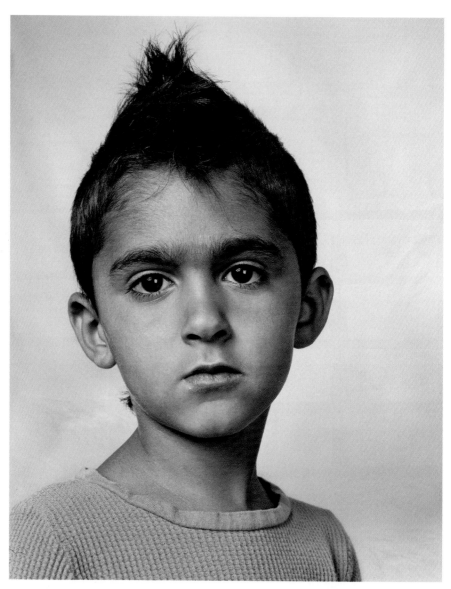

▲ Jivan is four years old. He lives with his parents in a skyscraper in Brooklyn, New York. From his bedroom window, he can see across the East River to New York's Manhattan Island and the Williamsburg Suspension Bridge, which connects it to Brooklyn. Jivan has his own bedroom with an en-suite bathroom and a toy cupboard. The room was designed by Jivan's mother, who is an interior designer. His father is a DJ and music producer. Jivan's school is only a ten minute walk away. To gain a place at his school, Jivan had to take a test to prove that he can mix socially with other children. He found this quite stressful as he is a very shy boy. His parents were also interviewed before he was accepted by the school. Jivan's favorite foods are steak and chocolate. He would like to be a fireman when he grows up.

Where Children Sleep by © James Mollison, published in 2010

Where Children Sleep by © James Mollison, published in 2010

▲ Kaya is four years old. She lives with her parents in a small apartment in Tokyo, Japan. Most apartments in Japan are small because land is very expensive to buy and there is such a large population to accommodate. Kaya's bedroom is every little girl's dream. It is lined from floor to ceiling with clothes and dolls. Kaya's mother makes all Kaya's dresses — up to three a month, usually. Now Kaya has thirty dresses and coats, thirty pairs of shoes, sandals and boots, and numerous wigs. (The pigtails in this picture are made from hairpieces.) Her friends love to come around to try on her clothes. When she goes to school, however, she has to wear a school uniform. Her favorite foods are meat, potatoes, strawberries, and peaches. She wants to be a cartoonist when she grows up, drawing Japanese anime cartoons.

Where Children Sleep by © James Mollison, published in 2010

Where Children Sleep by © James Mollison, published in 2010

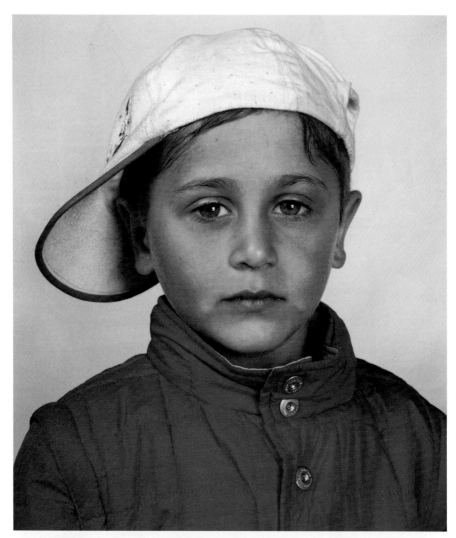

▲ Home for this four-year-old boy and his family is a mattress in a field on the outskirts of Rome, Italy. The family came from Romania by bus, after begging on the streets for enough money to pay for their tickets (€100 per adult and €80 per child). When they first arrived in Rome, they camped in a tent, but the police threw them off the site because they were trespassing on private land and did not have the correct documents. Now the family sleeps together on the mattress in the open. When it rains, they hastily erect a tent and use umbrellas for shelter, hoping they will not be spotted by the police. They left Romania without identity documents or work papers and so are unable to obtain legal employment. This boy sits by the curbside while his parents clean car windshields at traffic lights, to earn thirty to fifty cents a time. No one from the boy's family has ever been to school. His parents cannot read or write.

Where Children Sleep by © James Mollison, published in 2010

Where Children Sleep by © James Mollison, published in 2010

▲ Indira lives with her parents, brother and sister near Kathmandu in Nepal. Her house has only one room, with one bed and one mattress. At bedtime, the children share the mattress on the floor. Indira is seven years old and has worked at the local granite quarry since she was three. The family is very poor so everyone has to work. There are 150 other children working at the quarry, some of whom will lose their sight because they do not have goggles to protect their eyes from stone splinters. Indira works five or six hours a day and then helps her mother with household chores such as cleaning and cooking. Her favorite food is noodles. She also attends school, which is a thirty minute walk away. She does not mind working at the quarry but would prefer to be playing. She would like to be a Nepalese dancer when she grows up.

Where Children Sleep by © James Mollison, published in 2010

Where Children Sleep by © James Mollison, published in 2010

▲ Li is ten years old and lives in an apartment block in Beijing, China, with her parents. She is an only child — as a result of the Chinese government's "one child per family" policy, introduced to control population growth. Families with more than one child are usually penalized. Li goes to a school nearby, where she enjoys learning math, singing, and music. She is a perfectionist and will spend up to three hours each night completing her homework to the highest standard. She also attends ballet classes twice a week after school. Three times during her school life, she will have to attend a compulsory army summer camp organized by the People's Liberation Army. In preparation for this she has to attend army training. Li does not want to be in the army when she grows up. She wants to be a policewoman so that she can protect people.

Where Children Sleep by © James Mollison, published in 2010

Where Children Sleep by © James Mollison, published in 2010

Starting a
Conversation:
Respond to
"Where
Children
Sleep"

In your writer's notebook, reflect on the ideas presented in Mollison's photo essay by responding to the following questions:

1. A reflective photo essay such as this one might not have a strictly defined thesis statement. But how would you describe the main idea of Mollison's work? What is the dominant impression created by his mix of words and pictures?

2. While he acknowledges the issues of poverty and wealth that inform his photos, Mollison says, "There is no agenda to the book other than my own journey and curiosity, and wanting to share in pictures and words the stories that I found interesting, or that moved me." In what ways does this statement fit with the purpose of a reflective document? What changes do you think Mollison would have made to his approach if he had, in fact, been creating an analytical or argumentative photo essay?

3. As you look at the photographs and their accompanying text, consider this statement from Mollison: "The book is written and presented for an audience of 9–13 year olds . . . intended to interest and engage children in the details of the lives of other children around the world, and the social issues affecting them, while also being a serious photographic essay for an adult audience." How successfully do you think Mollison's work reaches each of those audiences? What do you see in Mollison's writing style and in the composition of his photographs that would appeal to adults and to older children? What do you think members of each audience — nine-to thirteen-year-olds, older teens, and adults — would take away from his work?

4. Why do you suppose that Mollison chose to use color images? Would black-and-white photographs have had as much impact, more impact, or less impact? Why do you think so?

5. **Reflection:** Consider how Mollison's photographs might have been different if he had chosen to focus on one country or region of the world. How do you think his audience and their expectations of his work would have changed, and how would they have remained the same?

Literacy Narratives

Literacy narratives allow writers to reflect on the people, ideas, and events that have shaped them as writers and readers. What distinguishes literacy narratives from other reflective documents is not their design — they are often indistinguishable in appearance from essays or brief memoirs — but their purpose. They exist solely to help writers share their reflections about their relationship with reading and writing. Some literacy narratives, such as the following one, focus on a critical event or series of events that influenced a person's identity as a writer. Others offer a comprehensive overview of the experiences that shaped the writer's relationship with words. Because of their focus on the writer's life, most literacy narratives use details drawn from personal experience to support points. In some cases, writers draw on information from published sources to provide a context for their narrative.

Literacy narratives are often assigned in college classes because they give students an opportunity to examine their past experiences with written expression and, in doing so, to overcome any assumptions or fears they might have. Experienced writers, too, frequently write literacy narratives, sometimes to share their joy of reading or their reasons for writing, but just as often to connect with their readers by exploring the challenges and rewards of learning to read and write.

 Salvatore Scibona

Where I Learned to Read

Salvatore Scibona has won numerous awards for his fiction. His first novel was a finalist for the National Book Award, and his work has been published in many newspapers, magazines, and journals. As he discusses in this piece, Scibona graduated from St. John's College, whose curriculum focuses entirely on classic works of literature. He later received a master of fine arts from the Iowa Writers' Workshop. "Where I Learned to Read" appeared in the June 13, 2001, issue of *The New Yorker*.

Where I Learned to Read

by Salvatore Scibona

I did my best to flunk out of high school. I failed English literature, American literature, Spanish, precalculus, chemistry, physics. Once, in a fit of melancholic vanity, I burned my report card in the sink of the KFC where I worked scraping carbonized grease from the pressure cookers. I loved that job the way a dog loves a carcass in a ditch. I came home stinking of it. It was a prudent first career in that I wanted with certainty only one thing, to get out of Ohio, and the Colonel might hire me anywhere in the world. The starting wage was $3.85 an hour. I was saving for the future.

But wasn't it far-fetched, this notion of a future, when I could hardly get through eleventh grade? I always showed up at that job; why couldn't I show up at the desk in my room and write a C-minus summary of the life of Woodrow Wilson? The television stayed on day and night, singing like a Siren in the crowded house. "Come sit by me and die a little," it said.

I didn't know what I was doing or what I believed in, except the United States of America and the Cleveland Browns. Sometimes, to break my addiction to the tube, I spent the night in a derelict shed with mushrooms growing from the rafter boards. Backyard rehab. I used to read in there, or, anyway, swing my eyes over the pages of library books: *Out of Africa* (the girl I was in love with loved the movie); Donald Trump's autobiography; Kierkegaard; *Leaves of Grass*; a book about how to make a robot from an eight-track player. As long as nobody had assigned the book, I could stick with it. I didn't know what I was reading. I didn't really know *how* to read. Reading

messed with my brain in an unaccountable way. It made me happy; or something. I copied out the first paragraph of Annie Dillard's *An American Childhood* on my bedroom's dormer wall. The book was a present from an ace teacher, a literary evangelist in classy shoes, who also flunked me, of course, with good reason. Even to myself I was a lost cause.

Early senior year, a girl in homeroom passed me a brochure that a college had sent her. The college's curriculum was an outrage. No electives. Not a single book in the seminar list by a living author. However, no tests. No grades, unless you asked to see them. No textbooks — I was confused. In place of an astronomy manual, you would read Copernicus. No books about Aristotle, just Aristotle. Like, you would read *book*-books. The Great Books, so called, though I had never heard of most of them. It was akin to taking holy orders, but the school — St. John's College — had been secular for three hundred years. In place of praying, you read. My loneliness was toxic; the future was coleslaw, mop water; the college stood on a desert mountain slope in Santa Fe, New Mexico, fifteen hundred miles from home; I could never get into such a school; my parents couldn't pay a dollar. And I loved this whole perverse and beautiful idea. I would scrap everything (or so I usefully believed) and go to that place and ask them to let me in. It felt like a vocation. It *was* a vocation.

Reader, I married it.

The summer before I started, the dean had the arriving students read the *Iliad* and memorize the

Greek alphabet. A year before, I had not known that ancient Greek still existed. I had assumed that all we knew of the Greeks was hearsay. The other students came from Louisiana, Alaska, Malaysia. I could not recognize any of the splintery plant life here. After Greek, we would learn to read French. A teacher, a soft-spoken giant from Colorado in a yarmulke and a worn wool jacket, pointed to a figure in a differential equation from Newton's *Principia* and said, "This is where our upper-middle-class prejudices about time and space begin to break down."

Loans. Grants from the college and the government. Jobs from asbestos remover to library clerk. I carried bricks and mortar to rooftops during the summers, but if I hadn't made time to read the night before, my legs wore out by noon. Even my body needed to read.

By senior year at St. John's, we were reading Einstein in math, Darwin in lab, Baudelaire in French tutorial, Hegel in seminar. Seminar met twice a week for four years: eight o'clock to ten at night or later, all students addressed by surname. On weekends, I hung out with my friends. The surprise, the wild luck: I had friends. One sat in my room with a beer and *The Phenomenology of Spirit*, reading out a sentence at a time and stopping to ask, "All right, what did that mean?" The gravity of the whole thing would have been laughable if it hadn't been so much fun, and if it hadn't been such a gift to find my tribe.

In retrospect, I was a sad little boy and a standard-issue, shiftless, egotistical, dejected teen-ager. Everything was going to hell, and then these strangers let me come to their school and showed me how to read. All things considered, every year since has been a more intense and enigmatic joy.

Starting a Conversation: Respond to "Where I Learned to Read"

In your writer's notebook, consider Scibona's reflections on his reading life by responding to the following questions:

1. How does Scibona re-create the voice of his teenage self throughout this piece? Do phrases such as this one — "Like, you would read *book-books*" (para. 4) — seem realistic to you? Why or why not?

2. Scibona describes studying at St. John's as "akin to taking holy orders" and "a vocation" (para. 4). What do these descriptions suggest about Scibona's attitude toward reading or toward college life in general?

3. In the middle of the essay, Scibona includes a short, one-line paragraph: "Reader, I married it," which is a slight variation of a famous line at the end of Charlotte Brontë's *Jane Eyre* ("Reader, I married him."). Why might Scibona have chosen to include this line? What does it say about his expectations of his readers?

4. Literacy narratives focus on moments or events that shape a person's relationship with words. How would you describe the change in Scibona's attitude toward reading and toward a successful future?

5. **Reflection:** In what ways does Scibona's essay lead you to reflect on your own development as a reader? If you had the opportunity to sit down with Scibona, what stories might you share with him? What would those stories say about you as a reader?

Memoirs

A memoir is a narrative that presents and reflects on personal experience, usually from a writer's past. Memoirs can vary greatly in length, from a few hundred words to multiple-volume books. Writers of shorter memoirs often focus on a specific moment and address readers of a particular publication, such as a newspaper, magazine, journal, or website. Writers of longer (book-length) memoirs usually address a more general audience of readers who share their interest in a certain aspect of their lives. Regardless of the length of their works, writers of memoirs usually employ the first-person point of view (*I*, *me*, *we*), emphasize text over visuals, and look for ways to make their personal stories relevant for readers.

 ### Margo Jefferson
Are We Rich?

"Are We Rich?" is an excerpt from Margo Jefferson's 2015 memoir *Negroland*. A personal reflection, but also a meditation on the larger discussion of race in America, the memoir recounts Jefferson's experience as a young black girl in an affluent Chicago family. Her experience in Negroland, her term for "the colored elite" or privileged, educated African Americans of the 1950s, reveals fraught comparisons between "us" and "them" — comparisons not only between blacks and whites but also between well-to-do blacks and working-class blacks. In retelling a story from her childhood, Jefferson explores class through the complication of race, juxtaposing her childhood questions with her now adult knowledge. Jefferson is a Pulitzer Prize winner and a professor of writing at the Columbia University School of the Arts. She has also taught at Eugene Lang College and New York University. Formerly a cultural critic for *The New York Times* and a staff writer for *Newsweek*, Jefferson has also been published in *Vogue*, *Harper's*, and other magazines. Her first book was *On Michael Jackson* (2006).

Are We Rich?

I

Are we rich?

Mother raises those plucked, deep-toned eyebrows that did such good, expressive work for women in the 1950s. Lift the penciled arch by three to four millimeters and you had bemused doubt, blatant disdain, or disapproval just playful enough to lure the speaker into more error. Mother's lips form a small, cool smile that mirrors her eyebrow arch. She places a small, emphatic space between each word—"Are We Rich?"—then adds, "Why do you ask?"

I ask because I have been told that day: "Your family must be rich." A schoolmate told me and I faltered, then stalled—flattered and ashamed to be. We are supposed to eschew petty snobberies at the University of Chicago Laboratory School: intellectual superiority is our task. Other fathers are doctors. Other mothers dress well and drive stylish cars. Wondering what stirred that question has left me anxious and a little queasy.

Mother says: "We are not rich. And it's impolite to ask anyone that question. Remember that. If you're asked again, you should just say 'we're comfortable.'" I take her words in and push on, because my classmate has asked a second question.

Are we upper class?

Mother's eyebrows settle now. She sits back in the den chair and pauses for effect. I am about to receive general instruction in the liturgies of race and class.

"We're considered upper-class Negroes and upper-middle-class Americans," Mother says. "But most people would like to consider us Just More Negroes."

II

"D. and J. asked me if we know their janitor, Mr. Johnson. They think he lives near us." (They had spoken of him so affectionately that I wished I could say I knew our janitor that well and that he liked me as much as Mr. Johnson seemed to like them. They had rights of intimacy with their janitor that I lacked.)

I have to stop here, though. My policy in these pages is to use initials when I recall the mishaps or misdeeds of my peers. Their words and acts belong to me; their names belong to them. I know initials look silly in dialogue that aims for realism. But I didn't want to use their names. They were my dear friends—one from sixth grade on, the other from our twenties on—and we grew into talking honestly about these matters. They were twins and now they're dead, killed by cancer. I didn't want them to be so starkly flawed here. But for now, they must be. And so:

"Debi and Judi asked me if we know their janitor, Mr. Johnson. They think he lives near us."

"It's a big neighborhood," Mother says. "Why would we know their janitor? White people think Negroes all know each other, and they always want you to know their janitor. Do they want to know our laundryman?"

That would be Wally, a smiling, big-shouldered white man who delivers crisply wrapped shirts and cheerful greetings to our back door every week.

"Good morning, Mrs. Jefferson," he says. "Good morning, Doctor. Hello, girls."

"Hello, Wally," we chime back from the breakfast table. Then, one weekend afternoon, I was in the kitchen with Mother doing something minor and domestic, like helping unpack groceries, when she said slowly, not looking at me: "I saw Wally at Sears today. I was looking at vacuum cleaners. And I looked up and saw him—" (Here she paused for the distancing Rodgers and Hammerstein irony, *"across a crowded room."*) "He was turning his head away, hoping he wouldn't have to speak. Wally the laundryman was trying to cut me." If this had been drama, she would have paused and done something with a telling prop—one of the better brands of an everyday food, or a nice-looking piece of flatware. Then she said, "And I don't even shop at Sears except for appliances."

Humor is laughing at what you haven't got when you ought to have it—the right, in this case, to snub or choose to speak kindly to your laundryman in a store where he must shop for clothes and you shop only for appliances.

Still, Wally went on delivering laundry with cheerful deference, and we responded with cooler—but not intrusively cool—civility.

Was there no Negro laundry to do Daddy's shirts as well or better? Our milkman was a Negro. So were our janitor, our plumber, our carpenter, our upholsterer, our caterer, and our dressmaker. Though I don't remember all their names, I know their affect was restful. Comfortable. If a Negro employee did his work in a sloppy or sullen way (and it did happen), Mother and Daddy had two responses. One was your standard folk wisecrack, something like "Well, some of us *are* lazy, quiet as it's kept." *Humor is laughing at what you haven't got when you ought to have it:* in this case, a spotless race reputation.

The second response was disquieting. "Some Negroes prefer to work for white people. They don't resent their status in the same way."

All right then, let's say you are a Negro cleaning woman, on your knees at this moment, scrubbing the bathtub with its extremely visible ring of body dirt, because whoever bathed last night thought, *How nice. I don't have to clean the tub because*

Cleo / Melba / Mrs. Jenkins comes tomorrow! Tub done, you check behind the toilet (a washcloth has definitely fallen back there); the towels are scrunched, not hung on the racks, and you've just come from the children's bedroom, where sheets have to be untangled and almost throttled into shape before they can be sorted for the wash.

Would you rather look at the people you do this for and think: *I will never be in their place if the future is like the past.* Or would you rather look at your employers and think: *Well, if I'd been able to get an education like Dr. and Mrs. Jefferson, if I hadn't had to start doing housework at fifteen to help my family out when we moved up here from Mississippi, then maybe I could be where they are.*

Whose privilege would you find easier to bear?

Who are "you"? How does your sociological vita — race or ethnicity, class, gender, family history — affect your answer?

Whoever you are, reader, please understand that neither my parents, my sister, nor I ever left a dirty bathtub for Mrs. Blake to clean. (My sister and I called her Mrs. Blake. Mother called her Blake.) She was broad, not fat. She had very short, very straightened hair that she patted flat and put behind her ears. When it got humid in the basement, where the washer and dryer were, or in the room where she ironed clothes, short pieces of hair would defy hot comb and oil to stick up and out. We never made direct fun of her hair — we would have been punished. But we regularly mocked Negro hair that blatantly defied rehabilitation. Mrs. B.'s voice was Southern South Side: leisurely and nasal. Now that I've given my adult attention to the classic blues singers, I can say she had the weighted country diction of Ma Rainey and the short nasal tones of Sippie Wallace. Vowels rubbed down, end-word consonants dropped or muffled.

Mother made it clear that we were never to leave our beds unmade when Mrs. Blake was coming. She was not there to pick up after us. When we were old enough, we stripped our own beds each week and folded the linen before putting it in the hamper for her to remove and wash.

Mother's paternal grandmother, great-aunt, and aunt had been in service, so she was sensitive to inappropriate childish presumption.

Mrs. Blake ate her lunch (a hot lunch that Mother had made from dinner leftovers) in the kitchen. When her day was done, Mr. Blake and their daughters drove to our house. He sent his daughters to the front door to pick her up. They had the same initials we did. Mildred and Diane. Margo and Denise. Mother brought us to the front door to exchange hellos with them. Sometimes Mrs. Blake left carrying one or two bags of neatly folded clothes. Did Mildred and Diane enjoy unfolding, surveying, and fitting themselves into our used ensembles and separates?

Starting a Conversation: Respond to "Are We Rich?"

In your writer's notebook, reflect on the ideas presented in Jefferson's memoir by responding to the following questions:

1. The primary question, "Are we rich?" suggests that Jefferson is reflecting on social class. Yet she does more than this. What are the other underlying themes that she calls into question? How do these other themes change the implication of the question, "Are we rich?" Does Jefferson answer the question? If so, in what ways is the question answered? If not, how does she leave the question unanswered?

2. The essay is divided into two sections. What is the effect of this structure? How do the sections complement or contrast with one another?

3. The essay begins and ends with a question, and there are a number of questions throughout the narrative. Do you find this pattern effective? Why or why not? Why do you think Jefferson thought it would be a good way to engage her readers?

4. Note a few of the moments in which the narrator switches from the past to the present. How does the narrator's voice change? Why do you think Jefferson alternates between reporting and reflecting? In what ways does this engage the reader?

5. **Reflection:** Think back on whether you were aware of your family's social or economic standing as a child. How has your understanding changed since then?

GENRE TALK

| Reflective Writing | Informative Writing | Analytical Writing | Evaluative Writing | Problem-Solving Writing | Argumentative Writing |

In the post–9/11 era, stories of returning home from war are gaining attention as more and more veterans decide to speak out about the lasting effects — both physical and psychological — of war. While some veterans opt for persuasive or problem-solving writing in the form of editorials or opinion columns, many prefer reflective documents, such as short stories, documentaries, and feature films. Run by the American Folklife Center at the Library of Congress, the Veterans History Project is a multimedia effort to collect and preserve the reflections of those who have fought in the United States armed services. The project contains letters, diaries, scrapbooks, drawings, photographs, videotaped interviews, and audio interviews with veterans from World War I up through the Iraq War. One such audio interview is featured here.

LaunchPad
macmillan learning

Test your knowledge of genre with the Genre Talk quiz in the LaunchPad for *Joining the Conversation*.
launchpadworks.com

A quotation by Gunnery Sgt. Noël and a photograph of her in uniform emphasize the difference between her civilian identity ("Rosie") and her identity as a marine ("Gunny Noël").

The record contains biographical information, details of Gunnery Sgt. Noël's deployments, and a brief description of her war experience.

Both the full audio interview and clips of highlights are available on the Web as part of the Library of Congress Veterans History Project.

Links to additional documents, including photos and correspondence

Veterans History Project, Library of Congress

How Can I Write a Reflective Essay?

For some writers, the greatest challenge in writing a reflective essay is getting past the idea that no one would be interested in reading their reflections on a subject. In fact, readers show a great deal of interest in reflective writing. They buy memoirs and autobiographies, visit blogs, and read opinion columns. They read articles and essays in which writers share their thoughts about their experiences and ideas. Some readers even try to pick the locks on their sisters' diaries.

Reflective writing is popular not only among readers but also among writers. Reflective essays allow you to share your insights with instructors and classmates, people who are likely to have an interest in your perspective on a subject.

Writing a reflective essay involves choosing and reflecting on a subject, preparing a draft, and reviewing and improving what you've written. As you work on your essay, you'll follow the work of Caitlin Guariglia, an Italian American student who wrote a reflective essay about a family trip to Italy.

Find a Conversation and Listen In

Reflective essays allow you to share your thoughts about a subject with readers who might have a common interest in it. You might reflect on a personal experience, an idea you've encountered in a book or a blog, a photograph or other physical object that holds special meaning for you, a person you've met or read about, a troubling conversation with a friend, or a recent event. In fact, you can reflect on almost anything. To get started on your reflective essay, spend some time thinking about your purpose, your readers, and the context in which your writing will be read (see p. 116). Then generate some ideas about possible subjects for your reflection, choose one that seems promising, and learn more about it by observing it closely or discussing it with others.

In Process

A Reflective Essay about a Family Vacation

Caitlin Guariglia wrote a reflective essay for her introductory composition course. Caitlin based her reflection on a family trip to Italy, using her observations of the people she met in Rome to consider how cultural influences affect her Italian American family's behavior. Follow her efforts to write the essay as you read the In Process boxes throughout this chapter.

EXPLORE YOUR EXPERIENCES

Brainstorming (see p. 41) provides a good way to generate ideas for the subject of a reflective essay. Start by asking questions about your past or recent experiences, such as the following:

- Why is my favorite childhood memory so special to me?
- Did I learn anything about myself this weekend?
- What surprised me in my history class this week?
- What story that is currently in the news annoys me the most?
- What is the last thing that made me laugh?
- What do I worry about most?
- What experiences in my life do I wish had gone differently?
- What am I most proud of, and why?

Use your imagination to come up with questions about your personal, academic, and professional experiences. Quickly jot down answers to your questions. Then review your answers to identify a subject that will meet your purpose, interest your readers, and be suitable for the context, requirements, and limitations of your writing assignment. If you're still not sure you've found the right inspiration for a topic, check the writing project ideas at the end of this chapter for additional suggestions (p. 167).

ASK QUESTIONS ABOUT PROMISING SUBJECTS

You can begin to focus on a subject by asking questions about it (see p. 48). If you were considering writing a reflective essay about online communities such as Facebook or Twitter, for example, you might use the following strategies to identify interesting aspects of the subject.

- **Ask *why, why not, when, where,* and *who.*** You might ask why so many parents react negatively to social-networking sites such as Facebook, or you might ask who is likely to cause difficulties for members of online communities.
- **Ask how your subject functions as a whole.** You might ask how websites such as Facebook are changing how people communicate, whether they represent a distinctly different kind of community, or why they're so popular with a particular age group.

- **Ask about parts of a whole.** You might ask which aspects of online communities are more attractive than others or whether one subgroup in an online community is likely to behave differently than another subgroup.

- **Ask questions about degree and extent.** You can ask about the degree to which something affects something else or about the extent of a problem. For instance, you might ask how friendships formed at a school direct the formation of online communities or whether the dangers associated with teenage use of social-networking sites are as widespread as reported.

CONDUCT AN OBSERVATION

If you've chosen a subject that lends itself to observation, you might find it useful to conduct one. Observing a subject firsthand can provide you with valuable insights that simply aren't possible when you're learning about the subject secondhand — for example, through discussion or through reading a book, magazine, or Web page. In addition, conducting an observation can increase your credibility as a writer. A reflective essay usually carries more weight if the writer has taken the time to observe the subject personally.

Want to know more about field research? See Chapter 14.

Although some observations can involve a significant amount of time and effort, an observation need not be complicated to be useful. (You can learn more about observation on pp. 503–505.)

Working Together: Try It Out Loud

Before you start writing a reflective essay, try having a conversation with your classmates about a common experience. Form small groups, and list the subjects each of you is considering writing about. Choose one that most people in the group can relate to (such as an embarrassing moment, a fight with a friend, or the first day of class). Take turns sharing your memories about the experience while the other members of the group listen, respond, and ask questions. Your purpose is to connect with the other members of your group,

so try to present an honest, personal view of the event.

When you are finished, take a few minutes to reflect on the exercise. What did you learn about your audience? Did you have to adapt what you said based on their interest level or on those parts of your story they didn't understand? What did you discover about what you have in common and what you do not?

Reflect on Your Subject

Perhaps you've had the opportunity to listen to musicians jamming during a concert, or perhaps you're a musician yourself. If so, you know about the ebb and flow of the music, how one line of melody plays off another, how the music circles and

In Process

Conducting an Observation

Caitlin Guariglia's reflective essay was based on a series of informal observations of strangers in Rome and family members at home. She recorded her observations in a journal.

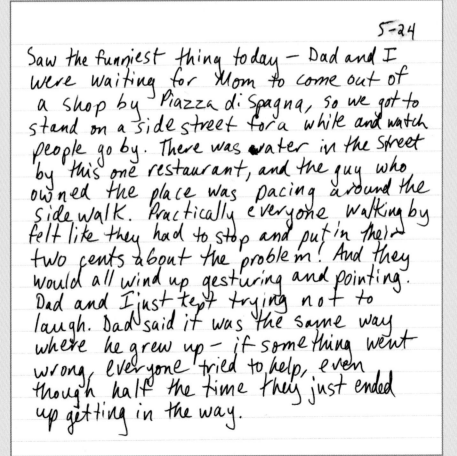

5-24

Saw the funniest thing today — Dad and I were waiting for Mom to come out of a shop by Piazza di Spagna, so we got to stand on a side street for a while and watch people go by. There was water in the street by this one restaurant, and the guy who owned the place was pacing around the sidewalk. Practically everyone walking by felt like they had to stop and put in their two cents about the problem! And they would all wind up gesturing and pointing. Dad and I just kept trying not to laugh. Dad said it was the same way where he grew up — if something went wrong, everyone tried to help, even though half the time they just ended up getting in the way.

▲ Caitlin reviewed her notes as she planned and then began to draft her essay.

builds. Reflection is similar to this process. As you reflect on a subject, your thinking moves from one aspect to another, flowing smoothly forward at some times and circling back at others. Reflection can involve seeking understanding, making connections, and exploring contrasts. In the same way that a jam session offers surprises not only to listeners but also to the musicians, reflection can lead you in unexpected directions. The key to reflecting productively is a willingness to be open to those new directions.

Reflection is most effective when you record your thoughts. Writing them down as notes in a writer's notebook or as entries in a journal allows you to keep track of your thinking. As you make decisions about your writing project, you can turn to your notes to review your reflections.

Reflection begins with viewing your subject from a particular perspective. It also involves collecting details and finding significance. To prepare to reflect, place yourself in a relaxing situation that will allow you to think. Take a walk, ride a bike, go for a run, enjoy a good meal, listen to music, lie down — do whatever you think will free you from distractions.

EXAMINE YOUR SUBJECT

Begin to reflect on your subject by viewing it through a particular lens, such as how it compares to something else, what caused it or what effects it might have, or what challenges and difficulties you associate with it. Although some perspectives are likely to be better suited to your subject than others, try to look at your subject from more than one angle.

Explore processes   Thinking of something as a process can help you understand how it works as well as how it contributes to the context in which it takes place. For example, instead of reflecting on text-messaging as a social phenomenon, reflect on the processes involved in text-messaging. Ask how it works, what steps are involved in composing and sending a message, and how people understand and respond to messages.

Consider implications   Considering the implications of a subject can help you understand its impact and importance. You can ask questions such as what is likely to happen, what if such-and-such happens, what will happen when, and so on. As you reflect on implications, stay grounded: don't get so carried away by speculation that you lose track of your reason for reflecting.

Examine similarities and differences Use comparison and contrast to find points of connection for your subject. You might examine, for example, the similarities and differences between new communication technologies, such as e-mail and text-messaging, and older means of staying in touch, such as letter writing and passing notes in class. Or you might compare and contrast the ways in which people get to know one another, such as hanging out together, joining organizations, and dating.

Trace causes and effects Thinking about causes and effects can help you better understand a subject. For example, you might reflect on the origins of complaints — some dating back to the ancient Greeks — that the latest generation of young people is not only impolite and uncultured but also likely to undo the accomplishments of previous generations. You might also reflect on the effects that this attitude has on relationships between the old and the young.

Consider value Reflection often involves considering factors such as strengths and weaknesses, costs and benefits, and limitations and opportunities. For example, you might reflect on the relative strengths and weaknesses of a candidate for political office. Or you might weigh the costs and benefits of a proposed law to make the Internet safer for children. Similarly, you might consider the limitations and opportunities associated with proposals to increase funding for higher education.

Identify challenges and difficulties Getting to the heart of an issue or idea often involves determining how it challenges your assumptions or values or identifying the nature of the difficulties it poses for you. For example, ask yourself why an idea bothers you, or ask why it might bother someone else.

Reflect on your experiences As you reflect on your subject, search for connections to your own life. Ask whether your personal experiences would lead you to act in a particular way. Ask how they are likely to influence your reactions and attitudes. Ask whether you've found yourself in situations that are relevant to your subject.

COLLECT DETAILS

People are fond of saying, "It's all in the details." Although this is true for nearly all types of writing, it's especially true for reflective essays. Without details, even the best essay can fall flat. You might get a laugh out of the following story, for example, but few people will find it truly satisfying:

> Once upon a time, they all lived happily ever after.

To collect details for a reflective essay, use the following strategies.

Describe your subject If you can, use observation to collect details about your subject (see p. 148). If you have firsthand experience with the subject, freewrite or brainstorm about it to refresh your memory: write down what you saw and heard, what you felt, even what you smelled. Provide as much detail as possible.

Compare your subject with something else Many subjects are best understood in relation to others. Darkness, for example, is difficult to understand without comparing it to light. Success is best understood in the context of its alternatives. And for those who live in colder climates, spring is all the more welcome because it follows winter. To find useful points of comparison, create a two-column log: place your subject at the top of one column and a contrasting subject at the top of the other, and then record your reflections on the similarities and differences between the two subjects in each column. Use the results to provide details for your essay.

Discuss your ideas If you talk about your subject with other people, you might be able to use their comments to add detail to your essay. You might want to set up a formal interview with someone who is an expert on the subject or with someone who has been affected by it (see Chapter 14), but you can also simply bring up your subject in casual conversations to learn what others think. If they tell a story about their experiences with your subject, ask whether you might add their anecdote to your reflection. Similarly, if you hear an interesting turn of phrase or a startling statement related to your subject, consider quoting it. (See Chapter 21 to learn more about integrating quotations into an essay.)

Learn more about your subject As you gain a better idea of how you'll focus your essay, look for opportunities to add to your understanding of the subject. Browse newspapers and magazines in your library's periodical room to pick up bits of information that will add depth to your essay, or see what's been written recently about your subject on news sites and in blogs (see Chapter 13). As you read about your subject, take note of interesting details that might grab your readers' attention.

FIND SIGNIFICANCE

Every good story has a point. Every good joke has a punch line. Every good reflective essay leaves its readers with something to think about. As you reflect on your subject, consider why it's important to you, and think about how you can make it important for your readers. Then ask whether they'll care about what you've decided to share with them. The main idea of your reflective essay should hold some significance for your readers. Ideally, after reading your essay, they'll continue to think about what you've written.

By now, you'll have reflected a great deal on your subject, and you'll be in a good position to identify the most significant aspects of what you've learned. To find significance, freewrite or brainstorm about your subject for ten or fifteen minutes. Ask yourself what your readers will need or want to know about it. Ask what will spark their imaginations. Ask what will stir their emotions. Then ask whether the ideas you've come up with will help you accomplish your goals as a writer.

Making Comparisons

Caitlin Guariglia used comparison to reflect on her experiences with strangers in Rome and with her family. She used a two-column table to make direct comparisons.

Strangers in Rome	Family in America
get involved in other people's business if they feel like they know how to do it better and can help	get involved in your business, whether you like it or not!
cool, confident, witty, LOUD	not always so cool, but definitely loud, full of themselves, and usually really funny
passionate about their city, its history, and its food	love NY, but not all are passionate about it, definitely opinionated about Italian food
beautiful Italian accents	only speak a little Italian, NY accents
really big on family, and like to make you feel like part of theirs	exactly the same

Caitlin used her notes to shape a point in her final essay:

> Our ancestors may have brought the food, the expressions, and the attitudes with them to the United States a few generations ago, but it is safe to say that over the years we have lost some of the style and the musical language that Italians seem to possess from birth.

Prepare a Draft

As you prepare to draft your reflective essay, you'll think about how to convey your main idea, how to shape your reflection, which details to include, and what point of view to take. You'll also make decisions about how to design and craft your essay. You can read about other strategies related to drafting academic essays, such as writing strong paragraphs and integrating information from sources, in Part Four.

CONVEY YOUR MAIN IDEA

Reflective essays, like other kinds of academic essays, should have a point. Before you begin writing, try to express your main idea in the form of a tentative thesis statement, a single sentence that articulates the most significant aspect of your reflections on your subject. By framing your main idea in a particular way, you can focus your efforts and help your readers see why your reflection should matter to them.

Consider the differences among the following tentative thesis statements about pursuing a career as a writer:

> Without commitment and discipline, pursuing a career as a writer would be a waste of time.

> Without a genuine love of words and a desire to share your ideas with others, pursuing a career as a writer would be a waste of time.

> The paths that lead to a career in writing are as varied as the writers who follow them.

Each of these statements would lead to significantly different reflective essays. The first frames becoming a writer as a test of character. It implies that writers can't succeed unless they are prepared to dedicate themselves to the hard work of writing. The second thesis statement shifts the focus from discipline and commitment to the writer's relationship with words and readers. It paints a warmer, less intimidating picture of what it takes to become a writer. The third thesis statement shifts the focus completely away from the qualities shared by successful writers, suggesting instead that each writer has different reasons for pursuing a career in writing. You can read more about developing a thesis statement in Chapter 16.

Need help with main ideas? See Chapter 16.

Even though having a main idea is necessary, the final draft of a reflective essay doesn't always include a formal thesis statement. Depending on the nature of the reflection, writers sometimes choose to use their observations to create a dominant impression of a subject. That is, they tell a story or build up details to show — rather than state outright — why the subject is significant.

TELL A STORY

Almost every type of writing — at least, writing that's interesting — tells a story. An autobiography tells readers about events in the writer's life. An opinion column uses an anecdote — a brief description of an event or experience — to personalize an abstract issue. An article on ESPN.com describes what happened in a game — and speculates about what it means for the playoffs. In fact, some people have said that everything we do can be understood as a story.

If the subject of your reflection is an event in your past, shaping your essay as a story (that is, a chronological narrative with a beginning, a middle, and an end) is a natural way to proceed. But other kinds of subjects also lend themselves to story-telling. For example, because writers of reflective essays often share their thinking about a subject by explaining how they arrived at their conclusions, they essentially tell a story about their reflections.

As you draft, think about what kind of story you want to share. Will it be a tale of triumph against all odds? Will it lead to a surprising discovery? Will it have a happy ending? Will it be a tragedy? A comedy? A farce?

To create a story, consider the following elements:

- **Setting.** Where does your story take place? What are the characteristics of the setting? How does the setting affect the story?

- **Character.** Who is involved in your story? What motivates them? What do they want to accomplish? What are their hopes and dreams?

- **Plot.** What happens in your story? In what order do the events take place?

- **Conflict.** Do the characters in your story disagree about something? What do they disagree about? Why do they disagree?

- **Climax.** What is the defining event in the story? What does the story lead the reader toward?

- **Resolution.** How is the conflict resolved in your story?

- **Point of view.** Who is telling this story? How is it told?

Even if you don't present your reflection as a traditional story, the elements of storytelling can help you shape your observations in a more concrete manner. For example, by asking who is involved in your subject and how they have dealt with conflicts, you can decide whether you should focus on a character's actions or on the reasons leading to a conflict. By asking about the climax of your story, you can decide whether to focus your reflection on a single event or on the results of that event.

GO INTO DETAIL

Experienced writers are familiar with the advice "Show. Don't tell." This advice, more often applied to creative writing than to academic writing, is founded on the belief that characters' words and actions should be used to convey a story. Simply learning what happened is far less satisfying for readers than viewing it through a series of unfolding events.

In the sense that a reflective essay conveys the story of your thinking about a subject, showing how you came to your main idea can be preferable to telling readers what it is. As you reflect, consider sharing what you've seen and heard about your subject that places others — the characters in your story — at the center of your essay. Use details to convey their actions. Use dialogue to convey their words.

Each point you present in your essay, each event you describe, and each observation you make should be illustrated with details. As you reflected on your subject, you collected details that helped you understand the subject. Now, return to those details, and decide which ones to include in your essay. You can go over your notes, reread your brainstorming and freewriting, and review the events and experiences associated with your subject. As you do so, select those details that will best help your readers understand your subject and grasp its significance, and add new ones as they occur to you.

CHOOSE YOUR POINT OF VIEW

In academic writing, point of view refers to the perspective the writer takes. Sometimes a writer will choose to reflect on a subject as a *detached observer*. Rather than participating in the action, the writer stands outside it, making observations or showing what happened without becoming a part of the story. This detached point of view is characterized by the use of third-person pronouns (*he, she, they*) and a seemingly objective relationship with the subject. James Mollison, for example, adopts a detached point of view for his photo essay "Where Children Sleep" (p. 123). By distancing himself from the lives of the children he has photographed, Mollison enables readers to consider his observations in a broader context.

At other times, a writer will reflect on a subject as a *participant observer*, someone who is centrally involved in the story being told. In this case, the writer shares experiences and observations from a personal perspective. This participatory point of view is characterized by the use of first-person pronouns (*I, me, we*) and a more personally involved relationship with the subject. By adopting this perspective, writers become key players in their own stories and can connect with their readers on a more intimate level. Consider, for example, "Are We Rich?" (p. 140), in which Margo Jefferson uses the first-person point of view to convey her childhood questions about her family's class status among Chicago's black elite in the 1950s.

Your decision about point of view will depend on the subject of your reflection, your relationship to the subject, and the amount of information you want to reveal about yourself. If you are reflecting on a subject with which you have little or no personal experience, or if you want to downplay your involvement, it's usually more effective to adopt the role of a detached observer. If, on the other hand, you want to directly convey your experiences with and perceptions of an event, or if you want to make an abstract subject more personal for readers, writing as a participant observer is often the better choice.

CONSIDER GENRE AND DESIGN

Reflective essays, like other academic essays, use design elements to make it easier for instructors and classmates to read and comment on drafts. As you draft your essay, consider how decisions about fonts, line spacing, margins, and illustrations will help your readers respond to your ideas.

- **Choose a readable font.** If you've ever read a document formatted with a decorative font, such as **MAVERICK** or Felt Tip Woman, you know how difficult it can be to read. Now imagine that you're an instructor reading twenty-five, fifty, or even a hundred essays over a weekend. Think about how you would feel if you found yet another essay printed in a decorative script, in a bright color, in CAPITAL LETTERS, or in an *italic* face. It's generally best to choose a simple font that's easy to read, such as Times New Roman or Helvetica.

- **Provide generous margins and double-spacing.** If you are asked to submit your essay on paper, your instructor will usually make comments in the margins. Leave plenty of room for handwritten comments. Your margins should be at least one inch wide, and lines should be double-spaced.

- **Consider using illustrations.** Depending on your subject, your reflective essay might benefit from illustrations. Photographs and other images can set a mood and help your readers understand the subject more completely. If you do decide to include illustrations, be sure that they contribute to your reflection; purely decorative images are usually more distracting than helpful.

You can learn more about these and other elements of document design in Chapter 18.

FRAME YOUR REFLECTIONS

Once you've made decisions about the content and design of your essay, consider how you'll frame it, or direct your readers' attention to particular aspects of your reflections rather than to others. Framing your reflections allows you to influence your readers' understanding of, and attitudes toward, what's most important to you.

Organization   The organization of a reflective essay is typically determined by the nature of the subject. Most stories, for instance, are arranged chronologically so that readers can easily follow the sequence of events. Reflections on a place or an object, on the other hand, might be arranged spatially, tracing the way a reader's eyes would take in the subject in person: top to bottom, left to right, near to far, and so on. If your reflections consider similarities and differences between your subject and something else, ordering your ideas by points of comparison and contrast might be most effective. (For more on these and other organizing patterns, see Chapter 17.)

Introduction and conclusion   Your introduction and conclusion provide the framework within which your readers will understand and interpret your reflections, so spend some time experimenting with them until they feel right. (Because these elements of an essay often prove the most challenging to draft, you might want to put them off until you finish the rest of the essay.) Several strategies are available for writing introductions and conclusions, but a few are particularly useful for reflective essays. For instance, you might open with a surprising statement or an anecdote — a brief, pointed story — that sets the stage for your main idea. As you close your essay, consider circling back to a detail from the beginning or reiterating the significance of your reflections. (For advice on drafting introductions and conclusions, see Chapter 18.)

Review and Improve Your Draft

Completing your first draft is a major milestone. However, additional consideration of your subject and a careful review of your draft will no doubt provide numerous opportunities to improve your essay. As you review your draft, pay particular attention to how you've presented and framed your main idea, the order in which you've presented your reflections, any use of dialogue, and your inclusion of details that show rather than tell.

ENSURE THAT YOUR MAIN IDEA IS CLEAR

Readers should be able to identify the point of your essay, even if you haven't provided a thesis statement. As you review your essay, ask whether your reflections support the tentative thesis statement you drafted before writing (see p. 154), and ask if everything you wrote helps your readers understand your subject in the way you intended. You might find that you need to revise your thesis statement to reflect your draft, or that you need to adapt your draft to better support your main idea.

EXAMINE THE PRESENTATION OF YOUR OBSERVATIONS

Reflective essays frequently rely on narrative, or storytelling. Review your draft to find out whether the order in which you've told your story makes sense and whether the details you have included will lead readers to be sympathetic to your observations. Upon review, you might decide that you should change the order, add important ideas or observations, or remove details that seem unnecessary or irrelevant.

REVIEW DIALOGUE

Many reflective essays use dialogue — spoken exchanges between key figures in a story — to help readers better understand a subject. Dialogue can underscore the significance of your subject and help readers gain insight into how people are affected by or react to the subject. Dialogue can also add interest to a story or allow others to make a point that you might not want to state outright. If you've included

In Process

Adding Dialogue

As she reviewed her first draft, Caitlin worried that a particularly important passage felt less interesting than it should:

> Anytime our group slowed down or started to get tired, Marco would yell to us to keep going, and suddenly we were revived. He knew everything about Rome, and everywhere we went, he knew someone. He loved his city and loved sharing it with all of us.

By adding dialogue, she created a better sense of Marco's personality and helped readers imagine themselves on a tour with him:

> Anytime our group slowed down or started to get tired, Marco would yell, "Andiamo! (Let's go!)," and suddenly we were revived. He knew everything about Rome, and everywhere we went, he knew someone. All day he was calling out to friends, "Ciao bella!" or "Come stai?" He loved his city and loved sharing it with all of us.

dialogue, ask whether you've used it effectively. For example, have you relied too heavily on other people's words? Are the right people engaged in dialogue? Does what they say make sense in the context of your story? If you haven't used dialogue, ask yourself where you might include it to liven up your essay or engage readers with your subject.

SHOW, DON'T TELL

As you review your draft, think about how you can bring your observations to life by placing the people and events involved with your subject at the center of your essay. Have you done more than simply summarize your points? Will adding details help your readers better understand and connect to your subject? Can you make your points more effectively by quoting dialogue among the characters in your story? Can you illustrate key ideas by showing characters in action?

After reviewing your essay, ask yourself how you might polish and edit it so that your readers will find it easy to read (see Chapter 22).

Do you know why you should document sources? See Chapter 15.

Finally, if you've drawn on ideas, information, or examples from written works, such as essays or stories, or cultural productions, such as movies or concerts, make sure that you've documented those sources in the body of your essay and in a works cited or references list.

For guidelines on the MLA and APA documentation systems, see Chapters 23 and 24.

Peer Review: Improve Your Reflective Essay

One of the biggest challenges writers face is reading a draft of their own work as a reader rather than as the writer. Because you know what you're trying to say, you find it easy to understand your draft. To determine how you should revise your draft, ask a friend or classmate to read your essay and to consider how well you've adopted the role of observer (see p. 116).

Purpose	1. Did you understand the significance of my observations? Do I need to state my main idea more directly or say anything more to clarify what's important about my subject?
	2. Does my subject seem relevant to you personally? Why or why not? Is there anything I can do to forge a better connection with readers?
	3. How did you respond to my reflections and observations? Do you accept what I had to say? Have I left you with something to think about?
Readers	4. Did the story of my experiences and insights make sense to you? Do you want to know anything else about them?
	5. Does my personality come through in my writing? Should I put more (or less) of myself into the essay?
	6. Have I offered you a fresh or an unusual perspective on my subject?
Sources	7. Is it clear which experiences and observations are my own and which I brought in from other sources?
	8. If I have referred to any published works or recent events, have I cited my source(s) appropriately?
	9. How well does my use of details show, rather than tell, the significance of my subject? Should I add or remove any details?
	10. Have I used dialogue effectively? Is there too little or too much?
Context	11. Did you understand any references I made to cultural, political, or social contexts? Do I need to explain anything more directly?
	12. Is the physical appearance of my essay appropriate? Did you find the font easy to read? Did you have enough room to write down comments? Did I use illustrations effectively?

For each of the points listed above, ask your reviewers to offer concrete suggestions for improving your essay. You might want to ask them to adopt the role of an editor — someone who is working with you to improve your draft. You can read more about peer review in Chapter 5.

✳ Student Essay

Caitlin Guariglia, "Mi Famiglia"

The following reflective essay was written by featured writer Caitlin Guariglia.

Guariglia 1

> **Information about the writer, class, and submission date is formatted according to MLA guidelines.**

Caitlin Guariglia

Professor Edwards

ENG 1011.04

September 28, 2016

> **Following MLA guidelines, the title is centered.**

Mi Famiglia

> **The opening paragraph grabs the reader's attention.**

Crash! The sound of metal hitting a concrete wall is my first vivid memory of Rome. Our tour bus could not get any farther down the tiny road because cars were parked along both sides. This, our bus driver told us, was illegal. He did not tell us, exactly; he grumbled it as he stepped out of the bus. He stood there with his hands on his hips, pondering the situation. Soon, people in the cars behind us started wandering up to stand next to the bus driver and ponder along with him. That, or they honked a great deal.

> **The writer begins to reflect on the experience.**

This is when I found out that Italians are resourceful people. They do not stand around waiting for someone else to fix a problem for them. They take initiative; they do what needs to be done to get things moving. Our bus driver and three other men started rocking the small cars parked crookedly along the sides of

> **The writer returns to the image in the opening paragraph.**

the narrow road, with every push moving them toward the concrete wall that lined the road. CRASH! The sound of the car hitting the wall was their signal that they were done pushing that car. And then they'd move to the next one in their way.

> **Details help the reader visualize the writer's experience.**

Angry people on Vespas sped by, making various hand gestures; some I knew and understood, but others I did not. The bus driver boarded the bus, his sleeves rolled up, sweat pouring down his face, and told us that these kind people on their Vespas were wishing us good luck. He moved the bus up about ten feet before he encountered another car he could not pass. The process repeated itself. CRASH! Another car moved. Soon a police officer walked up, talked to the bus

Guariglia 2

driver, looked around, shrugged, and helped them shove the cars into the wall. People who had parked there began to come back and move their cars before it was done for them. When we finally made it the hundred feet down the rest of the road, everyone on our tour bus cheered. Our bus driver smiled sheepishly, as if to say, "Eh, it was nothing."

This was the sort of thing I hoped to see in Italy. I wanted to see how Italians live. My dad's side of the family is Italian, so I wanted to understand more about our heritage and our family traits, like why my family is so loud and concerned with everyone else's business. Was it a cultural thing? Or was it a family thing? Was it just something about the region of Italy where my family is from? I smiled when I read Elizabeth Gilbert's memoir *Eat, Pray, Love*. Gilbert writes, "The Neapolitan women in particular are such a gang of tough-voiced, loud-mouthed, generous, nosy dames, all bossy and annoyed and right up in your face just trying to friggin' help you for chrissake, you dope — *why they gotta do everything around here?*" (78). This sounds exactly like almost all of my great-aunts, and I was curious to find out if the women in Rome would have the same attitude.

And the obsession with eating! My grandmother feeds us constantly. My dad and I always laugh at that scene in *Goodfellas* where the mobsters show up at two in the morning after killing someone, and one mobster's mother whips up a full pasta meal for them. We know that my grandmother would do the same thing: "Are you hungry? Here, sit, eat!" Grandma holds interventions over pasta. If she is unhappy with something someone in the family is doing, she invites everyone over for pasta, and we hash it out together. Was this something all Italians do? Or was my idea of a typical Italian person all wrong? Our time in Rome clarified some of these questions for me.

When we finally got to our hotel, we met our tour guide Maresa. This small, stout, sweet Italian woman said we could call her Mama. Mama looked up our reservation, glanced at it, and said our last name. Normally, that would be nothing to celebrate. But she said our last name perfectly. Actually, not just perfectly, she said it *beautifully*. After listening to Americans butcher my difficult Italian last name my entire life, hearing this Italian woman say it was music to my ears. My grandfather would have given her a standing ovation.

The next morning we met our tour guide Marco. A large, sturdy man who looked like my grandmother cooked for him, he was confident and full of life.

The writer explains what she hoped to gain from traveling to Italy.

A quotation from another writer places the writer's questions about her heritage in a larger context.

The page number for the quotation is provided, following MLA guidelines.

The writer connects questions about her heritage to her trip to Italy.

The writer uses text formatting (italics) to emphasize her point.

A transition indicates that time has passed.

Guariglia 3

He took us to the main historical sites that day: the Vatican, the Colosseum, the Pantheon, the Roman Forum. While all of that was spectacular, I enjoyed listening to Marco more than anything we saw. He was a true Roman, big, proud, and loud. The Italian accent made it seem like he was singing everything he said, making it all seem that much more beautiful. Anytime our group slowed down or started to get tired, Marco would yell, "Andiamo! (Let's go!)," and suddenly we were revived. He knew everything about Rome, and everywhere we went, he knew someone. All day he was calling out to friends, "Ciao bella!" or "Come stai?" He loved his city and loved sharing it with all of us. He had such a passion for Rome, and it made me passionate about it, too. He was also an entertainer; he enjoyed making us laugh. When our group reached a crosswalk near the Vatican, he knew all of us would not make it across in one light, so he told us to try to hurry up across the street. He told us if we did not make it before the light changed, it's okay, the cars won't hit us. "And if they beep at you," he added, "it's because they like-a the music."

> The writer uses dialogue to make the scene more vivid.

Marco fit into what my family came to know as the image of the quintessential Roman man. All of the men have two-day stubble, enough to look chic and sophisticated, but not so much as to look scruffy or messy. They also have half-smoked cigarettes hanging from their mouths. It is never a freshly lit cigarette, or a little butt, but right at that perfect halfway mark. There is a confidence, but not arrogance, in their walk. In essence, Roman men are eternally cool. In *Eat, Pray, Love*, Elizabeth Gilbert remembers watching a group of Roman men outside a bakery on their way home from a soccer game. They are "leaning up against their motorcycles, talking about the game, looking macho as anything, and eating *cream puffs*" (Gilbert 70). She is surprised at how cool they can look while eating something like cream puffs, but I have definitely seen what she means. Somehow they are manly without even having to try.

> The writer returns to her reflections about the connections between her family and her Italian heritage.

> The writer draws on a source to illustrate a point.

Romans, like many Italian Americans I've known, also have an opinion on everything and want you to know what that opinion is. Walking by the Spanish Steps on our second day in Rome, we saw a restaurant with a water leak that had spilled out into the street. It was a narrow street with mostly pedestrian traffic. As the water trickled between the cobblestones, the restaurant owner stood over the mess, looking a lot like our bus driver with his hands on his hips. Every Italian walking by had to stop and talk to this man, and then give him advice

Guariglia 4

on how to go about fixing it. The two would wave their hands at each other, sometimes nodding in agreement, sometimes yelling and waving their hands harder. This reminded me of many of my own family. When any problem arises, all the men in the house stand around looking at it saying, "No! What you gotta do is . . ." None of them are listening to each other, but each of them wants their point to be heard. It felt like déjà vu watching the same thing happen on this street in Rome. It was funny that they were all being stubborn and acting like know-it-alls, but I saw underneath it that the people stopping by really thought they were helping. They were not being rude or bossy in their minds; they were just looking out for their fellow Roman.

The last morning, Mama herded our tour group onto a bus to take us to the train station. When she got to my family, she gave us all a kiss on the cheek and a hug. She told us, "You must come back again and visit!" Then she looked at my sister and me, winked, and said, "And bring some husbands!" She must have channeled my grandmother at that moment, telling us to settle down with a nice Italian boy. We laughed and thanked Mama for her kindness during our visit.

As we pulled away from the station, I thought of all the wonderful people we met in Rome. I imagined them coming to our family reunion barbecue that takes place every summer. I think they'd fit right in. Mama would sit with Grandma and my father's aunts and talk about how beautiful their family is. Marco would sit with my dad and his cousins, drinking scotch and smoking cigars and cigarettes. Everyone would have a place.

> The writer begins her conclusion by sharing her thoughts as her trip comes to a close.

But then I thought of my cousin with two-day stubble, sitting on a Vespa, and I giggled. The image was ridiculous. Our ancestors may have brought the food, the expressions, and the attitudes with them to the United States a few generations ago, but it is safe to say that, over the years, we have lost some of the style and the musical language that Italians seem to possess from birth. Then why did so much of what I saw and heard in Italy feel strangely familiar? It seems that for Italians and Italian Americans, the traits we share are not just a cultural thing or just a family thing; they are both. It is impossible to separate the two. My time in Rome showed me that to Italians, a shared culture is a kind of family, one that extends even across the ocean.

> The conclusion offers reflections on differences between Italians and Italian Americans.

Guariglia 5

Works Cited

Gilbert, Elizabeth. *Eat, Pray, Love: One Woman's Search for Everything across Italy, India and Indonesia.* Viking, 2006.

Goodfellas. Directed by Martin Scorsese, performances by Robert De Niro, Ray Liotta, Joe Pesci, and Lorraine Bracco, Warner Bros., 1990.

> Following MLA guidelines, the title of the works cited section is centered on its own line.

> Sources used in the essay are cited and formatted according to MLA guidelines.

Project Ideas

The following suggestions provide ways to focus your work on a reflective essay or another type of reflective document.

Suggestions for Essays

1. REFLECT ON A PERSONAL EXPERIENCE

Write a reflective essay about something you've done, or something that happened to you, within the last month or so. (Choosing a recent experience enables you to focus on the interaction itself, rather than on its aftermath.) Provide sufficient details about the experience so readers will be able to picture it. Consider whether you need to supply background information as well. Support your reflections with personal observation and reasoning. You might also consider discussing the experience with friends or family members to gain their perspectives on it. If the experience was of a public nature or was related to a public event, consult news reports for background information and alternate perspectives.

2. REFLECT ON A PUBLIC EVENT

Reflect on a recent event covered in your local newspaper, a local television or radio news program, or a local news website. You might choose a cultural event, such as a local music festival; a civic event, such as a Labor Day celebration; or a school event, such as a lecture or campus protest. In your essay, describe the event and offer your reflections on its significance for you and your readers. Use details, and perhaps even dialogue, to convey the flavor of the event. Depending on the context, consider who your primary audience might be. Does the event have more significance for particular groups of readers? If so, how do you think it affects them? Support your reflection with examples from personal experience, information published in news media, or an interview with someone associated with the event (see Chapter 14). If you attended the event or participated in it yourself, be sure to include your observations of what happened.

3. REFLECT ON A POEM, SHORT STORY, NOVEL, PLAY, OR MOVIE

Respond to a work of literature that you've read recently, or attend a play or movie and reflect on it. Support your reflection by describing your reactions to the work, drawing on any relevant personal experiences or knowledge, or your own reasoning. You might also read published reviews, analyses, or comments posted to online forums to get an idea of other readers' reactions, or discuss the work with a friend, a family member, a classmate, or an instructor who has read it or seen it. In your essay, briefly describe the work to which you're responding, summarizing the plot and any key themes. Then offer your reflections on it: share with your readers why it affected you the way it did and consider how it relates to your own experiences or beliefs. Offer your reflections on the meaning of the work, its larger significance, or its emotional impact.

4. REFLECT ON AN ISSUE OF INTEREST

Reflect on an issue in a discipline, profession, or current news topic that interests you. For example, a writer interested in nuclear technology might reflect on the political or environmental implications of plans to store nuclear waste in Nevada. Or a student curious about allegations of voter suppression (denying or discouraging citizens from exercising their right to vote) might visit a local polling place on Election Day and offer her reflections. Ask who your audience might be. Are they already interested in the issue, as you are, or are they affected by it? Are they unfamiliar with the issue? Are they unfamiliar but likely to want to understand it more deeply? Support your reflection by drawing on your personal knowledge, experiences, and concerns, referring to information or arguments from published sources as necessary to inform your readers about the issue at hand. (Observers often need to adopt the role of reporter, at least initially, to ensure that their readers have a thorough understanding of the subject.) If appropriate, you might also interview an expert on the issue or conduct an observation to get a firsthand look at your subject. In your essay, introduce the issue and offer your reflections on it. Be careful to avoid composing an argument. Instead, focus on how the issue affects you and how it might affect your readers.

5. WRITE A LITERACY NARRATIVE

Write a focused literacy narrative that identifies and reflects on a personal experience (or a series of closely related experiences) that strongly influenced you as a writer or reader. You might focus on an experience in early childhood, or one from college or later, as Salvatore Scibona does (see p. 137). Shape your reflection as a story, building to a moment of insight to which your readers will relate. Conclude with a brief assessment of your current relationship with literacy. Discuss whether your feelings about reading and writing have changed since that experience and explore how this has taken place.

Alternatively, rather than focusing on a specific experience that relates to literacy, you might write a literacy narrative that reflects on your overall attitudes about reading and writing. Do you enjoy reading and writing, avoid them, struggle with them, find strength from engaging with them? Have your attitudes toward reading and writing changed over time? Are your feelings about reading similar to your feelings about writing, or do you have a stronger relationship with one or the other? Perhaps you have been surprised by the development of your literacy throughout the course of your life. Support your reflections on your experiences with reading and writing by drawing on your memories of events that have shaped your attitudes. Offer an assessment of your current relationship with writing and reading. Consider including a few telling comments by family members or teachers about your experiences with literacy to support your reflections.

Suggestions for Other Genres

6. WRITE A MEMOIR

Write a brief memoir that reflects on a key event in your life. Carefully describe the event and offer your insights into its meaning and significance, keeping in mind the need to help readers understand, connect to, and benefit from your reflections. Be sure to choose a discrete event or a limited time period — a move to a new town, for example, or a particularly memorable trip. A strong memoir has a narrow focus; if you try to address too much — for example, your complicated relationship with a relative — your writing might become abstract and lose both emotional power and narrative detail. Choose narrowly for the best result. Although the event will undoubtedly be significant in your life, consider why your readers would care about it. Does the event have larger significance? Is it something shared by others? Is it a universal experience or personal and particular?

Your memoir should be based primarily on your memories. You can use description to evoke the time and place of the event, and you might even choose to re-create dialogue. If you like, discuss the event with friends or family members and include some of their recollections and insights, or draw on published sources to give readers background information and context. Even if you make use of other sources, remember that your own memories should serve as the foundation for your memoir.

7. CREATE A PHOTO ESSAY

Take or gather several photographs that illustrate an important aspect of your life or a public issue that intrigues you. The pictures might be from your personal collection of photographs or from published sources such as history books, magazines, or websites. Select five to seven images that create a dominant impression of your subject. Think about what links the images you have chosen. How do they work together to tell a story, convey a mood, or offer a commentary on a subject? The images need not be chronological, but they should invite readers to make connections among them.

Introduce the photos with a few paragraphs that reflect on what they show, or else write an introduction along with a sentence-length caption for each image. As you write the introduction, consider whether your readers will be familiar with the subject. Is there something you want them to know or understand before they view the photographs? The introduction allows you to provide a framework or lens through which they will view the photo essay. The final mix of images and words should lead your readers to think about the subject from a perspective they wouldn't have developed on their own. You can learn about photo essays on page 123.

8. SHARE A BLOG POST

Like an essay, a blog post (see p. 242) can share your reflections on a personal or public event or on a work of art. Unlike an essay, which is often shared only with an instructor or classmates, a blog post is available to a wide audience and invites immediate responses from readers. Choose your topic carefully, as a result, with an awareness that your reflections might be read by people who will know little about you or the contexts that shaped your experiences.

As you draft a blog post reflecting on an experience, consider the opportunities afforded to you by the context, genre, and design of a blog. Consider as well the wide range of sources you can use to share your reflections and illustrate your ideas. Blog posts can include not only your insights and ideas from personal experiences but also images and photographs, video and audio, and links to other Web-based documents. Finally, consider the capabilities offered by the platform on which you choose to share your reflections. Blog tools such as WordPress and Tumblr allow you to choose a wide range of designs. Think carefully about how the design choices you might make will shape the impressions of your readers.

In Summary: Writing a Reflective Essay

* **Find a conversation and listen in.**
  * Explore your experiences (p. 147).
  * Ask questions about promising subjects (p. 147).
  * Conduct an observation (p. 148).

* **Reflect on your subject.**
  * Examine your subject (p. 150).
  * Collect details (p. 151).
  * Find significance (p. 152).

* **Prepare your draft.**
  * Convey your main idea (p. 154).
  * Tell a story (p. 155).

* Go into detail (p. 156).
* Choose your point of view (p. 156).
* Consider genre and design (p. 157).
* Frame your reflections (p. 158).

* **Review and Improve your draft.**
  * Ensure that your main idea is clear (p. 158).
  * Examine the presentation of your observations (p. 159).
  * Review dialogue (p. 159).
  * Show, don't tell (p. 160).

07 Writing to Inform

When I take on the role of a **reporter**, I focus on informing my readers about a topic.

What Is Writing to Inform?

Many of the documents you encounter on a regular basis are informative: newspaper and magazine articles, manuals, brochures, and books (including this textbook) are among the genres — or types of documents — that allow writers to add information to conversations about a wide range of subjects. In writing and writing-intensive courses, typical informative-writing assignments include essays, reports, and websites. You might also be asked to create pamphlets, multimedia presentations, memos, or posters.

Writing to inform involves adopting the role of reporter. Reporters make others aware of the facts central to a written conversation. They might provide background information for people just starting to learn about a subject or might present new information to those with a long-standing interest in it. One reporter, for example, might describe the events leading to elections in a new democracy, while another might explain the United Nations' role in monitoring those elections.

Reporters typically refrain from interpreting or analyzing the information they provide, and they seldom ask their readers to respond in a particular way. Instead, reporters allow readers to draw their own conclusions and to decide whether — and how — to act on what they've learned.

Readers of informative documents might be interested in a subject for personal or intellectual reasons, but they are usually looking for an answer to a question — whether it's a simple quest for a fact or a more general desire to understand an issue. They look for a focused treatment of a subject, and they find that visual elements — such as photos, images, charts, graphs, and tables — can help them understand key points. Readers want writers to be fair and reasonable, they appreciate clarity, and they expect that sources will be documented.

In most cases, reporters spend time learning about a subject to ensure that they have enough information to share. Whether they interview experts, collect information from published materials, or use data to create graphs and tables, reporters ensure that their sources are reliable and check that the evidence they provide is accurate.

Writers of informative documents often connect the information they provide to the social, cultural, and historical contexts they share with their readers. For example, they might refer to events or people who have recently been featured in the news media, and they might mention important sources that address the

subject. At the same time, reporters take into consideration what their readers might already know, leaving out details and explanations that are unnecessary for their purposes and focusing instead on what they want readers to understand about their subject.

Writers of informative documents are concerned primarily with helping readers and other writers advance their understanding of a subject. They do this in a variety of ways. They might report original research or provide a broad summary of existing knowledge, or offer a detailed discussion of a narrow area of interest. Regardless of their focus on the subject or the originality of their research, their contributions to a written conversation are essential to moving the conversation forward.

The Writer's Role: Reporter

PURPOSE
- To share information
- To answer questions

READERS
- Want to be informed
- Expect a fair and reasonable presentation of information, ideas, and arguments
- Need clear explanations of important ideas and concepts

SOURCES
- Information can be drawn from published studies and reports, news media, and personal experience.
- Information can be obtained firsthand, through interviews, observation, surveys, correspondence, and attendance at public events.
- Reporters check that their sources are credible and accurate.

CONTEXT
- The level of detail is adjusted to anticipate what readers are likely to know already and to make new information easier to follow.

- Informative documents often use illustrations — such as charts, tables, graphs, and images — to help readers understand concepts and ideas.

What Kinds of Documents Are Used to Inform?

Whether you are writing for a course, for publication, or in the workplace, you'll find yourself turning to — and creating — informative documents on a regular basis. If you are new to a conversation, informative documents can help you learn about a subject. As you prepare to contribute to the conversation, they can help you understand what is generally agreed upon about the subject and what remains unknown or open to debate. And as you draft your contribution, you can use information and ideas from informative documents to introduce your subject, to support your points, or to illustrate alternative perspectives.

Good writers select a genre that allows them to best address their purpose, their readers, and the context of the conversation they want to join. In the following sections, you'll find examples and discussions of some of the most common types of documents used to inform readers: informative essays and articles, infographics, profiles, and news reports.

Informative Essays and Articles

Informative essays and articles share information about a subject in a well-organized, well-supported, readable form. Essays are frequently written for academic settings, such as classes, but they are also often shared in anthologies and in magazines. Articles can appear in a wide range of publications, including magazines, newspapers, websites, and newsletters.

When essays are written for academic purposes, student writers often view instructors as their primary readers. Yet it is quite common for teachers to ask their students to address a different audience, such as other students, parents, politicians, or members of a particular profession. For example, in courses that use service learning, the primary audience for informative essays might be the director of an organization, employees of a government agency, or the members of a community group. In some cases, the choice of audience is left to the writer.

In academic settings, such as writing and writing-intensive classes as well as scholarly publishing, informative essays draw on sources (articles, books, websites, interviews, and so on) to provide evidence for the information the writer presents. Those sources should always be cited using a documentation system, such as MLA or APA (see Chapters 23 and 24). Writers frequently study the writing and design conventions of articles that have appeared in the publication for which they are writing. They also follow the conventions for citing sources used by the publication. In general, writers of informative articles tend to cite their sources in a more journalistic manner and typically do not provide a works cited or references list to identify their sources. Writers of articles often use illustrations to highlight key information or to explain complicated concepts; most also draw on quotations from interviews to present or expand on important points. Writers of informative essays and articles typically attempt to present a subject fairly, although their experiences with and attitudes toward the subject are likely to influence their approach to the subject and their selection and presentation of information from sources.

Liana Aghajanian
Stealth Generation

Liana Aghajanian is a widely published journalist whose work has been featured in such publications as *The New York Times*, *Los Angeles Times*, *The Atlantic*, *The Guardian*, the BBC, *Marie Claire*, *Foreign Policy*, *LA Weekly*, and *Mental Floss*, among others. She is the recipient of the International Reporting Project Fellowship in Global Religion Reporting, the MetLife Foundation Journalists in Aging Fellowship, and the California Health Journalism Fellowship. In this article, published in *Newsweek*,

Aghajanian focuses on a topic that has frequently been in the news and popular media: transgender individuals. Long before Caitlyn Jenner and Laverne Cox made headlines, people have identified with a gender other than the one assigned to them at birth and have decided to transition. Aghajanian reports on the aging transgender population and the ways in which these individuals' needs are often overlooked by the health care system. By recounting the stories of a few trans individuals, she challenges readers to wonder what other inequalities have forced Americans to be "stealth."

Stealth Generation

The oldest American trans people stayed invisible for decades. Now they need health care but can't get it.

by Liana Aghajanian

In the rural Pacific Northwest, 50 miles from the nearest city, lives a man who does not want to be found. He came of age during the 1950s, when saying you felt as if you were trapped in a body that you didn't belong in—you were assigned female at birth, but you identified as a boy, say—would be met with at best dismay and confusion, and at worst brutal abuse.

At 14, with no support system in sight, he attempted suicide, depressed at the physical changes taking place in his adolescent female body. At 19, he began taking testosterone, starting the transition into the person he knew he really was. His family told friends "she" had disappeared and then introduced him as a male cousin who had moved to the area. He married, became a stepfather and went off to live his life as a man. He never told anyone about his past. Now in his 70s, he remains deeply closeted (even members of his own family aren't aware of his transition) and deeply isolated (his wife passed away).

Reid Vanderburgh received a call seven years ago from the man, who asked Vanderburgh—a 60-year-old retired therapist and writer who is trans and has worked with close to 500 people on their gender transitions—to help find him a doctor who wouldn't record his transition in his medical notes. Even a confidential paper trail of his past seemed too frightening to face. Vanderburgh eventually referred him to a physician and began to visit him regularly, making the 160-mile round trip from Portland, Oregon, with his wife, bringing groceries and providing a rare hour of social interaction here and there.

The man, whose identity Vanderburgh hasn't disclosed to anyone, is part of a lost generation within the transgender population, even in a new age of visibility, where Caitlyn Jenner is largely praised and Amazon Studios' *Transparent,* a dramatic Web series about a father and retired professor coming out as transgender, wins awards.

They are the ones who transitioned in the 1950s, '60s and early '70s—from around the time the first plastic Coke bottles appeared in stores through John F. Kennedy's presidency and the Watergate scandal, and long before the advance of sexual-reassignment surgical techniques. This was before *transgender* was even a word in the American lexicon; they never called themselves trans or dared associate with those who did. They made up backstories about their lives, moved away and acquired new jobs. Researchers call it "going stealth." Now they remain cut off from the LGBT community: They cannot be found at community meetings or pride parades, and they don't show up in surveys or research studies.

Evidence of sex change operations can be found as early as the 1920s in Europe, but it wasn't until the 1950s that they were known in the U.S. In 1952, an Army veteran from the Bronx named Christine Jorgensen became the first widely known trans woman in the U.S. Born George Jorgensen, she underwent surgery in Denmark and made headlines the minute she stepped off a plane when she returned ("Ex-GI Becomes Blonde Beauty," New York's *Daily News* said on its front page in 1952). Soon gender identity clinics opened in the U.S. at universities on both coasts, offering evaluations, hormone therapy and sex-reassignment surgery operations.

But discrimination against trans people remained rampant. Even the doctors who performed sex-reassignment surgeries presented it as a treatment to get people from one gender to the next (mostly male to female). After the surgery, individuals were expected to disappear into their new body, if they wanted to live a happy and productive life. Socializing with other transgender individuals or even discussing the transition was discouraged. Instead, blending into society was emphasized. So thousands who underwent procedures back then ended up going "stealth" for most of their lives.

> "Violence and abuse is a kind of radiation background of our lives."

Those who attempted to live more openly were often pummeled. Marc, a clinical psychologist who works in the Los Angeles area, transitioned in 1979 at the age of 20. (He asked that his real name not be used in order to protect his identity.) A few years later, he started to come out in the comfort of a community led by two trans activists, Jude Patton and Sister Mary Elizabeth Clark, who were based in Orange County, California. They formed support groups and threw pool parties and barbecues with a wide array of gender-nonconforming people at every stage in their transitions. But then a horrific event convinced Marc it would be better to disappear.

In 1986, his best friend, a trans man, was shot while he showered by the disgruntled ex-husband of his girlfriend. The killer testified at his trial that "a person that appeared to be a man with no penis or testicles scream[ed] at me, telling me to get the fuck out of his house, threatening me, and I had a shotgun in my hand."

Traumatized, Marc retreated and went stealth for over a decade. It wasn't until the late '90s that he re-emerged and noticed that he had somehow become the oldest trans person people knew—and that there was no one talking about the health problems faced by senior trans people. For the past few years, he has been educating LGBT care providers on the subject, covering awareness of special needs and the heightened risk of abuse and neglect this population faces in settings like assisted living facilities. "Trans people don't have families of origin. They don't have spouses, family or children," he says. "If you don't have those people advocating for you, you're far more likely to be abused in a living facility or nursing home."

For this highly marginalized group, the idea of going into an assisted living facility is a nightmare.

Michelle Evans's worst fears about care facilities came true just after she transitioned. Evans, a 59-year-old trans woman from Orange County, knew from a young age that her body and mind were at odds, though it took her nearly a lifetime — over 50 years — to fully transition. About a year after she did, she broke both legs in an accident and was forced to stay in a nursing home after surgery. Except that no nursing home would take her, she says.

When she finally found one that would, it insisted on putting her in the men's ward. Evans protested and eventually ended up with a room of her own, but she says the doctor in charge told her that identifying as a female was "wrong." The doctor eventually stopped Evans's hormone treatments and even, in a fit of pique, took her off blood thinners — medication she needed after her surgery. Soon Evans developed dangerous blood clots in her legs. A friend finally intervened and took her back to the hospital, where she was told she had only 24 hours to live — the clots had made it to her lungs.

She survived, but the experience left her traumatized. "It's changed the way I view doctors. I don't view [care facilities] as a safe place anymore, but a place where I'm cut off from people and that they can do whatever they want." (She also ended up suing the doctor for malpractice; a settlement was reached in Evans's favor.)

In 2013, Tarynn Witten, a professor at the Center for the Study of Biological Complexity at Virginia Commonwealth University (VCU), led a survey investigating chronic illnesses and end-of-life matters in trans-identifying baby boomers. Thirty-nine percent responded that they had no or little confidence in being treated with dignity and respect as trans people by health care professionals at the end of their life. "I do not want to rely on strangers in the medical field that have little to no experience helping people with bodies like mine," one survey respondent wrote. "The day that I need a caregiver, I will implement my end-of-life suicide plan," another declared.

"This is a group of people who are very suspicious because they've been abused, and one of the main abusers is the health care system," says Witten, who transitioned in the 1990s. "Violence and abuse is a kind of radiation background of our lives."

It also has a severe health trickle-down impact: By avoiding health care professionals, these people put themselves at higher risk of dying from normally treatable conditions like high blood pressure and diabetes. In fact, studies have confirmed that transgender older adults suffer far higher levels of depression, disability and loneliness than nontransgender older adults. Seventy-one percent of transgender older adults have contemplated taking their own lives, compared with just 3.7 percent of the general U.S. population, according to the Institute of Multigenerational Health.

Advocacy groups and researchers are increasingly aware of the unique challenges faced by an aging transgender population. For example, Services and Advocacy for Gay, Lesbian, Bisexual and Transgender Elders, or SAGE, the country's only national LGBT organization concentrated on aging, published a report in 2012 on improving the lives of older transgender adults. Witten has also introduced a course on transgender medicine at VCU, which will begin this coming semester.

But the patients will also need to become better health advocates. Walter Bockting, co-director of the LGBT Health Initiative and

> "The day that I need a caregiver, I will implement my end-of-life suicide plan."

a professor of medical psychology at Columbia University, says success in later life for trans people can partially depend on increased interaction with members of their unique community. "The people who have more support and are connected to other transgender people do better," he says. "They are better able to cope with the stigma and discrimination that is out there."

Evans, who has mostly recovered from her ordeal (though there's permanent damage to her leg), is attempting to help facilitate these crucial connections. On the third Friday of every month, she leads a group called TG Rainbow, which meets in the Church of the Foothills in Santa Ana, one of the biggest cities in Orange County. Having come from all over the region, members sit on mismatched couches, sharing homemade cookies and stories of their past and current lives. The meetings include transgender people at all stages in their lives: the man who grew up in the Midwest knowing he was different for 58 years is finally transitioning at 70; the person who identifies as a woman inside but doesn't feel comfortable dressing as one, except at these meetings; the 20-something college student who is there with his mother and says he's finally made an appointment with an endocrinologist to begin the process.

"The only thing you need to transition to is yourself," Evans says. They all nod in agreement.

Almost 1,000 miles away, Vanderburgh prepares for a visit to the stealth trans man, the one he's taken groceries to for close to a decade. Vanderburgh desperately wants to reach more trans people like him. He's contemplating putting an ad in AARP's magazine. But for now, as he makes the drive to visit his friend, something simpler and more immediate is on his mind: What if he arrives at the front steps with groceries in hand and the knock at the front door goes unanswered?

Starting a Conversation: Respond to "Stealth Generation"

In your writer's notebook, consider how Aghajanian responds to her writing situation by answering the following questions:

1. Informative essays often begin with a question that readers might have about a subject. What question(s) does "Stealth Generation" attempt to answer?

2. Who is the intended audience for this article? What clues lead you to that conclusion? What assumptions does Aghajanian make about her readers?

3. What types of evidence does Aghajanian use to build her article? Which type is most effective? Why?

4. Aghajanian notes that even while we praise Caitlyn Jenner and celebrate television shows like *Transparent,* individuals who transitioned in the 1950s through the early 1970s are part of a "lost generation." What is the implication of the phrase "lost generation," and why is it especially important in the context of the article?

5. **Reflection:** Acceptance of trans people has advanced significantly since the 1950s, but as Aghajanian's article suggests, there is still a great deal of progress to be made. In May 2016, for example, North Carolina passed a controversial law restricting which bathroom or locker room transgender individuals can use. What are some ways your school could help create a more inclusive environment for trans students?

Infographics

An infographic is a visual representation of a set of facts or data. As informative documents, infographics typically present information in a seemingly unbiased way, and they sometimes include a list of sources for the facts and data presented. Timelines are among the most common infographics, but in recent years innovative designers have taken advantage of easy-to-use graphic tools to create a slew of infographics that present information in unusual and unexpected ways. Because of their versatility and ability to present complex data in a format that is easy for readers to parse, infographics are useful in magazines and newspapers, on websites and blogs, in journal articles, and in a variety of other contexts. An infographic's design contributes in large part to its effectiveness, and a clear, cohesive design is key to its success.

 International Network Archive, Princeton University
The Magic Bean Shop and *The Fries That Bind Us*

These infographics were created by Jonathan Harris of Flaming Toast Productions for the International Networks Archive (INA) at Princeton University. Led by sociology professor Miguel Angel Centeno, the INA uses network analysis to explore our globalized world. *The Magic Bean Shop* and *The Fries That Bind Us* use text, images, corporate logos, graphs, maps, and statistics to visualize the global reach of both Starbucks and McDonald's. Specifically, the infographics illustrate the incredibly large multinational presence of these companies and the way in which they connect the wealthiest and the poorest nations.

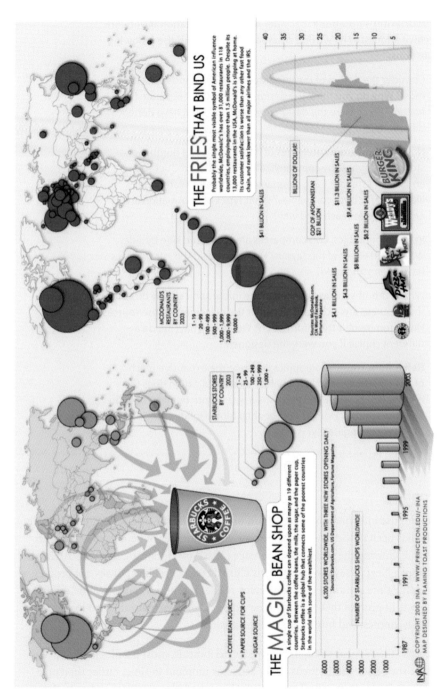

International Network Archive, Princeton University

Starting a
Conversation:
Respond to
"The Magic
Bean Shop"
and "The Fries
That Bind Us"
Infographics

In your writer's notebook, consider how the International Network Archive addresses its writing situation by answering the following questions:

1. Consider the design of the infographics. What stands out to you most? Why do you think the designer chose to incorporate that feature? If you were the designer, what would you have done differently?

2. Notice the different categories of information (the number of stores/restaurants by company, sales numbers, product sources, and so on) listed for each company. Are the same categories illustrated for both companies? What types of information are emphasized for each, and why?

3. In the infographics, two companies are compared side by side. What is the effect of this layout? How else could the infographics have been structured?

4. What kinds of sources are cited in the infographics? Why do you think sources are included? Consider the placement of the sources. How prominent is the information? Would you have made a different choice if you were the designer?

5. **Reflection:** These infographics illustrate the expansive reach of both Starbucks and McDonald's. What implication does this information have for you as a consumer? In your opinion, how do Starbucks and McDonald's utilize their global influence — either positively or negatively?

Profiles

Profiles use information to describe a place, a group, or a person, often someone who has been in the news or who represents a number of people affected by an issue. Following the widespread damage caused by Hurricane Sandy in 2012, for example, New Jersey governor Chris Christie was the subject of several profiles; at the same time, a number of New Jersey residents with no claim to fame were the subjects of profiles that conveyed the experiences of people who had lost family, friends, homes, and businesses to the disaster.

Because they appear so often in popular periodicals, most profiles are relatively brief. They also tend to focus on a particular moment in time, rather than on a lifetime. Profiles typically draw on interviews and observations, and sometimes on published sources such as biographies or news reports, to give readers a thorough understanding of the subject. Photographs of the subject of a profile are another common feature of this genre — although such images are not always strictly factual.

Rivka Galchen
An Unlikely Ballerina: The Rise of Misty Copeland

Rivka Galchen is the author of *Atmospheric Disturbances* (2008), *American Innovations: Stories* (2014), and *Little Labors* (2016). Galchen's writing has been featured in such publications as *Harper's* and *The New York Times Magazine*. She is also a regular contributor to *The New Yorker*, where this article was first published in 2014. In the excerpt provided here, Galchen traces Misty Copeland's improbable rise to the top of the ballet world. Using a mix of observation and interviews, Galchen's profile reveals not only Copeland's tenacity but also the challenges that she has had to address to reach her dream. In June 2015, less than a year after Galchen's profile was published, Misty Copeland was promoted to principal dancer with the American Ballet Theatre — the first African American woman to achieve this title.

An Unlikely Ballerina

The Rise of Misty Copeland

by Rivka Galchen

On a recent August afternoon, near Nineteenth Street, two young girls with blond hair pulled back in ponytails ran past me, one of them calling out, "Daddy, Daddy, I just saw Misty Copeland!" The tone of voice might as well have been used to announce a sighting of Katy Perry, or Snow White. A few steps later, I entered the tiny lobby of a building on Broadway, where an old electric fan was not quite keeping the doorman cool.

A caged elevator took me up to the third floor, where I passed through a low-ceilinged hallway crowded with unlabelled posters of ballet greats, until I reached an expansive fluorescent-lit room with two walls of slightly warped mirrors and air-conditioning units sealed into the windows with black electrical tape. The American Ballet Theatre soloists Misty Copeland and Alexandre Hammoudi were rehearsing the pas de deux from Act II

© RIA Novosti/The Image Works

of *Swan Lake*, the scene in which we first meet Odette; an evil sorcerer's spell has left her a swan by day and a human by night. Prince Siegfried is poised to kill the swan, but then witnesses its transformation into a beautiful young woman. "It's not that you turn her," Kevin McKenzie, A.B.T.'s artistic director since 1992 and a former principal dancer, told Hammoudi. "It's that she's startled, so she turns to you." In the movement they were practicing, Odette is downstage left and Prince Siegfried walks up behind her. Odette is naïve,

uncannily beautiful, and destined to die, but she is also, in each production, a very particular dancer. McKenzie continued, "And then you're near this creature, and you're both surprised by your proximity."

Although ballet fans never lack for darlings, rarely does a dancer become an old-fashioned star, one recognized outside the realm of people with nuanced opinions about the alternative endings to *Swan Lake*. But Misty Copeland, who is thirty-two, has not only performed some of the most coveted and challenging roles in classical ballet; she has also danced atop a grand piano during Prince's 2010 Welcome 2 America tour and starred in a Diet Dr Pepper commercial, and, a few days before the *Swan Lake* rehearsal, was featured in a commercial for Under Armour that within a week of its release had more than four million views on YouTube. In the ad, a voice-over reads a rejection letter detailing why "the candidate" is not a good fit for ballet — the letter is a fiction, albeit one not unrelated to Copeland's career — while Copeland, who is wearing a sports bra and underwear, slowly rises onto pointe. In chiaroscuro lighting that is usually reserved for boxers' bodies, the camera focusses on Copeland's substantial, sinewy musculature. "I Will What I Want" is the tagline; a billboard in SoHo features a similar muscles-and-determination image. While it is disheartening to be reminded that product endorsement is the strongest measure of mainstream success, it feels good to see a woman who is doing more than being pretty become the kind of idol commonly associated with the stars of ESPN. Most ballerinas don't have pensions, they rarely dance past the age of forty (injuries often end their careers earlier than that), and a soloist at A.B.T. earns between fifty thousand and a hundred thousand dollars a year. The great Anna Pavlova endorsed Pond's Vanishing Cream. . . .

Copeland grew up in Los Angeles, as one of six children. Her memoir, *Life in Motion*, written with Charisse Jones, portrays her childhood as having been in some ways idyllic: swimming at the beach, a circle of loving and talented siblings, a charismatic and beautiful mother, and a gift for responsibility and leadership. But another version of Copeland's childhood, which also comes through in her memoir, is the hardship tale: not knowing her real father, a succession of differently difficult stepfathers, and uncertainty about whether there would be dinner on any given night.

As a young girl, Copeland loved dancing to Mariah Carey videos, rewatching a movie about the gymnast Nadia Comaneci, and being very prepared for school, where she was a hall monitor and the class treasurer. She usually showed up an hour early. Until the age of thirteen, she took no gymnastics or dance classes, though she did take and love a woodworking class at the local Boys & Girls Club.

Copeland is considered an unlikely ballerina: she is curvy and she is black, neither of which is a common attribute in the field. But it is her very late beginning and rapid attainment of virtuosity that are arguably without precedent for a female ballerina. (Rudolf Nureyev had a famously late and chaotic start, his early training having been limited by the vagaries of the post–Second World War Soviet Union.) Many professional ballet dancers begin their training around the age of three. Every dancer is a synthesis of givens — height, limb length, natural turnout — and intense effort, but Copeland's late start can exaggerate the tendency we might have to regard a ballerina as simply touched by something divine.

When she was thirteen, and very shy, Copeland followed the lead of her older sister Erica and tried out for the middle-school drill team. She choreographed her own piece, set to George Michael's "I Want Your Sex." The closing move was a split, head held high. The evening after the audition, she received a call saying that she had been named captain of the squad of sixty.

The team's coach, Elizabeth Cantine, was new, and Erica, who had been a drill-team star, told Misty that this was unfortunate; the old coach had led the team to wins all over the state, while Cantine was an unknown, just someone who'd been hired to teach history and English. But Cantine had a background in classical dance, and, after working with Misty for a short time she suggested that she try the ballet class at the Boys & Girls Club. "I wasn't excited by the idea of being with people I didn't know, and though I loved movement, I had no particular feelings about ballet," Copeland said. "But I didn't want to displease Liz."

Cindy Bradley, who taught the class, told me, "I remember putting my hand on her foot, putting it into a tendu pointe, and she was definitely able to go into that position — she was able to go into all the positions that I put her into that day — but it wasn't about that." Bradley said she had a kind of vision, "right then, that first day, of this little girl becoming amazing."

Copeland recalls her first class differently: "I was so embarrassed. I didn't know anything that the other girls in the class knew; I thought I was doing everything wrong."

But she kept attending the class. Copeland had an unusual body: her shoulders were sloped, her legs were long, her knees were hyperextended, and she was effortlessly flexible and strong even as she was very slight. She was in the habit of entertaining her siblings (and slightly weirding them out) by linking her hands together, putting them over her head behind her ears, and then getting her elbows to bend in the wrong direction. She also had a natural ability to quickly memorize and mimic any movement she saw. She began attending ballet classes five days a week, at Bradley's studio in San Pedro. "One day, it just clicked," Copeland told me. "I began to understand what it was." . . .

Copeland says that eating disorders are not as pervasive among ballerinas as people think. Nearly every woman has at times felt that the shape of her body has determined an overwhelming proportion of someone's response to her; ballet dancers, so much more intimately aware of their bodies' appearance and ability both, might — through professionalism, through necessity — have a healthier way of relating to their bodies than the rest of us. Then again, the stakes are higher. Copeland had never given much thought to her diet, but when it was suggested to her that she needed to "lengthen" — balletspeak for losing weight — she rebelled. This was pretty much the first time in her life that she had done so, and, in the way of a young person, she mostly damaged herself.

"I didn't want to be seen ordering huge amounts of food, but the local Krispy Kreme would do deliveries if the order was large enough," Copeland said. "After practice, I would order two dozen doughnuts and then, alone in my apartment, eat most of them." She felt that her ballet career was getting away from her, that she was far from family, that she was alone. "I was barely over a hundred pounds, but I felt so fat, and even a stranger at a club, when I told him I was a ballerina, said, 'No way,'" Copeland recalled. "It took me about five years to figure out how my body worked, and to understand how to make my muscles more lean."

Even though Copeland now has a more elongated — more classical — physique, and no longer has a double-D chest, she remains more buxom than most ballet dancers, and also more visibly athletic. A significant part of what distinguishes her is her unclassical body. Marie Taglioni, the nineteenth-century ballerina, is thought to have had special appeal because her proportions didn't conform to the ideal; her rounded back made her lean forward a tiny bit, so that she seemed on the verge of losing her balance; her physical limitations ended up shaping what became her definitive style. And it was arguably with Taglioni that ballet — a man's game until a hundred years before, with men "*en travesti*" even playing the roles of women in most serious productions — began to be about ballerinas. . . .

When I visited Copeland backstage after *La Bayadère*, I met a friend of hers, eighty-year-old Raven Wilkinson, an elegant older woman who wore her hair twisted into a topknot. Wilkinson was born in Harlem, and in 1955 joined the Ballet Russe de Monte Carlo for its American tours. "I had been told not to try out, that they wouldn't take me, because they toured through cities in the South," Wilkinson said to me, when we met for lunch a while later. She has African, Native American, and European ancestors; she is pale, and onstage she wore powder. "But I thought, Well, if I don't even try out I know I'll never have what I want." . . .

The original dream of a uniquely American ballet was of a company that mixed whites and "Negroes" — the term used by George Balanchine, one of the cofounders of New York City Ballet. Balanchine had been influenced by working with Josephine Baker, the black American dancer who became a celebrity in France during the twenties. His vision was only occasionally realized: in his famous *Agon*, he choreographed a pas de deux for Diana Adams and Arthur Mitchell, a white woman and a black man. *Agon* was performed in 1957, to critical celebration, even though it could not be shown on television until

1968. Balanchine also made Maria Tallchief, who was of Osage heritage, an early star of the New York City Ballet. (For a time, he also made her his wife.)

Many black ballet dancers, including Wilkinson, were encouraged to concentrate on "African dance," or maybe modern dance or musical theatre—even if they had spent years training in classical ballet. Virginia Johnson, long a lead ballerina and now the artistic director of Dance Theatre of Harlem, a predominantly African-American ballet company, once said she had been told by someone with good intentions that she could never be a ballerina because there aren't any black ballerinas.

That is not quite true today, but it's in the neighborhood of true. "Let's be honest," Susan Fales-Hill, a writer and a philanthropist who served on the board of A.B.T., says. "Most ballet companies look like an Alabama country club in 1952." There is a small number of Asian-American ballerinas, and a small number of black ones. The reasons usually cited include the holdover of antiquated ideas of beauty, the lack of role models, the preference for a uniform look among the corps dancers in a company, and the high cost of years of training. (Pointe shoes, for example, are around seventy dollars a pair, and a serious dancer can easily go through a pair a week.) Lauren Anderson, a longtime principal dancer with the Houston Ballet, was the first African-American woman to reach the rank of principal ballerina with a major American company other than D.T.H. (Principal is the highest rank for a dancer, above soloist.) She played Odette/Odile a number of times before she retired, in 2006. "When we think of ballerinas, we think of pink and pale and fluffy," she told me. "We're not accustomed to thinking of black women's bodies in that context. We're accustomed to thinking of black women as athletic and strong. But all ballerinas are athletic, all ballerinas are strong.". . .

Copeland acts as a mentor to aspiring dancers, including Makeda Roney, a young woman who wrote Copeland a letter while she was in tenth grade, after seeing her perform. Roney, who was recently accepted into a yearlong program with the Joffrey Ballet, in Chicago, says that she calls or writes to Copeland whenever she feels anxious or discouraged. "She's like a sister to me," Roney said. Copeland has also been a public face for A.B.T.'s recent Project Plié initiative, which provides training and scholarships for kids who live in communities where there is little exposure to ballet.

Copeland's artistic and commercial successes make us all feel good—about ballet, about America—and yet that feeling is somewhat tendentious. It is impossible to distill the current role of race in ballet (or in any field) from one woman's career. Copeland's race makes her immediately distinctive in the ballet world, and this has undoubtedly helped her commercial career, but murmurings, on some online dance-discussion threads, that she has been excessively promoted within A.B.T. because of her race overlook not just her virtuosity but also the many years in which she wasn't a soloist, or even a lead dancer. . . .

In addition to its practice space on Broadway, A.B.T. has a rehearsal space several floors below the stage of the Metropolitan Opera House. One afternoon, I went to see Copeland rehearse a pas de deux with Herman Cornejo for a production of Kenneth MacMillan's ballet *Manon*, which they were to perform for the first time the next day. . . .

I never used to be easily drawn in by the long storybook standards of classical ballet; it was as if the salmon sandwiches and the bubbly rosés served during intermission got in the way. It was easier to access the more immediately legible expressiveness of abstract, modern pieces. But many dancers have told me that they revere the long classical pieces. When I asked why, they talked about how freeing the strict constraints of classical ballet are, from its most basic positions to its thirty-two-fouetté extremes; from other forms of dance, one couldn't transition to classical ballet, but from classical ballet one could do anything.

Dance is not like the other arts. The words in a book stay in place, paintings barely fade, musical performances can be recorded. But watching a recording of dance is about as close to the real thing as reading *Eugene Onegin* in Google Translate. Dancers often restrain themselves, necessarily, during practice, but Cornejo and Copeland seemed to be leaping higher, and moving more articulately, than they did onstage. I had just seen three grand ballet performances in a row, but this harshly lit, uncostumed, and repeatedly interrupted performance was my favorite. It wasn't simply the proximity, the sound of the shoes, the soothingly minor comments — "Your back arm tends to get behind you"; "A little more shoulder at the beginning, so it's not so flat" — it was more the juxtaposition of the mundane and the magnificent: "Be careful when you do the relevé; don't crank her leg too much"; "The second pirouette — did you just do left?"

"People are surprised to hear that I still go to class," Copeland told me. "But that's what dancers do." In a studio class one Thursday morning, there were dancers from all ranks of A.B.T., as well as dancers not yet in the company, stretching, chatting. One dancer asked for a recommendation for a travel agent. Another replied that no one has used travel agents since the eighties. Copeland sat on the floor beside them, in a purple leotard, applying glue to the inside of her pointe shoes. The director of A.B.T.'s studio company, a former dancer named Kate Lydon, called the class to attention: "We'll start with sixteen swings, port de bras forward." The pianist accompanying the class played some Dvořák, then some Bach, then "The Girl from Ipanema." After the barre exercises, there were floor exercises, then jumps, then more exercises moving across the room.

Starting a Conversation: Respond to "An Unlikely Ballerina: The Rise of Misty Copeland"

In your writer's notebook, consider Galchen's profile by answering the following questions:

1. In informative writing, the writer generally acts as a reporter or an observer but not as an interpreter. How well does Galchen fulfill this role? Look for specific examples in the essay that demonstrate this role.

2. As a reader of this informative document, what question do you believe Galchen is trying to answer? How well is that question answered? What other information do you need to answer that question?

3. Galchen's profile relies heavily on interviews and on Copeland's own words. Why are firsthand quotations from the subject of the profile important to this piece of writing? Could the piece have worked without as many direct quotes from Copeland? Who else does Galchen quote, and why are these other voices important?

4. **Reflection:** As the title of the article asserts, Copeland's success as a ballerina is considered "unlikely" for many reasons — her race, her physical shape, her background. Have you ever worked toward a goal that seemed "unlikely"? What aspects of Copeland's journey could help you overcome obstacles to your goals?

News Reports

News reports provide information about an issue, event, or individual. News reports can appear in a variety of forms, from written articles and essays to television broadcasts and videos or podcasts presented on the Web or the radio. News reports are usually written or presented in a straightforward, seemingly objective voice. Sources of information used in news reports are clearly identified and cited in a manner consistent with the form in which it appears. A written report may include in-text citations and a formal works cited list, while a video or audio report is more likely to identify sources in a more conversational manner. Written news reports generally identify sources of information in a journalistic manner, most often by citing individuals and organizations by name in the body of the text. In some cases, sources might be cited in a works cited list or bibliography, but this is rare. Video or audio news reports are likely to identify the authors of sources in a similar manner, identifying individuals or organizations by name.

Bill Chappell
4 New Elements Are Added to the Periodic Table

"4 New Elements Are Added to the Periodic Table" is a feature story from National Public Radio's news report *The Two-Way*. NPR writer and producer Bill Chappell reports on the breaking science news story. Chappell has been on staff at NPR since 2003, and his accomplishments include establishing the Peabody Award–winning site StoryCorps on NPR.org. Though brief, this informative radio news report includes detailed information, interviews, and scientific facts.

npr.com

4 New Elements Are Added to the Periodic Table

By Bill Chappell

For now, they're known by working names, like ununseptium and ununtrium — two of the four new chemical elements whose discovery has been officially verified. The elements with atomic numbers 113, 115, 117 and 118 will get permanent names soon, according to the International Union of Pure and Applied Chemistry.

With the discoveries now confirmed, "The 7th period of the periodic table of elements is complete," according to the IUPAC. The additions come nearly five years after elements 114 (flerovium, or Fl) and element 116 (livermorium, or Lv) were added to the table.

The elements were discovered in recent years by researchers in Japan, Russia and the United States. Element 113 was discovered by a group at the Riken Institute, which calls it "the first element on the periodic table found in Asia."

Three other elements were discovered by a collaborative effort among the Joint Institute for Nuclear Research in Dubna, Russia, the Lawrence Livermore National Laboratory in California. That collaboration has now discovered six new elements, including two that also involved the Oak Ridge National Laboratory in Tennessee.

Classified as "superheavy" — the designation given to elements with more than 104 protons — the new elements were created by using particle accelerators to shoot beams of nuclei at other, heavier, target nuclei.

The new elements' existence was confirmed by further experiments that reproduced them — however briefly. Element 113, for instance, exists for less than a thousandth of a second.

"A particular difficulty in establishing these new elements is that they decay into hitherto unknown isotopes of slightly lighter elements that also need to be unequivocally identified," said Paul Karol, chair of the IUPAC's Joint Working Party, announcing the new elements. The working group includes members of the International Union of Pure and Applied Physics.

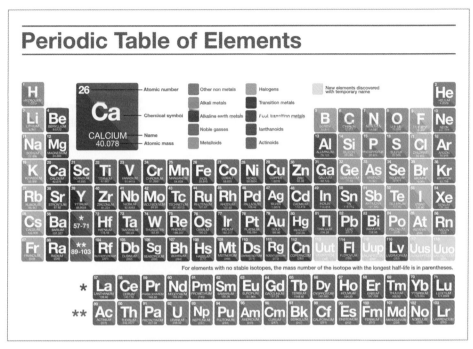

▲ **The seventh period of the periodic chart is now complete, thanks to the addition of four new elements in yellow.** © Irina Kostyuk/Shutterstock

The elements' temporary names stem from their spot on the periodic table — for instance, ununseptium has 117 protons. Each of the discovering teams have now been asked to submit names for the new elements.

With the additions, the bottom of the periodic table now looks like a bit like a completed crossword puzzle — and that led us to get in touch with Karol to ask about the next row, the eighth period.

"There are a couple of laboratories that have already taken shots at making elements 119 and 120 but with no evidence yet of success," he said in an email. "The eighth period should be very interesting because relativistic effects on electrons become significant and difficult to pinpoint. It is in the electron behavior, perhaps better called electron psychology, that the chemical behavior is embodied."

Karol says that researchers will continue seeking "the alleged but highly probable 'island of stability' at or near element 120 or perhaps 126," where elements might be found to exist long enough to study their chemistry.

International guidelines for choosing a name say that new elements "can be named after a mythological concept, a mineral, a place or country, a property or a scientist," according to the IUPAC.

In 2013, Swedish scientists confirmed the existence of the Russian-discovered ununpentium (atomic number 115). As *The Two-Way* described it, the element was produced by "shooting a beam of calcium, which has 20 protons, into a thin film of americium, which has 95 protons. For less than a second, the new element had 115 protons."

While you're not likely to run into the new elements anytime soon, they're not the only ones that have short existences. Take, for instance, francium (atomic number 87) and astatine (atomic number 85).

As Sam Kean, author of a book about the periodic table called *The Disappearing Spoon*, wrote of those elements:

> If you had a million atoms of the longest-lived type of astatine, half of them would disintegrate in 400 minutes. A similar sample of francium would hang on for 20 minutes. Francium is so fragile, it's basically useless.

As for why scientists keep pursuing new and heavier elements, the answer, at least in part, is that they're hoping to eventually find an element — or a series of elements — that is both stable and useful in practical applications. And along the way, they're learning more and more about how atoms are held together.

Starting a Conversation: Respond to "4 New Elements Are Added to the Periodic Table"

In your writer's notebook, consider how Chappell addresses his writing situation by answering the following questions:

1. What question (or questions) does Chappell answer in this news report? Who is the intended audience? How does Chappell address this audience in the answer(s) he gives?

2. One of the goals of informative writing is to make connections to contemporary issues. In what ways does Chappell highlight the importance of discovering new elements? How does the report's organization make the connection apparent to the reader or listener?

3. Identify the types of evidence that Chappell uses. What makes this evidence compelling? What impact does it have?

4. NPR is an independent news organization supported by listeners. In what ways might this affect its reporting, either positively or negatively? Why is it important to know about an organization's mission when interpreting a news report?

5. **Reflection:** Imagine you are writing a news report on an important topic. Which aspects of Chappell's report would you emulate? Which would you avoid? Explain your choices in detail.

GENRE TALK

Readers of informative documents often have a specific purpose or interest in the subject. Residents of California, scientists, environmentalists, and the general public can benefit from the information presented in this *L.A. Times* article about the severity of the 2015 drought in Southern California. Additionally, writers of informative documents may have certain aspects of the topic that they want to publicize or details they want to share. They may make use of various media, such as images, slide shows, maps, or infographics to share that information most effectively.

LaunchPad
macmillan learning

Test your knowledge of genre with the Genre Talk quiz in the LaunchPad for *Joining the Conversation.*
launchpadworks.com

The headline announces the topic of the article in a straightforward manner.

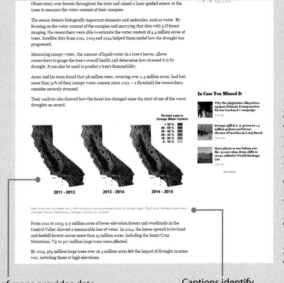

Both images: Gregory Asner, Carnegie Institution for Science

The writer reports on research published in a scholarly journal, describing how the scientists performed their study and collected their measurements.

The writer includes quotations from an expert (the study's lead author) as well as statistics to put the findings in perspective.

A set of maps provides data visualization to illustrate the rising percentages of water loss in the forest canopy since the beginning of the drought. A color-coded legend helps readers understand the information presented.

Captions identify what the images show and name the source of that information.

How Can I Write an Informative Essay?

The first step in writing a successful informative essay is recognizing that you don't have to be an expert on something to write about it — you simply have to know how to learn enough about it to share your findings with your readers. The second step is understanding how to collect and work with information. This doesn't mean that an informative essay needs to look like a research paper. As you've seen throughout this chapter, the amount and type of information used in informative documents can vary widely. What it does mean, however, is that you should understand where you can find information — for example, through interviews, published documents, the Web, direct observation, or personal experience — and how to work with it once you've collected it.

This section helps you tune in to the conversations around you and take on the role of reporter as you choose a subject, gather information, prepare your draft, and review and improve your draft. As you work on your essay, you'll follow the work of Ellen Page, a first-year student who wrote an informative essay about the use of DDT in the prevention of malaria.

In Process

An Informative Essay about the Use of DDT to Prevent Malaria

Ellen Page wrote an informative essay for her first-year seminar course in medical geography. To learn about her topic, Ellen read articles about malaria prevention and the effects of DDT. She also searched the Web for information from agencies such as the World Health Organization and the Centers for Disease Control and Prevention. Follow Ellen's efforts to inform her readers in the In Process boxes throughout this chapter.

Find a Conversation and Listen In

Informative essays offer a good opportunity to learn more about something that intrigues you and to report what you've learned to readers who share your interest in the subject. To get started on your informative essay, prepare yourself to take on the role of reporter, and spend some time thinking about your purpose, your readers, and the context in which your writing will be read (see p. 174). Look around for a topic of conversation that will interest both you and your readers — and that you can investigate in the time available to you.

EXPLORE YOUR INTERESTS
Nobody knows everything, but most of us know a little (or a lot) about a few things — especially if they involve us personally. As you search for ideas for an informative essay, examine your daily life for inspiration.

- **Personal interests and hobbies.** What do you like to do in your spare time? What magazines do you read? What television shows do you like to watch? What are your favorite websites? What makes you happy? Curious? Angry? What frightens you? Amuses you?

- **Academics.** Your major and your favorite classes are rich sources for essay ideas. Think about recent class discussions that interested you, questions that puzzled you, or information that surprised you when you first learned it.

- **Work.** Any past or current job, volunteer activity, or career you hope to enter involves specialized knowledge of some sort, from learning how to fill a soda machine to getting to know the U.S. tax code. Ask yourself whether you would be interested in informing others about this specialized knowledge.

- **Reading.** What have you read recently that interested or surprised you? What annoyed you or made you angry? What have you read that made you think?

Any of these areas can serve as a jumping-off point for generating ideas for an informative essay. Spend some time brainstorming or freewriting about these aspects of your life (see pp. 41–42), and then review your notes to identify the areas that seem most promising. (For additional suggestions, see the writing project ideas at the end of this chapter.) As you think about your ideas, remember that the best subjects are usually out of the ordinary. Instead of writing about the broad issue of capital punishment, for example, you would do better to consider a little-known but potentially important aspect of the subject, such as how inmates on death row spend their last day before execution or the role of DNA testing in overturning convictions. Once you've identified a few possible subjects, select one or two that interest you most, and jot down your thoughts about what you already know and what you need to learn before you start writing.

USE YOUR LIBRARY

Learn more about promising subjects by using your library. You can gain a preliminary understanding of a subject by searching the library catalog, browsing library shelves, searching library databases, and consulting librarians. Begin by generating a few keywords and phrases related to the subject, and then search the catalog with them. Your search results will give you an overview of the subject. The titles of books and journals on the subject will give you insights into what other writers think is important about it. You'll also be able to learn whether the subject is too broad to tackle on its own — or whether it's so specialized that you'll need to expand your focus.

If you are still interested in the subject after this preliminary research, spend a few minutes browsing the shelves in your library. Jot down or print out the call numbers for books and journals that appear promising, and locate them on the shelves. Skim these publications, and then look for nearby books and journals on the same subject. Spending as little as ten or fifteen minutes browsing the shelves can either confirm that a subject is worth pursuing or help you decide to look at others.

Some subjects are so recent that few books or journals focus on them. If so, try to gain an overview of your subject by searching news and article databases such as LexisNexis Academic or Academic Search Premier using the keywords and phrases you generated for your catalog search. Examine the titles and descriptions of the sources you find. In some cases, you might find links to full-text articles. If so, skim them to learn about the subject.

You can read more about searching libraries and databases in Chapter 13.

Working Together: Try It Out Loud

Before you start writing to inform, start a conversation with your classmates about something that interests you. Form small groups and choose a familiar subject (such as sports, family, your hometown, or the work of a favorite artist or musician). Take turns speaking while the other members of the group listen, respond, and ask questions. Your purpose is to inform the rest of the group, so try to present a fair and accurate view of your subject.

When you are finished, take a few minutes to reflect on the exercise. What did you learn about your audience? Did you have to adapt what you said based on their interest level and what they already knew? What kind of questions did they ask? What seemed to interest them the most about the subject?

Using the Library Catalog

To learn more about the issue of DDT use in the prevention of malaria, Ellen Page
searched her library's catalog for sources that addressed her subject.

Ellen searched for the
phrase *malaria
prevention*. She placed
quotation marks
around the phrase.

▲ **Ellen's search of the library catalog**

Ellen's searches produced several promising sources, including the following.

Clicking on the title
will show the
complete record for
the source.

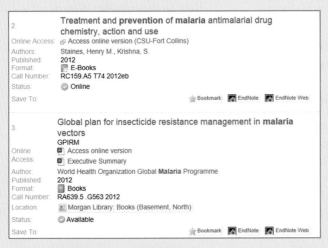

The results show
whether the source is
available, its location,
and (if available) a link
to its website.

▲ **Results of Ellen's library catalog search**

Finally, consider talking with a librarian about the subjects you've identified. Reference librarians or subject-area specialists can direct you to relevant sources, suggest related subjects, or help you narrow your focus.

ASK QUESTIONS ABOUT PROMISING SUBJECTS

Writers who adopt the role of reporter often find themselves confronted with a seemingly endless amount of information on their subject. Before you begin examining sources closely, narrow your focus by determining which subjects interest you the most and which conversation you want to join. Each of the following questions focuses your attention on a general subject in a different way, and each provides a useful starting point for an informative essay. Depending on the subject, you'll find that some questions are more relevant than others.

- **Importance.** Why is this an important subject? Who believes that it is important? Why do they believe it is important?

- **Process.** How does _____ work? What steps are involved?

- **History.** What is the origin of _____ ? What recent events are related to it? What are the implications of those events?

- **Limitations.** What is limiting the use of _____ ? What has kept _____ from succeeding? What must happen before _____ is accepted?

- **Benefits.** Who benefits from _____ ? How do they benefit? Why do they benefit?

- **Advantages and disadvantages.** What are the advantages of _____ ? What are the disadvantages?

Gather Information

No matter how much you already know about a subject, you'll want to learn more about it before you begin planning and drafting your essay. Informative essays tend to draw extensively on information from other sources and, to a lesser extent, on personal knowledge and experience. To learn more about your subject, create a search plan, collect sources, evaluate those sources, take notes, and consider conducting interviews.

CREATE A SEARCH PLAN

Depending on your subject and the kinds of information you are seeking, you might search library catalogs, databases, or the Web (see Chapter 13); browse library shelves and visit periodicals rooms (see Chapter 13); or conduct interviews, observations, or surveys (see Chapter 14). Creating a search plan before you begin will save time and keep you focused.

In Process

Asking Questions

After Ellen Page chose the general subject of "malaria prevention" and searched her library catalog to get a feel for the kinds of information available on her subject, she used clustering to consider which conversations she might join (see p. 44). She placed the words *malaria prevention* at the center of her cluster and then wrote questions about her subject. She used the questions to explore strategies that had been used in the past century to prevent malaria, the advantages and disadvantages of those strategies, and approaches that are now in use. She represented her answers to these questions as words or phrases linked to each question.

After considering her assignment and writing situation, Ellen decided to focus on the advantages and disadvantages of using DDT to prevent malaria. She felt that this focus would allow her to accomplish her purpose of informing her readers about an important issue and believed that it would interest both her and her readers. She knew that the effects of DDT in agriculture had led to a ban on its use in most of the developed world, but she had also found articles that showed how it was being used to prevent malaria in developing countries. She decided that it would be possible to present a balanced, informed assessment of the use of DDT.

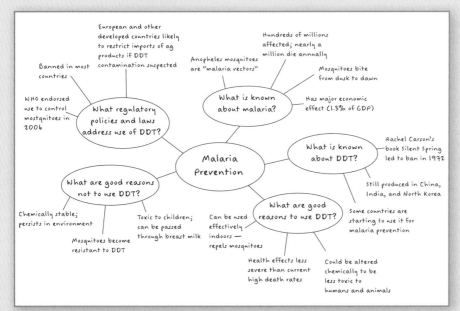

Ellen placed her general topic — malaria prevention — at the center of her cluster.

Ellen asked questions about her topic. Her questions focused on past and current strategies for malaria prevention, their benefits, their drawbacks, factors affecting their use, and so on.

Ellen wrote brief answers to her questions.

▲ **Ellen's cluster**

To develop a search plan, think about what you need to know and how you plan to use what you find. Then try to identify the types of sources most likely to provide the information you are looking for. If you are writing about recent developments in consumer robotics, for example, you want the most up-to-date information you can find. As a result, you should look in library databases focusing on the subject and search the Web. You might also want to interview an expert on the subject, such as a professor of engineering or computer science. In contrast, if you are writing about the influence of Greek culture on the Roman Empire, you would probably focus on books and scholarly journals that you find by searching your library catalog, browsing the shelves, and visiting periodicals rooms.

If you're not sure where to start, a reference librarian can suggest search strategies and relevant resources. You can learn more about creating a research plan and locating and using sources in Part Three.

Working Together: Plan Your Search for Sources

Before you visit the library, search a database, or browse the Web, sit down with a group of classmates to generate ideas for a search. To carry out this activity, follow these steps:

1. Explain your subject and discuss your purpose for informing readers. If your readers go beyond the instructor and your classmates, describe your readers and their needs, interests, knowledge, and backgrounds. Talk briefly about specific ideas you have for gathering information on your subject.

2. Once you've explained your subject, the other members of your group should brainstorm ideas about useful resources for locating sources, such as the library catalog, specific databases, useful websites and directories, and relevant field research methods.

3. For each resource that has been identified, the group should brainstorm suggestions for using it effectively. For example, the group might generate a list of specific keywords and phrases to use in your search, create a list of good candidates for an interview and useful interview questions, and make suggestions about what to look for in an observation.

4. At the end of the discussion, ask any questions you have about the resources and search strategies your classmates have suggested.

If you are working face-to-face, take notes on the discussion. If you are using a chat or instant-messaging program, record a transcript of the session. The goal of the session should be to generate as many useful search resources and strategies as possible. Don't rule out any ideas, no matter how trivial or ridiculous they might seem at first. When the exchange is completed, turn to the next writer and repeat the process.

COLLECT SOURCES

To collect sources, search for them in library catalogs, in databases, and on the Web. Visit your library to check out books and government reports, browse the shelves, and use the periodicals room. You can learn more about these activities in Part Three.

EVALUATE YOUR SOURCES

Depending on your subject, you might find yourself confronted with a dizzying array of promising sources, or you might find yourself gritting your teeth as one search after another comes up empty. In most cases, you'll collect at least a few useful sources, from books and scholarly articles to websites and blogs to video clips and news articles. Be aware, however, that not all information is created equal and that some sources will be more appropriate for an academic essay than others. Before you decide to use a source, assess its credibility and usefulness for your purposes. To evaluate print and digital sources for an informative essay, focus in particular on the following:

- **Relevance.** Be sure the information in a source will help you accomplish your purposes as a writer. It should address your subject directly, and it should help you learn more about aspects of the subject that are important to you. Your readers will also want to find information that meets their needs. If they know little about your subject, you'll need to provide them with information that will help them understand it. If they are already familiar with the subject, you'll want to locate information that will allow them to learn more about it.

- **Evidence.** Reliable sources provide details and supporting information to back up a writer's statements and assertions. Be wary of any source that makes sweeping generalizations without providing evidence.

- **Authority.** Look for sources written by experts on your subject. Scholarly sources (such as peer-reviewed journal articles) are usually more reliable than popular ones (such as general-interest magazines) because they go through an extensive peer-review process before being published. On the Web, information found on government (.gov), educational (.edu), and nonprofit (.org) domains is likely to be more reliable than information provided on business (.com) sites and personal pages.

Need a refresher on evaluating sources? See Chapter 4.

- **Timeliness.** In most cases, the more recently a source was published or updated, the more pertinent the information will be for your purpose.

TAKE NOTES

Once you've located enough reliable and credible sources to inform your essay, spend time taking notes on them. Because note taking often involves putting information about a subject into your own words, it can help you learn more about your subject and the writers who have been contributing to the conversation you want to join. Taking notes can also help you identify the most important information in your sources.

By studying a source and noting important information, ideas, and arguments, you'll gain a clearer understanding of the source and your subject. Careful note taking also helps you avoid plagiarism and lays the foundation for drafting your document. You can learn more about taking notes in Chapter 4.

In Process

Evaluating Sources

To learn more about the challenges associated with the use of DDT to prevent malaria, Ellen Page read several articles she found through her library's periodical databases to get a thorough understanding of the issue. She also searched the Web for up-to-date news and information. Not surprisingly, her searches of the Web pulled up several unreliable sources, such as this one.

Clip art and template design suggest an amateur Web author.

Web page provides no indication of authorship or authority to write on the subject.

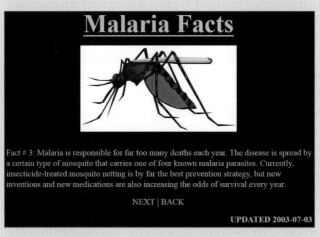

Assertions are not backed up with evidence.

Site has not been updated in several years.

▲ An unreliable source

Ellen's searches of the Web also brought her to the malaria page of the Centers for Disease Control and Prevention. On the site; she found an extensive collection of information about malaria, including reports about malaria control.

Ellen bookmarked the Web pages, saved copies of the pages on her laptop, and printed them.

A menu provides easy navigation to pages on the diagnosis, treatment, and impact of malaria.

Layout and illustrations are carefully thought out and look professional.

Contact information for the organization is provided.

References and related resources are provided.

▲ **A reliable source**

Centers for Disease Control

CONDUCT AN INTERVIEW

Interviews — in which one person seeks information from another — can provide firsthand accounts of an event, authoritative interpretations of an issue, and thoughts on a subject from the people who have been affected by it. You can conduct interviews face-to-face, over the telephone, via e-mail, and even through a chat program.

The decision to conduct an interview should be based on the kinds of information you need to support your argument, although it can also be a result of having access to someone who has specific expertise or experience relevant to your subject or issue. As you prepare for an interview, consider your purpose, develop a limited set of main questions, and draft follow-up questions for each main question. If possible, record the interview. In all cases, take notes. (You can learn more about conducting interviews on pages 499–503.)

Prepare a Draft

Writers of informative essays focus on reporting information to their readers. As you prepare a draft of your informative essay, you'll decide which information, ideas, and arguments to present and how you will share them with your readers.

Your decisions about what to focus on, which points to make, and what evidence to use will influence what your readers learn about your subject and how they are likely to understand it. Although reporters strive for objectivity in their writing, experienced writers recognize the difficulty of presenting information in a completely unbiased manner. They understand that their choices can (and will) lead readers to think about a subject in a particular way. Consider a writer selecting details for an informative essay about the impact of a recent ban on smoking in bars and restaurants. Statistical information about cash register receipts would focus readers' attention on financial implications of the ban for small business owners; a photograph of an asthmatic bartender might encourage readers to consider the positive public health effects of such a ban; and an interview with a smokers' rights advocate could emphasize concerns about eroding personal freedoms. No matter how objectively the writer presents the information, the final mix of statistics, images, and quotations will affect the conclusions readers draw from the document.

It's best to begin by choosing a main point and expressing it as a thesis statement. Then you can decide what supporting points and evidence will most effectively support your main point. During the drafting process, you should also decide whether to include visual information, how to organize your ideas, and how to frame your introduction and conclusion.

PRESENT YOUR MAIN POINT

In an informative essay, the main point is usually presented in the form of a thesis statement. A thesis statement, typically no more than a single sentence, directs readers' attention to what you want them to learn about a subject. Consider how the following thesis statements about voter turnout among younger Americans direct readers' attention in a particular way:

> The high turnout among younger voters in the last presidential election — and in particular in Democratic primaries and caucuses — underscores the growing importance of young Americans on the political scene.

> The growing political commitment of voters under the age of twenty-five has led to higher voter turnout, which, in turn, has reduced the historic imbalance in the relative political influence of younger and older Americans.

> Regardless of the causes, the overall pattern of increasing voter turnout among younger voters should be cause for celebration among voters — young and old alike.

Although each of these thesis statements would provide a sound foundation for an informative essay, the essays would have little in common. By focusing on distinctly different aspects of the subject, they require the writer to provide different supporting points and evidence.

Is your thesis focused enough for your purpose? See Chapter 16 for more info.

Your thesis statement will be shaped by what you've learned about your subject; your purpose; your readers' purposes, needs, and interests; your readers' knowledge and backgrounds; and the requirements and limitations of your writing project.

DEVELOP SUPPORTING POINTS AND EVIDENCE

Most readers want more than a thesis statement — they want to know why they should accept it. If readers who are thinking about purchasing a car come across a thesis statement such as "For many drivers, renting a car on an occasional basis is a cost-effective alternative to owning one," they'll want to know why renting could be a better choice. If readers interested in financing a college education read a thesis statement such as "Today's college students have a wide range of options for reducing the overall cost of a college education," they'll want to know what those options are. To convince readers to accept your thesis statement, you'll need to provide supporting points and offer evidence for each point.

Choose your supporting points Supporting points are the reasons you give readers to accept your main point. They are usually expressed as topic sentences in the form of general statements, such as "Renting a car means you can pay less in car insurance" or "If your family qualifies, Pell Grants can significantly reduce the cost of a college education." Consider, for instance, the way Liana Aghajanian presents the supporting points for her essay about the aging transgender population (p. 175). Each paragraph opens with a clearly stated topic sentence (for example, "But discrimination against trans people remained rampant.") that announces the supporting point Aghajanian makes in that paragraph. As you choose your supporting points, keep in mind that not only should they serve as reasons to accept your main point but they should also be consistent with how you've presented your thesis statement. In short, you should resist the urge to include every idea you've come across. You can find more advice on developing support for a thesis statement in Chapter 16.

Identify evidence for each supporting point Without evidence to support them, even the most clearly expressed supporting points will not be enough to inform your readers fully. You need evidence to help them understand why they

In Process

Developing Support

For her informative essay on the use of DDT to prevent malaria, Ellen Page identified the following supporting points:

1. The history of DDT use in preventing malaria

2. The effects of DDT on humans and the environment

3. The relative risks of using — and not using — DDT

4. Alternatives to DDT

For her first draft, she expressed the third point as a general statement and offered evidence from a source to support it.

> Ellen drew on information from a scholarly journal article. She used APA in-text citation style to acknowledge her sources.

> In the face of uncertainty about the effects of DDT on human health, the fundamental issue of "the right of people to a safe environment" demands that research continue on its effects (Bouman et al., 2011, p. 746). Simply put, we must weigh the question of whether people should be exposed to a chemical that, although it prevents malaria, might cause physical harm later on. Here lies the main ethical argument in which the health risks and benefits must be weighed. To do this, we must understand not only the risks but also the benefits of using DDT.

> Ellen's third supporting point

should accept the reasons you've used to support your thesis statement. In a profile of Misty Copeland (p. 183), for instance, writer Rivka Galchen uses evidence to illustrate a point about Copeland's unusual status as an African American ballerina:

> Virginia Johnson, long a lead ballerina and now the artistic director of the Dance Theatre of Harlem, a predominantly African-American ballet company, once said she had been told by someone with good intentions that she could never be a ballerina because there aren't any black ballerinas.

Writers of informative essays also use information from sources to present ideas and clarify statements. You might amplify a statement by providing examples from sources. You might qualify a statement by noting that it applies only to specific situations and then use a quotation or paraphrase from a source to back that up. Or you might define a concept or term, as Bill Chappell does in his news report about the discovery of four new elements on the periodic table (p. 189):

> Classified as "superheavy" — the designation given to elements with more than 104 protons — the new elements were created by using particle accelerators to shoot beams of nuclei at other, heavier, target nuclei.

As you select information from sources for your essay, consider your writing situation (see p. 12). Be sure that the evidence you choose will help you accomplish your

Working Together: Brainstorm Supporting Points and Evidence

You can use group brainstorming sessions to help generate supporting points and evidence. You can work in person or online (using chat, instant messaging, or a threaded discussion forum). To carry out the activity, follow these steps:

1. The writer should describe his or her writing project, main point, and ideas for supporting points.

2. Each member of the group should make suggestions about the supporting points the writer mentions.

3. Each member of the group should suggest additional supporting points.

4. Each member of the group should make suggestions about potential sources of evidence to support each point.

If you are working face-to-face, ask one member of the group to take notes on the discussion. If you are using a chat or instant-messaging program, be sure to record a transcript of the session. The goal of the session is to generate as many potential supporting points as possible. Take care not to rule out any ideas, no matter how trivial or ridiculous they might seem at first. When the exchange is completed, turn to the next writer and repeat the process.

purpose; that you provide enough detail and explanation to help readers understand the information, ideas, or arguments you present to them; and that you present the evidence in a way that won't conflict with your readers' values and beliefs.

To identify evidence to support your points, follow these guidelines:

1. List your supporting points.

2. Review your notes to identify evidence for each point.

3. If necessary, review your sources (or find new ones) for additional information.

4. Avoid relying too heavily on one type of information.

5. Avoid relying too heavily on information from a single source.

6. Consider how the evidence fits your writing situation.

CONSIDER GENRE AND DESIGN

As is the case with other academic essays, the basic design of your informative essay will reflect the formatting requirements of your assignment and the expectations of your readers, particularly your instructor. Typically, those requirements specify the use of wide (one-inch) margins, double-spaced lines, page numbers, and a readable font. These design features make it easier for instructors and classmates to read and comment on the essay.

Other design elements can help you clarify information for your readers and add visual interest to your essay. As you think about how you will present information to your readers, consider the benefits of using visual evidence to support your points.

- **Illustrations** such as photographs and drawings allow you to clarify abstract concepts and demonstrate processes that might be difficult to follow were they presented in the main text of your essay.

- **Charts, graphs, and tables** let you convert dense numerical information or statistical data into more easily understood visual summaries.

You can draw on your sources for visual evidence in two ways. You might borrow an illustration from a print or an online source to help readers understand a complex concept or process, such as the steps involved in cellular respiration. Or you might use data from one or more sources to create an original chart, graph, or table to clarify a point, such as the growth of the Asian American population in the chart on the next page.

As you draft your informative essay, carefully consider the use and placement of illustrations. You must acknowledge the source of any images or numerical information (see Chapter 15). Images, graphs, and tables should appear as close as possible

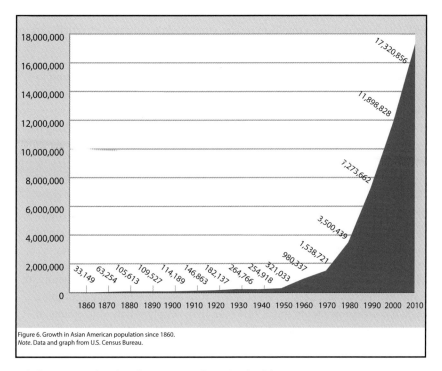

Figure 6. Growth in Asian American population since 1860.
Note. Data and graph from U.S. Census Bureau.

▲ A chart converting data from a source into visual evidence

to the point where they are mentioned in the text, and a title or caption should identify or explain the illustration.

You can read more about document design in Chapters 18, 19, and 20.

FRAME YOUR INFORMATION
After you've settled on the supporting points you want to make and the evidence you'll use to develop your ideas, spend some time thinking about how you will put everything together for your readers.

Introduction Your introduction sets the tone for your essay and influences how your readers understand and interpret the information that you give them. Most informative essays present the thesis statement in the introduction so that readers will grasp the writer's main idea from the start. Beyond stating your thesis, you can use a range of strategies to introduce your ideas. Two effective options are providing a historical account and asking a question. Historical accounts, such as the one Liana Aghajanian offers in the fifth and sixth paragraphs of "Stealth Generation" (p. 175), can help your readers understand the origins of a subject and how the situation has changed over time. Asking a question invites your readers to become participants in the conversation.

Organization The organization of your essay also affects how readers respond to your points. Your organizing strategy should take into account your purposes and your readers' needs and interests, as well as the nature and amount of evidence you've assembled to support your points. To organize your essay, choose an organizing pattern and create an outline or a map. You can use a wide range of organizing patterns in an informative essay, but some are better suited to the genre than others. If you are informing your readers about an event or a series of events, for instance, you might want to use chronological order to structure your essay. If you are providing an overview of competing ideas about an issue, you might choose comparison and contrast. And if you are explaining the defining characteristics of a subject, such as the typical attitudes of college-age voters, description might be a useful pattern to follow.

Conclusion You've probably read conclusions that simply summarize a document. These summaries can be effective, especially if your essay has presented complex concepts. A conclusion can do more, however, than simply restate your points. If you asked a question in your introduction, for instance, consider answering it in your conclusion. And if you want your readers to continue thinking about your subject after they've finished reading your essay, you might conclude by offering additional insights about what the information you've provided might mean for readers, as featured writer Ellen Page does in her finished essay (p. 213).

Chapter 18 provides additional strategies for writing introductions and conclusions. Chapter 17 provides information about organizing patterns, outlines, and maps.

Review and Improve Your Draft

Writing an informative essay involves juggling information, identifying main and supporting points, providing evidence for those points, and framing your ideas to accomplish your purposes. Any one of these activities can pose a significant challenge to a writer. Add them together and you've created a complex task that is sure to require additional work beyond a first draft. As you review your draft, pay particular attention to how well you've focused your discussion of the main point, the clarity of your discussion, your use of information from sources, and the effectiveness of your introduction and conclusion.

FOCUS YOUR DISCUSSION

Maintaining a clear focus is one of the most difficult challenges faced by writers of informative essays. Even when dealing with the most obscure subjects, the amount of information available to writers is still likely to be so large that it can be difficult to decide what to use and what to set aside. As you review your essay, make sure that your draft focuses on a single main point, that your thesis statement clearly conveys that point, and that every supporting point is relevant and well defined.

ENSURE CLARITY

Readers invest time in an informative document because they want to learn about a subject. If the document is unclear or difficult to follow, they'll look elsewhere. Review your essay to ensure that you've discussed your subject as clearly as possible. To ensure clarity, make certain that you use information from sources accurately and that you refer to concepts and ideas consistently. Make your prose as economical as possible, and choose the right words for your purpose, readers, and subject. In addition, vary the structure of your sentences and paragraphs without making them overly complex. You can read more about strategies for ensuring a clear discussion in Chapters 18 and 22.

REVIEW YOUR USE OF SOURCES

The effectiveness of your informative essay depends heavily on your selection and use of sources. As you revise, ask yourself these questions: Have you chosen the right sources to support your points? Have you used enough sources to make your points effectively? Have you used the right amount of evidence from your sources? Have you clearly differentiated your own ideas from those of your sources? Have you clearly identified the sources from which you've drawn information? Have you provided appropriate citations in both the text and the works cited list? Have you paraphrased accurately and fairly? Have you quoted properly?

You can learn more about using information from sources in Chapter 21. For a fuller discussion of why you should document sources, see Chapter 15. For guidelines on the MLA and APA documentation systems, see Chapters 23 and 24.

ASSESS YOUR INTRODUCTION AND CONCLUSION

Your introduction and conclusion serve not only as the beginning and end of your essay but also as a means of framing your discussion. Your introduction calls your readers' attention to specific aspects of your subject — while turning their attention away from others — and your conclusion reinforces their understanding of the points you've made in the essay. If your introduction, conclusion, supporting points, and evidence are inconsistent with one another, your essay will be ineffective. To avoid inconsistencies, review your introduction and conclusion, keeping in mind your main point, supporting points, and use of evidence from sources. You can read more about framing your introduction and conclusion in Chapter 18.

Once you've revised your essay, ask yourself how you might polish and edit it so that your readers will find it easy to read — and ask a friend, relative, or classmate to proofread your final draft to make sure that it is free of distracting errors. For a discussion of editing and proofreading strategies, see Chapter 22.

Peer Review: Improve Your Informative Essay

One of the biggest challenges writers face is reading a draft of their own work as a reader rather than as the writer. Because you know what you're trying to say, you find it easy to understand your draft. To determine how you should revise your draft, ask a friend or classmate to read your essay and to consider how well you've adopted the role of reporter (see p. 174).

Purpose	1. Did you find the essay informative? Did you learn anything new? 2. What questions does the essay answer? Do I need to address any other questions?
Readers	3. Did you find the essay interesting? Why or why not? 4. Does the information I've included in my essay address my readers' needs, interests, knowledge, and backgrounds? 5. Does the essay seem fair? Did you detect any bias or agenda in the way I presented information?
Sources	6. Does the information make sense? Can I add, clarify, or rearrange anything to help you understand the subject better? Do you think any of the details are unnecessary? 7. Do my sources strike you as reliable and appropriate? Does any of the information seem questionable?
Context	8. Is my subject sufficiently narrow and focused? Is my thesis statement clear? 9. Would any of the information be better presented in visual form? 10. Is the physical appearance of my essay appropriate? Did you find the font easy to read? Did you have enough room to write down comments?

For each of the points listed above, ask your reviewers to provide concrete advice about what you should do to improve your draft. It can help if you ask them to adopt the role of an editor — someone who is working with you to improve your draft. You can read more about peer review in Chapter 5.

Student Essay

 Ellen Page, "To Spray or Not to Spray: DDT Use for Indoor Residual Spraying"

The following informative essay was written by featured writer Ellen Page.

To Spray or Not to Spray:

DDT Use for Indoor Residual Spraying

> APA notes that requirements for title pages on student essays vary. Check with your instructor first.

Ellen Page

Medical Geography

Professor Pratt

December 5, 2016

> Information about the writer, course, and submission date is provided on the cover page.

To Spray or Not To Spray: DDT Use for Indoor Residual Spraying

The essay's title is repeated and centered.

In many parts of the world, mosquitoes are far more than just a nuisance. When mosquitoes infected with the *Plasmodium* parasite bite humans, they transmit the often fatal disease malaria. Vector control — killing the mosquitoes that spread the disease — is the primary strategy in reducing malaria deaths worldwide. Currently, the most frequently implemented methods for malaria vector control include insecticide-treated bed nets and indoor residual spraying with pesticides (World Health Organization [WHO], 2015, p. 4). But such pesticides carry risks of their own. One insecticide in particular, DDT, has offered both the most success and the greatest risk in malaria vector control. Scientists and governments devising approaches to eradicating malaria consider three main factors in determining whether DDT should be used in IRS: health consequences, environmental consequences, and degree of resistance.

Ellen's thesis statement

Since the discovery of the insecticide dichlorodiphenyltrichloroethane (DDT) in 1939, a long and controversial battle has waged over its use in the prevention of malaria. DDT was first used during World War II, when it was sprayed over large areas of the southern United States to kill mosquitoes, and in 1955, the World Health Organization (WHO) proposed a global malaria eradication program in which DDT would be a key player (CDC, 2016). According to Sadasivaiah, Tozan, and Breman (2007), following the 1962 release of Rachel Carson's book *Silent Spring*, which questioned DDT's safety and environmental consequences, public support for spraying DDT declined dramatically (p. 250). This lack of support, combined with signs of developing resistance to the chemical, brought widespread spraying of DDT to a halt in 1969 (Sadasivaiah et al., 2007, p. 249).

The writer frames the subject with an overview of the history of using DDT to treat malaria.

When the authors are named in a signal phrase, the parenthetical citation provides only the page number.

In APA style, subsequent references to the source use "et al." in place of all but the first author's name.

Although DDT's use in agricultural applications largely diminished, it continued to be used in insecticide-treated bed nets and indoor residual spraying. While bed nets only protect those individuals sleeping under the nets, indoor residual spraying protects all the members of a household. It is applied to the interior surfaces of a dwelling and "keeps mosquitoes out of and away from sprayed houses and reduces feeding rates and shortens resting periods" of malaria-carrying mosquitoes (Sadasivaiah et al., 2007, p. 249). Furthermore, a major benefit of indoor residual spraying is its "applica[bility] in many epidemiological settings" (WHO, 2015, p. 6); it works regardless of factors such as geographic location, climate, and housing structure. Currently

Brackets are used to modify a quotation.

TO SPRAY OR NOT TO SPRAY   2

WHO (2015) has estimated that 59% of residents of sub-Saharan Africa
are protected from malaria transmission by these two types of vector control
involving DDT (p. 4).

> Per APA style, the year of publication is put in parenthesis after the author.

  Given the huge health and economic impact of malaria, renewed global
efforts to fight the disease have caused divisions among many countries,
researchers, and organizations over the appropriate use of DDT. Governments
and non-governmental organizations must assess the considerable risks of DDT,
including adverse effects on human health, environmental consequences, and
chemical resistance. They must also weigh the considerable benefits afforded by
DDT, including its proven effectiveness and its low cost.

  First, there are unanswered questions about how the DDT in indoor residual
spraying affects human health. The health outcomes of DDT exposure from spraying
inside the home are less well understood than the harmful effects of large-scale
agricultural spraying. WHO's report *DDT in Indoor Residual Spraying: Human Health
Aspects* (2011a) stated that "in terms of potential risks at levels of exposure of
the general population in countries using [indoor residual spraying], research is
needed on reproductive effects in females and certain child developmental effects
to better evaluate risks that were suggested in the studies that were reviewed"
(p. 16). Many studies have suggested that DDT causes "early pregnancy loss,
fertility loss, leukemia, pancreatic cancer, neurodevelopmental deficits, diabetes,
and breast cancer," yet conflicting outcomes in experiments on lab rats and human
case studies have left researchers with a lack of definitive evidence regarding
human health risks associated with DDT exposure (van den Berg, 2009, p. 1658).
Collectively, these studies point to a need for further research into many of the
human health concerns related to DDT exposure via indoor residual spraying.

> The writer explains the first risk of DDT (health effects).

> A partial quotation is integrated into the text.

  The second factor that scientists must critically examine is the
environmental consequences of DDT. DDT is chemically very stable; it doesn't
break down in the environment but persists for long periods of time and can
bio-accumulate in a food chain (WHO, 2011b, p. 2). The toxicity of DDT in the
environment is clear; the pesticide's negative effects have been documented by
a host of researchers since the 1960s, with the majority of concern involving
the contamination of agricultural crops. It is unclear, however, whether indoor
residual spraying with DDT causes the same environmental harm, especially
since the amount of DDT used in spraying does not come close to the amount
used for agriculture in the mid to late 1900s (Sadasivaiah et al., 2007, p. 250).

> The writer explains the second risk of DDT (environmental effects).

TO SPRAY OR NOT TO SPRAY 3

Figure 1 shows the gradual decline of DDT use worldwide from 6,800,000 kg to 900,000 kg between 1995 and 2005 (Sadasivaiah et al., 2007, p. 252). The strict management of indoor residual spraying virtually eliminates overuse of the pesticide to a degree that would cause harm (WHO, 2011b, p. 5). Given the low levels of DDT used in indoor residual spraying and the careful enforcement of global policies concerning DDT, there is little risk that this method of vector control could contaminate agricultural crops.

Figure 1. Quantities of commonly used insecticides for malaria vector control

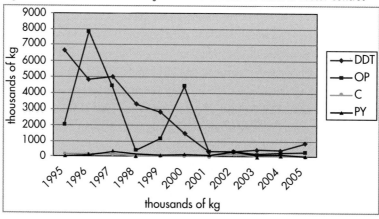

A caption describes the figure, and information about the source of the data is provided in a note.

Note. Data is adapted from "Dichlorodiphenyltrichloroethane (DDT) for Indoor Residual Spraying in Africa: How Can It Be Used for Malaria Control?" by Shobha Sadasivaiah, Yesim Tozan, and Joel G. Breman, 2007, *American Journal of Tropical Medicine and Hygiene 77*(6), p. 251. DDT = dichlorodiphenyltrichloroethane; OP = organophosphate; C = carbamate; PY = pyrethroid.

Finally, as with all pesticide use, one major threat to malaria vector control is the development of resistance to the chemical. The more pesticide used and the larger the area it is used to treat, the more likely resistance is to occur (Sadasivaiah et al., 2007, pp. 252-253). If the pesticides used to kill mosquitoes are rendered useless, the number of malaria cases worldwide would almost certainly escalate. To prevent the development of resistance, the World Health Organization recommends not "using the same insecticide for multiple successive IRS cycles" and instead implementing "a system of rotation with a different insecticide class being used each year" (WHO, 2015, p. 6). It is

TO SPRAY OR NOT TO SPRAY   4

unlikely that pesticide use will ever be discontinued, but the enforcement of pesticide regulation and limiting its use can reduce the possibility of resistance and increase the efficacy of the pesticide in protecting human health.

    To understand the controversy over DDT in indoor residual spraying, we must understand not only its risks but also its benefits. Cost is an extremely important aspect of malaria control. When compared with other pesticides available for use in indoor residual spraying, the cost of DDT is significantly lower. As shown in Table 1, the pesticide Deltamethrin ranks similarly to DDT as far as cost is concerned, but it is slightly more expensive to produce and does not last as long as DDT. Other pesticides cost as much as six times more than DDT and are not yet as effective (Sadasivaiah et al., 2007, p. 254). Furthermore, DDT does not have to be reapplied for six months whereas other pesticides used have to be reapplied every two or three months. When these considerations are coupled with the health costs of malaria, DDT appears to be the most cost-effective pesticide choice at this time.

Table 1. WHO Insecticide Cost Comparison in U.S. Dollars

Insecticide	Approximate duration of residual effect on mud surfaces (months)	Number of spraying rounds per 6 months	Approximate amount of formulated product required per house per 6 months (kg)	Approximate cost of formulated product (US$ per kg)	Cost per house per 6 months (US$)	Cost ratio (DDT = 1)
DDT	6	1	0.5	3.0	1.6	1.0
Deltamethrin	3	2	0.4	4.0	1.6	1.0
Malathion	2	3	2.4	3.4	8.2	5.1
Lambda-cyhalothrin	3	2	0.1	72.0	8.6	5.4
Bendiocarb	2	3	0.3	46.0	13.8	8.6
Fenitrothion	3	2	2.0	7.4	14.8	9.3
Propoxur	3	2	1.0	18.8	18.8	11.8

Note. Data is adapted from "Dichlorodiphenyltrichloroethane (DDT) for Indoor Residual Spraying in Africa: How Can It Be Used for Malaria Control?" by Shobha Sadasivaiah, Yesim Tozan, and Joel G. Breman, 2007, *American Journal of Tropical Medicine and Hygiene 77*(6), p. 254.

> A table provides statistical information in a readable format. A note indicates the source of the data.

TO SPRAY OR NOT TO SPRAY   5

The concerns around DDT have caused many countries to forgo using it for
vector control, but switching to a different pesticide can have its own drawbacks.
In 1996, Kwa-zulu Natal, a province in South Africa, abandoned DDT because
of health concerns and switched to pyrethrenoid pesticides (Sadasivaiah et al.,
2007, p. 256). Unfortunately, this measure which was taken to improve health
ended up doing more harm than good. Mosquitoes became resistant to the
new pesticides and malaria cases increased; when DDT was reintroduced, cases
plummeted 90% (Sadasivaiah et al., 2007, p. 256). Because of such dramatic
results, in 2006 the World Health Organization announced a policy change and
endorsed the use of DDT in indoor residual spraying throughout Africa. Dr. Anarfi
Asamoa-Baah, the assistant director-general for the organizations's HIV/AIDS, TB,
and malaria division, explained, "Indoor residual spraying is useful to quickly
reduce the number of infections caused by malaria-carrying mosquitoes. Indoor
residual spraying has proven to be just as cost effective as other malaria prevention measures, and DDT presents no health risk when used properly" (as cited in
WHO, 2006).

> In her conclusion, the writer emphasizes the main question posed by the essay.

Given "the right of people to a safe environment," researchers and
governments consider whether people should be exposed to a chemical that
prevents malaria but might cause physical harm down the road (Bouwman
et al., 2011, p. 746). Do the health risks of malaria outweigh the health risks
of using DDT? Unfortunately, it is a difficult question to answer. The continued
evolution of resistance in malaria-carrying mosquito species, the substantial
environmental consequences of DDT, and the uncertain effects on human
health are all serious concerns. However, the health risks posed by malaria
cannot be ignored. Although infection and mortality rates have declined, an
estimated 214 million cases of malaria occurred in 2015, with 438,000 of
them resulting in death (WHO, 2015, p. 8). Compounded by poor healthcare
systems in many of the countries faced with malaria, the overall health effects
of the disease can be severe. For countries with high rates of malaria and little
funding available for expensive control strategies, DDT may continue to be the
answer.

TO SPRAY OR NOT TO SPRAY   6

References

Bouwman, H., van den Berg, H., & Kylin, H. (2011). DDT and malaria prevention: Addressing the paradox. *Environmental Health Perspectives, 119*(6), 744-747.

Centers for Disease Control and Prevention. (2016, March 11). *About malaria.* Retrieved from http://www.cdc.gov/malaria/about/history/

Sadasivaiah, S., Tozan, Y., & Breman, J.G. (2007, December). Dichlorodiphenyltrichloroethane (DDT) for indoor residual spraying in Africa: How can it be used for malaria control? *The American Journal of Tropical Medicine and Hygiene, 77*(6), 249-263. Retrieved from http://www.ncbi.nlm.nih.gov/books/NBK1724/#pg249.r73

Van den Berg, H. (2009). Global status of DDT and its alternatives for use in vector control to prevent disease. *Environmental Health Perspectives, 117*(11), 1656-1663.

World Health Organization. (2006, September 15). *WHO gives indoor use of DDT a clean bill of health for controlling malaria.* Retrieved from http://www.who.int/mediacentre/news/releases/2006/pr50/en/

World Health Organization. (2011a). *DDT in indoor residual spraying: Human health aspects.* Retrieved from http://www.who.int/ipcs/publications/ehc/ehc241.pdf

World Health Organization. (2011b). *Malaria factsheet.* Retrieved from http://www.who.int/mediacentre/factsheets/fs094/en/index.html

World Health Organization. (2015). *World malaria report 2014.* Retrieved from http://www.who.int/malaria/publications/world_malaria_report_2014/en/

In APA style, the references are listed on a separate page, with a centered heading.

Sources are alphabetized by the author's last name and are formatted with hanging indents.

A Web source

An article from a scholarly journal

In APA style, multiple works by the same author are listed chronologically.

In APA style, works by the same author in the same year are distinguished by letters.

Project Ideas

The following suggestions offer ideas for writing an informative essay or another type of informative document.

Suggestions for Essays

1. DESCRIBE A SITUATION TO YOUR CLASSMATES

Inform your classmates about a situation that is likely to affect them. For example, you might report on changes to your school's course registration system, or you might let them know about a proposed student fee increase. Identify the main point you want to share with your readers. You might, for example, focus on the likely effects of the situation, the individuals or groups who are supporting it, or the events that led to the situation. Then identify supporting points that you'll share with your readers. For example, if you are looking at a fee increase, you could talk about how the money generated by the fee might be used and how (and how many) students might benefit from the service provided through the fee. You might also look at the impact of not providing the service. In your essay, describe the situation clearly, drawing on personal observation, an interview with someone who is familiar with the situation, or written sources (see Chapters 13 and 14).

2. EXPLAIN HOW SOMETHING WORKS

Explain how something works to an audience of your choice, such as your classmates, other college students, your instructor, your parents, or members of the community. For example, you might explain how a new technology improves the performance of wireless headphones, or how a new diet supplement affects the health of those who use it. In your essay, identify the key features or processes that allow the subject of your essay to accomplish its purpose and provide evidence to support your main points. Consider supporting your explanation by using observation, interviews, media sources and Web-based video, or written sources (see Chapters 13 and 14).

3. CHRONICLE A SEQUENCE OF EVENTS

Write an informative essay that describes a series of events. You might choose a historical event, such as the first Gulf War or the decision to send manned missions to the moon, or a more recent event, such as the decision to fire the coach of a local professional sports team, a major layoff at a national high-technology firm, or a recently passed law that has caused some controversy. In your essay, identify the event you will chronicle and lay out the sequence of events that led up to it. Provide information about the event by drawing on sources from experts who have written or spoken about the event, by examining news reports that came before or after the event, and by conducting field research (see Chapter 14) such as interviews, observation, and correspondence (e-mail messages, text messages, social media posts, or letters).

4. WRITE A PROFILE

Select a friend, family member, or public figure and write a profile for a newspaper, magazine, journal, blog, or website. If you are writing about a friend or family member, interview the subject of your profile and, if possible, interview friends or family members who are well acquainted with him or her. Your profile should offer insights into the person's character and contributions.

If you are writing about a public figure, ask for an interview. If you cannot conduct an interview, locate sources that offer information about the person. Your profile should offer insights into his or her accomplishments, interests, and plans. You should reflect on the person's impact on society and the implications of his or her work for the future. Base the profile on personal experience, information from a published source or an interview with someone who is aware of or acquainted with the person, and your own reasoning.

5. REPORT THE NEWS

Share news of a recent event, discovery, or disaster with an audience of your choice. You might direct your essay to your instructor, your classmates, other college students, your friends, or people from your hometown. Choose a subject that would interest your readers but that they are unlikely to know about. For example, if you are writing to people from your hometown, you might choose to write about something that has occurred at your college or university. If you are writing to your instructor or classmates, you might choose something that recently occurred in your hometown. Provide information about the event by conducting field research (see Chapter 14) such as interviews, observation, and correspondence (e-mail messages, text messages, social media posts, or letters). You should also review and use accounts from news services that have reporters in place at an event or a disaster or that provide information about a new discovery through experts or knowledgeable reporters.

Suggestions for Other Genres

6. CREATE AN INFORMATIVE BROCHURE

Begin working on your brochure by considering your purpose and your readers. Identify the single most important message you want to convey to your readers, and determine how you would like them to react to your message. Then brainstorm the organizing patterns and design strategies you might use to convey that message.

Once you've decided on the content, organization, and design of your brochure, create a mockup and ask for feedback from a friend, a classmate, a relative, or an instructor. Keep their feedback in mind as you revise and edit your brochure. Pay attention to the design principles discussed in Chapter 18. In particular, think carefully about how you stage information and how you use illustrations and colors to frame your most important messages and convey a specific mood to readers.

7. DEVELOP AN INFORMATIVE WEBSITE

Begin working on your website by considering your purpose and your readers. Once you've identified the information you want to provide, consider how best to present it. Give some thought to the overall structure of your site — that is, the number of and relations among the pages on your site. Then determine which information you will present on each page, and choose the type of navigation tools you'll provide so that your readers can easily move from page to page.

Once you've worked out the overall structure of the site, spend time developing a consistent look and feel for your pages. Your pages should have a similar design (such as a standard color scheme, consistent placement of navigation tools, consistent fonts for headers and body text, and so on). Finally, decide on the type of illustrations and the nature of communication tools, if any, that you'll use on the site. As you develop your design and create your pages, consider the design principles discussed in Chapter 18. To learn more about designing websites, see Chapter 19.

8. DRAFT AND DESIGN AN INFORMATIVE ARTICLE FOR A PRINT PUBLICATION

As you prepare to write your article, decide whether you want to focus on a particular subject or publish in a particular magazine, journal, or newspaper. If you want to write about a particular subject, search your library's databases and the Web for relevant articles (see Chapter 13). This search can also help you identify publications that might be interested in your article. If you want to publish your article in a particular publication, read it carefully to determine the kinds of subjects it normally addresses. Once you've selected a target publication, analyze it to determine its writing conventions (such as level of formality and the manner in which sources are acknowledged) and design conventions.

Provide information about the subject of your article by conducting field research (see Chapter 14) such as interviews, observation, and correspondence (e-mail messages, text messages, social media posts, or letters) and by drawing on written sources published in print and on the Web and media sources such as videos on news sites or YouTube. You can learn more about searching for digital and print sources in Chapter 13.

As you learn about your subject and plan, organize, and design your article, keep in mind what you've learned about the writing and design conventions of the articles you've read. Your article should reflect those conventions. You can learn more about design principles in Chapter 18. You can learn about the distinctive design features of articles in Chapter 19.

In Summary: Writing an Informative Essay

* **Find a conversation and listen in.**
  - Explore your interests (p. 194).
  - Use your library (p. 195).
  - Ask questions about promising subjects (p. 198).

* **Gather information.**
  - Create a search plan (p. 198).
  - Collect sources (p. 201).
  - Evaluate your sources (p. 201).
  - Take notes (p. 201).
  - Conduct an interview (p. 204).

* **Prepare a draft.**
  - Present your main point (p. 205).
  - Develop supporting points and evidence (p. 205).
  - Consider genre and design (p. 208).
  - Frame your information (p. 209).

* **Review and improve your draft.**
  - Focus your discussion (p. 210).
  - Ensure clarity (p. 211).
  - Review your use of sources (p. 211).
  - Assess your introduction and conclusion (p. 211).

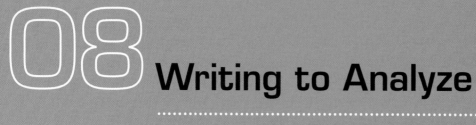

08 Writing to Analyze

When I analyze a topic, I take on the role of **interpreter**.

What Is Writing to Analyze?

Analytical writing begins with a question: To what extent does government surveillance of suspected terrorists affect the civil liberties of ordinary citizens? How will new environmental regulations affect plans to drill for oil near a state park? Why do animated films from Pixar Studios appeal to so many adults? The types of documents — or genres (see p. 271) — writers create to share their answers are as varied as the questions they ask. And each document, in turn, reflects aspects of the writing situations in which writers find themselves: their purposes for analyzing a subject, the interests and expectations of their intended readers, the sources used to support the analysis, and the context in which the document will be read.

Analysis involves adopting the role of *interpreter*. Writers who adopt this role help readers understand the origins, qualities, significance, or potential impact of a subject. An interpreter might address the causes of a recent economic downturn, for example, while another might explore the cultural implications of a new album by Kanye West. Another writer might present a historical analysis of U.S. involvement in foreign wars, while yet another might try to help college students understand the impact of proposed legislation on the cost of attending college.

In many cases, interpreters are already knowledgeable about their subjects. More often, however, they spend time learning about a subject to ensure that they can offer a well-grounded interpretation. Whether they draw on the subject itself, interview experts, collect information from published sources, or use statistical evidence, effective interpreters provide even knowledgeable readers with enough information about a subject to explain the focus of their analyses and to ensure that their interpretations will make sense in the context in which they're read.

Readers of analytical documents usually share the writer's interest in the subject and want to understand it in greater depth, either because it affects them in some way or because they are curious about it. They expect a clear introduction to the subject, focused interpretation, thorough explanations of how the writer arrived at his or her conclusions, and reasonable support for those conclusions. Readers also tend to expect that an analytical document will use an interpretive framework that is appropriate to the subject and similar to those typically used by other writers in the field. For example, readers with a literary background would be surprised if an analysis of a major novel was based on the book's sales history, rather than on some form of textual interpretation. Similarly, readers with a background in political science might find an article that focused on the aesthetic qualities of a speech by a presidential candidate less interesting than one that analyzed the political implications of the candidate's arguments.

Interpreters' choices about interpretive framework, sources, and perspective can and do lead to different — sometimes extremely different — conclusions about a subject. As a result, analytical documents not only serve as significant contributions to a conversation but also provide a foundation for further contributions to the conversation.

What Kinds of Documents Are Used to Present an Analysis?

The Writer's Role: Interpreter

PURPOSE
- To find patterns of meaning
- To trace causes and effects
- To determine significance

READERS
- Want to understand the subject
- Expect a careful and appropriate use of analytical techniques
- Expect coherent, focused reasons and evidence for the writer's interpretation

SOURCES
- Especially in the case of textual analysis, the subject itself is often the main source.
- Data, background information, and other writers' interpretations are often obtained from published material.
- Field research (interviews, observation, surveys, correspondence) and personal experience can add details and support.

CONTEXT
- Analytical questions, interpretive frameworks, and genres are shaped by reader expectations and disciplinary standards and expectations.

- Interpreters usually need to frame a subject for readers before analyzing it.

Writers share their interpretations of subjects through a strikingly large array of genres. Soldiers and aid workers in Iraq and Afghanistan, for example, have interpreted the events in which they are involved through books, blogs, and social-networking sites. Commentators analyze the political landscape through columns, editorials, and data analyses. Scholars examine subjects as diverse as Shakespeare's sonnets, the possibility of life on Mars, and the potential for electoral college reform through journal articles and conference presentations. And students are frequently asked to share their interpretations through essays, reports, and presentations.

Regardless of the genre a writer decides to use, most analytical writing begins with an attempt to understand how other writers have approached the challenges of analyzing a particular subject. Examining analytical documents can spark ideas about how to focus an analysis, offer insights into the kinds of interpretive frameworks that have been used to direct past analyses, and provide an understanding of the conclusions other writers have drawn. In the following sections, you'll find examples and discussions of magazine and newspaper articles, rhetorical analyses, and analytical blog posts.

Articles

Magazine and newspaper articles often provide analyses of issues, events, or problems. Because most articles are written for a specific publication, writers typically have a clear picture of their readers (in terms of age, income, education, hobbies, and so forth) and can target their analysis to the needs and interests of a narrowly defined group. An article about an election, for example, might analyze turnout among younger voters, analyze the campaign of a recently elected senator from the Midwest, or analyze the impact of organizations such as the Teamsters or the National Rifle Association.

Authors of magazine and newspaper articles typically rely on information gathered through observations, interviews, correspondence, and personal experience. They also draw frequently on published sources. Writers of these articles are less likely than writers in academic or professional settings to use works cited or references lists, although they typically identify their sources in the body of the article.

Carly Lewis
The Writing on the Virtual Bathroom Wall

In "The Writing on the Virtual Bathroom Wall," Carly Lewis explores the increase in "rape list" postings, both online and in the real world. These listings of alleged sexual abusers have been widely controversial. While supporters say that an unreliable legal system leaves no other way for their voices to be heard, critics contend that such postings are defamatory and, as such, illegal. In a careful analysis, Lewis brings a larger issue to light: we do not yet have an effective way to handle sexual assault. Lewis is a writer whose work has been featured in *Maclean's* (where this article was published) as well as *New York* magazine, *The Guardian, Interview, Spin, The Globe and Mail, Flair,* and *The National Post,* among others.

The Writing on the Virtual Bathroom Wall

In the post–Cosby era, women are reviving a controversial tactic: naming names.

by Carly Lewis

Last month, a stack of loose papers with the title "s--t list" appeared in the women's washroom of a Toronto concert venue. On the first page was a handful of names, written in black marker, of alleged sexual abusers, most of them well-known figures in Toronto's music and west-end nightlife scenes. One of the people named on the list had been acquitted in two sexual assault cases this year. (In the second trial, the judge noted that the man's testimony and the complainant's were "equally plausible.")

Before social media, the list would have been viewed by a limited contingent of clubgoers. (The venue's capacity is around 1,400.) But the velocity of digital sharing being what it is, a photo of the first page spread via Twitter, Facebook and Instagram. The names of the alleged aggressors were later posted to a dedicated Tumblr page, which featured — for an evening — additional names that had been emailed to the page's creator.

The creator says she was not involved in the bathroom list, but says she started the Tumblr as a way to share its warnings with people who weren't at the concert. She has since removed the site due to fear of legal repercussions. She can't vouch for the accuracy of the list, she acknowledges, but her perspective is simple: she believes the accusers, despite their anonymity, and the absence of other details. "The men on the list are popular, respected members of the community, and I am sick of their actions being excused," she said by email. "The law isn't really on our side. It's important that we look out for each other as best we can."

Post–Jian Ghomeshi — and the highly public allegations against Bill Cosby et al. — it's become impossible to ignore both the reluctance of women to report sexual assault, given the uphill battle they face in the legal system, and the fact that people often know about allegations of abuse for years, even decades before they become public. In the cases of Cosby and Ghomeshi, it took years for accusers' voices to be heard. When they were, it was because they joined forces to amplify one another. These were landmark moments: women speaking about sexual assault to media rather than to police, and being heard in the absence of any charges.

Women are also speaking out in "rape lists," such as the one in the Toronto club — and not just between bathroom stalls. There was at least one other Toronto Tumblr that named names and ran accounts of alleged assaults and other aggressive behavior. It, too, was taken down recently. In September 2014, rape lists showed up in women's washrooms at the University of Chicago, and a corresponding Tumblr page that named "people known to commit varying levels of gender-based violence" appeared around the same time.

According to *Jezebel*, the Tumblr, which has since been removed, stated that its aim was "keeping the community safe — since the university won't." In 2012, a Kentucky high school student revealed the names of her convicted abusers on Twitter (for which she faced a contempt-of-court charge, later dropped). In 2013, a dating app called Lulu, which allowed users to rate the bad dates they'd gone on, quickly became a space for women to warn other women about creepy or uncomfortable encounters they'd had with men — much the way an Uber driver's low rating functions as a warning to potential customers.

Rape lists, online or off, are a way to help women bypass an unfriendly legal system. They are also "seriously defamatory," says Toronto-based defamation lawyer Peter Downard, senior litigation counsel at Fasken Martineau. It's not unusual for people to take matters into their own hands when official structures fail to protect them. "In the face of that failure, there is going to be great frustration," says Downard, who considers rape lists a form of civil disobedience expressed through vigilantism.

The creator of the Toronto Tumblr page says that, as a survivor of abuse herself, her mission is to warn women. "My intentions are not to incite a witch hunt against the named," she says. "I simply want a safe space for survivors to share information." This strategy echoes a controversial suggestion made by Germaine Greer a few years ago. "I wish there were an online rapists' register, and that it was kept up-to-date, because we know the courts can't get it right," said the well-known feminist academic and author of *The Female Eunuch*.

The legal route comes, undeniably, with serious challenges. Sexual assault survivors who do come forward often face re-traumatization, as well as a legal system perceived to be stacked in favor of the accused. Not surprisingly, Statistics Canada estimated that only around eight percent of sexual assaults in Canada are reported to police.

Hence the prevalence of anonymous rape lists — and all the issues they raise. Women have been plumbing the ethics of underground symposia for decades. In autumn 1990, a list of alleged rapists appeared in a women's washroom at Brown University. At its fullest — the list stayed intact for months — it contained roughly 30 names, some of which had been reported to officials.

A story about the list in the student newspaper alerted the rest of campus. At the time, Brown's executive vice-president of university relations, Robert Reichley, called the list "anti-male" and branded its contributors "Magic Marker terrorists." Custodians were instructed to remove selected graffiti from campus washrooms. "Men who've assaulted me or a woman I know," in the women's washroom was scrubbed away. Meanwhile, misogynistic graffiti remained. Later that year, a new list appeared: "Women who need to be raped." One of the students named on that list was prominent campus feminist Jesselyn Radack.

"If officials had actually listened to what the women graffitists had to say," Radack wrote later in the collection of essays *Just Sex: Students Rewrite the Rules on Sex, Violence, Activism, and Equality*, "they would have realized that the motivation was to protect women in the absence of a judicial board willing to hear complaints of sexual violence."

Today, Radack is better known as a legal adviser to Edward Snowden, as well as a former ethics adviser to the U.S. Department of Justice, and the whistleblower who disclosed what she believed to be a violation of ethics during the FBI's interrogation of enemy combatant John Walker Lindh during America's 2001 invasion of Afghanistan. "Women are going to engage in guerrilla tactics," Radack told *Maclean's,* "but I would much rather have a legal system that adequately [and] confidently handles sexual assault."

Twenty-five years after the Brown controversy, it's hardly better inside the law. "Within a criminal-court context, it is very difficult to get a conviction," says Simona Jellinek, a Toronto-based lawyer whose firm specializes in representing sexual assault survivors. Jellinek argues that false accusations of rape are "absolutely rare." But "if the judge hears both sides and thinks they're both credible, the judge actually has no other option but to acquit, even if the judge believes the survivor."

In May 2014, the names of four alleged assailants appeared in various women's washrooms at Columbia University, a month after 23 students filed a federal complaint in one month against Columbia. "We needed some way to warn people that these people are violent," one of the activists involved told the *Guardian*. (According to the *Guardian*, one student complained that, though her attacker confessed to assaulting her, he was merely suspended for one semester, then returned to school. The paper noted that his father made a financial contribution to Columbia.)

For all the cultural progress we've made, the Sharpie marker—and its online equivalent—remains, somehow, mightier than the law. In fact, the online version of the bathroom wall is even more powerful: It can warn more women faster, but it can also change a person's reputation

> The online version is more powerful: it can warn more women but also change a reputation permanently.

permanently and without an accuser coming forward.

Of course, it is defamatory to scribble the name of one alleged rapist on a wall; it is defamatory to scribble the names of 30, and it is certainly defamatory to tweet it. That's one reason the Ontario Civil Liberties Association feels defamation should be abolished from Canadian law completely. "Defamation is a tool that the powerful use to silence criticism," says Joseph Hickey, executive director of the non-profit organization. "I would rather see members of society independently assess information they receive, and not feel the need to depend on legal authority to decide whether they approve of someone's reputation or not." That position is considered by many to be extreme. "They would have to remove the Supreme Court of Canada if they wanted to do that," says Downard.

But if preventive measures rely on abuses that have already taken place, and if official institutions are not remedying the problem, women may continue to turn to unofficial watch lists. "It's a matter of ensuring effective measures for bringing [abusers] to justice, so that women don't have to write on bathroom walls," says Radack. "It's such a desperate thing to have to do."

Late last month, the creator of the Toronto Tumblr emailed to say she was no longer in pursuit of a legally sound way to keep the list of names online. "I can't believe how hard it is to speak up about abusers," she says.

"To me, the problem clearly indicates a serious barrier in the way in which we deal with sexual assault," says Downard, of rape lists. "An act like this, if it is emblematic of a dysfunction in our society, it's just the canary in the coal mine."

Starting a Conversation: Respond to "The Writing on the Virtual Bathroom Wall"

In your writer's notebook, reflect on Lewis's analysis by responding to the following questions:

1. Consider the tone of "The Writing on the Virtual Bathroom Wall." Does Lewis fairly represent both sides of the issue? Who is not represented, and why?

2. What sources does Lewis use? How does she draw on sources to lend credibility to her argument? Why do you think Lewis chose the sources that she did?

3. Lewis utilizes the highly publicized allegations against Jian Ghomeshi and Bill Cosby as a framework for the perhaps lesser publicized "rape lists." Why is this context important? What other strategies does Lewis use to establish context for what she calls a "controversial tactic: naming names"?

4. Lewis writes, "For all the cultural progress we've made, the Sharpie marker — and its online equivalent — remains, somehow, mightier than the law" (para. 15). How does Lewis support this claim? How does this claim inform Lewis's ultimate analysis?

5. **Reflection:** In paragraph 2, Lewis remarks on the power of social media: "Before social media, the list would have been viewed by a limited contingent of clubgoers. . . . But the velocity of digital sharing being what it is, a photo of the first page spread via Twitter, Facebook and Instagram." How has digital sharing affected the ways in which we converse about controversial issues like the one Lewis documents in this essay? In this sense, is social media a positive or negative force? Why?

Issue Analyses

Articles and essays that analyze issues often begin with a question, or a problematic fact or puzzling situation that leads to a question. Writers of these kinds of documents need to know about and understand the history and significance of their subjects. Depending on the specific publication and writing situation, they might rely on statistical evidence, personal experience, or direct observation. In many cases, they must clearly explain unfamiliar background material to their readers or interpret complex data for them.

Issue analyses can draw on a variety of sources, ranging from interviews, surveys, published studies, and scholarly works to popular culture and personal observation. These sources are usually identified in the text, although formal works cited lists typically are not provided. In this sense, issue analyses resemble the articles that appear in popular magazines. And like magazine articles, they usually make use of design elements such as columns, headings and subheadings, and illustrations.

 Peter C. Baker
Reform of the Nerds, Starring Arthur Chu

In this excerpt from a 2015 article published in *Pacific Standard*, Peter C. Baker analyzes the underbelly of "nerd-dom" and Arthur Chu's rising role as a voice of positive change in what's grown to be a contentious, even dangerous culture. Baker chronicles how Chu has become a perhaps surprising advocate for reining in the aggressive, misogynistic culture of the online gaming world. By questioning how nerd culture became so angry, Baker sheds light on the larger issues of gender in gamer culture, self-expression, and the reappropriation of the "nerd." Baker's work has also been featured in publications such as *The New Yorker*, *The Nation*, and *The Times Literary Supplement*. His short stories have been published in such literary journals as *Granta* and *New World Writing*.

Reform of the Nerds, Starring Arthur Chu

How a game-show champion became the embattled conscience of American male geekdom.

by Peter C. Baker

In January of 2014, I started getting text messages from my college friends asking whether I was following our old classmate Arthur Chu on *Jeopardy!* I wasn't — I hadn't watched the show for years — but I tuned in the next day.

From then on, I watched rapt as Chu racked up what was, at the time, the third-longest winning streak in the show's history, drawing attention not only for the size of his haul (almost $400,000 in the end), but also for his supremely stereotypical nerdiness. He used an unorthodox strategy that drew on both game theory and statistical analysis of the *Jeopardy!* board. He was slightly pudgy, with glasses, and his hair was cut in a harsh horizontal line across his forehead. His shirts were rumpled, his ties poorly knotted. He spoke in a monotone and sometimes interrupted *Jeopardy!* host Alex Trebek, cutting off Trebek's patter so they could move on to the next question.

I had barely known Chu in college, but I loved watching him win. He seemed to simultaneously embody nerd stereotypes and vindicate them — by raking in a fortune. I especially liked his attitude toward his detractors: When people mocked him on Twitter, he re-tweeted their jibes, as if to demonstrate how little they hurt.

After Chu's run ended, I found myself missing it. Several months later, checking his Twitter feed, I saw him announce he would be appearing on a panel at a gaming convention in Maryland called MAGFest, where he would be talking about "the general unpleasantness in the nerd community this year," including "the Gamergate fiasco." This had the ring of familiarity, but I would have been hard pressed to say what any of it meant.

It didn't take much research for me to pick up that 2014 had been a tumultuous year in American nerd-dom. Long-simmering tensions built into the very concept of "the nerd" had reached a boiling point, with shockingly vicious results: death threats, rape threats, and torrents of online abuse, most of them made by nerds themselves against those perceived to be finding fault with nerd culture.

To my surprise, some of the most interesting and well-circulated analyses of the mayhem had been written by none other than Arthur Chu, who had leveraged his 15 minutes of game-show fame into, of all things, a national platform for his opinions about nerds: What America gets wrong about nerds; what nerds — especially male nerds — get wrong about themselves; and why it matters. In Chu's view, nerd-dom has a toxic, intolerant fringe, one that has gone unchecked in large part because nerds are awful at policing their own subculture, especially online. In an era when the nerds are increasingly ascendant, Chu wants to make nerd culture better — and to stop more of his fellow nerds from getting drawn into the worst of it. . . .

Before *Jeopardy!*, Chu was working as an insurance compliance analyst in Broadview Heights, a small city outside of Cleveland, where he also acted and did improv on the side. Waiting for his *Jeopardy!* episodes, which were pre-taped, to air, he hoped that the publicity might help him get gigs as a voice actor, a side career he's been trying to build for years. (It sounded quixotic to me, until Chu told me he'd had several voice-over gigs already, including a video for Safeway.)

When the *Jeopardy!* episodes were broadcast, they triggered a tsunami of media attention. Chu had never anticipated that people would care so much about his clothes, weight, or way of speaking. It was his introduction to a peculiarly modern form of exposure, one in which you can watch in real time as thousands of people entertain themselves by talking about you as if you weren't there. Some deemed Chu smug; others opted for digs about his weight. ("Looks like he just ate a pizza in bed," tweeted one nonfan.) Many deemed his aggressively money-focused strategy unsportsmanlike. The media started calling him "the *Jeopardy!* villain."

But the notoriety also had more agreeable results. Chu gained fans, many of them Asian Americans happy to see a nerdy Chinese American kicking unapologetic ass on the national stage.

TV shows wanted to interview Chu, and reporters wanted to profile him. Chu said yes to almost everything, intrigued by the possibility of finding his way into a new career—something, he told me, "that sort of goes with the rhythm of my interests, instead of getting orders from corporations." He thought it was absurd that a person could get famous from a game show, but—as he puts it in the trailer for *Who Is Arthur Chu?*, an upcoming documentary—"I'd rather be famous for that than for nothing."

Chu also began to find his voice as a writer, as Web publications took an interest in his byline. In May, Chu was asked to review *The Big Bang Theory*, the popular sitcom about nerds, for the *Daily Beast*. It was his fourth assignment for the site (on which his author bio describes him as a "Chinese-American nerd" who is "shamelessly extending his presence in the national spotlight by all available means"). But Chu never wrote the review. On the Friday before it was due, a 22-year-old named Elliot Rodger went on a violent rampage in Isla Vista, California, killing six people and injuring 14 others before committing suicide. On the day of his killings, Rodger had emailed a 141-page manifesto to family and acquaintances that described the violence he was about to commit as revenge on the female gender for ruining his life and on sexually active men for besting him.

When Chu read Rodger's manifesto, he found much of it to be terribly familiar. Except for the parts about murder, it read like a standard-issue litany of complaints by a lonely male nerd blaming women for his loneliness. "It's all girls' fault for not having any sexual attraction towards me," Rodger wrote. Instead of writing a review of *The Big Bang Theory*, Chu stayed up past dawn writing a different piece—an angry one—in which he insisted that, though Rodger was mentally ill, his attitudes toward women were common, especially among aggrieved male nerds. Chu confessed to having spent much of his own life as a lonely nerd and to having contributed to a culture that excused bad behavior. He said he had known nerdy male stalkers, even nerdy male rapists, but to his disgust had never confronted them.

"So, a question, to my fellow male nerds," he wrote. "What the fuck is wrong with us?"

The term "nerd" has come a long way since the 1980s, when it simply denoted an awkward social loser, usually a bespectacled, physically graceless male too book-smart for his own good. Today, it encompasses ever more subtypes: the loser; the intense (or even just mildly intense) fan of this or that pop-culture phenomenon; and the wealthy Silicon Valley coder or CEO wielding power over the American zeitgeist. The idea that "we are all nerds now" is increasingly common: See *The Guardian* in 2003, *New York* magazine in 2005, *Esquire* in 2013, and *The New York Times* last year.

Chu recognizes that many nerds are thriving in the post-industrial economy and that many once-nerdy interests are now mainstream. But he is careful to stress that the more painful variety of nerd-dom, the kind you don't adopt by choice, still exists. He knows there is still such a thing as not fitting in, or being unable to get a date. And he knows how much it sucks, because he's been there himself.

Chu's parents are fundamentalist Christians who immigrated to America from Taiwan. They lived in Rhode Island until Chu was 12, then moved to Boise, and by the time Chu was in high school they had settled in Cerritos, California, near Los Angeles. "Growing up evangelical was a real double bind," he says. He didn't accept religion easily, arguing the fine points of C. S. Lewis with his

Sunday school teachers, which made him an outsider in the evangelical community. Meanwhile, being an evangelical Christian — not to mention an Asian-American child with an advanced vocabulary and precise diction — marked him as an outsider everywhere else.

"I was the kid who probably spent fully 10 times as many hours reading books at school [as] exchanging words with any of my classmates," he wrote last year in *Salon*. "It was years before I learned to talk something like a normal human being and not an overly precise computerized parody of a 'nerd voice.' People felt uncomfortable around me, disliked me instinctively."

Chu joined a clique of what he calls "bitter angry guys" who desperately wanted female attention and felt antipathy toward women for not giving it to them. Even when Chu managed to get a high school girlfriend, he resented her for being, as he saw it, above him, as an automatic result of being female. He says he and his friends had "tunnel vision" and couldn't understand that "it could suck to be sexually wanted as much as to be sexually invisible."

After high school, he moved east to attend Swarthmore, a Pennsylvania liberal arts college with fewer than 1,600 students. He promptly joined a storied campus club, devoted to science fiction, fantasy, and the general embrace of nerddom, called SWIL — the Swarthmore Warders of Imaginative Literature. Chu felt he'd arrived in utopia: an in-the-flesh version of the online message boards he'd frequented through high school.

But SWIL did not feel so welcoming to all of its members. Chu says several male SWILlies were guilty of behavior that ranged from off-putting (sexist jokes) to predatory (dating a local high school student). A larger group of SWILlies turned a blind eye to it. In Chu's view, this was because

of nerd indulgence, born of a reluctance among people who have been ostracized to set standards that might exclude others. What one group of SWILlies viewed as misogyny and harassment got written off by the other group of SWILlies as awkwardness, or autism, or misunderstanding. (Both factions were made up of males and females.)

By his own reckoning, Chu spent most of college as part of the second group. But over time, thanks in part to friendships with some of the female SWILlies who felt uncomfortable, he came to think the club had a problem. Among the issues were club events that attracted creepy alumni — guys who had a habit of, as Chu puts it, "serially sleeping" with freshmen — and, in 2007, a group of reformers within SWIL voted not only to change the club's name (to Psi Phi — get it?) but also to ban alumni from its meetings and parties, an act of nerd exclusion that caused serious rifts among club members. Chu strongly supported the ban, eagerly debating its merits. (Jillian Waldman, who was co-president of SWIL in 2004 and 2005, disputes Chu's characterizations of "old-school SWIL," which she says was the more tolerant club.)

The SWIL civil war coincided with a general unraveling in the rest of Chu's life. Freed from his strict home, Chu was suddenly free to stay up all night playing video games, fine-tuning the SWIL newsletter, writing his campus newspaper column ("Chu on This"), editing Wikipedia articles, and indulging his insatiable appetite for debate on any subject under the sun. He was also spending more and more time in campus theater productions.

Chu's GPA dropped, and he got kicked out of a seminar, setting in motion a chain reaction that made him unable to graduate on time. He spent an extra year living in Philadelphia and taking classes, and another finishing his course work from his parents' house in California. He used the public library there to research his thesis and to try to launch his voice-over career, or, when that didn't work, to just find a job, any job, in the crashing economy. He sank into depression, played too many video games, and wondered how much longer he could go on.

Chu's choice last May to surprise his *Daily Beast* editor with an article about nerds and the Isla Vista killings ended up paying off. Headlined "Your Princess Is in Another Castle," a reference to *Super Mario Bros.*, the article went viral. Chu started getting calls from the media once more. This time, CNN and NPR didn't want to talk about his "Daily Double" *Jeopardy!* strategy. They wanted to hear about "nerd lust."

Chu found himself with a new sense of purpose. Other people had made similar observations about nerd culture before, but thanks to *Jeopardy!*, Chu had a shot at taking the issues to a bigger audience. In the months that followed, he wrote more about the dark currents within nerd-dom. One article discussed nerd power-lust. ("The creepy nerd fantasy that remains alive and well in today's Age of the Nerd Triumphant is not of making peace with the popular kids but taking their throne.") Another called out blockbusters like *Game of Thrones* and *Avatar* for nerd ethnic chauvinism. ("We repeatedly tell stories about a white protagonist who goes on a journey of self-discovery by mingling with exotic brown foreigners and becoming better at said foreigners' culture than they themselves are.")

Then came the controversy dubbed Gamergate, which was to raise Chu's profile even further. To explain Gamergate simply — or at all — is no easy task, but it began last August, when a 24-year-old man named Eron Gjoni posted a rambling, 9,000-plus-word blog post about the game developer Zoe Quinn, an ex-girlfriend whom he accused of cheating on him with a video-game journalist in order to advance her career. Quinn had often criticized the way women are portrayed and treated by mainstream gaming culture, so a contingent of hardcore gamers viewed Gjoni's allegations against her as emblematic of a corrupt journalistic culture that was out to undermine traditional games that were fun but non-PC: too violent, the bad guys too dark-skinned, the women too scantily clad. The angriest of them bombarded Quinn with online harassment, including death and rape threats. Some of Quinn's detractors broke into her accounts for online services like Tumblr, posted nude photos of her, and published her home address, leading her to move out of her residence. Online campaigns also sprang up targeting other female game developers and gaming writers.

Chu was horrified by the online Gamergate mobs, but also energized. He sparred with Gamergate supporters — meaning those who sided with gamers against people like Quinn — on Twitter, and he wrote articles categorizing Gamergate supporters as part of a "reactionary" movement doomed to eventual failure. If his hope was to become a nerd pundit, here was the ideal cultural moment.

Chu often stressed that he understood first-hand the pain of persistent social and romantic rejection. He assured readers that he, too, loved video games and well knew how powerful a refuge they could provide. But he also insisted that not all injustices merit equal pity. Yes, he wrote, he sympathized with some of the aggrieved feelings out there, but he could not endorse the self-pitying militancy they generated, calling it a "toxic swell of nerd entitlement that's busy destroying everything I love." . . .

In Chu's view, nerds created much of what we love about Internet culture but also much of what we hate about it. Intended as a refuge from real-world hierarchies and prejudices, the Internet has often wound up simply reproducing, even exaggerating, the power dynamics of the "real world," complete with bullying. Chu feels that if nerds were more willing to set some community standards, like the SWILlies did at Swarthmore, and behave with less indifference to the worst of their peers, they could make the world a lot more pleasant and protect the best of nerdiness — the joyful obsessions, the embrace of outsiders, the indifference to convention.

One challenge for Chu's conversion efforts is that he has trouble accounting for his own recovery from nerdy bitterness. When I asked him about this during one of our conversations, he shook his head, looking genuinely mystified. "I don't know," he said. "That's, you know, 'there but for the grace of God.'" But he was quick to point to one development his younger, angrier self could barely have imagined: wedlock.

Chu met his wife-to-be, Eliza Blair, at Swarthmore during his sophomore year; she was one of the SWILlies (a co-president, eventually) who led the reform charge. They didn't hit it off. "He was a huge blowhard jerk and I hated him on sight," she wrote me in an email. "It was all insecurity, immaturity."

Over time, though, Blair became Chu's biggest fan. In 2006, she made drawings of all her SWIL friends, representing their futures. Chu was depicted standing on a podium, speaking to an enthralled audience of thousands. "I knew that under the shitty nerd veneer was a guy with a lot of depth and a lot to say about the way the world works," Blair wrote. "I loved that guy and wanted to give him every chance to succeed." . . .

Chu has seen enough of the world to know he can't convince Gamergate obsessives that their outrage is absurd. Indeed, despite his love of debate, he has only limited faith in argument *per se*, which is one reason he has softened since college on his view of activists, whom he used to disdain because they weren't as committed as he was to exhaustive skeptical argument. If lonely nerds are to be wooed away from defeatism and rage, he believes, they must be reached with camaraderie as much as reason. "You can have someone who wants to be a good role model for you," Chu says, "but if they don't speak the same language, you're just not going to take influence from them."

At the reconvened MAGFest panel, it was clear that people were speaking the same language, reveling in both the debate and the shared obsessions. Chu stayed on stage for two hours more, then announced that he wanted a drink and invited anyone who wanted to keep talking upstairs to a hotel suite. A dozen nerds skipped the video-game hall, the board- and card-game rooms, and the live-action role-play zone and instead squeezed into an elevator together and headed up to keep debating, college-style, nerd culture's glory and excesses, its past and future. It felt optimistic, passionate, welcoming, and, sure, a little awkward: Chu's ideals made manifest. There was music playing from tiny laptop speakers, and someone had set up a disco ball. The crowd stayed for hours, nerding into the night.

In your writer's notebook, reflect on Baker's analysis by responding to the following questions:

Starting a Conversation: Respond to "Reform of the Nerds, Starring Arthur Chu"

1. How does Baker establish a brief history of the term "nerd"? At what point in the article does Baker introduce this term? Why might defining terms be an important aspect of analytical writing?

2. *Pacific Standard* is a print and online magazine "for affluent and influential readers interested in working toward forward-looking changes." How is the intended audience for this publication reflected in "Reform of the Nerds"? Consider Baker's tone — how do you think it would change for a different publication?

3. How does Baker connect Chu's personal experiences with the evolution of the larger nerd culture? Why is this connection important? What purpose does it serve in Baker's analysis?

4. **Reflection:** As he nears his conclusion, Baker writes, "Intended as a refuge from real-world hierarchies and prejudices, the Internet has often wound up simply reproducing, even exaggerating, the power dynamics of the 'real world,' complete with bullying." In what ways have you observed or experienced this aspect of online life? Baker describes several of Chu's strategies for confronting this problem in the online gaming world — how could these strategies be applied to other instances of the "exaggerated power dynamics" online?

Rhetorical Analyses

Rhetorical analyses take numerous forms, from articles and essays to blogs, Web pages, and — as in the case of Brooke Gladstone's graphic analysis — comics. Rhetorical analyses typically address factors such as the writer's purpose and background, the nature of the audience involved in a particular communication situation, the context in which a particular communication act took place, or the source of the information used in a particular exchange. Writers of rhetorical analyses often draw on sources of information that reflect the knowledge and interests of their intended readers. A rhetorical analysis written for a scholarly journal in political science, for example, might rely more heavily on scholarly articles and books than would an analysis directed to a general audience, which might rely more heavily on observation, interviews, and references to news articles or broadcasts.

Brooke Gladstone
The Goldilocks Number

"The Goldilocks Number" first appeared in Brooke Gladstone's book *The Influencing Machine: Brooke Gladstone on the Media*, illustrated by Josh Neufeld, and it was adapted from a radio segment Gladstone produced for NPR in 2010. Gladstone, a journalist and media analyst, calls *The Influencing Machine* a "media manifesto" in which she challenges readers' common assumptions about media. As you read, pay attention to how the illustrations enhance Gladstone's analysis and help distinguish her own ideas from those of her sources.

From *The Influencing Machine: Brooke Gladstone on the Media*. Illustrated by Josh Neufeld. Copyright 2011 by Brooke Gladstone and Josh Neufeld. Used by permission of W. W. Norton and Company, Inc.

Starting a Conversation: Respond to "The Goldilocks Number"

In your writer's notebook, reflect on Gladstone's analysis by responding to the following questions:

1. "The Goldilocks Number" begins by inquiring into the story behind a seemingly improbable statistic. What leads Gladstone to question the numbers she keeps hearing? Why do you think she chooses the sources she does to find answers?

2. Gladstone traces her evidence back through several layers in order to find out the truth behind the statistic, and in the last panel of the first page, Neufeld depicts Gladstone in a detective's outfit with a magnifying glass. In what ways does Gladstone's research resemble that of a detective? What questions does she return to as she tracks down each new source? How do those questions — and the answers she finds — shape her analysis?

3. Rhetorical analysis is a specific type of analysis (see p. 238 for more information). In what ways is Gladstone's analysis of the Goldilocks number a rhetorical analysis? How does she take into consideration the context and audience around her questions?

4. Many of the experts Gladstone cites in her analysis were also cited in a 2006 *National Law Journal* article by Jason McClure that addresses the very same misuse of the number 50,000. How might Gladstone have better acknowledged this article in her work?

5. **Reflection:** Gladstone concludes with the comment, "Sometimes the simplest reasons are the scariest." What do you think she means? In what ways are the "simplest reasons" the most frightening in this situation, and to whom?

Analytical Blog Posts

Blogs — short for Weblogs — are online forums that allow writers to present their opinions, observations, and reflections to a broad readership. They can consist of the contributions of a single writer, or they can draw on contributions from multiple writers. Blogs can be published and maintained by individuals, in a manner similar to putting material on a personal website. They can also be sponsored by news organizations, public interest groups, government agencies, corporations, and other organizations. When a blog is sponsored by an organization or a publication, the writer takes into account the purpose of the organization or publication and the interests, needs, and backgrounds of readers who visit the blog.

Blogs are frequently used in analytical and informative writing. Entries typically are brief and often present a personal perspective on an issue. However, because blogs have fewer length limitations than a newspaper, magazine, or journal article might have, blog entries are more likely to rely on evidence from other sources than are opinion columns and letters to the editor. Because of their digital format, they can also use multimedia illustrations, such as video and audio clips or interactive polls, and link to other sources. And because readers can reply publicly to a blog entry by posting responses and analyses of their own, conversations can be extended over time and can involve readers and writers more actively.

 Scott Barry Kaufman
Why Creativity Is a Numbers Game

In this blog post on the *Scientific American* Blog Network, Scott Barry Kaufman claims that inherent creative genius is a myth. Kaufman is the scientific director of the Imagination Institute, a professor of psychology at the University of Pennsylvania, and a researcher at the Positive Psychology Center. He is also a regular contributor to *Scientific American*; the author of *Ungifted: Intelligence Redefined* (2015) and *The Complexity of Greatness: Beyond Talent or Practice* (2013); the coauthor of *The Cambridge Handbook of Intelligence* (2011) and *Mating Intelligence Unleashed: The Role of the Mind in Sex, Dating, and Love* (2013); and the coeditor of *The Psychology of Creative Writing* (2009) and *The Philosophy of Creativity: New Essays* (2014). Kaufman's most recent book, coauthored by Carolyn Gregoire, is *Wired to Create: Unraveling the Mysteries of the Creative Mind* (2016), from which this blog post was adapted.

Why Creativity Is a Numbers Game

By Scott Barry Kaufman

December 29, 2015

It's a great myth that creative geniuses consistently produce great works.

They don't. In fact, systematic analyses of the career trajectories of people labeled geniuses show that their output tends to be highly uneven, with a few good ideas mixed in with many more false starts. While consistency may be the key to expertise, the secret to creative greatness appears to be doing things differently — even when that means failing.

According to Dean Keith Simonton, true innovation requires that creators engage in a sort of Darwinian process in which they try out many possibilities without fully knowing what their eventual public reception will be. Especially during the idea-generation stage, trial and error is essential for innovation. Simonton's theory does not mean that creators are working completely in the dark; ideas are not generated in complete ignorance of their ultimate value to society. Instead, new ideas just aren't guaranteed to be fruitful.

So how are creative masterminds so successful, if they don't really know what they're doing? Simonton's extensive analysis of geniuses found two major factors to be critical in explaining the creative process of geniuses. First, creative geniuses simultaneously immerse themselves in many diverse ideas and projects. Second, and perhaps even more important, they also have extraordinary productivity. Creators create. Again and again and again. In fact, Simonton has found that the quality of creative ideas is a positive function of quantity: The more ideas creators generate (regardless of the quality of each idea), the greater the chances they would produce an eventual masterpiece.

Thomas Edison — one of the greatest inventors of all time — had roughly a one-third rejection rate for all the patents he led. Even among the 1,093 patents he did get accepted, most went nowhere. In fact, the number of truly extraordinary creative feats he achieved can probably be counted on one hand. As Simonton points out, a look at Edison's entire body of patents might not reflect his creative genius as much as his creative failures.

During the peak years of Edison's career, between the ages of thirty-five and thirty-nine, the inventor was working on the electric light and power distribution system. As part of this process, he attempted to develop fuel cells to power the lightbulbs. However, these efforts faced repeated difficulties, including one experiment in which the windows were blown out of his lab.

Edison *was* unlucky — he failed to invent fuel cells. The first commercially successful fuel cells were developed in the mid-twentieth century, long after Edison moved on to pursuing other ideas. Edison accepted the inevitable frustrations of the creative process and turned his attention to other projects that would eventually lead to the invention of the electric lightbulb — the source of his recognition as a genius today.

Such frequent shifts among projects may have primed Edison's mind to consider options he might have otherwise ignored. By taking on a range of projects, Simonton notes, "Edison always had somewhere to channel his efforts whenever he ran into temporary obstacles — especially any long series of trials followed only by consecutive errors." Despite having failed more than he succeeded, Edison's few successes were so great that they surpassed all of the other inventors in the history of technology.

A very similar pattern can be found within Shakespeare's creative output. The variability in quality of his large body of work is in itself impressive! Simonton computed a popularity score for each of Shakespeare's thirty-seven plays and found that the most popular plays were created around mid-career (age thirty-eight). At this time, he composed his masterpiece *Hamlet*, which received a popularity rating of 100 percent.

However, right before and after *Hamlet*, Shakespeare produced a few duds. For instance, soon after *Hamlet*, the Bard wrote *Troilus and Cressida*, which has a popularity rating of just 23 percent. But after *Troilus and Cressida*, he produced his three greatest tragedies since *Hamlet* — *Othello* (rating of 74 percent), *Lear* (rating of 78 percent), and *Macbeth* (rating of 83 percent). Then, once again, he fell well below expectations with *Timon of Athens* (rating of 3 percent) and *Pericles* (rating of 8 percent).

Even Beethoven left a trail of musical failures in his wake. While none of Beethoven's compositions could be considered worthless, they aren't all masterpieces either. Beethoven sometimes composed inferior works around the same time he was working on a major masterpiece. One analysis found that even a computer could tell that his even-numbered symphonies were of a markedly different quality than his odd-numbered symphonies. Beethoven himself recognized this, referring to some of his nine symphonies as "little."

One reason for variable quality is the need to innovate. All creators — whether inventors, actors, or choreographers — are under constant pressure to avoid doing things the exact same way. In this quest for originality, creative geniuses fail and fail often. Indeed, the creative act is often described as a process of failing repeatedly until something sticks, and highly creative people learn to see failure as simply a stepping-stone to success. Doing things differently sometimes involves doing things badly or wrong.

Even today's most successful innovators — including Steve Jobs, who was fired from his own company at age thirty — tend to have as many stories of failure as they do of success. Or take J. K. Rowling — likely one of the only authors who holds a claim to making billions as an author — who has become an outspoken advocate for the importance of creative failure. As many Harry Potter fans know, the first book in Rowling's series was rejected by twelve publishers before being accepted by Bloomsbury — and only then because the chairman's eight-year-old daughter insisted on it.

Rowling later said, "Some failure in life is inevitable. It is impossible to live without failing at something, unless you live so cautiously that you might as well not have lived at all — in which case, you fail by default."

Starting a Conversation: Respond to "Why Creativity Is a Numbers Game"

In your writer's notebook, reflect on Kaufman's analytical blog post by responding to the following questions:

1. In paragraph 2, Kaufman outlines both the major question for the analysis and the structure with which he intends to analyze the question. What is his question? What is the structure he uses to analyze it? Why do you think Kaufman chose this structure? How effective (or ineffective) is it?

2. Analytical writing often identifies a pattern and then establishes its meaning. What pattern does Kaufman identify, and how does he interpret it? How does he use sources to reach his goals?

3. Who is the intended audience for this blog post? How can you tell? How might the analysis have differed for another audience?

4. Blog posts often use a more conversational tone than a formal article. Evaluate Kaufman's tone throughout this document. Is it conversational? Scholarly? How does the tone influence his analysis?

5. **Reflection:** Kaufman writes that "the secret to creative greatness appears to be doing things differently — even when that means failing" (para. 2). Describe a time when you achieved something great by doing something differently. Did you fail along the way?

GENRE TALK

Reflective Writing | Informative Writing | **Analytical Writing** | Evaluative Writing | Problem-Solving Writing | Argumentative Writing

2015 and 2016 saw millions of immigrants fleeing Syria and Iraq and seeking safety and asylum in Greece, Turkey, Hungary, and other parts of Europe, and eventually the United States. Immigrants from the Middle East have added yet another frontier to the conversation about immigration, in addition to the heated debates over the U.S.-Mexican border. Because it is a complicated topic with many vexing issues, immigration is well suited to analytical writing, which aims to answer questions, identify causes and effects, and consider future significance or consequences. Analytical writing on the topic of immigration considers how issues such as personal safety, national security, religious tolerance, cultural assimilation, and moral obligation fit together, overlap, and sometimes contradict each other.

This report from the Pew Research Center analyzes how immigration continues to change American demographics fifty years after the 1965 Immigration and Nationality Act. It also examines how the American public views immigrants from various parts of the world and how it values their impact on various aspects of American life, from the economy and crime to food, music, and the arts. Drawing on recent census data and online surveys conducted in English and Spanish of more than three thousand Americans, this report offers a complex portrait of how immigration is shaping the makeup and the attitudes of the country today.

 LaunchPad
macmillan learning

Test your knowledge of genre with the Genre Talk quiz in the LaunchPad for *Joining the Conversation*.
launchpadworks.com

The title page clearly lists the title, publication date, and sponsoring organization of the report.

The individual authors and their roles are identified, and contact information is provided.

Pew Research Center

Section headings help organize the information in the report.

Figures illustrate census data and survey responses. Figures are labeled, numbered, and set off from the main text with rules.

Color, italics, boldface, and distinct fonts contribute to a formal but eye-catching design.

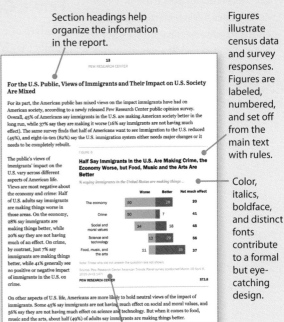

Source information is cited at the bottom of each figure.

How Can I Write an Analytical Essay?

Got questions? Got an inquiring mind? Got the discipline to follow up on a question carefully and thoroughly? If you answered "yes" to these questions, you've got what it takes to start writing an analytical essay.

That's not all it takes, of course. Writing an analytical essay also involves refining your question, gaining a fuller understanding of your subject, applying an appropriate interpretive framework, and drafting your response to your analytical question. But the foundation of an analytical essay — and of all analytical documents, for that matter — is developing and responding to a question about a subject.

As you work on your analytical essay, you'll follow the work of Mackenzie Owens, who wrote a rhetorical analysis of an article written by Jason Lee Steorts and published in *The Atlantic* about the use of deadly force by police.

In Process

A Rhetorical Analysis of a Magazine Article

Mackenzie Owens wrote an analytical essay for her introductory composition course. She used rhetorical analysis to explore an argument made by author Jason Lee Steorts about police use of deadly force. Follow Mackenzie's efforts to write her analytical essay by reading the In Process boxes throughout this chapter.

Find a Conversation and Listen In

Analytical essays allow you to share your interpretation of a subject with your readers. Your analysis will reflect not only your analytical question and interpretive framework but also what other writers involved in the conversation about your subject have written and the types of analyses they've conducted. It will also reflect the demands of your writing assignment. To get started on your analytical essay, review your assignment and spend some time thinking about your writing situation: your purposes for writing; your readers' needs, interests, knowledge, and background; potential sources of evidence; and the contexts that might affect your analysis (see p. 13). Then start generating ideas about the kinds of questions you might ask, find a conversation worth joining, and learn more about it.

EXPLORE YOUR SURROUNDINGS

Analysis is largely a search for patterns — and searching for patterns is something we do on a daily basis. As we learn to drive, for example, we start noticing the typical behaviors of other drivers as they approach an intersection. It doesn't take long to learn that we can reliably predict whether other drivers are planning to go through the intersection, stop, turn left, or turn right — even when they fail to use turn signals. When we see behaviors that are unusual or unexpected, we go on alert, making sure that we aren't hit by a driver who isn't paying attention. Similarly, we look for patterns in everything from playing tennis (noticing, for instance, how a player grips the racket before returning a shot) to reading the newspaper (learning where we can find stories that interest us or how to distinguish news from advertisements).

Humans are quite good at identifying and responding to patterns. But it takes time to notice them and even more time to figure out how they work. Before choosing a specific focus for your analytical essay, identify general topics that might interest you enough to explore in depth. One good way to begin is to brainstorm (see p. 41), freewrite (see p. 42), or loop (see p. 43) about the objects and events that surround you.

- **Your shelves.** Scan your collection of music, books, and movies, and think about anything you've listened to, read, or watched that grabbed your attention. You might be rewarded by looking beneath the surface for meaning or themes, or you might find yourself intrigued by a plot line or a style that appears to be part of a larger trend.

- **The daily news.** Whether you follow current events in newspapers, on television, or on the Web, recent and ongoing news stories offer rich opportunities for analysis: Why were some groups offended by a magazine cover? Is third-party health insurance to blame for the high cost of medical care? How do "bad girl" celebrities influence children's behavior? Be alert to the questions that occur to you as you read, to reactions (other people's and your own) that surprise you, and to themes that seem to pop up from one day to the next. You're likely to notice something you want to investigate further.

- **Your leisure activities.** No matter what you do for fun — participate in a sport, play video games, take photographs — you can probably find some aspects of your lifestyle that raise questions or suggest a trend. For instance, perhaps you've wondered whether the X Games will become more popular than the Olympics, or noticed that massively multiplayer online games have become more popular than first-person shooters.

- **Your physical environment.** Take a look around you. A favorite poster in your bedroom, for instance, might be a good candidate for interpretation. A new bank in town might inspire questions about interest rates, community service, or architectural style. An overflowing trash bin might suggest an analytical essay on recycling or municipal waste management.

As you consider possible topics for your writing project, look for new or surprising ideas that interest you and your readers and lend themselves to analysis. If you come across a subject or a question that makes a good candidate for your essay, add it to your writer's notebook.

You'll find additional writing project ideas at the end of this chapter (p. 280).

ASK INTERPRETIVE QUESTIONS

The foundation for analysis is a question that is open to interpretation. For example, asking whether you have enough money to purchase a ticket to the latest Jennifer Lawrence movie would not require an interpretive response. Either you have enough money or you don't. Asking whether Lawrence's performance breaks new ground, however, would require an analysis of her work in the film. Similarly, while a driver wouldn't need to conduct an analysis to determine whether a car has a full tank of fuel, a city planner might find it necessary to carry out an analysis to anticipate how high the cost of fuel must rise before commuters leave their cars at home and take public transportation.

You can generate potential interpretive questions about promising topics by brainstorming, freewriting, or clustering in response to the following prompts. Each prompt focuses your attention on a general topic in a different way, and each provides a useful starting point for an analytical essay. Depending on your topic, you'll find that some prompts are more productive than others.

- **Elements.** Think about the subject in terms of its parts. How does it break down into smaller pieces, or how can it be divided in different ways? Which parts are most important, and which are less significant?

- **Categories.** What groups does the subject belong to? How is it similar to or different from other subjects in a particular group? How can comparing the subject to related subjects help you and your readers understand it in a new way?

- **History.** Look into the origins of the subject. What recent events are related to the subject, and what are the implications of those events? Does your subject build on previous events? Will it continue to have influence in the future, and if so, how will it do so?

- **Causes and effects.** What caused the subject, and why is it the way it is? What are the subject's influences on people, events, and objects? Who or what affects the subject? What effects is the subject likely (or unlikely) to cause in the future?

- **Relationships.** How is the subject connected to other ideas, events, or objects? For example, are changes in the subject related to changes in related ideas, events, or objects?

- **Meaning.** What is the subject's significance and implications? Can different people find different meanings in the subject, and if so, why? Does a close examination of the subject reveal a new way of looking at it?

As you ponder ways to turn a general topic area into the subject of your analytical essay, spend time learning about other people's answers to the most promising questions you've generated. You can discuss the subject with people you know, skim sources published on the subject, or even observe the subject firsthand. You can learn more about gathering information in Chapter 2 and in Part Three.

Working Together: Try It Out Loud

Working in a small group, choose a popular song that everyone in your group likes, or choose one of the top songs of the week on Billboard or the iTunes store. Then use one set of the interpretive question prompts in the preceding section to analyze the song. If you are doing this activity during class, the class might choose a single song, and each group might choose a different set of prompts. Take turns asking questions about the song while the other members of the group try to answer them. Record your answers, noting both agreements and disagreements. Your purpose is to interpret, so don't get distracted by whether the song is good or bad; instead, focus on its significance and implications. If you are doing this activity during class, each group should report its results to the class.

When you are finished, take a few minutes to reflect on the activity. What did you learn about different ways of approaching an analysis? Did some interpretive question prompts produce more useful or interesting results than others? How did examining the song from multiple perspectives affect your interpretation of it?

SEARCH DATABASES

Once you've identified a promising question, learn whether — and how — other writers have attempted to answer it. Analytical essays tend to draw on information and analyses from other sources in addition to the writer's personal knowledge and interpretation, so even if you already know a great deal about a subject, be sure to review other writers' contributions to the conversation and to look for sources you can use to support your analysis.

Databases can give you an in-depth understanding of your subject, as well as a sense of useful interpretive frameworks, existing interpretations, and unanswered questions. They allow you to search for analyses that have been published on a particular subject or in a particular discipline. Although some databases, such as

In Process

Searching Databases

Mackenzie Owens used her interpretive question — *How does the writer Jason Lee Steorts convey an argument about the use of deadly force by police?* — to develop search terms for research in her library's databases. She knew from exploring her subject that it had been addressed in newspapers and magazines, so she searched databases such as LexisNexis Academic and Newspaper Source. Because she also wondered whether sociological and psychological studies had been conducted on the subject, she searched the Sociological Abstracts, PsychInfo, and Academic Search Premier databases.

Mackenzie used the search terms *police*, *deadly force*, and *shooting*. She searched all fields in the database and used Boolean operators (AND and OR) to require that *police* and either *deadly force* or *shooting* be present (see Chapter 13).

> **ProQuest**
>
> All databases | Change databases
>
> **Sociological Abstracts**
> Basic Search   Advanced Search   About
>
> **Advanced Search**   Command Line   Thesaurus   Field codes   Search tips
>
> police   In   Anywhere ▾
>
> AND ▾   deadly force   OR   shooting   In   Anywhere ▾
>
> ● Add a row
>
> Limit to: ☑ Peer reviewed ❶
>
> Publication date: Last 12 months ▾
>
> Search   Clear form

▲ **Mackenzie's search of the Sociological Abstracts database**

ERIC (eric.ed.gov), can be accessed publicly through the Web, most are available only through a library's computers or website.

To identify databases that might be relevant to the subject you are analyzing, review your library's list of databases or consult a reference librarian. Generate keywords and phrases that are related to your interpretive question, and search a few different databases for potential resources. Using the citation information provided by the database, check your library's online catalog for the title of the publication in which the article appears. Your library might own many of the sources you'll identify through a database search, but if it doesn't, you can usually request promising materials through interlibrary loan.

You can read more about searching databases and using interlibrary loan in Chapter 13.

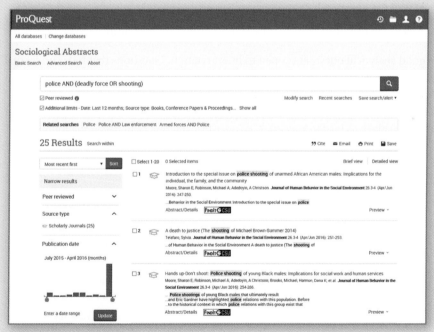

The search produced 25 results. The database allowed her to view abstracts (summaries of the source) and complete reference information.

The database allowed Mackenzie to narrow her search.

▲ Mackenzie's search results

Mackenzie's database searches produced sources in several scholarly publications. She located one of the articles, which focused on the shooting death of Michael Brown in Ferguson, Missouri, and downloaded it.

Conduct Your Analysis

An analytical essay helps readers understand the origins, qualities, significance, or potential effects of a subject. A successful essay builds on a carefully crafted analytical question, a thorough understanding of the subject, and a rigorous and fair application of an appropriate interpretive framework. It also builds on a clear understanding of your writing situation.

REFINE YOUR QUESTION

Begin your analysis by reviewing the interpretive questions you generated about your subject (see p. 250). Choose one that interests you and will allow you to carry out your assignment. Then review and refine your question. Ask yourself:

- How might I respond to this question? Will my response be complex enough to justify writing an essay about it? Will it be too complex for my assignment?

- Is the question appropriate for the conversation that I'm planning to join?

- Will the question help me accomplish my purposes?

- Will my response interest my readers or address their needs?

A good analytical question is open to interpretation. Questions that focus on factual or yes/no answers seldom provide a strong foundation for an analytical essay. In contrast, questions that lead you to investigate the origins or potential impacts of a subject, to consider its qualities, to weigh its significance, or to explore its meaning are more likely to lead to success. Consider the differences between the following sets of questions.

Questions Leading to Factual or Yes/No Answers	Questions Open to Interpretation
When did the Iraq War begin?	What caused the Iraq War?
Has NASA's annual budget kept pace with inflation?	How can NASA pursue its mission on a reduced annual budget?
Who were the villains in the first Indiana Jones movie?	In what ways do the key themes of the first Indiana Jones movie reflect changes in American foreign relations?
Who won the last World Series?	What contributed to the success of the last World Series champions?

You should also consider how a question will direct your thinking about your subject. For example, you might want to understand the potential effects of a proposal to reduce the cost of attending your state's public colleges and universities by increasing class size and laying off faculty and staff. Asking a question about the plan's impact on education might direct your attention toward students and the trade-offs between lower costs and the quality of instruction. In contrast, asking a question about the plan's impact on the state budget might lead you to view the subject through the lens of business concerns and economic forecasts. Although the questions are related, they would lead to significantly different analyses.

SEEK A FULLER UNDERSTANDING OF YOUR SUBJECT

If you've ever talked with people who don't know what they're talking about but nonetheless are certain of their opinions, you'll recognize the dangers of applying an interpretive framework before you thoroughly understand your subject. To enhance your understanding of your subject, use division and classification. Division allows you to identify the elements that make up a subject. Classification allows you to explore a subject in relation to other subjects and to consider the similarities, differences, and relationships among its elements.

Division Division breaks a subject into its parts and considers what each contributes to the whole. A financial analyst, for example, might examine the various groups within a company to understand what each group does and how it contributes to the overall value of the company. Similarly, a literary critic might consider how each scene in a play relates to other scenes and how it contributes to the play's major theme.

As you use division to examine a subject, keep in mind the following guidelines:

- **Pick a focus.** Division can take place on many levels. Just as you can divide numbers in different ways (100, for example, can be seen as ten 10s, five 20s, four 25s, and so on), you can divide subjects differently. A government agency, for instance, might be considered in terms of its responsibilities, its departments, or its employees. Trying to understand all of these aspects at once, however, would be difficult and unproductive. Use your analytical question as a guide to determine how best to divide your subject.

- **Examine the parts.** Most subjects can be thought of as a system of interrelated parts. As you divide your subject, determine what role each part plays, individually and in relation to other parts.

- **Assess contributions to the whole.** As you divide a subject, be sure to consider the contributions that each part makes to the larger whole. In some cases, you'll find that a part is essential. In other cases, you'll find that it makes little or no contribution to the whole.

Even though you can divide and reassemble a subject in a variety of ways, always take into account your purpose and your readers' needs, interests, and expectations. It might be easier to focus on a government agency's departments than on its functions, but if your question focuses on how the agency works or what it does, you'll be more successful if you examine its functions.

Classification Classification places your subject — or each part of your subject — into a category. By categorizing a subject or its parts, you can discover how and to what extent your subject or a part of your subject is similar to others in the same category and how it differs from those in other categories. Identifying those similarities and differences, in turn, allows you to consider the subject, or its parts, in relation to the other items in your categories. As you use classification to gain a better understanding of your subject, consider the following guidelines:

- **Choose a classification scheme.** The categories you work with might be established already, or you might create them specifically to support your analysis. For example, if you are analyzing state representatives, you might place them in standard categories: Democrat, Republican, Libertarian, Green, and so on. Or you might create categories especially for your analysis, such as who voted for or against particular types of legislation.

- **Look at both similarities and differences.** When you place an item in a category, you decide that it is more similar to the other items in the category than to those in other categories. However, even though the items in a broad category will share many similarities, they will also differ in important ways. Botanists, for example, have developed a complex system of categories and subcategories to help them understand general types of plants (such as algae, roses, and corn) as well as to consider subtle differences among similar plants (such as corn bred for animal feed, for human consumption, and for biofuels).

- **Justify your choices.** Your decisions about what to place in a given category will be based on your definition of the category, if you've created it yourself, or your understanding of categories that have been established by someone else. In most cases, you'll need to explain why a particular category is the best fit for your subject. If you want readers to accept your classification of Walmart as a mom-and-pop retailer, for instance, you have to explain that your category is defined by origin (not current size) and then inform readers that the chain started as a single discount store in Arkansas.

Classification and division are often used in combination, particularly when you want to consider similarities and differences among different parts of your subject. For example, if you are examining a complex organization, you might use division to analyze each department; in addition, you might use classification so that you can analyze groups of departments that have similar functions, such as customer service and technical support, and contrast those departments with departments in other categories, such as sales, marketing, and research and development.

APPLY AN INTERPRETIVE FRAMEWORK

An interpretive framework is a set of strategies for identifying patterns that has been used successfully and refined over time by writers interested in a given subject area or working in a particular field. Writers can choose from hundreds (perhaps thousands) of specialized frameworks used in disciplines across the arts, sciences, social sciences, humanities, engineering, and business. A historian, for example, might apply a feminist, social, political, or cultural analysis to interpret diaries written by women who worked in defense plants during World War II, while a sociologist might conduct correlational tests to interpret the results of a survey. In a writing course, you'll most likely use one of the broad interpretive frameworks discussed here: trend analysis, causal analysis, data analysis, text analysis, and rhetorical analysis.

By definition, analysis is subjective. Your interpretation will be shaped by the question you ask, the sources you consult, and your personal experience and perspective. But analysis is also conducted within the context of a written conversation. As you consider your choice of interpretive framework, reflect on the interpretive frameworks you encounter in your sources and those you've used in the past. Keep in mind that different interpretive frameworks will lead to different ways of seeing and understanding a subject. The key to success is choosing one that can guide you as you try to answer your question.

> *Need help with context? See Chapter 1 for more information.

Trend analysis Trends are patterns that hold up over time. Trend analysis, as a result, focuses on sequences of events and the relationships among them. It is based on the assumption that understanding what has happened in the past allows us to make sense of what is happening in the present and to draw inferences about what is likely to happen in the future.

Trends can be identified and analyzed in nearly every field, from politics to consumer affairs to the arts. For example, many economists have analyzed historical accounts of fuel crises in the 1970s to understand the instability of fuel prices. Sports and entertainment analysts also use trend analysis — to forecast the next NBA champion, for instance, or to explain the reemergence of superheroes in popular culture during the last decade.

To conduct a trend analysis, follow these guidelines:

- **Gather information.** Trend analysis is most useful when it relies on an extensive set of long-term observations. News reports about NASA since the mid-1960s, for example, can tell you whether the coverage of the U.S. space program has changed over time. By examining these changes, you can decide whether a trend exists. You might find, for instance, that the press has become progressively less positive in its treatment of the U.S. space program. However, if you don't gather enough information to thoroughly establish the trend, your readers might lack confidence in your conclusions.

- **Establish that a trend exists.** Some analysts seem willing to declare a trend on the flimsiest set of observations: when a team wins an NFL championship for the second year in a row, for instance, fans are quick to announce the start of a dynasty. As you look for trends, cast a wide net. Learn as much as you can about the history of your subject, and carefully assess it to determine how often events related to your subject have moved in one direction or another. By understanding the variations that have occurred over time, you can better judge whether you've actually found a trend.

- **Draw conclusions.** Trend analysis allows you to understand the historical context that shapes a subject and, in some cases, to make predictions about the

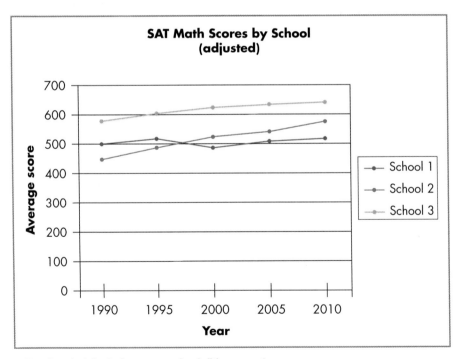

▲ Trend analysis looks for patterns that hold up over time.

subject. The conclusions you draw should be grounded strongly in the evidence you've collected. They should also reflect your writing situation — your purposes, readers, and context. As you draw your conclusions, exercise caution. Ask whether you have enough information to support your conclusions. Search for evidence that contradicts your conclusions. Most important, on the basis of the information you've collected so far, ask whether your conclusions make sense.

Causal analysis Causal analysis focuses on the factors that bring about a particular situation. It can be applied to a wide range of subjects, such as the dot-com collapse in the late 1990s, the rise of terrorist groups, or the impact of calorie restriction on longevity. Writers carry out causal analysis when they believe that understanding the underlying reasons for a situation will help people address the situation, increase the likelihood of its happening again, or appreciate its potential consequences.

In many ways, causal analysis is a form of detective work. It involves tracing a sequence of events and exploring the connections among them. Because the connections are almost always more complex than they appear, it pays to be thorough. If you choose to conduct a causal analysis, keep in mind the following guidelines:

- **Uncover as many causes as you can.** Effects rarely emerge from a single cause. Most effects are the results of a complex web of causes, some of which are related to one another and some of which are not. Although it might be tempting, for example, to say that a murder victim died (the effect) from a gunshot wound (the cause), that would tell only part of the story. You would need to work backward from the murderer's decision to pull the trigger to the factors that led to that decision, and then further back to the causes underlying those factors.

  Effects can also become causes. While investigating the murder, for instance, you might find that the murderer had long been envious of the victim's success, that he was jumpy from the steroids he'd been taking in an ill-advised attempt to qualify for the Olympic trials in weight lifting, and that he had just found his girlfriend in the victim's arms. Exploring how these factors might be related — and determining when they are not — will help you understand the web of causes leading to the effect.

- **Determine which causes are significant.** Not all causes contribute equally to an effect. Perhaps our murderer was cut off on the freeway on his way to meet his girlfriend. Lingering anger at the other driver might have been enough to push him over the edge, but it probably wouldn't have caused the shooting by itself.

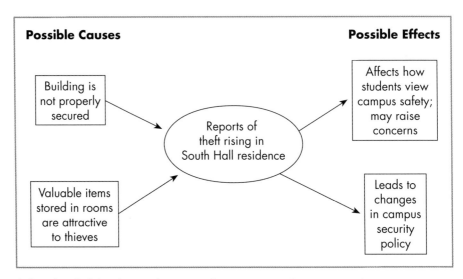

Possible Causes

Building is not properly secured

Valuable items stored in rooms are attractive to thieves

Reports of theft rising in South Hall residence

Possible Effects

Affects how students view campus safety; may raise concerns

Leads to changes in campus security policy

▲ Causal analysis involves tracing connections among events.

- **Distinguish between correlation and cause.** Too often, we assume that because one event occurred just before another, the first event caused the second. We might conclude that finding his girlfriend with another man drove the murderer to shoot in a fit of passion — only to discover that he had begun planning the murder months before, when the victim threatened to reveal his use of steroids to the press just prior to the Olympic trials.

- **Look beyond the obvious.** A thorough causal analysis considers not only the primary causes and effects but also those that might appear only slightly related to the subject. For example, you might consider the immediate effects of the murder not only on the victim and perpetrator but also on their families and friends, on the wider community, on the lawyers and judges involved in the case, on an overburdened judicial system, and even on attitudes toward Olympic athletes. By looking beyond the obvious causes and effects, you can deepen your understanding of the subject and begin to explore a much wider set of implications than you might have initially expected.

Data analysis Data is any type of information, such as facts and observations, and is often expressed numerically. Most of us analyze data in an informal way on a daily basis. For example, if you've looked at the percentage of people who favor a particular political candidate over another, you've engaged in data analysis. Similarly, if you've checked your bank account to determine whether you have enough money for a planned purchase, you've carried out a form of data analysis. As a writer, you can analyze numerical information related to your subject to better understand the subject as a whole, to look for differences among the subject's parts, and to explore relationships among the parts.

To begin a data analysis, gather your data and enter the numbers into a spreadsheet or statistics program. You can use the program's tools to sort the data and conduct tests. If your set of data is small, you can use a piece of paper and a calculator. As you carry out your analysis, keep the following guidelines in mind:

- **Do the math.** Let's say you conducted a survey of student and faculty attitudes about a proposed change to the graduation requirements at your school. Tabulating the results might reveal that 52 percent of your respondents were female, 83 percent were between the ages of eighteen and twenty-two, 38 percent were juniors or seniors, and 76 percent were majoring in the biological sciences. You might also find that, of the faculty who responded,

Use of Social-Networking Sites		
	# surveyed	% who use social networking regularly
Gender		
Male	48	56%
Female	42	65%
Age		
16–20	20	85%
21–30	31	71%
31–45	28	46%
45+	11	27%
Education		
Some high school	12	35%
High school graduate	25	56%
Some college	34	65%
College graduate	16	64%
Graduate school	7	62%

▲ Data analysis can involve assessing information from a variety of sources.

75 percent were tenured. Based on these numbers, you could draw conclusions about whether the responses are representative of your school's overall population. If they are not, you might decide to ask more people to take your survey. Once you're certain that you've collected enough data, you can draw conclusions about the overall results and determine, for example, the percentage of respondents who favored, opposed, or were undecided about the proposed change.

- **Categorize your data.** Difference tests can help you make distinctions among groups. To classify the results of your survey, for example, you might compare male and female student responses. Similarly, you might examine differences in the responses between other groups — such as faculty and students; tenured and untenured faculty; and freshmen, sophomores, juniors, and seniors. To carry out your analysis, you might look at each group's average level of agreement with the proposed changes. Or you might use statistical techniques such as T-Tests, which offer more sensitive assessments of difference than comparisons of averages. You can conduct these kinds of tests using spreadsheet programs, such as Microsoft Excel, or statistical programs, such as SAS and SPSS.

- **Explore relationships.** Correlation tests allow you to draw conclusions about your subject. For example, you might want to know whether support for proposed changes to graduation requirements increases or decreases according to GPA. A correlation test might indicate that a positive relationship exists — that support goes up as GPA increases. Be cautious, however, as you examine relationships. In particular, be wary of confusing causation with correlation. Tests will show, for example, that as shoe size increases, so do scores on reading tests. Does this mean that large feet improve reading? Not really. The cause of higher reading scores appears to be attending school longer. High school students tend to score better on reading tests than do students in elementary school — and, on average, high school students tend to have much larger feet. As is the case with difference tests, you can use many spreadsheet and statistical programs to explore relationships. If your set of data is small enough, you can also use a piece of paper to examine it.

- **Be thorough.** Take great care to ensure the integrity of your analysis. You will run into problems if you collect too little data, if the data is not representative, or if the data is collected sloppily. Similarly, you should base your conclusions on a thoughtful and careful examination of the results of your tests. Picking and choosing evidence that supports your conclusion might be tempting, but you'll do a disservice to you and your readers if you fail to consider all the results of your analysis.

Text analysis   Today, the word *text* can refer to a wide range of printed or digital works — and even some forms of artistic expression that we might not think of as documents. Texts open to interpretation include novels, poems, plays, essays, articles, movies, speeches, blogs, songs, paintings, photographs, sculptures, performances, Web pages, videos, television shows, and computer games.

Students enrolled in writing classes often use the elements of literary analysis to analyze texts. In this form of analysis, interpreters focus on theme, plot, setting, characterization, imagery, style, and structure, as well as the contexts — social, cultural, political, and historical — that shape a work. Writers who use this form of analysis focus both on what is actually presented in the text and on what is implied or conveyed "between the lines." They rely heavily on close reading of the text to discern meaning, critique an author's technique, and search for patterns that help them understand the text as fully as possible. They also tend to consider other elements of the wider writing situation in which the text was produced — in particular, the author's purpose, intended audience, use of sources, and choice of genre.

> In the song "What Is New Orleans, Part 2," recorded by Kermit Ruffins and the Rebirth Brass Band, a call-and-response pattern structures both the lyrics ("What is New Orleans? New Orleans is . . .") and also the interaction between Ruffins and the musicians. Frequently, after Ruffins sings a pattern of syllables, the musicians echo or answer him, as though the music itself is to be considered a sufficient response. Meanwhile, the song's lyrics highlight the importance of food in the city's culture by beginning with a list of meals. Each meal is associated with a specific time and day of the week, giving the impression that the rest of the week's events are scheduled around these meals. Ruffins then lists musicians and locations, moving from the specific to the general, from individual lounges to entire neighborhoods.

▲ Text analysis can focus on a wide range of artistic expression.

If you carry out a text analysis, keep the following guidelines in mind:

- **Focus on the text itself.** In any form of text analysis, the text should take center stage. Although you will typically reflect on the issues raised by your interpretation, maintain a clear focus on the text in front of you, and keep your analysis grounded firmly in what you can locate within it. Background information and related sources, such as scholarly articles and essays, can support and enhance your analysis, but they can't do the work of interpretation for you.

- **Consider the text in its entirety.** Particularly in the early stages of learning about a text, it is easy to be distracted by a startling idea or an intriguing concept. Try not to focus on a particular aspect of the text, however, until you've fully reviewed all of it. You might well decide to narrow your analysis to a particular aspect of the text, but lay the foundation for a fair, well-informed interpretation by first considering the text as a whole.

- **Avoid "cherry-picking."** Cherry-picking refers to the process of using only those materials from a text that support your overall interpretation and ignoring aspects that might weaken or contradict your interpretation. As you carry out your analysis, factor in *all* the evidence. If the text doesn't support your interpretation, rethink your conclusions.

Rhetorical analysis In much the same way that you can assess the writing situation that shapes your work on a particular assignment, you can analyze the rhetorical situation (see p. 13) that shaped the creation of and response to a particular document. A rhetorical analysis, for example, might focus on how a particular document (written, visual, or some other form) achieved its purpose or on why readers reacted to it in a specific way. Featured student writer Mackenzie Owens wrote a rhetorical analysis of political writer Jason Lee Steorts's article on police use of deadly force (see p. 275).

Rhetorical analysis focuses on one or more aspects of the rhetorical situation.

- **Writer and purpose.** What did the writer hope to accomplish? Was it accomplished and, if so, how well? If not, why not? What strategies did the writer use to pursue the purpose? Did the writer choose the best genre for the purpose? Why did the writer choose this purpose over others? Are there any clear connections between the purpose and the writer's background, values, and beliefs?

- **Readers/audience.** Was the document addressed to the right audience? Did readers react to the document as the writer hoped? Why or why not? What aspects of the needs, interests, backgrounds, values, and beliefs of the audience might have led them to react to the document as they did?

- **Sources.** What sources were used? Which information, ideas, and arguments from the sources were used in the document? How effectively were they used?

How credible were the sources? Were enough sources used? Were the sources appropriate?

- **Context.** How did the context in which the document was composed shape its effectiveness? How did the context in which it was read shape the reaction of the audience? What physical, social, cultural, disciplinary, and historical contexts shaped the document's development? What contexts shaped how readers reacted to it?

Rhetorical analysis can also involve an assessment of the argument used in a document. It is common to examine the structure of an argument, focusing on the writer's use of appeals — such as appeals to logic, emotion, character, and so on (see p. 436) — and the quality of the evidence that was provided. In many courses, such as the one for which Mackenzie Owens wrote her rhetorical analysis, these appeals are referred to using the classical Greek terms *logos* (logic), *pathos* (emotion), and *ethos* (character). Courses that use these rhetorical concepts might also explore the

In Process

Applying Interpretive Frameworks

Mackenzie Owens used a rhetorical analysis in her essay about Jason Lee Steorts's efforts to address the use of deadly force by police. After reading widely about the issue, she focused on Steorts's article that appeared in *The Atlantic*, "When Should Cops Be Able to Use Deadly Force?" She highlighted words and phrases and wrote notes in the margin about her evolving understanding of how Steorts constructed his argument.

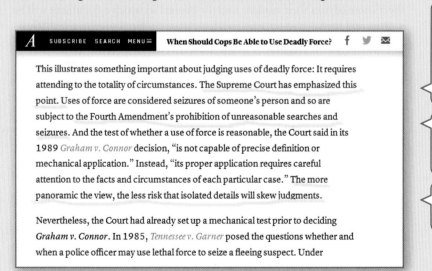

When Should Cops Be Able to Use Deadly Force?

This illustrates something important about judging uses of deadly force: It requires attending to the totality of circumstances. The Supreme Court has emphasized this point. Uses of force are considered seizures of someone's person and so are subject to the Fourth Amendment's prohibition of unreasonable searches and seizures. And the test of whether a use of force is reasonable, the Court said in its 1989 *Graham v. Connor* decision, "is not capable of precise definition or mechanical application." Instead, "its proper application requires careful attention to the facts and circumstances of each particular case." The more panoramic the view, the less risk that isolated details will skew judgments.

Nevertheless, the Court had already set up a mechanical test prior to deciding *Graham v. Connor*. In 1985, *Tennessee v. Garner* posed the questions whether and when a police officer may use lethal force to seize a fleeing suspect. Under

He's bringing in an appeal to authority here. And it doesn't get much more authoritative than the Supreme Court. Good use of ethos (even if it isn't his ethos).

He's linking his argument to the Constitution. Another appeal to authority.

Logical appeal: if this, then that. Good use of logos.

notion of *kairos*, which refers to timing or opportunity. It is also common, in rhetorical analysis, to ask whether the argument contains any logical fallacies, such as sweeping generalizations or questionable analogies (see p. 432). In general, when examining an argument is a key part of a rhetorical analysis, the writer will typically connect the analysis to one or more of the major elements of the rhetorical situation. For example, the writer might explore readers' reactions to the evidence used to support an argument. Or, as Brooke Gladstone does in her analysis of the Goldilocks number (p. 238), you might focus on how evidence migrates from one document to another.

Carrying out a rhetorical analysis almost always involves a close reading (or viewing) of the document (see p. 263 for a discussion of text analysis). It can also involve research into the origins of the document and its effects on its audience. For example, a rhetorical analysis of the Declaration of Independence might focus not only on its content but also on the political, economic, and historical contexts that brought it into existence; reactions to it by American colonists and English citizens; and its eventual impact on the development of the U.S. Constitution.

As you carry out a rhetorical analysis, consider the following guidelines:

- **Remember that the elements of a rhetorical situation are interrelated.** Writers' purposes do not emerge from a vacuum. They are shaped by their experiences, values, and beliefs — each of which is influenced by the physical, social, cultural, disciplinary, and historical contexts out of which a particular document emerges. In turn, writers usually shape their arguments to reflect their understanding of their readers' needs, interests, knowledge, values, beliefs, and backgrounds. Writers also choose their sources and select genres that reflect their purpose, their knowledge of their readers, and the context in which a document will be written and read.

- **If you analyze the argument in a document, focus on its structure and quality.** Rhetorical analysis focuses on the document as a means of communication. It might be tempting to praise an argument you agree with or to criticize one that offends your values or beliefs. If you do so, however, you won't be carrying out a rhetorical analysis. This form of analysis is intended to help your readers understand your conclusions about the origins, structure, quality, and potential impact of the document.

- **Don't underestimate the complexity of analyzing rhetorical context.** Understanding context is one of the most challenging aspects of a rhetorical analysis. Context is multifaceted. You can consider the physical context in which a document is written and read. You can examine its social context. And you can explore the cultural, disciplinary, and historical contexts that shaped a document. Each of these contexts will affect a document in important ways. Taken together, the interactions among these various aspects of context can be difficult to trace.

In fact, a full analysis of context is likely to take far more space and time than most academic documents allow. As you carry out your analysis, focus on the aspects of context that you determine are most relevant to your own writing situation.

Prepare a Draft

As you prepare to draft your analytical essay, you'll decide how to present the results of your analysis to your readers. Your draft will reflect not only your conclusions and your interpretive framework but also what others involved in the conversation have written about your subject and the types of analyses they've conducted. As you write, you'll focus on making an interpretive claim, explaining your interpretation, designing your essay, and framing your analysis.

MAKE AN INTERPRETIVE CLAIM

Your interpretive claim is a brief statement — usually in the form of a thesis statement (see Chapter 16) — that helps readers understand the overall results of your analysis. Essentially, it's a one- or two-sentence answer to your interpretive question. Just as your question should be open to interpretation, your claim should be open to debate. If it simply repeats the obvious — either because it is factually true or because it has long been agreed to by those involved in your written conversation — it will do little to advance the conversation.

Your claim will frame your readers' understanding of your subject in a particular way. It will also reflect the interpretive framework you've decided to use. Consider the differences among the following claims about distance running:

> Evidence collected since the mid-1990s suggests that distance running can enhance self-image among college students.

> Although a carefully monitored exercise program built around distance running appears to have positive effects for most cardiac patients, heart attack survivors who engage in at least two hours of running each week have a 30 percent higher survival rate than coronary artery bypass surgery patients who engage in the same amount of distance running.

> Since 2000, distance running has undergone a resurgence in the United States, allowing the country to regain its standing as a leader in the international running community.

> Distance running, when it is addressed at all in contemporary novels, is usually used to represent a desire to escape from the pressures of modern life.

Each of these interpretive claims would lead a writer to focus on different aspects of the subject, and each would reflect a different interpretive framework. The first calls readers' attention to a causal relationship between distance running and mental health. The second explores differences in the effect of distance running on two groups of cardiac patients. The third directs attention to a trend analysis of increasing competitiveness among elite distance runners. And the fourth makes a claim about how distance running is treated in literature.

EXPLAIN YOUR INTERPRETATION

People who read analyses are intelligent, curious people. They want to know more than just what you think of a subject; they want to know how you arrived at your interpretation and why your analysis is reasonable. Your readers won't always agree with your interpretation, and that's fine — but even if you can't persuade them to accept your analysis, you do want to convince readers that your take on the subject is insightful and well considered.

Provide relevant reasons for your interpretation Build on your interpretive claim by presenting reasons for your readers to accept your analysis. The overall results of your analysis form your main point, and the reasons to accept your analysis become your supporting points.

Look over the results of your analysis, and ask yourself why readers should agree with your interpretation. You might come up with more reasons than you can possibly use — or you might find yourself struggling to find enough reasons to support your claim. Either way, try to generate as many potential reasons as possible, taking care not to rule out any at first, no matter how trivial or ridiculous they might seem.

Working Together: Generate Reasons for Your Interpretation

The goal of this collaborative activity is to generate potential reasons supporting your interpretation of your subject. You can work in person or online (using chat, instant messaging, or a threaded discussion forum). If you are working face-to-face, one member of the group should take notes on the discussion. If you are using a chat or instant-messaging program, be sure to record a transcript of the session.

To carry out the activity, follow these steps:

1. One writer should describe his or her writing project, the overall results of the analysis, and the reasons that will be offered to support the analysis.

2. Each member of the group should help evaluate the reasons identified by the writer. Are the reasons sound, appropriate, and credible?

3. Each member of the group should also suggest additional reasons the writer might consider.

When the exchange is completed, turn to the next writer and repeat the process.

Once you have generated a substantial list of potential reasons, select the ones that seem most likely to convince your readers that your analysis is sound. Some reasons will be more relevant than others. Rather than list every possible reason to accept your analysis, identify those reasons that are most directly related to your interpretive claim. The reasons you choose should also be consistent with the interpretive framework you've decided to follow. For example, you might find several reasons to support your analysis of a new novel's significance, among them comments published in literary journals such as *PMLA* and endorsements by celebrities such as Oprah Winfrey and Gwyneth Paltrow. If you are using text analysis as your interpretive framework, you might find commentary offered by authorities in the field of literary studies more useful than celebrity endorsements.

Support your reasons with evidence No matter which reasons you choose, each of them must be supported by evidence. Analytical essays tend to rely on a mix of evidence from the subject itself (particularly in the case of text analyses and rhetorical analyses), from the writer's reflections and personal experience, and from published or field sources. Evidence can include the following:

- language or images from a text that is being analyzed
- quotations, paraphrases, and summaries from published sources such as reports and journal articles
- illustrations in the form of images, charts, graphs, and tables
- statements from personal interviews
- notes from an observation
- numerical information

You can use evidence to provide examples and illustrations, to define ideas and concepts, to illustrate processes, and to associate particular ideas and concepts with authorities, such as political leaders, subject-matter experts, or people who have been affected by the subject.

To organize your evidence, list all the reasons you will use to support your overall analysis, review your notes to find evidence that supports each reason, and then list the evidence below each reason. You might need to review your sources to locate additional evidence or even obtain additional sources. If you are conducting a text analysis, be careful to avoid cherry-picking your evidence (see p. 264). If you are conducting another type of analysis, make sure that you haven't relied too heavily on a single source of evidence.

You can read more about how to use evidence to support your analysis in Chapter 21.

Establish the context It's quite possible — even likely — that others involved in a conversation will have conducted their own analyses of your subject. Be sure to check for those analyses so that you can place your analysis in a larger context. Ideally, you'll be able to present your interpretation as a contribution to a growing understanding of the subject rather than simply as an isolated set of observations.

As you draft your analytical essay, keep in mind the other interpretations you've encountered. Review the sources you consulted as you learned about your

In Process

Supporting Reasons with Evidence

Mackenzie identified four major reasons to support the interpretive claim of her rhetorical analysis — that Jason Lee Steorts addresses a contentious issue in an evenhanded and effective manner:

> Reason 1: Steorts reflects an awareness of kairos (timeliness).
>
> Reason 2: Steorts uses pathos (appeals to emotion) to create an emotional argument and establish a serious and thoughtful tone.
>
> Reason 3: Steorts uses ethos (appeals to character) to portray himself and his argument as credible.
>
> Reason 4: Steorts uses logos (appeals to logic) to support his argument.

Mackenzie used each of these reasons as the basis for a general statement in her draft. Here is her preliminary list of evidence to support her second reason, that Steorts uses pathos effectively:

> Uses of emotional appeals:
>
> — The killing of Milton Hall, a homeless man with a history of mental illness, who died from a "volley of 74 bullets" after stealing a cup of coffee and walking toward police officers with a knife
>
> — The killing of Walter Scott, who was unarmed and running away from a police officer when the officer fired eight shots at Scott's back
>
> — The killing of Darrien Hunt, who had a history of emotional problems and had shown signs of mental illness, who was shot after swinging a sword at police officers and then killed with a shot to the back as he was running away

As she drafted her essay, Mackenzie used her lists of evidence to remind herself of sources she might turn to while making her points.

subject and conducted your analysis. If you find reasonable interpretations that support — or contradict — yours, consider how to address them in your essay. You might offer similar interpretations to back up one or more of your reasons, or you might explain why another writer's analysis is less adequate than your own. In either case, you should briefly define significant existing analyses for your readers and explain how your interpretation complicates or improves on what's been said before. You might also need to draw on evidence from other sources or from the subject itself.

CONSIDER GENRE AND DESIGN

A well-written analytical essay uses design for three primary reasons: to improve readability, to simplify the presentation of complex concepts and information, and to enhance the writer's ability to achieve his or her goals. As is the case with other academic essays, you'll need to consider the expectations of your readers about design elements such as wide margins, double-spaced lines, page numbers, and a readable body font. But you can also use page layout elements as well as color, shading, borders, and rules to enhance the effectiveness of your essay.

- **Page layout elements,** such as marginal glosses, pull quotes, and headings and subheadings, can draw readers' attention to key points in your essay. For example, a pull quote — a passage of text set off from the body of your essay using borders or white space — can highlight an important idea. Similarly, headings and subheadings can help readers understand at a glance the main idea of a section in your essay.

- **Color, shading, borders, and rules** can be used to call attention to key information and ideas in your essay. For instance, you might use a shaded box to present a dramatic example or related information that doesn't fit well within the body of your essay, or you might use a contrasting color to draw the reader's eye to an important passage.

Other design elements — such as illustrations and captions, tables and figures, and bulleted and numbered lists — can also contribute to the effectiveness of your essay. As you consider how best to connect with your readers, reflect on which design strategies will help you accomplish your purpose. Chapters 18, 19, and 20 provide a detailed discussion of document design principles and elements.

FRAME YOUR ANALYSIS

The results of your analysis will be strongly influenced by your interpretive question, interpretive framework, and sources of evidence. You can increase the odds that your readers will accept your conclusions if you help them understand your choices.

Introduction Rather than launching immediately into your interpretation, begin by introducing readers to your subject and explaining its significance. Provide enough information about your subject — in the form of a summary or description of a text, an overview of a trend, or a report of a recent event — to help readers understand your focus and follow your line of thinking. Another useful strategy is to start by offering some context about the conversation you've decided to join. Consider, for example, how Peter C. Baker starts his essay, "Reform of the Nerds, Starring Arthur Chu," by narrating how he first came in contact with his subject.

> In January of 2014, I started getting text messages from my college friends asking whether I was following our old classmate Arthur Chu on *Jeopardy!* I wasn't — I hadn't watched the show for years — but I tuned in the next day.
>
> From then on, I watched rapt as Chu racked up what was, at the time, the third-longest winning streak in the show's history, drawing attention not only for the size of his haul (almost $400,000 in the end), but also for his supremely stereotypical nerdiness. He used an unorthodox strategy that drew on both game theory and statistical analysis of the *Jeopardy!* board. He was slightly pudgy, with glasses, and his hair was cut in a harsh horizontal line across his forehead. His shirts were rumpled, his ties poorly knotted. He spoke in a monotone and sometimes interrupted *Jeopardy!* host Alex Trebek, cutting off Trebek's patter so they could move on to the next question.

Conclusion Because analytical essays so often begin with a question, interpreters frequently withhold the thesis statement (the answer) until the end — after they've given readers sufficient reasons to accept their conclusions as reasonable. You might also wrap up your analysis by raising a related question for the reader to ponder, speculating about the future, or contemplating the implications of your interpretation, as Mackenzie Owens does in her essay (p. 275).

> The public outcry against recent cases of deadly force leads Steorts to conclude that it may be time for law enforcement to change its standards for applying deadly force. For the families of Milton Hall, Eric Garner, and Walter Scott, and for many other Americans, this is welcome news.

You can learn more about using your introduction and conclusion to frame the results of your analysis in Chapter 18.

Organization The organization of your essay can also help frame your analysis because it will affect the order in which you present your reasons and evidence. Your choice of organizing pattern should take into account your purposes and your readers' needs and interests. For instance, if you are reporting the results of a trend analysis, you might want to use chronological order as your organizing pattern.

If, by contrast, you are conducting a causal analysis, you might use the cause-and-effect organizing pattern. Creating an outline or a map (see p. 542) can also help you organize your thoughts, especially if your assignment calls for a relatively long essay, if you are combining interpretive frameworks, or if you expect to present a lot of reasons or evidence to support your interpretive claim. You can read more about organizing patterns and outlines in Chapter 17.

Review and Improve Your Draft

Creating the first draft of an analytical essay is a complex and rewarding process. In the course of learning about a subject, you've developed an interpretive question, chosen an interpretive framework, and conducted an analysis; you've made and supported an interpretive claim; and you've organized your reasons and evidence and framed your essay. Once you complete your first draft, you should step back and assess its strengths and weaknesses. A careful review — done individually and with the help of others — can help you pinpoint where you should invest time in improving your essay.

ENSURE THAT YOUR CLAIM IS DEBATABLE

If your interpretive claim is not debatable (see p. 267), it will do little to advance the conversation about your subject. As you review your essay, focus on your interpretive claim, and ask how your readers will react to it. For example, will your interpretive claim lead readers to disagree with you, or will it surprise or shock them? Will it make them think about the subject in a new way? Will it force them to reconsider their assumptions? If you think that your readers might respond by asking "so what?" you should take another look at your claim.

CHALLENGE YOUR CONCLUSIONS

As you review your essay, challenge your findings by considering alternative explanations and asking your own "so what?" questions. Your initial impressions of a subject will often benefit from additional reflection. Those impressions might be refined, or perhaps even changed substantially, through additional analysis. Or they might be reinforced, typically by locating additional evidence.

EXAMINE THE APPLICATION OF YOUR INTERPRETIVE FRAMEWORK

Ask whether you've applied your interpretive framework fairly and rigorously to your subject. If you are carrying out a causal analysis, for example, ask whether you've ruled out the possibility that the causal relationships you are exploring are simply correlations. If you're conducting a text analysis, ask whether you've fully and fairly represented the text and whether you have considered alternative interpretations. Review how you've used your interpretive framework to make sure that you've applied it carefully and evenhandedly to your subject.

Peer Review: Improve Your Analytical Essay

One of the biggest challenges writers face is reading a draft of their own work as a reader rather than as the writer. Because you know what you're trying to say, you find it easy to understand your draft. To determine how you should revise your draft, ask a friend or classmate to read your essay and consider how well you've adopted the role of interpreter (see p. 226).

Purpose	1. Is my interpretive claim clear and easy to understand? Is it debatable? 2. Have I offered a careful and thorough analysis to support my claim?
Readers	3. Did the essay help you understand my subject in a new way? Why or why not? 4. Does the analysis seem fair to you? Did you notice any cherry-picking? Can you think of any aspects of my subject that I neglected to consider?
Sources	5. Are the reasons I've offered for my interpretation coherent? Have I provided enough evidence to support each reason? Should I add or drop anything? 6. Do my sources strike you as reliable and appropriate? Does any of the evidence I've used seem questionable?
Context	7. Did I provide enough (or too much) information about my subject to ground the analysis? 8. Does the interpretive framework I've chosen seem like an appropriate choice for analyzing my subject? Would a different framework have been more effective?

For each of the points listed above, ask your reviewers to provide concrete advice about what you could do to improve your draft. It can help if you ask them to adopt the role of an editor — someone who is working with you to improve your draft. You can read more about peer review in Chapter 5.

ASSESS YOUR ORGANIZATION

When readers can anticipate the sequence of reasoning and evidence that appears in your analytical essay, they'll conclude that the essay is well organized. If an essay is confusing or difficult to follow, however, they'll conclude that it is poorly written or, worse, that the analysis is flawed. As you review your essay, ask whether your reasons and evidence seem easy to follow. If you find yourself growing puzzled as you try to read your essay, take another look at your choice of organizing pattern. Check, as well, whether your reasons are presented in an order that allows them to build on one another. If you have difficulty figuring out how you've organized your essay, consider creating a backward outline, an outline based on an already written draft. You can read more about organizing your essay and outlining in Chapter 17.

Once you've revised your essay, ask yourself how you might polish and edit your writing so that your readers will find your analysis easy to read. For an overview of editing strategies, see Chapter 22.

 ## Student Essay

Mackenzie Owens, "Deadly Force: A Conservative Political Writer Takes on a Quickly Evolving Issue"

The following analytical essay was written by featured writer Mackenzie Owens.

Owens 1

Information about the writer, class, and date is formatted properly.

Mackenzie Owens

September 8, 2015

CO 301C — Project 1

Professor Amidon

Deadly Force: A Conservative Political Writer Takes on a Quickly Evolving Issue

The stark opening sentence begins the essay with a dramatic punch.

Tamir Rice. Walter Scott. Michael Brown. Eric Garner. Freddie Gray. These individuals, killed by police officers in recent years, have become ingrained in the public consciousness as representing the problematic balance between law enforcement's need for self-defense and the civil rights of American citizens.

The writer identifies the article that she will be analyzing in this essay.

Political writer Jason Lee Steorts tackles this issue in the essay he published in *The Atlantic*, "When Should Cops Be Able to Use Deadly Force?" Steorts uses appeals to pathos, ethos, and logos to establish his claim: that the police should only be able to use deadly force in situations that unequivocally and unambiguously demand it, or at least be able to prove beyond a reasonable person's doubt that the killing was necessary. Steorts acknowledges in his essay how difficult it can be to prove that deadly force is necessary, and he notes that many situations in which police must resort to using force are not clear-cut. Gathering evidence from legal precedents, interviews with law enforcement members, and research conducted by the police, Jason Lee Steorts analyzes a contentious issue in an evenhanded manner.

Beginning the rhetorical analysis, the writer provides background information about the author of the article and discusses his previous publications.

Steorts is the managing editor of *National Review*, a conservative magazine that focuses on politics and culture. He has written multiple articles for the magazine and its website on such topics as the meaning of patriotism, political correctness, and being pro-life. Despite the conservative leanings of *National Review,* Steorts has at times asserted surprisingly more liberal views. In one article he wrote, for example, Steorts acknowledged the Justice Department's report on racism in the Ferguson police department and encouraged fellow conservatives to reflect on its findings ("Ferguson"). This position is not shared by many of Steorts's fellow *National Review* authors. In fact, at least eight other conservative columnists dismissed the report and condemned its findings (Friedersdorf). Perhaps even more divisive, in yet another article Steorts argued that conservatives should recognize same-sex marriage ("Equal"). Research has shown that Americans who identify as Republican tend to be less likely than those who identify as liberals to support same-sex marriage (Enten). Taken as a whole, then, Steorts's publications show that he is capable of looking at political issues

Owens 2

from both sides of the aisle, even while writing for a conservative magazine, and that he is not afraid to take stances that go against the party line.

As far as the venue in which the article was published, *The Atlantic* has a prestigious reputation and is known for being politically moderate ("The Atlantic Monthly"). Its target audience includes so-called thought leaders, or authorities who have expertise in a specialized field, and serious readers, or people who are interested in current events and politics and want to read articles that are not pushing a political agenda. By publishing his article in *The Atlantic*, Steorts shows that he is willing to write for a more moderate audience than *National Review* generally attracts.

> The writer analyzes the publication in which the article appeared.

The exigence for this article is drawn straight from the news, given the greater media attention to police killing unarmed citizens, although the actual number of shootings has increased only slightly in the past few years (Wines and Cohen). Steorts clearly states his purpose in writing: "After more than a year of debate and protest and occasional riots in response to particular police killings, it would be well to take a scrutinizing look at use-of-force rules themselves" ("Cops"). With this sensible and cautious statement of purpose, Steorts announces his interest in responding to this increased media coverage of police shootings and the outrage that they have sparked. By questioning the circumstances around which police officers are actually allowed to use deadly force, and by doing so in a more moderate publication than his usual venue, Steorts reflects an awareness of *kairos*.

> The writer focuses on the exigence of the article.

Steorts uses *pathos* throughout the article to create an emotional argument for his claim and establish a serious and thoughtful tone through his diction. Opening the article with a detailed account of the 2012 police shooting of Milton Hall, a mentally ill homeless man, Steorts notes that "the officers shot Hall to death in a volley of 47 bullets" ("Cops"). The appeal to pathos here is subtle, since the reader cannot help being affected by the extreme number of bullets ("a volley") that killed Hall. He goes on to acknowledge that ambiguities are present in each case police encounter and that applying a universal standard to all cases "can lead to horrifying results" (Steorts, "Cops"). The choice of the word "horrifying" here is meant to urge the audience to take a stance against such results, as it has obvious negative connotations and evokes feelings of fear and disgust. Such diction allows Steorts to establish his claim by illustrating to his audience that these deaths are awful and that no good person could possibly support a system that allows unnecessary deaths like these to happen. Importantly, Steorts does not necessarily condemn *all* deadly force used by police

> The first rhetorical appeal, *pathos*, is identified.

> A partial quotation is integrated into a sentence and is properly cited. Because the source was read online, a page number is not provided.

Owens 3

but instead shows that he believes it is wrong to apply the same kind of deadly force standard to every situation. He is willing to find common ground with law enforcement as he is implicitly admitting that, on certain occasions, deadly force is justified.

> The writer turns to the second rhetorical appeal, *ethos*.

Steorts also uses *ethos* in order to portray himself and his evidence as credible. He makes his most convincing appeal to credibility when he references the ultimate authority in the judicial system: the Supreme Court. He examines several cases involving questionable murders by the police, such as *Graham v. Connor* and *Tennessee v. Garner*, and although the cases are conflicting, he uses both to justify his claim. In the *Graham v. Connor* case, the court said that it is impossible to have a universal standard for use of force when it "is not capable

> The writer includes evidence from a source quoted in the Steorts article, noting in her citation where she encountered it.

of precise definition or mechanical application" (qtd. in Steorts, "Cops"). However, in *Garner*, the court gave broad permission to use deadly force "when the officer has probable cause to believe that the suspect poses a threat of serious physical harm, either to the officer or to others" (qtd. in Steorts, "Cops"). Steorts then discusses why the former decision makes more sense and why a lenient standard for the use of deadly force by the police results in unwarranted deaths. By citing these Supreme Court cases, Steorts both shows that he has done his research and strengthens his claim because he has specific court rulings to back it up.

> *Logos*, or logic, is the third rhetorical appeal the writer analyzes.

Finally, Steorts uses appeals to logic to support his claim. He uses logical reasoning throughout the article, even when discussing morality, or as he calls it, "moral logic." He establishes this moral logic: "Two requirements must be met for a use of force to be justified—a 'proportionality' requirement and a 'necessity'

> A shortened title is included in the parenthetical citation to distinguish more than one work by the same author.

requirement"—and then brings in a criminal law expert to talk about these requirements (Steorts, "Cops"). By using moral logic, Steorts depicts his claim as not just reasonable but moral as well, and shows that it is not arbitrary. He is drawing on moral rules—rules that have been previously established and widely accepted for the greater civil good—and is thus being logical when he insists that shooting deaths committed by the police must be unambiguously necessary if they do occur.

Steorts goes on to examine several complicating factors in the use of deadly force by police, including when and how police dogs are used, and to what effect, and how police treat car chases differently than a single individual who poses a danger, simply because car chases have the potential to endanger many more lives

> The writer identifies a weakness in the article's analysis.

due to traffic accidents. One factor Steorts does not fully investigate, however, is

Owens 4

the issue of race. Since in many, but not all cases, the police officers have been white, while the offender has been black, a more forthright examination of racial bias would be warranted. Ultimately, though, Steorts circles back to his fundamental belief about the use of deadly force: given the huge potential for abuse and the urgency and speed with which police must act, "it is difficult to justify authorizing the use of deadly force for anything but unambiguous and compelling reasons" ("Cops"). The public outcry against recent cases of deadly force leads Steorts to conclude that it may be time for law enforcement to change its standards for applying deadly force. For the families of Milton Hall, Eric Garner, and Walter Scott, and for many other Americans, this is welcome news.

> The writer restates the article's main conclusion

> The conclusion returns to victims invoked in the essay's introduction.

Works Cited

> Per MLA style, the Works Cited title is centered.

"The Atlantic Monthly." *Encyclopaedia Britannica*. 14 Jan. 2016, www.britannica
    .com/topic/The-Atlantic-Monthly.

Enten, Harry. "The GOP May Regret Its Lasting Battle against Gay Marriage."
    FiveThirtyEight. ESPN, 30 June 2015, fivethirtyeight.com/features/
    the-gop-may-regret-its-lasting-battle-against-gay-marriage/.

> The citation for an online article includes the URL.

Friedersdorf, Conor. "Where's the Conservative Outcry on Ferguson Police
    Abuses?" *The Atlantic*, 10 Mar. 2015, www.theatlantic.com/politics/
    archive/2015/03/the-conservative-ambivalence-about-abuses-in-ferguson
    -department-of-justice-michael-brown/387196/.

Steorts, Jason Lee. "An Equal Chance at Love: Why We Should Recognize Same-
    Sex Marriage." *National Review*, 19 May 2015, www.nationalreview.com/
    article/418515/yes-same-sex-marriage-about-equality-courts-should
    -not-decide.

---. "The Ferguson Report and the Right." *National Review*, 13 Mar. 2015, www
    .nationalreview.com/corner/415349/ferguson-report-and-right-jason-lee-steorts.

> Three dashes are used to show that these documents have the same author.

---. "When Should Cops Be Able to Use Deadly Force?" *The Atlantic*. 27 Aug. 2015,
    www.theatlantic.com/politics/archive/2015/08/use-of-deadly-force-police/
    402181/.

Wines, Michael, and Sarah Cohen. "Police Killings Rise Slightly, though Increased
    Focus May Suggest Otherwise." *The New York Times*, 30 Apr. 2015, www
    .nytimes.com/2015/05/01/us/no-sharp-rise-seen-in-police-killings-though
    -increased-focus-may-suggest-otherwise.html.

Project Ideas

The following suggestions can help you focus your work on an analytical essay or another type of analytical document.

Suggestions for Essays

1. ANALYZE AN ACADEMIC TREND

Identify a trend in a field of study that interests you. For instance, you might have noticed the increasing use of statistical methods and advanced mathematics in biology courses, a decreasing emphasis on politics and great leaders in history courses, or a new focus on ethics in business courses. Confirm that the trend exists, through reading, viewing, observing, or interviewing (see Chapter 14). Then choose a main point and express it as a thesis statement (see Chapter 16).

Ask yourself whether the trend has implications for how the field of study addresses issues central to that field and whether it will affect how work is shared with audiences inside or outside the field. To support your analysis, consult scholarly journals, survey instructors in the field, or interview students who are majoring in the field. Provide evidence in the form of quotations, paraphrases, and summaries (see Chapter 21). You can learn how one student writer, Elisabeth Layne, explored an academic trend and used evidence from sources by reading her argumentative essay about trigger warnings in college courses (see p. 444).

2. INTERPRET A RECENT EVENT OR A POPULAR TREND

Interpret a recent event or the rise of a popular trend for an audience of your choice, such as your classmates, other college students, your instructor, your parents, or members of the community. You might focus on an event such as a local ballot initiative, a natural disaster affecting your region, an incident involving law enforcement officers and college students, or anything you've read about in the news that intrigues or worries you. Or you might focus on a trend such as the rise in popularity of a particular kind of music or growing interest in a particular area of study. In your essay, describe the event or trend and explain why your readers might be interested in it or need to know about it. To support your analysis, draw on written sources (see Chapter 13), or conduct field research using interviews, observations, or surveys (see Chapter 14).

3. ASSESS THE EFFECTS OF A HISTORICAL EVENT

Analyze the long-term consequences of a historical event for an audience of your choice. You might direct your essay to your instructor, your classmates, other college students, your friends, or people working in a particular profession. Choose a historical event that has implications for your audience. For example, if you are writing for people from your hometown, you might choose to write about something that occurred when the town was founded. If you are writing for your instructor or classmates, you might choose something related to education, such as the passage of Title IX, which banned discrimination on the basis of sex in educational programs that receive federal funding, or the Morrill Act, which established public land-grant universities. In your essay, describe the event clearly, identify the sources you used to learn about it, and discuss the implications of the event for your readers.

4. ANALYZE AN ADVERTISEMENT

Write an essay that uses rhetorical analysis to interpret an advertisement. Address your essay to your instructor. Choose an ad that interests you, and develop an interpretive question to guide your analysis. For example, you might ask how ads for a credit card company use appeals to character or logic to elicit a positive response from readers, or you might ask how an ad for a popular brand of beer uses emotional appeals to distinguish the beer from its competitors. If possible, include part or all of the ad as an illustration in your essay. To support your analysis, draw on written sources (see Chapter 13), or conduct field research using interviews, observations, surveys, or correspondence (see Chapter 14).

5. CONDUCT A RHETORICAL ANALYSIS

Write an essay that uses rhetorical analysis to analyze a published source, such as a speech, a video, a television show, or a documentary. You might use elements of the writing situation to analyze how a writer crafted a document — focusing on the writer's purpose, the readers' needs and interests, the context in which the document was read, and the sources used to help the writer accomplish his or her purpose. Or you might explore how readers of the document or viewers of a media source are likely to react to the writer's attempts to achieve his or her purpose. Like Mackenzie Owens (see p. 275), you might also analyze how the writer crafted his or her argument, focusing on the quality, appropriateness, and organization of the reasons offered to support the argument, the evidence provided to support the reasons, and the writer's use of appeals to logic, emotion, or character. If you focus on the writer's argument, consider examining the document or media source for use of logical fallacies.

Your essay should show clear links between the points you make in your analysis and relevant passages from the document or media source that is the subject of your analysis. Ideally, you will use quotations, paraphrases, summaries from a written document, or media clips to illustrate the points you make in your essay.

Suggestions for Other Genres

6. DRAFT AND DESIGN A COLUMN FOR A MAGAZINE

Decide whether you want to write about a particular subject or submit your column to a particular magazine. If you have a specific subject in mind, search your library's databases and the Web for articles that address it. This can help you identify magazines that might be interested in your column. If you want to publish your column in a particular magazine, read two or three issues cover-to-cover to determine the kinds of subjects it normally addresses. Once you've selected a target magazine, analyze it to determine its writing conventions (such as the level of formality and the manner in which sources are acknowledged) and design conventions. You can read more about design principles in Chapter 18. As you learn about your subject and plan, organize, and design your column, keep in mind what you've learned about the columns you've read. Your column should reflect those writing and design conventions.

While most columns rely heavily on personal experience, support your analysis by drawing on published sources and, if appropriate, by using observation, interviews, surveys, and correspondence. If you provide evidence from published sources, use the strategies for integrating sources discussed in Chapter 21. As you plan and draft your column, be careful to avoid shifting from analyzing your subject to reporting on it. While it will be important — even necessary — to help readers understand that subject, you should focus the majority of your column on analysis.

7. CREATE A NEWS ANALYSIS

Begin working on your news analysis by identifying an event to analyze. Consider whether analyzing this event will help you accomplish your purposes as a writer. Then reflect on whether your readers will want or need to know about the event. Finally, identify the newspaper, magazine, or website where you'd like to publish your news analysis.

Once you've made these preliminary decisions, learn more about the event by using your library's databases to identify relevant news reports and commentaries by other analysts. For more information about using databases, see Chapter 13. Consider using correspondence (see Chapter 14) to reach out to experts on the issue or to contact individuals who might be familiar with the event. Use what you learn about the event to plan, organize, and design your news analysis.

As you plan and draft your news analysis, be careful to avoid focusing largely on providing information about the event. While it will be important — even necessary — to help readers understand the event, you should focus most strongly on analysis. To check on your success in providing your analysis, seek feedback on your drafts from other writers (friends, classmates, relatives) and from your instructor.

8. ANALYZE A POEM, SHORT STORY, OR NOVEL

Analyze a poem, short story, or novel that you've read recently. Address your analysis to your instructor and other readers who share your interest in this work of literature. Focus on a clearly stated interpretive question, and use text analysis as your interpretive framework.

As you carry out your analysis, consider which elements of literary analysis you might use. You might focus on common literary elements, such as theme, plot, setting, characterization, imagery, style, and structure. You might also focus on the writing situation in which the author worked. For example, you could explore the social, cultural, political, and historical contexts that shaped the author's efforts. Or you might focus on what you can learn about the author's purpose for creating the work and his or her understanding of how readers would react to the work. Base your analysis not only on what is clearly present in the work but also on what can be found "between the lines" (see p. 263).

Support your analysis by drawing on the work of literature and published reviews or journal articles. In your essay, identify and briefly describe the work you're analyzing. Then offer your interpretation of the work.

In Summary: Writing an Analytical Essay

* **Find a conversation and listen in.**
  - Explore your surroundings (p. 248).
  - Ask interpretive questions (p. 250).
  - Search databases (p. 252).

* **Conduct your analysis.**
  - Refine your question (p. 254).
  - Seek a fuller understanding of your subject (p. 255).
  - Apply an interpretive framework (p. 257).

* **Prepare a draft.**
  - Make an interpretive claim (p. 267).
  - Explain your interpretation (p. 268).

- Consider genre and design (p. 271).
- Frame your analysis (p. 271).

* **Review and improve your draft.**
  - Ensure that your claim is debatable (p. 273).
  - Challenge your conclusions (p. 273).
  - Examine the application of your interpretive framework (p. 273).
  - Assess your organization (p. 275).

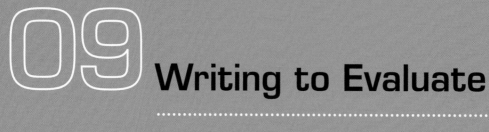

09 Writing to Evaluate

As an **evaluator**, I write with certain criteria in mind.

What Is Writing to Evaluate?

As readers, we seek out evaluative documents as much as any other type of writing. We search for reviews of new movies and restaurants; we surf the Web to learn about the strengths and weaknesses of products ranging from treadmills to smart-phones to insect repellents; and we read editorials, letters to the editor, and columns in online magazines in the hope that they will help us develop an informed opinion about recent issues and events.

Writing to evaluate involves adopting the role of *evaluator*. Writers who adopt this role focus on reaching an informed, well-reasoned conclusion about a subject's worth or effectiveness and clearly conveying their judgments to readers. Their writing is usually balanced, and they generally offer clear reasoning and ample evidence to support their judgments.

Writers typically evaluate a subject with one of three general goals: to determine whether something has succeeded or failed, to help readers understand how something might be improved or refined, or to help readers choose among alternatives. They form their conclusions by learning about their subject and considering how well it meets a given set of *criteria* — the standards or principles on which judgments are based.

Readers of evaluations typically share the writer's interest in a subject and hope to learn more about it. They often share the writer's assumptions about which criteria are appropriate — few readers, for example, expect movie reviewers to justify their choice of criteria. Readers expect the writer to provide evidence and reasoning to support his or her judgments, and readers usually want the writer to acknowledge and address alternative opinions about the subject. In fact, not only are readers likely to know that alternative opinions exist (usually through reading other evaluations) but they might also hold those opinions themselves. As a result, readers are likely to dismiss an evaluation that seems unfair or unaware of different points of view.

Writers' decisions about criteria and evidence are shaped by the contexts in which they find themselves. Writers who address a general audience, for example, might need to define their criteria carefully, while those who write to professionals in a particular field might reasonably expect their readers to be familiar with the criteria they've selected. Similarly, a writer's choice of evidence reflects the nature of the subject and readers' knowledge, expertise, and social and cultural backgrounds. For instance, an evaluation of a creative production such as a movie or a television

documentary will usually draw most heavily on the subject itself for evidence, citing examples from the work and referring to expectations about the genre to support the writer's judgments. An evaluation of a building restoration project, on the other hand, is likely to bring in evidence from outside sources — such as budget reports, building codes, and interviews with community members and architects — to support the writer's assessment of the project's relative success or failure and recommendations for improving it.

Evaluative documents make important contributions not only to our personal lives but also to written conversations. On an individual level, evaluations help us make decisions that can affect everything from the brand of car we drive to how we vote in the next election to where we attend college. Within a written conversation, evaluations provide the basis for making collective judgments about how to move the conversation forward.

The Writer's Role: Evaluator

PURPOSE

- To determine whether something has succeeded or failed
- To improve or refine something
- To provide a basis for choosing among alternatives

READERS

- Want another person's opinion
- Expect judgments to be based on appropriate criteria and supported with evidence and analysis

SOURCES

- The subject itself is often an important source of evidence.
- Published documents, personal experiences, and, in some cases, interviews and observations provide additional support.
- Reviewing other sources alerts evaluators to alternative opinions and perspectives.

CONTEXT

- Decisions about criteria and evidence reflect a writer's knowledge of readers, of the subject, and of its background and setting.
- Effective evaluations balance positive and negative assessments and acknowledge alternative perspectives.

What Kinds of Documents Are Used to Share Evaluations?

Writers can draw on a wide range of documents to share their judgments. Their evaluations might appear in print, as is often the case with articles and editorials, or on the Web, which is increasingly home to reviews, many of them posted to discussion boards and electronic mailing lists. In writing and writing-intensive courses, the most frequently assigned evaluative projects include essays, reports, blog entries, and source evaluations.

Evaluative documents make important contributions to conversations that focus on the relative merits of products, media, policies, proposals, and artistic works, and they often stand on their own as assessments, opinions, or advice that readers seek out as they try to form their own judgments. Evaluations can also contribute to broader conversations that focus less on judgment alone and more on problem solving or argument. For example, an evaluative report on a U.S. government program might help a writer support a proposal to change foreign policy. The following sections offer discussions and examples of four of the most common evaluative genres: scholarly articles, Web-based articles, media reviews, and progress reports.

Scholarly Articles

Scholarly articles convey a writer's judgment to readers who share an interest in an academic discipline, such as biochemistry, sociology, or art history. The criteria that direct the writer's evaluation are usually identified early and are influenced by several factors, including the subject itself, the writer's purpose and perspective, and recent scholarship on the subject.

In most cases, evidence from sources (such as published articles and books, personal interviews, direct observation, experimental studies, and government documents) provides the basis for determining whether the subject of an evaluative scholarly article measures up to the criteria. For example, details about the effectiveness of an inner-city summer jobs program might be obtained from an interview with the program director, from a study conducted by researchers, or from published government reports.

Readers of scholarly articles expect the writer's evaluation to be well organized, well supported, and methodologically rigorous. Readers also expect the evaluation to be presented in a fair and unbiased manner.

 Eileen Ferrer et al.
Playing Music to Relieve Stress in a College Classroom Environment

The following excerpt is from a scholarly article published in *College Student Journal*, a peer-reviewed journal that focuses on how college students think and learn. The authors of the study present their findings regarding the impact of music therapy on college students. The participants, students at California State University, were asked to rate their stress levels after listening to a song. While the "Introduction" presents the overall goals of the study, the "Discussion" is a deeper analysis of the results, evaluating whether or not music did have a stress-reducing effect. The complete article contains detailed information on the methodology and design of the study, the data that was collected, and evidence from other studies that have similarly investigated how students' stress levels were affected by music.

PLAYING MUSIC TO RELIEVE STRESS IN A COLLEGE CLASSROOM ENVIRONMENT

EILEEN FERRER

School of Kinesiology and Nutrition Science, California State University

POLONG LEW

Los Angeles Chinatown Senior Citizen Center

SARAH M. JUNG

School of Kinesiology and Nutrition Science, California State University

EMILIA JANEKE

School of Kinesiology and Nutrition Science, California State University

MICHELLE GARCIA

School of Kinesiology and Nutrition Science, California State University

CINDY PENG

School of Kinesiology and Nutrition Science, California State University

GEORGE POON

Los Angeles Chinatown Senior Citizen Center

VINISHA RATHOD
SHARON BECKWITH
CHICK F. TAM

School of Kinesiology and Nutrition Science, California State University

INTRODUCTION

Time spent in college can be a priceless experience, but it can also be a stressful one. In recent years, the academic circle has noted stress to be an important topic of interest, due to the many stresses of daily life (Agolla & Ongori, 2009). There are a variety of reasons students experience stress, which may include: being away from home for the first time; trying to balance the demands of classes, work, extracurricular activities, and a social life; the pressure to perform well academically. Even though some of these may be perceived as positive changes, any departure from a familiar routine can bring about some degree of stress (Richlin-Klonsky & Hoe, 2003).

Some students may not know how to effectively cope with the demands of college life. As a result, having severe and/or prolonged stress may lead to reduced academic performance. This type of stress can potentially hinder a student's level of contribution and participation in campus life, and increases the likelihood of substance abuse and other destructive behaviors (Ross, Neibling & Hecker, 1999). Coping with unhealthy stress begins with recognizing the signs of building stress levels and the stressors that cause them. While stress can be caused by external events, the events themselves may not necessarily be stressful. In fact, it is the way in which an individual interprets and reacts to a stressor that is responsible for producing stress (Busari, 2012). Consequently, although various methods exist to help college students cope with stress, the appropriate method must be selected for the individual.

According to Romano (1992), the interactions between an individual's perception and reaction to stressors are what result in stress. While many may be unaware of the danger of stress, the American Institute of Stress (2012) claimed stress to be the number one health problem for Americans. While stress itself can be debilitating, its main effect on public health involves increasing risk for diseases such as cancer, diabetes mellitus, and cardiovascular disease. Stress can also lead to depression and its related conditions. Moreover, overall health and wellness is a matter of concern among populations with elevated levels of stress. College students, subject to pressure from many areas, fit into this category.

Music Therapy—Interventions for Health

Music therapy (MT) is defined by the American Music Therapy Association (2011) as the clinical and evidence-based use of music interventions to accomplish individualized goals within a therapeutic relationship by a credentialed professional who has completed an approved music therapy program. According to the American Music Therapy Association (2011), music therapy is a well-established health program and it is used therapeutically to address an individual's physical, emotional, cognitive, and social needs. Furthermore, a study by Lu and colleagues (2010) defined MT as a form of psychotherapy that is safe, enjoyable, and inexpensive.

The goal and purpose of this study was to examine the role of music as a potentially stress-alleviating therapy among college students. The correlation between music therapy and stress was examined, and research was conducted to investigate the effectiveness of stress reduction via music within an academic population in classroom settings. . . .

PURPOSE OF THE PROJECT

The purpose of this study is therefore to investigate the effectiveness of music therapy, and demonstrate how different forms of music influence stress levels before and after a musical selection in a college classroom environment. Specifically, this study aims to investigate how music can affect stress by observing changes in levels of stress among students before and after listening to a music selection. It is hypothesized that music self-selected by the participant will reduce stress levels. . . .

MATERIALS AND METHODS

Design of the Project

Participants

Participants consisted of college students attending California State University, Los Angeles, enrolled in an annual Alternative Nutrition class designed to study mind and body medicine, as well as stress management using music therapy and nutritional supplementation. . . . All student participants remained anonymous and strictly confidential.

Procedures

As a required project of this class, participants were to select any song, and present it to their cohort during the class period (3 hours, 50 minutes). . . . Songs varied in genre, from classical, pop, alternative/rock, to cultural/ethnic music and more.

Participants were asked to listen to each song, and provide written feedback at the end. . . .

DISCUSSION

As it has been emphasized, music can be used to produce health benefits, especially for the study population. There are many potential stressors affecting college students.

MUSIC THERAPY SURVEY FORM

1. AGE_____YRS

2. GENDER_____

3. WEIGHT_____LBS   HEIGHT_____ FT/INS

4. MAJOR_____

5. SUBJECTIVELY, WHAT IS YOUR CURRENT "STRESS LEVEL" (WITH 10 BEING THE HIGHEST LEVEL)?
CIRCLE ONE: 1 2 3 4 5 6 7 8 9 10

6. DID YOU LIKE THE MUSIC?
CIRCLE ONE: VERY MUCH [1]   GOOD [2]   SOMEWHAT [3]
DISLIKE [4]

7. DID YOU FIND ANY MEANING IN THE SONG?
CIRCLE ONE: HAS MEANING [1]   NO MEANING [2]
DON'T KNOW [3]

8. DO YOU FEEL HAPPIER AFTER LISTENING TO THE SONG?
CIRCLE ONE: YES [1]   NO [2]   DON'T KNOW [3]

9. SUBJECTIVELY, WHAT IS YOUR STRESS LEVEL AFTER THE SONG (WITH 10 BEING THE HIGHEST LEVEL)?
CIRCLE ONE: 1 2 3 4 5 6 7 8 9 10

▲ Music therapy survey form

Pressured with balancing academics and a personal life, many students can fall victim to stress. Listening to music for a short period can alleviate the effects of these stressors.

Research has proven that music may be an effective medium to help college students reduce the effects of negative emotional states (Labbé, Schmidt, Babin, & Pharr, 2007). Results have suggested that listening to at least ten minutes of soothing music has a relaxing effect (Lai, 2004). However, stress-related changes such as those that occur in serum hormone levels, which can affect mood, can be seen in as few as six minutes (Mockel, Rocker, Stork, Vollert, Danne, Eichstadt, & Hochrein, 1994). Thus, music is an easily accessible and efficient therapy to utilize for college students that is also cost-effective. Listening to music does not require a licensed musical therapist and can be done at the time and location that is convenient to the individual. The only requirement is equipment for playing music, which is already accessible to many students.

In some study participants, listening to music did not produce any effect. Among individual responses, there were some songs that appeared to have caused participant stress levels to increase or have no effect at all. But as the results show, for the overall study population, self-perceived stress levels were reduced in multiple categories from the pre-selected songs to the songs chosen by the instructor. One possible explanation for this reduction in stress levels is that music therapy utilizes the power of the mind to express emotions, potentially influencing all aspects of health and well-being. As it shows in the results, listening to personally selected music had the most impact on stress levels following each song. It could be that hearing the various types of music provided an emotional response.

There were a few limitations for this music therapy intervention. Because this was a self-administered experiment, the length of the experimental period for listening to all individual songs was limited to only a couple of class meeting days. Due to time constraints, each participant had to introduce and play their songs consecutively with minimal breaks in between, which could have prohibited full focus on each musical selection. Limiting the amount of songs to be played per day to approximately ten or less could provide additional time to respond to each participant's choice of music before reflecting on one's own self-perceived levels of stress; fewer songs played per day may also allow for additional time to prepare for the next song to be played. Conducting a longer study on a single population during the entire length of the academic quarter would demonstrate music's effectiveness over a period of time, and possibly provide a more truthful perception of stress level from participants.

In addition, the effect of music genre was not specifically explored in depth for this intervention. It was mentioned briefly that music genre did not have much influence; however, most studies have demonstrated that soothing, pleasant music, such as classical, has shown to reduce stress levels the most. Further study assessing music genre would provide insight as to which genre is most effective against stress and anxiety or to prove if genre selection makes any difference at all within the same study population. These limiting factors present an opportunity for future studies to be conducted.

Overall, listening to music is a functional, inexpensive, and effortless intervention to utilize in various stressful situations. As this intervention has evidently proven to be successful amongst college students, research has sufficiently established the efficacy and benefit of music for diverse populations in varying age groups.

As more people and healthcare professionals become aware and accepting of mind-body therapies and other complementary and alternative medical treatments, music can be widely utilized as a complement to all areas of conventional healthcare. . . .

REFERENCES

Agolla, J. E., & Ongori, H. (2009). An assessment of academic stress among undergraduate students: The case of University of Botswana. *Educational Research and Review, 4,* 63-70.

American Institute of Stress. (2012). What is stress? Retrieved from http://www .stress.org/what-is-stress/

American Music Therapy Association. (2011). Definition and quotes about music therapy. Retrieved from http://www.musictherapy.org/about/quotes/

Brattico, E., & Pearce, M. (2010). The neuroaesthetics of music. *Psychology of Aesthetics, Creativity, and the Arts, 7*(1), 48-61.

Busari, A. O. (2012). Identifying difference in perceptions of academic stress and reaction to stressors based on gender among first year university students. *International Journal of Humanities and Social Science, 2,* 138-146.

Labbé, E., Schmidt, N., Babin, J., & Pharr, M. (2007). Coping with stress: The effectiveness of different types of music. *Applied Psychophysiology and Biofeedback, 32,* 163-168. doi: 10.1007/s10484-007-9043-9

Lai, H. L. (2004). Music preference and relaxation in Taiwanese elderly people. *Journal of Geriatric Nursing, 25,* 286-291.

Lu, Y., Liu, M., Shi, S., Jiang, H., Yang, L., Liu, X., Zhang, Q., & Pan, F. (2010). Effects of stress in early life on immune functions in rats with asthma and the effects of music therapy. *Journal of Asthma, 47,* 526-531. doi: 10.3109/02770901003801964

Mockel, M., Rocker, L., Stork, T., Vollert, J., Danne, O., Eichstadt, H., & Hochrein H. (1994). Immediate physiological responses of healthy volunteers to different types of music: cardiovascular, hormonal and mental changes. *European Journal of Applied Physiology and Occupational Physiology, 68,* 451-459.

Richlin-Klonsky, J., & Hoe, R. (2003). Sources and levels of stress among UCLA students. Student Affairs Briefing, 2.

Romano, J. L. (1992). Psychoeducational interventions for stress management and well-being. *Journal of Counseling and Development, 71,* 199-202.

Ross, S. E., Niebling, B. C., & Hecker, T. M. (1999). Sources of stress among college students. *College Student Journal, 33,* 312-317.

Starting a Conversation: Respond to "Playing Music to Relieve Stress in a College Classroom Environment"

In your writer's notebook, consider how Ferrer et al. respond to their writing situation by answering the following questions:

1. How do the authors incorporate into the article preexisting research on the benefits of music for reducing stress? Why is this acknowledgment important in a piece of scholarly writing?

2. How do Ferrer and her coauthors measure the effect of music as a source of stress relief? What is their ultimate conclusion?

3. Limitations are included as a part of the discussion. Why do you think the authors address the study's limitations? What purpose does this serve? Why is the information important to the overall evaluation?

4. **Reflection:** As a current student, how do you relate to the findings of this study? Does your personal experience align with the study's findings? Why or why not?

Web-Based Articles

Most major magazines, such as *Time*, *The Atlantic*, and *Wired*, offer online versions of their publications, providing electronic copies of print articles along with material written specifically for the Web edition. Many newer magazines, however, publish exclusively on the Web. Some of these online publications, such as *Slate* and *Salon*, appeal to a general audience. Others, such as *Pedal Pushers Online* (pedalpushersonline.com) or *Gather* (gatherjournal.com), a food magazine, cater to readers with specific interests. In either case, Web-based magazines typically offer a mix of traditional articles and essays, blogs, video entries, news feeds, and reader-response forums.

Analytical Web-based articles often begin with a question or a problematic fact or puzzling situation that leads to a question. Writers of such articles need to know about and understand the history and significance of their subjects. Depending on the specific publication and writing situation, they might rely on statistical evidence, personal experience, or direct observation. In many cases, they must clearly explain unfamiliar background material or interpret complex data for their readers.

Articles in online magazines can draw on a variety of sources, ranging from interviews, surveys, published studies, and scholarly works to popular culture and personal observation. Writers of online articles often embed links to their sources within the text of their documents instead of listing them at the end, allowing readers to jump directly to cited works as they read. Commenting functions encourage readers to respond to writers in a public forum, creating an ongoing written conversation that anyone can join. In these and other ways, analytical discussions usually move forward more quickly and more unpredictably online than they do in print journals.

Kathryn Edin and Luke Shaefer
The Truth about Food Stamps (Hint: They Work and Help Millions)

This interview with two academic experts on SNAP (Supplemental Nutrition Assistance Program) was published in *The New Republic,* a progressive monthly publication that aims to educate and enact change around the most important issues of the day. Readers of *The New Republic* are typically open-minded and interested in social and political issues. Kathryn Edin is a Bloomberg Distinguished Professor at Johns Hopkins University. Luke Shaefer is an associate professor of social work and associate professor of public policy at the University of Michigan. Edin and Shaefer are widely published and have coauthored the book *$2 a Day: Living on Almost Nothing in America* (2015).

---

newrepublic.com

The Truth about Food Stamps (Hint: They Work and Help Millions)

SNAP has halved the number of children living in extreme poverty.

By Kathryn Edin and Luke Shaefer

July 29, 2014

Editor's Note: Conservatives love to beat up on food stamps. It happened again last week, when Paul Ryan called for overhauling the program and converting it into a "block grant." How does the program actually work? Does it actually need reform? What would happen if conservatives got their way? As part of the QEDecide series, we put those questions to a pair of the nation's most trusted researchers on the subject: Kathryn Edin from Johns Hopkins University and Luke Shaefer from the University of Michigan. Here's what they said:

What is the food stamp program and why is it actually called SNAP?

The Supplemental Nutrition Assistance Program, or "SNAP," the new name for the Food Stamp Program, is America's largest and most important nutrition assistance program. It provides low-income people with money they must use to purchase food. The modern program was established as part of the War on Poverty in the 1960s, but it has undergone a ton of changes since then. For example, the government now gives recipients electronic debit cards, rather than stamps, for buying food. Those changes are one reason Congress decided in 2008 to rename the program — to signal a fresh start.

If I were eligible for SNAP, how would I get it — and how would I use it?

These days an individual on SNAP with zero net income would get a maximum monthly benefit of $189 per month; for a family of four it'd be $632. The more money you make, the less food assistance you get. But the decline isn't one-to-one — you lose only about 30 cents for every extra net dollar you earn. If you were on SNAP, you would take your benefits card with you to the grocery store and fill your shopping cart with food just like you always do. When you check out, you'd slide your card through a machine just like a credit or ATM card, enter your pin, and the store would deduct your grocery total from your balance. The only complication is that SNAP doesn't cover non-food purchases, like diapers or toothpaste. To pay for those, you have to check out a second time and pay cash.

How many people are on SNAP — and how does that compare to the past?

As of March 2014, there were about 46.1 million people in households receiving SNAP. That's roughly one in every seven people living in the United States. The

single largest subgroup of recipients is households with children, although the program also serves working-age adults with no children, as well as the elderly.

Today's SNAP caseload is quite a bit larger than the rolls have ever been before. The previous peak, of 27 million, was in the early 1990s. The SNAP caseload fell after that, thanks to the booming economy and some new

Andrew Burton/Getty Images

restrictions on eligibility introduced by welfare reform. As of 2000, the total caseload was down to 17.2 million. Do the math and you'll see that, since that time, the caseload has risen almost 170 percent.

The primary reason SNAP caseloads have swelled is the economy. Recent research has shown that with so many people out of work for so long, many more people needed the help. Of course, the economy has started to improve recently, ever so slowly. Sure enough, SNAP rolls are starting to come back down a little.

Another, albeit less significant factor that's contributed to the rising SNAP caseload is a set of relatively recent changes to the program, some that made it easier for the working poor in particular to qualify for benefits. Most of these changes didn't take place under President Obama, they took place under George W. Bush. Among the changes: encouraging states to allow people to stay on the program for longer periods of time, without submitting new evidence of their eligibility. The Bush Administration also encouraged states to conduct outreach campaigns to sign people up, and rolled back some restrictions on benefits for legal immigrants that were enacted in the 1990s.

How much does the program cost today? And how has that changed over the years?

In 2013, the federal government, which finances every dollar in benefits, paid $76.1 billion in benefits. The feds also split the cost of program administration with the states, and their part came to $3.9 billion that year. In all, then, the federal government spent about $80 billion on the program, with the states chipping in a few billion more.

Wow, that sounds like a lot of people — and a lot of money.

Eighty billion dollars ain't nothing, that's for sure. But it's still a tiny portion of the annual federal budget. In 2013, out of every $100 the federal government spent, a little over $2 went to SNAP. In contrast, about $22 dollars in every $100 went to our major health insurance programs for the poor and elderly (Medicaid, CHIP, and Medicare), and $19 went to defense and international security assistance spending. SNAP's expensive, but it isn't busting the federal budget.

What's the evidence that the program is actually helping people?

Assessing SNAP's effects is actually pretty difficult, because the people getting benefits aren't just a random portion of the population. It's people who have opted to be part of it — and, as you can imagine, it's the group of people having the most trouble getting food. Thus, if you just compare poor families on SNAP to similarly poor families not on SNAP, you would find that those getting benefits have worse outcomes. That's the sort of finding that keeps policy researchers like us up all night.

But over the past few years, social scientists have found some solid ways to address these "selection" issues. A number of recent studies using those methods find that SNAP benefits have a big and positive effect on the food security of recipients, making it easier for them to get the food they need. There's also evidence (by Shaefer) that SNAP allows families to redirect some of the dollars they previously spent on food to other essential household expenses, which can keep them from falling behind on their rent and utilities. Perhaps the most exciting recent study finds that program benefits improve the long-term health outcomes of children.

Our own research finds that SNAP gets to many of the families who need it most. We find that the program reduces the number of households with children in the U.S. living in extreme poverty (at $2 per person, per day or less) by about half. SNAP is a lifeline for families with virtually nothing else. We see this especially in the administrative SNAP data. Starting in 2001, more and more families with children who were receiving SNAP (food stamps) began to report that they had no other source of income to live on — not from work, not from public assistance. By 2006, the number of such families had grown 143 percent from a decade before. By 2011, 1.2 million families on SNAP told eligibility workers they had no other income. The big question is, how are they paying their rent? How are they getting to job interviews?

I've heard there is a lot of waste — is there?

SNAP is actually a pretty efficient program. About 95 percent of all federal dollars spent on the program goes directly into benefits. Even adding in what the states spend, SNAP remains pretty efficient. Imagine if America's health care system spent that little on administration and overhead! Also, the U.S. Department of Agriculture (USDA), which oversees the program and the states that administer it is very serious about making sure only people who are eligible for the program get it — and that they only get the amount for which they are eligible.

Yeah, but what about fraud? I keep hearing stories about people misusing it. Are they?

As you might imagine, it is hard to get good estimates of fraud. It certainly exists, and can take a lot of different forms. But USDA and the states also take fraud very, very seriously. Families can face big fines and jail time if they are found to have intentionally engaged in fraud. Even if there was an honest mistake (by a state, or an applicant) in determining how much they should be awarded, they can be forced to pay back the overage.

Every few years, USDA conducts audits to try to estimate the prevalence of "trafficking." This is a kind of fraud where the merchants would ring up, say, $100 in fake groceries, and give the purchaser, say, $60 in cash. Thus, the SNAP recipient gets unrestricted cash, while the merchant pockets $40. Over the years, according to the USDA audits, the prevalence of SNAP trafficking has fallen, so that now only about 1.3 percent of benefits are trafficked. This is down from about 3.8 percent in the early 1990s and is likely the result of the switch over to electronic debit cards from paper stamps, as well as USDA's focus on antifraud efforts.

Conservatives and Republicans want to change the program. What do they have in mind?

There have been some efforts in recent years to roll back some of the changes made by President Bush and others that make it easier for families to get SNAP benefits. Other proposals would allow states to drug test SNAP recipients, deny anyone convicted of a violent crime at any point in their life access to the program, impose a work requirement on all working-age adult SNAP recipients, and strengthen the one that already exists for able-bodied adults without children. Recently, Paul Ryan suggested a change that would consolidate SNAP with some other programs into a block grant to states, giving them more flexibility on how to spend the money, but at the same time cap federal spending. This would be a radical change that would end SNAP in its current form.

What would happen if they succeeded?

If existing research is correct, then imposing more restrictions on the program will cause people to drop off the rolls and would increase rates of food insecurity and other material hardship. This increased hardship would be concentrated among families with children, although it would affect childless working-age adults and the elderly as well. In a lot of ways, SNAP is the only game in town when a family hits a hard spell of unemployment or experiences a big crisis. Also, historical evidence suggests that when you block grant a program and cap its funding, it can lose its responsiveness to changes in the economy. The funding stays the same unless Congress acts, which sometimes can take a while. So a program might not be able to serve everyone who applies and is eligible when, say, the unemployment rate spikes and a lot of people need help.

I'm sure the program isn't perfect. What could we do to improve it?

Some exciting programs implemented by some states do things like increase benefits if they are spent at local farmer's markets or otherwise used for fresh local foods. It would be great to expand these even further, across states, and invest in the infrastructure needed to make them successful. These are good for families and good for local farmers and local economies.

With so many families surviving on no other income but SNAP, it would be nice somehow to give these families some more flexibility to buy some other essential household goods, like diapers or toothpaste and toothbrushes.

But, in the end, SNAP is a critical foundation of the safety net. It's the closest thing we've ever had to a guaranteed minimum income. We have solid evidence that it reduces food insecurity and improves child health outcomes. It is run efficiently. And for a lot of people, it's all they've got.

So while the economy is still experiencing sluggish growth, perhaps the best thing to do is just not mess with it. SNAP is not perfect, but on the whole it works, in fact quite well. For the time being, maybe we should just let it do its job.

Starting a Conversation: Respond to "The Truth about Food Stamps (Hint: They Work and Help Millions)"

In your writer's notebook, record your thoughts on "The Truth about Food Stamps (Hint: They Work and Help Millions)" by responding to the following questions:

1. The outcome of the evaluation is clearly stated in the title. Why do you think the authors made this style choice? What impact does it have on the reader?

2. Unlike most evaluations, this piece is structured as an interview. How does this format affect the content of the evaluation? How does it affect its tone?

3. How do Edin and Shaefer leverage the interview structure to address counterarguments to their claim? What are the benefits of this approach? Are there drawbacks? How effectively are the counterarguments addressed?

4. What types of evidence are supplied to support the claim of the evaluation? How do the authors use each type of evidence? Did you find the evidence convincing? Why or why not?

5. **Reflection:** What was your opinion of food stamps before reading this evaluation? Did the evaluation change your opinion? What aspect of the evaluation was most persuasive?

Media Reviews

Media reviews present an evaluation of a work of art, a song or music album, a television program, a book, a movie or play, a computer game, a DVD, a website, or any of a number of other cultural productions. The subject of the review reflects the shared interests of the group of writers and readers involved in a written conversation. For example, a group of horror fans might be interested in a new film based on one of Dean Koontz's novels, while people who play a particular video game will probably be interested in the latest version of the game.

Because media reviewers expect their readers to understand what's necessary for success in a particular medium, they often do not define their criteria. For example, a movie critic will assume that readers are familiar with the importance of acting, plot, and cinematography. The evidence used to determine whether the subject of a review has met the criteria for success is most often drawn from the subject itself and from the reviewer's personal interpretation, although writers sometimes include evidence from interviews, surveys, or published sources to support their evaluations.

Jon Dolan
Adele, 25

This review of Adele's album *25* was published in *Rolling Stone* in 2015. An English singer and songwriter, Adele experienced meteoric success in the United States after an appearance on *Saturday Night Live* in 2008. Her first album, *19,* was a success both critically and commercially, and she continued to garner accolades with subsequent releases. Her powerful voice and emotional, relatable lyrics have captured the attention of listeners and critics alike. In this review, music critic Jon Dolan considers *25* in light of its predecessor, the 2011 album *21.* Music reviews are intended to help the reader decide whether or not to buy an album, and Dolan builds a clear case for his readers.

Adele, *25*

by Jon Dolan

Adele's 2011 blockbuster, *21*, was all about turning pain into power. Four years and 30 million albums sold later, remorse is still her muse. But where *21* was the sound of a woman soldiering through bad romance, *25* finds her queenly and resolute, lamenting the past on songs with titles like "Water under the Bridge" and "When We Were Young." Even "Hello" is a goodbye. The nostalgic mood is the perfect fit for an artist who reaches back decades for her influences, even as her all-or-nothing urgency feels utterly modern.

> The pop superstar makes a case for greatness on her most self-assured LP yet.

Some of pop's biggest names, from Max Martin to Bruno Mars, join familiar faces like Paul Epworth and Ryan Tedder in *25*'s dream team of producers and co-writers. They help create a rich set of songs without getting in the way of the lady in charge. "River Lea," a collaboration with Danger Mouse, is an organ-heavy soul shouter, and "Water under the Bridge" builds to gospel-steeped ecstasy. Adele is more somber on "Million Years Ago," a gorgeous acoustic reverie that suggests Caetano Veloso writing for Dusty Springfield. "I feel like my life is flashing by," she sings, her voice deepening with regret and sounding decades beyond her years.

The music feels more mature, too, on torchy ballads like "When We Were Young" and "Love in the Dark." The most powerful moment is "All I Ask," a silken tempest co-written with Mars, where Adele addresses a lover on what she knows will be their final night, processing the end of an affair in what feels like slow motion. When she sings, "Give me a memory I can use," it's like she's already imagining the heartrending song she'll craft from the experience. There's vulnerability in that moment, but there's also grace and resilience.

Throughout *25*, there's a deeper sense of artistic command. In a great, intimate bit before the start of "Send My Love (To Your New Lover)," she issues orders to the guys in the studio: "Just the guitar." The Martin-helmed song that follows — built on a nimble acoustic figure — is a farewell to an ex who couldn't deal with Adele's fire, sung with chill composure.

Whether she's holding notes with the strength of a suspension bridge or enjoying a rare lighthearted "whoo-hoo!" on "Sweetest Devotion," her incredible phrasing — the way she can infuse any line with nuance and power — is more proof that she's among the greatest interpreters of romantic lyrics. "No river is too wide or too deep for me to swim to you," she sings on the gently lifting "Remedy." On *25*, no feat of strength comes as a surprise. Let's just hope the next one is called *28*, and not, say, *30*. Each new chapter of her story is too good to wait for.

Kevin Mazur/Getty Images

Starting a Conversation: Respond to "Adele, *25*"

In your writer's notebook, record your thoughts on Jon Dolan's review by responding to the following questions:

1. Describe the tone Dolan uses in his review. Is his writing style formal or casual? What kind of language does he use to describe Adele's album? How do these descriptions reflect Dolan's evaluation of the album?

2. Dolan uses comparison and contrast to explain the ways in which, in his opinion, Adele has evolved as an artist. To whom or what does he draw the comparison? Does this comparison reveal his personal preference in music? What do you think that preference is?

3. In paragraph 5, Dolan uses a musical term, *phrasing*, that not all readers are likely to be familiar with. How does Dolan handle this term? How, if at all, does this affect the accessibility of the review? What does it tell us about Dolan's expected audience?

4. Ultimately, what is Dolan's position on *25*? How can you tell? Explain in a few sentences why you agree (or disagree) with his review.

5. **Reflection:** Consider times in your life when you rely on reviews. Perhaps you have consulted reviews during a major event like purchasing a car or even for the more routine question of where to eat dinner. What kind of information is important to you in a review? What makes you trust a review or take its judgment seriously?

Progress Reports

Progress reports provide an assessment of a project or an initiative. For example, a state environmental agency might issue a report on its efforts to reduce pesticide and fertilizer runoff from farmland into state watersheds. Similarly, an account team at an advertising agency might report on its efforts to increase sales of a product through a national advertising campaign, while the development manager at a charitable organization might report on her efforts to increase donations through corporate subscriptions. Because most reports focus narrowly on a subject, they often use criteria that might be unfamiliar to readers, particularly those, such as supervisors and managers, who might not be as well versed in the subject as the specialists who wrote the report. As a result, the criteria used in the evaluation are often defined in detail and, when applied in the report, discussed at length. Longer reports, particularly those that assess the effectiveness of a project or an initiative, often rely on information gathered by researchers associated with the project. The source of this kind of evidence might include surveys, interviews, testing, observation, and reviews of published sources.

The formats in which reports are written and read vary widely. Government reports, for example, are often distributed as bound documents that resemble books, as well as in downloadable formats. In contrast, reports written for a company or a political group might be distributed to only a small group of readers, and great care might be taken to ensure that the document does not receive wide distribution. Regardless of the number of readers, however, the writers of these documents often put a great deal of effort into the report's design.

 ### High HOPES Campaign
Restorative Justice in Chicago Public Schools

Restorative justice is a community-oriented approach to disciplinary action, and it has become an increasingly popular method of addressing conflict. The restorative justice model emphasizes the impact of the misconduct rather than the behavior itself. The goal of this approach is to create a community where individuals take responsibility for their mistakes and then work with those directly affected and the community at large to repair damages caused by the behavior. While traditional disciplinary programs emphasize punishment, restorative justice programs emphasize ownership and improvement. The High HOPES (Healing Over the Punishment of Expulsion and Suspension) Campaign, a coalition of community organizations in Chicago, published the report "Restorative Justice in Chicago Public Schools" in 2012, to examine the impact of restorative justice practices as opposed to traditional disciplinary action in public schools in Chicago. This excerpt highlights both the data collected and the evaluation of the restorative justice model as an effective method of addressing disciplinary issues in schools.

FROM POLICY TO STANDARD PRACTICE

Restorative Justice in Chicago Public Schools

EXECUTIVE SUMMARY

In 2006, the Board of Chicago Public Schools officially stripped the language of "zero-tolerance" from the CPS Student Code of Conduct and declared that it "recognizes and embraces the philosophy of restorative justice." The dramatic change in official discipline policy was noted in the press and celebrated by the students, parents, and advocates who had been calling for an end to the punitive practices and policies that push children out of school.

The 2006 declaration, however, has yet to change the culture of "zero-tolerance" in our schools. Indeed, most CPS schools still treat suspensions, expulsions, and school-based arrests as a matter of routine, while restorative justice methods remain underutilized. The High HOPES Coalition, made up of students, parents, educators, and community members, believes that it is time for true change.

We spent a year researching, with the input of many stakeholders, to create this report, which shines a light on the ongoing crisis of suspensions, expulsions and school-based arrests and proposes a course for the full implementation of restorative justice in CPS.

Specifically, our report finds that:

- Suspensions and expulsions do not make schools safer but instead negatively affect the school environment; have long-damaging effects on student behavior, learning and academic achievement; and contribute to higher dropout rates and violence.
- Restorative justice has been shown to make schools safer and help to lower suspension and expulsion rates.
- Integrating restorative justice practices is a critical way to improve the culture and climate of a school by supporting the social and emotional development of students and strengthening partnerships among all stakeholders.

We therefore recommend that CPS take the following concrete steps:

- Commit to and proactively pursue a district-wide reduction in suspensions and expulsions by 40% in the coming school year.

- Overcome current barriers to the implementation of restorative justice by developing a sustainable, district-wide plan for rolling out these practices in schools.
- Fully fund and support implementation by creating full-time restorative justice coordinator positions in each school, and offering ongoing training and technical assistance.
- Reprioritize its spending on school safety by diverting costly investments in policing and zero-tolerance strategies to the implementation of restorative justice. We estimate that such a full-scale investment in restorative justice would cost around $44 million, much less than the $67 million budget of the CPS Office of School Safety and Security.
- Create monitoring and evaluation mechanisms to track the reduction in punitive discipline methods and the success of restorative justice implementation, and make that information available in an ongoing, public manner. . . .

> "If we're going to equip students to handle adulthood, we need to give them chances to remedy their harms, rather than kicking them out of school all the time."
> *Principal Ernesto Matias of Wells High School*

Conclusion

In the 2011–2012 Student Code of Conduct, CPS states that "out-of-school suspensions should be used as a last resort, unless necessary due to the severity of a student's misconduct." Moreover, CPS encourages principals and administrators to adopt and implement restorative justice philosophy and practices to address student misconduct. This report has outlined concrete steps that CPS leadership must take in order for restorative justice to become a reality in our schools. With this shift in priorities and investment, we can create the culture shift necessary to transform CPS into a truly restorative system and lower the dangerously high rates of suspensions and expulsions of Chicago students. . . .

FROM POLICY TO STANDARD PRACTICE: RESTORATIVE JUSTICE IN CHICAGO PUBLIC SCHOOLS

The Problem: Suspensions, Expulsions, and Arrests in Chicago Public Schools

In the 2008 to 2009 school year, 43,972 students were suspended from CPS[1], and, in 2010, there were 5,574 juvenile school-based arrests at CPS locations.[2] CPS has been suspending and expelling students at a higher rate than other big-city districts.[3] Many of these suspensions have been for low-level, minor behavior.[4] African American male students, who represented only 23% of CPS students from 2008 to 2009, represented over 48% of suspensions and 57% of expulsions.[5] New data released by the U.S. Department of Education shows that, from 2009 to 2010, "CPS's African American students were five times as likely to be suspended as their white peers."[6] On a national level, studies have also indicated that Latino, LGBTQ, special education, and other minority students are suspended and/or expelled at higher rates, and may thus be at a higher risk in Chicago, as well.[8]

> "Minority students across America face much harsher discipline than non-minorities — even within the same school . . . some of the worst discrepancies are in my home town of Chicago."
> **US Education Secretary Arne Duncan[7]**

High levels of suspensions and expulsions are highly correlated to high levels of dropouts.[9] In 2010, only 55.8% of CPS students earned their diploma within five years.[10] CPS is referred to as an epicenter of the dropout crisis.[11] As long as CPS continues to rely on suspensions, expulsions, and arrests, the more accurate way to describe CPS is as an epicenter of the pushout crisis. This pushout crisis feeds into the violence problem devastating Chicago as unaddressed conflicts in school spill over into the streets and as pushed out students turn to the street economy when educational doors close.

> According to CPS CEO Brizard, "400-plus kids were killed in this city over the past few years, and I'll be the first to tell you, I think there is a direct correlation between kids dropping out or being pushed out of school, and crime in the city."[12]

Suspensions and expulsions are ineffective at addressing behavioral, achievement, and school safety issues.[13] Independent research by education and psychology professionals has proven that:

> Suspensions and expulsions do not make schools safer and do not improve students' behavior.

- Suspensions and expulsions do not make schools safer and do not improve students' behavior.[14]
- Suspensions and expulsions have long-damaging effects on student behavior and learning.[15]
- The higher a school's rate of suspension and expulsion, the lower the academic achievement of its students — even when taking socioeconomic status out of the equation.[16]

- High levels of suspension do not make students and teachers feel safer, and, instead, can negatively affect the school environment by creating distrust.[17]
- School districts which have focused on decreasing suspensions have seen an increase in graduation rates. For example, Baltimore City Public Schools lowered suspensions from 26,000 to 10,000 and experienced an increase in their graduation rate of 20%.[18]

Using Restorative Justice in Schools

Research has proven that stronger relationships between students, staff, and parents make a school safer, even if a school is at a disadvantage in other ways,[19] and efforts focused on developing trust and respect among all in the school community are more likely to succeed.[20] Restorative justice is designed to repair and strengthen relationships, so it should be used as a tool for creating school safety.

Within the discipline context, restorative justice philosophy and practices bring together the student who misbehaved with those people who were affected in order to hold the student accountable, repair the harm that was caused, and prevent similar actions in the future by addressing needs.

Restorative justice philosophy and practices based upon it are also much more than an alternative way to respond to disciplinary infractions. Integrating restorative justice practices into the everyday school life is a critical way of improving the culture and climate of a school in order to support the social and emotional learning and the academic performance of all students and strengthen partnerships among all stakeholders.

Using restorative justice makes schools safer, improves relationships between staff, students, parents, and the community, helps to lower suspension, expulsion, and arrest rates, and provides social-emotional support, so that all can be successful. . . .

Successful Implementation of Restorative Justice in CPS

In the CPS Student Code of Conduct, the Chicago Board of Education "embraces the philosophy of restorative justice"[21] and "encourages principals and administrators to adopt and implement restorative justice philosophies and practices."[22] In addition, the Student Code of Conduct "is intended to be **instructional and corrective**, not punitive."[23] Chicago public schools that have holistically and consistently implemented restorative justice programs have seen benefits in school culture and performance paired with a decrease in violence and disciplinary issues. Restorative justice programs in CPS include circles, peer juries, and victim offender conferencing.[24]. . .

Best Practices

When the restorative justice philosophy is implemented effectively in CPS, it can be a powerful tool for avoiding suspensions, improving student achievement, and creating a safer and more peaceful school environment. According to independent research (such as that presented in the previous sections of this report), interviews conducted with restorative justice practitioners and other stakeholders, and the information gathered at the High HOPES Summit from different stakeholders, the most effective models of implementation have included:

- Commitment and buy-in from the entire school leadership team;
- A full-time position within the school, either a school employee or a community partner, to coordinate restorative justice programs, as well as the shift of school culture toward restorative principles;
- Collaboration between school leadership (including local school council members, principals, and other administrators), students, parents, and community members and partners in creating and planning for restorative justice;
- Ongoing hands-on training and technical assistance for a critical number of students, parents, community members, and school staff (including substitute teachers) in restorative justice practices;
- Space and time within the school dedicated to restorative justice practices;
- Ongoing and transparent monitoring, evaluation, and adjustment with the participation of all stakeholders, such as principals, students, parents, community members, and local school council members, and making sure there is local oversight; and
- Clear and sustained funding, support, and accountability.

Current Barriers to Implementation District-Wide

Unfortunately, through our yearlong review process, we have found that CPS' official adoption of the philosophy of restorative justice in 2006 has not translated into a sustained, system-wide effort to actually put the philosophy into practice. A number of individual schools have implemented restorative justice of their own initiative or in partnership with community-based partners with outside funding sources, but the best practices listed above are missing in CPS as a whole. Even where they do exist, restorative justice programs are sometimes marginalized, so that the whole school does not see the positive effect.

In the midst of the transition to a new CPS administration, the lack of coherent infrastructure has become even more apparent. Some schools that want to implement restorative justice are not getting a clear response on what to do or the resources with which to do it. . . . . These barriers indicate that even schools with a strong interest in restorative justice cannot appeal to CPS for effective support, while other schools can continue and are even encouraged to implement CPS-sanctioned and financed zero tolerance strategies. Therefore, all schools can continue to suspend and expel students at high rates (even if they do not want to do so). Independent research and practice (such as that presented in this report) has shown that zero tolerance strategies not only fail to make schools safer, but also bring down academic achievement and have long-damaging effects on student behavior, learning, and the school environment.

Restorative Justice Saves Money and Makes Schools Safer

We are often told that the financial woes of CPS prevent it from making commitments to new initiatives. But, shifting funds to restorative justice would mean that schools could actually become safer and save on security costs. In the 2010–2011 school year alone, the CPS central office budget gave more than $67 million to the Office of School Safety and Security to fund "school security," which included security officers, metal detectors, and surveillance cameras.[25] These $67 million did not "even include school-level spending on security."[26]

There are also huge additional costs associated with enforcing zero tolerance policies, which require significant time and resources to process tens of thousands of suspensions, expulsions, arrests, and referrals to alternative schools. Most of the $1.4 million given in 2010–2011 to the Office of Student Support and Engagement included $1.1 million to be spent on expulsion hearings, appeals, and officers.[27] In addition, the City of Chicago has "administrative costs associated with questioning, processing, charging and detaining the thousands of youth who are arrested in school every year. Moreover, because these policies contribute to Chicago's high truancy and dropout rates, they result in a loss of state and federal funding for CPS, which are based on attendance and enrollment numbers. . . . .

ENDNOTES

1. Catalyst-Chicago. (2010, September). Reaching black boys. *Catalyst in Brief,* Retrieved December 1, 2011 from http://www.catalyst-chicago.org/sites /catalyst-chicago.org/files/inbrief-blackboys.pdf.

2. Kaba, M. and Edwards, F. (2012, January). Policing Chicago Public Schools: A Gateway to the School-to-Prison Pipeline. *Project Nia.* 9, 19, 22, 23. Retrieved February 4, 2012 at http://policeinschools.files.wordpress.com/2011/12/policing -chicago-public-schools-final2.pdf.

3. Catalyst-Chicago. (2010, September).

4. Voices of Youth in Chicago Education. (2011, July). *Failed Policies, Broken Futures: The True Cost of Zero Tolerance in Chicago.* 1, 8, 9. Retrieved December 1, 2011 from http://www.publicinterestprojects.org/wp-content/uploads/downloads/2011 /08/VOYCE-report-2011.pdf. Advancement Project. (2005). Education on Lockdown: The Schoolhouse to Jailhouse Track. 31–36. Retrieved February 5, 2012 from http://www.advancementproject.org/sites/default/files/publications /FINALEOLrep.pdf.

5. Catalyst-Chicago. (2010, September).

6. Rossi, R. and Golab, A. (2012, March 6). Black students face tougher discipline in Chicago and the U.S. *Chicago Sun-Times.* Retrieved March 8, 2012 from http://www.suntimes.com/news/metro/11087696-418/black-students-face -tougher-discipline-in-chicago-and-the-us.html. U.S. Department of Education. (2011, March). Civil Rights Data Collection. Retrieved March 8, 2012 from http://ocrdata.ed.gov/.

7. St. George, D. (2012, March 5). Federal data show racial gaps in school arrests. *The Washington Post.* Retrieved March 8, 2012 from http://www .washingtonpost.com/national/federal-data-show-racial-gaps-in-school -arrests/2012/03/01/glQApbjvtR_story.html; Rossi, R. and Golab, A. (2012, March 6). Black students face tougher discipline in Chicago and the U.S. Chicago Sun-Times. Retrieved March 8, 2012 from http://www.suntimes .com/news/metro/11087696-418/black-students-face-tougher -discipline-in-chicago-and-the-us.html.

8. Losen, D. (2011, October). *Discipline Policies, Successful Schools, and Racial Justice.* Boulder, CO: National Education Policy Center. 12–13. Retrieved December 1, 2011 from http://nepc.colorado.edu/publication/discipline-policies. ACLU of Northern California. (2008, November). *Schools for All Campaign: The School Bias & Pushout Problem.* San Francisco, CA: ACLU of Northern California. 2–7.

Retrieved December 1, 2011 from http://www.aclunc.org/s4a/full_report.pdf. Himmelstein, K. and Brückner, H. (2010, December). Criminal-Justice and School Sanctions Against Nonheterosexual Youth: A National Longitudinal Study. *Pediatrics*, 127(1). 49, 55. Retrieved February 4, 2012 from http://pediatrics.aappublications.org/content/127/1/49.full.

9. Advancement Project. (2010, March). *Test, Punish, and Push Out: How "Zero Tolerance" and High-Stakes Testing Funnel Youth into the School-to-Prison Pipeline.* 5. Washington, DC: Advancement Project. Retrieved December 1, 2011 from http://www.advancement-project.org/sites/default/files/publications /rev_fin.pdf. Catalyst-Chicago. (2010, September).

10. Ahmed-Ullah, N. (2011, June 21). Making the grade—in life—despite long odds—South Side teen's story illustrates what some CPS students contend with. *Chicago Tribune.* Retrieved from http://articles.chicagotribune.com /2011-06-21/news/ct-met-cps-grad-20110621_1_cps-students-eighth-grade -graduation-guidance-counselor.

11. Swanson, C. (2010, June 2). U.S. Graduation Rate Continues Decline. *Education Week.* Retrieved December 1, 2011 from http://www.edweek.org/ew /articles/2010/06/10/34swanson.h29.html.

12. Forte, L. and Karp, S. (2011, December 7). Q&A with Jean-Claude Brizard. *Catalyst-Chicago.* Retrieved February 8, 2012 from http://www.catalyst-chicago .org/notebook/2011/12/07/19695/qa-jean-claude-brizard.

13. American Academy of Pediatrics. (2003, November). Policy Statement: Out-of-school suspension and expulsion. *Pediatrics*, 112(5), 1206–1209. Retrieved December 1, 2011 from http://aappolicy.aappublications.org/cgi/content/full /pediatrics;112/5/1206. American Psychological Association Zero Tolerance Task Force. (2008, December). Are zero tolerance policies effective in the schools? An evidentiary review and recommendations. *American Psychologist,* 63(9), 852–862. Retrieved December 1, 2011 from http://www.apa.org/pubs /info/reports/zero-tolerance.pdf. Advancement Project. (2010, March). 16–17

14. Steinberg, M., Allensworth E. & Johnson D. (2011, May). *Student and Teacher Safety in Chicago Public Schools: The Roles of Community Context and School Social Organization.* 2, 8, 33–35. Chicago, IL: Consortium on Chicago School Research at the University of Chicago Urban Education Institute. Retrieved December 5, 2011 from http://ccsr.uchicago.edu/downloads/8499safety_in _cps.pdf. American Psychological Association Zero Tolerance Task Force. (2008, December). 853–854; Legal Aid Justice Center's Just Children Program (2011, November 17). *Educate Every Child: Promoting Positive Solutions to School*

Discipline in Virginia. 7. Charlottesville, VA: Author. Retrieved December 5, 2011 from http://www.justice4all.org/sites/default/files/Educate%20Every%20 Child%20Report.pdf.

15. American Academy of Pediatrics. (2003, November). 1206–1209; American Psychological Association Zero Tolerance Task Force. (2008, December). 852–862; Advancement Project. (2010, March). 14, 16.

16. American Psychological Association Zero Tolerance Task Force. (2008, December). 854; Gregory, A., Skiba, R. and Noguera, P. (2010, January/February). The Achievement Gap and the Discipline Gap: Two Sides of the Same Coin? *Educational Researcher.* Retrieved December 9, 2011 from http://www.aera .net/uploadedfiles/publications/journals/educational_researcher/3901/059 -068_02edr10.pdf.

17. Steinberg, M., Allensworth E. & Johnson D. (2011, May). 47.

18. Rojas, R. (2011, October 6). Zero Tolerance Policies Pushing Up School Suspensions, Report Says. *Los Angeles Times.* Retrieved December 1, 2011 from http:// articles.latimes.com/2011/oct/06/local/la-me-1006-discipline-20111006. Losen, D. (2011, October).

19. Steinberg, M., Allensworth E. & Johnson D. (2011, May). 47.

20. *Id.*

21. Chicago Public Schools. (2011, September 15). *Student Code of Conduct.* 11.

22. *Id.* at 3.

23. *Id.* at 6.

24. *Id.* at 57–62, Appendix H.

25. Voices of Youth in Chicago Education. (2011, July).

26. *Id.* at 5.

27. Voices of Youth in Chicago Education. (2011, July). 21.

Starting a Conversation: Respond to "Restorative Justice in Chicago Public Schools"

In your writer's notebook, analyze the evaluation presented in the progress report by responding to the following questions:

1. What kinds of sources are included in this report? How do these sources support the credibility of the evaluation?

2. Why is it important to establish credibility in an evaluation?

3. What do you think is the primary reason this progress report includes suggestions for best practices to successfully enact restorative justice? How does this serve the purpose(s) of the report?

4. Consider the examples and reasons used to support the implementation of restorative justice. Based on the examples and reasons cited, who do you think is the intended audience for this report? Which examples and reasons lead you to this conclusion?

5. **Reflection:** Is restorative justice practiced at your school? If it is, how successful do you think it is? If it is not, did reading this article convince you that it should be used in your school? Why or why not?

How Can I Write an Evaluative Essay?

If you regularly make purchases online, you've almost certainly run into reviews on sites such as Amazon or NexTag. Chances are also good that you've turned to your local newspaper or searched the Web for help deciding which movie to watch or which new restaurant to try. It turns out that product and media reviews are both plentiful and easy to locate. That's not the case, however, for other types of evaluations. For instance, if you're hoping to learn whether it would be better to work an extra ten hours per week or take out a college loan, or if you're trying to determine whether your community should invest in renewable energy credits or start its own wind farm, you're likely to find that the best place to look for answers is in the mirror.

Evaluative essays allow you to address subjects — some as complex as genetic engineering in agriculture and others as seemingly straightforward as deciding how to travel between home and school — that connect to your personal, academic, or professional life. Like other academic essays, they also present some intriguing

GENRE TALK

| Reflective Writing | Informative Writing | Analytical Writing | **Evaluative Writing** | Problem-Solving Writing | Argumentative Writing |

Recent innovations in wearable technology and a growing range of fitness apps have yielded the next generation of technology tools for better health. As a student, you are likely juggling classes, a job, extracurricular activities, volunteer work, your social life, and maybe even a family, all while trying to stay healthy. The new smart watches, monitors, and trackers not only count your steps, measure your heart rate, monitor your sleep, and keep track of your calories but also offer GPS tracking to map your runs or bike rides and integrate smoothly with other fitness apps. This online article evaluates the Microsoft Band 2, a wearable fitness tracker, first defining what the product does ("What is it?"), then listing positive and negative features ("Like" and "No like"), and finally offering an evaluative judgment ("Should you buy it?").

LaunchPad
macmillan learning

Test your knowledge of genre with the Genre Talk quiz in the LaunchPad for *Joining the Conversation.*
launchpadworks.com

The title of the article provides an attention-grabbing summary of the writer's evaluation of the product.

Section headings divide the article, for clear and easy reading.

The comments section invites readers to extend the conversation, share their own experiences, or include links to other reviews or products.

A close-up photograph gives readers a detailed view of the product.

In Process

An Evaluative Essay about Programs to Reduce College Drinking

Dwight Haynes wrote an evaluative essay for his introductory composition course. Dwight learned about his topic by reading articles about approaches to reducing alcohol consumption by college students. Follow Dwight's efforts to write his evaluative essay by reading the In Process boxes throughout this chapter.

challenges for writers. In addition to choosing an appropriate subject for evaluation, you must identify criteria on which to base your judgment, learn enough about your subject to make an informed judgment about how well it measures up to your criteria, and convey your judgments in a well-written, well-organized, readable manner.

This section helps you tune in to the conversations around you and take on the role of evaluator as you choose a subject, conduct your evaluation, prepare your draft, and review and improve your draft. As you work on your essay, you'll follow Dwight Haynes, a first-year student who wrote an evaluative essay about approaches to reducing alcohol consumption by college students.

Find a Conversation and Listen In

Evaluative essays allow you to share your judgments with readers who will consider your conclusions seriously and, in many cases, act on your recommendations. Your decision about which conversation to join should reflect your interests and your writing assignment. For example, were you surprised by a government plan to regulate the banking industry? Are you wondering whether a promising new television show has a future? Are you skeptical about claims that a new battery technology will finally usher in the age of the electric car? If so, ask yourself what interests you most about the subject, and then start listening to what others have had to say about it.

EXPLORE YOUR NEEDS, INTERESTS, AND CONCERNS

Evaluative documents are most successful when their subject matches up with readers' needs, interests, or concerns. Readers of *Skiing* magazine, for instance, typically view the sport as an important part of their lives and are interested in new developments in equipment and techniques. An evaluation of the latest skis from Rossignol is likely to address the needs and interests of these readers, many of whom might be in the market for new equipment. Similarly, readers of the magazine might be interested in an evaluation of the effectiveness of conditioning techniques or energy bars.

Readers are also likely to read evaluative documents that address their concerns. Subscribers to *Skiing*, for example, might be concerned about the impact of climate change on skiing or about plans to allow oil shale excavation in areas near ski resorts.

Engaging and effective evaluative essays deal with subjects that address not only your readers' needs, interests, and concerns but also your own. As you consider potential subjects for your essay, ask yourself what has caught your attention lately — or better yet, what has long been a matter of interest or concern to you. And be sure to consider your current needs. If you can write about a subject that will help you address your needs, you'll be more invested in conducting the evaluation. To explore your needs, interests, and concerns, cast a wide net. Use idea-generating strategies such as brainstorming, freewriting, or clustering (see pp. 41–44) to respond to questions like these:

- **Products.** Take an inventory of your personal interests, such as hobbies, outdoor activities, or sports. What new products have been introduced lately? Are you thinking of buying (or have you bought) any of them? Are they truly useful, or has the manufacturer overhyped them? Would you recommend them to others?

- **Media.** What's new and interesting in books, movies, television, music, video games, or the Web? What have you read, watched, or listened to that made you think? Have you noticed any developments that trouble you? Have you heard or read criticisms that you think are unfair?

- **Campus life.** Are you thinking about joining a club, team, or group but can't decide if it's worth your time? Do your peers engage in any behaviors that seem dangerous or unhealthy to you? Have you attended a guest lecture or student performance that you felt was overrated or underappreciated? Has a new building or work of public art sparked controversy?

Working Together: Try It Out Loud

Before you conduct an evaluation, start a conversation with your classmates about the advantages and disadvantages of majoring in a particular subject. Form small groups and choose a subject area to evaluate, such as English, history, business, psychology, chemistry, math, art, or sociology. As a group, identify the kinds of criteria you will use to evaluate each major, such as personal rewards, academic challenges, skill development, or future employment opportunities. Then take turns applying the criteria to your major (or the major that currently interests you most) while the other members of the group listen, respond, and ask questions. After everyone has had a chance to speak, revisit your criteria. Were they useful in helping you evaluate the majors? Would you consider changing these criteria?

If you are doing this activity during class, share your conclusions about your criteria with other groups. Then, as a class, take a few minutes to reflect on the exercise. Did every group use the same criteria? If not, what might account for the differences?

- **Ideas.** Have you been worried or intrigued by a new development you read about in a professional or trade journal? Have you heard an unusual proposal for a new public policy or business incentive? How have you responded to the different teaching methods you've encountered in your high school and college classes? What do you make of conflicting arguments in your course readings?

You'll find additional ideas for evaluative writing projects at the end of this chapter (p. 339).

SEARCH THE WEB

The World Wide Web is a rich source of information and ideas for writers conducting evaluations. Product and media reviews are among the most popular items on the Web, and online editions of newspapers and magazines offer a seemingly endless collection of commentary and critique on everything from the latest diets to pending legislation to new techniques for studying and taking exams. If you're interested in whether professional soccer has a future in the United States, for example, you could find data and opinions on websites such as SoccerTimes.com and USSoccer.com, check out developments reported in the sports sections of newspapers that have a Web presence, and read the online versions of magazines such as *SoccerAmerica* and *90:00*. To search for information and evaluations for just about any subject that intrigues you, consult the following Web search resources.

General web search The easiest way to learn about a subject through the Web is to visit an established search site, such as Google (google.com), Ask (ask.com), Bing (Bing.com), or Yahoo! (yahoo.com). In response to your keywords and phrases, these sites present ranked lists of sites they judge relevant to your search terms. These sites also provide advanced search forms that allow you to specify which keywords and phrases must, might, or should not appear on a page; to limit search results to particular domains such as .gov or .org; and to limit your search to websites updated within a specific time period, such as the last week or month.

Meta search Meta search sites, such as Dogpile (dogpile.com) and WebCrawler (webcrawler.com), allow you to conduct a single search and return results from several Web search sites at the same time. These sites typically search leading general search sites and directories and then present a limited number of results on a single page.

News search To conduct focused searches for current and archived news reports, try sites such as Google News (http://news.google.com) and Digg (digg.com).

Reference search Sites such as Encyclopedia.com (encyclopedia.com) and Information Please (infoplease.com) allow you to search for information that has been collected in encyclopedias, almanacs, atlases, dictionaries, and other reference resources.

Media search   The Web is home not only to textual information but also to a growing collection of other types of media, such as photographs, podcasts, and streaming video. You can locate useful information about your subject by searching for recordings of radio broadcasts, television shows, documentaries, podcasts, and other media using established search sites, such as Ask, Google, and Yahoo!, as well as specialized sites such as YouTube (www.youtube.com) for video, Picsearch (www .picsearch.com) for images, and Find Sounds (www.findsounds.com) for audio.

You can learn more about searching the Web in Chapter 13.

In Process

Searching the Web

Dwight Haynes learned about promising subjects by searching for information on the Web.

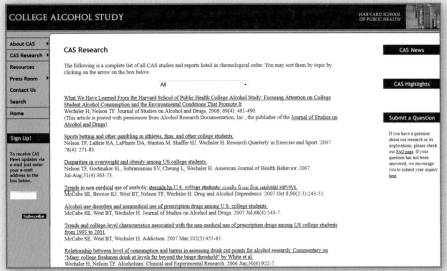

Dwight used the search terms *alcohol* and *college*. He found several journal articles on the Harvard School of Public Health's College Alcohol Study website.

Dwight used a search engine to look for websites with keywords such as *alcohol, higher education, drinking, college, students*, and *awareness*. His searches allowed him to identify and locate enough sources that he was able to get a good initial understanding of the subject. Because he was particularly interested in how colleges respond to student drinking, he decided to download a study written by E. R. Weitzman and her colleagues at the Harvard School of Public Health, who had found correlations between a particular type of alcohol prevention campaign — the environmental approach — and reduced alcohol consumption among students.

NARROW YOUR FOCUS BY ASKING QUESTIONS

As you learn about possible subjects for your evaluation, use the following questions to identify which ones capture your interest and best meet the needs of your assignment. Each question focuses your attention on a subject in a different way, and each provides a useful starting point for an evaluative essay. Depending on the subject, you'll find that some questions are more relevant than others.

- **Importance.** Do you think this is an important subject? If so, why? Who else believes that it's important? Why do they believe that it's important? What would readers do with an evaluation of this subject?

- **Appropriateness.** What aspects of this topic lend themselves to evaluation? Do you have the resources and the time to learn about it and examine it closely?

- **Effectiveness.** Is _____ an effective response to _____? Is it designed well? Is it likely to produce the intended results?

- **Costs/benefits.** What are the benefits of _____? What are the costs? Are the benefits worth the costs?

In Process

Focusing on a Subject

Dwight Haynes brainstormed in response to the questions above about a subject he was considering for his evaluative essay: binge drinking among college students. As he asked and answered questions, two promising focuses emerged: the costs and benefits that college students associate with drinking and the effectiveness of different approaches to reducing drinking on college campuses.

> Costs: delayed graduation, failure to graduate, health problems, social problems (losing friends), poorer academic performance/lower GPA, less learning (just getting by)
>
> Benefits: fun, relaxation, less difficult to talk with people, being part of the group, looking cool
>
> Effectiveness of approaches for stopping or reducing drinking:
>
> — education (might work)
>
> — punishment/prevention (hasn't worked very well)
>
> — alternative activities (might work for some)

Dwight used two sets of questions to guide his brainstorming. He generated lists of ideas in response to each approach.

After reviewing the results of his brainstorming, Dwight decided that it would be difficult to evaluate the costs and benefits of drinking. Instead, he chose to focus on the effectiveness of approaches to reducing drinking on campus.

- **Prevailing opinion.** How have others responded to this subject? How did they reach their conclusions? What have they neglected to consider?

Conduct Your Evaluation

Far too many evaluators tell readers little more than "this is good (or bad or ineffective or the best choice) because I say so." It's as if these writers believe that readers will accept their conclusions without question or doubt.

As a reader, when was the last time you did that?

If you're like most readers, you probably expect evaluators to provide sound reasoning and appropriate evidence to back up their judgments. As a writer, you should strive to offer the same things to your readers. The judgments you reach in your evaluation should move beyond knee-jerk reactions or general pronouncements. For example, rather than saying a baseball manager should be fired merely because the team failed to win the division, you should also consider the quality of players available throughout the season, the strength of the competition, and the decisions made during key games.

An effective evaluative essay is based on a clear understanding of your subject, a carefully chosen set of criteria, and well-supported judgments — first, about how well the subject of your evaluation meets each criterion and, second, about the overall results of your evaluation. As you conduct your evaluation, start by choosing a set of criteria that is relevant and clearly defined. Then review what you've learned about your subject, and consider whether you've collected enough evidence to make an informed judgment. Finally, use your criteria and evidence to make your judgments, making an effort to ensure that your evaluation is balanced and fair.

DEFINE YOUR CRITERIA

Criteria are the factors on which your judgments about a subject are based. In many written conversations, criteria are well established. Movie reviewers, for example, typically base their judgments on plot, characterization, cinematography, editing, and directing, while restaurant reviewers tend to use criteria such as the taste and presentation of the food, the attentiveness and courteousness of the waitstaff, the cleanliness and attractiveness of the restaurant, and the cost of a meal. Similarly, writers of progress reports tend to focus on a fairly consistent set of criteria, most often results, responses to unexpected challenges, and cost-effectiveness.

Even when evaluating well-established subjects, however, writers often depart from the norm. A movie reviewer might focus on the use of product placement in a film, while a music reviewer might draw criteria from poetry or drama to evaluate a new rap album.

Often, you will have the option of choosing among a wide range of evaluative criteria. Consider, for example, the criteria you might use to evaluate competing health plans for employees at a small company:

- overall cost to the company
- cost per employee to participate in the plan
- deductibles
- coverage
- choice of health care providers
- ease of access to plan information
- access to plan administrators
- required paperwork
- speed of reimbursement to employees

If you chose all these criteria, your evaluation would be quite lengthy. To keep the evaluation brief and to the point — and, of course, useful for readers — you would focus on fewer criteria. If you were creating a brief overview of competing health care plans for managers, you might focus on overall cost to the company, employee costs, coverage, required paperwork, and access to plan administrators. If you were creating a report for employees, on the other hand, criteria might include employee costs, deductibles, coverage, choice of health care providers, ease of access to plan information, and speed of reimbursement. The key is to choose those criteria most relevant to your subject, your purpose, and the needs, interests, and backgrounds of your readers.

IDENTIFY EVIDENCE

Evidence provides evaluators with a basis for making their judgments. Evaluative essays tend to rely on a mix of evidence from published sources, observations, and personal experience.

Some evidence is quantitative — that is, it can be measured. For instance, the rate of inflation over the past decade or the number of people participating in a noon-time activity program can be found through sources such as public documents or direct observation. Other evidence is qualitative — that is, it is based on the writer's experiences with and reactions to the subject. Music reviewers, for example, usually base their evaluations on the originality of the music, the quality of the performance, and the quality of the recording and production. Some criteria, such as cost, can be judged on both quantitative and qualitative evidence. For instance, you can calculate the amount of money that would be required to pay for a particular program or solution, but you can also view cost in terms of its impact on quality of life or on the environment.

To identify evidence for your evaluation, list the criteria you'll use to conduct your evaluation. Determine whether each criterion will rely on quantitative or qualitative evidence. Then pinpoint potential sources of evidence for your evaluation by reviewing your initial research and any notes you've taken. Next to each criterion, list the evidence on which you'll base your judgments. If you find that you don't have enough evidence to support a thorough evaluation, look for more information.

MAKE YOUR JUDGMENTS

Once you've identified and organized your evidence, you're ready to determine how well your subject measures up to the criteria you've selected. The quality of your judgments depends not only on the number and kinds of criteria you've defined and the amount and types of evidence you've collected but also on your commitment to being fair and reasonable. If you are applying quantitative evidence to a small number of criteria, making your judgments might be a fairly straightforward process. However, if you are making multiple judgments on the basis of qualitative evidence, it might take significantly more time and effort to complete your evaluation. The challenge you face in making your judgments will also depend on how much impact your decision has on your life or the lives of others. For example, weighing which of three job offers to accept is of far greater consequence than comparing the features and costs of two video game systems.

To make judgments about your subject, list your criteria and examine the evidence you've assembled. Write down your judgments in as much detail as possible so that you can draw on them as you draft your essay.

Prepare a Draft

Writers of evaluative essays focus on conveying the results of their evaluation processes to their readers. As you prepare your draft, you'll decide how to convey the overall result of your evaluation, present and define your criteria, share the evidence on which you've based your judgments, design your essay, and frame your evaluation for your readers.

In Process

Making Judgments

For his evaluation of approaches to reducing college drinking, Dwight Haynes selected two criteria: the overall effectiveness of programs that used a particular approach and the effort required to create programs based on an approach. To sort through his notes and decide what information would best support his evaluation, he created a table that identified possible evidence for his criteria as they applied to two competing approaches and then made preliminary judgments about each approach.

Approach	Criterion	Evidence	Judgment
Social norms	Effort	Relatively low effort. Turner says it focuses on marketing and education, using ads on Facebook, campus posters, etc.	Easy to start and maintain without tons of work.
	Effectiveness	Some research raises concerns about effectiveness (Wechsler et al.), but DeJong et al. found it associated with lower perceptions of student drinking levels and lower alcohol consumption.	Effective. Good choice for smaller schools or those without the resources for another approach.
Environmental	Effort	Larger and more ambitious than social norms programs. Includes collaborations with local law enforcement agencies, the local business community, and local health care providers (Weitzman et al.).	Complex, but justified by effectiveness.
	Effectiveness	Effective because it addresses more of the factors involved in student drinking (Weitzman et al. and Dowdall interview).	Most effective.

Your draft will be strongly influenced by the purpose of your evaluation. If your intention is to help readers understand whether something has succeeded or failed, for example, consider how your readers will react to your judgments. If you are arguing that a project has failed, you might want to discuss whether the project should be carried out with specific changes or whether it should be abandoned altogether. If you are offering your judgments about which of several options is best, you might want to discuss the trade-offs associated with accepting your judgment. And if you are trying to help readers understand how your subject might be improved or refined, you might want to include guidance about how to put those improvements or refinements into practice.

STATE YOUR OVERALL JUDGMENT

The goal of an evaluative essay is to share your judgment about a subject, often with the intention of helping readers make a decision. It's usually a good idea, then, to give readers a summary of your overall judgment — your verdict — in the form of a thesis statement. In some cases, you'll want to mention the criteria on which your judgment is based so that readers understand the thinking behind your evaluation. Your thesis statement can also frame your subject in a way that helps achieve your purpose and address the needs and interests of your readers. Consider, for example, how the following thesis statements about locally grown produce set up different expectations among readers.

> **Thesis statement 1:** Buying your fruits and vegetables at a farmer's market might be a little less convenient and a little more expensive than going to the supermarket, but you'll be rewarded with healthier, tastier food.

> **Thesis statement 2:** Importing fruits and vegetables carries hidden environmental costs that outweigh the benefits of having year-round access to seasonal produce.

> **Thesis statement 3:** By insisting on produce that has been grown nearby, consumers can support family farms and have a positive impact on their local economies.

Each of these thesis statements focuses on different aspects of the same subject. The first one emphasizes consumer concerns about price, convenience, and quality. The second thesis statement directs attention to the environmental consequences of shipping food long distances. The third one points to the economic benefits of supporting local businesses. These thesis statements would lead to quite different evaluative essays.

Where you place your thesis statement depends largely on your understanding of your readers' needs and interests. Sharing your overall judgment at the beginning

Is your thesis statement focused enough? See Chapter 16 for help.

of the essay allows readers to follow the logic of your evaluation process and better understand how the criteria and evidence relate to the evaluation's overall result. However, if your overall judgment is likely to be seen as unusual or controversial, it might be best to share it later in the essay, after allowing evidence to unfold in a way that helps readers understand the reasons underlying your conclusions.

PRESENT YOUR EVALUATION

To be effective, your evaluative essay must do more than present a straightforward report of criteria, evidence, and judgments. It should help readers understand your subject in a particular way and show them that you've chosen appropriate criteria and evidence. Equally important, your essay should prove to your readers that you've based your judgments on sound and thorough reasoning and that you've conducted a balanced evaluation.

Explain your criteria Criteria are an essential part of any evaluation (see p. 321). Your readers should understand not only what your criteria are but also why you've selected them. In some cases, you can rely on general knowledge to supply the rationale for your choice of one or more of your criteria. If you were evaluating an advertising campaign for a new soft drink, for example, you could probably rely on a widespread understanding that sales figures are an important factor in the evaluation. Similarly, you wouldn't need to justify your use of nutrition and weight loss in an evaluation of diet programs.

In most cases, however, you should define your criteria explicitly. For example, if you were evaluating a new state program that encourages high school students to take additional driver education courses after receiving their licenses, you might use criteria such as teenagers' willingness to sign up for the courses and the effectiveness of the program. But how would you define a criterion such as effectiveness? In the context of continuing education courses for newly licensed drivers, it might mean lowering the number of accidents attributable to inexperience, or preventing injuries or deaths associated with teenage drivers, or increasing drivers' awareness of the problems caused by distraction or impatience, or some combination of these factors. Your readers should understand how you've defined your criteria so that they can follow — and, ideally, accept — your evaluation.

Support your judgments with evidence Providing evidence to explain the reasoning behind your judgments helps readers accept your evaluation as valid and carefully thought out. Evidence can also help deepen your discussion of the overall results of your evaluation. In general, you'll want to apply evidence to each of your criteria to show readers how your subject measures up. You can also use evidence to

- introduce your subject
- define your criteria
- provide examples and illustrations
- associate particular ideas and concepts with authorities, such as political leaders, subject-matter experts, or people who have been affected by your subject

In Process

Using Evidence to Support Judgments

Dwight Haynes drew on information and opinions from his sources to support his judgment that the social norms marketing approach to reducing alcohol consumption among college students is not as effective as it might seem.

> The environmental approach involves a mix of strategies designed to reduce or eliminate alcohol consumption, using the resources of both the campus community and the surrounding town or city. According to Weitzman et al. (2004), "Drinking-related norms and behaviors result from interactions over time and space between individuals and their environments" (p. 188). By changing the "contextual forces," like availability of alcohol, that encourage students to drink, this approach more strongly emphasizes policies that directly put a stop to excessive drinking — unlike the social norms marketing approach, which relies on influencing individual behavior (p. 187). As George W. Dowdall, author of *College Drinking: Reframing a Social Problem*, has argued, "Informational approaches used alone simply don't work. Trying to deal with college drinking as only an individual's choice doesn't work either. Instead, colleges should try to shape the entire environment that shapes college drinking" (as cited in Jaschik, 2009). By cracking down on when and how alcohol is available on campus, and by taking steps to keep underage students from accessing alcohol off campus, colleges that adopt the environmental approach tend to be more successful in decreasing the overall rate of student drinking and the negative consequences that can come from excessive alcohol use.

Dwight cites information from a journal article, identified by the authors' names. He includes the page on which the quotation can be found.

An expert is identified in an attribution.

Using APA style, Dwight notes that one source is cited in another.

Whether you draw your evidence from print, broadcast, or digital sources or from field research, be sure to identify your sources. Evaluative essays typically rely on citation systems such as those provided by the Modern Language Association and the American Psychological Association to identify sources. If you are unsure about which citation system to use, consult your instructor. (You can read more about how to use evidence to support your evaluation in Chapter 21.)

Be fair To be effective, your evaluation must be fair. The notion of fairness is sometimes confused with objectivity. In fact, being truly objective is difficult — and perhaps impossible. Each writer approaches an evaluation with a particular set of experiences, values, and beliefs that leads to a particular outlook on a subject. These differences among writers — even the most disciplined and rigorous — lead to minor and sometimes major differences in their judgments, even when they work with the same criteria and evidence. Being fair and reasonable, as a result, does not necessarily mean coming to the same conclusion as another writer. Instead, it means taking the time to consider different points of view, weighing evidence carefully, and being as consistent in your judgments as possible.

One way to ensure fairness is to provide a context for your evaluation. By making it clear to your readers what you've evaluated, what you've considered during the evaluation process, and how you've approached the evaluation process, you can help them understand how and why you've come to your conclusions. If a reviewer has concerns about the size of a new phone, for example, she might point out that she has small hands or that she prefers to send texts using one hand. By providing context, you'll increase the likelihood that your readers will view your evaluation as sound and well supported.

Working Together: Ask Whether Your Judgments Are Fair

Use feedback from other writers to assess the fairness of your judgments. Describe your subject, briefly define your criteria, present your evidence, and discuss your judgments. The other members of the group should pose reasonable questions about your choice of criteria, selection of evidence, and judgments, paying particular attention to the reasonableness of your judgments. Whenever possible, they should also suggest alternative judgments. Take notes on the doubts expressed by other members of the group so that you can consider them during revision.

CONSIDER GENRE AND DESIGN

Like other academic essays, evaluative essays can benefit from thoughtful consideration of design. Bear in mind your readers' expectations about design elements such as wide margins, double-spaced lines, page numbers, and a readable body font. In addition, consider the benefits of using headings and subheadings and bulleted and numbered lists.

- **Headings and subheadings** can help readers understand the organization of the essay, serve as transitional devices between sections and subsections, and add visual interest to what would otherwise be pages of unbroken text.

- **Numbered and bulleted lists** display brief passages of related information using numbers or symbols (usually round "bullets"). The surrounding white space draws the eye to the list, highlighting the information for your readers, while the brief content in each entry can make concepts or processes easier to understand.

These design elements can make significant contributions to the readability and overall effectiveness of your essay. Headings and subheadings identify and briefly summarize the sections of your essay, helping readers compare the judgments you've made in different sections of your essay. Numbered and bulleted lists allow you to present evidence or a series of judgments about a subject in a compact form. If you use similar lists — for example, of strengths and weaknesses or of costs and benefits — in different sections of your essay, readers will find it easier to locate and compare the lists.

You can find discussions of document design in Chapters 18, 19, and 20.

FRAME YOUR EVALUATION

The choices you make as you structure your essay will affect how your readers understand and interpret your evaluation. Your strategies for organizing, introducing, and concluding your essay should take into account your purposes — for example, whether you are assessing success and failure or making a recommendation, and what you hope readers will do after they've read your essay — as well as your readers' needs and interests. They should also take into account your criteria and the nature and amount of evidence you've assembled to support your judgments.

Organization To decide how to organize your criteria, evidence, and judgments, create an outline or a map (see p. 542). Most evaluative essays are organized either according to the items that are being evaluated or by the criteria used to evaluate them. If you are evaluating a single item, such as a proposed change to class registration procedures or the performance of a musical group on a recently released album, you are likely to present your evaluation as a series of judgments, applying one criterion after another to your subject. If you are evaluating more than one item, you can use your criteria to organize your discussion, or you can discuss each item in turn. Evaluative essays can also employ several of the organizing patterns discussed in Chapter 17, such as comparison and contrast, costs and benefits, or strengths and weaknesses.

Introduction Most evaluative essays begin with some explanation of the context and a description of the subject. In some cases, your readers will be unfamiliar with particular aspects of the subject — or even with the subject as a whole. For example, if you are evaluating a new technology for distributing movies online, your readers will probably appreciate a brief discussion of how it works. Similarly, if you are reviewing a movie, it can help to provide some details about its plot, characters, and setting — although not, of course, its ending or surprising plot twists. Once you've established the parameters of your evaluation and decided how to frame your introduction, you can use a range of strategies to put it into words, including asking questions, leading with a quotation, or telling a story. You can read more about strategies for introducing your essay in Chapter 18.

Conclusion Your conclusion offers an opportunity to highlight or even to present the overall results of your evaluation. If you've already presented your overall results in the form of a thesis statement earlier in the essay, you might use your conclusion to reiterate your main judgment or to make a recommendation for your readers. You can also turn to other strategies to conclude your essay, such as linking to your introduction, asking a question, or speculating about the future. Chapter 18 provides more strategies for using your conclusion to frame the results of your evaluation.

Review and Improve Your Draft

Writing a successful evaluative essay depends on choosing an appropriate subject, considering your writing situation, selecting appropriate criteria and evidence, making fair judgments, and deciding how to frame and organize your evaluation. Don't be surprised if your first draft doesn't successfully address all of these challenges: few first drafts do. Instead, take advantage of the opportunity to revise. As you review your draft, pay particular attention to your choice of criteria, your selection of evidence, and the fairness of your judgments.

REVIEW YOUR CRITERIA

Once you've written a first draft, read it carefully. Then step back and ask questions about your criteria. Ask whether you've used enough — or too many — criteria (generally, evaluative essays include between two and five). Most important, ask whether you've considered the most significant criteria. For example, an evaluation of competing approaches to funding intercollegiate athletic programs that doesn't consider the impact of those approaches on tuition and fees is missing an important criterion.

RECONSIDER YOUR EVIDENCE

Good criteria and reasonable judgments are the heart of an effective evaluative essay, but they are seldom sufficient to convince readers to accept your point of view. Presenting an evaluation — even a careful one — that lacks well-chosen evidence is like telling your readers, "Look. I'm really smart, and I'm making good judgments. Trust me." Few readers, of course, give their trust so easily. As you review your essay, ask whether you've provided enough evidence to support your judgments. Then ask whether you've chosen the right evidence. As you conduct your review, make sure that you haven't relied so heavily on a single source of evidence that it appears as though you're simply borrowing someone else's evaluation. Try to draw evidence from multiple sources, such as published documents and personal experience.

ENSURE THAT YOUR JUDGMENTS ARE FAIR AND REASONABLE

The most important question you can ask about your evaluative essay is whether your judgments are well grounded and convincing. Individual judgments should reflect the criteria and evidence you've presented to your readers. And your overall conclusion should reflect your judgments as a whole. If your judgments do not line up with your criteria and evidence, your readers will question your conclusions. Similarly, if your judgments are based on poorly chosen criteria or inadequate evidence, your readers will also question your conclusions. On the other hand, if your readers see your criteria as appropriate and your judgments as reasonable and well supported, they'll be far more likely to act on your evaluation.

Peer Review: Improve Your Evaluative Essay

One of the biggest challenges writers face is reading a draft of their own work as a reader rather than as the writer. Because you know what you're trying to say, you find it easy to understand your draft. To determine how you should revise your draft, ask a friend or classmate to read your essay and consider how well you've adopted the role of evaluator (see p. 286).

Purpose	1. What subject does the essay address? Is it a subject that readers will need or want to know about? 2. Does the thesis statement clearly convey an overall judgment? 3. What role does this essay take on? Is it recommending improvements or making a final judgment?
Readers	4. Did you find the essay interesting? Why or why not? 5. Does the evaluation address my readers' needs, interests, and backgrounds? 6. Do the criteria seem appropriate for the subject? Did I use too many criteria? Too few? Should I add or remove any criteria?
Sources	7. Have I provided enough evidence to support my judgments? Too much? 8. Have I relied on a particular source — or a particular type of source — too heavily? 9. Do my sources strike you as reliable and appropriate? Does any of the evidence I've used seem questionable?
Context	10. Have I provided enough information about the subject? About my reasons for evaluating it? 11. Do the judgments made in the essay seem fair? Did you detect any bias or agenda in the way I presented my evaluation? Do you know of any alternative points of view that I should take into consideration? 12. Is the physical appearance of my essay appropriate? Should I consider adding headings or lists?

For each of the points listed above, ask your reviewers to provide concrete advice about what you should do to improve your draft. It can help if you ask them to adopt the role of an editor — someone who is working with you to improve your draft. You can read more about peer review in Chapter 5.

✳ Student Essay

Dwight Haynes, "Making Better Choices: Two Approaches to Reducing College Drinking"

The following evaluative essay was written by featured writer Dwight Haynes. Dwight's essay follows the requirements of the sixth edition of the *APA Publication Manual*. However, this edition does not include specific instructions for formatting student essays, so Dwight's essay has been formatted to fit typical requirements for undergraduate student writing.

MAKING BETTER CHOICES   1

Making Better Choices: Two Approaches to Reducing College Drinking
Dwight Haynes
CO150 College Composition
Professor Palmquist
March 20, 2016

A cover page provides the essay title and information about the writer, class, and submission date.

MAKING BETTER CHOICES 2

Making Better Choices: Two Approaches to Reducing College Drinking

> The writer contrasts humorous depictions of college drinking with sobering statistics about drinking-related deaths, injuries, and crimes.

Over the past few decades, alcohol consumption among college students has received a great deal of attention. Despite humorous portrayals of college parties and the drunken antics depicted in movies and on television, serious concerns have been raised about health, safety, and academic issues associated with heavy drinking on campus. Most alarming, excessive levels of drinking are thought to cause between 1,400 and 1,700 student deaths each year (Jaschik, 2009). Also significant are the physical harm and violent behavior that tend to arise from heavy drinking: 500,000 students each year sustain injuries as a result of alcohol use, and another 600,000 per year report being victims of alcohol-fueled assaults,

> Following APA style, source information is cited in parentheses.

including rape (Wechsler et al., 2003). Heavy drinking has been blamed for a host of other problems as well, including vandalism, alcohol poisoning, and academic failure. Rather than waiting until after students suffer the consequences of alcohol abuse to intervene, colleges have found that preventative programs can teach better habits and help students avoid the problems caused by underage or irresponsible drinking. What kinds of approaches are colleges using to reduce student drinking, and how well do they work?

> The writer identifies and defines the two leading approaches that he will evaluate.

Two current strategies being tried on college campuses are the social norms marketing approach and the environmental approach. The *social norms marketing* approach assumes that college students drink heavily because they think everyone else does it. Supporters of this approach argue that telling students about normal drinking behaviors, typically through mass marketing campaigns, will lead them to drink less (Turner, Perkins, & Bauerle, 2008). The *environmental* approach focuses on changing the factors within the campus and community—like discount drink specials at local bars and inconsistent enforcement of underage drinking laws—that may encourage college students

> An overview of the essay is provided.

to drink (Weitzman, Nelson, Lee, & Wechsler, 2004). Supporters of the environmental approach believe that students are unlikely to change their behavior in an environment that supports harmful levels of drinking. This essay will look at each of these approaches in turn, examining their effectiveness by

> The evaluation criteria—effectiveness and ease of implementation—are introduced and defined.

comparing the reported rates of student drinking and harmful consequences after each approach is used, and by considering how easily their strategies can be implemented.

MAKING BETTER CHOICES 3

The Social Norms Marketing Approach

The social norms marketing approach is based on the theory that correcting a person's misperceptions will lead to a change in behavior (Turner et al., 2008). This approach is popular and relatively easy to implement, since it focuses largely on standard education and marketing techniques — something colleges and universities are well equipped to provide (Turner et al., 2008). DeJong et al. (2006) found that, when done with pervasive and consistent marketing messages, social norms campaigns were associated not only with lower perceptions of student drinking levels but also with lower alcohol consumption. Turner et al. (2008) used posters, Facebook ads, student newspaper articles, and e-mails over the course of six years to inform students at one college how often their fellow students consumed alcohol (and how much), as well as how often they showed "protective behaviors" like helping friends avoid driving while drunk (p. 86). Between 2001 and 2005, the percentage of students who reported experiencing negative consequences of drinking, like performing poorly in class or being the victim of assault, dropped significantly (Turner et al., 2008). Likewise, DeJong et al. (2006) found that social norms marketing campaigns at 18 colleges and universities across the country provided a "meaningful . . . effect," with students consuming fewer drinks per week and at parties than before the campaign (p. 878). These results indicate that students absorbed the social norms messages put forth by their schools, and although they didn't stop drinking entirely, they did change their behavior to match their perceptions of other students' drinking habits.

However, Wechsler et al. (2003) analyzed trends at schools using social norms marketing and revealed that the campaigns did not necessarily decrease student drinking; in some cases, schools even reported higher alcohol consumption, according to seven criteria that measured whether students drank, how much, and how often. The team of the Harvard School of Public Health's College Alcohol Study suggested that because social norms marketing was first developed at a small school that wasn't very diverse, it might not be as suitable for schools with many different kinds of people. As the researchers explained, "Individual student's drinking behaviors align more closely to the drinking behaviors of their immediate social group rather than to the overall student population at a given school" (p. 492). Students at larger schools, then, might

---

A heading is set off from body text using bold formatting.

A source is cited using APA style.

A partial quotation indicates that the phrase is taken from the source named in the attribution. The page number of the quotation is provided.

An evaluation of the effectiveness of the approach is provided.

A summary of contrasting evidence is provided, indicating that the approach might not be effective at all schools.

A quotation conveys conclusions offered by the researchers who conducted the study. The page number is provided.

MAKING BETTER CHOICES   4

The writer offers his interpretation of the results of the study.

not be as receptive to the social norms marketing approach as other studies indicated, especially if their personal experience contradicts the messages distributed in a campaign.

Additional information is offered regarding the potential positive effects of the approach.

Unexpected factors may also complicate the perceived success of social norms marketing campaigns. One study noted that campaigns at several schools resulted in only "relatively small changes in [heavy] drinking behavior, from a 1.1% decrease to a 10.6% increase" over three years, while a control group of schools not using any kind of alcohol prevention experienced surprising increases in heavy drinking — between 17.5% and 24.7% (DeJong et al., 2006, p. 877). Although social norms marketing in this case did not appear to reduce consumption, the fact that alcohol use increased so much in the control group indicates that the social norms marketing may have served to keep drinking levels steady at schools that might have otherwise experienced a similar jump in alcohol use.

An overall judgment on the approach is provided.

Given this evidence, it seems clear that social norms marketing is not a one-size-fits-all solution. Students might ignore statistics and facts in social norms advertisements because they don't believe the ads represent the peers whose opinions they care about most. But for smaller schools looking to curb heavy drinking and its consequences, social norms marketing might be a good strategy, especially where colleges want to change student behavior without making significant changes to school or community alcohol policies.

The Environmental Approach

A detailed definition of the second approach is provided.

The environmental approach involves a mix of strategies designed to reduce or eliminate alcohol consumption, using the resources of both the campus community and the surrounding town or city. According to Weitzman et al. (2004), "Drinking-related norms and behaviors result from interactions over time and space between individuals and their environments" (p. 188). By changing the "contextual forces," like availability of alcohol, that encourage students to drink, this approach more strongly emphasizes policies that directly put a stop to excessive drinking — unlike the social norms marketing approach, which relies on influencing individual behavior (p. 187). As George W. Dowdall, author of *College Drinking: Reframing a Social Problem*, has argued, "Informational approaches used alone simply don't work. Trying to deal with college drinking as only an

MAKING BETTER CHOICES   5

individual's choice doesn't work either. Instead, colleges should try to shape the entire environment that shapes college drinking" (as cited in Jaschik, 2009). By cracking down on when and how alcohol is available on campus, and by taking steps to keep underage students from accessing alcohol off campus, colleges that adopt the environmental approach tend to be more successful in decreasing the overall rate of student drinking and the negative consequences that can come from excessive alcohol use.

> Following APA style, information cited in a source is identified using the phrase "as cited in."

One drawback of the environmental approach is that it can be more time-consuming and difficult to implement than social norms marketing, as it relies on the cooperation of campus administrators, faculty, community members, law enforcement, and business owners in enforcing sometimes unpopular changes in alcohol policies. However, Dowdall pointed out that harmful levels of drinking among students already result in arrests and disciplinary actions, which involve community and campus resources after the fact (as cited in Jaschik, 2009). Instead of using these resources in reaction to drinking-related problems, schools and towns that adopt an environmental approach can use them proactively to prevent problems from happening in the first place.

> A weakness of the approach is considered in light of the implementation criterion.

> A summary of a source provides evidence about the effectiveness of the approach.

In fact, research suggests that environmental changes are needed for consistent and lasting change in student drinking levels. Weitzman et al. (2004) looked at an environmental approach program that decreased the availability and appeal of alcohol at several colleges through many different, simultaneous methods like police enforcement of party regulations, substance-free residence halls, and parental notification for alcohol-related violations. The team found that significantly fewer students experienced drinking-related problems, like missed classes and alcohol-fueled fights, after the program was implemented. Just as important, and in contrast with the results of some social norms marketing programs, students across the sample also reported lower amounts of drinking overall. The study looked at public and private colleges of different sizes across the nation, showing that the environmental approach works for a range of different student populations (Weitzman et al., 2004). Environmental changes reach beyond the individual student to shape the community as a whole, making sure that the campus and its surroundings are not contributing to the problem of student drinking but helping to solve it.

> The conclusion focuses on the higher level of overall effectiveness of the environmental approach, despite the complexities involved with its implementation.

MAKING BETTER CHOICES 6

Conclusions

While social norms marketing appears to offer a strong combination of positive outcomes and ease of implementation, the environmental approach is more effective overall. Despite being more complicated and demanding more school and community resources, it delivers stronger results by involving students' entire college community. The environmental approach has a much greater scope than that of the social norms marketing approach and is suitable for schools of all sizes and types. Therefore, it has the potential to affect not only students who drink heavily because they think that's the normal thing to do but also students who either are unaware of the dangers of using alcohol or will moderate their drinking only in the face of severe consequences for not doing so. Given appropriate resources, a program based on the environmental approach to curb heavy drinking is likely to be the best choice.

> Following APA style, the list of works cited is titled "References."

> Entries in the list are formatted with hanging indents.

> A news article retrieved from the Web

> Journal article

> A journal article with a Digital Object Identifier (DOI)

References

DeJong, W., Schneider, S. K., Towvim, L. G., Murphy, M. J., Doerr, E. E., Simonsen, . . . Scribner, R. A. (2006). A multisite randomized trial of social norms marketing campaigns to reduce college student drinking. *Journal of Studies on Alcohol, 67*(6), 868-879.

Jaschik, S. (2009, February 26). College drinking: Reframing a social problem. *Inside Higher Ed*. Retrieved from http://www.insidehighered.com/

Turner, J., Perkins, H. W., & Bauerle, J. (2008). Declining negative consequences related to alcohol misuse among students exposed to a social norms marketing intervention on a college campus. *Journal of American College Health, 57*(1), 85-93. doi:10.3200/JACH.57.1.85-94

Wechsler, H., Nelson, T. F., Lee, J. E., Seibring, M., Lewis, C., & Keeling, R. P. (2003). Perception and reality: A national evaluation of social norms marketing interventions to reduce college students' heavy alcohol use. *Journal of Studies on Alcohol, 64*(4), 484-494.

Weitzman, E. R., Nelson, T. F., Lee, H., & Wechsler, H. (2004). Reducing drinking and related harms in college: Evaluation of the "A Matter of Degree" program. *American Journal of Preventive Medicine, 27*(3), 187-196. doi:10.1016/j.amepre.2004.06.008

Project Ideas

The following suggestions provide means of focusing your work on an evaluative essay or another type of evaluative document.

Suggestions for Essays

1. EVALUATE THE EFFECTIVENESS OF A PUBLIC OFFICIAL OR GROUP

Write an essay that evaluates the effectiveness of an elected official or group, such as a mayor, a state legislator, or a city council. Your evaluation might focus on overall performance, or on performance related to a specific issue, such as addressing urban growth. Identify and define the criteria you'll use to conduct your evaluation. Collect information from published sources (see Chapter 13). If you can, interview or correspond with the official or a representative of the group (see Chapter 14).

2. EVALUATE A PERFORMANCE

Review a public performance, such as a concert, a play, or a poetry reading, for your classmates. To prepare, read reviews that have appeared in print and online publications, and familiarize yourself with the criteria that other reviewers have used. In your review, describe the performance and evaluate it, keeping in mind the characteristics of your readers. Take notes and, if possible, interview others who attended the performance. If you can, interview one of the performers. Your review should focus primarily on your personal assessment of the performance. You should draw on your notes and interviews to introduce ideas, illustrate a point, or support your conclusions.

3. EVALUATE A PRODUCT

Select a product you are thinking about purchasing, such as a kitchen gadget, television, laser printer, cosmetic, or piece of athletic equipment. Evaluate it using the criteria of effectiveness, cost, and quality. Provide clear definitions of each criterion in terms of the product you've chosen to evaluate. Your evaluation should draw on written sources, interviews with people who have used the product, and, if possible, your own use of the product.

4. EVALUATE AN ATHLETE OR A COACH

Evaluate the performance of a professional athlete, such as a basketball or baseball player, or evaluate the effectiveness of a coach. Select criteria such as the contributions made to the team's success, leadership qualities, entertainment provided to fans, contributions to the community, and so on. In your essay, identify the athlete or coach, explain the contributions the individual has made to his or her team or sport, identify and define the criteria you are using to evaluate his or her performance, and present your evaluation to your readers. To support your evaluation, draw on your observations of the athlete or coach, interviews or surveys of other sports fans familiar with the athlete or coach, and published sources that discuss the athlete or coach. If possible, you might also interview the athlete or coach.

5. EVALUATE A PROPOSED SOLUTION TO A PROBLEM

Think of a proposed solution to a problem that you have read or heard about recently. You might focus on proposed legislation for addressing problems with public schools in your state or on a proposal for addressing a foreign policy problem. Alternatively, you might evaluate a new means of dealing with copyright on digital media such as music or videos. Be sure to define the problem, outline the proposed solution, identify and define a set of criteria on which to base your evaluation, and collect information about the problem and its proposed solution by gathering sources or interviewing an expert.

Suggestions for Other Genres

6. POST A MOVIE OR RESTAURANT REVIEW

Review a recently released movie or a new restaurant for the readers of a specific blog or website. To prepare, read reviews that have appeared on the site you have selected, and familiarize yourself with its conventions. If you are reviewing a movie, describe the movie and evaluate it, keeping in mind the interests of your readers. Take notes and, if possible, interview others who have seen the movie. Visit the movie's website to learn about the movie, its director, and its cast. If you are reviewing a restaurant, have a meal at the restaurant with one or more friends. Order a variety of items, examine the decor, and keep track of the quality of the service provided by the waitstaff. After you leave the restaurant, take notes to remind yourself of your impressions of the food, decor, and service. Ask your friends for their reactions, and take note of them as well. In your review, describe the restaurant and evaluate it, keeping in mind the interests of readers who read the blog or visit the site.

Your review should focus primarily on your personal assessment of the movie or restaurant. Draw on your notes to introduce ideas, illustrate a point, or support your conclusions.

7. WRITE A PROGRESS REPORT

Write a report that evaluates the progress that a group or organization you belong to has made during a particular period of time, such as the last six months or the last year. To develop the criteria for your progress report, interview key members of the group or organization, or locate any written documents that define its goals. Draw on your personal experience with the group, interviews, and documents (such as funding proposals or a website) as sources of evidence for your evaluation. Your report should define the group's or organization's goals and assess its progress in meeting them. The report might also include recommendations about strategies for enhancing the group's or organization's efforts to meet its goals.

8. WRITE A REVIEW OF LITERATURE

A literature review offers your assessment of relevant published sources in a given area, such as the use of social media to support writing instruction or approaches to funding presidential campaigns. The goal of a literature review is to share your understanding of the range of ideas, information, and arguments you find in a body of published work. For example, you might find that the work you've read about the use of social media in writing instruction focuses on three areas: (1) supporting interaction among members of a given writing class, (2) allowing instructors to share course materials with students, and (3) helping instructors and students share feedback on writing projects.

In your literature review, locate sources using the search strategies discussed in Chapters 12 and 13. Read your sources carefully and identify general approaches to the subject. Provide an overview of each approach you've identified; then discuss some of the most important or representative sources. Use quotations, paraphrases, and summaries to share information from the sources with your readers. Use in-text citation and a works cited list to identify your sources.

In Summary: Writing an Evaluative Essay

* **Find a conversation and listen in.**
  - Explore your needs, interests, and concerns (p. 316).
  - Search the Web (p. 318).
  - Narrow your focus by asking questions (p. 320).

* **Conduct your evaluation.**
  - Define your criteria (p. 321).
  - Identify evidence (p. 322).
  - Make your judgments (p. 323).

* **Prepare a draft.**
  - State your overall judgment (p. 325).
  - Present your evaluation (p. 326).
  - Consider genre and design (p. 329).
  - Frame your evaluation (p. 329).

* **Review and improve your draft.**
  - Review your criteria (p. 331).
  - Reconsider your evidence (p. 331).
  - Ensure that your judgments are fair and reasonable (p. 331).

10 Writing to Solve Problems

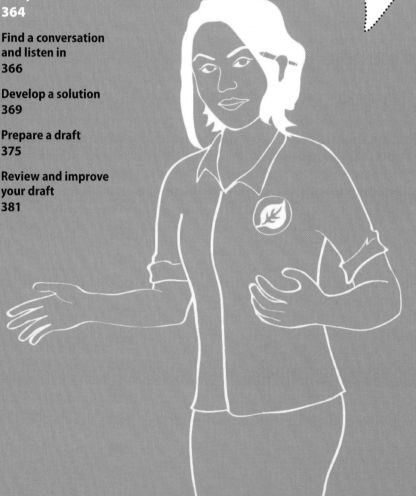

Problem solvers like me define a problem and offer possible solutions.

What Is Writing to Solve Problems?

The word *problem* is slippery. When a problem affects us directly, it might take on the dimensions of a crisis: we want to know how to solve it — and the sooner the better. When a problem affects someone else, it might seem, to us, more like an interesting challenge than an imminent disaster. And sometimes a problem is nothing of the sort. It's simply a label for lack of knowledge. For example, when a research scientist says that she's working on an interesting problem, she usually means that she's investigating an intriguing puzzle, which, when solved, will advance our knowledge in a specific area.

Writers who adopt the role of *problem solver* carry out activities such as calling readers' attention to problems, discussing the nature and extent of those problems, or proposing solutions. Whether a writer focuses on defining, discussing, or proposing a solution to a problem depends on how much is known about it. Consider, for example, the evolution of our understanding of the HIV/AIDS epidemic. In the early 1980s, when little was known about HIV — the virus that causes AIDS — it wasn't clear that the growing number of illnesses caused by HIV were related to one another. As a result, the first writers who addressed the problem focused largely on defining the symptoms and arguing that a problem existed. Later, as more information became available about the origin and effects of the disease, medical researchers began writing reports and scholarly articles that discussed its potential impact on people who carried the virus and on society. As researchers began to understand how the disease was spread and what might be done to prevent infection, writers proposed solutions to reduce the spread of HIV. Eventually, as the nature of HIV became better understood, writers began proposing programs of medical research that might be carried out to develop a way of preventing, and perhaps even eradicating, the spread of the virus.

A writer's decisions about how to address a problem depend largely on context. Until the nature and significance of a problem are understood, it does little good to propose a solution. Because of the critical role played by writers who help define and understand problems, they are actively involved in solving these problems — even when they don't propose a fully developed solution.

No matter how aware readers are of a problem, however, more often than not they are seeking a solution. Readers expect a clear definition of the problem and a thorough discussion of options for addressing it. And although readers might not be surprised when a writer uses emotionally charged language, they usually prefer that problem-solving documents discuss the problem in a straightforward, balanced manner.

Most readers also expect writers not only to explain and discuss the benefits of their proposed solution but also to address its advantages over other solutions. They expect a fair and reasonable presentation of a subject, clear explanations of important ideas and concepts, and thorough documentation of sources. Readers usually react favorably to the use of visual elements — such as photos, images, charts, graphs, and tables — that help them understand the problem and its solution.

The Writer's Role: Problem Solver

PURPOSE

- To identify or define a problem
- To explain the significance of a problem
- To propose solutions

READERS

- Expect information, ideas, and insights to be presented fairly
- Expect a clear explanation of a proposed solution

SOURCES

- Published information (such as studies, reports, blogs, websites, and news media), personal experience, and field research (including interviews, observation, surveys, and correspondence) help writers define and learn about previous attempts to solve problems.

CONTEXT

- Writers consider what readers are likely to know, assume, and value, and they focus on what readers want or need to understand about the problem.
- Illustrations — such as charts, tables, graphs, and images — can improve readers' understanding.

Writers of problem-solving documents are concerned primarily with helping readers understand the nature of and potential solutions to a problem. Sometimes they define and discuss the origins or impact of a problem. Sometimes they reflect on the strengths and weaknesses of potential solutions to a problem. In most cases, however, they analyze a problem and offer readers a thoroughly considered, well-supported solution. In doing so, they play a critical role in advancing our understanding of and response to problems.

What Kinds of Documents Are Used to Solve Problems?

It's rare to spend a day without running across documents that promise to solve a problem: advertisements alert us to solutions for problems (with our health, our love lives, our breath) that we might not know we have; e-mail messages ask us for our help with problems ranging from hunger to funding for the arts; and entire websites, such as VoteSmart.org and GlobalWarmingSolutions.org, promote solutions to problems. Unfortunately, the number of unsolved problems far exceeds those with solutions. As a result, writing to solve problems is a common occurrence.

In your work writing a problem-solving essay, you might turn to sources as varied as books, reports, pamphlets, posters, memos, opinion columns, and blog entries — any of which might define a problem or advance solutions to a problem. The following examples illustrate four of the problem-solving documents you're likely to encounter: problem-solving articles and essays, proposals, opinion pieces, and advice.

Problem-Solving Articles and Essays

Like other types of problem-solving documents, articles and essays can define problems and offer solutions for readers who share a writer's interest in an issue. Problem-solving articles and essays, however, tend to offer a more reflective and comprehensive treatment of a problem than shorter genres, such as advice or opinion columns, typically do. In addition, articles are also likely to offer the writer's personal insights into a problem, the situation out of which it emerges, and the reasons why the proposed solution is preferable to competing solutions. While writers of problem-solving essays typically do their best to define a problem and propose a solution as fairly as possible, they can also allow their experiences with and attitudes toward the problem to influence both their presentation of the problem and their selection and presentation of information from sources, such as websites, blog posts, and interviews.

Readers of problem-solving essays and articles might be part of a broad audience, such as subscribers to a general-interest magazine such as *Time* or *The Atlantic*, or they might be part of a more narrowly defined group, such as community college administrators, parents of children with autism, small-town mayors, or members of a particular church. In academic settings, instructors are usually the primary readers, although students are often asked to address a different audience, such as fellow students, politicians, or the members of a particular community.

 Anneke Jong
Leveling the Playing Field: How to Get More Women in Tech

"Leveling the Playing Field: How to Get More Women in Tech" is the final part of a three-part series written by Anneke Jong and published on themuse.com. Jong encourages girls to pursue success in the tech field by exposing them to potential career paths in Part One and by celebrating role models in the field in Part Two. Part Three questions why more girls aren't encouraged to build coding skills and considers the positive changes that would likely result if they were encouraged to develop such skills. Anneke Jong is the vice president of operations and marketing at Reserve, an online services company. She is also a speaker and tech writer, with several articles featured on themuse.com.

themuse

Leveling the Playing Field: How to Get More Women in Tech

By Anneke Jong

This article is part of a three-part series, "Solving the Pipeline Problem: How to Get More Women in Tech." Check out Part 1: Girls Don't Know What Computer Science Is _and_ Part 2: You Can't Be What You Can't See.

The Problem: Girls Haven't Coded Before

Omosola Obetunde was lucky. Her parents sent her to computer science camp in 8th grade. "I didn't know it was computer science. I just thought it would be cool to make things." Seven years later, she's a computer science major at Stanford University.

Sara Haider's parents also exposed their daughter to technology early — she learned to program at age 9. "I had no idea I could do this for a job until I took computer science in high school and my teacher told me, 'there's a career in this.'" Today, Haider is a software engineer at Twitter, and sees her family's encouragement as a key influencer in her career.

When I talked to women who have decided to pursue a career in computer science, I was surprised to learn that nearly all of them credited early exposure to programming as the greatest factor in their decision to become engineers. Conversely, they cited a lack of early exposure to computer science as the primary deterrent for women who leave — or never join — the field.

"There's a competitive showiness in the classroom that intimidates some women who don't have experience," says Kathy Cooper, a master's candidate in computer science. "Even in intro classes, the guys seem like they've been programming before."

Cooper's instinct is right: Boys really are more prepared. Although most of the female computer science students I spoke to had taken Advanced Placement (AP) Computer Science classes in high school, they're part of a small minority. According to the most recent reporting from the College Board, female enrollment in AP Computer Science is as low as 14%, making it the most gender-skewed AP class in the country.

And the uncommon ground starts even before that. "There's an impression that guys start coding when they're little. Boys play with robots, and girls play with dolls," says J. J. Liu, a sophomore computer science major. "[It] feels like the guys have been 'speaking code' for a long time."

This sense that boys have a head start creates a high competence threshold for women in computer science, even those who have prior experience in the field.

"Because of the stereotype that women do worse in computer science, a lot of high-achieving women get a B on their first exam and think they're just not good enough. They feel behind already, so they quit," laments Obetunde.

Angie Schiavoni, who teaches programming to underserved middle school girls, has observed a similar mind-set among her students: "I've seen that girls feel like they have to be super good at something to pursue it."

The Solution: Teach Computer Science to Middle School Girls

So, solving the pipeline problem requires giving our girls the confidence they need to go head-to-head with their male classmates. Unless we put our female and male students on equal footing going into college, young women are at risk of perceiving their efforts as a failure, feeling behind, and quitting early to pursue something else.

Key to this is getting middle school girls to think programming is cool. As the College Board stats show, reaching girls in high school is too late — at that point, they're already opting out of studying programming. Plus, the earlier they start learning, the better their chance of success in the field will be.

"Kids are like sponges with foreign languages, and programming languages are no different," Schiavoni says. "We can't leave girls behind in an industry that will be the forefront of our economy for years to come."

Silicon Alley venture capitalist and father of two Fred Wilson agrees. On his blog, _AVC_, he openly called for more computer science curriculum in schools: "We continue to teach our kids French but we don't teach them Ruby on Rails. Which do you think will help them more in the coming years?"

Schiavoni's solution is Code Ed, a program that trains middle school girls to code HTML and build their own websites. "It's inspiring to see how engaged our students are," explains Schiavoni. "The girls jump up and down and cheer when they change the background color."

She wants girls to see programming not as work, but as a creative process to pursue their passions. (Just what kinds of passions do 5th graders pursue? Schiavoni jokes that 90% of her students make Justin Bieber fan sites.)

Say what you will about Bieber, Code Ed works — and girls' opinions on computer science change dramatically after they go through the program. "I used to hear about boys and men doing all the websites," said 12-year-old Taiya Edwards, who went through Code Ed's program in the Bronx. "But now I know that girls can do anything a guy can do."

When asked if she'll make another website, she responded with an emphatic, "Yeah! I'll probably make one with advice for teens."

Code Ed isn't the only organization teaching girls about computer science — there are regional groups like Black Girls Code and Code Now, Microsoft's national Digigirlz program offers high school girls hands-on workshops, camps, and online training in technical topics like building a website, and the UN has launched a Girls in ICT portal. And these are all extremely important efforts. We just need more.

We're All Part of the Solution

Some say that teaching girls to code isn't that important. "Women can always hire someone to code for them," the skeptics say.

But why should women go find someone else to code for them? Relying on someone else to build your ideas means you need to have funding or be willing to give up equity in your company. Knowing how to program means the difference between spending months finding the right technical cofounder and being able to go home and build your idea tonight.

Plus, making investments to improve the pipeline of women in tech doesn't just benefit the next generation of girls, but it primes our economy for a boost in innovation. The female Mark Zuckerberg is out there, and it's within our power to make sure she follows her dream.

Starting a Conversation: Respond to "Leveling the Playing Field: How to Get More Women in Tech"

In your writer's notebook, reflect on the problems and solutions presented in Jong's article by answering the following questions:

1. Identify and evaluate the organizing pattern (p. 536) used in the article. How does the organization of the article reinforce the author's purpose? Would a different organizing pattern have been more effective? Why or why not?

2. Themuse.com is designed to help readers explore different career options. What does the design of the site allow you to infer about its intended audience?

3. What is the "pipeline problem" (para. 10)? Why is it problematic, according to Jong? What are the causes of this problem?

4. In presenting her solution, how does Jong address potential counterarguments? Does she effectively address roadblocks to achieving her solution? What additional information could have been included? What information, if any, might she have left out? Why do you think she approaches potential opposition to her proposed solution in this manner?

5. **Reflection:** Jong argues that girls need more access to learning coding skills, as well as more opportunities to see coding as "cool." How is coding perceived in your peer group? Do you think your friends, family, and classmates believe that tech has a gender problem? Explore two or three ways that coding could become more accessible or more popular with young girls.

Proposals

Proposals offer a plan for solving a specific problem. They are usually presented to groups or individuals who have resources that might be used to address the problem or who can grant permission for putting a plan into effect. For example, a nonprofit organization might propose that a charitable foundation fund an after-school tutoring program for children of one-parent families. Or a research center at a university might request approval from a city council for a pilot program to improve wheelchair access in local parks.

Proposals typically define a problem, describe a plan for addressing the problem, and argue that the person or group making the proposal has the capacity to carry out the plan. They might also include budgets, plans for evaluating outcomes, and information about the person or group making the proposal.

The structure and general appearance of proposals vary widely and tend to reflect the interests of the intended audience; often, proposals must follow strict guidelines outlined in grant application instructions or a call for proposals. Some proposals resemble academic essays, with wide margins, double-spaced lines, headings and subheadings, and limited use of color and illustrations. Others more closely resemble magazine articles or brochures, with heavy use of color, illustrations, columns, and other design elements.

Dan Hughes
Proposal for Skateparks under Bridges

Skateboarding enthusiast Dan Hughes submitted the following proposal to the city of Seattle. The proposal offers background on the benefits of skateboarding for young people and identifies a problem in the lack of appropriate venues for young skateboarders in the city. The proposal then offers a detailed plan for solving the problem by creating skateparks under bridges and highway overpasses. In structure, style, and tone, the proposal anticipates potential objections from city officials and offers persuasive details to support the plan as a viable solution.

PROPOSAL FOR SKATEPARKS UNDER BRIDGES

BACKGROUND

Skateboarding is a high-energy activity that builds both physical and mental strength, as it requires an individual to be self-reliant while sharing space with other individuals.

Part of what makes skateboarding a positive activity is that it allows people to focus on their personal abilities and skills. As a sport, skateboarding has no prescribed rules, no governing body, and no restrictions that require a team effort. Kids who are not served by team sports are attracted to skateboarding because it doesn't require them to join a team and compete until a winner and a loser are declared. It is an activity in which there are no losers, only winners. Anyone can simply grab a board and skate anytime to improve his or her skills.

Skateboarding has other positive attributes, as older skaters can attest. It builds confidence, and often it's this confidence in oneself that allows one to make the right choices in life. It also teaches kids that they can do things they never thought possible. For parents and kids alike, skating also provides opportunities for learning and acting as positive role models. One only has to look at champion skater Tony Hawk to see how skateboarding has become a way for him to connect with his kids.

It is well known that social problems occur in cities when adequate facilities and challenging activities for young people are not available. Skateboarding offers one solution, but skateboarding cannot occur in the rain, or when it's excessively hot, or in the dark winter months. Ultimately, a well-designed and well-built skatepark is necessary to provide a challenging and safe environment for young skaters. Older skaters would also use and enjoy such a park, and this mix of age groups would give younger skaters the opportunity to learn and grow, not only as skaters but also as people.

PROPOSAL

This proposal puts forth a plan for building skateparks in underutilized spaces under bridges and overpasses in Seattle. Skateparks can take organic, asymmetrical forms; they need not be bound in squares like other sports fields. This key feature allows for more efficient use of space that otherwise may be rendered useless (such as land under bridges or freeways).

Using land under a bridge has two main advantages compared to other skatepark locations. First, it largely eliminates the "N.I.M.B.Y." (Not In My Back Yard) problem, which happens when local residents do not want loud or disruptive activities near their houses. Because these areas already accommodate a freeway or a noisy bridge, skatepark-generated noise is no longer an issue. Second, skateparks discourage illegal activities that often occur under bridges of this sort. A good example is the area under the Burnside Bridge in Portland. This location was home to all kinds of criminal activity (drug deals, prostitution, abandoned cars, and so on) before Mark Scott and other skaters started building a skatepark there in 1990. The skaters cleaned up the area and kept the criminals out, to the point that the surrounding businesses took notice and volunteered their time and money toward expanding the skatepark. Even the local police chief donated money toward the effort. (This information was taken from a personal interview with Joanne Ferrero, who is owner and operator of Ferrero Equity Inc., a company right next to the Burnside Skatepark.)

In addition to these advantages for cities, using land under bridges and over-passes also provides an advantage for skaters. The bridge provides protection from rain in the winter and excessive heat in the summer. With the addition of lights, the skatepark can be used after dark as well.

OBJECTIVES

1. Give skaters a good, covered place to skate that can be used rain or shine, day or night, throughout the year.

2. Effectively use space that most wouldn't think to use as park land. Effective use of this space fulfills the goals of the City by providing a designated area for skateboarders and serves the community by freeing up more land to be used for other types of parks.

3. Provide kids with a healthy and intense activity. At skateparks, kids learn how to skateboard and are given a positive kinesthetic and creative outlet for their energy.

PROJECT DETAILS

Suggested Locations

1. <u>Under I-90 along Royal Brougham.</u> This area is centrally located with access to public transportation. It features a large covered space that is largely unused.

Dan Hughes

2. <u>Under I-5 between NE 40th Street and NE 42nd St.</u> This area is close to the University District, where there are lots of students who skateboard. It, too, features access to public transportation and a very large covered area that is largely unused.

Dan Hughes

Clientele

Two different groups would be likely to use skateparks in the suggested locations. The first and most important group is made up of young people who live nearby and who frequently skate in the area already. The second group is made up of skaters of all ages who live in various parts of the city and who would travel to this park (either by car or bus) because it is usable even in the rain, unlike most other outdoor skate parks.

Both clientele groups are essential components of this project, and it is expected that both would make significant use of the skatepark. Skateboarding is currently one of the fastest growing sports, and facilities such as these are used more heavily than basketball courts or baseball fields in similar locations.

Methods

The primary methods for achieving these objectives:

- The design and construction of a skatepark using concrete as its surface material.
- The use of experienced design and contracting companies comprised of skateboarders.
- The development of the area under a bridge as a full-fledged city park, complete with restrooms, trash cans, and lights.

Potential Objections and Responses

Skateparks under bridges are hidden, allowing for illegal activities. As the Burnside skatepark has proven, skateparks under bridges actually discourage crime in these areas. Skateboarders concentrate on their skateboarding, not on illegal activities. Lights, restrooms, picnic tables, a play area for toddlers, and vending machines will attract parents of the kids who are skateboarding. In Newberg, Oregon, this adult-friendly approach has been very successful at promoting self-policing of the skatepark.

Seismic safety. Traffic safety engineers design such bridges specifically to withstand the weight and stress of consistent car travel. If the bridge is safe for auto travel, one can reasonably assume it is safe for skateboarders beneath the bridge.

The land is not the property of the city. Currently there is a skatepark under I-90 in Spokane, Washington, which sets a precedent that Seattle can follow.

A park that attracts people from surrounding cities doesn't serve Seattle. In fact, it does. A good example is the skate bowl in Ballard Commons Park. Skaters come from all around to skate there, and the surrounding businesses, such as the QFC and Texaco, benefit—as does the city. The bottom line is that skaters spend money when they travel, and if they travel to Seattle, they will spend money in Seattle.

Lights are expensive. Darkness arrives early during Seattle's winter, just after the school day ends. This causes skaters to look for lighted places to skate, such as the streets or parking garages, both of which are illegal. It's far better to have the kids in one place like a skatepark, where their parents and the authorities can keep track of them. If lights can be used at a tennis court, then they can be used in the same way for a skatepark. Lights need not stay on all night. They can shut off automatically at a designated time or have a coin-operated switch to turn them on (to help offset the cost).

Needed Resources

- **Site Acquisition/Lease from Washington State Department of Transportation or the City of Seattle**
- **Personnel**: No personnel will be needed to staff the park.
- **Facilities Maintenance**: Emptying trash, cleaning restrooms, changing lights, and so on.
- **Design and Construction Costs**: Central Contractors Association estimates approx. $15/sq ft.
- **Infrastructure Maintenance Costs**:
    - Skate-only and concrete with steel coping: $0
    - Skate-only with pool coping: about $3000 the first year and $2000 a year thereafter
    - BMX: about $5000 a year

Additional Possibilities for Sites in Seattle

1. Under the Ballard Bridge
2. Under Interstate 5 in Seattle along Airport Way
3. Under the 12th Street Bridge and Dearborn Ave.
4. Under 45th St. next to University Village

5. Under Highway 509 at the intersection of Highway 99 and 509 and W. Marginal Way

6. Under Highway 99 at South Hanford St.

7. Under Hwy 99 at South Atlantic St.

8. Under I-5 and Spokane St.

9. Under I-5 at Shelby St.

10. I-90 next to Rainer Ave. and Goodwill

11. Under West Seattle Bridge at Duwammish St.

Dan Hughes
NorthwestSkater.com

Starting a Conversation: Respond to "Proposal for Skateparks under Bridges"

In your writer's notebook, evaluate Hughes's proposal by responding to the following questions:

1. What elements of Hughes's proposal demonstrate his sensitivity to the concerns of skateboarders? What elements demonstrate his awareness of the concerns of city officials?

2. How would you characterize the structure of this proposal? In what ways does the form — background, problem definition, proposed solution, and so on — help the writer achieve his purpose?

3. Hughes addresses possible objections to his proposed solution in the section "Potential Objections and Responses." Where else in the proposal does he address potential objections, and how does he refute them? Can you think of additional possible objections? What questions might remain in readers' minds?

4. At several points in his proposal, Hughes refers to examples such as the Ballard Skatepark and the Burnside Skatepark. How do these sources support his claims? What important details, if any, are missing?

5. **Reflection:** Think about your city and its recreation options. Do you think a proposal like this one would be popular in your city? Is there a different local recreation problem that you could imagine drafting a proposal to address?

Opinion Pieces

Opinion pieces—often in the form of columns, letters to the editor, or guest editorials— present focused arguments supported by analysis and evidence. They usually appear in magazines or newspapers, and to a lesser extent in journals and on the Web. Opinion pieces often advance arguments about a problem or a proposed solution that has been covered elsewhere in the publication. It is common, for example, to find an opinion column in a newspaper responding to an event reported in a front-page story. The problems and issues addressed in opinion columns generally reflect the interests of regular readers of the publication in which they appear. A column in *The New Yorker,* for instance, is far more likely to focus on literature or the arts than would a column in *Field & Stream.*

Compared to other problem-solving genres, such as essays and articles, opinion pieces tend to rely more heavily on personal experience and reflection than on evidence from other sources, although it is not unusual for a writer to advance an argument about a claim made in another publication or to offer reflections on a problem or proposed solution. In general, they are designed simply, often as a single column of text.

 Patrik Jonsson

Five Ways to Reduce Mass Shootings in the US

Patrik Jonsson is an Atlanta-based correspondent for *The Christian Science Monitor,* where he covers issues related to the southern United States. A native of Sweden, he immigrated to the United States at the age of ten. He has written for newspapers, including *The Boston Globe* and *The Portsmouth Herald,* since he was a teenager. In his opinion piece "Five Ways to Reduce Mass Shootings in the US," Jonsson identifies some of the ways in which the United States has tried (and at times failed) to reduce mass shootings and points out where further improvements might be made. Jonsson makes a clear call for change while addressing both sides of the gun control debate.

Five Ways to Reduce Mass Shootings in the US

By Patrik Jonsson, Staff writer | December 5, 2015

Afraid. Helpless. Numb.

According to news reports, those are some feelings shared by Americans after a wave of disturbing mass shootings, including the one Wednesday in San Bernardino, Calif., where 14 people were killed and 21 others wounded in a hail of bullets.

By unofficial counts the 355th mass shooting in 2015, the mayhem in Southern California was preceded hours earlier by a mass shooting in Savannah, Ga. Before that, the list goes on: Roseburg, Colorado City, Isla Vista, Chattanooga, Charleston, Phoenix, Aurora, Newtown.

This is how the news makes Tampa, Fla., resident Wendy Malloy feel: "It is a constant, grinding anxiety. And it gets louder every day," she told *The New York Times*.

The US is dealing with what appears to some experts to be an increasingly greater willingness by disturbed or ideologically motivated individuals to lash out at perceived injustices by meting out maximum damage to strangers.

In the past four years, the pace of such attacks has accelerated, by some measures. According to a Harvard University study based on a database compiled by *Mother Jones* magazine, what used to be an average of 200 days between mass shooting deaths in the US has dropped to just over 60 since 2011.

To address the roots of this trend in a substantive way, experts say, will require shifts in attitude and political thought.

While it often is left out of political rhetoric, America has seen dramatic successes in quelling violent crime in the past century— from the elimination of lynchings to decreases in domestic violence and child abuse, from declines in cop shootings and gun homicides, which have dropped 49 percent since a peak in 1993, according to Pew. Considering progress made in reducing other forms of violence, Americans and their institutions aren't quite as powerless as it may sometimes seem to, if not eliminate, dramatically curb what's become a numbing kind of new normal.

At the same time, it's clear that any broad-based attempt to address mass shootings as a societal ill will have to involve several factors. Chief among them is compromise among political partisans and a greater willingness to accept advances in science, forensics, mental health screening, and gun safety features.

"The choice between the blood-soaked status quo and the politically impossible is a false one," Evan DeFilippis and Devin Huges, the founders of Armed With Reason, wrote recently in *The Washington Post*.

Experts see five areas in which progress could be made in reducing mass shootings:

1. Threat assessment

In a nondescript FBI building near Washington, D.C., sits Behavioral Unit No. 2, a federal threat assessment laboratory that disseminates its strategies to pinpoint potential havoc-makers to local police departments. Its mission to spot potential domestic mass shooters was added onto the FBI's profiling wing in 2010, as an outgrowth of counter-terror activities going back to 9/11. Many of its interventions don't involve arrest, but rather helping someone get help to address mental health issues.

It is not a perfect system. Santa Barbara police supposedly versed in threat assessment visited Elliot Rodger on a so-called welfare, or check-up, call from his mother. Everything seemed fine to the officers, but they failed to ascertain whether he had recently purchased a gun, a standard question that threat assessment professionals say can be crucial in stopping a shooter in the planning stages. A few days later, Mr. Rodger killed six people during a campus rampage in Isla Vista.

But despite such failures, the American government, as well as states, already has investigators combing leads for any common thread of danger. It's a strategy in its infancy, but proponents say the tactics, which when used correctly don't violate individual constitutional rights, can be further shifted from terrorism to mass shootings.

Unit No. 2 has been involved in at least 500 interventions that might have ended in mass shootings. "Threat assessment has been America's best and perhaps only response to the accelerating epidemic of active shooters and mass shootings," Tom Junod reported for *Esquire* last year.

2. Common sense gun controls

No, the science is not settled on whether stronger gun control laws actually quell mass gun violence. In the case of San Bernardino, the weapons were bought legally. Also, California already has some of the strongest gun control laws in the country.

But "there's such a clear middle ground" in the gun control debate "because you can stem gun violence without taking away guns," says Jonathan Metzl, director of the Center for Medicine, Health and Society, at Vanderbilt University, in Nashville, Tenn.

Experts would like to see more of that middle ground employed.

The 2009 Heller decision by the US Supreme Court did guarantee the right of Americans to have access to firearms for personal protection, but left municipalities and states with room to regulate weaponry among the citizenry. And some of those legal checks on gun ownership have proven effective in saving lives.

When Connecticut enacted a law in 1995 that required that people purchase a permit before purchasing a gun, studies found a 40 percent reduction in the state's homicide rate.

When Missouri in 2007 repealed a similar permit-to-purchase law, the state saw a 16 percent increase in suicides with a gun.

3. Citizen defenders

In terms of compromise, if gun owners cede new checks on gun ownership, then gun control proponents may have to concede points of their own, specifically that lawful gun-carry by responsible Americans can have a role in deterring, or in certain cases, stopping mass killers once an attack has begun.

One of the victims in the San Bernardino attack told CNN on Thursday that he wished he had been armed as he hunkered in a bathroom with bullets whizzing through the wall.

It is, without question, a controversial proposition. Sheriffs in Arizona and New York have called for concealed carry permit holders and retired police officers to carry their weapons with them to rebuff any attack. But other law enforcement officers have said they oppose having untrained bystanders step in to active shooter situations, possibly resulting in more loss of innocent life.

While rare, there have been cases, often involving off-duty police officers, where someone has been able to successfully intervene.

- In 2007, an off-duty police officer having an early Valentine's Day dinner with his wife shot and killed an 18-year-old gunman at an Ogden, Utah, mall, stopping a rampage where five people died. "There is no question that his quick actions saved the lives of numerous other people," then–police chief Chris Burbank said at the time.

- In 2010, another off-duty police officer drew his personal weapon and fired when a man attacked an AT&T store in New York Mills, N.Y. The attacker was killed before he could carry out a plan to murder several employees at the store.

- And in 2012, a young shooter killed two people and wounded three others during a rampage at Clackamas Town Center before a man carrying a lawful personal weapon drew it and pointed it at the man. At that point, the assailant retreated, and then killed himself in a stairway.

Many Americans don't like how widespread gun-carry has become in recent years.

But it's already a fact of life, and one that some law enforcement experts believe can be corralled into a potential bulwark the next time someone decides to go on a shooting spree.

4. The science of violence

Why is America, one of the bastions of scientific breakthroughs on the globe, so hesitant to better understand the fundamental dynamics of how guns, if at all, promote violence?

Partisan politics is the obvious answer to why Congress has for 20 years blocked the Centers for Disease Control from using public funds to study gun violence, worried that the data will be used for gun control advocacy. But even deeper is a long-running distrust between the NRA and gun control advocates about each other's true intentions.

One symptom of the lack of systematic study is that there is currently no common standard for tracking mass shootings. Most news reports this week, including this one, have cited crowdsourced data from two online tracking sites that rely on news reports, in conjunction with studies such as the Harvard one and an FBI report on "active shooter" situations.

The NRA rebuffs even the most minor check on guns on the idea that it's part of a disarmament end game rather than an effort to save lives. The other side reflexively paints the gun lobby as a puppet for culpable weapons manufacturers, indeed as coconspirators to violence, rather than as a politically active firearms safety organization.

That means any movement on research funding will require both sides to ease up their rhetoric and open their eyes to the emerging facts.

For example, one key question is whether laws that make it easier to carry guns reduce crime or increase it. Studies have found trends, but causation has remained elusive.

"Fundamental questions of whether you are safer carrying a gun around with you or not have not been answered adequately," Daniel Webster, the director of the Johns Hopkins Center for Gun Policy and Research in Baltimore, told the *Post* recently.

After all, applying scientific research to other societal dangers has had dramatic impacts on human safety.

As highway death tolls rose in the US decades ago, studies of car crashes showed that younger people were particularly prone to serious accidents. In response, states raised standards for younger adults, improved car safety, and saved thousands, if not millions, of lives.

"We learned that you could design cars to be safe . . . [and] we could do the same with guns and save some lives," said Mr. Webster at Johns Hopkins. Having deeper knowledge "opens you up to having fuller understanding of the problem and what you can do to solve it."

5. Celebrate victims, shun shooters

A free, vigorous press is enshrined in the Constitution as one of the highlights of American democracy. Yet studies have shown that current coverage of mass shootings likely fuels what experts call a "contagion effect," given that many modern mass shooters emulate their "heroes" and yearn for their own infamy.

There are strategies that responsible media enterprises can employ without abandoning their fact-finding missions, says Ron Astor, a professor of social work at the University of Southern California.

"I'm like everybody else, I want to know who the person is, who his wife was, why they did it—that's human nature," he says. "But focusing intently on victims and what was lost here in a meaningless and random way . . . sends a really clear message that the sanctity of human life is so high that it's unacceptable to shoot somebody as a way to send a message. Yes, it's a news story that needs to include important information, but talking about the lives that were destroyed, what good they did, why that was taken away from us for no reason, that's important, and will change how we think and how we feel."

Starting a Conversation: Respond to "Five Ways to Reduce Mass Shootings in the US"

In your writer's notebook, record your analysis of Jonsson's opinion piece by responding to the following questions:

1. Gun control is one of the most controversial topics in American culture. How does Jonsson address both sides of the issue? What examples of pro–gun control and anti–gun control arguments are included? Does Jonsson present both sides fairly?

2. Consider the opening of this opinion piece. How would you describe its purpose? Is it what you would expect in a problem-solving document? Why do you think Jonsson begins this way? Is the approach effective? Why or why not?

3. How does Jonsson use car crashes (para. 37) as supporting evidence, and for which side of the gun control debate? How effective is citing a parallel example from a different issue? What strategy does Jonsson employ to tie the two issues together?

4. What can you infer about Jonsson's political beliefs from the manner in which he addresses failures at the government level and from his proposed solution? What does this suggest about the politics of the intended audience?

5. **Reflection:** The ability to carry guns with a permit, either openly or concealed on one's person, is especially contentious on college campuses. What is the gun policy on your campus? Do you agree or disagree with the policy? Why?

Advice

Writers offer advice in a variety of forms, from advice columns to speeches and presentations to essays and articles. What distinguishes documents that offer advice is the writer's purpose and role: writers who offer advice believe that a problem exists, that they understand the problem, that their readers have an interest in the problem (and most likely are affected by it), and that their advice — their solution to the problem — is worth sharing.

Keeping in mind the observation that free advice is usually worth what you pay for it, readers can sometimes gain a great deal from the writers and presenters who offer it, particularly when the advice is supported by hard-won experience and insights gained through careful reflection and analysis. But how can you determine whether the advice is trustworthy and useful? To some extent, you can base your trust on the reputation of the publisher. Well-established publishers — such as reputable magazines, major news channels, and many of the larger book publishers — guard their reputations vigorously, and readers or viewers can expect that the advice they make available will have gone through a careful vetting process. You can also make judgments about the quality of advice by comparing what is being said with your understanding of the problem and by reflecting on your experiences. If you find that the advice seems applicable, you might have greater confidence in following it.

The evidence and analysis offered as support for advice varies widely. Advice is often based on analysis or personal experience, but it can also include results from studies, statistical analysis of survey data, excerpts from interviews, and reports from observation. In most cases, the sources of advice are identified within the text or presentation in relatively general forms, most often by referring to the author or title of the source. Formal, in-text citation and works cited lists are seldom used.

 ## Chris Colin
Carpe FOMO

With a heavy dose of humor, Chris Colin's article challenges our culture's fear of missing out (FOMO). Colin suggests that perhaps FOMO doesn't deserve its negative reputation and that perhaps FOMO should really be considered a positive experience. This article appeared in *Pacific Standard* magazine in 2015. Chris Colin's work has been featured in *The New York Times Magazine*, *Pop-Up Magazine*, *Outside*, *Wired*, *Smithsonian*, *Mother Jones*, and *McSweeney's*, and he is a contributing writer for *Afar*. He is the coauthor of *What to Talk About: On a Plane, at a Cocktail Party, in a Tiny Elevator with Your Boss's Boss* (2014), and the author of *What Really Happened to the Class of '93* (2004) and *Blindsight* (2011).

Carpe FOMO

Fretting over your options is part of a life well lived.

by Chris Colin

No American should have to choose between kickball and potato printing. But this was the bleak conundrum faced by arrivals at Camp Grounded, a place for grown-ups wishing to unplug for a weekend. It was a bright California morning, the redwoods towered overhead, and a dozen of us stood clustered around a sign listing available electives: capoeira, solar carving, archery, creek walk. So dizzying was the smorgasbord that everyone sailed right through enthusiasm and into anguish.

I watched several campers locate a counselor and deliver a frantic earful. By signing up for one fun activity, they explained, they'd miss out on another.

Preacher-style, the counselor lifted his arms.

"Guys," he said. "No FOMO. No fear of missing out."

And then something magical happened. It worked. Simply stamping an acronym on this familiar pang diminished it. We saw that the problem lay not with poorly scheduled events but with ourselves. The campers visibly unclenched, signed up for their activities, and drifted away, some of them amusedly repeating the new word to themselves. I was on hand as a reporter, but I'd felt something, too. A whole species of discomfort had been identified and, for the moment, cured.

As it happens, I've come to reject that cure. I stand here for pain. But we'll get to that.

The day at Camp Grounded was a few summers ago. Since then, FOMO has exploded and splintered across the Internet and beyond. In 2013,

Oxford Dictionaries defined FOMO as "anxiety that an exciting or interesting event may currently be happening elsewhere, often aroused by posts seen on a social media website." Sites like Lifehacker were on the case, with posts such as "How Can I Overcome My Fear of Missing Out?" FOMO has become a marketing strategy and a teen's lament, a Facebook side effect and a half-ironicccri de coeur.

Of course, the fear of missing out on something is hardly new. Postwar advertisers loved to stoke it: "If you're not smoking Winston, you're missing out on the best taste in filter cigarettes." The 19th-century Romantics surely nursed an early FOMO, desperate to feel all the feels. Walk back far enough and I reckon there were Neanderthals fearing they'd miss out on the mammoth. What's new is the amperage. Before the Internet, we couldn't see over the hedge quite so easily. Today, our vast connectedness is a buffet of all the dishes everyone else is trying (and Instagramming).

In 2013, an article in *Computers in Human Behavior* assessed the motivational, emotional, and behavioral correlates of FOMO, which was defined as "a pervasive apprehension that others might be having rewarding experiences from which one is absent." (You can take a version of the test they designed online; I scored "high.") The article's lead researcher, the behavioral scientist Andrew Przybylski, says the people hit hardest by FOMO are those whose basic psychological needs aren't satisfied and who don't feel competent, autonomous, or connected in daily life. *Homo sapiens*, in other words.

For many of us, FOMO is so built in to our daily lives, so *no-duh*, that it's become as invisible as it is wearying. The articles we click on are packaged to elicit FOMO. Dare you miss the "Ten Must-Read Tweets about Last Night's Oscars"? The architecture behind those articles is designed for FOMO, too. Look at Facebook, Twitter, Instagram, Reddit. Where once the Internet was an encircling sea, we now encounter it in river form, forever passing us by. A friend of mine who's single says FOMO has infected the online dating world, each face simply obscuring the next. Then there's economic FOMO, unless you had the good sense to invent a Twitter of your own.

Backlash was inevitable. Transcending FOMO has become both a cottage industry and quasi-spiritual movement. There are No FOMO life hacks and No FOMO apps. You can attend a No FOMO party, receive a No FOMO public-relations pitch, and absorb earnest No FOMO sermons. Even advertisers, some of the most egregious FOMO-igniters of all, have brazenly started to include be-more-present, put-down-your-phone messages in their commercials.

Such efforts may be temptingly consoling, like the camp counselor's directive of "No FOMO." But that doesn't make them wise. On the contrary, I suggest you pick that phone back up. Grab a ladder to look over your neighbor's hedge. If someone builds a better ladder, trash yours and buy that one. Is FOMO a piggish affliction of the decadent, the gluttonous inevitability of a nation premised on endlessly pursuing happiness? Of course it is. It's also philosophically sound.

Faced with a million life choices, we'll often choose wrong. The No-FOMOers would have us accept that with equanimity. No thanks—I'll equanimize when I'm dead. Longing isn't just another inconvenience for today's eager solutionists to disrupt. It is a vital biological tool. To put this in programmer-speak, FOMO's a feature, not a bug. Life is a miracle. If we're not heartbroken over all we're not experiencing, I daresay we haven't gotten our arms around the situation.

The other day, in a small San Francisco redwood grove, I found myself gazing up at the wild geometry of branches. The very perfection of the moment made me start wanting more. What would it be like to lead a different life, here under this canopy? What would it be like to be that park ranger over there? Or that bird screaming overhead? This marvelously infinite universe we confront—how shatteringly bogus it is to have access to just one sliver of it! And how much more bogus it would be, for the sake of pretending that FOMO doesn't bother you, to make do with an inferior sliver.

You can't pine after every stupid thing. But to declare yourself happiest without the pleasures that passed you by is to be guilty of either fragile self-deception or sad resignation. Civilization was built on FOMO. Carpe diem is FOMO. Literature and its attempt to deliver us lives beyond our own—that's FOMO. Banishing it keeps Jacques Cousteau on deck and our Mars rovers on Earth and Adam and Eve in Eden.

There's beauty in acceptance, but there's also beauty in the jones for more. In the end, the only thing worse than the fear of missing out is, you know, missing out.

> Life is a miracle. If we're not heartbroken over all that we're not experiencing, I daresay we haven't gotten our arms around the situation.

In your writer's notebook, record your analysis of "Carpe FOMO" by responding to the following questions:

Starting a Conversation: Respond to "Carpe FOMO"

1. Who do you think Colin's intended audience is? Who else, outside of the intended audience, might this article appeal to? Why?

2. Colin alternates between first-person (*I, me, we*) and third-person (*he, she, they*) points of view. Why do you think he does this? What effect does it have on his relationship to his readers?

3. How does Colin build support for his solution to the problem of "FOMO"? What sort of reasons or examples does he use? How effective are they in developing a solution? If you were writing an article on this topic, what other information would you include?

4. In paragraph 13, Colin writes, "The No-FOMOers would have us accept [making wrong choices] with equanimity. No thanks — I'll equanimize when I'm dead." What do you think *equanimity* means in this context? How would you paraphrase what Colin is saying?

5. **Reflection:** Based on your experience of FOMO, do you agree with what Colin has identified as the problem with FOMO? Do you agree with the solution that Colin proposes? Why or why not? Do you have other solutions to add?

How Can I Write a Problem-Solving Essay?

We all have problems. Some of us have more than others. You've probably heard someone say, "I've got a problem. My taxes are due." Or "I'm about to be evicted from my apartment." Or "My hard drive crashed." When people make statements like these, they are assuming that you share their understanding of the problem. Unfortunately, that's not always the case. You might assume that the person who has a problem paying taxes lacks the money to do so and that the best solution is to get a loan or pick up a part-time job. In fact, the problem might be based on a moral objection to how the government uses funds raised through taxes.

Until people share an understanding of a problem, it can be difficult to develop a solution and put it into effect. A successful problem-solving essay begins with the recognition that explaining a problem to others involves far more than saying, "I've got a problem with that. You know what I mean?" In this chapter, we'll work from the assumption that a problem is best understood as a situation

GENRE TALK

In recent years, more attention has been drawn to the problem of child labor on cocoa farms. According to the U.S. Department of Labor, more than two million cocoa laborers in Ivory Coast and Ghana are between five and fourteen years old. To harvest the cocoa, laborers must perform extremely hazardous work, including clearing forests with chainsaws, cutting down cocoa bean pods with machetes, and carrying heavy sacks of cocoa beans. Labor analysts and policy researchers have found that many children are trafficked into slavery in the cocoa industry, with little hope of earning their freedom. As global demand for chocolate increases, several fair trade companies have created partnerships with cocoa farmers to pay them a fair wage, allowing them to hire legal adult workers and ensure safe working environments.

These Halloween cards from the International Labor Rights Forum offer hard facts about the problem and ask readers to become part of the solution.

 LaunchPad
macmillan learning

Test your knowledge of genre with the Genre Talk quiz in the LaunchPad for *Joining the Conversation*.
launchpadworks.com

Tag line identifies the dilemma facing consumers.

Point-by-point explanation of how direct trade companies address the problem of slave labor in the cocoa industry.

A photograph personalizes the plight of cocoa farmers.

Design elements remind the reader that laborers are often children.

An attention-getting appeal to readers.

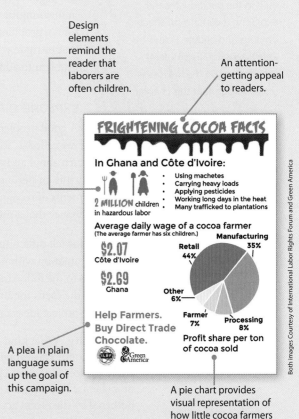

A plea in plain language sums up the goal of this campaign.

A pie chart provides visual representation of how little cocoa farmers earn from their labor.

Both Images Courtesy of International Labor Rights Forum and Green America

In Process

A Problem-Solving Essay about Puppy Mills

James Hardjadinata wrote a problem-solving essay about puppy mills for his introductory composition course. James learned about his topic by reading articles about the role of puppy mills in the pet industry and exploring their harmful effects on dogs and people. Follow his efforts to write his problem-solving essay in the In Process boxes throughout this chapter.

that has negative consequences for an individual or a group. To address such a situation in writing, you need to carefully define your problem, consider its significance for readers, review past efforts to address it, and either develop your own solution or argue for the adoption of one that's been proposed by someone else.

As you work on your own problem-solving essay, you'll follow the work of James Hardjadinata, a first-year student who wrote a problem-solving essay about the heartbreaking impact of puppy mills in the United States.

Find a Conversation and Listen In

Taking on the role of problem solver requires you to understand the nature of problems — an understanding that a surprisingly large number of writers appear to lack. By learning about problems, you can begin to identify and understand them and even to address them in meaningful ways. Once you gain an understanding of what constitutes a problem, you can begin to look for and learn about problems that intrigue you. In the process, you'll position yourself to choose a problem to address in your essay.

EXPLORE DIFFICULTIES

A good problem-solving essay begins with what educational philosopher John Dewey called a "felt difficulty" — the recognition that something isn't right. As you learn about an issue, you might find yourself wondering why something is the way it is, or perhaps you'll say to yourself, "That's not right." Treasure these early moments of recognizing a problem. If you feel that something isn't right, there's a good chance that a problem is near at hand.

As you search for felt difficulties in the world around you, keep in mind the idea that a problem is a situation with negative consequences for an individual or a group. Your responses to the following sets of questions can help you identify subjects that might serve as the focus for a problem-solving essay. (For additional suggestions, see the writing project ideas on p. 393.)

- **Community.** What kind of difficulties have you encountered or noticed in your neighborhood? Have you been stuck in long lines at a bank or post office? Have you volunteered at a food pantry that has been overwhelmed by an influx of new clients? Run across a pothole so deep that it ruined one of your tires? Been bothered by the recent actions of local politicians or law enforcement officials?

- **Economy.** Are any of your friends or relatives having financial difficulties? Have you worried about what the future holds for you? For your parents? For your children?

- **Work.** Do any issues at your workplace need to be addressed? Is the industry in which you work facing any challenges? Have you grown aware, through your course work or general reading, of difficulties facing people in your field of study?

- **News.** What have you read recently that surprised or worried you? What annoyed you or made you angry? What have you read that made you think? What controversies have you noticed on the evening news or on the websites you visit?

To begin turning a felt difficulty into a defined problem, jot down what doesn't feel right and then brainstorm or freewrite about it (see pp. 41–42). As you list ideas or write about your felt difficulty, the problem will begin to come into focus.

It can take time to sketch the outlines of a problem. You might find it helpful to think about the problem over a period of a few days or a week. During that time, you might read more about the problem or talk with others about it. As you reflect on the problem, keep track of your ideas by recording them in your writer's notebook or in a word-processing file.

ASK QUESTIONS ABOUT PROMISING SUBJECTS

Even if you think you know a great deal about each of the problems you've identified as potential subjects for your essay, check them out thoroughly before you begin trying to solve one. To learn more about a promising problem, reflect on your own experiences with it, discuss it with others, and find and review relevant published sources through your library or the Web. (You can learn more about locating, collecting, and managing information in Part Three.)

Once you've learned about the most promising problems, select those that continue to hold your interest, and then spend a few minutes responding to the following questions. Each set of questions focuses your attention on a problem in a different way, allowing you to think not only about the problem but also about its potential as the focus of your problem-solving essay. Depending on the problem you work with, you'll find that some questions are more useful than others.

- **Relevance.** Is this problem widespread, or does it involve only a small group of people? Who is affected by it, and how are they affected? Will my readers think it's important? Can I address it within the limits of my assignment?

- **Definition.** What, exactly, is the problem? How can I explain it? What kinds of information will readers need to understand it?

- **Context.** When and where did this problem begin? How much is known about it? What solutions have been tried? Why haven't they worked?

- **Causes and effects.** What caused this problem? What must happen before it can be solved? What is likely to happen if it isn't solved?

As you think about your ideas, remember that the best problems to tackle in an essay are usually highly specific. For example, instead of writing about the general problem of encouraging college students to become teachers, you might focus on how to encourage students in a particular discipline, such as math or biology, to become high school teachers in rural school districts.

CONDUCT A SURVEY

A survey can help you learn about the beliefs, attitudes, or behaviors of people associated with a problem. For example, you might use a survey to discover whether the attitudes and beliefs about education differ among students who stay in school and those who drop out. Or you might use a survey to explore whether students who put a high value on community involvement are highly engaged in volunteer activities.

Typically, surveys help you answer *what*, *who*, or *how* questions — such as "What kinds of exercise do you engage in at least once a week?" — rather than more

Working Together: Ask Whether Your Judgments Are Fair

Before you start working on your problem-solving essay, start a conversation with a small group of your classmates about a minor problem that affects you. Explain the problem as clearly as you can, and tell the members of your group about how you think you might solve it. Ask them whether your preliminary solution seems likely to work and why. Then ask them to suggest additional solutions you should consider trying. Take turns speaking while the members of the group listen, respond, and ask questions.

When you are finished, take a few minutes to reflect on the exercise. What did you learn about your audience? Did they understand the problem right away, or did you have to adapt your initial explanation to overcome their assumptions? How much detail did you have to give them before your solution made sense? Did they think your solution was reasonable? What kinds of solutions did they suggest as alternatives? Did their questions and suggestions help you develop a better understanding of your problem or give you new ideas about how to solve it?

analytical *why* questions. For example, the California State University professors who were interested in the effect of music on stress conducted a survey to record students' experiences (see p. 291). They included questions to measure stress levels before and after the students listened to music.

You can learn more about surveys in Chapter 14.

Develop a Solution

Once you've identified a promising problem and learned about it, you can begin to develop a solution to the problem. If your problem has already attracted the attention of other writers, the solution you choose might be one that another writer has already advanced, or it might be an improved version of someone else's proposed solution. If the problem has remained unresolved for some time, however, you might find it best to develop a new solution. If your problem is relatively new or is one that has not yet attracted the attention of other writers, you might develop your own solution to the problem, or you might look at how similar problems have been addressed and then adapt one of those solutions.

Whatever approach you take, remember that a clear problem definition is the single most important element in a problem-solving essay. Without it, even the most elegant solution won't be convincing. A problem definition enables you to take a problem apart, examine its causes and effects, and understand whom or what it affects. It also influences how your readers understand the problem and how they are likely to react to your solution.

In addition, remember that a solution must be practical. Few readers will be impressed by a solution that costs too much or takes too long to put into effect or that causes even more problems than it solves. As you consider potential solutions to your problem, carefully assess their feasibility and potential consequences.

DEFINE THE PROBLEM

Some people define a problem with a particular solution in mind. As a result, their solution usually looks good in theory. But a solution based on a weak problem definition seldom works well in practice, and it is unlikely to convince your readers. For this and other reasons, you should define your problem as clearly and accurately as possible.

You can define your problem by exploring situation and effects, focusing on actions, examining severity and duration, and considering goals and barriers.

Situation/effects Explore the effects a problematic situation has on people or things. Ask yourself:

- What is the situation?
- What are its effects?
- Who or what is affected?

Agent/goals/actions/results Focus on actions that have unwanted results. Ask yourself:

- Who or what is the *agent* (the person, group, or thing that acts in a manner that causes a problem)?
- What are the agent's *goals*?
- What *actions* does the agent carry out to accomplish the goals?
- What are the *results* of the agent's actions?

Severity and duration Analyze the severity and duration of the effects of a problematic situation. Ask yourself:

- What is the situation?
- What effects are associated with the situation?
- How severe are the effects?
- What is the duration of the effects?

Goals and barriers Identify goals, and ask what obstacles stand in the way of accomplishing them. Ask yourself:

- What are the goals?
- What barriers stand in the way of accomplishing the goals?

Most of these methods of defining a problem focus on cause/effect relationships, and many involve unintended consequences. However, each one allows you to view a problem from a different perspective. Because your problem definition has powerful effects on the development of a solution to your problem, it can be useful to experiment with different ways of defining the problem.

CONSIDER POTENTIAL SOLUTIONS

Use your problem definition to weigh potential solutions. If your problem definition focuses on the causes of the problem or barriers to achieving a goal, for example, consider solutions that address those causes or barriers. If your problem definition

In Process

Developing a Survey

As part of his problem-solving essay about puppy mills, James Hardjadinata wanted to launch a social media campaign to raise awareness about this issue. James created a survey to find out more about students' social media habits. He kept it brief so that more students would respond.

1. Which social media platform do you use the most? (Check one.)

    ____ Facebook

    ____ Twitter

    ____ Snapchat

    ____ Tumblr or other blogging tool

    Comment:

> A multiple-choice question asks respondents to pick one answer.

> Room is provided for brief comments.

2. Which topics do you tend to write about frequently on social media? (Check as many as apply.)

    ____ College life (academics, campus life)

    ____ News and politics (local, state, and national)

    ____ Sports and entertainment (sports, books, music, movies, video games)

    ____ Lifestyle (food, entertaining, pets)

    ____ Science and technology

    ____ Other: _____

    Comment:

> A multiple-choice question asks respondents to pick multiple answers.

3. How likely are you to favorite or retweet a post that you find relevant or informative?

    ____ Very likely

    ____ Somewhat likely

    ____ Neither likely nor unlikely

    ____ Somewhat unlikely

    ____ Very unlikely

    Comment:

> A Likert-scale question asks students to indicate the likelihood that they would retweet a favorite post.

focuses on actions that have had unexpected or undesired effects, explore solutions that might address those effects. If your problem definition focuses on the duration and severity of a problem, ask yourself how the duration and severity of the problem might be reduced or perhaps even eliminated.

As you generate ideas for possible solutions, keep in mind what you've learned about your problem. If you're dealing with a problem that other writers have

In Process

Defining a Problem

James Hardjadinata used the situation/effects questions (p. 370) to develop his problem definition. He started by identifying the problematic situation of overcrowded puppy mills and examining its effects on puppies, pet owners, and puppy shelters.

What is the situation? Puppy mills are breeders that mass-produce upwards of 1 million puppies per year by subjugating their mothers to constant reproduction and forcing mothers and offspring to live in small, inhumane enclosures (The Humane Society of the United States). Although there are state and federal laws that attempt to regulate puppy mills, many define puppy mills poorly and cannot be fully enforced.

What are the effects? Due to their mistreatment, dogs from puppy mills are more likely to suffer behavioral and mental conditions that make them much less likely to be adopted. They end up in animal shelters, which often euthanize the dogs they believe are "unadoptable" to save money and space for the dogs that are more likely to be adopted (Rudy 62). As many as 60% of the animals admitted to shelters are euthanized annually (Protopopova et al.).

Who is affected? Millions of puppies across the United States, both in puppy mills and in shelters, are victims of puppy mills. Adoptive families are also affected, when they realize the puppies they have purchased have physical and behavioral problems far greater than they can handle. While these animals live in miserable conditions for much of their short lives, their breeders suffer few consequences (Shaw).

Because James was trying to approach the problem of puppy mills as a situation that affects a broad segment of the American public, the situation/effects questions worked well for him. Since he was also interested in assessing the severity of the problem and its long-term impact, he might also have used the questions that address severity and duration. If he had been trying to identify the causes of the problem, he might have used the agent/goals/actions/results questions.

addressed, pay attention to the solutions they've proposed. Even if those solutions have failed to solve the problem — which is likely, given the continuing existence of the problem — they might have helped address at least some of its effects. Consider the impact of these earlier solutions, weigh their negative consequences, and ask whether you might adapt them — or parts of them — for your own use.

In your writer's notebook, create a list of potential solutions — both your own and those of other writers — and briefly describe them. Evaluate each solution by answering the following questions:

- How well does this solution address the causes of the problem?
- How well does this solution address the effects of the problem?
- To what extent does this solution address the needs of the people or things affected by the problem?
- What costs would be associated with this solution?
- What advantages does this solution have over other solutions?
- What disadvantages does this solution have?

Review your responses to the questions, and identify your most promising solutions. If you've identified more than one solution, ask whether the best features of each might be combined into a single solution. As you consider each solution, you'll gain a better understanding of the problem itself. Your problem-solving essay will be most effective if you clearly connect your solution to your problem definition, so you might find it useful to revise your definition to reflect the additional thinking you've put into the problem. Remember that your problem definition isn't set in stone. It can be revised and improved throughout the process of writing your essay.

ASSESS THE PRACTICALITY OF YOUR SOLUTION

Most problems can be solved given unlimited time, vast sums of money, revisions to the laws of physics, or changes in human nature. If your solution requires any or all of these, however, your readers are likely to question its practicality. Before you start drafting your essay, ensure that your solution is feasible by asking whether your solution can be implemented

- in a reasonable amount of time
- with available funding
- with available resources
- given current knowledge and technology
- without causing additional problems

In Process

Developing a Solution

To begin solving the problem he had defined, James Hardjadinata created a cluster map. He used the situation/effects and severity/duration questions on page 370 to explore causes, effects, severity, and potential solutions to the problem of puppy mills.

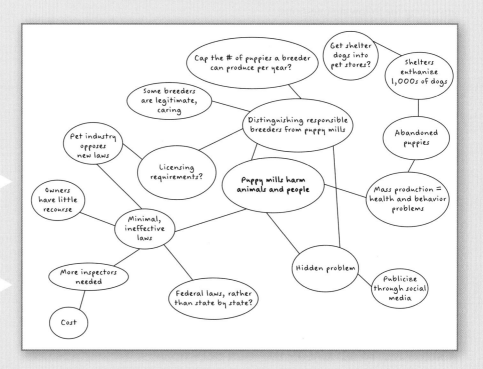

> James placed his issue — the dangers of puppy mills — in a bubble at the center of his cluster.

> Each cause, effect, level of severity, and solution generated more specific ideas.

James's cluster map helped him lay out solutions to prevent puppy mills from over-producing and harming puppies in the future and to help dogs who have been abandoned to animal shelters already. With that in mind, he used freewriting to generate ideas that might solve both aspects of the problem.

> The most practical option is to match up adoptive families with the puppies who are already in animal shelters. Cutting out the breeder as middleman makes sense, both for the families and for the puppies. Especially once people learn about the horrors of puppy mills, they will not want to buy their dogs there. We need to make the general public more aware of this problem.

Consider as well how your readers' needs, interests, and backgrounds will affect their responses to your solution. For example, if your readers have strong religious beliefs about the use of birth control, they probably won't react favorably to a proposal to reduce teenage pregnancies by requiring public schools to dispense contraceptives.

Finally, consider potential objections to your solution. If your solution requires funding or resources that might be used for other purposes, for example, ask whether readers will object to reducing funding for those purposes. If you think that your readers will not accept the trade-offs associated with your solution, take another look at it. You might be able to modify your solution to account for likely objections, or you might want to prepare an argument about why the trade-offs are better than just leaving things as they are.

Prepare a Draft

As you get ready to draft your essay, review your problem definition, the solutions you've examined, and your notes on your proposed solution. You'll need to decide how to explain the problem, present your solution, and convince readers that your solution is worth pursuing. You'll also want to consider the role of document design in your essay, how you'll organize your ideas, and how you'll frame your introduction and conclusion.

EXPLAIN THE PROBLEM

Your problem definition is the single most important element of your problem-solving essay. It sets up your solution and shapes your thesis statement (see Chapter 16). It also affects your choice of sources and evidence to support the points you make in your essay. As is the case with so many aspects of writing, however, you should pay attention not only to the content of your problem definition but also to how you present it to readers.

For example, consider how a reader might react to the statement "Teachers are the reason education is in trouble." Which of the following thoughts flashed through your mind?

- Teachers are lazy.
- Teachers are poorly prepared.
- Teachers are spreading left-wing propaganda and infecting the minds of our youth.
- Teachers are extraordinarily boring.
- Good teachers are quitting to become stockbrokers or advertising executives.

All of the above? None of the above? Now substitute "students" or "parents" or "politicians" or "television" or "video games" in the same statement. What flashes through your mind?

Statements like these are unclear because they don't define the problem. They don't explain, for example, what it is about teachers that causes education to be in trouble.

Consider the differences between "Teachers are the reason education is in trouble" and the following problem definitions.

> **Problem definition 1:** The lack of certified science teachers in public schools has limited the development of a general understanding of key scientific concepts among Americans. Without that understanding, it will be difficult to carry out informed debates about policies that rely on an understanding of scientific concepts, such as the development of a hydrogen economy or decisions about how we deal with the causes of global climate change.

> **Problem definition 2:** The relatively low salaries offered to beginning teachers, combined with the growing cost of higher education and the high debt burden incurred by many college graduates, have reduced the attractiveness of pursuing a career as an educator. The result is a growing shortage of qualified teachers in key areas, such as the sciences, mathematics, and the arts. Because of this shortage, students are not receiving the education they deserve.

Each of these problem definitions calls attention to the effects of a particular situation on specific groups or individuals. In the first example, the situation — a lack of certified science teachers — affects Americans' ability to understand and participate in debates about scientific issues. In the second example, the economic situation faced by beginning teachers affects college students' willingness to pursue careers as teachers, which in turn affects the education of students. Through their clarity and detail, both of these problem definitions offer significant advantages over "Teachers are the reason education is in trouble."

As you consider how best to explain your problem definition to your readers, reflect on what they already know about it. If they are already familiar with the problem, you might be able to convey your problem definition in one or two sentences that frame the solution that will follow. If they are unfamiliar with the problem, however, you might need to devote a significant portion of your essay to establishing the existence of the problem and explaining its consequences.

PROPOSE YOUR SOLUTION

Most problem-solving essays frame the problem in a way that prepares readers to accept the proposed solution. The problem of skyrocketing college tuition costs, for example, might be framed so that the best solution would seem to involve more online learning opportunities, while the problem of a growing national debt might be framed so that the best solution would appear to rely on changes in tax laws.

After you introduce a problem to your readers, you can present a thesis statement that summarizes your proposed solution. Your thesis statement should be closely tied to your problem definition, and it should suggest a logical and reasonable means of addressing the problem. Because your thesis statement will frame readers' understanding of your solution in a certain way, it serves as a powerful tool for influencing your readers. Consider the differences among the following thesis statements addressing the problem of low salaries for teachers who leave college with high levels of debt:

> **Thesis statement 1:** If we are to ensure an adequate supply of qualified teachers, we must increase their starting salaries.

> **Thesis statement 2:** The most promising approach to ensuring an adequate supply of qualified teachers is paying the tuition and fees for college students who promise to spend at least five years teaching in our public schools.

> **Thesis statement 3:** A public-private partnership designed to identify and support promising new teachers is the key to ensuring an adequate supply of qualified teachers in our public schools.

Each of these thesis statements calls attention to a different solution to the problem. The first focuses on salaries, suggesting that the promise of higher salaries will lead more students to consider a career in teaching and perhaps will encourage those who do become teachers to stay in the profession. The second thesis statement focuses on the cost of attending college, borrowing an approach used successfully to attract new doctors to rural parts of the country. The third focuses on recruiting students into the teaching profession. Each thesis statement offers a reasonable solution to the problem as it has been defined, yet each would also lead the writer to produce a significantly different essay.

Is your thesis statement focused enough? See Chapter 16 for help.

EXPLAIN YOUR SOLUTION

Your solution is what most readers will remember about your essay. Once you've defined the problem and proposed your solution, explain your solution by going into detail, offering support for your ideas, and considering your solution in light of promising alternatives.

Go into detail A surprising number of problem-solving essays spend several pages defining and discussing the consequences of a problem, only to offer a skimpy discussion of a proposed solution. However, readers are rarely satisfied by such an approach, so be sure to spend some time identifying the key aspects of your solution. Help your readers understand, in detail, how you would implement the solution, how much it would cost to put into effect, what kinds of effects the solution would have on the problem, and how you would judge its effectiveness in addressing the problem.

Provide support for your points Most problem-solving essays rely heavily on evidence to establish the existence of a problem, support a proposed solution, and dismiss alternative solutions. Your solution should offer a reasonable and thoughtful response to the problem, and it should be clear that your proposed solution is superior to alternatives.

You can use evidence to

- identify and frame your solution
- provide examples and illustrations
- illustrate processes that might be required to put the solution in place
- associate particular ideas and concepts with authorities, such as political leaders, subject-matter experts, or people who have been affected by the problem

To develop support, list the key points you are making about your proposed solution. For each point, review your sources and notes to identify relevant evidence, and then list the evidence below each point. If your sources support your solution, draw on evidence from them to show your readers why your solution is likely to be effective. If your sources do not directly address your solution, consider using personal experience. You can read more about how to use evidence to support your points in Chapter 21.

Address promising alternative solutions As you draft your problem-solving essay, be sure to consider alternative solutions that are likely to occur to your readers. In proposing a solution to a problem, you are essentially making an argument that your solution is preferable to others. If your readers can think of alternatives, especially alternatives that might be less expensive or more effective than yours, they might wonder why you haven't mentioned them.

To address (and dismiss) alternative solutions, you can do the following:

- Identify the strongest alternative solution, explain why it's the best of several alternatives, and then explain why your solution is better.

- Identify a group of alternative solutions that share the same weakness, such as high cost or impracticality, and explain why this group of solutions is weaker than your solution.
- Identify a group of promising alternatives, and dismiss each solution, one after the other.

You can gain insights into effective strategies for organizing your response to alternative solutions by reading about organizing patterns in Chapter 17.

CONSIDER GENRE AND DESIGN

Depending on the complexity of the problem you're addressing and the nature of the solution you propose, design can contribute greatly to the overall effectiveness of your essay. As you contemplate design options for your essay, make note of any

In Process

Providing Support for Key Points

James Hardjadinata identified support for his key points by listing each point, then reviewing his notes to find sources that would support those points. He wrote the relevant sources next to each point.

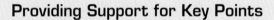

Key Points	Support
Through overbreeding and poor living conditions, puppy mills harm hundreds of thousands of puppies each year.	Humane Society
Dogs from puppy mills suffer from health problems and behavioral problems, and many end up euthanized.	Humane Society, Rudy
Pet stores and individual buyers can't always tell a puppy mill from a reputable breeder.	Widner, Tushaus
Existing laws are minimal, unenforced.	Humane Society, Burger, Tushaus
Possible new legislation: quantity caps for individual breeders; funneling puppies from shelters to adoption via pet stores; more inspectors and licensing requirements.	Widner, Tushaus
We must raise awareness and educate the public about this situation, especially via social media.	Tushaus, Shirky

formatting requirements specified in your assignment (such as margins, spacing, font, and the like). Consider as well the expectations of your readers, particularly your instructor. You might also think about including visual evidence such as figures and images.

- **Figures,** such as charts and graphs, can help readers better understand complex concepts or see trends that would be difficult to discern through textual descriptions alone. A chart, for example, can clearly show comparative cost figures for a state plan to subsidize public transportation. A graph could show changes over time in ridership of those who use trains, buses, subways, or private automobiles.

- **Images,** particularly when you are analyzing a visual text such as a photograph, video, or painting, can help readers better understand the subject and increase the likelihood that they'll accept your interpretation as valid and well founded.

- **Captions** are a necessary complement to figures and images. Be sure to include a caption for each figure or image in your essay. At a minimum, a caption should provide a figure number cross-referenced in the text, a descriptive label, and source information. You can also use the caption to briefly describe what is shown and to explain what it contributes to your analysis.

If you use figures and images in your essay, place them near their first mention in the text. You can learn more about figures, illustrations, captions, and other aspects of document design in Chapters 18, 19, and 20.

FRAME YOUR ESSAY

Once you've worked out how to define the problem and present your proposed solution, decide how you'll organize, introduce, and conclude your essay.

Organization Most problem-solving essays start with an introduction, then define the problem and explain the proposed solution, and finish with a conclusion. Longer problem-solving essays often make use of the organizing patterns discussed in Chapter 17. For instance, process explanation can offer a helpful outline for explaining the steps involved in implementing a solution. The costs/benefits and strengths/weaknesses patterns provide a practical structure for both analyzing a problem and examining a solution's potential. And problem-solving essays that address several alternative solutions often take advantage of the comparison/contrast pattern.

Introduction Your introduction creates a framework within which you can present your thesis statement and prepare your readers to understand how you've defined your problem. You can draw on a number of strategies to draw your readers in:

- Use an anecdote (a brief story) to personalize the problem.

- Use dramatic statistics, as James Hardjadinata does in his essay, to illustrate the scope of the problem.

- Use quotations from experts, or from people who have been affected by a problem, to make the problem hit home with your readers.

- Draw comparisons between this problem and other, more widely understood problems.

You can read more about strategies for introducing your essay in Chapter 18.

Conclusion In much the same way that you can use your introduction to direct readers toward a particular understanding of a problem, you can use your conclusion to encourage them to accept your ideas for solving it. Most problem-solving essays end with a call to action, in which the writer urges readers to do something specific to help put the solution into effect. Other strategies you can employ to conclude your essay include summarizing your problem definition and proposed solution, circling back to the introduction, and speculating about the future. You can learn more about framing your conclusion in Chapter 18.

Review and Improve Your Draft

The success of your problem-solving essay rests heavily on how well you can define your problem, present your solution, convince readers that your solution is feasible, and consider alternatives and potential objections to your solution. Few writers can manage all these tasks in a first draft, so keep them in mind as you assess your draft and revise your essay.

REASSESS YOUR PROBLEM DEFINITION

Now that your essay is in draft form, consider how well you present your problem definition and how effectively it leads to your proposed solution. Your problem definition should direct your readers' attention to the problem in a particular way. If not, they'll find it difficult to understand how your definition of the problem is related to your proposed solution. As you draft your essay — and spend additional time thinking about the problem — you will almost certainly deepen your understanding of the problem. Take a few moments now to ask whether your problem definition fully reflects that understanding.

Then ask some harder questions: Have you defined your problem in the best way (with *best* defined in light of the solution you've proposed and the needs, interests, and backgrounds of your readers)? Will your readers accept the problem definition

In Process

Using a Figure to Support a Point

James Hardjadinata found a figure on the website of the Humane Society of the United States. He included it in his essay as evidence to support a point about the inadequacies of laws regulating puppy mills.

Laws exist to regulate these problematic puppy mills, but they are insufficient. Burger points out that states with "lemon laws" offer stricter consumer protections, requiring breeders to guarantee the health of their puppies or replace them (Burger 262, Widner 220). However, as shown in figure 1, the laws vary by state, with some states requiring both licensure and inspection, others requiring only licensure, and still others having no laws at all (Humane Society, "State"). As a result, breeders often move to those states with laxer laws. This predicament is perhaps best exemplified by Missouri, known as the "Puppy Mill Capital" of the US, with 33% to 40% of the country's mill-bred dogs originating from that state (Burger 265).

> James refers to the figure in the text of his essay. He places the figure close to where he mentions it.

> Text is "wrapped" around the figure.

> The figure has a caption. The source of the figure is identified in parentheses after the caption.

Figure 1. A graphic of states with puppy mill laws and the extent to which they are defined. As the legend indicates, those states in purple are the most stringent in their definitions with required licensing and inspection, those in blue only require licensing and limits without inspections, while those in gray have no laws that specifically address puppy mills. (Humane Society, "State")

▲ A figure used as evidence

you've developed? If you suspect that they'll object to it or find it inadequate, how can you change it to address their likely concerns?

REVIEW THE PRESENTATION OF YOUR SOLUTION

When you're in the midst of drafting, it's normal to spend more time on some aspects of your solution than others or to overlook key steps that will be required to put the solution into effect. As you review your draft, take a careful look at how you've presented your solution. Have you explained it logically and clearly? Have you provided your readers with a sufficiently detailed understanding of what the solution involves and how it could work? Have you presented sufficient evidence to support your points?

CHECK THE FEASIBILITY OF YOUR SOLUTION

When you're caught up in the details of presenting a solution, it's easy to lose sight of whether the solution will actually work. During your review, ask whether the solution you've proposed can be put into practice given the time, funding, and resources that are available. If you suspect that you've proposed a solution that might not be cost-effective — such as solving the problem of rising tuition costs by giving everyone who wants to attend college a $100,000 scholarship, a solution that would cost taxpayers roughly $1.8 trillion — reconsider your solution. Similarly, if the time and resources necessary to achieve a solution are simply not available, take another look at your options.

CONSIDER OBJECTIONS AND ALTERNATIVE SOLUTIONS

Put yourself in the position of your readers, and ask some hard questions. Why is this solution better than another? What are the major drawbacks of your proposed solution? Under what conditions would your solution be likely to fail? Identify the objections your readers might have to your solution, and address them in your essay. Look as well for challenges to your solution that your readers might not consider but that you've become aware of in the course of your reading. Then address each challenge, explaining clearly why your solution is preferable to the alternatives you've identified.

Peer Review: Improve Your Problem-Solving Essay

One of the biggest challenges writers face is reading a draft of their own work as a reader rather than as the writer. Because you know what you're trying to say, you find it easy to understand your draft. To determine what you should do to revise your draft, ask a friend or classmate to read your essay and to assess how well you have adopted the role of problem solver (see p. 344) by answering the following questions.

Purpose	
	1. Is my problem definition sufficiently narrow and focused? Is it clear and easy to understand?
	2. Do you believe the problem is significant? Why or why not?
	3. Is my solution clearly presented? Does it seem like a reasonable response to the problem I've defined?
Readers	
	4. Were you aware of the problem before you read the essay? Are other readers likely to be familiar with it? Do I need to say more about it to help readers understand?
	5. Are you convinced that my solution can work? Does it seem feasible? Why or why not?
	6. Have I presented ideas fairly? Are you aware of any potential objections or alternative solutions that I should have addressed?
Sources	
	7. Does the evidence I've offered to define the problem and support my proposed solution make sense? Can I add or clarify anything to help you understand the problem and solution better? Do you think any of the evidence is unnecessary?
	8. Do my sources strike you as reliable and appropriate? Does any of the evidence I've used seem questionable?
Context	
	9. Have I taken my readers' knowledge, assumptions, and values into consideration?
	10. Would any of the information I've drawn on in this essay be better presented in visual form? Could I make changes in page layout, color, shading, or rules to improve the essay's appearance?

For each of the points listed above, ask your reviewers to provide concrete advice about what you should do to improve your draft. It can help if you ask them to adopt the role of an editor — someone who is working with you to improve your draft. You can read more about peer review in Chapter 5.

✳ Student Essay

James Hardjadinata, "The Truth about Puppy Mills: Exposing a Heartrending Industry"

The following problem-solving essay was written by featured writer James Hardjadinata.

Hardjadinata 1

James Hardjadinata

Writing 39C

Professor Lynda Haas

May 30, 2016

The Truth about Puppy Mills: Exposing a Heartrending Industry

As the famous aphorism goes, a dog is "man's best friend." It might not surprise anyone, then, that nearly 40% of US households own dogs, for a total population of about 72 million dogs (ASPCA). Many pet owners, however, are clueless about the origins of their beloved companions. Sadly, a surprisingly large number of dogs are likely to have started their lives in puppy mills. Puppy mills are breeders that mass-produce dogs to maximize profits, with little regard for quality of care. The Humane Society of the United States estimates that puppy mills churn out upwards of 1 million puppies per year by subjugating their mothers to constant reproduction and forcing mothers and offspring to live in small, inhumane enclosures ("Puppy Mills").

Although state and federal laws attempt to regulate puppy mills, many of these laws are ineffective in their definitions and cannot be fully enforced. Solutions to this hidden problem require addressing why these malicious puppy mills continue to thrive, tightening existing laws, and imposing punishments on breeders who violate those laws. In order to overcome the objections of pet industry lobbyists, we must raise awareness so that the public can advocate for

Annotations (right margin):

- Information about the writer, class, and date is formatted according to MLA guidelines.
- The title is centered.
- The writer begins with a familiar quotation to frame the issue.
- The writer discusses situation/effects to define the problem of puppy mills.
- The writer makes a key point.
- An overview of the solutions the writer will discuss

Hardjadinata 2

regulations on puppy mills and stop buying from pet stores that source from them. Through social media outlets, we can collectively make rapid progress in raising awareness and stopping these enslaving and exploitive breeders.

Of Puppy Mills, Pet Stores, and Animal Shelters

> Headings use boldface type.

Although precise numbers are hard to determine, experts estimate that animal shelters euthanize between 2 and 4 million dogs every year, with puppy mills a major contributing cause of pet overpopulation (ASPCA; Humane Society, "Pets"). How did we end up in this predicament? Puppy mills emerged after World War II, when farmers were desperate for alternatives to the conventional crops that began to fail them. A rise in the supply of dogs and pet shops established to sell them was backed by the USDA, under the pretense that puppies would be their new "crops" (qtd. in Tushaus 504). Kailey Burger, writing for the *Washington University Journal of Law*, explains that many of these former crop farmers consider the puppies to be commodities, a substitute for farming amidst hard economic times: "They do not share the same sense of moral responsibility or duty that animal welfare activists infer from their own relationships with animals" (264-65).

> A brief history of the problem

> The writer indicates that the quoted material appeared in another source.

With profit their main motive, puppy mills crowd dogs into small cages, maximize the number of dogs they hold, and skimp on veterinary care, food, heat, and other necessities. Such conditions lead to the spread of diseases, and foster increased aggression, nervousness, and other behavioral problems for the dogs that live there. Puppy mills sell in volume to national pet store chains and to consumers via newspaper ads and online, often posing as small family breeders with innocent names like "Tanni's Precious Paws" and "Rainbow Ranch" (Humane Society, "Horrible"). In this way, even informed buyers may unsuspectingly buy from disreputable puppy mills.

Intense behavior training and expensive vet bills are required to normalize these cute yet abused puppies, and many are inevitably abandoned or sent to shelters. When damaged mill dogs are sent into animal shelters, often their behavioral and mental conditions worsen and their hopes of adoption lessen.

Hardjadinata 3

Again, estimates vary, but as many as 60% of the animals living in shelters are euthanized annually due to overpopulation (Rudy 43).

> The writer uses elements of a severity/duration problem definition to show the end result of the problem.

Laws exist to regulate these problematic puppy mills, but they are insufficient. Burger points out that states with "lemon laws" offer stricter consumer protections, requiring breeders to guarantee the health of their puppies or replace them (Burger 262, Widner 220). However, as shown in figure 1, the laws vary by

Figure 1. A graphic of states with puppy mill laws and the extent to which they are defined. As the legend indicates, those states in purple are the most stringent in their definitions with required licensing and inspection, those in blue only require licensing and limits without inspections, while those in gray have no laws that specifically address puppy mills. (Humane Society, "State")

> A figure provides an effective visual presentation of information. The figure is captioned, and its source is cited.

state, with some states requiring both licensure and inspection, others requiring only licensure, and still others having no laws at all (Humane Society, "State"). As a result, breeders often move to those states with laxer laws. This predicament is perhaps best exemplified by Missouri, known as the "Puppy Mill Capital" of the United States, with 33% to 40% of the country's mill-bred dogs originating from that state (Burger 265).

> The author's name and page number of a source

While state laws remain a patchwork, there is a federal animal protection law, the 1966 Animal Welfare Act (AWA). Unfortunately, the AWA is poorly defined and difficult to enforce. First, as a federal law designed to regulate interstate transactions, it requires inspections of animal dealers — breeders who sell to pet stores or other outlets — only. Puppy mills who sell directly to the public circumvent these inspections (Burger 263). Furthermore, the AWA sets no limits on the number of dogs living in a facility, it does not define the ratio of

> Information from a source is paraphrased.

Hardjadinata 4

caregivers to animals, and it does not stipulate a minimum size of their cages. The law does not offer clear definitions or limits, leaving it up to breeders to determine what "adequate" conditions are (Humane Society, "Puppy"). Without such clear guidelines, many puppy mills remain unheated in the winter, uncooled in the summer, and overcrowded year-round.

Finally, even if we set aside the law's shortcomings, there is neither enough federal funding nor staffing for proper oversight. Although the USDA has not released its staffing numbers, estimates suggest that only 70 to 110 USDA inspectors oversee the thousands of puppy mills nationwide, as well as zoos, circuses, and laboratories (Widner 222). With such deficiencies on the federal level and disparities on the state level, many breeders continue to operate with no repercussions.

> The writer begins to discuss potential solutions and identifies precedents.

Attacking the Problem through Legal Avenues

If aging federal laws like the Animal Welfare Act are ineffectual, then we must consider new alternatives to address this problem. One suggestion involves new standards for puppy mill laws that can be easily applied from state to state. Christina Widner points to legislation, recently passed in Colorado, that classifies breeders as low, medium, or high risk, assigning a metric based on the size of the litters produced and the size of the breeding operation. Under this new law, breeders in higher-risk categories are inspected more frequently (228). This sliding scale notion could be applied to licensing fees on breeders as well. Several other states have adopted laws that cap the number of puppies living in any one location, a moderate solution that at the very least remediates the mistreatment of animals in these facilities due to overcrowding (Widner 235). In these states, law-abiding backyard breeders need not be penalized, while the bigger establishments will be subjected to more frequent inspections and higher fees, yielding more revenue to support puppy mill inspections.

Although these recommendations are stringent, they do not address the current lax enforcement, particularly for large-scale offenders. They also require significant effort. Katherine C. Tushaus, writing for the *Drake Journal of Agricultural Law*, notes an easier alternative proposed overseas, which

Hardjadinata 5

would eliminate outright the sale of pets in pet stores throughout the state. The Animals (Regulation of Sales) Bill introduced in the Australian state of New South Wales gets to the root of the puppy mill problem by mandating that pet stores can only match customers with pets from pet shelters, rather than selling those sourced from puppy mills. However, the bill stipulated that breeders could still sell animals directly to families if they followed the regulations and accepted the responsibilities the state has established for dog breeders (Tushaus 515). This radical solution works twofold: puppy mills would no longer have a market for their mass-produced puppies, and overpopulated shelters would find homes for their puppies. Additionally, the state would not need to keep checking on smaller breeders, because breeders would be required go to the state for licensing (Tushaus 515).

   Tushaus argues that a law like this, if passed in the United States, could yield major gains in the effort against puppy mills. By shifting the source of puppies in pet stores from puppy mills to shelters, breeders would no longer have the financial incentive to maximize the litter and confine their puppies in enclosed spaces to optimize profits. Their businesses could thrive if they adhere to regulations and become recognized by the state to continue selling pets. Pet stores could still reasonably continue business by selling pet care products instead of pets, while directing people to shelter facilities to adopt pets (Tushaus 516-17). Furthermore, violation of the law would be obvious, making enforcement easy. If the people see a pet store selling pets instead of facilitating adoptions from animal shelters, they can easily report it to local authorities (Tushaus 516).

   The logical obstacle to this effective solution is how to pass such a radical bill in the United States. Even though these policies would benefit many parties (breeders, buyers, animal shelters), proponents of the pet industry would surely lobby against it. In fact, as Burger notes, agricultural industries are often quite powerful in state government, and their interest groups have been able to influence state law in their favor (269). Admittedly, the Australian bill failed to pass. After years of debate, however, it raised awareness in the government and the public regarding the issue of puppy mills and resulted in a call for a scientific review of unwanted companion animals in the state (Australian Veterinary Association). Likewise, the mere proposal of such a radical bill in the United States could, as Tushaus asserts, "set the stage for more public to support and

> An online source without page numbers is cited by the author's name only.

Hardjadinata 6

even demand for legislation dealing with the industry as people become aware of the cruelty the sale of puppy mill dogs perpetuates" (518).6

Using the Power of Social Media

Federal and state legislation are not the only ways to crack down on puppy mills. Spreading awareness of what puppy mills do and how their animals suffer will help galvanize the movement against them. In her law journal note, Burger cites the 2010 Puppy Mill Cruelty Prevention Act, a ballot initiative in Missouri, as an example of a successful publicity campaign, including pamphlets, Web videos, and commercials (275). She makes an analogy to free-range chicken or humanely raised beef: just as shoppers are willing to pay more for the additional benefits and quality of life afforded to those animals, they will likely be willing to buy humanely bred dogs.

Social media is one of the best ways today to accomplish such a campaign. With the rapid expansion of social media sites like Twitter and Facebook, ideas can rapidly be shared en masse with little effort. As one media scholar describes it, social media is "the first medium in history that has native support for groups and conversation at the same time . . . [and] gives us the many-to-many pattern," the ability for almost anyone to communicate with anyone else about anything and to reach a large audience (Shirky). Moreover, social media provides this ability to broadcast at almost no cost. For these reasons, it is a powerful tool for supporting advocacy efforts for animals and for raising awareness of the puppy mill problem.

With other members of a group carrying out research on puppy mills, I collaborated on the development of a simple campaign to spread awareness about the fraud perpetrated by popular pet food brands, which rely on unhealthy ingredients. As we discovered, it only took a few tweets a day to garner an extensive following on Twitter, our most successful platform. With enticing titles and as many relevant hashtags as could fit in the span of 140 characters, our tweets were favorited and retweeted by many in support of our hashtag #FeedingFido. We quickly amassed more than 200 followers. Some read through our past tweets and retweeted them, while others gave automated courtesy tweets thanking us for following them. Still other followers sent passionate messages in support of their respective animal advocacy efforts. All of these

---

> The writer argues that new legislation is not enough. Awareness is needed, too.

> The writer describes his success raising awareness via social media platforms.

Hardjadinata 7

posts, tweets, and retweets publicized our cause in small increments. We found the campaign effective in that it only took a few, well-worded tweets per day to expand awareness of our cause.

Given our limited actions, the possibilities for a more active campaign against puppy mills are boundless. The effort to spread awareness could go international via social media outlets, educating people to give more thought to the pets they buy and where they buy them from, but also giving recognition to existing efforts against puppy mills. By helping current and future generations become more aware of the origins of those cute puppies they fawn over in pet store windows, we can ensure a healthier future for all.

Conclusion

Puppy mills have existed since the 1940s as a means to support struggling farmers. They have become even more prevalent, however, due to the ease with which these unscrupulous producers can trick consumers into buying unhealthy, neglected puppies — so many of which eventually end up in shelters waiting to be euthanized. Without question, we should morally oppose puppy mills. Yet current state and federal laws are ineffective due to inadequate funding. Consequently, the most promising solutions are creating laws that are easier to enforce. As with the New South Wales Animals bill, this might mean stopping the sale of animals in pet stores altogether, a policy under which small breeders would earn government recognition to continue sales instead of hiding in rural areas.

Pushing for such radical bills to be passed into law requires broad public awareness and education on the matter, which we can readily accomplish through the use of social media. Now more than ever we are able to spread the word as groups and individuals alike worldwide, through media outlets like Twitter, Facebook, YouTube, and Reddit, with little to no cost and effort. By harnessing the power of social media, the general public, not just animal rights' groups, can collectively advocate for laws and government attention, creating a future without puppy mills.

> The writer's conclusion summarizes how he thinks his solution will succeed.

Hardjadinata 8

Works Cited

Organization as author

ASPCA. "Pet Statistics." *American Society for the Prevention of Cruelty to Animals*, 2015, www.aspca.org/animal-homelessness/shelter-intake-and -surrender/pet-statistics.

Australian Veterinary Association. "Animals (Regulation of Sale) Bill 2008."

URLs are provided for Web sources.

Australian Veterinary Association, 2015, www.ava.com.au/node/1065.

Burger, Kailey A. "Solving the Problem of Puppy Mills: Why the Animal Welfare Movement's Bark Is Stronger than Its Bite." *Washington University Journal of Law and Policy*, vol. 43, 2014, pp. 259-84.

For multiple works by the same author, only the first entry lists the author's name. Subsequent entries use three hyphens and a period.

Humane Society of the United States. "A Horrible Hundred Selected Puppy Mills in the United States." *Humane Society of the United States*, May 2013, www.humanesociety.org/assets/pdfs/pets/puppy_mills/100-puppy-mills -list.pdf.

---. "Pets by the Numbers." *Humane Society of the United States*, www .humanesociety.org/issues/pet_overpopulation/facts/pet_ownership _statistics.html. Accessed 10 May 2016.

---. "Puppy Mills: Frequently Asked Questions." *Humane Society of the United States*, www.humanesociety.org/issues/puppy_mills/qa/puppy_mill_FAQs.html. Accessed 10 May 2016.

---. "State Puppy Mill Laws." *Humane Society of the United States*, May 2015, www.humanesociety.org/assets/state-puppy-mill-laws.pdf.

Rudy, Kathy. *Loving Animals: Toward a New Animal Advocacy*. U of Minnesota P, 2011.

Shirky, Clay. "How Social Media Can Make History." *TED*, June 2009, www.ted .com/talks/clay_shirky_how_cellphones_twitter_facebook_can_make_history.

Tushaus, Katherine C. "Don't Buy the Doggy in the Window: Ending the Cycle That Perpetuates Commercial Breeding with Regulation of the Retail Pet Industry." *Drake Journal of Agricultural Law*, vol. 14, 2009, pp. 504-17, www .animallaw.info/article/dont-buy-doggy-window-ending-cycle-perpetuates

For articles accessed on the Web, volume number, page numbers, and URL are all provided.

-commercial-breeding-regulation-retail-pet.

Widner, Christina. "Channeling Cruella De Vil: An Exploration of Proposed and Ideal Regulation on Domestic Animal Breeding in California." *San Joaquin Agricultural Law Review*, vol. 20, 2010, pp. 217-36.

Project Ideas

The following suggestions provide a means of focusing your work on a problem-solving essay or another type of problem-solving document.

Suggestions for Essays

1. DEFINE A PROBLEM AT YOUR SCHOOL

In a brief essay, define a problem at your college or university. You might choose a problem related to your major, your residence hall, a campus neighborhood, an extracurricular activity, or your school's student government. Using one of the sets of problem-definition questions provided on page 370, describe the problem in as much detail as possible, and define the consequences if it were to be left unaddressed. Use observation, interviews, or a survey of affected students to collect information about the problem (see Chapter 14). If the problem might be common to other institutions, locate and review published sources that address the problem (see Chapter 13).

2. PROPOSE A SOLUTION TO A LOCAL PROBLEM

Identify and define a problem in your community or local school district and then propose a solution. You might, for example, choose a problem related to conducting local elections or funding local schools. Similarly, you might look at issues such as homelessness in your community or school district. Collect information about the problem from published sources, such as a community newspaper, a local magazine, or local-area websites. Conduct research to locate other communities with a similar problem and find out how they've addressed it. If possible, interview or correspond with someone who knows about or has been affected by the problem (see Chapter 14).

3. TRACE THE DEVELOPMENT OF A PROBLEM

Identify a problem that has not yet been solved, and trace its development. Discuss its causes, factors that contribute to its ongoing status as a problem, and factors that have worked against the creation of a successful solution. To support your discussion, locate published sources that have considered the problem. If you can, collect evidence firsthand through observation, surveys, or interviews (see Chapter 14). Although you are not required to offer a solution, consider using your conclusion to suggest directions that might be pursued to solve the problem.

4. EVALUATE PROPOSED SOLUTIONS TO A PROBLEM

Evaluate solutions that have been proposed to solve a problem. In your essay, briefly define the problem, and discuss the long-term consequences of the problem if left unsolved. Then identify approaches that have been proposed to solve the problem. Choose two to four proposed solutions to evaluate. Define your evaluation criteria (see p. 321), and discuss how well each of the proposed solutions measures up. In your conclusion, offer your assessment of whether the solution you deem most likely to succeed will actually be implemented. To support your discussion, locate published sources that have addressed the problem (see Chapter 13).

5. EVALUATE A SOLUTION THAT HAS GONE WRONG

Identify an attempt to solve a problem that has produced unintended consequences or failed to adequately address the problem. You might find, for example, that mandatory sentencing requirements for possession of alcohol or drugs have led to a significant increase in incarceration, which in turn has harmed otherwise law-abiding citizens and placed a significant burden on the state budget. In your essay, define the problem that gave rise to the solution, explain the intent of the solution, and analyze how it went wrong. Offer an alternative approach to addressing the problem. To support your argument, locate published sources that have addressed the problem (see Chapter 13). If the problem lends itself to field research (see Chapter 14), consider using observation, interviews, surveys, or correspondence to gather information about the problem and the solution that was put into place.

Suggestions for Other Genres

6. DRAFT AND DESIGN A PROBLEM-SOLVING ARTICLE FOR A NEWSPAPER OR MAGAZINE

Begin by deciding whether you want to write about a particular problem or publish in a particular newspaper or magazine. If you want to write about a particular problem, search your library's databases for articles about the problem. This can help you identify newspapers and magazines that have published articles dealing with the problem. If you want to publish your article in a particular newspaper or magazine, read a few issues of the publication carefully to determine the kinds of problems it normally addresses. Analyze its writing conventions (such as level of formality and the manner in which sources are acknowledged) and design conventions. Your article should reflect those writing and design conventions. In your article, define the problem you are addressing, argue for the importance of solving the problem, propose your solution, and consider and dismiss alternative solutions. You should support your argument with evidence from other sources, such as journal and magazine articles, newspaper articles, blogs, and websites (see Chapter 13). You can also interview an expert or correspond with someone who has been affected by the problem (see Chapter 14).

7. WRITE A PROPOSAL TO SOLVE A PROBLEM

Choose an issue of interest to you and define a problem associated with it. Then develop a potential solution and identify an organization or government agency that might provide funding for your solution. Before drafting your proposal, conduct research on the problem and on the organization or agency. In your proposal, frame the issue (see p. 380) in a way that helps your potential funder understand the importance of the problem, explain how addressing the problem will support the mission of the organization or agency, and describe how your proposal will solve the problem. Be sure to identify the likely outcomes of implementing your proposed solution. You should draw on published sources (see Chapter 13) and interviews with experts to support your proposal (see Chapter 14). You should also provide a budget and an evaluation plan. If you have questions about how best to complete the proposal, ask your instructor.

8. WRITE A LETTER OF COMPLAINT

Write a letter that identifies and complains about a problem you've experienced with a product or service. Your letter should be addressed to a person, a group, or an agency that has the capacity to address the problem. To prepare your letter of complaint, conduct research on the problem and on the person, group, or agency (see Chapters 13 and 14). Your letter should be no longer than 1,000 words. It should clearly define the problem, explain why the recipient of the letter is in a position to address the problem, and explain how to address the complaint. If you have questions about how best to compose the letter, discuss them with your instructor.

In Summary: Writing a Problem-Solving Essay

✱ **Find a conversation and listen in.**
- Explore difficulties (p. 366).
- Ask questions about promising subjects (p. 367).
- Conduct a survey (p. 368).

✱ **Develop a solution.**
- Define the problem (p. 369).
- Consider potential solutions (p. 370).
- Assess the practicality of your solution (p. 373).

✱ **Prepare a draft.**
- Explain the problem (p. 375).
- Propose your solution (p. 377).

- Explain your solution (p. 377).
- Consider genre and design (p. 379).
- Frame your essay (p. 380).

✱ **Review and improve your draft.**
- Reassess your problem definition (p. 381).
- Review the presentation of your solution (p. 383).
- Check the feasibility of your solution (p. 383).
- Consider objections and alternative solutions (p. 383).

11 Writing to Convince or Persuade

As an **advocate**, I write to convince or persuade my readers to see my perspective on a subject.

What Is Writing to Convince or Persuade?

Some people love a good argument. Others go out of their way to avoid conflict. Regardless of where you stand, it's hard to deny the important role that debate and discussion play in our daily lives. Unfortunately, few of the arguments we encounter on a daily basis are well grounded and fully thought out. Whether you're listening to a talk show, reading the lunatic ravings of a misinformed blogger, or streaming a clever clip on YouTube about the issue of the day, it can be almost comically easy to pick out the flaws in a weak argument.

An effective argument, on the other hand, makes a well-supported, well-considered point about an issue in an attempt to convince or persuade readers. *Convincing* involves gaining readers' agreement that a position on an issue is reasonable and well founded. *Persuading* involves getting them to take action. One writer, for example, might seek to convince readers that the drinking age should be lowered to eighteen, while another might attempt to persuade teenagers to take a vow of sobriety.

Whether they attempt to convince or persuade, writers who make arguments adopt the role of *advocate*. An effective advocate considers not only the argument he or she will advance but also how best to formulate and express that argument for a particular audience. Although readers of arguments typically share the writer's assumption that an issue is important and are willing to consider new ideas, they bring their own values, beliefs, and experiences to the conversation. A writer who wants to change readers' minds or persuade them to act must give careful thought to who readers are and where they come from, what they value, how resistant or receptive they might be to an argument, and what kinds of argumentative strategies — such as appeals to logic, emotion, or authority — are most likely to sway them.

Sources of evidence used in argumentative documents include numerical data, reports of a writer's direct observation, and statements by experts, to name just a few. Advocates sometimes use charged language, but more often than not they adopt a straightforward, reasonable tone. They typically offer evidence and reasoning to align their arguments with authorities and with other writers, provide background information, support their claims and reasoning, and refute opposing arguments. Advocates might also offer evidence in the form of illustrations, such as images, video and audio clips, or tables and charts, to set a mood or call attention to specific points. Their decisions about the type of evidence they use are shaped by

both the type of document they choose to write and the context in which they find themselves.

Argumentative documents are the means through which many written conversations make progress on an issue. By stating a claim and providing evidence to support it, advocates help readers understand options for addressing an issue. By pointing out the drawbacks of competing arguments, they help participants in the conversation weigh alternatives. More than any other type of document, written arguments help us decide — individually and as a group — what we should believe and how we should act. In doing so, they have a profound effect on how we live our lives.

The Writer's Role: Advocate

PURPOSE

- To stake a position on an issue
- To convince others to agree with the position
- To persuade readers to take action

READERS

- Want thoughtful consideration of an issue that is important to them
- Look for a clearly stated claim supported by ample reasons and reliable evidence
- Expect a fair and reasonable presentation of information, ideas, and competing arguments

SOURCES

- Advocates appeal to readers' reason, emotion, and trust as they present arguments.
- Evidence can come from personal observation, print and digital documents, or field research.
- Supporting information is often presented in visual form.

CONTEXT

- Effective writers consider opposing points of view and choose argumentative strategies that establish common ground with readers.
- Advocates might use color and images to set a mood and often present supporting information in visual forms — such as charts, tables, and graphs — to help readers understand an issue.

What Kinds of Documents Are Used to Convince or Persuade?

Argumentation involves making a claim, supporting it with reasons and evidence, addressing reasonable alternatives, and urging readers to accept or act on the writer's main point. Virtually any type of writing, then, can contain an argument — and even documents that serve primarily to reflect, inform, analyze, evaluate, or solve problems often contain some elements of argumentation.

Understanding the genres that can be used to convince or persuade can help you prepare to write your own argument. In this section, you'll find examples of common argumentative documents: argumentative essays, advertisements, point/counterpoint editorials, and open letters. As you read these documents, reflect on the contexts in which the writers found themselves. Ask, for example, what readers need to know about an issue to be convinced or persuaded. Ask about the kinds of evidence that readers interested in a particular issue might accept — or reject. And ask about the design elements that might influence readers — positively or negatively — as they consider an argument.

Argumentative Essays

To some extent, argumentative essays resemble written debates. Writers typically advance a thoroughly considered and well-supported argument that addresses competing positions on the issue and explains why the writer's position is preferable to the others. Argumentative essays almost always draw on information from other sources (articles, books, websites, statistics, interviews, and so on) to provide evidence that supports the effort to convince readers of the merits of a particular stance on an issue or to persuade them to take action. Argumentative essays can also draw extensively on a writer's personal experience with an issue.

Writers of argumentative essays must carefully consider readers' needs, interests, backgrounds, and knowledge of an issue. A thorough understanding of readers' familiarity with the issue, their purposes for reading the essay, and the values, beliefs, and assumptions they bring to a reading of the essay can help a writer make thoughtful, strategic choices about how to present and support an argument. It can also help a writer determine how best to acknowledge and argue for the comparative inadequacy of competing positions on the issue.

 Anu Partanen

What Americans Keep Ignoring about Finland's School Success

In comparing and contrasting Finland's education policies with America's, Anu Partanen sets up evidence for compelling claims about equity in education. This argumentative essay originally appeared in *The Atlantic*, a monthly magazine devoted to political, cultural, and literary topics. Partanen, a journalist born in Finland and currently based in New York, has written for several American and Scandinavian publications and is writing a book about lessons from Nordic society that can help Americans.

What Americans Keep Ignoring about Finland's School Success

by Anu Partanen

Everyone agrees the United States needs to improve its education system dramatically, but how? One of the hottest trends in education reform lately is looking at the stunning success of the West's reigning education superpower, Finland. Trouble is, when it comes to the lessons that Finnish schools have to offer, most of the discussion seems to be missing the point.

The small Nordic country of Finland used to be known — if it was known for anything at all — as the home of Nokia, the mobile phone giant. But lately Finland has been attracting attention on global surveys of quality of life — *Newsweek* ranked it number one last year — and Finland's national education system has been receiving particular praise, because in recent years Finnish students have been turning in some of the highest test scores in the world.

Finland's schools owe their newfound fame primarily to one study: the PISA survey, conducted every three years by the Organization for Economic Co-operation and Development (OECD). The survey compares 15-year-olds in different countries in reading, math, and science. Finland has ranked at or near the top in all three competencies on every survey since 2000, neck and neck with superachievers such as South Korea and Singapore. In the most recent survey in 2009 Finland slipped slightly, with students in Shanghai, China, taking the best scores, but the Finns are still near the very top. Throughout the same period, the PISA performance of the United States has been middling, at best.

Compared with the stereotype of the East Asian model — long hours of exhaustive cramming and rote memorization — Finland's success is especially intriguing because Finnish schools assign less homework and engage children in more creative play. All this has led to a continuous stream of foreign delegations making the pilgrimage to Finland to visit schools and talk with the nation's education experts, and constant coverage in the worldwide media marveling at the Finnish miracle.

So there was considerable interest in a recent visit to the U.S. by one of the leading Finnish authorities on education reform, Pasi Sahlberg, director of the Finnish Ministry of Education's Center for International Mobility and author of the new book *Finnish Lessons: What Can the World Learn from Educational Change in Finland?* Earlier this month, Sahlberg stopped by the Dwight School in New York City to speak with educators and students, and his visit received national media attention and generated much discussion.

And yet it wasn't clear that Sahlberg's message was actually getting through. As Sahlberg put it to me later, there are certain things nobody in America really wants to talk about.

During the afternoon that Sahlberg spent at the Dwight School, a photographer from the

New York Times jockeyed for position with Dan Rather's TV crew as Sahlberg participated in a roundtable chat with students. The subsequent article in the *Times* about the event would focus on Finland as an "intriguing school-reform model."

Yet one of the most significant things Sahlberg said passed practically unnoticed. "Oh," he mentioned at one point, "and there are no private schools in Finland."

This notion may seem difficult for an American to digest, but it's true. Only a small number of independent schools exist in Finland, and even they are all publicly financed. None is allowed to charge tuition fees. There are no private universities, either. This means that practically every person in Finland attends public school, whether for pre-K or a Ph.D.

The irony of Sahlberg's making this comment during a talk at the Dwight School seemed obvious. Like many of America's best schools, Dwight is a private institution that costs high-school students upward of $35,000 a year to attend — not to mention that Dwight, in particular, is run for profit, an increasing trend in the U.S. Yet no one in the room commented on Sahlberg's statement. I found this surprising. Sahlberg himself did not.

Sahlberg knows what Americans like to talk about when it comes to education, because he's become their go-to guy in Finland. The son of two teachers, he grew up in a Finnish school. He taught mathematics and physics in a junior high school in Helsinki, worked his way through a variety of positions in the Finnish Ministry of Education, and spent years as an education expert at the OECD, the World Bank, and other international organizations.

> Finland's experience shows that it is possible to achieve excellence by focusing not on competition, but on cooperation, and not on choice, but on equity.

Now, in addition to his other duties, Sahlberg hosts about a hundred visits a year by foreign educators, including many Americans, who want to know the secret of Finland's success. Sahlberg's new book is partly an attempt to help answer the questions he always gets asked.

From his point of view, Americans are consistently obsessed with certain questions: How can you keep track of students' performance if you don't test them constantly? How can you improve teaching if you have no accountability for bad teachers or merit pay for good teachers? How do you foster competition and engage the private sector? How do you provide school choice?

The answers Finland provides seem to run counter to just about everything America's school reformers are trying to do.

For starters, Finland has no standardized tests. The only exception is what's called the National Matriculation Exam, which everyone takes at the end of a voluntary upper-secondary school, roughly the equivalent of American high school.

Instead, the public school system's teachers are trained to assess children in classrooms using independent tests they create themselves. All children receive a report card at the end of each semester, but these reports are based on individualized grading by each teacher. Periodically, the Ministry of Education tracks national progress by testing a few sample groups across a range of different schools.

As for accountability of teachers and administrators, Sahlberg shrugs. "There's no word for accountability in Finnish," he later told an audience at the Teachers College of Columbia University. "Accountability is something that is left when responsibility has been subtracted."

For Sahlberg what matters is that in Finland all teachers and administrators are given prestige, decent pay, and a lot of responsibility. A master's degree is required to enter the profession, and teacher training programs are among the most selective professional schools in the country. If a teacher is bad, it is the principal's responsibility to notice and deal with it.

And while Americans love to talk about competition, Sahlberg points out that nothing makes Finns more uncomfortable. In his book Sahlberg quotes a line from Finnish writer Samuli Paronen: "Real winners do not compete." It's hard to think of a more un-American idea, but when it comes to education, Finland's success shows that the Finnish attitude might have merits. There are no lists of best schools or teachers in Finland. The main driver of education policy is not competition between teachers and between schools, but cooperation.

Finally, in Finland, school choice is noticeably not a priority, nor is engaging the private sector at all. Which brings us back to the silence after Sahlberg's comment at the Dwight School that schools like Dwight don't exist in Finland.

"Here in America," Sahlberg said at the Teachers College, "parents can choose to take their kids to private schools. It's the same idea of a marketplace that applies to, say, shops. Schools are a shop and parents can buy whatever they want. In Finland parents can also choose. But the options are all the same."

Herein lay the real shocker. As Sahlberg continued, his core message emerged, whether or not anyone in his American audience heard it.

Decades ago, when the Finnish school system was badly in need of reform, the goal of the program that Finland instituted, resulting in so much success today, was never excellence. It was equity.

Since the 1980s, the main driver of Finnish education policy has been the idea that every child should have exactly the same opportunity to learn, regardless of family background, income, or geographic location. Education has been seen first and foremost not as a way to produce star performers, but as an instrument to even out social inequality.

In the Finnish view, as Sahlberg describes it, this means that schools should be healthy, safe environments for children. This starts with the basics. Finland offers all pupils free school meals, easy access to health care, psychological counseling, and individualized student guidance.

In fact, since academic excellence wasn't a particular priority on the Finnish to-do list, when Finland's students scored so high on the first PISA survey in 2001, many Finns thought the results must be a mistake. But subsequent PISA tests confirmed that Finland — unlike, say, very similar countries such as Norway — was producing academic excellence through its particular policy focus on equity.

That this point is almost always ignored or brushed aside in the U.S. seems especially poignant at the moment, after the financial crisis and Occupy Wall Street movement have brought the problems of inequality in America into such sharp focus. The chasm between those who can afford $35,000 in tuition per child per year — or even just the price of a house in a good public school district — and the other "99 percent" is painfully plain to see.

Pasi Sahlberg goes out of his way to emphasize that his book *Finnish Lessons* is not meant as a how-to guide for fixing the education systems of other countries. All countries are different, and as many Americans point out, Finland is a small nation with a much more homogeneous population than the United States.

Yet Sahlberg doesn't think that questions of size or homogeneity should give Americans reason to dismiss the Finnish example. Finland *is* a relatively homogeneous country — as of 2010, just 4.6 percent of Finnish residents had been born in another country, compared with 12.7 percent in the United States. But the number of foreign-born residents in Finland doubled during the decade leading up to 2010, and the country didn't lose its edge in education. Immigrants tended to concentrate in certain areas, causing some schools to become much more mixed than others, yet there has not been much change in the remarkable lack of variation between Finnish schools in the PISA surveys across the same period.

Samuel Abrams, a visiting scholar at Columbia University's Teachers College, has addressed the effects of size and homogeneity on a nation's education performance by comparing Finland with another Nordic country: Norway. Like Finland, Norway is small and not especially diverse overall, but unlike Finland it has taken an approach to education that is more American than Finnish. The result? Mediocre performance in the PISA survey. Educational policy, Abrams suggests, is probably more important to the success of a country's school system than the nation's size or ethnic makeup.

Indeed, Finland's population of 5.4 million can be compared to many an American state — after all, most American education is managed at the state level. According to the Migration Policy Institute, a research organization in Washington, there were 18 states in the U.S. in 2010 with an identical or significantly smaller percentage of foreign-born residents than Finland.

What's more, despite their many differences, Finland and the U.S. have an educational goal in common. When Finnish policymakers decided to reform the country's education system in the 1970s, they did so because they realized that to be competitive, Finland couldn't rely on manufacturing or its scant natural resources and instead had to invest in a knowledge-based economy.

With America's manufacturing industries now in decline, the goal of educational policy in the U.S. — as articulated by most everyone from President Obama on down — is to preserve American competitiveness by doing the same thing. Finland's experience suggests that to win at that game, a country has to prepare not just some of its population well, but all of its population well, for the new economy. To possess some of the best schools in the world might still not be good enough if there are children being left behind.

Is that an impossible goal? Sahlberg says that while his book isn't meant to be a how-to manual, it is meant to be a "pamphlet of hope."

"When President Kennedy was making his appeal for advancing American science and technology by putting a man on the moon by the end of the 1960s, many said it couldn't be done," Sahlberg said during his visit to New York. "But he had a dream. Just like Martin Luther King a few years later had a dream. Those dreams came true. Finland's dream was that we want to have a good public education for every child regardless of where they go to school or what kind of families they come from, and many even in Finland said it couldn't be done."

Clearly, many were wrong. It is possible to create equality. And perhaps even more important — as a challenge to the American way of thinking about education reform — Finland's experience shows that it is possible to achieve excellence by focusing not on competition, but on cooperation, and not on choice, but on equity.

The problem facing education in America isn't the ethnic diversity of the population but the economic inequality of society, and this is precisely the problem that Finnish education reform addressed. More equity at home might just be what America needs to be more competitive abroad.

Starting a Conversation: Respond to "What Americans Keep Ignoring about Finland's School Success"

In your writer's notebook, record your analysis of Partanen's essay by responding to the following questions:

1. Partanen begins her argument with a question: "Everyone agrees the United States needs to improve its education system dramatically, but how?" What assumptions is Partanen making about her readers? How do you think readers are likely to respond to these assumptions?

2. Partanen notes that when it comes to education, "there are certain things nobody in America really wants to talk about" (para. 6). To what things, specifically, does she refer? Why do you think she says Americans don't want to talk about them?

3. Aside from advocate, what roles does Partanen take on as she presents her argument? How does she signal to her readers when she is changing roles?

4. What counterarguments does Partanen raise in her essay? How does she respond to ideas and information that don't seem to support her argument? How effective would you say her responses are, and why?

5. **Reflection:** Partanen quotes Pasi Sahlberg as saying that his book isn't intended as a "how-to manual" for reforming American education; rather, "it is meant to be a 'pamphlet of hope'" (para. 34). What do you think this statement means? How might a "pamphlet of hope" be a better approach than a "how-to manual"?

Advertisements

Advertisements seek to persuade the people who see or hear them to take a specific action — whether it's purchasing a product, supporting a cause, applying for a job, donating to a nonprofit organization, or voting for a political candidate. The argument usually takes the form of a simple claim, which might be conveyed through a brief slogan, such as "The Best Food in Texas"; through an image, such as a photo of people having a good time while they use a particular product (an adult beverage, for example, or a new sports car); or through an endorsement in which a celebrity extols the virtues of a particular product. The argument might even take the form of a detailed list of features and benefits, such as you might see in a brochure for a smartphone or a new prescription drug. In some cases, such as political campaigns or the battle between cable and satellite television providers, advertisements can also make negative claims.

Few readers seek out advertisements. They usually encounter them as they flip through a magazine, browse the Web, watch television, listen to the radio, or drive along a highway studded with billboards. Because most readers don't devote a great deal of time to considering an advertisement, most ads are designed to capture the reader's or viewer's attention and convey their claim as quickly as possible. As a result, they typically rely on images and limit the amount of written text. For example, the long-running advertising campaign originated by the California Milk Processors Board asks the simple question "Got Milk?" Another, developed by the U.S. Marines, urges enlistment with the slogan "The few. The proud. The Marines." Yet another ad, used so heavily in the 1980s and 1990s that it has become part of our cultural landscape, urges youth to "Just say no to drugs."

 ## Men Can Stop Rape
Where Do You Stand?

The advertisements beginning on the next page, developed by the nonprofit organization Men Can Stop Rape for its "Where Do You Stand?" campaign, challenge men to help prevent rape with a mix of imagery and brief passages of text. Representing an effort to model effective intervention strategies, the ads are designed to appear as banners, postcards, and posters. They target young adults on college campuses.

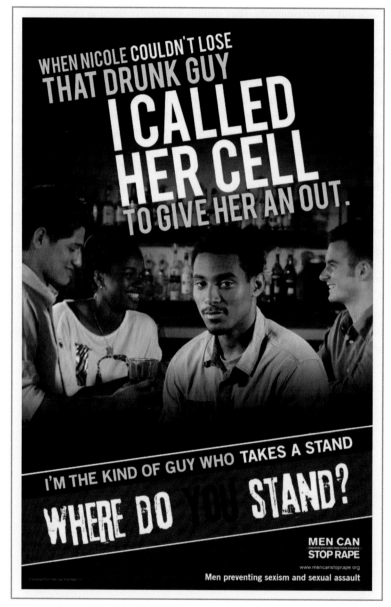

© 2011 Men Can Stop Rape

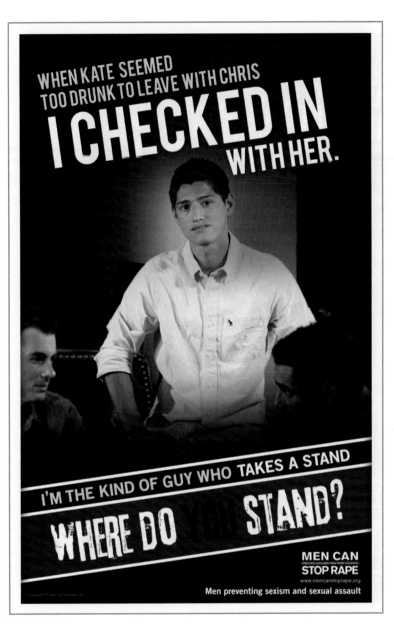

© 2011 Men Can Stop Rape

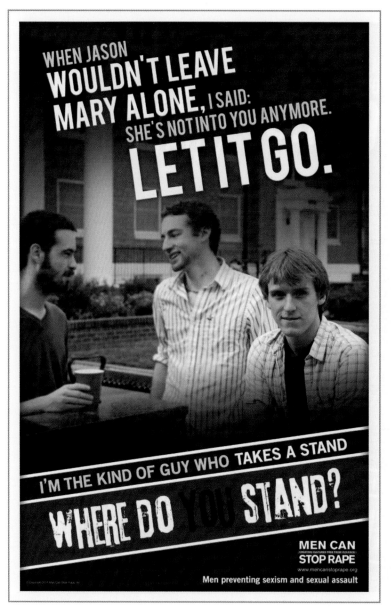

© 2011 Men Can Stop Rape

4 THINGS YOU CAN DO TO TAKE A STAND

1 Distraction

Call your friend's cell to ask her a question or suggest it's time to go. You can also distract the guy harassing her: "Hey man, didn't I see you at [fill in the blank]?"

2 Group Intervention

Ask your/her friends to help out with distraction or separation. They can pull her aside to check in. Or they can say to him: "We see what you're doing and it's not okay."

3 Get an authority

Ask the bartender, bouncer, or any other authority figure to help support the intervention.

4 Prepare Yourself

Be aware of the pressures men face not to take a stand and choose what kind of man you want to be.

WHERE DO YOU STAND?

Starting a Conversation: Respond to "Where Do You Stand?" Advertisements

In your writer's notebook, record your analysis of the "Where Do You Stand?" advertisements by responding to the following questions:

1. Although the four advertisements are part of the same campaign, their specific messages are different. What particular actions does each advocate? What characteristics do they share?

2. How would you describe the relationship between text and image in these advertisements? What effect does the design of the ads and the images used in them have on their overall message?

3. This campaign was aimed at college students and young adults between the ages of eighteen and twenty-five. How are these ads meant to appeal to that audience? In what ways do the ads reflect the culture and values of their presumed readers?

4. **Reflection:** The "Where Do You Stand?" campaign represents one of many Men Can Stop Rape initiatives. Have you seen similar campaigns? How have you reacted to them? Do you agree with the assumptions they make about college age men and women? Why or why not?

Point/Counterpoint Editorials

Point/counterpoint editorials are used by newspapers, magazines, and other news media to illustrate opposing views about an issue. If disagreement exists about a proposed amendment to a state constitution, for example, a newspaper might invite proponents and opponents of the amendment to contribute to a point/counterpoint editorial. The two editorials might be placed side by side on a single page, or, depending on the size of the page and the amount of space given to their writers, they might be placed on facing pages.

Like other editorials and opinion columns, point/counterpoint editorials are typically brief, usually containing fewer than a thousand words. Because they tend to address issues of larger public interest, however, point/counterpoint editorials are more likely than are opinion columns to include evidence such as quotations or paraphrases from published sources, quotations from interviews, or statistical data drawn from published studies. In this sense, point/counterpoint editorials are more similar to reports and essays than they are to opinion columns and letters to the editor.

In general, point/counterpoint editorials are designed simply. In some cases, they might include charts, tables, photographs, and other illustrations — should the editors of the newspaper, magazine, or website wish to call attention to the relative importance of the issue being addressed. Most often, however, they do not include illustrations or headings.

David W. Kreutzer

Point: Solar Power Presents Significant Environmental Problems

David W. Kreutzer, research fellow in energy economics and climate change at the Heritage Foundation, wrote the following opinion piece on solar energy. The Heritage Foundation is a research institution and educational center that aims to identify and promote conservative public policies. In his role at the Heritage Foundation, it is Kreutzer's primary goal to research the economic effects of energy and climate change. Kreutzer argues that solar energy is not the best energy solution, and furthermore, that the government's involvement in solar energy has unfairly burdened consumers.

Point: Solar Power Presents Significant Environmental Problems

By David W. Kreutzer | December 12, 2015

Pollyanna and a pile of money make for bad energy policy. Yes, American ingenuity and entrepreneurial spirit are famously creative and productive. However, simply repeating that mantra while heaping subsidies on the politically well-connected and mandates on the rest won't make solar power more affordable or reliable.

For sure, solar power makes sense in certain applications. If you're far from the grid with low power demand, solar can work for you. Want to charge cell phones in the middle of Chad? Solar panels could be the right answer. And my solar-powered watch has kept perfect time for over five years with no battery changes. But when it comes to providing reliable, utility-scale, baseload power, solar faces formidable technical and environmental hurdles.

The most daunting, perhaps, is sunset. Clouds, snow and other weather changes also significantly limit solar power output. Since every power grid must continuously balance supply and demand, spikes and dips in solar power output must be offset with instantaneous cuts or additions from other sources, such as natural gas.

"Green energy" may conjure images of butterflies and national parks, but solar power presents significant environmental problems, from the toxic wastes of solar-panel production to the incineration of flying wildlife at concentrating solar plants. And solar farms require far more land than a conventional power plant generating the same output.

Many, if not all, of the problems can be addressed, but it will cost. Like growing tomatoes in Antarctica, it's possible, but why bother when most of the rest of the world is much better suited to agriculture? We face a similar problem with ramping up solar power from wristwatch scale to utility scale — there are other sources of power that are much more reliable and affordable.

The Pollyanna response is that we should use government to make solar energy affordable and reliable. However, government policies promoting solar energy are in opposition to the we-can-do-it American spirit. The can-do attitude and freedom to pursue it were the driving forces behind the greatest energy innovation of the past 50 years — the smart drilling technology that gives us access to so much new natural gas and petroleum that we have reversed the trend of manufacturers moving production overseas and we have broken the back of OPEC.

Instead of putting faith in free minds and inventiveness to provide Americans with the affordable and reliable energy they demand, our solar-energy policies have imposed huge costs on consumers and threaten to cause electricity rates to skyrocket (to borrow a term from President Obama). Solar-energy policies range from the infamous to the insidious.

The owners of Solyndra used their political connections to get more than $500 million in loan guarantees. The Department of Energy put millions into Solyndra even as the proprietors knew the company was crashing and burning. In a hilarious fit of understatement, the department's inspector general concluded, "We also found that the Department's due diligence efforts were less than fully effective." Hey, what do you expect? It wasn't their money, it was the taxpayers' money, and they lost it all on that one loan.

Solyndra's was far from the only green-energy loan that went sour, but an even more disturbing aspect of the loan program was that it channeled billions to companies that don't need taxpayer support. Solar projects owned by companies such as Goldman Sachs, BP and Chevron were propped up by billions of dollars in special federal loans. Another large corporation, the Spanish Abengoa, received $2.7 billion in loan guarantees. This loan is now at risk as Abengoa is threatened with bankruptcy.

The Abengoa bankruptcy highlights why green-energy subsidies are a bad idea. In his first term, President Obama pointed to Spain as a role model for our own energy policy. The European Union provides similar object lessons. Germany and Denmark have the highest share of electricity from renewable sources (wind and solar), but they also have the highest electricity prices in the EU. Their citizens pay about three times what the average American pays. Because of the unaffordability of subsidizing and mandating renewable energy, Germany, Denmark, Britain and Spain are cutting way back on their support for solar power. The cut in subsidies is the prime cause of Abengoa's impending demise, which lays bare solar's claim of competitiveness.

History proves that America can solve its energy problems when producers and consumers are free to make their own best choices and get rid of government meddling that blesses the powerful with largesse and burdens the powerless with higher costs.

Don Kusler
Counterpoint: We Need to Continue to Invest in Solar

Don Kusler is the executive director of Americans for Democratic Action and the Americans for Democratic Action Education Fund. Americans for Democratic Action is an independent liberal lobbying organization that promotes progressive change for social and economic justice. Kusler, in opposition to Kreutzer, contends that while solar energy may not be a perfect solution, it is the best one given the alternatives. Solar energy's benefits, according to Kusler, outweigh the negatives.

Counterpoint: We Need to Continue to Invest in Solar

By Don Kusler | December 12, 2015

There is no such thing as a perfect energy source. Unless you're watching a sci-fi Hollywood movie. That being said, while solar and other renewable energies are not perfect, when compared to traditional energy sources they are safe, clean, inexhaustible, naturally abundant and the best way forward.

The benefits of solar energy are extensive. In short, solar energy is not only sustainable, it is renewable; this means that we will never run out of it.

The use of solar over traditional energy sources also curbs greenhouse gas emissions and reduces our collective dependence on fossil fuels. It's gaining popularity both commercially and in residential use; therefore the best plan forward is to continue to invest and improve this natural clean energy source. According to the Energy Information Administration, solar energy will grow faster than any other renewable source, averaging an annual growth rate of 11.7 percent through 2035.

While there have been some unwanted environmental effects, the important thing is that we learn the lessons from these mistakes and work continuously to improve how we plan and build this 21st-century renewable infrastructure. One way the industry is doing this is by working with experts, such as those from the Bureau of Land Management's Western Solar Program, to understand the potential effects and plan accordingly so that we can limit the impact on natural resources.

There are countless examples of solar companies taking the right steps to ensure that solar development causes minimal effects to the natural environment. As environmental lawyer and author Philip Warburg points out, projects like the California Valley Solar Ranch worked with teams of experts to relocate sensitive species during the construction of the ranch and then reintroduce them afterward with migratory corridors and additional land mapped out to allow for the least amount of environmental impact.

Other large-scale solar projects are taking place on top of large commercial buildings and airports. Last week Minnesota's largest solar power generator was turned on at the

Minneapolis–St. Paul International Airport. The 3 million-watt system is expected to supply 20 percent of the electricity used in the airport terminal and to cut an estimated 7,000 tons of carbon emissions per year. While the initial investment is expensive, this new solar generator is estimated to save $10 million over 30 years.

It's important to understand that every action causes a reaction. Our agricultural economy requires huge amounts of water, fuel, fertilizers and pesticides. Does that mean we should stop growing crops? The truth is we live in a chaotic society. One town builds a dam to utilize the water to improve farming, harness the energy to create power, and improve their communities. That decision will no doubt cause a domino effect, which causes another area downstream to suffer.

While there are complications to consider while installing the infrastructure to allow solar energy to thrive, when are there not? And what is our alternative? Does it mean we should continue to rely on oil, coal, natural gas and other energy sources that are limited, dangerous, and adding more toil to our already threatened environment?

We need to continue to invest in solar and other renewable resources so we can create a future for our children where energy will be naturally abundant, without the wars that we have witnessed for centuries fighting over the earth's declining natural resources.

Starting a Conversation: Respond to Point/ Counterpoint Editorials

In your writer's notebook, record your analysis of Kreutzer's and Kusler's editorials by responding to the following questions:

1. Briefly summarize each writer's claim. On what major points do Kreutzer and Kusler disagree? On what, if anything, do they agree?

2. Both the point and counterpoint were published on *InsideSources*, which describes itself as a nonpartisan news source that aims to present new, compelling, fact-based information to readers who are seeking informed opinions. What types of facts and evidence does each writer use to support his claim? How well is each claim supported? Are the articles nonpartisan? How can you tell?

3. What does Kreutzer mean by "the Pollyanna response" in paragraph 6? Though Kusler doesn't use the same phrasing, how does he refute Kreutzer's position on "the Pollyanna response"?

4. **Reflection:** After reading both the point and the counterpoint, which article was more convincing? Why? Were you surprised by your reaction?

Open Letters

Open letters are written to an individual or group of individuals, organization, corporation, or government agency and are published in a public forum, such as a newspaper, magazine, or website. Open letters often respond to an action taken or a decision made (or not made) by the recipient of the letter. Sometimes the letter writers are well-known authors or local (or national) figures; sometimes they're representatives of an organization with a stake in an issue; and sometimes they are average citizens who want to voice their opinion on an issue that affects them. When open letters are published in newspapers or magazines, they usually appear in the form of paid advertising or as public service announcements. They are also likely to reflect issues covered by the publication. Similarly, open letters published on the Web usually reflect the issues addressed by the website on which the letter appears.

The format of an open letter is typically simple, consisting of a salutation (Dear . . .), one or more paragraphs of plain text, and the name of the writer or group (in place of a signature). Letters are often brief, because of length limitations specified by the publication in which they appear, but many magazines and websites publish longer letters. Although brief letters typically provide little in the way of formal evidence to support an argument, longer letters might offer a thorough discussion that is carefully supported by evidence from personal experience, observation, interviews, and published sources.

Barack Obama
An Open Letter to America's Law Enforcement Community

Barack Obama was the 44th President of the United States and the first African American president, serving from January 2009 to January 2017. He was born in Honolulu, Hawaii, to an American mother and a Kenyan father. He graduated from Columbia University in 1983 and Harvard Law School in 1991, where he was the first African American editor of the *Harvard Law Review*. Obama received the Nobel Peace Prize in 2009 "for his extraordinary efforts to strengthen international diplomacy and cooperation between peoples." The open letter that follows reflects the civic strife between whites and blacks, and between police and civilians, going back to the 2012 shooting of Trayvon Martin, an unarmed black teenager. The letter was sent to the National Fraternal Order of Police in response to the 2016 shootings of police officers in Dallas and Baton Rouge. In the letter, Obama offers his gratitude and support to America's law enforcement community and calls on the American people to come together as a community, trust one another, and recognize what we have in common rather than what divides us.

An Open Letter to America's Law Enforcement Community

THE WHITE HOUSE
WASHINGTON

July 18, 2016

To the brave members of our Nation's law enforcement community:

Every day, you confront danger so it does not find our families, carry burdens so they do not fall to us, and courageously meet test after test to keep us safe. Like Dallas officer Lorne Ahrens, who bought dinner for a homeless man the night before he died, you perform good deeds beyond the call of duty and out of the spotlight. Time and again, you make the split-second decisions that could mean life or death for you and many others in harm's way. You endure the tense minutes and long hours over lifetimes of service.

Every day, you accept this responsibility and you see your colleagues do their difficult, dangerous jobs with equal valor. I want you to know that the American people see it, too. We recognize it, we respect it, we appreciate it, and we depend on you. And just as your tight-knit law enforcement family feels the recent losses to your core, our Nation grieves alongside you. Any attack on police is an unjustified attack on all of us.

I've spent a lot of time with law enforcement over the past couple of weeks. I know that you take each of these tragedies personally, and that each is as devastating as a loss in the family. Sunday's shooting in Baton Rouge was no different. Together, we mourn Montrell Jackson, Matthew Gerald, and Brad Garafola. Each was a husband. Each was a father. Each was a proud member of his community. And each fallen officer is one too many. Last week, I met with the families of the Dallas officers who were killed, and I called the families of those who were killed in the line of duty yesterday in Baton Rouge. I let them know how deeply we ache for the loss of their loved ones.

Some are trying to use this moment to divide police and the communities you serve. I reject those efforts, for they do not reflect the reality of our Nation. Officer Jackson knew this too, when just days ago he asked us to keep hatred from our hearts. Instead, he offered—to protestors and fellow police officers alike—a hug to anyone who saw him on the street. He offered himself as a fellow worshipper to anyone who sought to pray. Today, we offer our comfort and our prayers to his family, to the Geralds and the Garafolas, and to the tight-knit Baton Rouge law enforcement community.

As you continue to serve us in this tumultuous hour, we again recognize that we can no longer ask you to solve issues we refuse to address as a society. We should give you the resources you need to do your job, including our full-throated support. We must give you the tools you need to build and strengthen the bonds of trust with those you serve, and our best efforts to address the underlying challenges that contribute to crime and unrest.

As you continue to defend us with quiet dignity, we proclaim loudly our appreciation for the acts of service you perform as part of your daily routine. When you see civilians at risk, you don't see them as strangers. You see them as your own family, and you lay your life on the line for them. You put others' safety before your own, and you remind us that loving our country means loving one another. Even when some protest you, you protect them. What is more professional than that? What is more patriotic? What is a prouder example of our most basic freedoms—to speech, to assembly, to life, and to liberty? And at the end of the day, you have a right to go home to your family, just like anybody else.

Robert Kennedy, once our Nation's highest-ranking law enforcement official, lamented in the wake of unjust violence a country in which we look at our neighbors as people "with whom we share a city, but not a community." This is a time for us to reaffirm that what makes us special is that we are not only a country, but also a community. That is true whether you are black or white, whether you are rich or poor, whether you are a police officer or someone they protect and serve.

With that understanding—an understanding of the goodness and decency I have seen of our Nation not only in the past few weeks, but throughout my life—we will get through this difficult time together.

We will do it with the love and empathy of public servants like those we have lost in recent days. We will do it with the resilience of cities like Dallas that quickly came together to restore order and deepen unity and understanding. We will do it with the grace of loved ones who even in their grief have spoken out against vengeance toward police. We will do it with the good will of activists like those I have sat with in recent days, who have pledged to work together to reduce violence even as they voice their disappointments and fears.

As we bind up our wounds, we must come together to ensure that those who try to divide us do not succeed. We are at our best when we recognize our common humanity, set an example for our children of trust and responsibility, and honor the sacrifices of our bravest by coming together to be better.

Thank you for your courageous service. We have your backs.

Sincerely,

Starting a Conversation: Responding to "An Open Letter to America's Law Enforcement Community"

In your writer's notebook, record your analysis of "An Open Letter to America's Law Enforcement Community" by responding to the following questions:

1. Why do you think Obama uses an open letter format? Why is this structure meaningful in his effort to address both the law enforcement community and general readers? What is the effect of Obama's use of *we* and *us*?

2. Obama alludes to recent civic tension, writing that "some are trying to use this moment to divide police and the communities you serve" (para. 5). What examples to the contrary does Obama provide? Throughout his letter, how does Obama rhetorically bridge the gap between police officers and community members?

3. In paragraph 5, Obama writes, "As you continue to serve us in this tumultuous hour, we again recognize that we can no longer ask you to solve issues we refuse to address as a society." To what issues is he referring? How do you know? How does his letter try to address those issues?

4. The letter ends with the simple statement, "We have your backs." Why does Obama use this phrasing? What is it meant to invoke?

5. **Reflection:** Obama quotes Robert Kennedy in paragraph 7. Why does he use this quote about the disparity between city and community? How does Obama convey a sense of "community"? After reading this letter, consider your own city or town. Does it feel unified as a community, or are there divisions? Explain why, and if there are divisions, reflect on what community leaders and law enforcement might do to help repair those divisions.

GENRE TALK

Reflective Writing | Informative Writing | Analytical Writing | Evaluative Writing | Problem-Solving Writing | **Argumentative Writing**

Zara. H&M. Forever 21. These popular clothing retailers are the heart of "fast fashion," the latest trend in consumer buying habits. Fast fashion retailers price their goods very low and receive new shipments every day, including knock-offs of high-end designs. The combination of low prices (plus sales that slash the prices even further) and the constant influx of trendsetting goods is hard to resist, so shopping at stores like these can become a constant habit.

There is a hidden price for such cheap apparel, however. The workers who manufacture these goods are paid meager, often unlivable, wages. They toil twelve- or fourteen-hour shifts in unsafe working conditions, as the 2012 fire in a Bangladeshi sweatshop illustrated. Our wear-and-toss shopping habits also take an environmental toll, as landfills hold ever-growing piles of discarded clothing.

Slowly, the problem of fast fashion is being brought to light. The documentary film *The True Cost* (2015), an exposé of garment sweatshops and the fashion industry, argues that fast fashion is hardly fun, cheap, or benign.

LaunchPad
macmillan learning

Test your knowledge of genre with the Genre Talk quiz in the LaunchPad for *Joining the Conversation*.
launchpadworks.com

Bright colors grab the viewer's attention.

Navigation menu offers opportunities to learn more about the problem.

A tagline argues the film's main point.

Viewers can watch the film immediately online.

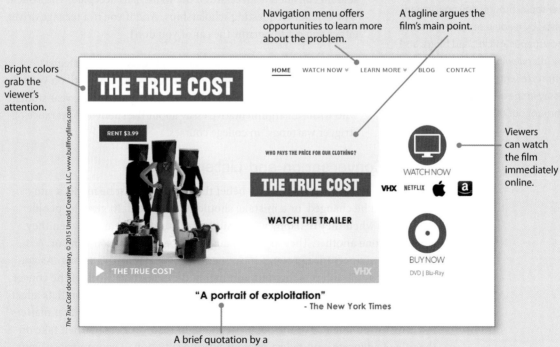

The True Cost documentary, © 2015 Untold Creative, LLC, www.bullfrogfilms.com

A brief quotation by a well-known source lends authority to the film.

How Can I Write an Argumentative Essay?

Many people believe that an argument is effective only if it's won, that unless they convince or persuade someone, they've failed in their mission to change the world — or their community or the minds of people they hang out with or the people who read their Facebook pages. In fact, most written arguments aren't so much about winning or losing as about sharing the writer's perspective with others who are interested in an issue. Think of it as exploring alternative ways of thinking, acting, and believing — as advancing a conversation about an issue. If you follow this line of thinking, you'll recognize that the effectiveness of your essay isn't based on whether you win the argument. It is based on your ability to affect the community of readers and writers to whom you direct your argument.

Then again, sometimes winning is all that matters. Application essays for medical or business school, no matter how well written, are seldom considered successful if the writer isn't accepted. The same is true of letters requesting scholarships. And if you're a teenage driver, either you get to borrow the car or you don't.

In this section, you'll learn about the processes and strategies involved in writing an argumentative essay. As you work on your essay, you'll follow the work of Elisabeth Layne, a third-year student who wrote an argumentative essay about the sudden appearance of "trigger warnings" in college courses.

In Process

An Argumentative Essay about Trigger Warnings

Elisabeth Layne wrote an argumentative essay for her composition course. Elisabeth learned about her topic through personal experience; by reading magazine articles, newspaper articles, and blogs; and by interviewing friends. Follow her efforts to write her argumentative essay in the In Process boxes throughout this chapter.

Find a Conversation and Listen In

Argumentative essays grow out of a belief that a choice must be made, a situation should be changed, or a mistake should be corrected. In general, people don't argue when they're happy with a situation, nor do they argue when they agree with one another. They argue because they believe that someone or something — a person, a group, a movement, a government — is wrong. As you consider possible subjects for your argumentative essay, take stock of the conversations taking place around you. Ask what bothers you. Ask what conflicts affect you, individually or as a member of a community. Look for an issue that matters not only to you but also to the people who might read your essay. Then take on the role of advocate, and reflect on your writing situation — your purpose, your readers, and the contexts in which your writing will be read (see p. 398).

EXPLORE DISAGREEMENTS

Unless they're deeply conflicted, few people carry on extended arguments with themselves. The kinds of arguments that are worth addressing in academic essays revolve around issues that affect a larger community. To identify issues that might interest you and your readers, explore popular, professional, and academic conversations. In almost every case, you'll find points of disagreement and debate that bring people together in discussions — sometimes polite and sometimes anything but — about the challenges that confront us.

- **Popular conversations.** What's new in the media and the popular press? What's new on the Web? You can visit the opinion sections on websites such as CNN.com and National Public Radio (www.npr.org) to learn about issues

In Process

Generating Ideas about Conversations

Seeing trigger warnings move from online discussion boards to college campuses led Elisabeth Layne to explore conversations related to trigger warnings in academia.

> It feels like trigger warnings are suddenly popping up everywhere in college. I'd seen them before on feminist discussion boards and blog comments. People would use them to warn other commenters that they were about to post something disturbing, something that might "trigger" a post-traumatic stress reaction. Usually it was for really upsetting episodes of violence or sexual assault, or maybe even a graphic description of a suicide attempt or anorexia. That way, readers could choose to scroll past and not read the triggering comment. But lately, trigger warnings have started appearing in college assignments, warning students that an assigned reading or film might contain a scene that's disturbing. And a lot of writers are saying that trigger warnings are too close to censorship, or that they show how students today are too "fragile" and want to avoid dealing with difficult topics. I'm not sure how I feel about this. On one hand, college should be a place that opens our minds to new ideas and facts, even difficult ones; on the other hand, shouldn't we respect students who have reasons to be sensitive to traumatic topics?

Elisabeth used the results of her freewriting to explore how common trigger warnings really are in college courses. The articles she found in newspapers, magazines, and on higher education websites and blogs helped her learn more about both students' and instructors' perspectives.

that have sparked discussion. On sites such as these, you can read commentary from other visitors to the site, read blogs and opinion columns, and view the latest news reports on issues that have spurred popular debate.

- **Professional conversations.** If you are involved or are planning to become involved in a particular profession, tune in to the conversations taking place in your field of interest. If you're working as an intern or at a part-time job, for example, listen to what your coworkers are talking about. Skim some trade and professional journals to find points of disagreement. Read some blogs that focus on your profession, and notice what people are arguing about.

- **Academic conversations.** Just as you will find disagreements in public and professional life, you will find them in academic disciplines. Look for disagreements in course readings, and pay attention to controversies addressed during class discussions and lectures. Ask professors and graduate students what's "hot" in their fields. Scan the tables of contents of recent issues of academic journals. Visit websites that focus on your discipline.

Recognizing ongoing conversations can give you insights into debatable issues that might serve as the basis for your argumentative essay. Try listing issues from one or more of these areas — or from the writing project ideas at the end of this chapter — and then explore your thoughts about them (see pp. 41–48 for an overview of strategies for generating ideas). When you've finished, review what you've written to identify the areas that seem most promising, and then select one or two that interest you most. Jot down your thoughts about what you already know and what you would need to learn before you can develop your argument.

Working Together: Try It Out Loud

Before you start developing your argument, hold an informal debate with your classmates about an issue that affects all of you. Form small groups, and choose an issue you're familiar with and that lends itself to argument, such as a disagreement affecting your hometown, school, or state. You might scan the school paper or a local publication for current issues worth discussing. Explain your perspective on the issue, and then state your position. Offer reasons and, if possible, evidence from personal experience or readings to support your argument. Ask the other members of your group to identify counterarguments, giving their own reasons and evidence. Take turns speaking while the other members of the group listen, respond, and ask questions.

When you are finished, take a few minutes to reflect on the exercise. What did you learn about presenting an argument? Did you have to adapt what you said based on your classmates' values, beliefs, and concerns? What kind of questions did they ask? What seemed to interest them the most about the issue? How did they react to your argument? What reasoning and evidence did they find most convincing? Least convincing?

TRACK ONLINE CONVERSATIONS

Issues worth arguing about almost always become a topic of conversation. Increasingly, that conversation takes place online, through blogs and social media sites. These resources are designed specifically to support exchanges among writers and readers. By following these online conversations, you can not only learn more about your subject but also discover what other writers and readers think about it.

Blogs consist of chronologically ordered entries on a website and most closely resemble entries in a diary or journal. Blog entries usually include a title and a text message and can also incorporate images, audio, video, and other types of media. Many entries provide links to other pages on the Web. Blogs allow readers to post their responses to entries, so a single blog entry might be accompanied by several — sometimes hundreds — of responses.

You can find blogs that address your subject by turning to sites such as BlogCatalog (blogcatalog.com) and IceRocket (icerocket.com). Read more about blogs in Chapter 13.

Social media sites such as Facebook, Google+, Tumblr, Twitter, and LinkedIn provide opportunities to identify people who share your interest in an issue. By searching these sites, you can identify individuals who might be knowledgeable about an issue or have been affected by it. If you have an account with a social media site such as Facebook, you can use its search tools to locate individuals and groups that share your interest. Facebook's Graph Search, for example, allows you to create complex searches of Facebook members and events.

Even though these resources can be helpful as you explore potential issues for your essay, take the time to learn more about the conversations you find online. You can locate print and digital sources through your library's catalog and through Web search sites and directories. If the sources you collect leave you with unanswered questions, you can conduct additional searches, talk to a librarian, or collect information through observations or interviews. Depending on your issue, you might also want to search for government documents.

Do you know how to locate online sources? See Chapter 13 for help.

ASK QUESTIONS ABOUT PROMISING ISSUES

Before you begin constructing an argument, determine which aspect of an issue interests you most. The best written arguments are usually focused and narrow. Be wary of writing about something as broadly defined as climate change or ethics in politics. Instead, try to find a subtopic that you can manage in the space and time available to you. For example, if you're interested in climate change, take a look at issues such as the carbon emissions that result from producing the batteries used in hybrid cars and trucks. Each of the following questions focuses your attention on a general issue in a different way, and each provides a useful starting point for an argumentative essay. Depending on the subject, you'll find that some questions are more relevant than others.

- **Values.** Why is this important to me? What about it will matter to readers? Can I make an argument without letting my emotions run away with me?

- **Definition.** Why do people disagree about this issue? What, exactly, is at stake?

- **Possibilities.** What could be accomplished if this issue is addressed? What might happen if it is not addressed?

- **Positions.** What positions have been taken on this issue? What intrigues me about those positions?

- **Strengths and weaknesses.** What are the strengths of other writers' arguments? What are the weaknesses?

As you narrow your focus, ask yourself one last question: Is your goal to convince your readers to agree with you or to persuade them to act? Be aware that getting people to act can be a far greater challenge than getting them to agree with you. For example, it's easy to convince someone that it's a good idea to spend more time studying. It can be far more difficult to persuade that person to set aside two more hours each day to do so. As you consider how you'll focus your argument, remember that it will take a strong argument to persuade your readers to act.

Build Your Argument

Putting together an effective argumentative essay starts with knowing what you want others to believe or how you want them to act. But that's just the beginning. To build your argument, you must develop a strategy for achieving your goal. Your strategy should reflect not only your overall goal but also a thorough understanding of your readers — their purposes in reading your essay, their knowledge of the issue, and their needs, interests, and backgrounds.

In short, you'll need to figure out how to get your readers to accept your argument. To do so, start by defining your overall claim, and then identify the reasons and supporting evidence that will be most convincing or persuasive to your readers. In addition, consider how opposing positions affect your argument, and make sure that your reasoning is sound.

In Process

Locating Sources

Elisabeth Layne was interested in learning how common trigger warnings were on college campuses. She also wanted to find out what other students and instructors thought about them. Her Web searches led her to an online article that offered a first-person response to the issue of trigger warnings and that had a series of comments from readers.

THE CUT

FASHIONS   FAME   BEAUTY   GOODS

TRIGGER WARNINGS

Why I Stopped Rolling My Eyes at Trigger Warnings

By Kat Stoeffel   Follow @kstoeffel

May 21, 2014
12:40 p.m.

698
Shares

Share   617
Tweet   81
Share   0
Pin It   0
Email
Print

Photo: Shutterstock

The perennially controversial blog convention of trigger warnings made it into the *New York Times* this week, thanks to a growing movement of college students calling for such warnings on graphic classroom materials. For the uninitiated, trigger warnings are a quick heads-up at the top of a post alerting readers to sensitive matters below, somewhat like the title card before *Law and Order: Special Victims Unit*. They were popularized in the feminist blogosphere, to warn participants of the self-designated safe spaces about stories involving rape, abuse, or self-harm that might induce flashbacks to their own past traumas. But they were soon applied to blog posts about racism, classism, heterosexism, cissexism, dyadism, and other lesser-known Tumblr-isms, at which point they became kind of a joke, and were eventually declared dead (at least in certain corners of the internet) two years ago. Their sudden appearance in academia has become

> Elisabeth located an article by Kat Stoeffel on the *New York* magazine website.

> Stoeffel refers to a recent newspaper article about the topic. Later in the article Stoeffel quotes from other newspapers and magazine articles criticizing trigger warnings on campus.

Elisabeth saved a copy of this article. Then she followed the links in it to related materials and saved those as well. Later, she printed a copy and highlighted key passages.

From TheCut.com. Photo © Vladimir Gjorgiev/Shutterstock

DEFINE YOUR OVERALL CLAIM

It's important that you understand precisely what you want your readers to believe or do before you begin drafting. Your overall claim — the heart of the argument you want to make — will serve as a touchstone as you juggle the complexities of crafting an argument. Your claim should take into account your purpose as a writer, the conversation you've decided to join, and the readers you hope to convince or persuade.

You can begin to define your overall claim by brainstorming or freewriting (see pp. 41–42) in response to the following questions:

- What is my position on this issue?

- Which aspects of this issue interest me most?

- Which aspects of this issue do I feel most strongly about?

- What do I want my readers to believe or do as a result of reading my essay?

- What are my readers likely to think about this issue? What will it take to change their minds or get them to act?

- How does my position differ from those advanced by other writers? How is it similar?

Review what you've written. Then try to express, in one or two sentences, your overall claim. Later, your claim can serve as the basis for a thesis statement (see Chapter 16). For now, use it to direct your thinking about the argument you want to formulate.

DEVELOP REASONS TO ACCEPT YOUR OVERALL CLAIM

Few readers will accept "because I'm right" as a good reason to accept your position on an issue. They expect you to explain why you're right. Developing an explanation begins with identifying reasons that are consistent with your own perspective on the issue. At this stage of your writing process, don't worry about whether your readers will be convinced or persuaded by your reasoning. Instead, treat your efforts to develop reasons to accept your overall claim as you would any other form of brainstorming. As you generate a list of potential reasons, you can certainly begin to ask whether the reasons you've identified are well grounded, logical, and consistent with the values and beliefs held by you and your readers. And later, as you draft your essay, you can decide how to present your reasons to your readers. For now, though, your primary goal is to generate as many potential reasons as possible to support your overall claim.

Generate ideas about potential reasons Your understanding of an issue and the conversations surrounding it will provide a framework within which you can develop a set of reasons to support your overall claim. To guide your efforts, ask questions such as the following, and respond to them by brainstorming, freewriting, blindwriting, looping, clustering, or mapping:

- **Costs.** What costs are associated with not accepting and acting on your overall claim? Are there monetary costs? Will time and effort be lost or wasted? Will valuable resources be wasted? Will people be unable to lead fulfilling lives? Will human potential be wasted? Will lives be lost?

- **Benefits.** What will be gained by accepting and acting on your overall claim? Who or what will benefit if the claim is accepted and acted on? What form will these benefits take?

- **Alternatives, choices, and trade-offs.** What is gained by accepting and acting on your overall claim? What is lost by not doing so? In what ways are the potential costs or benefits associated with your overall claim preferable to those associated with rejecting it?

- **Parallels.** Can you find similarities between the overall claim you are making about this issue and claims made about other issues? Can you argue that, if your claim is accepted and acted on, the outcomes will be similar to those found for other issues? What consensus, if any, exists among experts on this issue about what similar situations have led to in the past?

- **Personal experience.** What does your personal experience tell you is likely to happen if your claim is accepted and acted on? What does it tell you might happen if it is rejected?

- **Historical context.** What does history tell you is likely to happen—or not happen—if your claim is accepted and acted on? What does it tell you might happen if it is rejected? What consensus, if any, exists among experts on this issue about what similar situations have led to in the past?

- **Values and beliefs.** In what ways is your overall claim consistent with your values and beliefs? With those of your readers? In what ways is it consistent with larger societal and cultural values and beliefs? How might it further those values and beliefs?

Examine the list of reasons you've generated to determine which ones fit best with your overall claim, your purpose, and what you know about your readers. Select the reasons that, individually and as a group, best support your overall claim.

Decide how your reasons support your overall claim Effective arguments make connections (sometimes called **warrants**) between the overall claim and the reasons offered to support it. Sometimes readers accept a connection because they share the writer's values and beliefs or have similar experiences with and knowledge of an issue. In other cases, readers accept a connection because the writer explains it effectively. This explanation (sometimes called **backing**) provides readers with information and analysis that help them understand and accept the connection.

Warrant: Colleges and universities should show respect for the different personal circumstances of their students.

Backing: Colleges try to attract more diverse student populations, including veterans, nontraditional students, international students, and students from all socioeconomic backgrounds, so the different physical and emotional needs of those students need to be considered.

Claim

Reason

Evidence

Trigger warnings in college courses should not be controversial because they show respect for the personal circumstances of a diverse student population, as students noted in the comments on a recent *New York Times* article.

The reasons you choose to support your overall claim should reflect your understanding of the conversation you've decided to join. Your reasons should emerge from careful thought about the information, ideas, and arguments you've encountered in your reading. Your reasons should reflect your purpose and goals. And they should take into account your readers' needs, interests, backgrounds, and knowledge of the issue.

As you consider your reasons, ask how clearly they connect to your overall claim. Ask whether you should explain each connection or leave it unstated. Your answers will depend in part on the extent to which your readers share your values, beliefs, experience, and knowledge of the issue. If your readers' backgrounds and knowledge differ from yours, connections that make sense to you might not be clear to them.

CHOOSE EVIDENCE TO SUPPORT YOUR REASONS

Your argument will be effective only if you back up each of your reasons with evidence. Most readers will expect you to provide some sort of justification for accepting your reasons, and their assessment of your evidence will affect their willingness to accept your argument. The form your evidence takes will depend on your overall claim, the reasons themselves, and your readers' values and assumptions. In general, however, consider drawing on the following types of evidence to support your reasons:

- textual evidence, in the form of quotations, paraphrases, and summaries
- numerical and statistical data
- images, including photographs, drawings, animations, and video
- tables, charts, and graphs
- information and ideas from interviews, observations, and surveys
- personal experience
- expert opinion

Take the following steps to identify evidence to support your reasons:

1. List the reasons you are using to support your overall claim.
2. For each reason, review your notes to identify relevant evidence.
3. List your evidence below each point.
4. Identify reasons that need more support, and locate additional evidence as necessary.
5. Consider dismissing or revising reasons for which you don't have sufficient evidence.

Effective arguments typically provide evidence that is both plentiful and varied in type. A writer arguing about the need to improve the U.S. health care system, for example, might draw on personal experience, interviews with friends and relatives, policy briefs from the American Medical Association, commentary by bloggers, reports issued by government agencies, and articles in popular and scholarly journals.

As you choose evidence to support your reasons, think about whether — and, if so, how — you will show the connections between reasons and evidence. These connections, often called appeals, help readers understand why a reason is appropriate and valid. Common appeals include citing authorities on an issue; using emotion to sway readers; calling attention to shared principles, values, and beliefs; asking readers to trust the writer; and using logic.

You can read more about using appeals on page 436. You can read about how to identify evidence to support your reasons in Chapter 16.

Claim: Trigger warnings in college courses should not be controversial **because**

Reason: they show respect for the personal circumstances of a diverse student population, as students noted in their comments on a recent *New York Times* article.

Appeal: The principle is that members of a college community should respect each other.

Evidence

In Process

Choosing Evidence

Elisabeth Layne chose the evidence she would use in her essay by creating a list of reasons to support her overall claim that trigger warnings were helpful and respectful of student diversity, rather than repressive. She reviewed the notes she took on her sources, listing sources next to each reason, and deciding whether she needed more or better evidence for each reason. She created a simple table in a word-processing file to keep track of her evidence.

Reason	Evidence/Source	Notes
Student populations are diverse today; colleges should respect that diversity of experience.	*Columbia Spectator* opinion column: http://columbiaspectator.com/opinion/2015/04/30/our-identities-matter-core-classrooms	"Students need to feel safe in the classroom, and that requires a learning environment that recognizes the multiplicity of their identities."
Trigger warnings are minimal and unobtrusive. They only help those who need them and don't harm anyone else.	Kat Stoeffel: http://nymag.com/thecut/2014/05/stop-rolling-your-eyes-at-trigger-warnings.html	A trigger warning on course material is not the same as censoring that material. It's simply warning those students who need advance notice about the graphic content.
Post-traumatic stress disorder is a real syndrome with terrible, intrusive effects.	Mental Health America: http://www.mentalhealthamerica.net/conditions/post-traumatic-stress-disorder	For individuals with PTSD, being reminded of their trauma can itself be a traumatic experience.

IDENTIFY AND CONSIDER OPPOSING CLAIMS

A critical part of developing and supporting your argument is identifying opposing claims, or counterarguments. You might assume that calling attention to competing positions in your essay will weaken your argument. Nothing is further from the truth. Identifying opposing claims provides opportunities to test and strengthen your reasons and evidence by comparing them with those put forth by other writers. Considering counterarguments also allows you to anticipate questions and concerns your readers are likely to bring to your essay. And later, as you are writing your draft, your responses to these opposing claims will provide a basis for clearly explaining to your readers why your argument is superior to others.

Remember that you're making an argument about your issue because people disagree about how to address it. If reasonable alternatives to your argument didn't exist, there would be no need for an argument in the first place. As a writer contributing to an ongoing conversation, you have a responsibility to indicate that you're aware of what has been said and who has said it. More important, you have a responsibility to consider carefully how your argument improves on the arguments made by other members of the conversation.

To identify opposing claims, review the sources you encountered as you learned about your issue. Identify the most compelling arguments you found, and ask how the reasons and evidence offered to support them compare to yours. Then ask whether you can think of reasonable alternative positions that haven't been

Working Together: Identify and Consider Opposing Claims

Working with a group of two or more classmates, carry out a "devil's advocate" exercise to identify and consider opposing claims. First, briefly describe your issue, overall claim, and reasons. Other members of the group should offer reasonable alternative arguments. One member of the group should serve as a recorder, taking careful notes on the exchange and listing opposing claims, reasons supporting those claims, and your response to the claims. Once the exchange (which might last between three and ten minutes) is

completed, switch roles and repeat the activity for every other member of the group.

This activity can be carried out face-to-face, online, or on the phone. If you are working on the activity using a chat program or a threaded discussion forum, you can record your exchange for later review. Most chat programs allow you to create a transcript of a session, and threaded discussion forums will automatically record your exchange.

addressed in the sources you've consulted. Finally, talk with others about your issue, and ask them what they think about it.

For each reason you expect to use in support of your overall claim, create a list of opposing points of view, briefly describing each one and noting where you found it. To determine whether you're making the best possible argument, consider each of these opposing claims in turn. Take notes on your response to each one, considering both its merits and its faults. Use what you've learned to reflect on and refine your overall claim and the reasons and evidence you've identified to support it. Later, you can use what you've learned to address counterarguments in your essay (see p. 439).

ENSURE THE INTEGRITY OF YOUR ARGUMENT

If you're familiar with the "buy this car and get a date with this girl (or guy)" school of advertising, you know that arguments often lack integrity. Although weak arguments might be easier to develop, they usually backfire (setting aside the enduring success of automobile ads filled with attractive young men and women). Readers who recognize errors in reasoning or the use of inappropriate evidence are likely to reject an argument out of hand.

Acquainting yourself with common logical fallacies can help you not only ensure the integrity of your argument but also identify and address counterarguments based on fallacious reasoning and weak or inappropriate forms of evidence.

Some of the most common logical fallacies are described below.

Fallacies based on distraction

- **A red herring** is an irrelevant or a distracting point. The term originated with the practice of sweeping a red herring (a particularly fragrant type of fish) across the trail being followed by a pack of hunting dogs to throw them off the scent of their prey. For example, the question *Why worry about the rising cost of tuition when the government is tapping our phones?* is a red herring (government surveillance has nothing to do with increases in college tuition).

- **Ad hominem attacks** attempt to discredit an idea or argument by suggesting that a person or group associated with it should not be trusted. These kinds of attacks might be subtle or vicious. If you hear someone say that a proposed wind farm should be rejected because its main supporter cheated on her taxes, or that school vouchers are bad because a principal who swindled a school district supports them, you're listening to an ad hominem attack.

- **Irrelevant history** is another form of distraction. For example, arguing that a proposal is bad because someone came up with the idea while they were using cocaine suggests that the state of mind of the person who originates an idea has something to do with its merits. It might well be the case that the idea is flawed, but you should base your assessment on an analysis of its strengths and weaknesses. Otherwise, you might as well say that an idea is undoubtedly sound because someone thought of it while he or she was sober.

Fallacies based on questionable assumptions

- **Sweeping generalizations**, sometimes known as *hasty generalizations*, are based on stereotypes. Asserting that the rich are conservative voters, for example, assumes that everyone who is rich is just like everyone else who is rich. These kinds of arguments don't account for variation within a group, nor do they consider exceptions to the rule.

- **Straw-man attacks** oversimplify or distort another person's argument so it can be dismissed more easily. Just as a boxer can easily knock down a scarecrow, a writer who commits this fallacy might characterize an opposing position as more extreme than it actually is, or might refute obviously flawed counterarguments while ignoring valid objections.

- **Citing inappropriate authorities** can take several forms: citing as an authority someone who is not an expert on a subject, citing a source with a strong bias on an issue, suggesting that an individual voice represents consensus when that person's ideas are far from the mainstream, or treating paid celebrity endorsements as expert opinion.

- **Jumping on a bandwagon**, also known as *argument from consensus*, implies that if enough people believe something, it must be true. This type of argument substitutes group thinking for careful analysis. The idea of jumping on a bandwagon refers to the practice, in early American politics, of parading a candidate through town on a bandwagon. To show support for the candidate, people would climb onto the wagon.

Fallacies based on misrepresentation

- **Stacking the deck** refers to the practice of presenting evidence for only one side of an argument. Most readers will assume that a writer has done this deliberately and will wonder what he or she is trying to hide.

- **Base-rate fallacies** are commonly found in arguments based on statistics. If you read that drinking coffee will triple your risk of developing cancer, you might be alarmed. However, if you knew that the risk rose from one in a billion to three in a billion, you might pour another cup.

- **Questionable analogies**, also known as *false analogies*, make inappropriate comparisons. They are based on the assumption that if two things are similar in one way, they must be similar in others. For example, a writer might argue that global warming is like a fever, and that just as a fever usually runs its course on its own, so too will the climate recover without intervention.

Fallacies based on careless reasoning

- **Post hoc fallacies**, formally known as *post hoc, ergo propter hoc* fallacies ("after this, therefore because of this"), argue that because one event happened before a second event, the first event must have caused the second event. For example, a student might conclude that she received a low grade on an essay exam because she argued with an instructor during class. In fact, the real cause might be the poor quality of her exam responses.

- **Slippery-slope arguments** warn that a single step will inevitably lead to a bad situation. For instance, one of the most common arguments against decriminalizing marijuana is that it leads to the use of stronger narcotics. Indeed, some heroin or cocaine addicts might have first tried marijuana, but there is no evidence that *all* marijuana users inevitably move on to harder drugs.

- **Either/or arguments** present two choices, one of which is usually characterized as extremely undesirable. In fact, there might be a third choice, or a fourth, or a fifth.

- **Non sequiturs** are statements that do not follow logically from what has been said. For example, arguing that buying a particular type of car will lead to a successful love life is a non sequitur.

- **Circular reasoning**, also known as *begging the question*, restates a point that has just been made as evidence for itself. Arguing that a decline in voter turnout is a result of fewer people voting is an example of circular reasoning.

As you build your argument — and in particular, as you consider counterarguments and check your reasoning for fallacies — you might find that you need to refine your overall claim. In fact, most writers refine their arguments as they learn more about an issue and consider how best to contribute to a conversation. As you prepare to write a first draft of your argumentative essay, take another look at your overall claim, reasons, and evidence. Do they still make sense? Do they stack up well against competing arguments? Do you have enough evidence to convince or persuade your intended readers? If you answer "no" to any of these questions, continue to develop and refine your argument.

Prepare a Draft

Building your argument prepares you to draft your essay. It allows you to decide how to frame your thesis statement, appeal to your readers, address counter-arguments, take advantage of design opportunities, and organize your reasons and evidence.

MAKE AN ARGUMENTATIVE CLAIM

The overall claim you developed as you built your argument (p. 426) provides the foundation for your thesis statement — a brief statement that conveys the main point you want to make about your issue. In an argumentative essay, a thesis statement should be debatable, plausible, and clear.

- **A debatable thesis statement is one with which readers can disagree.** Saying that we should take good care of our children, for example, isn't particularly debatable. Saying that we need to invest more public funding in mandatory immunization programs, however, would almost certainly lead some readers to disagree. Even though your goal in writing an argumentative essay is to convince readers to accept or act on your argument, there's little to be gained in arguing for something with which everyone will agree. An argumentative essay is useful only if it makes people think and, ideally, change their attitudes, beliefs, or behaviors.

- **A plausible thesis statement appears at the very least to be reasonable, and in fact the claim it makes might appear to be convincing or persuasive on its own.** That is, although your claim should be debatable, don't make it so extreme that it comes across as ridiculous or absurd. For example, it's one thing to argue that the news media should pay more attention to political candidates' platforms and leadership qualities than to their personal failings; it's quite another to argue that a candidate's criminal record should be ignored.

- **A clear thesis statement advances a claim that is easy to follow.** It explains what readers should believe or how they should act. Typically, this involves using words such as *should*, *must*, or *ought*. It's important to remember that you are attempting to convince or persuade your readers. Unless you tell them what to believe or how to act, they won't be sure of your position.

An effective thesis statement will shape your readers' understanding of the issue, directing their attention to particular aspects of the issue and away from others. Consider, for example, the following thesis statements about athletes' use of performance-enhancing drugs.

Thesis statement 1: If for no other reason, athletes should avoid the use of performance-enhancing drugs to safeguard their personal health.

Thesis statement 2: To eliminate the use of performance-enhancing drugs, athletes themselves must take the lead in policing their sports.

Thesis statement 3: National and international governing bodies for sports should engage in a coordinated effort to educate aspiring athletes about ethics and sportsmanship.

Is your thesis statement focused enough? See Chapter 16 for help.

These thesis statements would lead to significantly different argumentative essays. The first thesis statement directs readers' attention to the health consequences for athletes who use performance-enhancing drugs. The second suggests that athletes themselves should take charge of efforts to eradicate this form of cheating. The third thesis statement focuses attention on the contributions that might be made by what are essentially large corporate and government agencies. Each thesis statement is plausible and debatable, and each one tells readers what they should believe or act on. Yet each leads the reader to view the issue in a significantly different way.

APPEAL TO YOUR READERS

As you work on your draft, consider the strategies you'll use to convince or persuade your readers to accept your argument. These strategies are essentially a means of appealing to — or asking — your readers to consider the reasons you are offering to support your overall claim and, if they accept them as appropriate and valid, to believe or act in a certain way.

Fortunately, you won't have to invent strategies on your own. For thousands of years, writers and speakers have used a wide range of appeals to ask readers to accept their reasons as appropriate and valid. Much of the work of ancient Greek and Roman thinkers such as Aristotle and Cicero revolved around strategies for presenting an argument to an audience. Their work still serves as a foundation for how we think about argumentation.

You can ask readers to accept your reasons by appealing to authority; emotion; principles, values, and beliefs; character; or logic. Most arguments are built on a combination of these appeals. The combination you choose will reflect your issue, purpose, readers, sources, and context.

Appeals to authority When you present a reason by making an appeal to authority, you ask readers to accept it because someone in a position of authority endorses it. The evidence used to support this kind of appeal typically takes the form of quotations, paraphrases, or summaries of the ideas of experts in a given subject area, of political leaders, or of people who have been affected by an issue. As you consider whether this kind of appeal might be appropriate for your argumentative essay, reflect on the notes you've taken on your sources. Have you identified experts, leaders, or people who have been affected by an issue? If so, can you use them to convince your readers that your argument has merit?

Appeals to emotion attempt to elicit an emotional response to an issue. The famous "win one for the Gipper" speech delivered by Pat O'Brien, who portrayed Notre Dame coach Knute Rockne in the 1940 film *Knute Rockne: All American*, is an example of an appeal to emotion. At halftime during a game with Army, with Notre Dame trailing, he said:

> Well, boys . . . I haven't a thing to say. Played a great game . . . all of you. Great game. I guess we just can't expect to win 'em all.
>
> I'm going to tell you something I've kept to myself for years. None of you ever knew George Gipp. It was long before your time. But you know what a tradition he is at Notre Dame. . . . And the last thing he said to me — "Rock," he said, "sometime, when the team is up against it — and the breaks are beating the boys — tell them to go out there with all they got and win just one for the Gipper. . . . I don't know where I'll be then, Rock," he said — "but I'll know about it — and I'll be happy."

Using emotional appeals to frame an argument — that is, to help readers view an issue in a particular way — is a tried-and-true strategy. But use it carefully, if you use it at all. In some types of documents, such as scholarly articles and essays, emotional appeals are used infrequently, and readers of such documents are likely to ask why you would play on their emotions instead of making an appeal to logic (see p. 438) or an appeal to authority.

Appeals to principles, values, and beliefs rely on the assumption that your readers value a given set of principles. Religious and ethical arguments are often based on appeals to principles, such as the need to respect God, to love one another, to trust in the innate goodness of people, to believe that all of us are created equal, or to believe that security should never be purchased at the price of individual liberty. If you make an appeal to principles, values, or beliefs, be sure your readers share the particular principle, value, or belief you are using. If they don't, you might need to state and justify your underlying assumptions at the outset — or you might want to try a different kind of appeal.

Appeals to character Writers frequently use appeals to character. When politicians refer to their military experience, for example, they are saying, "Look at me. I'm a patriotic person who has served our country." When celebrities endorse a product, they are saying, "You know and like me, so please believe me when I say that this product is worth purchasing." Appeals to character can also reflect a person's professional accomplishment. When scientists or philosophers present an argument, for example, they sometimes refer to their background and experience, or perhaps to their previous publications. In doing so, they are implicitly telling their readers that they have been accurate and truthful in the past and that readers can continue to trust them. Essentially, you can think of an appeal to character as the "trust me" strategy. As you consider this kind of appeal, reflect on your character, accomplishments, and experiences, and ask how they might lead your readers to trust you.

Appeals to logic A logical appeal refers to the concept of reasoning through a set of propositions to reach a considered conclusion. For example, you might argue that a suspect is guilty of murder because police found her fingerprints on the murder weapon, her blood under the murder victim's fingernails, scratches on the suspect's face, and video of the murder from a surveillance camera. Your argument would rely on the logical presentation of evidence to convince jurors that the suspect was the murderer and to persuade them to return a verdict of guilty. As you develop reasons to support your claim, consider using logical appeals such as deduction and induction.

- **Deduction** is a form of logical reasoning that moves from general principles to a conclusion. It usually involves two propositions and a conclusion.

    Proposition 1 (usually a general principle): Stealing is wrong.

    Proposition 2 (usually an observation): John stole a candy bar from the store.

    Conclusion (results of deductive analysis): John's theft of the candy bar was wrong.

    Deduction is often used to present arguments that have ethical and moral dimensions, such as birth control, welfare reform, and immigration policy.

- **Induction** is a form of logical reasoning that moves from specific observations to general conclusions, often drawing on numerical data to reveal patterns. Medical researchers, for example, typically collect a large number of observations about the effectiveness and side effects of new medications and then analyze their observations to draw conclusions about the effectiveness of the medications. Induction is based on probability — that is, whether something seems likely to occur in the future based on what has been observed. Three commonly used forms of induction are trend analysis (see p. 257), causal analysis (see p. 259), and data analysis (see p. 260).

You can use different types of appeals to support your claim. Emotional appeals can be mixed with appeals to character. A coach's address to a team before an important athletic competition often relies not only on appeals to emotion but also on appeals to character, asking the players to trust what the coach has to say and to trust in themselves and their own abilities. Similarly, appeals to principle can be combined with appeals to emotion and logic.

To choose your appeals, reflect on your purpose, readers, sources, context, and overall claim. In your writer's notebook, do the following:

1. Put your overall claim in the form of a thesis statement.
2. List the reasons you will offer to accept your overall claim.
3. Identify the evidence you will use to accept each reason.
4. Ask what sort of appeals will help you connect each reason to the evidence you have chosen.
5. Sketch out promising appeals. Ask, for example, how you would appeal to authority, or how you would appeal to logic.
6. Ask how your readers are likely to respond to a given appeal.
7. Ask whether each appeal is appropriate in light of your overall argument. An emotional appeal might seem effective by itself, for example, but if the argument you've developed relies largely on appeals to logic and authority, an emotional appeal might surprise your readers.

ADDRESS COUNTERARGUMENTS

Your readers will expect you to consider and address reasonable alternatives to your overall claim. They'll do so not only because it is appropriate to acknowledge the contributions of other authors who have written about an issue but also because they want to understand why your argument is superior to the alternatives. If your readers are aware of opposing claims but notice that you haven't addressed them, they'll question your credibility. They might conclude that you haven't thought carefully about the issue, or they might wonder whether you haven't addressed opposing claims in your essay because you think the other claims are stronger than yours.

To address counterarguments, review the work you did to identify and consider opposing claims as you built your argument (see p. 431). Consider the strengths and weaknesses of each claim in relation to your argument and in relation to the other opposing claims you identified. Then decide whether to concede, refute, or ignore each claim.

Concede valid claims Show your readers that you are being fair — and establish common ground with readers who might otherwise be inclined to disagree with you — by acknowledging opposing points of view and accepting reasonable aspects of counterarguments. For example, if you are arguing that your state government should spend more to repair roads and bridges, acknowledge that this will probably mean reducing funding for other state programs or increasing state taxes.

You can qualify your concession by explaining that although part of a counter-argument is sound, readers should consider the argument's weaknesses. You might note, for example, that reducing funding for some state programs could be offset by instituting fees for those who use those programs most.

Refute widely held claims A counterargument might be widely advocated or generally accepted yet still have significant weaknesses. If you identify widely held claims that have weaknesses such as cost, undesirable outcomes, or logical flaws, describe the counterargument, point out its flaws, and explain why your claim or reason is superior. For example, you might note that although it is costly to maintain roads and bridges, allowing them to fall into disrepair will cost far more in the long run — in terms of both funding and loss of life.

Ignore competing claims Don't assume that addressing counterarguments means giving every competing claim equal time. Some counterarguments will be much stronger than others, and some will be so closely related to one another that you can dismiss them as a group. Once you've addressed valid and widely held competing claims, you can safely ignore the rest. Even though your sense of fairness might suggest that you should address every counterargument, doing so will result in a less effective (and potentially much longer) essay.

As you present your discussion of counterarguments, maintain a reasonable and polite tone. You gain little, if anything, by insulting or belittling writers with whom you disagree, particularly when it's possible that some of your readers think a certain counterargument has merit. It is preferable — and generally more effective in terms of winning your argument — to carefully and politely point out the limitations of a particular counterargument.

CONSIDER GENRE AND DESIGN

A well-written argumentative essay uses design to help readers understand your argument more clearly, usually by simplifying the presentation of reasons and evidence or by setting a mood through the use of carefully selected illustrations. The design of your essay should reflect the formatting requirements of your assignment and the expectations of your readers, particularly your instructor.

In many cases, the appeals you choose to make to your readers will suggest design elements that can enhance your argument.

- **Photographs** can strengthen (or serve as) an emotional appeal. For instance, an argument in favor of tightening lending restrictions might show a family in front of the home they've lost to foreclosure.

- **Headings and subheadings** can help readers follow your reasoning about an issue.

- **Color** and **pull quotes** can underscore appeals to values, beliefs, and principles by calling a reader's attention to shared assumptions and important ideas.

- **Sidebars** can highlight an appeal to character by giving related information about a writer or a source without interfering with the flow of the argument.

- Appeals to authority often present statistical data in the form of **tables**, **charts**, and **graphs**.

Consider the placement of visual evidence carefully. In general, place illustrations as close as possible to the point where they are mentioned in the text, provide a title or caption that identifies or explains the illustration, and cite the source of the information.

You can find discussions of document design in Chapters 18, 19, and 20.

FRAME YOUR ARGUMENT

Most written arguments rely on a well-established set of elements: a clearly expressed thesis statement, a thorough discussion of the reasons and evidence supporting the overall claim, careful consideration of counterarguments, and an introduction and a conclusion. The presentation of these elements, however, is as varied as the issues addressed in argumentative essays and the writers who tackle them.

Organization As you organize your argumentative essay, give some thought to the sequence in which you present your reasons and evidence and discuss counterarguments. If you are drawing heavily on emotional appeals, for example, you might lead with a particularly striking appeal, one designed to outrage or excite your readers — or at least to get them to continue reading your essay. Similarly, you might end with a reason that would leave your readers feeling that they must do something about the issue you've raised. If you are crafting an argument that relies heavily on logical analysis, you should ask whether any of your appeals build on (or logically follow) other appeals. You should also ask whether some appeals are easier to understand and accept than others. If so, be sure to present them before you advance more complex or objectionable appeals. Counterarguments might all be addressed early on, discussed in turn, or withheld until you've established the reasons in support of your overall claim. Refer to Chapter 17 for additional guidelines on organizing and outlining an essay.

Introduction and Conclusion Pay particular attention to your introduction and conclusion. These important elements not only provide the framework within which your readers will understand the issue you are addressing but also influence their willingness to accept your argument. Once you've decided how to frame your introduction and conclusion, you can use a range of strategies to put them into words. In their introductions, writers of argumentative essays frequently rely on strategies such as asking a question, leading with a quotation, and telling a story. In their conclusions, they often use strategies such as speculating about the future, asking a question, and closing with a quotation. You can read more about strategies for introducing and concluding your essay in Chapter 18.

Review and Improve Your Draft

An effective argumentative essay makes its claim in such a manner that readers will understand an issue in a particular way, provides plausible and well-supported appeals to accept that claim, addresses likely counterarguments, and avoids the traps posed by logical fallacies and other forms of argument that lack integrity. Few writers can fully address all these elements in a first draft, so don't expect to produce a finished essay in one sitting. Set aside enough time to review your draft and to revise it at least once. Allowing at least a day or two between completing your draft and reviewing it makes it easier to recognize opportunities for improvement and to clarify your thinking.

CONSIDER YOUR OVERALL CLAIM

Before you review any other part of your draft, spend some time reassessing your overall claim. Is it presented in such a manner that your readers will understand the issue in a specific way? Have you stated it clearly? Is it possible that your readers might reasonably misinterpret your claim, or might think of the issue differently than you do? Finally, is the claim stated in a way that is consistent with how you've framed your introduction and conclusion?

REVIEW YOUR REASONS, EVIDENCE, AND APPEALS

How you present your overall claim will set up expectations among your readers about how you're likely to support it. For example, if you've said that the city council needs to increase funding for a flood mitigation program, your readers are likely to expect that at least some of your reasons for making the claim will touch on the consequences of failing to fund the program at a reasonable level. As you review your draft, ask whether your reasons make sense individually, and then ask whether they work well together. Most important, ask how your readers are likely to react to each reason and whether you've provided enough evidence to support it.

Peer Review: Improve Your Argumentative Essay

One of the biggest challenges writers face is reading their own work as a reader rather than as the writer. Because you know what you're trying to say, you'll find it easy to understand your draft. To determine what you should do to revise your draft, ask a friend or classmate to read your essay and to assess how well you have adopted the role of advocate (see p. 398) by answering the following questions.

Purpose	1. How do you interpret my purpose for writing? Does my goal seem to be to convince or to persuade?
	2. Is my overall claim plausible and debatable? Do you agree with what I am saying? If not, what should I do to convince you?
	3. Do the reasons I've offered to support my claim seem sufficient and appropriate?
Readers	4. Do you accept the connections I've made (or have assumed to exist) between my reasons and my overall claim?
	5. Do you find the issue significant? Why or why not?
	6. Does my reasoning seem sound? Did you catch any fallacies?
	7. Have I used argumentative appeals appropriately and effectively? Should I consider making any other kinds of appeals?
Sources	8. Does the evidence I've offered to support my appeals make sense? Can I add or clarify anything to help you understand the argument better? Do you think any of the evidence is unnecessary?
	9. Do my sources strike you as reliable and appropriate? Does any of the evidence I've used seem questionable? Have I relied on any sources too heavily?
	10. Is it clear which ideas and information are my own and which came from my sources?
Context	11. Have I clearly introduced and effectively handled counterarguments? Did I present them fairly?
	12. How familiar were you with this issue before reading my essay? Do I need to provide more (or less) background information or context? Did I fail to include any reasons or evidence that you expected?
	13. Could I strengthen any of my appeals by bringing in design elements, such as photographs or tables?

For each of the points listed above, ask your reviewers to provide concrete advice about what you should do to improve your draft. It may help if you ask them to adopt the role of an editor — someone who is working with you to improve your draft. You can read more about peer review in Chapter 5.

In addition, ask whether your readers are likely to accept the kinds of appeals you've used to present your reasons and evidence. Always consider your readers' needs, interests, backgrounds, and knowledge of the issue. You might conclude, for instance, that an emotional appeal will backfire, or that your readers will expect more evidence from authorities, or that you could strengthen an appeal to values by explaining an underlying assumption.

EXAMINE YOUR TREATMENT OF COUNTERARGUMENTS

As you review how you've addressed counterarguments, put yourself in your readers' place. Doing so allows you to pose reasonable arguments that contradict your overall claim about the issue. If you believe a counterargument is plausible and likely to be raised by your readers, make sure you've responded to it. Your response need not be lengthy, but it should let readers know that you've considered the counterargument and found it less effective than the argument you're making.

ENSURE THE INTEGRITY OF YOUR ARGUMENT

Carefully review the reasons and evidence you've offered to support your overall claim. Then review the list of common logical fallacies starting on page 432. Make sure that your argument is free of these fallacies. Even an otherwise strong argument can fail to convince or persuade readers if it relies in part on questionable argumentative strategies.

 ## Student Essay

Elisabeth Layne, "Trigger Warnings on College Campuses"

The following argumentative essay was written by featured writer Elisabeth Layne.

Layne 1

Elisabeth Layne

ENG 1011

Prof. Prince

April 10, 2016

Trigger Warnings on College Campuses

Nearly overnight, the term "trigger warning" went from relative obscurity to the center of a heated debate in academic spheres around the country. From *The Washington Post* and *The New York Times* to *Forbes* and *Slate*, prominent media outlets have jumped on the use of trigger warnings as a sign of the decline of higher education. Among the frequent critiques of their academic use is that trigger warnings coddle overly sensitive students, discourage the critical thinking that is essential in college, and lead to censorship in academia. Such conclusions are simplistic, rarely taking into account what trigger warnings provide for students and whether their presence actually limits or detracts from class discussion. Because they honor the traumatic experiences of some students, trigger warnings should be a noncontroversial option for college professors and students.

A trigger warning is a short and easy way to caution the reader or viewer about the more difficult aspects of a written or visual text, much like the brief notices that appear on television before a show with explicit violence or sex. Trigger warnings came into recent, regular use online, especially on feminist blogs and in forums. When survivors of sexual assault or other traumas would share their experiences, they would often post a warning to let readers know in advance of any explicit or upsetting content — for instance, "TW: sexual violence, suicidal ideation." Encountering depictions of the traumatic events can be very difficult for trauma survivors or those suffering from a clinical condition, such as anorexia, because they can cause — or trigger — the individual to reexperience the trauma. Trigger warnings simply allow readers to prepare themselves for upcoming content; they are valuable in many different contexts, including academic spaces.

In a 2015 article in *The Atlantic,* Greg Lukianoff and Jonathan Haidt dismiss trigger warnings as unnecessary and even harmful in college courses. They argue that "classroom discussions are safe places to be exposed to incidental reminders of trauma" because "a discussion of violence is unlikely to be followed

---

Sidebar annotations:

Information about the writer, class, and submission date is formatted according to MLA guidelines.

The title is centered.

The writer begins with a brief overview of the controversy surrounding trigger warnings.

The writer explains what trigger warnings are and describes their origin.

The writer gives an example of a trigger warning.

The writer summarizes a critique of trigger warnings and integrates a partial quotation.

Layne 2

by actual violence" (Lukianoff and Haidt). While it's true that actual violence is thankfully rare in the classroom, the authors ignore the effects of exposure to such triggers on individuals suffering from post-traumatic stress disorder, or PTSD. PTSD sufferers who encounter a trigger can experience panic attacks, sweating, increased heart rate, muscle tension, shortness of breath, nausea, and other physical symptoms, along with suicidal thoughts, feelings of guilt and shame, and hopelessness ("Post-Traumatic Stress Disorder"). In their blanket declaration that the college classroom is always safe, Lukianoff and Haidt disregard the toll these physical and emotional experiences take on students. In fact, as Cornell professor Kate Manne argues, the problem with triggered experiences of trauma is not just that they are unpleasant but that they impede learning. Pointing out that "it's impossible to think straight" in the throes of a panic attack, Manne argues that trigger warnings can protect and support learning in her classroom. Trigger warnings are measures requested by students to protect themselves so they can be challenged *by* their coursework, and not primarily by their reaction *to* it.

> *When a document has no author, the parenthetical citation gives the title in quotation marks.*

> *An authority is cited to support the writer's claim.*

Critics of trigger warnings allege that they dampen intellectual pursuit by catering to students who are too sensitive. The American Association of University Professors (AAUP), for instance, worries that trigger warnings violate the true purpose of higher education: "The presumption that students need to be protected rather than challenged in a classroom is at once infantilizing and anti-intellectual" (qtd. in Lukianoff and Haidt). Another critic goes so far as to call the students of this generation "an insufferable breed of self-centered Care Bears" (qtd. in Miller). Such mockery aside, the AAUP, like Lukianoff and Haidt, makes an unwarranted leap from warning students about difficult content to removing that content from the syllabus. Professors who give trigger warnings and students who appreciate them aren't censoring a disturbing film or reading. Rather, they are acknowledging the complex experiences that students bring to the classroom. Insensitivity toward students' identities and formative experiences will only obstruct higher education, rather than achieve its goals.

> *Information cited in a source is identified using the abbreviation "qtd. in."*

At the heart of this issue are students' sense of identity and the role that sense plays in their education. As four Columbia students — members of the university's Multicultural Affairs Advisory Board — explain, "Students need to feel safe in the classroom, and that requires a learning environment that

Layne 3

recognizes the multiplicity of their identities" (Johnson et al.). What the AAUP criticizes as being overprotective, these students deem necessary for feeling safe. Another convert to the use of trigger warnings, writer Kat Stoeffel, is aware of the power dynamics at work here. "[T]he trigger-warning backlash feels like part of a larger reaction against the needs of marginalized groups — even when they're perfectly easy to accommodate — simply because they are the minority," she writes. It is difficult to imagine requests from the majority being met with such resistance.

A third criticism lodged against the use of trigger warnings is that violence and trauma are unfortunately everywhere, making trigger warnings impossible and impractical. As Conor Friedersdorf writes, colleges shouldn't — and in fact, can't — help students avoid trauma when studying the world around them:

> How to study slavery, or the Rwandan genocide, or the Communist purges, or the Holocaust, or the Crucifixion, or the prose of Toni Morrison or James Joyce, or the speeches of MLK, or the debate that surrounds abortion, or psychological experiments about the human willingness to take orders, without risking trauma?
>
> Surely college students should know what's coming when they set out to plumb human civilization. A huge part of it is a horror show.
> To spare us upset would require morphine.

Friedersdorf rightly acknowledges the violence and oppression at the root of these significant moments in historical, literary, economic, and political study, but he misconstrues the goal of trigger warnings. They are not intended to shield students from harsh truths (numbing them like "morphine") but rather to support students whose personal experiences echo those being depicted in their academic study. While some critics decry those who treat students as delicate children, Friedersdorf does the opposite, expecting them to be hardened, to "know what's coming," before they step foot in a college classroom. Is that really a fair expectation?

History instructor Angus Johnston, who teaches at a community college, believes that it's not. He defends the use of trigger warnings because a college classroom is different than a blog or discussion post or an episode of The

---

Three or more authors are cited using the first author's name, followed by "et al."

A block quotation is indented.

The writer quotes a source's words to make her point.

Layne 4

Sopranos. It is

a shared space — for the 75 minutes of the class session and the 15 weeks of the semester, we're pretty much all stuck with one another, and that fact imposes interpersonal obligations on us that don't exist between writer and reader. Second, it's an interactive space — it's a conversation, not a monologue, and I have a responsibility to encourage that conversation as best I can. Finally, it's an unpredictable space — a lot of my students have never previously encountered some of the material we cover in my classes, or haven't encountered it in the way it's taught at the college level, and don't have any clear sense of what to expect.

The gap between Friedersdorf's and Johnston's expectations of college students is striking. Friedersdorf lays responsibility squarely on the shoulders of eighteen- and nineteen-year-olds, who are "plumbing human civilization" for perhaps the first time, while Johnston, the community college instructor, emphasizes his responsibilities to his students. Manne makes a similar point about an instructor's responsibilities in the classroom, noting that trigger warnings remind students who don't need them to be sensitive to the experiences of those who do. Beneficial to those who need them as well as those who don't, trigger warnings bring empathy into the classroom.

Although trigger warnings can be advantageous, they are also limited. A 2014 editorial by seven humanities professors objects that sometimes trigger warnings don't go far enough. "Institutions seriously committed to caring for traumatized students ought to be directing students, from their first days on campus, to a rich array of mental health resources. Trigger warnings are not an adequate substitute for these resources" (Freeman et al.). Mental health or disability issues are beyond the purview of college professors, and trigger warnings should not give colleges and universities a pass on true mental health care for their students.

Despite their shortcomings, trigger warnings do help ease students into engaging with difficult academic material. Simple, unobtrusive, and effective, they honor student experiences and facilitate learning — one of the main goals of colleges and universities. As this generation of students speaks up more and more about mental illness, sexual assault, war-related PTSD, and other difficult experiences, trigger warnings affirm that trauma must not be left at the classroom door.

The writer quotes a different source to provide evidence.

The writer paraphrases a point from a source.

Works Cited

Freeman, Elizabeth, et al. "Trigger Warnings Are Flawed." *Inside Higher Ed*, 29 May
2014, www.insidehighered.com/views/2014/05/29/essay-faculty-members
-about-why-they-will-not-use-trigger-warnings.

Friedersdorf, Conor. "What HBO Can Teach Colleges about 'Trigger Warnings.'" *The
Atlantic*, 20 May 2014, www.theatlantic.com/education/archive/2014/05/
what-trigger-warning-activists-and-critics-can-learn-from-hbo/371137/.

Johnson, Kai, et al. "Our Identities Matter in Core Classrooms." *The
Columbia Spectator*, 30 Apr. 2015, http://columbiaspectator.com/opinion/
2015/04/30/our-identities matter core classrooms.

Johnston, Angus. "Why I'll Add a Trigger Warning." *Inside Higher Ed*, 29 May
2014, www.insidehighered.com/views/2014/05/29/essay-why-professor
-adding-trigger-warning-his-syllabus#sthash.3AiFHg3f.dpbs.

Lukianoff, Greg, and Jonathan Haidt. "The Coddling of the American Mind."
The Atlantic, Sept. 2015, www.theatlantic.com/magazine/archive/
2015/09/the-coddling-of-the-american-mind/399356/.

Manne, Kate. "Why I Use Trigger Warnings." *The New York Times*, 19 Sept. 2015,
www.nytimes.com/2015/09/20/opinion/sunday/why-i-use-trigger-warnings
.html.

Miller, Michael E. "Columbia Students Claim Greek Mythology Needs a Trigger
Warning." *The Washington Post*, 14 May 2015, www.washingtonpost.com/
news/morning-mix/wp/2015/05/14/columbia-students-claim-greek-mythology
-needs-a-trigger-warning/.

"Post-Traumatic Stress Disorder." *Mental Health America*, www
.mentalhealthamerica.net/conditions/post-traumatic-stress-disorder.
Accessed 10 Apr. 2016.

Stoeffel, Kat. "Why I Stopped Rolling My Eyes at Trigger Warnings." *New York*,
New York Media LLC, 21 May 2014, nymag.com/thecut/2014/05/stop
-rolling-your-eyes-at-trigger-warnings.html.

Following MLA guidelines, the Works Cited heading is centered.

Entries are listed alphabetically by author and formatted with hanging indents.

A source with more than three authors is listed by the first author's name, followed by "et al."

Entries for online sources include URLs.

A source without an author is listed by its title.

Since no publication date is available for this online source, the writer includes her date of access.

Project Ideas

The following suggestions provide means of focusing your work on an argumentative essay or another type of argumentative document.

Suggestions for Essays

1. ARGUE ABOUT A SOCIAL TREND

Identify and discuss the relevance of a social trend, such as the increasing focus on wellness and healthy lifestyles, changes in home-ownership patterns, or dressing in a particular manner. Then make an argument about (a) the advisability of following the trend, (b) the likely effects — short- or long-term — of the trend on society, or (c) the likelihood that the trend will have a lasting impact on society. Use evidence from online conversations and your personal observations to support your argument.

2. ARGUE AGAINST A COMMONLY HELD BELIEF

Urge your readers to reject a commonly held belief. For example, you might argue that the widespread belief that writing ability is a gift rather than an acquired skill causes students to give up too easily on efforts to improve their writing. Or you might argue that a particular belief about American families is inaccurate. For example, you might focus your argument on the belief that only children are more likely to be "spoiled," that a woman's life will be less rich if she chooses not to become a mother, or that siblings are friends for life. In your essay, define the belief and make an overall claim about the effects of accepting it. Offer reasons and evidence to support your claim. Base your appeals on logic and on principles, values, and beliefs.

3. URGE READERS TO WIDEN THEIR CULTURAL HORIZONS

Make an argument about the value of attending a play or concert, viewing a movie or watching a television show, attending a poetry reading or an art exhibition, or purchasing a new music album or video game. Your argument should be based on the benefits of appreciating and supporting cultural events, literature, artistic work, music, or games. To support your argument, draw on your observations and interpretations of your subject. You might also use evidence from interviews or surveys and read published work that reviews or analyzes the subject of your essay.

4. ARGUE ABOUT A DEFINITION

Make an argument about a definition, such as how a problem or an issue has been defined or how a particular standard has been developed and applied. For example, you might argue that characterizations of state support for public education as a financial issue are inappropriate, and that it would be better to understand the issue as one of ensuring that citizens are well prepared to participate in a democracy. Or you might argue that your state's definition of intoxication (for example, .08 percent blood alcohol content) is inappropriate, and that it ought to be higher or lower. Use evidence from published sources to support your argument (see Chapter 13). Depending on the subject of your essay, consider using field research methods such as interviews, observations, surveys, and correspondence (see Chapter 14) to support your argument. Think about the type of evidence you've collected to support your argument and consider which types of appeals are likely to be most effective with your readers.

5. ARGUE ABOUT AN ISSUE IN YOUR AREA OF STUDY

Write an argumentative essay about an issue in a discipline or profession in which you have an interest. For example, if you are interested in human resources, you might argue about the implications of allowing employers to access employees' genetic profiles. The issue you choose should be under debate in the discipline or profession, so be sure to search professional or academic journals and online conversations among members of the discipline or profession for prevailing arguments (see Chapter 13). Depending on the subject of your essay, consider using field research methods such as interviews, observations, surveys, and correspondence (see Chapter 14) to gather information to support your argument. For example, you might locate online discussion forums or subscribe to e-mail lists within your discipline. As you craft your argument, consider the type of evidence you've collected to support your argument and consider which types of appeals are likely to be most effective with your readers.

Suggestions for Other Genres

6. WRITE AN OPINION COLUMN ABOUT A NEW LAW OR REGULATION

In an opinion column, identify a recently passed law or a new regulation (federal, state, or local), and discuss its potential impact. You might, for example, take a look at changes in election laws, such as requirements that state-issued IDs be provided at polling stations. Or you might explore laws that address labeling of genetically modified foods. Offer a brief summary evaluation of the appropriateness or likely effects of the new law or regulation, and then make recommendations to your readers about how to respond. For example, you might argue that a new law is so flawed that it should be repealed. Or you might argue that only by providing adequate funding to a local or state agency can a regulation be enforced effectively. Use evidence from government documents, other published sources, and field research to support your argument.

7. WRITE A BLOG ENTRY ABOUT AN ISSUE RAISED IN ANOTHER BLOG

In a blog, argue about an issue addressed by the author of another blog. For example, you might object to an argument about the economic and political trade-offs of government rescues of failed financial institutions. Or you might argue about the advisability of joining social-networking websites such as Facebook or LinkedIn. Your blog entry should link to the blog entry that raised the issue, as well as to other relevant blogs. Use evidence from blogs and other published sources to support your argument. You should refer to your sources by using phrases such as "in an article published in *Time* on July 23, 2013, Ann Smith argues" or by linking directly to the source.

8. CREATE A PUBLIC SERVICE ADVERTISEMENT

Create a full-page ad suitable for a magazine or website that urges readers to take action on a social issue, such as adoption or hunger. Your ad should use visual images and only enough text to clearly identify the issue and convey your argument to your readers. For inspiration, examine the ads shown on pages 406–409.

In Summary: Writing an Argumentative Essay

* **Find a conversation and listen in.**
  - Explore disagreements (p. 421).
  - Track online conversations (p. 423).
  - Ask questions about promising issues (p. 423).

* **Build your argument.**
  - Define your overall claim (p. 426).
  - Develop reasons to accept your overall claim (p. 426).
  - Choose evidence to support your reasons (p. 428).
  - Identify and consider opposing claims (p. 431).
  - Ensure the integrity of your argument (p. 432).

* **Prepare a draft.**
  - Make an argumentative claim (p. 435).
  - Appeal to your readers (p. 436).
  - Address counterarguments (p. 439).
  - Consider genre and design (p. 440).
  - Frame your argument (p. 441).

* **Review and improve your draft.**
  - Consider your overall claim (p. 442).
  - Review your reasons, evidence, and appeals (p. 442).
  - Examine your treatment of counterarguments (p. 444).
  - Ensure the integrity of your argument (p. 444).

PART THREE

Conducting
Research

Beginning Your Search

Given the amount of information available through library collections, databases, and the Web, writers have become less worried about finding enough sources and far more concerned about finding the right sources. This chapter explores strategies for collecting information for a writing project and then looks at how you can keep track of that information.

How Should I Focus My Search for Sources?

As you prepare to do your research, it's best to have an idea of what you're looking for. Focus your efforts to collect, read, evaluate, and take notes on sources by developing a *research question* — a brief question that asks about a specific aspect of your subject, reflects your writing situation, and is narrow enough to allow you to collect information in time to meet your deadlines.

To develop your research question, generate ideas for potential questions and assess them in light of your interests, role, and writing situation.

Generate Potential Research Questions

Most research questions begin with the words *what, why, when, where, who,* or *how.* Some research questions use the words *would* or *could* to ask whether something is possible. Still others use the word *should* to analyze the appropriateness of a particular action, policy, procedure, or decision. Questions can focus on the following:

- **Information:** what is known — and not known — about a subject
- **History:** what has occurred in the past that is relevant to a subject
- **Assumptions:** what conclusions — merited or not — writers and readers have already made about a subject
- **Goals:** what the writers and readers involved in this conversation want to see happen (or not happen)
- **Outcomes:** what has happened so far, or what is likely to happen
- **Policies:** what the best procedures are for carrying out actions or for making decisions

Questions can also lead you to engage in the following kinds of thinking processes. These processes will be shaped, in turn, by your purpose and role as an author (see Part Two).

- **Reflecting:** considering the significance of a subject
- **Reporting:** seeking information; conveying what is known about a subject
- **Analyzing:** looking for similarities and differences among subjects or aspects of a subject; asking what leads to a specific result; asking about a series of events
- **Evaluating:** asking about strengths and weaknesses, advantages and disadvantages, or appropriateness

- **Problem solving:** defining problems, considering the outcomes of a problem, assessing potential solutions, and/or offering solutions

- **Advocating:** advancing arguments about a subject

By combining a specific focus, such as assumptions or policies, with a specific type of thinking process, such as problem solving, you can create carefully tailored research questions, such as the ones that featured writer James Hardjadinata considered for his essay about puppy mills (see p. 385).

> What factors have contributed to the increase in puppy mills?
>
> What policies have tried but failed to resolve this problem?
>
> Why have officials been unable (or unwilling) to enforce current legislation?
>
> Why do so many families buy puppies from unreputable breeders?
>
> What can the government do to protect animals and consumers?
>
> What can animal lovers do to help?

Use specific question words to start generating potential research questions. If you are interested in conducting an analysis, for example, ask questions using the words *what*, *why*, *when*, *where*, *who*, and *how*. If you want to explore goals and outcomes, use the words *would* or *could*. If the conversation focuses on determining an appropriate course of action, generate questions using the word *should*. Consider the differences among these questions:

> **What** are the dangers of puppy mills?
>
> **Would** it be feasible to require pet stores to investigate the breeders they use to source their puppies?
>
> **Should** the U.S. Congress pass federal legislation to regulate breeders?

Each question would lead to differences in how to search for and select sources of information, what role to adopt as a writer, and how to organize and design the document.

Select and Refine Your Question

Once you have a list of potential research questions, select a question that interests you, is consistent with the role you have adopted, and is appropriate for your writing situation. Then refine your question by referring to shared assumptions and existing conditions, narrowing its scope, and conducting preliminary searches.

REFLECT ON YOUR WRITING SITUATION

As you consider potential research questions, pay attention to your purpose and role. Your efforts to collect information should help you accomplish your purpose and address your readers' needs, interests, values, and beliefs. Keep in mind, however, that as you learn more about your subject, you might refine your purpose. In turn, that might lead to changes in your research question. If you think of your research question as a flexible guide — as a question subject to revision — you can be open to new ways of thinking about the conversation and your contribution to it.

REFER TO SHARED ASSUMPTIONS AND EXISTING CONDITIONS

You can refine your research question by calling attention to assumptions that have been made by the community of writers and readers who are addressing your subject or by referring to existing conditions relevant to your subject. Note the difference among these three versions of featured writer Ellen Page's research question about malaria prevention.

Original Question:

What role, if any, can insecticides such as DDT play in preventing malaria?

Alternative 1:

Given the damaging effects of insecticides such as DDT on the environment, why would health professionals consider using it in preventing malaria?

Alternative 2:

In the face of hundreds of millions of cases of malaria worldwide each year — including more than one million annual fatalities — why are proven insecticides such as DDT still banned in the United States?

As you refine your research question, experiment with using qualifying words and phrases such as the following:

Mix . . .	and Match
Although	we know that . . .
Because	it is uncertain . . .
Even though	it is clear that . . .
Given that	studies indicate . . .
If	recent events . . .
Now that	it has been shown . . .
Since	the lack of . . .
While	we cannot . . .

NARROW YOUR SCOPE

Early research questions typically lack focus. You can narrow the scope of your question by looking for vague words and phrases and replacing them with more specific words or phrases. The process of moving from a broad research question to one that might be addressed effectively in an academic essay might produce the following sequence:

Original Question:

> What is behind the increased concern about how we fund election campaigns?

Refined:

> What has led to the increased attention to the amount of corporate funding for national election campaigns?

Further Refined:

> How has the Supreme Court's Citizens United ruling changed the role and influence of corporate funders in presidential elections?

In this example, the writer has narrowed the scope of the research question in two ways. First, the writer has shifted the focus from concerns about the funding of election campaigns to the role of corporate funding in national campaigns. Second, the writer has moved from a general focus on campaign funding to a more specific focus on the effects of a Supreme Court ruling on the role played by funders in presidential elections.

✈ TECH TIP: CONDUCT PRELIMINARY SEARCHES

One of the best ways to test your research question is to conduct some preliminary searches in an online library catalog or database or on the Web. If you locate a vast amount of information in your searches, you might need to revise your question so that it focuses on a more manageable aspect of the subject. In contrast, if you find almost nothing, you might need to expand the scope of your question.

How Can I Develop a Search Plan?

Once you've created your research question, you'll need to decide how to search for and collect information. Use your research questions and your writing situation to shape your search plan — a brief, informal plan that records your ideas about how to locate and collect information.

Identify Relevant Types of Sources

Writers use information found in a variety of sources — digital, print, and field — to support the points they make in their documents. To identify relevant sources for your writing project, consider the scope of the conversation you are joining, the timeliness of your subject, the information you'll need to develop your ideas, and the evidence you'll need to support your points.

CONSIDER THE SCOPE OF YOUR CONVERSATION

If the conversation focuses on a highly specialized issue within a scholarly discipline, such as a discussion of gene splicing in biology, the best sources usually are scholarly books and journal articles. If it addresses a subject that has broad appeal, such as transportation problems in your state or region, you can draw on a much wider range of sources, including newspaper and magazine articles, editorials and opinion columns, blogs, and websites.

CONSIDER THE TIMELINESS OF YOUR SUBJECT

Some subjects, such as funding for higher education or reducing alcohol consumption by college students, tend to be discussed over an extended period of time in a wide range of sources. If your subject focuses on a recent event, however, it might be best to turn to magazine and newspaper articles, the Web, blogs, observation, surveys, or interviews.

CONSIDER WHAT YOU NEED TO LEARN

If your subject is unfamiliar to you, look for sources that offer general overviews or discuss important aspects of the subject. Such sources tend to include magazine articles, professional journal articles, and articles on the Web.

CONSIDER THE EVIDENCE YOU'LL NEED

Think about the kind of evidence other writers have used to make their points. Have they used numerical data from scholarly research reports? Have they referred to expert opinion? If so, search for sources that can provide these kinds of evidence.

Identify Appropriate Search Tools and Research Methods

In general, you can use three sets of resources to locate information.

- **Digital search tools**, such as library catalogs, databases, and Web search sites, allow you to search and browse for sources using a computer. Digital search tools provide access to publication information about — and in some cases to the complete text of — print and digital sources.

- **Print resources**, such as bibliographies, indexes, encyclopedias, dictionaries, handbooks, almanacs, and atlases, can be found in library reference and periodical rooms. Unlike digital search tools, which typically cover recent publications, many print resources provide information about publications over several decades — and in some cases over more than a century.

- **Field research methods** allow you to collect information firsthand. These methods include conducting observations, interviews, and surveys; corresponding with experts; attending public events and performances; and viewing or listening to television and radio programs.

Featured writer Ellen Page, who wrote an informative essay about the use of DDT in the prevention of malaria (see p. 213), knew that her topic would require recent sources. As she put together her search plan, she decided to search databases for recent scholarly articles and to look for websites that reported recent research. To obtain the most up-to-date information, she also scheduled an interview with a professor at her university who had expertise in the area.

Review and Refine Your Plan

Your search plan might be an informal set of notes or a list of step-by-step instructions complete with details such as keywords to search, interview questions to ask, and observation forms to fill out. No matter how informal it is, you should write it down. A written plan will help you remember the decisions you've made as you've prepared to collect your sources.

Use your plan to schedule time to search for and collect information. Next to each activity — such as searching a database or conducting an interview — identify start dates and projected completion dates. Creating a schedule will help you budget and manage your time.

Share your plan with your instructor, your supervisor, your classmates, or a librarian. Each might suggest additional search tools, research methods, shortcuts, and alternative research strategies for your project. Take notes on the feedback you receive, and if necessary, revise your plan.

How Can I Keep Track of My Sources?

If you've ever forgotten to save a phone number, e-mail address, or password, you know how frustrating it can be to lose something. It can be just as frustrating to lose your interview notes or forget where you found a quotation or fact. Your writer's notebook is a good place to keep track of the information you collect during a writing project. You can also organize and save your sources, create a working bibliography, and create an annotated bibliography.

Manage Print Materials

Depending on the scope of your writing project, you might accumulate a great deal of print information, such as

- your written notes (in a notebook, on loose pieces of paper, on sticky notes, and so on)
- printouts from Web pages and databases
- printed typed documents, such as your outline and rough drafts
- books, magazines, newspapers, brochures, pamphlets, and government documents
- photocopies of articles, book chapters, and other documents
- letters, printed e-mail messages, and survey results

Rather than letting all this material build up in messy piles on your desk, create a filing system to keep track of your print documents. Filing systems can range from well-organized piles of paper labeled with sticky notes, to three-ring binders, to file cabinets filled with neatly labeled file folders.

Regardless of the approach you take, keep the following principles in mind:

- **Make it easy to locate your print materials.** Decide whether you want to group materials by topic, by date, by argument, by type of material (Web pages, photocopies, original documents, field sources, and so on), or by author.
- **Stick with your organizing scheme.** You'll find it difficult to locate materials if you use different approaches at different points in your writing project.
- **Always include complete publication information.** If a source doesn't contain publication information, write it on the document. You'll need it later. Publication information includes author, title, publisher, place and date of publication, and — for a Web source — sponsoring organization and URL.
- **Write a brief note on each of your print materials.** Indicate how it might contribute to your project.
- **Record the date.** Indicating the date when you found a source can help you reconstruct what you might have been doing at the time. Dates are also essential for documenting Web sources and other online sources (see Chapters 23 and 24).

Manage Digital Materials

The single most important strategy for managing digital information is keeping it organized. Save your sources in a folder and use descriptive file names. Rather than naming a file "Notes 1.doc," for instance, name it "Interview Notes from John Garcia, April 22.doc." If you find that you are storing a large amount of information, use subfolders to group your sources.

DOWNLOADING

Downloading digital sources to a hard drive, a flash drive, or a cloud-based service such as Dropbox, OneDrive, or iCloud allows you to open them later in a Web browser or word-processing program. Downloading sources can save you time toward the end of your writing project, particularly when you are drafting or revising your document.

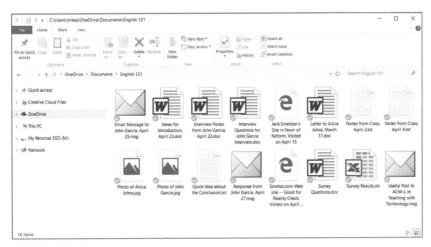

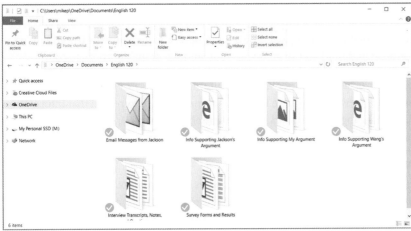

▲ Saving work in folders and subfolders

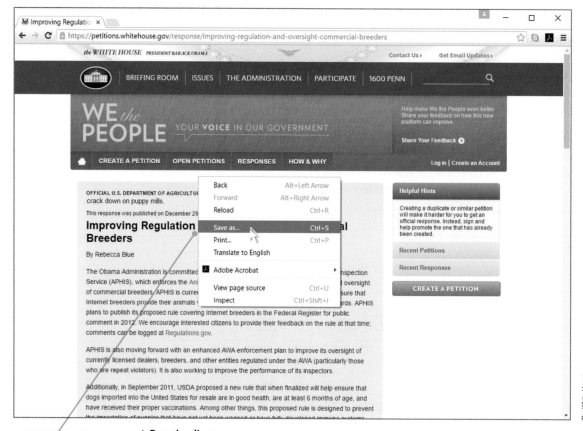

In Chrome, open the right-click menu and select Save as . . . to save a Web page.

▲ **Downloading a source**

The White House

To download entire Web pages, right-click (for Windows), Command-click (for Macs), or press and hold a finger (on phones and tablets) on the page, and choose the Save command. To download images and other media materials from the Web, click or press and hold on the item you want, and select the appropriate command.

Remember that saving a source does not automatically record the URL or the date on which you viewed the source for the first time. Be sure to record that information in your writing log, in your working bibliography (see p. 467), or in a document in the folder where you've saved your files.

COPYING AND PASTING

You can save text from relevant sources as notes in a word-processing document or programs such as Evernote or OneNote. Be sure to keep track of source information, such as the URL and the date you viewed a source, so that you can return to it if necessary and cite it appropriately.

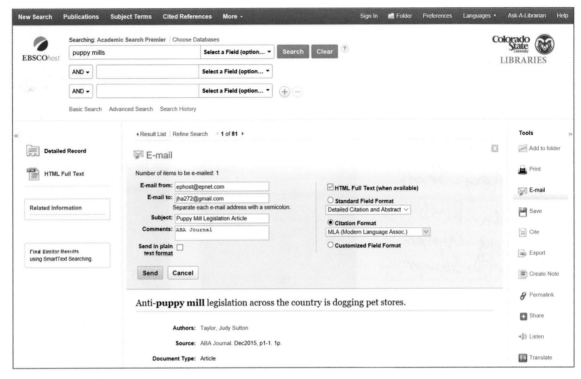

▲ Sending e-mail from a database

You can also use Web clipping tools, which work with your browser as toolbars or "add-ons" (a term used for programs that work within browsers) to copy all or part of a Web page. Leading, no-fee Web capture tools include Diigo (www.diigo.com) and Zotero (www.zotero.org).

USING E-MAIL

You can e-mail yourself messages containing digital documents you've found in your research. Some databases, such as EBSCO and OCLC's FirstSearch, allow you to e-mail the text of selected records directly from the database.

 TECH TIP: TAKING PHOTOS, MAKING RECORDINGS, AND SAVING NOTES

If you have a smartphone or a tablet, you can use apps to record conversations with others, record voice memos that contain ideas about your project, save video, take photos of sources you find in the periodical room (see p. 492), and surf the Web to locate sources. These apps allow you to collect and organize information, much as you would on a laptop or desktop computer.

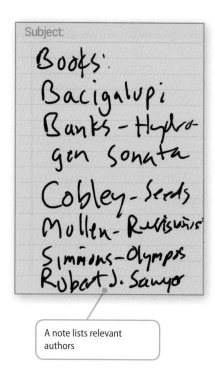

Subject:

Books:
Bacigalupi
Banks - Hydro-
gen Sonata
Cobley - Seeds
Mullen - Redisivus
Simmons - Olympos
Robert J. Sawyer

A note lists relevant authors

A photo records a location

Voice recording apps can be used to conduct interviews or record ideas

As you save information with these tools, keep your work well organized. Use descriptive names, save work in folders or albums, and include notes about where and when you found the information. Talk with other writers about the apps they've found useful, and if they're free, try them out yourself.

SAVING BOOKMARKS AND FAVORITES IN YOUR BROWSER

You can use a Bookmarks or Favorites list in a Web browser on your computer, tablet, or smartphone to keep track of online sources. Keep these lists organized by putting related items into folders and giving the items on your list descriptive names. If you use this strategy, however, remember that pages on the Web can and do change — perhaps before you finish your writing project. Be aware as well that some Web pages are generated by database programs, which can result in unwieldy URLs such as

http://newfirstsearch.oclc.org/WebZ/FSFETCH?fetchtype=fullrecord
:sessionid=fsapp2-49320-imjmp9sc-hoge4g:entitypagenum=9:0:recno
=4:resultset=3:format=FI:next=html/record.html:bad=error/badfetch
.html:entitytoprecno=4:entitycurrecno=4:numrecs=1

Although this long string of characters starts out looking like a normal URL, the majority of the characters are used by the database program to determine which records to display on a page. In many cases, the URL works only while you are conducting your search. If you add such a URL to your Bookmarks or Favorites list, there's a good chance it won't work later.

BACKING UP YOUR FILES

Whatever strategies you use to save and organize digital materials, replacing lost information takes time and effort. Avoid the risk of lost information by taking the time to make copies of your digital files, saved Web pages, e-mail messages, and Bookmarks or Favorites lists.

How Can I Create a Bibliography?

A bibliography is a list of sources with complete publication information, usually formatted according to the rules of a documentation system such as the Modern Language Association system (see Chapter 23) or the American Psychological Association system (see Chapter 24). As you start collecting information, create a working bibliography or an annotated bibliography to keep track of the sources you are using.

List Sources in a Working Bibliography

A working bibliography is a running list of the sources you've explored and plan to use in your writing project — with publication information for each source. The organization of your working bibliography can vary according to your needs and preferences. You can organize your sources in any of the following ways:

- in the order in which you collected your sources
- in categories
- by author
- by publication title
- according to an outline of your project document

The entries in a working bibliography should include as much publication information about a source as you can gather.

Your working bibliography will change significantly over the course of your writing project. As you explore and narrow your topic and, later, as you collect and work with your

Information You Should List in a Bibliography

Type of Source	Information You Should List
All Sources	• Author(s) • Title • Publication year • Brief note — or annotation — describing or commenting on the source, indicating how you might use it in your document, or showing how it is related to other sources (for annotated bibliographies only)
Book	• Editor(s) of book (if applicable) • Publication city • Publisher • Series and series editor (if applicable) • Translator (if applicable) • Volume (if applicable) • Edition (if applicable)
Chapter in an Edited Book	• Chapter title • Publication city • Publisher • Editor(s) of book • Book title • Page numbers
Journal, Magazine, and Newspaper Article	• Journal title • Volume number or date • Issue number or date • Page numbers
Website, Blog Post or Comment, Discussion Forum or Newsgroup Post, E-mail Message, and Chat Transcript	• URL • Access date (the date you read the source) • Sponsoring organization, if listed
Field Research	• Title (usually a description of the source, such as "Personal Interview with Ellen Page" or "Observation of Reid Vincent's Class at Dunn Elementary School") • Date (usually the date on which the field research was conducted)

sources, you will add potentially useful sources and delete sources that are no longer relevant. Eventually, your working bibliography will become one of the following:

- **a works cited or reference list** — a formal list of the sources you have referred to in a document
- **a bibliography or works consulted list** — a formal list of the sources that contributed to your thinking about a subject, even if those sources are not referred to explicitly in the text of the document

You can read more about works cited and reference lists in Part Five.

Keeping your working bibliography up-to-date is a critical part of your writing process. It helps you keep track of your sources and increases the likelihood that you will cite all the sources you use in your document — an important contribution to your efforts to avoid plagiarism.

The first six sources from featured writer James Hardjadinata's working bibliography are shown in the illustration below.

ASPCA. "Pet Statistics." *American Society for the Prevention of Cruelty to Animals*, 2015, www.aspca.org/animal-homelessness/shelter-intake-and-surrender/pet-statistics.

> Organization as author

Australian Veterinary Association. "Animals (Regulation of Sale) Bill 2008." *Australian Veterinary Association*, 2015, www.ava.com.au/node/1065.

> URLs are provided for Web sources.

Burger, Kailey A. "Solving the Problem of Puppy Mills: Why the Animal Welfare Movement's Bark Is Stronger than Its Bite." *Washington University Journal of Law and Policy*, vol. 43, 2014, pp. 259-84.

Humane Society of the United States. "A Horrible Hundred Selected Puppy Mills in the United States." *Humane Society of the United States*, May 2013, www.humanesociety.org/assets/pdfs/pets/puppy_mills/100-puppy-mills-list.pdf.

> For multiple works by the same author, only the first entry lists the author's name. Subsequent entries use three hyphens and a period.

---. "Pets by the Numbers." *Humane Society of the United States*, www.humanesociety.org/issues/pet_overpopulation/facts/pet_ownership_statistics.html. Accessed 10 May 2016.

---. "Puppy Mills: Frequently Asked Questions." *Humane Society of the United States*, www.humanesociety.org/issues/puppy_mills/qa/puppy_mill_FAQs.html. Accessed 10 May 2016.

▲ **Part of James Hardjadinata's working bibliography**

Summarize Sources in an Annotated Bibliography

In addition to complete citation information, an **annotated bibliography** provides a brief note — two or three sentences long — about each of your sources. Consider your purposes for creating an annotated bibliography, and tailor the content, focus, and length of your annotations accordingly.

- In some writing projects, you will submit an annotated bibliography to your instructor for review and comment. In this situation, your instructor will most likely expect a clear description of the content of each source and some indication of how you might use the source.

- In other writing projects, the annotated bibliography serves simply as a planning tool — a more detailed version of a working bibliography. As a result, your annotations might highlight key passages or information in a source, suggest how you can use information or ideas from the source, or emphasize relationships between sources.

- In still other projects, the annotated bibliography will be the final result of your efforts. In such cases, you would write your annotations for your readers, keeping their purposes, needs, interests, and backgrounds in mind.

An annotated bibliography is a useful tool even if you aren't required to submit it for a grade. By turning your working bibliography into an annotated bibliography, you can remind yourself of each source's information, ideas, and arguments and how the source might be used in your document.

The annotated bibliography that follows provides information that an instructor could use to assess a student's progress on a writing project.

Fumarola, Adam J. "With Best Friends Like Us Who Needs Enemies? The Phenomenon of the Puppy Mill, the Failure of Legal Regimes to Manage It, and the Positive Prospects of Animal Rights." *Buffalo Environmental Law Journal,* **vol. 6, no. 2, Spring 1999, pp. 253-89.**

A history of the problem of puppy mills in America and the current mass production of purebred dogs. Fumarola discusses the various attempts to restrict the growth of puppy mills, analyzing why legal attempts have failed. The end of the article focuses on the ethical considerations and the future of animal rights. This will be a good source for getting an overview of current and past legislation regarding puppy mills.

Humane Society of the United States, "State Puppy Mill Laws." *Humane Society of the United States,* **May 2015, www.humanesociety.org/assets/ state-puppy-mill-laws.pdf.**

A map of the United States showing three categories of existing legislation regarding puppy breeders: states requiring licensing and inspection; states requiring some degree of licensing but not mandatory inspections; and states with no specific laws regulating breeders. This map will be a strong visual for showing how many states lack legislation protecting animals from disreputable breeders.

Shaw, Anthony E. "Prisoners of Profit (Puppy Mills)." *Petfinder.* **www .petfinder.com/helping-pets/puppy-mills/prisoners-profit-puppy-mills/. Accessed 9 May 2015.**

Shaw is an executive at the American Society for the Prevention of Cruelty to Animals (ASPCA). His article describes the pitiful circumstances of female dogs in puppy mills, living in overcrowded conditions, forced to mate and bear litter after litter, regardless of the toll on their health. Shaw also notes the need for more inspectors of breeding facilities. He includes an anecdote about buying a sickly puppy from a breeder and the lies the breeder told to make the sale. This article will be useful for details about the atrocious living conditions of dogs stuck in puppy mills.

Entries include all citation information the writer will need for the final document.

Annotations provide brief summaries of the purpose and content of the sources.

Annotations are intended for the writer and the instructor. They indicate how and where the writer will use the source in the document.

▲ **Part of James Hardjadinata's annotated bibliography**

In Summary: Beginning Your Search

* Develop and refine a research question (p. 456).

* Plan your search for sources (p. 459).

* Review and refine your plan (p. 461).

* Save and organize print and digital sources (p. 462).

* Create a working bibliography (p. 467).

* Consider creating an annotated bibliography (p. 470).

Locating Sources

▶▶ Your search plan prepares you to start collecting sources. In this chapter, you'll learn how to generate search terms; use library catalogs, databases, the Web, and media search sites; and take advantage of the print resources in a library. As you start to locate sources, keep in mind your writing situation and the conversation you've decided to join. Focusing on your purpose, readers, and context can help you decide which resources and search techniques to use.

How Can I Locate Sources Using Digital Resources?

Writers can turn to four general sets of digital resources to locate information about their subjects: library catalogs, databases, the Web, and media search sites. You can search these resources using basic and advanced searches.

Generate Search Terms and Strategies

Regardless of which digital resource you use, the results of your searches will be only as good as your search terms. Even the best search tools can produce poor results — and all too often that's exactly what happens. To increase your chances of obtaining good results, spend time identifying search terms related to your subject and learning about the types of searches you might conduct.

IDENTIFY KEYWORDS AND PHRASES

You can identify useful search terms by building on your research question (see p. 456) or thesis statement (see Chapter 16) or by using a range of idea-generating techniques, such as brainstorming, freewriting, looping, and clustering (see p. 41). Dwight Haynes, for example, used freewriting to generate ideas for his searches. Then he highlighted promising keywords and phrases.

> I'm most interested in finding sources that can help me understand why some approaches to reducing college drinking — and binge drinking in particular, although it's not the only problem (date rape, drunk driving, and falling out of windows or trees, for example, are related to too much drinking) — work better than others. What's been done by schools with successful programs? How much do those programs cost? And why haven't schools made more progress on this problem? Is it just something that college students have to go through? But if that's the case, why do so many students swear off drinking altogether — or maybe it's just a case of extremes all around, with some people drinking too much and some people swearing off it even though they wouldn't mind having a beer now and then?

You can also generate search terms by using your research question or thesis statement as a starting point. One student, for example, typed her research question in a word-processing program, formatted the most important words and phrases in color, and then brainstormed a list of related words and phrases.

What barriers **stand in the way of** widespread use **of** hydrogen fuel **in the** United States?

limits	adoption	"fuel cells"	U.S.
limitations	utilization	"clean energy"	America
obstacles	usage	"hydrogen power"	American
hurdles		"clean power"	
difficulties			
impediment			
expense			

PLAN BASIC SEARCHES

A basic search allows you to look for documents that contain a single word or phrase in the subject, title, or text or, in the case of databases, in other parts of a database record (see p. 481 for more information about databases). Basic searches can return large sets of results. To find results that will be relevant to your subject, consider using additional keywords, exact phrases, and wildcards.

Use additional keywords In most cases, using more than one keyword will limit the number of results returned by your search. This strategy is especially helpful when searching the Web, which tends to produce thousands (sometimes millions) of hits for individual words or phrases.

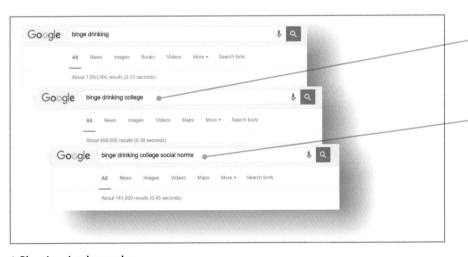

Adding *college* to a search for the keywords *binge* and *drinking* on Google reduces the number of results by roughly 25 percent.

Adding *students* reduces the number by an additional 80 percent.

To find out how a search tool treats multiple keywords, consult its help page, or conduct some test searches and review your results.

▲ **Planning simple searches**

Search for exact phrases Sometimes the best way to locate information is to search for an exact phrase. To further refine your search, you might use *binge drinking* and *college students* as phrases. This would eliminate sources in which the words *binge* and *drinking* appear but are separated by other words. The simple search format in many catalogs, databases, and Web search sites permits you to specify phrases using quotation marks.

In many catalogs, databases, and Web search sites, you can specify phrases using quotation marks.

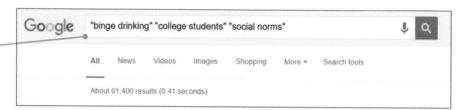

Google   "binge drinking" "college students" "social norms"

All   News   Videos   Images   Shopping   More ▾   Search tools

About 61,400 results (0.41 seconds)

▲ **A simple search with exact phrases**

Use wildcards Sometimes you might not be sure what form of a word is most likely to occur. Rather than conducting several searches for *drink*, *drinking*, *drinkers*, *drunk*, and *drunken*, for example, you can combine keywords into a single wildcard search. Wildcards are symbols that take the place of letters or strings of letters. By standing in for multiple letters, they allow you to expand the scope of your search.

The following are the most commonly used wildcard symbols:

* usually takes the place of one or more characters, such as *drink**

? usually takes the place of a single character, such as *dr?nk*

Other wildcard symbols include !, +, #, and $. To find out whether wildcard symbols are supported, consult the help section in a catalog or database or the advanced search page of a Web search engine.

🖅 TECH TIP: PLAN ADVANCED SEARCHES

You are probably fairly comfortable doing basic searches already, but they can take your research only so far. To make bigger strides on your research and find more targeted results, try out some advanced searches. Most library catalogs, databases, and Web search sites provide an advanced search page. These pages allow you to focus your searches in powerful ways using Boolean operators (which are used to search for all, some, or none of the words or phrases in a search box) and search limits (such as publication date and document characteristics).

Focus searches with Boolean operators Boolean operators let you narrow your search by specifying whether keywords or phrases can, must, or must not appear in the results. Some Boolean operators also allow you to search for keywords or phrases that appear next to, before or after, or within a certain distance from one another in a document. Here is a list of commonly used Boolean operators and their functions.

Boolean Operator	Function	Example
AND/+ (plus)	Finds sources that include both search terms (either keywords or phrases)	hydrogen AND economy
OR	Finds sources that include either search term	energy OR power
NOT/–	Finds sources that include one search term but not the other	gasoline NOT oil
ADJ (adjacent)	Finds sources in which the search terms appear next to each other	fuel ADJ cells
NEAR	Finds sources in which the search terms appear within a specified number of words from each other	alternative NEAR energy
BEFORE	Finds sources in which search terms appear in a particular order	clean BEFORE power
Parentheses ( )	Parentheses are used to group search terms and Boolean operators	hydrogen AND (fuel OR energy) AND (economy NOT economics)

Limit searches Search limits allow you to limit your searches to documents that have particular characteristics, such as publication date and document type. Common limits include publication date (or, in the case of Web pages, the date on which a page was last updated), type of document, and the availability of full text (for databases).

Search Library Catalogs

Online catalogs provide information about the author(s), title, publication date, subject heading, and call number for each source in the library's collection. Typically, they also indicate the location of the source in the library and whether the source is available for checkout.

AND requires *surveillance* to be present.

OR indicates that the keywords *government* or *federal* can be in the record.

NOT excludes records that include the keyword *Snowden*.

The "Limit your results" section provides numerous options for customizing a search.

Limit to documents available in full text.

Limit to scholarly journals.

Limit by document type.

Limit by publication date.

Limit by publication type.

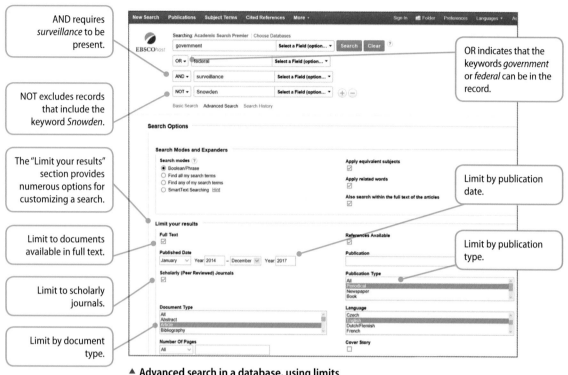

▲ Advanced search in a database, using limits

Equivalent to Boolean AND

Equivalent to Boolean NOT

Equivalent to Boolean OR

Limit to a particular language.

Limit to results from government websites.

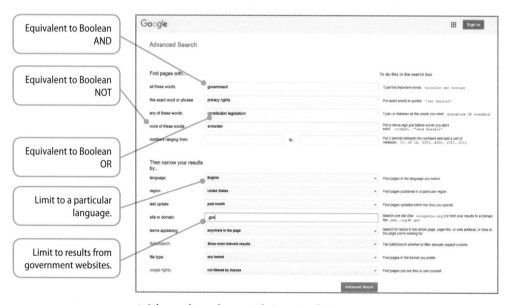

▲ Advanced search on a website, using limits

Library catalogs typically help you locate

- books
- journals owned by the library (although not individual articles)
- newspapers and magazines owned by the library (although not individual articles)
- documents stored on microfilm or microfiche
- videotapes, audiotapes, and other multimedia items owned by the library
- maps
- theses and dissertations completed by college or university graduate students

In addition to searching the library catalog at your college or university, you can also benefit from searching other catalogs available on the Web. The Library of Congress online catalog (catalog.loc.gov), for example, presents a comprehensive list of publications on a particular subject or by a particular author. Some sites, such as WorldCat (www.worldcat.org), allow you to locate or search multiple libraries. If you find a promising source that your library doesn't own, you can request it through interlibrary loan.

Most library catalogs allow you to search or browse for sources by keywords and phrases, author(s), title, subject, and call number. The following examples illustrate common types of searches.

Search by keyword You can search for a specific keyword or phrase.

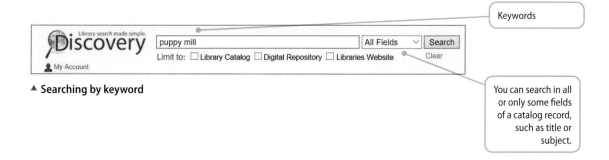

▲ **Searching by keyword**

Keywords

You can search in all or only some fields of a catalog record, such as title or subject.

Search by author If you search by author, you can find sources written by a particular person or organization.

Most library catalogs assume that you will enter the last name of the author first, followed by a first name or initial.

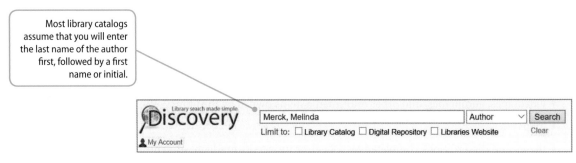

▲ **Searching by author**

Search by title If you know either the exact title of a source or some of the words in the title, you can search by title to find sources.

You can search for a complete or a partial title. Searching for partial titles produces a list of sources whose titles begin with the phrase or word you enter.

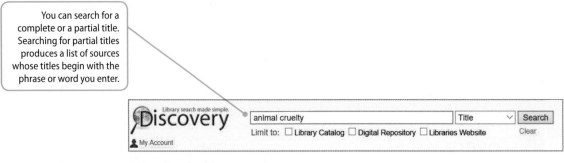

▲ **Searching by title**

Browse by call number or subject heading To locate sources related to a promising result, search by either call number or subject heading.

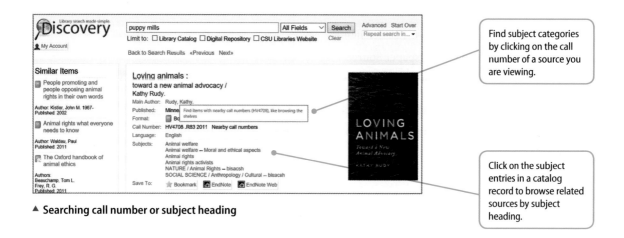

Find subject categories by clicking on the call number of a source you are viewing.

Click on the subject entries in a catalog record to browse related sources by subject heading.

▲ Searching call number or subject heading

Search Databases

Databases operate much like library catalogs, although they focus on a different collection of sources. While a library catalog allows you to search for publications owned by the library, a database allows you to search for sources that have been published on a particular topic or in a particular discipline regardless of whether the library owns the sources. Although some databases, such as ERIC, MedLine, and Science Direct, are available publicly via the Web (see p. 483), most are available only through library computers or a library website. Large research libraries often subscribe to hundreds of databases, while smaller libraries might subscribe to only a handful.

Databases supply publication information and brief descriptions of the information in a source; some — but not all — provide electronic copies of the source. Using the citation information provided by the database, you can check your library's catalog for the title of the publication in which the source appears. If your library does not own the publication, you can request it through interlibrary loan.

IDENTIFY RELEVANT DATABASES

Databases tend to specialize in particular subject areas and types of sources. To identify databases that might be relevant to your issue, review your library's list of databases or consult a reference librarian. Ask yourself the following questions.

Am I focusing on an issue that is likely to have been addressed in recent news coverage? If so, search *news and information databases* that focus on newspapers and weekly news magazines, such as

- Alternative Press Index
- LexisNexis Academic
- Newspaper Source
- ProQuest Newspapers

Am I focusing on a broad area of interest, such as business, education, or government? If so, search *subject databases* that focus on more general issues, such as

- Academic Search Premier
- Article First
- Catalog of U.S. Government Publications
- WorldCat

Am I focusing on an issue that is related to a particular profession or academic discipline? If so, consult *bibliographies* that focus on that area. Many library websites categorize databases by profession or discipline. For example, if you are interested in an issue related to sociology, you might consult the following databases:

- Family and Society Studies Worldwide
- Social Science Abstracts
- Sociological Abstracts

Have I already identified sources about my issue? If you have already located promising sources, search *citation indexes* to identify sources that refer to your sources. Depending on your area, you might search the following databases:

- Arts & Humanities Citation Index
- Science Citation Index
- Social Sciences Citation Index

Is the full text of the source available? *Full-text databases* offer the complete source for viewing or download. These databases cut out the middle step of locating the specific periodical that published the article. Databases that offer some of or all their sources in full text include

- Academic Search Premier
- ERIC
- IEEE Xplore
- LexisNexis Academic
- ScienceDirect

Am I searching for images, video, or audio? If you are seeking nontextual sources, turn to *media databases* such as the following:

- AccessScience
- ARTstor
- Mountain West Digital Library

SEARCH WITHIN DATABASE FIELDS

To search for sources using a database, type keywords and phrases in the database's search fields. If you are conducting a basic search, the process will be similar to a search on a Web search site (see p. 475). The following illustrations show an advanced search that featured writer Dwight Haynes conducted in ProQuest and the results that were returned.

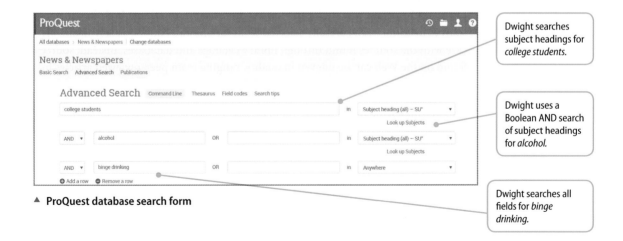

▲ **ProQuest database search form**

Dwight searches subject headings for *college students.*

Dwight uses a Boolean AND search of subject headings for *alcohol.*

Dwight searches all fields for *binge drinking.*

The search terms are displayed in Boolean form (see p. 476).

Search results can be sent via e-mail, printed, or saved.

Results are displayed in a list.

The search can be limited in a variety of ways.

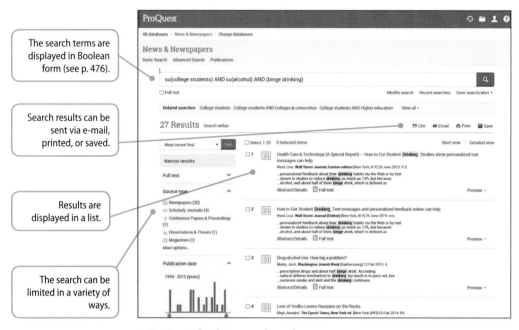

▲ **ProQuest database search results**

Search the Web

Web search sites can help you sift through the vast amount of information available on the Web, including Web pages, blogs, social-networking sites, magazine and journal articles, books, music, photos, and video. While Web search is among the easiest and quickest ways to locate information, keep in mind that Web-based sources have not been carefully selected by librarians and editors, as is typically the case with the sources found through library catalogs and databases. Instead, sources found on the Web can be uneven in quality, ranging from peer-reviewed articles in scholarly journals to blogs created by eighth graders.

To determine which search sites might be best suited to your writing situation, consider their areas of emphasis, which range from general to such focused areas as blogs or social-networking sites, and the tools they offer to support searching and working with results.

USE WEB SEARCH ENGINES

Web search engines keep track of Web pages and other forms of information on the Internet — including PDF files, PowerPoint files, Word files, blogs (see p. 487),

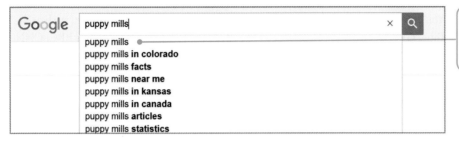

Google offers search suggestions as you type in the search box.

▲ **Google search**

and newsgroup posts — by locating documents on websites and entering them in a searchable database.

Leading Web search engines include

- Ask: ask.com
- Bing: bing.com
- Duck Duck Go: duckduckgo.com
- Excite: excite.com
- Google: google.com
- Yahoo!: search.yahoo.com

Keep two cautions in mind as you use Web search engines. First, because most search engines index only a portion of the Web — sometimes as much as 50 percent and sometimes as little as 5 percent — you should use more than one search engine. If you don't find what you're looking for in your first choice, you might find it in another. Second, Web pages can be moved, deleted, or revised. This means that a search engine's results can be inaccurate.

USE META SEARCH SITES

On a meta search site, you can conduct a search on several Web search engines or Web directories at the same time. These sites typically search the major search engines and directories and then present a limited number of results on a single page. Leading meta search sites include:

- Dogpile: dogpile.com
- Ixquick: ixquick.com
- Webcrawler: webcrawler.com

USE NEWS SEARCH SITES

You can search for news on most major Web search sites and directories, such as Bing, Google, and Yahoo!, as well as the sites for news providers such as BBC, CNN, and Reuters. In addition, specialized news search sites allow you to conduct focused searches for current and archived news reports, while social news sites such as Digg and StumbleUpon allow you to view news stories and videos that have been recommended by other readers. Leading news search sites include

- Bing News: bing.com/news
- Digg: digg.com
- Google News: news.google.com
- StumbleUpon: stumbleupon.com
- World News: wn.com
- Yahoo! News: news.yahoo.com

USE REFERENCE SITES

A reference site allows you to search for information that has been collected in encyclopedias, almanacs, atlases, dictionaries, and other reference resources. Some reference sites, such as Encyclopaedia Britannica Online, offer limited access to information from their encyclopedias at no charge and complete access for a fee. Other sites, such as Information Please and Bartleby.com, allow unrestricted access to recently published reference works, including the *Columbia Encyclopedia, The Encyclopedia of World History,* and *The World Factbook.*

One widely used reference site is Wikipedia, whose articles are collaboratively written by its readers. Because of its comprehensiveness, Wikipedia can serve as a useful starting point for research on a topic. However, because any reader can make changes to most of the pages on the site, it's best to double-check any information you find there.

Leading reference search sites include the following:

- Bartleby.com Reference: bartleby.com/reference
- Encyclopaedia Britannica Online: britannica.com
- Encyclopedia.com: encyclopedia.com
- Information Please: infoplease.com
- Wikipedia: en.wikipedia.org

USE GOVERNMENT SEARCH SITES AND DIRECTORIES

Most government agencies and institutions use the Web as the primary means of distributing their publications. USA.gov, for example, allows you to search the federal government's network of online resources, while the State and Local Government Directory provides access to a wide range of materials related to state and local government.

Leading government document sites include the following:

- Canadian Government Search Engines: recherche-search.gc.ca
- Government Printing Office: govinfo.gov
- GovSpot.com: govspot.com
- State and Local Government Directory: statelocalgov.net
- USA.gov: usa.gov

✈ TECH TIP: USE E-BOOK SITES

E-Books are available through a wide variety of sources, including Amazon, Apple, Barnes & Noble, and Google, as well as several open-access publishers, such as Project Gutenberg. You can locate (and often preview) e-Books by visiting sites such as Amazon (amazon.com), Barnes and Noble (bn.com), Google Books (books .google.com), and Project Gutenberg (gutenberg.org). You can also locate e-Books through the Apple iTunes and Google Play online stores.

E-Book sites include

- Amazon: amazon.com
- Barnes & Noble: barnesandnoble.com
- Google Books: books.google.com
- Internet Archive Community Books: archive.org/details/texts
- Kobo: store.kobobooks.com
- Online Books Page: onlinebooks.library.upenn.edu
- Project Gutenberg: gutenberg.org
- Wikibooks: wikibooks.org

SEARCH BLOGS

Blogs — short for Weblogs — consist of chronologically ordered entries on a website and most closely resemble entries in a diary or journal. Blog entries usually include a title and post and can also incorporate images, audio, video, and other types of media. Many entries provide links to other pages on the Web. Blogs have a number of purposes:

- Some blogs report on events and issues. The bloggers who provided daily — sometimes hourly — reports on the 2016 political conventions offered valuable, firsthand insights into aspects of the conventions that were not addressed through the mainstream media. Similarly, the bloggers who reported on the Syrian refugee crisis offered a perspective on events that would not have been available otherwise.

- Some blogs alert readers to information elsewhere on the Web. These blogs cite recently published news reports and articles, the latest developments in a particular discipline, and new contributions to an ongoing debate — and provide commentary on that information.

- Some blogs serve as public relations spaces for institutions and organizations, such as corporations, government agencies, and colleges. These blogs typically focus on services or activities associated with the institution or organization.

- Some blogs serve largely as a space for personal reflection and expression. A blogger might share his or her thoughts about daily life, current events, or other issues with friends and family.

Writers can use blogs as sources of information and commentary on an issue and as sources of firsthand accounts by people affected by an issue. If you find blogs by experts in the field, you can begin a discussion with people involved in or knowledgeable about your topic. To locate blogs that are relevant to your research question, use the following sites:

- Alltop: alltop.com

- BlogCatalog: blogcatalog.com

- IceRocket: icerocket.com

SEARCH SOCIAL MEDIA SITES

Sites such as Facebook, Google+, Reddit, LinkedIn, Tumblr, and Twitter provide opportunities to identify people who share your interest in an issue. By searching these sites, you can identify individuals who might be knowledgeable about an issue or have been affected by it. You can search social networks using the following sites:

- Facebook Search: search.fb.com

- Google+ Search: plus.google.com

- LinkedIn Search: linkedin.com

- Reddit Search: reddit.com/search

- Social Mention: socialmention.com

- Twitter Search: twitter.com/search-home

- Tumblr Search: tumblr.com/tagged/tumblr-search

Search Media Sites

The Web is home not only to textual information, such as articles and books, but also to a growing collection of other types of media, such as photographs, podcasts, and streaming videos. You can search for media using established search sites, such as Ask, Google, and Yahoo!, as well as newer search sites that focus on specific media.

USE IMAGE SEARCH SITES AND DIRECTORIES

Image searches have long been among the search tools available to writers. Using Google's image search, for example, you can search for images using keywords and phrases, and you can conduct advanced searches by specifying the size and kind of image you desire. The following search sites and directories allow you to locate images:

- Bing Image Search: bing.com/images

- Google Image Search: images.google.com

- PicFindr: picfindr.com

- Picsearch: picsearch.com

- Yahoo! Image Search: images.search.yahoo.com

USE AUDIO SEARCH SITES

Thinking of the Web as the first place to visit for new music has become second nature for many of us. But the audio content available through the Web includes more than just music. You can also find radio broadcasts, recordings of speeches, recordings of natural phenomena, and other forms of sound. Sites such as FindSounds allow you to search for sounds and listen to them before downloading. Leading audio search sites include the following:

- Audio Archive: archive.org/details/audio

- FindSounds: findsounds.com

- Freesound: freesound.org

- Library of Congress American Memory: memory.loc.gov/ammem

- Wav Central: wavcentral.com

USE VIDEO SEARCH SITES

Through sites such as YouTube and Yahoo! Video, Web-based video has become one of the fastest-growing parts of the Web. You can view everything from news reports on CNN.com, to a video about the effects of a recent earthquake, to documentaries about the Iraq War. Of course, much of the material will be of little use in a writing project. With careful selection and evaluation, however, you might find video that will help you better understand and contribute to the discussion of your subject. The following are some leading video search sites:

- Bing Video Search: bing.com/videos/browse
- Blinkx: blinkx.com
- Google Video: google.com/videohp
- Yahoo! Video Search: video.search.yahoo.com
- YouTube: youtube.com

Keep Track of Your Searches

One of the most important strategies you can use as you collect information is keeping track of your searches. Note the keywords or phrases and the search strategies you used with them (wildcards, Boolean search, author search, and so on), as well as how many sources the search turned up and whether those sources were relevant to your writing project. Keeping track of your searches will help you identify promising approaches; it will also ensure that you don't repeat your efforts.

In your writer's notebook, record the following information for each source you search:

Checklist for Recording Search Terms

✔ Resource that was searched

✔ Search terms used (keywords, phrases, names)

✔ Search strategies used (basic search, exact-phrase search, wildcard search, Boolean search)

✔ Date the search was conducted

✔ Number of results produced by the search

✔ Relevance of the results

How Can I Locate Sources Using Print Resources?

Contrary to recent claims, there is life (and information) beyond the World Wide Web. The print resources available in a library can help you locate a wealth of relevant material that you won't find online. If your writing project has a historical component, for example, bibliographies and indexes can point you toward sources that cannot be located using a database or a Web search site. By relying on the careful selections librarians make when adding to a collection, you will be able to find useful, credible sources that reflect your purpose and address your subject.

To locate information using print resources, discuss your search plan with a librarian, visit the library stacks, browse periodicals, and check reference works.

Discuss Your Search Plan with a Librarian

As you begin collecting information about your subject, use your search plan to capitalize on your library's print resources — and its librarians. Given the wide range of specialized print resources that are available, a few minutes of discussion with a knowledgeable librarian could save you a great deal of time or point you to key resources you might have overlooked.

Visit the Library Stacks

The library stacks — or shelves — house the library's collection of bound publications. By browsing the stacks and checking publications' works cited pages, you can locate related sources. Once you've decided that a source is relevant to your project, you can check it out or request it through interlibrary loan.

One of the advantages of the classification systems used by most libraries — typically the Library of Congress or Dewey decimal classification system — is that they are subject based. Because books on similar subjects are shelved together, you can browse the stacks to look for sources on a topic. For example, if your research takes you to the stacks for books about alcohol abuse, you're likely to find books about drug abuse, treatment programs, and codependency nearby. When you find a publication that seems useful, check the works cited list for related works. The combination of browsing the stacks for sources and checking those sources' works cited lists can lead you to publications relevant to your subject.

You can usually take library books — and some periodicals and media items — home with you to read or view at your own pace. In some cases, a publication you want might not be available because it has been checked out, reserved for a course, or placed in off-site storage. If a publication has been checked out, you might be able to recall it — that is, ask that it be returned to the library and held for you. If it has been placed on reserve, ask whether you can photocopy or take notes on it. If it has been placed in off-site storage, you can usually request it at the circulation desk.

✈ TECH TIP: USE INTERLIBRARY LOAN

If you can't obtain a particular book, periodical, or media item from your library, use interlibrary loan to borrow it from another library. Most libraries allow you to request materials through the library catalog. And you might be able to check the status of your request or renew interlibrary loan materials through the catalog as well. To learn how to use interlibrary loan, consult your library's website or ask a librarian.

Browse Periodicals

Periodicals include newspapers, magazines, and academic and professional journals. A periodicals room — or journals room — contains recent issues that library visitors may browse. Many libraries also have a separate room for newspapers published in the last few weeks or months. To ensure everyone's access to recently published issues, most libraries don't allow you to check out periodicals published within the last year, and they usually don't allow newspapers to be checked out at all.

Older periodicals are sometimes placed in bound volumes in the stacks. Few libraries, however, keep back issues of newspapers in paper form. Instead, you can often find back issues of leading newspapers in full-text databases or in microform. *Microform* is a generic name for both microfilm, a strip of film containing greatly reduced images of printed pages, and microfiche, film roughly the size of an index card containing the same kinds of miniaturized images. You view these images using a microform reader, a projection unit that looks something like a large computer monitor. Many microform readers allow you to print copies of the pages.

In addition to browsing periodicals, use databases to locate specific articles on your subject. They are more likely than print indexes and bibliographies to contain listings of recent publications. Once you've identified an article you want to review, you'll need to find the periodical in which it appears. Conduct a title search for the periodical in the same way you conduct a title search for a book. The library catalog will tell you the call number of the periodical and usually will give information about its location in the library. In addition, some libraries provide a printed list that identifies where periodicals are located. If you have difficulty finding a periodical or judging which publications are likely to be useful for your writing project, ask a librarian for assistance.

Check Reference Works

Reference rooms contain reliable print resources on a range of topics, from government to finance to philosophy to science. Although many of these reference books serve the same purposes as databases, others offer information not available in databases. Using reference books to locate print resources has several advantages over using databases.

- **Most databases have short memories.** Databases typically index sources only as far back as the mid-1980s and seldom index anything published before 1970. Depending on your subject, a database might not include some important sources. If you use a reference book, however, you might be able to locate print resources dating back a century or more.

- **Most databases focus on short works.** In contrast, many of the print resources in library reference rooms will refer you to books and longer publications as well as to articles in periodicals.

- **Many library reference resources are unavailable in digital form.** While a growing number of print reference books have become available in digital formats, a large number are accessible only in print form.

- **Entries in print indexes are easier to browse.** Despite efforts to aid browsing, databases support searching far better than they do browsing.

Some of the most important print resources you can consult in a reference room include bibliographies, indexes, biographies, specialized encyclopedias, handbooks, almanacs, and atlases.

CONSULT BIBLIOGRAPHIES

Bibliographies list books, articles, and other publications that have been judged relevant to a topic. Some bibliographies provide only citations, while others include abstracts — brief descriptions — of listed sources. Complete bibliographies attempt to list all the sources published about a topic, while selective bibliographies attempt to list only the best sources on a topic. Some bibliographies limit their inclusion of sources by time period, often focusing on sources published during a given year.

You're likely to find several types of bibliographies in your library's reference room or stacks.

- **Trade bibliographies** allow you to locate books published about a particular topic. Leading trade bibliographies include *The Subject Guide to Books in Print*, *Books in Print*, and *Cumulative Book Index*.

- **General bibliographies** cover a wide range of topics, usually in selective lists. For sources on humanities topics, consult *The Humanities: A Selective Guide* *to Information Sources.* For sources on social science topics, see *Social Science Reference Sources: A Practical Guide.* For sources on science topics, go to bibliographies such as *Information Sources in Science and Technology, Guide to Information Sources in the Botanical Sciences,* and *Guide to Information Sources in the Physical Sciences.*

- **Specialized bibliographies** typically provide lists of sources — often annotated — about a specific topic. For example, *A Research Guide to the Ancient World: Print and Electronic Sources* focuses on sources about ancient Egypt, southwestern Asia, and the Mediterranean.

Although most general and trade bibliographies can be found in the library reference room, specialized bibliographies are usually shelved in the library's stacks. To locate them, start by consulting a cumulative bibliography, such as *The Bibliographic Index: A Cumulative Bibliography of Bibliographies,* which identifies bibliographies on a wide range of topics and is updated annually. You might also search your library's catalog using keywords related to your subject plus the keyword *bibliography.* If you need help finding bibliographies that are relevant to your subject, ask a reference librarian.

REVIEW INDEXES

Indexes provide citation information for sources found in a particular set of publications. Many indexes also include abstracts — brief descriptions — that can help you determine whether a source is worth locating and reviewing. The following types of indexes can be found in libraries:

- **Periodical indexes** list sources published in magazines, trade journals, scholarly journals, and newspapers. Some periodical indexes, such as *The Reader's Guide to Periodical Literature,* cover a wide range of general-interest publications. Others, such as *Art Index,* focus on periodicals that address a single subject. Still others focus on a small set or even an individual periodical; *The New York Times Index,* for example, lists articles published only in that newspaper and organizes entries by subject, geography, organization, and references to individuals.

- **Indexes of materials in books** can help you locate articles in edited books. Turn to resources such as the *Essay and General Literature Index,* which indexes nearly five thousand book-length collections of articles and essays in the arts, humanities, and social sciences. You might also find subject-specific indexes. *The Cumulative Bibliography of Asian Studies,* for example, covers articles in edited books.

- **Pamphlet indexes** list the pamphlets that libraries frequently collect. If your subject is likely to be addressed in pamphlets, ask a reference librarian whether your library has a pamphlet index. You can also consult the *Vertical File Index*, which lists roughly three thousand brief sources on ten to fifteen newsworthy topics each month.

- **Government documents indexes** list publications from federal, state, and local governments. The most useful indexes include *Monthly Catalog of United States Government Publications*, *CIS Index to Publications of the United States Congress*, *Congressional Record* (for daily proceedings of the House of Representatives and the Senate), and *United States Reports* (for Supreme Court documents). These types of indexes might be found in either the reference room or a separate government documents collection in your library. Ask a reference librarian for help.

CHECK BIOGRAPHIES

Biographies cover key figures in a field, time period, or geographic region. *Who's Who in America*, for instance, provides brief biographies of important figures in the United States during a given year, while *Great Lives from History* takes a broader view, offering biographies of key figures in world history.

BROWSE SPECIALIZED ENCYCLOPEDIAS

While general encyclopedias, such as the *New Encyclopaedia Britannica*, have moved online and are generally no longer available in print, you can find a great deal of useful information in specialized encyclopedias. General encyclopedias present enough information about a subject to get you started on a more detailed search. Specialized encyclopedias, such as *Encyclopedia of Health Communication*, take a narrower focus, usually covering a field of study or a historical period. Articles in specialized encyclopedias are typically longer than articles in general encyclopedias and offer more detailed coverage of subjects.

CONSULT HANDBOOKS

Like encyclopedias, handbooks provide useful background information about a subject in a compact form. Unlike specialized encyclopedias, most handbooks, such as *The Engineering Handbook* and the *International Handbook of Psychology*, cover a specific topic area. The entries in handbooks are also much shorter than the articles found in specialized encyclopedias.

REVIEW ALMANACS

Almanacs contain lists, charts, and tables of information of various types. You might be familiar with *The Old Farmer's Almanac*, which is known for its accuracy in predicting weather over the course of a year. Information in almanacs can range from the average rainfall in Australia to the batting averages of the 1927 Yankees to the average income of Germans and Poles before World War II.

SCAN ATLASES

Atlases provide maps and related information about a region or country. Some atlases take a historical perspective, while others take a topical perspective.

In Summary: Locating Sources

* Generate search terms and choose search strategies (p. 474).

* Search your library's catalog (p. 477).

* Search relevant databases (p. 481).

* Use appropriate Web search sites (p. 484) and social media search sites (p. 488).

* Browse the library stacks (p. 491).

* Examine periodicals (p. 492).

* Check reference works (p. 493).

 # Conducting Field Research

When Should I Use Field Research Methods?

Some research writers think of field research as the next-best thing to learning about an issue through a published source. If they can't find anything relevant in books, articles, newspapers, blogs, Twitter, or the broadcast media, then perhaps field research might be worth considering.

These writers misunderstand the value and power of field research. Far from being a good fallback position, field research is sometimes the best way to learn about an issue or collect information to support a position.

Consider using field research methods if you find yourself in one of the following situations.

- If published sources address your issue from a perspective that you don't find useful, field research can provide another way of approaching the issue. For example, most discussions of gun rights and gun control focus on constitutional arguments. If you want to consider the issue from another perspective, such as differences in how people from rural areas and urban or suburban areas understand the issue, you might find it useful to collect information through interviews, surveys, or correspondence.

- If you are interested in an issue that most people think of as settled, published sources may not include information, ideas, and arguments to help you challenge the conventional wisdom about the issue. Field research, in contrast, can bring new voices into the conversation.

- If the issue you are addressing is so current that little authoritative information is available, field research can provide needed information about it.

- If you come up with a new idea or argument that seems reasonable and obvious but has not yet been addressed by your sources, field research can provide a useful reality check, allowing you to explore your idea or argument through interviews, observation, surveys, or correspondence.

- If your argument can be strengthened by including evidence from primary sources, turn to field research. Information from interviews, correspondence, or observation notes can bring a document to life, providing your readers with firsthand reports from people who know about or have been affected by an issue. Similarly, information from a survey can allow your readers to see trends and differences among groups that might not otherwise be clear.

Sometimes the decision to use a particular field research method is a natural extension of the kind of work you're doing. For example, a writer exploring the pressures that lead athletes to use performance-enhancing drugs might not only consult published sources but also interview friends and family members who played competitive sports. At other times, writers might use evidence collected firsthand to lend a sense of immediacy to their arguments.

Whether you rely primarily on field research or use it in combination with information from published sources, field research methods can be powerful tools for exploring your issue and developing your position. The strategies discussed in Chapter 12 for managing print and digital information will help you save and organize the information you collect so that you can locate it quickly and easily.

How Can I Conduct an Interview?

Interviews — in which one person seeks information from another — can provide firsthand accounts of an event, authoritative interpretations of events and issues, and reactions to an event or issue from the people who have been affected by it. Most interviews follow a question-and-answer format, but some more closely resemble a free-flowing discussion. You can conduct interviews face-to-face, over the telephone, via e-mail, and even through an instant-messaging program.

Plan Your Interview

The most important things to consider as you plan your interview are whom to interview, what to ask, and how to conduct your interview.

DECIDE WHOM TO INTERVIEW

Base your decisions on the kind of information you want for your research project.

- If you're trying to better understand a specific aspect of a conversation, interview an expert in the field such as a professor, government official, or member of the business community.

- If you want to learn what people in general think about an issue, interview a number of people who are affected by the issue in different ways.

- If you're hoping to collect quotations from people who are authorities on a subject, interview someone who will be recognized as knowledgeable by your readers.

Once you've decided what sorts of people you want to interview, you'll need to identify and contact interview candidates. Ask your instructor and classmates for suggestions. Then ask whether they can introduce you to the people they suggest. Before you call to set up an interview, make some preparations.

- Write a script to help you remember what to say.
- Prepare a list of dates and times that work for you.
- Estimate how much time you'll need to complete the interview.
- Be ready to suggest a location for the interview.
- Leave your phone number or e-mail address so that your interview candidate can get in touch with you if a conflict arises.

DECIDE WHAT YOU SHOULD ASK

Your interview questions should focus on the issue you want to address in your project. As you prepare your questions, keep the following principles in mind.

- *Consider your research question, the role you are adopting, and the kind of information you want to collect.* Are you seeking background information, or do you want someone's opinion? An answer to the question, "How did this situation come about?" will be quite different from an answer to the question, "What do you think about this situation?"
- *Ask questions that require more than a yes or no answer.* You'll learn much more from an answer to a question such as "What factors will affect your vote on referendum X?" than from an answer to "Will you vote for referendum X?"
- *Prepare a limited number of main questions and many follow-up questions.* Experienced interviewers know that each question can lead to several follow-up questions, such as "Why do you think this has happened?" or "How did your coworkers react to the new policy?"
- *Be flexible.* Be prepared to tailor your follow-up questions to the interviewee's responses.

DECIDE HOW TO CONDUCT YOUR INTERVIEW

You can conduct interviews face-to-face, over the telephone, and through e-mail, chat, and video communication programs.

- **Face-to-face interviews** conducted in person or through a computer-based video tool such as Skype, Google Hangouts, or FaceTime allow you to carry out a nearly normal conversation with the person you are interviewing.

As in regular conversations, pay close attention to nonverbal cues, such as facial expressions, body positions, and eye contact. These cues can help you understand whether your questions are clear, welcome, or surprising and can alert you to opportunities to ask useful follow-up questions.

- **Telephone interviews** also let you hold a fairly normal conversation, but they require a setting with relative peace and without distractions. You won't have visual cues to help you connect with the person you are interviewing, so be sure to listen for pauses, tone of voice, and changes in speaking volume that might indicate surprise, discomfort, or confusion. As in face-to-face interviews, you'll receive fairly direct answers and elaborations in response to questions.

- **Written interviews** conducted by e-mail, chat, text-messaging, or letter can be a good option if your subject is difficult to reach because of distance or a busy schedule. Written responses to interview questions are generally more precise than spoken responses. Written responses can be reviewed and revised by the person being interviewed to ensure that statements are clear and accurate, while spoken responses are usually more spontaneous.

DECIDE HOW TO RECORD AND TAKE NOTES ON YOUR INTERVIEW

Recording or saving a transcript of an interview, along with taking notes, provides you with a complete record of what was said, which helps you ensure the accuracy of quotations, paraphrases, and summaries.

- **Recordings.** If you plan to record the interview, seek permission in advance or at the start of the interview. Some people might be nervous about being recorded, so be prepared to explain how you'll use a recording. Choose initial questions that put them at ease and make them comfortable about the interview process.

- **Transcripts.** If you are conducting an interview via e-mail (or even via a series of text messages), you'll have a written record of all the responses to your questions. Similarly, you can save a transcript from most chat sessions and even Google Voice conversations, either by saving a file from the chat program or copying and pasting the transcript into a word-processing file. Transcripts can be used to create accurate quotations, and they make it relatively easy to review responses to your questions.

- **Taking Notes.** You should always take notes during an interview. Recordings and transcripts can be lost through technological glitches. More important, taking notes allows you to respond to new information and ideas, to consider how you might use the interview in your document, and to identify important parts for later review.

Conduct Your Interview

Consult the following checklist before you conduct your interview.

Checklist
for
Conducting
Interviews

✔ **Arrive early and review your questions.** If you are conducting your interview over the phone or with a computer, review your questions and then contact the person you are interviewing at the agreed-upon time.

✔ **Introduce yourself and ask for permission to record the interview.** Explain why you are conducting the interview. Ask for permission to record or generate a transcript and ensure that you will be allowed to use quotes from the interview.

✔ **Set up and test your recording equipment or computer.** Ideally, use an audio or video recorder to make a complete record of face-to-face or phone interviews and use the built-in recording or transcript-generating features in online communication tools. At a later time, you can review what was said and create exact quotations from the recording or transcript.

✔ **Ask your questions clearly and be ready to respond with follow-up questions.** Allow the person you are interviewing to answer your questions fully and without interruption. Don't insist on strictly following your list of interview questions; if discussion naturally flows in another useful direction, be prepared to shift your line of questioning.

✔ **Take notes, even if you are creating a recording or transcript.** Write down key points made during the interview as well as any important ideas that come to mind.

✔ **Be alert for related sources mentioned in the interview.** If specific sources that might be relevant to your writing project are mentioned during the interview, ask for copies of those sources or for the exact titles and where you might find them.

✔ **Leave your contact information when the interview is over.** Provide a way for the person you interviewed to reach you to change or add anything to his or her comments.

✔ **Send a thank-you note or e-mail message.** Let the person you interviewed know how much you appreciated the opportunity to learn from him or her.

Analyze Your Results

Treat your interview recording or transcript as you would any other source. Read it, listen to it, or view it critically.

- Look for new information, ideas, and arguments.
- Look for statements that confirm or contradict information from your other sources.
- Look for inconsistencies and contradictions within the interview as a whole.
- Ask whether the information, ideas, and arguments are relevant and credible.
- Determine whether the person you interviewed is as qualified as you'd expected when you planned the interview.
- Look for statements that provide context about the issue.
- Look for statements that might help your readers better understand the issue or view the issue in a particular way.

Then ask whether you can use the information, ideas, and arguments from the interview in your project document. If not, it may help you understand the issue more fully or raise questions that you could investigate in other ways.

How Can I Conduct an Observation?

Like interviewing, observing a setting can provide you with valuable insights you would not be able to find in other sources. Although some observations can involve a significant amount of time and effort, an observation need not be complicated to be useful.

Plan Your Observation

As you plan your observation, determine the following.

WHAT YOU SHOULD OBSERVE AND HOW OFTEN YOU SHOULD OBSERVE IT

If, for example, you've decided to observe children in a day-care center, you'll quickly learn that there are not only many day-care providers in your community but also several different kinds of providers. Observing a large day-care center won't tell you much about what happens in a small center operated out of a home. And there's no guarantee that what you'll see in one day-care center on any given day will be typical. Should you conduct multiple observations? Should you observe multiple types of day-care providers?

The answers to these questions will depend largely on how you will use the information you collect during your observations. If you want to learn more about the topic but don't need to collect a great deal of information, then you might want to conduct a fairly limited observation. If you decide to use evidence from your observations throughout your project, then you will need to conduct multiple observations, possibly in more than one setting. In this case, as you prepare for each observation, review your notes from previous sessions so that you can focus on the most important aspects of what you've observed so far.

WHETHER YOU NEED PERMISSION TO OBSERVE

Seeking permission to observe someone can be complicated. People have expectations about privacy, and they can (and often do) change their behavior when they know they are being observed. As you consider whether to ask for permission, imagine yourself in the position of someone who is being observed. If you are still uncertain, ask your instructor for advice.

Current School / Program Information

Name _____

Address _____

City _____   State _____

Phone _____

E-mail _____

I, the undersigned, hereby authorize [*observer name*] to observe [*the setting*] for the purposes of completing work on [*name of writing project*]. I understand that I may revoke this authorization, in writing, at any time.

Signature: _____

Date: _____

▲ **Sample permission form for observation sessions**

If you decide to seek permission by letter or e-mail, be sure to include a clear description of your writing project and explanations of why you believe observation will enhance the project, how you'll use the observations, and how you will ensure the privacy of the individuals, groups, or organization you observe. If you decide to contact the person by telephone, jot down some notes before you call.

In some cases, you might find it useful to use a permission form, such as the one shown on the previous page.

Conduct Your Observation

You'll find a number of similarities between collecting information in an interview and collecting information during an observation. The checklist that follows will help you conduct your observation.

Checklist for Conducting Observations

✔ **Arrive early.** Give yourself time to get prepared.

✔ **Review your planning notes.** Remind yourself what you're looking for and how you will record your observations.

✔ **Introduce yourself.** If you have asked for permission to observe a setting (such as a class or a day-care center), introduce yourself before you begin your observation. Use your introduction as an opportunity to obtain signatures or consent forms if you need them.

✔ **Set up your recording equipment.** You'll certainly want to make sure you've got a notepad and pens or pencils. You might also have an audio or a video recorder, a laptop computer, or a smartphone or tablet. Test whatever you've brought with you to make sure it's working properly.

✔ **Take notes.** As with interviews, take notes during your observation even if you're using an audio or a video recorder. Noting your impressions and ideas while conducting an observation can help you keep track of critical events. If you find yourself in a situation where you can't take notes — such as at a swimming lesson, when you're taking part in the lesson — try to write down your thoughts about what you've observed immediately after the session.

✔ **Leave contact information and send thank-you notes.** If you have asked someone for permission to observe the setting, give the person a way to contact you, and send a thank-you note after you have completed the observation.

Analyze Your Results

Treat your observation notes or recording as you would any other source. Ask whether you observed the setting thoroughly enough to feel confident about moving forward with an analysis. If so, do the following.

- Identify key features and patterns of behavior.

- Identify key individuals and describe their actions.

- Look for unusual and surprising patterns and actions.

- Ask what you've learned about the issue through observation.

- Look for patterns and actions that provide context about the issue.

- Look for patterns and actions that might help your readers better understand the issue or lead them to view the issue in a particular way.

Then ask whether you can use what you've learned in your project document. If you're unsure, consider whether your analysis can help you generate new questions and whether you should pursue another form of field research.

How Can I Conduct a Survey?

Surveys allow you to collect information about beliefs, attitudes, and behaviors from a group of people. Typically, surveys help you answer *what* or *who* questions — such as "Who will you vote for in the next election?" Surveys are less useful in obtaining the answers to *why* questions. In an interview, for instance, you can ask, "Why did you vote the way you did in the last election?" and get a reasonably well-thought-out answer. In a survey, you're unlikely to collect lengthy, carefully written responses. The strength of surveys lies in sheer numbers. A well-designed survey administered to a sizable group of people can provide insights into an issue that often can't be obtained easily using other methods.

Plan Your Survey

As you plan your survey, determine the following.

DECIDE WHOM TO SURVEY

Consider whom and how many people to survey. For instance, if you're interested in what students in a specific class think about an issue, survey all of them. Even if the class is fairly large (say, one hundred students), you can easily tabulate the results of a brief survey. However, most surveys aren't given to everyone in a group. National polls, for instance, seldom survey more than one thousand people, yet they are used to assess the opinions of everyone in the country. So how will you select your representative sample? One way is to choose people from the group at random. You could open your school's directory and then pick, say, every twentieth name. Another option is to stratify your sample. For example, you could randomly select a specific number of first-year, second-year, third-year, and fourth-year students — and you could make sure that the number of men and women in each group is proportional to their enrollment at the school.

DECIDE WHAT TO ASK AND HOW TO ASK IT WITH INTEGRITY

Designing effective surveys can be challenging. Start by considering the strengths and weaknesses of the different kinds of questions typically found on surveys:

- Yes/no items divide respondents into two groups.
- Multiple-choice items indicate whether a respondent knows something or engages in specific behaviors. Because they seldom include every possible answer, be careful when including them.
- True/false items more often deal with attitudes or beliefs than with behaviors or events.
- Likert scales measure respondents' level of agreement with a statement, their assessment of something's importance, or how frequently they engage in a behavior.
- Ranking forces respondents to place items along a continuum.
- Short-answer items allow greater freedom of response but can be difficult to tabulate.

Developing a good survey question is similar to writing an essay. The first drafts of survey questions serve to express your thoughts. Subsequent revisions help clarify questions for survey respondents. Keep your purpose in mind to be sure your question will elicit the information you need.

Consider how a writer created and refined a question about how students view heavy metal music.

1. Write a first draft of the question:

   • Do you listen to heavy metal music and why or why not?

> The question is too analytical. It will take a lot of time to answer and results will be hard to tally.

2. Simplify the question:

   • Why do you listen — or not listen — to heavy metal music?

> Combines both parts of the previous question ("do you" and "why"), but is still too analytical.

3. Consider alternative ways of asking a question — including whether it should be a question:

   • When you hear heavy metal bands like Slayer and Pantera, what do you think?

> The question focuses on respondents' reactions to the music, rather than on their reasons for listening.

4. Identify and then clarify key words and phrases:

   List five words to describe music by heavy metal bands like Pallbearer and Tool.

> The question is easy for respondents to answer and provides information that can be tallied.

As you create questions, keep in mind the importance of asking questions that do not cue the respondents to answer in a particular way. Ask yourself how you might respond to the following questions:

- Do you support increasing income tax rates to reduce the federal debt?
- Do you support increasing income tax rates to ensure that future generations are not crushed under the burden of a spiraling federal debt?
- Do you support increasing income tax rates to enable the federal government to continue its irresponsible and uncontrolled spending on entitlements?

DETERMINE WHETHER YOU ARE ASKING YOUR QUESTIONS CLEARLY

Test your survey items before administering your survey by asking your classmates or family members to read your questions. A question that seems perfectly clear to you might confuse someone else. Rewrite the questions that confuse your "testers" and then test them again. Consider the evolution of the following question.

Original Question:

• What can be done about voter turnout among younger voters?

> Does "about voter turnout" mean increasing voter turnout, decreasing voter turnout, or encouraging younger voters to be better informed about candidates? Does the phrase "younger voters" mean 18-year-olds or 30-year-olds?

Revised Question:

In your opinion, what can be done to increase turnout among 18- to 24-year-old voters?

Distribute Your Survey

Surveys are typically distributed via e-mail, the Web, or social media. Online surveys are easier to distribute and offer more choices of tools you can use to create surveys (such as SurveyGizmo, SurveyMonkey, and Quibblo). Online survey tools also make tabulating results easier, allowing you to break down responses and create charts from survey data. The disadvantages include low response rates and the likelihood that the people who respond will do so because of a specific interest in the issue. In other words, you might find that most of your respondents have some sort of interest or bias that leads them to want to respond and are not a representative sample of the group you hope to understand.

Paper-based surveys are most useful in situations where you can pass them out to a group, such as students in a class or people attending a meeting. Surveying people over the phone tends to result in a low response rate and might be prohibited by local and state laws regarding telephone solicitations. Telephone surveys are seldom a productive tool for collecting responses.

The sheer number of surveys people are asked to complete these days has reduced the public's willingness to respond to them. In fact, a "good" response rate for a survey is 60 percent, and many professional pollsters find lower response rates acceptable.

Analyze Your Results

For greatest flexibility, tabulate your survey responses using a spreadsheet program. When you analyze your results, look for trends and patterns. For example, ask whether age or experience seems to predict responses or whether groups respond differently to particular questions. Look as well for surprising results, such as unexpectedly high levels of agreement or disagreement with Likert-scale items or striking differences in the responses to short-answer questions.

As you conduct your analysis, keep in mind the need to ensure confidentiality for your respondents. Survey respondents usually expect anonymity. As you review your responses, be careful not to reveal personally identifiable information. A respondent might reveal, for example, that she is the only Iraq War veteran in a particular writing class. If you find this kind of information, do not include it in your report.

Checklist for Conducting Surveys

✔ **Keep it short.** Surveys are most effective when they are brief. Don't exceed one page.

✔ **Format and distribute your survey appropriately.** If your survey is on paper, make sure the text is readable and that there is plenty of room to write. For e-mailed surveys, you can either insert the survey questions into the body of your e-mail message or attach the survey file. If you are distributing your survey on the Web, use the formatting options in your Web survey tool to test out various layouts for your questions.

✔ **Explain the purpose of your survey.** Explaining who you are and how you will use the results of the survey in your writing project can help increase a respondent's willingness to complete and return your survey.

✔ **Treat survey respondents with respect.** People respond more favorably when they think you are treating them as individuals rather than simply as part of a mailing list. Address potential respondents by name in e-mail messages or cover letters.

✔ **Make it easy to return the survey.** Provide clear directions for submitting completed surveys on the Web or via e-mail. If you are distributing the survey to students in classes, provide a large envelope with your name and contact information into which the surveys can be placed.

✔ **Make your survey available.** Include a copy of your survey questions in an appendix to your project document.

How Can I Engage in Other Forms of Field Research?

Other common forms of field research include engaging in correspondence and attending public events. In addition, you can often collect more information by collaborating with others.

Engage in Correspondence

Correspondence includes any textual communication — such as letters and e-mail — as well as real-time communication using chat or text-messaging. If you use chat or text-messaging, be sure to save a transcript of the exchange. You can correspond with experts in a particular area; people who have been affected by or are involved with an issue or event; staff at corporations, organizations, and government agencies; or even journalists who have written about a subject. Always explain who you are, what you are writing about, and why you want to correspond.

Attend Public Events

Public events, such as lectures, conferences, and public meetings and hearings, often provide writers with useful information. You can take notes or record public events by using a smartphone or digital recorder (if permitted). If you attend a public event in person or on the Web, find out whether a transcript of the proceedings will be available.

Collaborate with Others

Conducting field research can be time intensive. Consider forming collaborative teams with your classmates to collect information. You can use one or more of the following strategies.

- If you and a classmate conduct an observation or attend a public event, you'll get more than a single perspective on the subject. You might observe at the same time as your classmate so that together you can see more of what is taking place. Or you and your classmate might observe the same setting at different times, effectively doubling the amount of information you can obtain. If you decide to work with a classmate, consider creating an observation checklist so that each observer will know what to look for.

- If you are conducting an interview, share your interview questions with a classmate before conducting the interview. Have your classmate role-play the interviewee. Then ask him or her how you might improve your questions.

- If you are gathering information through correspondence, ask a classmate to review your letter or message before you send it and to offer suggestions for improving it. Your classmate can follow the guidelines for conducting an effective peer review (see p. 106).

- If you are conducting a survey, share drafts of your survey with a few classmates. Ask them to note any questions that seem unclear, irrelevant, or ineffective. If they identify any questions that could be improved, ask them why they found the questions problematic and whether they have any suggestions for revision.

In Summary: Conducting Field Research

* Consider reasons for using field research (p. 498).

* Plan and conduct interviews (p. 499).

* Plan and conduct observations (p. 503).

* Design, conduct, and analyze a survey (p. 506).

* Use correspondence to collect information (p. 511).

* Attend public events that are relevant to your issue (p. 511).

* Enlist help in carrying out collaborative projects (p. 511).

Avoiding Plagiarism

Few writers intentionally try to pass off the work of others as their own. However, deadlines and other pressures can lead writers to take notes poorly and to cite sources improperly. In addition, access to documents through the Web and full-text databases has made it all too easy to copy and paste work from other writers without acknowledging its source.

Failing to cite your sources can lead to serious problems. Your readers will not be able to determine which information, ideas, and arguments are your own and which are drawn from your sources. If they suspect you are failing to acknowledge your sources, they might doubt your credibility and even stop reading your document. More seriously, submitting academic work that does not properly identify sources might result in a failing grade or other disciplinary action.

What Is Plagiarism?

Plagiarism is a form of intellectual dishonesty. It involves either unintentionally using someone else's work without properly acknowledging where the ideas or information came from (the most common form of plagiarism) or intentionally passing off someone else's work as your own (the most serious form of plagiarism).

Plagiarism is based on the notion of copyright, or ownership of a document or an idea. Like a patent, which protects an invention, a copyright protects an author's investment of time and energy in the creation of a document. Essentially, it assures authors that someone else won't be able to steal ideas from their work and profit from that theft without penalty.

In this sense, plagiarism in academic writing differs in important ways from the kind of mixing and remixing that can take place in popular culture. The expectations of readers and writers differ in important ways from those of composers and listeners. Musicians, for example, often use other songs as springboards or inspiration for their own work, sometimes sampling other songs or creating mixes. Writers of books, magazine articles, or academic journal articles, in contrast, don't have that freedom. Readers would be surprised to find an unattributed passage that they recognize as the work of another writer, while writers would be alarmed if they came across an unattributed passage of their own in someone else's document. In general, writers are pleased when someone else quotes their work. But they are quick to take offense — and have good reason to do so — when another writer uses their work without giving proper credit. Context matters, and in this case the context of academic writing differs significantly from that of popular culture.

Unintentional Plagiarism

In most cases, plagiarism is unintentional, and most cases of unintentional plagiarism result from taking poor notes or failing to use notes properly. You are plagiarizing if you

- quote a passage in a note but neglect to include quotation marks and then later insert the quotation into your document without remembering that it is a direct quotation
- include a paraphrase that differs so slightly from the original passage that it might as well be a direct quotation

- don't clearly distinguish between your ideas and those that come from your sources
- neglect to list the source of a paraphrase, quotation, or summary in your text or in your works cited list

Although unintentional plagiarism is, by definition, something that the writer hasn't planned to do, it is nonetheless a serious issue and, when detected, is likely to have consequences. Some instructors might require that an assignment be rewritten, others might impose a penalty, such as a lowered or failing grade.

Intentional Plagiarism

Intentional plagiarism can lead to serious academic penalties, ranging from a reduced grade on an assignment, to failure of a course, to expulsion. Intentional plagiarism includes

- engaging in "patchwork writing," or piecing together passages from multiple sources without acknowledging the sources of the passages and without properly quoting or paraphrasing
- creating fake citations to mislead a reader about the sources of information used in a document
- copying or closely paraphrasing extended passages from another document and passing them off as the writer's original work
- copying an entire document and passing it off as the writer's original work
- purchasing a document and passing it off as the writer's original work

Plagiarism in Group Projects

Peer review and other collaborative activities raise important, and potentially confusing, questions.

- If another writer suggests changes to your document and you subsequently incorporate them into your document, are you plagiarizing?
- What if those suggestions significantly change your document?
- If you work with a group of writers on a project, do you need to identify which parts each of you wrote?
- Is it acceptable to list yourself as a coauthor if another writer does most of the work on a collaborative writing project?

The answers to these questions will vary from situation to situation. In general, it's appropriate to use comments from reviewers in your document without citing them. If a reviewer's comments are particularly helpful, you might acknowledge his or her contributions in your document; writers often thank reviewers in a footnote or an end-note or in an acknowledgments section. It is usually appropriate to list coauthors on a collaboratively written document without identifying the text that each coauthor wrote, although some instructors ask that individual contributions be noted in the document or on a cover page. If you are uncertain about what is appropriate, ask your instructor.

What Are Research Ethics?

Research ethics are based on the notion that writing is an honest exchange of information, ideas, and arguments among writers and readers who share an interest in a subject. As a writer, you'll want to behave honestly and ethically. In general, you should do the following:

- Acknowledge the sources of the information, ideas, and arguments you use in your document. By doing so, you show respect for the work that others have done before you.

- Accurately and fairly represent the information, ideas, and arguments from your sources to ensure that you do not misrepresent other writers' work to your readers.

- Provide citation information for your sources. These citations help your readers understand how you have drawn your conclusions and where they can locate those sources should they want to consult them.

These three rules are the essence of research ethics. Ultimately, failing to act ethically — even when the failure is unintentional — reflects poorly on you and your document. If your readers suspect that you have acted unethically, they will question the accuracy and credibility of the information, ideas, and arguments in your document. If they suspect that you have sacrificed research ethics altogether, they'll probably stop reading what you've written.

By adhering to research ethics — acknowledging your sources, representing them fairly, and citing them accurately — you can earn the trust of your readers and increase the chances that they'll pay attention to your argument. The example on the next page, from James Hardjadinata's essay about the problem of puppy mills, demonstrates a writer's adherence to research ethics.

If aging federal laws like the Animal Welfare Act are ineffectual, then we must consider new alternatives to address this problem. One suggestion involves new standards for puppy mill laws that can be easily applied from state to state. Christina Widner points to legislation, recently passed in Colorado, that classifies breeders as low, medium, or high risk, assigning a metric based on the size of the litters produced and the size of the breeding operation. Under this new law, breeders in higher-risk categories are inspected more frequently (228). This sliding scale notion could be applied to licensing fees on breeders as well. Several other states have adopted laws that cap the number of puppies living in any one location, a moderate solution that at the very least remediates the mistreatment of animals in these facilities due to overcrowding (Widner 235). In these states, law-abiding backyard breeders need not be penalized, while the bigger establishments will be subjected to more frequent inspections and higher fees, yielding more revenue to support puppy mill inspections.

Although these recommendations are stringent, they do not address the current lax enforcement, particularly for large-scale offenders. They also require significant effort. Katherine C. Tushaus, writing for the *Drake Journal of Agricultural Law*, notes an easier alternative proposed overseas, which would eliminate outright the sale of pets in pet stores throughout the state.

> An attribution identifies the source of an idea.

> A parenthetical citation indicates a paraphrase and provides the page number.

Tushaus, Katherine C. "Don't Buy the Doggy in the Window: Ending the Cycle That Perpetuates Commercial Breeding with Regulation of the Retail Pet Industry." *Drake Journal of Agricultural Law*, vol. 14, 2009, pp. 504-17, www.animallaw.info/article/dont-buy-doggy-window-ending-cycle-perpetuates-commercial-breeding-regulation-retail-pet.

Widner, Christina. "Channeling Cruella De Vil: An Exploration of Proposed and Ideal Regulation on Domestic Animal Breeding in California." *San Joaquin Agricultural Law Review*, vol. 20, 2010, pp. 217-36.

> Complete source information is included in the works cited list.

> Sources are cited in MLA style.

▲ Adhering to research ethics

Understand Common Knowledge

Although crediting other authors for their work is important, you don't need to document every fact and idea used in your document because some of that information falls under the category of common knowledge. Common knowledge is information that is widely known, such as the fact that the Declaration of Independence was signed in 1776. Or it might be the kind of knowledge that people working in a particular field use on a regular basis.

If you're relatively new to your topic, it can be difficult to determine whether information in a source is common knowledge. As you explore your topic, however, you will begin to identify what is generally known. For instance, if three or more sources use the same information without providing a citation, you can assume that the information is common knowledge. However, if those sources provide a citation for that information, make sure you cite it as well.

Ask Permission to Use a Source

The concept of fair use deals with how much of a source you can borrow or quote. According to Section 107 of the Copyright Act of 1976 — the fair use provision (available at www.copyright.gov/title17/) — writers can use copyrighted materials for purposes of "criticism, comment, news reporting, teaching (including multiple copies for classroom use), scholarship, or research." In other words, writers generally don't need to seek permission to make brief quotations from a source or to summarize or paraphrase a source.

If you are working on an assignment for a course and do not plan to publish it on the Web or in print, you generally can use material from another source without seeking permission. Remember, however, that in all cases you must still cite the source of the material you use.

Writers who plan to publish their work — in a newspaper or magazine, in a blog, or on a public website, for example — should seek permission to use material from a source if they want to quote a lengthy passage or, in the case of shorter works such as poems and song lyrics, if they want to quote a significant percentage of the source. Writers who wish to use multimedia sources, such as images, audio, or video, should either seek permission to use the source or link directly to the Web page that displays it.

To seek permission to use a source, explain why and how you want to use it. Many authors and publishers allow academic use of their work but frown on commercial uses. When you contact an author or a publisher, include your name and contact

Dear Ms. Jackson:

I am a student and am writing an essay for my writing class, English Composition 200, at Colorado State University. The essay will be used only for educational purposes and will be distributed on our class website, which is available only to my instructor and members of my class, for a period of three weeks during April and May of this year.

> Or ". . . on the Web at www.myschool.edu"

I would like to include in my essay the following image, which is displayed on your site at www.westernliving.org/images/2302a.jpg, and would greatly appreciate your permission to do so:

> Insert or describe the passage or image. For example: "paragraphs 3 to 5 of the article," a thumbnail of the image, or the URL of a document or an image on the Web.

If you are able to grant me the requested permission, please respond to this e-mail message. My deadline for completing my project is April 22. I appreciate your quick response.

> Or ". . . sign the enclosed copy of this letter and return it to me."

If you are not the copyright holder or do not have authority to grant this request, I would appreciate any information you can provide concerning the current copyright holder.

Thank you for considering this request.

Sincerely,

Sara Petrovich
Sara.Petrovich@students.colostate.edu
(970) 555-1515

> Provide contact information, such as name, address, e-mail address, phone number.

▲ **Sample permission request**

information, the source you wish to use, the purpose for which you will use the source, and the time during which it will be used.

If you contact an author or a publisher by mail, include a self-addressed, stamped envelope. It will save the recipient the cost of responding by mail, indicates that you are serious, and perhaps most important, shows good manners.

How Can I Avoid Plagiarism?

In most cases, writers who plagiarize do so unintentionally. You can avoid unintentional plagiarism by learning how to

- conduct a knowledge inventory

- take notes accurately

- distinguish between your ideas and those drawn from your sources

- cite sources in the text and in a works cited or references list (see Chapters 23 and 24)

- recognize misconceptions about intentional plagiarism

Conduct a Knowledge Inventory

Having a clear understanding of your subject will help you avoid unintentional plagiarism. When you are just beginning to learn about a conversation, it might be difficult not only to express your own ideas clearly but also to restate or reframe the information, ideas, and arguments you've encountered in your sources. The result might be a document composed of passages that have been copied without attribution or paraphrased too closely. To prevent these difficulties, conduct a knowledge inventory by answering three questions:

- What do you already know about the subject?

- What don't you know?

- What do you want to know?

Your answers can serve as a starting point for brainstorming, collecting and working with sources, and planning. They can also serve as a guide for discussing the subject with others. Once you've completed your knowledge inventory, meet with your instructor, consult a librarian, or talk with people who are knowledgeable about the subject. Ideally, these discussions will help you determine the most productive way to learn more about your subject.

Take Notes Carefully

Unintentional plagiarism often results from sloppy note taking. Notes might contain direct quotations that are not surrounded with quotation marks, paraphrases that differ in only minor ways from the original passage, and summaries that contain original passages from a source. Quoting, paraphrasing, and summarizing accurately and appropriately as you take notes is the first — and arguably the most important — step in avoiding unintentional plagiarism.

For guidance on quoting, paraphrasing, and summarizing, see Chapter 4. To learn more about integrating quotations, paraphrases, summaries, numerical information, and illustrations into your document, see Chapter 21.

Attribute Ideas Appropriately

To distinguish between your ideas and those obtained from your sources, use attributions — words and phrases that alert your readers to the source of the ideas or information you are using. As you draft your document, use the author's name or the title of the source whenever you introduce ideas from that source. Phrases such as "According to Tom Siller . . ." or "As Heather Landers indicates . . ." let your readers know that information from a source will follow.

You can learn more about using attributions to identify the origin of quotations, paraphrases, and summaries in Chapter 21.

Identify Your Sources

Include a complete citation for each source you refer to in your document. The citation should appear both in the text of the document and in a works cited or references list.

In the following examples, the writer includes MLA-style parenthetical citations that refer readers to a works cited list at the end of the document. Both MLA style and APA style use a combination of attributions and parenthetical information to refer to sources.

> Jessica Richards argues, "We need to develop an efficient, cost-effective means of distributing hydrogen fuels before we can move to a hydrogen economy. If we don't, we'll be operating in crisis mode when the next serious oil shortage arrives" (322).

> "We need to develop an efficient, cost-effective means of distributing hydrogen fuels before we can move to a hydrogen economy" (Richards 322).

Be sure to cite the page or paragraph numbers for paraphrased and summarized information as well as for direct quotations. The following paraphrase of Jessica Richards's comments about energy needs includes the page number of the original passage in parentheses.

> Jessica Richards argues that we need to create an "efficient, cost-effective" system for delivering hydrogen fuels now, instead of while we are facing a critical oil shortage (322).

To learn how to document sources using the MLA and APA documentation systems, see Chapters 23 and 24.

Understand Why Writers Plagiarize

Although most plagiarism is unintentional, some students do plagiarize deliberately. The causes of intentional plagiarism range from running out of time to seeing little value in a course. The most common reasons offered to explain intentional plagiarism — and the steps you can take to avoid falling victim to the temptation to engage in it — are listed below.

- **"It's easier to plagiarize."** Some people believe that it takes less work to cheat than to create an original document. That's probably true — but only in the short term. If you are pursuing a college degree, you will probably work in a profession that requires writing ability and an understanding of how to work with information. When you're assigned to write a report or a proposal down the road, you might regret not taking the time to hone your writing and research skills.

- **"I ran out of time."** Most writers occasionally find themselves wondering where all the time has gone and how they can possibly complete an assignment on schedule. If you find yourself in this situation, contact your instructor about a revised deadline. You might face a penalty for turning in work late, but it will almost certainly be less severe than the penalty for intentional plagiarism.

- **"I couldn't care less about this assignment."** It's not unusual to put off assignments that don't interest you. Rather than avoiding the work, try to approach the assignment in a way that interests you (see p. 41). If that fails, ask your instructor if you can customize the assignment so that it better aligns with your interests.

- **"I'm no good at writing."** A lot of people have doubts about their ability to earn a good grade in a writing course. Occasionally, however, some students convince themselves that plagiarizing is a reasonable alternative to writing their own document. If you lack confidence, seek assistance from your instructor, a campus writing center, a tutoring center, one of the many writing centers on the Web (such as the Writing@CSU website at writing.colostate.edu), or a friend or family member. Even with only modest support, you'll probably do much better than you think you can.

- **"I didn't think I'd get caught."** Some students believe — and might even have experiences to support their belief — that they won't get caught plagiarizing. Most writing instructors, however, become familiar with their students' writing styles. If they notice a sudden change in style or encounter varying styles in the same document, they might become suspicious. The availability of plagiarism detection software also increases the likelihood that plagiarism will be detected.

- **"Everybody cheats."** Some students plagiarize because they believe that many of their classmates are doing so. They fear that if they don't plagiarize, they'll be at a competitive disadvantage. In fact, however, the number of students who plagiarize is quite low. Don't be persuaded by dramatic statistics showing that cheating is the norm. The reality is that few students plagiarize intentionally, and those who do still tend to earn lower grades than their peers.

- **"This course is a waste of my time."** If you view a course as little more than a box that needs to be checked, you might be tempted to put in as little effort as possible. However, turning in work that isn't your own can backfire. If you are caught plagiarizing, you'll probably receive a reduced — or failing — grade for the assignment or the course. Instead of plagiarizing, talk with your instructor or an academic adviser about your lack of interest. You might find that the course actually has some relevance to your interests and career plans.

What Should I Do If I'm Accused of Plagiarism?

If your instructor expresses concerns about the originality of your work or the manner in which you've documented information, ideas, and arguments from sources, ask for a meeting to discuss the situation. To prepare for the meeting, do the following:

- Review your document to identify passages that might have raised suspicions.
- Collect the materials you used in your writing project, such as copies of your sources, responses to surveys, interview transcripts, and so on.

- Collect materials you wrote during the project, such as the results of brainstorming and freewriting sessions; any outlines, clusters, or maps; and drafts of your document.
- Reflect on your writing process.

During the meeting, listen to your instructor's concerns before responding. It's natural to feel defensive, but you'll probably be more comfortable if you take notes and try to understand why your instructor has questions about your document. Once your instructor is finished expressing his or her concerns, think carefully about what has been said and respond as clearly as possible. Your instructor might ask follow-up questions, most likely about the sources you've used, your writing process, and the document you've written.

If you find that you have engaged in unintentional plagiarism, ask your instructor for guidance about how to avoid it in the future, and ask what sort of penalty you will face. If your instructor determines that you have plagiarized intentionally, ask what consequences you will face.

If you and your instructor are unable to resolve the situation, you might face a disciplinary process. To prepare for that process, learn as much as you can about the academic integrity policies at your institution.

In Summary: Avoiding Plagiarism

* **Understand the definition of plagiarism and the concept of copyright (p. 514).**

* **Understand and follow research ethics (p. 516).**

* **Understand what is meant by common knowledge (p. 518).**

* **Seek permission to use sources when necessary (p. 518).**

* **Conduct a knowledge inventory (p. 520).**

* **Cite and document your sources (p. 521).**

* **Resist temptations to plagiarize intentionally (p. 522).**

* **Know what to do if you are accused of plagiarism (p. 523).**

PART FOUR

Crafting and Polishing Your Contribution

# Developing and Supporting Your Thesis Statement

Your thesis statement provides a clear, focused expression of the position you've developed on your issue or subject. It is an important tool for sharing your best thinking about the conversation you've decided to join. Thesis statements emerge from your position on an issue — your reactions to what you've read so far.

How Can I Develop My Position on an Issue?

Writers take a position when they react to what they've learned about an issue or subject, form opinions about it, or decide to take actions because of it. When you're new to a conversation, your position is likely to be tentative and incomplete. As you learn more, your position will become more clearly defined and well thought out.

As you take a position on the issue or subject you've been reading about, review what you've learned and consider your writing situation. You need not express your position in writing, but you'll find that reflecting on how you are approaching the conversation will prepare you for the work of developing your thesis statement and, eventually, your contribution to your conversation.

Review Your Notes

As you consider the position you want to take, reread your notes and think about what you learned as you evaluated your sources. During your review, do the following:

- List important information, ideas, and arguments that you've come across in your reading.
- Consider what interests you about the information, ideas, and arguments you've identified in your notes.
- Review and elaborate on the ideas and arguments that you've come up with as a result of your own thinking about the subject.

When you complete your review, identify the ideas you would most like to address in your document.

Consider Your Writing Situation

Use the following questions about your writing situation to develop your position:

- How have the sources you've consulted changed your thinking about the subject?
- Have your purposes — the reasons you are working on this project — changed since you started the project? If so, how do you view your purpose now?
- Has your role as a writer — for example, to inform or to solve a problem — changed since you started your project? If so, how do you view your role now?

- Will focusing on a particular idea help you address your readers' purposes, needs, interests, and backgrounds?
- Can you address this idea given the requirements and limitations of your writing project?

After you've answered these questions, draft some position statements. Think of your position as you would the brainstorming you did early in your writing project. You need not write more than a sentence or two and you need not edit your position carefully. Focus, instead, on your overall take on the conversation and what you might want to say to the other readers and writers involved in it. Quinn Jackson, for example, wrote several draft position statements for the essay she planned to write about preparing teachers to teach writing:

> Teachers should have more classes about writing theory and classroom practice and more professional development on the job.
>
> No matter how much they learn about teaching writing in college (and that's not nearly enough), new teachers will have too many students and not enough time.
>
> Future teachers should have more classes on writing.
>
> Teachers should be writers.
>
> Students won't improve as writers unless they get good feedback.

These position statements are written in a casual manner.

The focus is on ideas and not on grammar or style.

These position statements provided a basis for the thesis statement Quinn eventually used in her essay:

> Because the feedback that teachers provide has a strong impact on students' development as writers, teacher training programs should incorporate best practices for responding to student writing.

How Can I Draft My Thesis Statement?

To develop your thesis statement, think about how your position relates to the type of document you will write and to the information, ideas, and arguments you want to include. Then try out different ways of phrasing your thesis statement. As you develop each new version, try to predict how your readers will react to it.

Consider Your Genre

An effective thesis statement will reflect the genre you plan to write in (see p. 21). Readers of an academic essay will expect a calm, clearly written statement of what you want them to learn, believe, or do. Readers of a newspaper article will expect to see information presented in a balanced and seemingly unbiased manner. Readers of an opinion column will expect you to be more assertive, and perhaps even more entertaining, about your position on an issue. Consider how the following thesis statements, all addressing problems with the recruitment of athletes at a university, reflect the type of document the writer plans to draft.

Argumentative Academic Essay

> A strong but formal assertion

The university should ensure that its recruiting practices are in full compliance with NCAA regulations.

Informative Newspaper Article

> A seemingly unbiased statement of fact

The university is taking steps to bring its recruiting practices in line with NCAA regulations.

Opinion Column

> An informal tone

The university's coaches need to get their act together before the NCAA slaps them with sanctions.

Identify Important Information, Ideas, and Arguments Related to Your Position

Begin developing your thesis statement by identifying important information, ideas, and arguments related to your position. When you first explored a conversation (see Chapter 2), you asked questions to learn about your subject. Review those questions and examine them for key words and phrases. Then look through your notes to see how your sources address those questions or use those key words and phrases. Consider the following example, which shows a list of Quinn Jackson's initial questions and the important information, ideas, and arguments she found in sources.

> Quinn circled key words and phrases in her initial questions about her subject and then identified which sources address those key words and phrases.

Questions about how writing teachers respond to student work:

What are the ways that teachers give students feedback on their written work?

Have different approaches common to writing feedback been studied? Are any proven to be more successful than others?

Is written feedback more effective than verbal feedback?

What is the goal of feedback on student writing?

Does the feedback students receive vary with the audience they are writing for?

What my sources say:

Feedback that makes observations is more valuable than feedback that evaluates whether writing is good or bad, successful or unsuccessful (Johnston para. 5).

Teacher feedback encourages students to do more than just improve their sentences; it helps them develop important habits of mind (Sommers para. 16).

What goes on in a successful classroom is far more than just "teaching writing"; it extends to what students learn about being citizens of the world (Sommers para. 19).

You can use the key words and phrases you've identified in your questions and notes in the various versions of thesis statements that you try out.

Draft Alternatives

An effective thesis statement can invite your readers to learn something new, suggest that they change their attitudes or beliefs, or argue that they should take action of some kind. Consider how the following thesis statements reflect these three ways of focusing a position statement.

Position Statement

Teachers should have more classes about writing theory and classroom practice and more professional development on the job.

Thesis Statement: Asking Readers to Learn Something New

Recent research on how teachers give feedback has identified students' most common writing problems and teachers' most common responses.

Thesis Statement: Asking Readers to Change Their Attitudes or Beliefs

When teachers give feedback on written work, they are communicating to students values and ideals that go beyond the classroom.

Thesis Statement: Asking Readers to Take Action

Parents should demand that school districts provide more research about and guidance for responding to student work.

Experiment with different approaches to determine which one works best for your writing situation. The thesis statement you choose should convey your position in a way that addresses your purpose and your readers' needs, interests, backgrounds, and knowledge of a subject. For example, if you're focusing on the causes of a problem, your thesis statement should identify those causes. If you're advocating a particular solution to a problem, your thesis statement should identify that solution.

Focus Your Thesis Statement

A broad thesis statement does not encourage your readers to learn anything new, change their attitudes or beliefs, or take action. The following thesis statement is too broad.

Broad Thesis Statement

The feedback that teachers provide on written work has a big impact on students' development as writers.

There's no conversation to be had about this topic because few people would argue with such a statement. A more focused thesis statement would define what should be done and who should do it.

Focused Thesis Statement

Because the feedback that teachers provide has a strong impact on students' development as writers, teacher training programs should incorporate best practices for responding to student writing.

To focus your thesis statement, ask what your readers would want to know about your subject, what attitudes should be changed, or what action should be taken. Consider their likely responses to your thesis statement, and attempt to head off potential counterarguments or questions.

How Can I Support My Thesis Statement?

Presenting your thesis statement effectively involves far more than knowing what you want others to understand or believe or how you want them to act. You must develop a strategy to accomplish your goal. Developing your strategy involves reflecting on your purposes, your readers, and the conventions typically used in the type of document you plan to write.

Choose Reasons to Accept Your Thesis Statement

In longer documents, such as essays, reports, and websites, writers usually present readers with several reasons to accept their thesis statement. The kinds of reasons will vary according to the types of documents they are writing. In informative documents (see Chapter 7), for example, writers might focus on the three or four most important aspects of the subject they want readers to understand. In analytical documents (see Chapter 8), they might choose points that help readers understand the results of the analysis. In argumentative documents (see Chapter 11), writers usually offer a series of claims that will lead readers to accept their arguments.

To choose the reasons you'll offer to support your thesis statement, consider brainstorming, freewriting, looping, or clustering (see p. 41). As you generate ideas, reflect on your purpose, your role as a writer, the type of document you intend to write, and your readers.

- **Writing to reflect.** Which of your observations are most significant? What kind of impression do you want to create? (See Chapter 6.)

- **Writing to inform.** What do you want to convey to your readers? What are they most likely to want to know about the subject? (See Chapter 7.)

- **Writing to analyze.** How will you present the results of your analysis? What questions might your readers have about each part of your analysis? (See Chapter 8.)

- **Writing to evaluate.** What is the best way to present your criteria and the results of your evaluation? (See Chapter 9.)

- **Writing to solve problems.** How will you define the problem, and how will you present your solution? What questions do you think your readers will have about your problem definition, proposed solution, and alternative solutions? (See Chapter 10.)

- **Writing to convince or persuade.** How can you convince your readers to accept your thesis statement? How do you think they might respond to your argument? What sort of counterarguments might they propose? (See Chapter 11.)

Select Evidence to Support Your Reasons

For each reason you offer to support your thesis statement, you'll need evidence — such as details, facts, personal observations, and expert opinions — to back up your assertions and help your readers understand your ideas. The evidence you choose plays a central role in gaining your readers' acceptance of your thesis statement.

You can draw evidence from your sources in the form of quotations, paraphrases, summaries, numerical data, and visual images. You can also gather evidence first-hand by conducting interviews, observations, and surveys or by reflecting on your personal experience. Chapters 6 through 11 offer detailed suggestions for locating and choosing evidence for specific purposes.

Use the following prompts to identify evidence to support your reasons:

1. List the reasons you are using to support your thesis statement.

2. Identify relevant evidence from your sources, personal experience, or your own field research, and then list that evidence below each reason. You might need to review your sources to locate additional evidence or even obtain additional sources.

3. Determine whether you are relying too heavily on information from a single source or on one type of evidence.

As you select supporting evidence, consider the genre of your document. Genre conventions (see p. 587) often determine how and how much evidence is used in a document. Articles in magazines, newspapers, and websites, for example, are more likely to rely on interviews, observation, and illustrations as primary sources of evidence than are academic essays, whose writers tend to draw information from published sources found in a library or database. Multimodal essays, in contrast, are likely to use not only textual information and images but also audio, video, and animation.

In Summary: Developing and Supporting Your Thesis Statement

* Take a position on your issue (p. 528).

* Draft your thesis statement (p. 529).

* Choose reasons to accept your thesis statement (p. 533).

* Select evidence to support your reasons (p. 533).

17

Organizing

⏩ A well-organized document allows a reader to predict what will come next. Choose an appropriate organizing pattern by reflecting on your writing situation, thesis statement, reasons, and evidence. With that pattern in mind, use labeling, grouping, clustering, and mapping to arrange your argument and informal and formal outlining strategies to organize your document.

How Can I Choose an Organizing Pattern?

Organizing patterns provide an overall principle for arranging your argument and document. The pattern you choose should help you organize your document in a manner that your readers can follow easily. It should also help you achieve your purpose and adapt to your readers and context.

Understand the Types of Organizing Patterns

Common organizing patterns include the following.

Chronology reflects the order in which events occur over time. For example, you might focus on a sequence of events in a recent election or during someone's life. Biographies and memoirs, for instance, are often organized chronologically, portraying early events first and moving forward in time.

Description provides a point-by-point account of the physical attributes of a subject. For example, you might focus on what you see as you walk the streets of a city. Description is best for documents that address physical spaces, objects, or people — things that we can see and observe — rather than theories or processes that are not visible.

Definition lays out the distinguishing characteristics of a subject and then provides examples and reasoning to explain what differentiates it from other subjects. For instance, an essay defining *pride* might begin by stating that it is an emotion and then move on to explain why that particular emotion is not as harmful as many people believe.

Cause/effect patterns focus on the factors that lead to (cause) an outcome (effect). For example, you might identify the reasons behind a recent strike by grocery store employees or the health risks that contribute to heart disease.

Process explanations outline the steps involved in doing something or explain how something happens. For example, you might help readers understand the stages of nuclear fission or teach them what to do to prepare for a hurricane.

Pro/con organizing patterns present arguments made for (pro) and against (con) a particular position. For example, you might consider the arguments for and against increased reliance on wind power.

Multiple perspectives organizing patterns arrange information, ideas, and arguments according to a range of perspectives about a subject. Writers who use this pattern frequently provide an analysis supporting one perspective. For example, a writer addressing the use of tidal power as an alternative energy source might present the perspectives of utility companies, environmentalists, oceanographers, legislators, and waterfront residents and ultimately favor one group over the others.

Comparison/contrast patterns can help you explore similarities and differences among the information, ideas, and arguments relevant to a subject. A writer analyzing a policy initiative to decriminalize marijuana possession, for example, might consider how current drug laws are like or unlike alcohol prohibition. Another writer might compare and contrast medical and recreational uses of marijuana.

Strengths/weaknesses patterns can help you examine positive and negative aspects of a subject, such as increasing federal funding for health care by instituting a national lottery, or the overall quality of life in a particular city. Writers who choose this organizing principle typically work toward a conclusion where one or two considerations outweigh the others.

Costs/benefits organizing patterns present the trade-offs associated with a subject, usually a choice or proposal of some sort. For example, the writer of an evaluative essay might discuss why the expenses associated with implementing a particular educational initiative are justified (or not) by the potential for higher test scores.

Problem/solution organizing patterns involve defining a problem and discussing the appropriateness of one or more solutions. If multiple solutions are proposed, the writer usually argues for the superiority of one over the others. For instance, an informative article might explain the problem of "brain drain," in which highly educated and skilled workers move out of state, and then argue in support of a proposal to retain and attract more skilled workers.

Reflect on Your Writing Situation

Your choice of organizing pattern will reflect your purpose and the role or roles you adopt as a writer (see Chapters 6 through 11). Consider which pattern will help you achieve your goals as a writer, meet the needs and interests of your readers, adapt to your context, and be consistent with the genre you've chosen. An organizing pattern should also highlight the reasons and evidence you offer to convince readers to accept your thesis statement.

Keep in mind that a writer may use more than one organizing pattern in a document. For instance, a process explanation often works in tandem with chronology, since both present steps in a sequence. Similarly, a document presenting multiple perspectives might use the strengths/weaknesses pattern to evaluate the merits of each perspective.

How Can I Arrange My Argument?

Once you have selected an organizing pattern, you can use strategies such as labeling, grouping, clustering, and mapping to determine how to present your argument. These strategies will also help you later as you develop an outline for your document.

Labeling

Labeling can help you understand at a glance how and where you will use your evidence. For example, you might label notes or sources containing the evidence you want to use in your introduction with "Introduction," those that you plan to use to define a concept with the name of that concept, and so on. Digital notes and sources can be labeled by changing a file name or editing the document text. Print notes and sources can be labeled with pen or pencil or with sticky notes.

Once you've labeled your notes and sources, you can organize them into groups and put them in order.

Label at the top of a note in a word-processing file

MLA style calls for including URLs in works cited lists.

Annotation captures the main point of the source.

MLA recommends using paragraph numbers only when paragraphs are numbered in the source. However, you can include them in your notes to help identify key passages.

Puppy Mill Conditions

Shaw, Anthony E. "Prisoners of Profit (Puppy Mills)." *Petfinder.* www.petfinder.com/helping-pets/puppy-mills/prisoners-profit-puppy-mills/. Accessed 9 May 2015.

Makes observations about living conditions of dogs in puppy mills, particularly female dogs used for breeding. Focuses on conditions, legal issues, regulation, and typical behaviors of owners of puppy mills.

Key Quotes:

"Given authority under the Animal Welfare Act since the 1970s to set and enforce federal standards for sanitation, nutrition, housing and general conditions for dog wholesalers, the short-staffed corps of USDA inspectors — only 73 nationwide — has tried to regulate puppy mills. But the results have been uneven at best" (para. 8).

▲ **Labeling digital notes and sources**

▲ **Grouping digital notes and sources in a browser**

Grouping

Grouping involves categorizing the evidence you've obtained from your sources. Paper-based notes and copies of sources can be placed in related piles or file folders; sources and notes in word-processing files or on a smartphone can be saved in larger files or placed in folders; items in Bookmarks or Favorites lists can be sorted by category. Placing things that are similar in groups allows you to locate the evidence you've collected more easily and helps you understand the range of evidence you might use to support a particular point.

Clustering

You can use clustering to explore the relationships among your thesis statement, reasons, and evidence. Clustering involves arranging these elements visually on a sheet of paper or on a computer, phone, or tablet screen (using a word-processing program or an app such as iThoughtsHD).

Mapping

Mapping allows you to explore sequences of reasons and evidence. For example, you might use mapping to create a timeline or to show how an argument builds on one reason after another. Mapping can be particularly effective as you begin to think about organizing your document, and it often relies on the organizing patterns discussed earlier in this chapter, such as chronology, cause/effect, comparison/contrast, costs/benefits, and problem/solution.

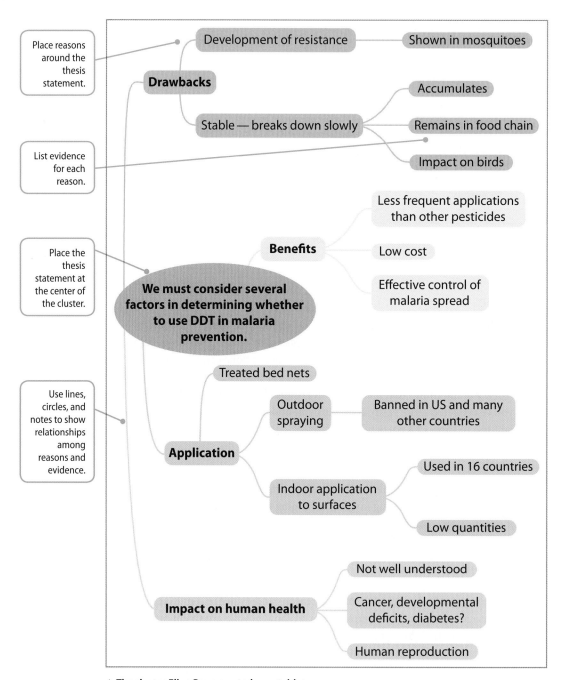

Place reasons around the thesis statement.

List evidence for each reason.

Place the thesis statement at the center of the cluster.

Use lines, circles, and notes to show relationships among reasons and evidence.

Development of resistance — Shown in mosquitoes

Drawbacks

Stable — breaks down slowly

Accumulates

Remains in food chain

Impact on birds

Benefits

Less frequent applications than other pesticides

Low cost

Effective control of malaria spread

We must consider several factors in determining whether to use DDT in malaria prevention.

Treated bed nets

Outdoor spraying — Banned in US and many other countries

Application

Indoor application to surfaces

Used in 16 countries

Low quantities

Impact on human health

Not well understood

Cancer, developmental deficits, diabetes?

Human reproduction

▲ The cluster Ellen Page created on a tablet

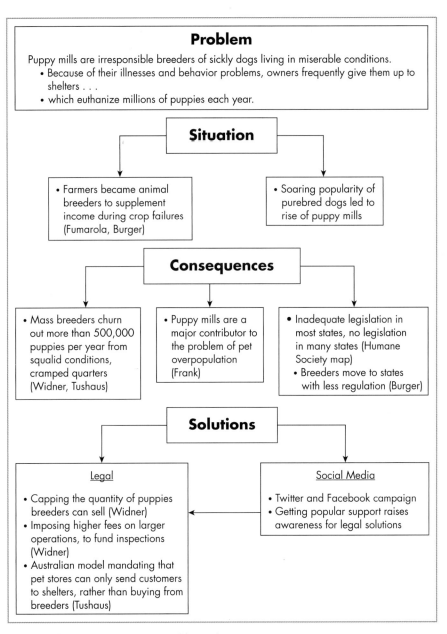

Problem

Puppy mills are irresponsible breeders of sickly dogs living in miserable conditions.
- Because of their illnesses and behavior problems, owners frequently give them up to shelters . . .
- which euthanize millions of puppies each year.

Situation

- Farmers became animal breeders to supplement income during crop failures (Fumarola, Burger)

- Soaring popularity of purebred dogs led to rise of puppy mills

Consequences

- Mass breeders churn out more than 500,000 puppies per year from squalid conditions, cramped quarters (Widner, Tushaus)

- Puppy mills are a major contributor to the problem of pet overpopulation (Frank)

- Inadequate legislation in most states, no legislation in many states (Humane Society map)
- Breeders move to states with less regulation (Burger)

Solutions

Legal
- Capping the quantity of puppies breeders can sell (Widner)
- Imposing higher fees on larger operations, to fund inspections (Widner)
- Australian model mandating that pet stores can only send customers to shelters, rather than buying from breeders (Tushaus)

Social Media
- Twitter and Facebook campaign
- Getting popular support raises awareness for legal solutions

▲ A map of James Hardjadinata's problem-solving essay

How Can I Create an Outline?

Not all documents require an outline, but creating one will usually help you put your thoughts in order. As you develop an outline, you'll make decisions about the sequence in which you'll present your reasons and the evidence you'll use to back them up.

Create an Informal Outline

Informal outlines can take many forms: a brief list of words, a series of short phrases, or even a series of sentences. You can use informal outlines to remind yourself of key points to address in your document or of notes you should refer to as you draft. Featured writer Dwight Haynes, who wrote an evaluative essay about anti-drinking campaigns on college campuses, created the following informal outline. Each item in his outline represents a section he planned to include in his essay.

Dwight identified sources he could use in each subsection.

1. Introduction
2. Establish two approaches to addressing binge drinking on campus
3. Evaluate each approach
   • Social norms (Turner, Wechsler, DeJong)
   • Environmental (Weitzman, Jaschik)
4. Conclusion

▲ Dwight Haynes's informal outline

You can also create a "thumbnail outline," a type of informal outline that helps you group your ideas into major sections. Featured writer Elisabeth Layne wrote the thumbnail outline on the following page as she worked on her argumentative essay about trigger warnings. Elisabeth identified the major sections she wanted to include in her essay and noted which sources she could use to provide background information and to support her argument.

Create a Formal Outline

A formal outline provides a complete and accurate list of the points you want to address in your document. Formal outlines use Roman numerals, letters, and Arabic numerals to indicate the hierarchy of information. An alternative approach, common in business and the sciences, uses numbering with decimal points.

Introduction

Critics both in and out of academia view trigger warnings as "too politically correct," catering to overly sensitive students, and resulting in censorship. However, many students welcome trigger warnings for the sensitivity they show to students' experiences in and out of the classroom.

Thesis Statement

Because they honor the traumatic experiences of some students, trigger warnings should be a noncontroversial option for course syllabi and assignments.

What Are Trigger Warnings?

Trigger warnings originated online in blogs, feminist discussion boards, and media. They caution readers (or viewers) about disturbing content (rape, mental illness, violence) that might trigger traumatic physical and emotional reactions, such as PTSD responses.

Arguments against Trigger Warnings

College is a place to encounter hard truths and think critically. Students are being indulged too much by trigger warnings. They represent the opposite of academic freedom.

In Defense of Trigger Warnings

They recognize that students come to class with varied experiences, some of them traumatic, and respect the whole student. Critics underestimate how strong PTSD symptoms can be.

Conclusion

Trigger warnings are easy to include and don't actually censor anything; they merely give advance warning and allow students to brace themselves if they need to.

▲ **Elisabeth Layne's thumbnail outline**

Thesis Statement: Scientists and governments devising approaches to eradicating malaria consider three main factors in determining whether DDT should be used in indoor residual spraying: health consequences, environmental consequences, and degree of resistance.

I. Introduction
   a. DDT first used for malaria vector control in World War II (CDC, 2016)
   b. WHO proposed global malaria eradication program in 1995, with DDT playing a key role (CDC, 2016)
   c. Publication of Rachel Carson's *Silent Spring*; agricultural use of DDT banned in 1969 (Sadasivaiah, Tozan, & Breman, 2007, p. 250)
   d. Despite ban, DDT continues to be used, particularly in poorer countries (Sadasivaiah, Tozan, & Breman, 2007, p. 252)
      i. Endorsed by WHO as main tool for fighting malaria (WHO, 2006)
      ii. Among most economical options for malaria prevention
   e. A key question is whether indoor use of DDT has the same impact on health as agricultural uses (WHO, 2011; WHO, 2015)
      i. Lower amounts of DDT used
      ii. Use strictly enforced
      iii. Mitigation strategies employed

II. Human health effects of DDT
   a. Highly toxic to children (Sadasivaiah, Tozan, & Breman, 2007, p. 255)

III. Environmental consequences of DDT
   a. Harmful to crops (WHO, 2011b)

IV. Resistance to DDT
   a. Resistance to the chemical is a major obstacle to all pesticide use
   b. Rotating insecticides during spraying cycles helps reduce resistance (WHO, 2015)

V. Risks versus benefits
   a. Research on DDT use must continue (Bouwman, van den Berg, & Kylin, 2011, p. 746)
   b. Currently used in 16 countries (WHO, 2015, p. 23)
   c. Resistance to alternative pesticides (Sadasivaiah, Tozan, & Breman, 2007, p. 256)

▲ **Ellen Page's topical outline**

VI. Conclusion
    a. Evaluation of benefits and risks is complex and difficult
    b. Malaria's health risks must be weighed against those associated with DDT
    c. We should use all tools available, including funding for health care and infrastructure

▲ **Ellen Page's topical outline (*continued*)**

Writers use formal outlines to identify the hierarchy of arguments, ideas, and information. You can create a formal outline to identify

- your thesis statement
- the reasons you offer to support your thesis statement
- the sequence in which your reasons should be presented
- evidence to support your reasons
- the notes and sources you should refer to as you work on your draft

The most common types of formal outlines are topical outlines and sentence outlines.

Topical outlines present the topics and subtopics you plan to include in your document as a series of words and phrases. Items at the same level of importance should be phrased in parallel grammatical form. In her topical outline for her informative essay about DDT use in the prevention of malaria, featured writer Ellen Page identified her main point, listed her reasons, mapped out the supporting evidence for her reasons, and used a conventional system of Roman numerals and letters.

Sentence outlines use complete sentences to identify the points you want to cover. Sentence outlines begin the process of converting an outline into a draft of your document. They can also help you assess the structure of a document that you have already written.

Using her topical outline as a starting point, Ellen Page wrote a sentence outline to test her ideas. Part of her sentence outline is shown below.

Thesis Statement: Scientists and governments devising approaches to eradicating malaria consider three main factors in determining whether DDT should be used in indoor residual spraying: health consequences, environmental consequences, and degree of resistance.

II. Human health effects of DDT
   a. The major concerns surrounding human health and the use of DDT are consumption of the pesticide by children (this has been deemed toxic) and exposure of the pesticide to pregnant women (Sadasivaiah, Tozan, & Breman, 2007, p. 251; WHO, 2011a, p. 9).
   b. Many studies have suggested that DDT causes pregnancy loss, fertility loss, leukemia, cancer, diabetes, and other health problems (van den Berg, 2009, p. 1658).

▲ **Part of Ellen Page's sentence outline**

In Summary: Organizing

✳ **Choose an appropriate organizing pattern (p. 536).**

✳ **Use labeling, grouping, clustering, and/ or mapping to organize your argument (p. 538).**

✳ **Create an informal or formal outline (p. 542).**

Drafting and Designing

As you've learned about your subject, you've encountered new information, ideas, and arguments. In response, you've considered how to craft your own contribution to the conversation you are joining. How you frame your contribution — that is, how you organize your argument,

(Continued)

construct your paragraphs, introduce and conclude your document, and design your document — can have a profound effect on readers' understanding of your subject and on their willingness to accept your main idea. This chapter offers guidance on how to use what you've learned to create an effective, readable document.

How Can I Use My Outline to Begin Drafting?

Your outline provides a framework you can use to draft your document. Your outline likely includes your plans for

- the points you will include in your document
- the order in which you will make your points
- the amount of space you plan to devote to each point

As you review your purpose and your outline, check that you have organized your document in a way that will allow you to achieve your purpose and address the needs and interests of your readers.

If you have listed information about the sources you will use to support your points, you can check whether you are

- providing enough evidence to support your points
- relying too heavily on a small number of sources
- relying too heavily on support from sources that favor just one side of the conversation

If you created an informal outline, you can begin to flesh it out by translating key points in your outline into sentences or paragraphs. If you created a formal outline, you can turn major headings in the outline into headings or subheadings in your draft and then use the points under each heading as the basis for topic sentences for paragraphs. If your outline is highly detailed, you can use minor points as the basis for supporting sentences within each paragraph.

Make sure that you use your notes and review the paraphrases, summaries, and quotations you wrote down. Take advantage of the time you spent thinking about which sources are most appropriate for a particular section of your document.

As you work on your draft, you might find it necessary to reorganize your ideas. Think of your outline as a flexible guide rather than a rigid blueprint.

How Can I Draft an Effective Document?

Effective documents contribute to the conversation in a way that reflects and adapts to your writing situation. Your document should help you accomplish your purpose, address your readers effectively, and help you take advantage of — or work within — the contexts in which it will be read.

Create Paragraphs That Focus on a Central Idea

Writers use paragraphs to present and develop a central idea. Depending on the complexity of your thesis statement and the type of document you are writing, a single paragraph might be all you need to present a supporting point and its associated reasoning and evidence — or it might play only a small role in conveying your thinking about your subject. You can draft a more effective document by creating paragraphs that are focused, organized, and well developed and by using transitions that clearly convey the relationships among paragraphs.

Each of your paragraphs should focus on a single idea. Paragraphs often have a topic sentence in which the writer makes an assertion, offers an observation, or asks a question. The rest of the sentences in the paragraph elaborate on the topic sentence. Consider the following paragraph, drawn from Rivka Galchen's profile of the ballet dancer Misty Copeland (p. 183).

The central idea of the paragraph is provided in the opening clause, and details about Copeland support it.

The second sentence analyzes why the central idea is significant.

The third sentence offers evidence by way of an exception to the rule, while the fourth sentence provides further information that illustrates why Copeland is "unlikely."

The fifth sentence builds on the second, extending the analysis of Copeland's fame.

> Copeland is considered an unlikely ballerina: she is curvy and she is black, neither of which is a common attribute in the field. But it is her very late beginning and rapid attainment of virtuosity that are arguably without precedent for a female ballerina. (Rudolf Nureyev had a famously late and chaotic start, his early training having been limited by the vagaries of the post–Second World War Soviet Union.) Many professional ballet dancers begin their training around the age of three. Every dancer is a synthesis of givens — height, limb length, natural turnout — and intense effort, but Copeland's late start can exaggerate the tendency we might have to regard a ballerina as simply touched by something divine.

Create Paragraphs That Use Appropriate Organizing Patterns

Effective paragraphs follow an organizing pattern, often the same one that the document as a whole follows, such as chronology, description, or costs/benefits (see p. 536). These common patterns help readers anticipate what you'll say. Readers who recognize a pattern, such as process explanation, will find it easier to focus on your ideas and argument if they understand how you are organizing your paragraph. Note how the following paragraph from featured student writer Ellen Page's essay focuses on the costs of DDT.

> First, there are unanswered questions about how the DDT in indoor residual spraying affects human health. The health outcomes of DDT exposure from spraying inside the home are less well understood than the harmful effects of large-scale agricultural spraying. . . . Many studies have suggested that DDT causes "early pregnancy loss, fertility loss, leukemia, pancreatic cancer, neurodevelopmental deficits, diabetes, and breast cancer," yet conflicting outcomes in experiments on lab rats and human case studies have left researchers with a lack of definitive evidence regarding human health risks associated with DDT exposure (van den Berg, 2009, p. 1658). Collectively, these studies point to a need for further research into many of the human health concerns related to DDT exposure via indoor residual spraying.

> The paragraph is organized around the health risks of DDT.

> A reputable source is quoted, providing evidence about the risks of DDT exposure.

> The final sentence concludes that DDT must be studied further.

Integrate Information from Sources Effectively

Information from sources can be used to introduce an important concept, establish the strength of your argument, and elaborate on the central ideas in your document. Writers frequently state a point, offer a reason to accept it, and support their reasoning with evidence from a source, typically in the form of quotations, paraphrases, and summaries. In the following example, a quotation and a paraphrase are used to support a point introduced in the first sentence of the paragraph:

> In fact, pollution from power plants may worsen as the demand for electric power continues to increase. The U.S. Department of Energy (2012b) notes that "it is likely that the nation's reliance on fossil fuels to power an expanding economy will actually increase over at least the next two decades even with aggressive development and deployment of new renewable and nuclear technologies" (para. 1). Moreover, demand in developing nations is expected to increase even more dramatically. Of the nearly 1,200 conventional, coal-fired power plants now on the drawing board worldwide, most are in developing countries (Plumer, 2012). The addition of so many new plants will almost certainly lead to more global air pollution in the near term.

Quoting an authority on the issue, the U.S. Department of Energy, lends strength to the argument. The quotation, along with a subsequent paraphrase of a passage from another source, serves as evidence to support the point. The writer follows the quotation and paraphrase with a sentence that restates the point. (See Chapter 21 for more about integrating information from sources.)

Write Clearly and Concisely

Readers don't want to work any harder than necessary to understand and engage with the information, ideas, and arguments in a document. They get unhappy if they have to put in extra effort to read a document — so unhappy, in fact, that they'll often give up.

To keep your readers engaged with your document, write clearly and concisely. Consider the following passages.

> Please join me, Dr. Watson. I have concluded that I am in a situation in which I require your assistance.

> Come here, Dr. Watson. I need you.

> Help!

The second example, reputed to be the first words ever spoken on a telephone, was spoken by Alexander Graham Bell after he'd spilled acid on his pants. Had he spoken the first sentence instead, he might have wasted crucial time while he waited for his assistant to figure out what he was being asked to do. The simple exclamation "Help!" might have been even more effective and would certainly have taken less time to utter. Then again, it might have been too vague for his assistant to figure out just what sort of help was required. In general, if two sentences provide the same information, the briefer sentence is usually easier to understand.

The following three techniques can help you write with economy:

- **Avoid unnecessary modifiers.** Unnecessary modifiers are words that provide little or no additional information to a reader, such as *fine, many, somewhat, great, quite, sort of, lots, really,* and *very.*

Example Sentence with Unnecessary Modifiers

The Volvo S90 serves as a really excellent example of a very fine performance sedan.

Revised Example

The Volvo S90 serves as an excellent example of a performance sedan.

- **Avoid unnecessary introductory phrases.** Avoid phrases such as *there are, there is, these have, these are, here are, here is, it has been reported that, it has been said that, it is evident that, it is obvious that,* and so on.

Example Sentence with Unnecessary Introductory Phrase

It goes without saying that drinking water should be clean.

Revised Example

Drinking water should be clean.

- **Avoid stock phrases.** Search your document for phrases that you can replace with fewer words, such as the following.

Stock Phrase	Alternative
as a matter of fact	in fact
at all times	always
at that point in time	then
at this point in time	now, currently
at the present time	now, currently
because of the fact that	because
by means of	by
due to the fact that	because
in order to	to
in spite of the fact that	although, though
in the event that	if

Example Sentence with Stock Phrase

Call the security desk in the event that the alarm sounds.

Revised Example

Call the security desk if the alarm sounds.

Engage Your Readers

As you draft your document, consider how you'll keep your readers' attention. One of the easiest things you can do is to write your sentences in *active voice*. A sentence written in active voice specifies an actor — a person or thing — who carries out an action.

Active Voice

Juan took an exam.

The tornado leveled the town.

Carmelo Anthony scored the game-winning basket with 0.2 seconds remaining in overtime.

In contrast, a sentence written in passive voice indicates that something was done, but it does not necessarily specify who or what did it.

Passive Voice

The exam was taken by Juan.

The town was leveled.

The game-winning basket was scored with 0.2 seconds remaining in overtime.

In general, sentences written in active voice are easier to understand and provide more information.

Passive voice, however, can be effective when active voice requires unnecessary information. For example, many scientific experiments are conducted by large teams of researchers. Few readers would want to know which members of the team carried out every task. Rather than using active voice (for example, "Heather Landers, assisted by Sandy Chapman and Shaun Beaty, anesthetized the mice, and then Greta Steber and Justin Switzer examined their eyes for lesions"), you can use passive voice ("The mice were anesthetized, and their eyes were examined for lesions") for a sentence that is clearer, easier to understand, and free of unnecessary information.

Passive voice is also useful if you wish to emphasize the recipient of the action, rather than the actor. Police reports, for example, often use passive voice ("The suspect was apprehended at the corner of Oak and Main Streets").

Use Details to Capture Your Readers' Attention

An effective document does more than simply convey information — it provides details that bring a subject to life. Consider the differences between the following versions of a passage from featured writer Caitlin Guariglia's essay on her family trip to Italy.

Example 1: Minimal Details

The next morning we met our tour guide. He was full of life. He took us to the main historical sites that day. They were spectacular, but I enjoyed listening to Marco more than anything we saw.

Example 2: Extensive, Concrete Details

The next morning we met our tour guide Marco. A large, sturdy man who looked like my grandmother cooked for him, he was confident and full of life. He took us to the main historical sites that day: the Vatican, the Colosseum, the Pantheon, the Roman Forum. While all that was spectacular, I enjoyed listening to Marco more than anything we saw. He was a true Roman, big, proud, and loud. The Italian accent made it seem like he was singing everything he said, making it all seem that much more beautiful.

Both examples convey the same main idea. The first example, however, does little more than state the facts. The second example, by providing details about the tour guide's physical appearance, personality, and voice, gives readers a more concrete and more intimate understanding of the subject. (For advice about integrating details from your sources effectively, see Chapter 21.)

Create Transitions within and between Paragraphs

Transitions help readers understand the relationships among sentences, paragraphs, and even sections of a document. Essentially, they smooth the way for readers, helping them understand how information, ideas, and arguments are related to one another. Transitions are most effective when they don't call attention to themselves, but instead move the reader's eye along to the next sentence, paragraph, or section. Consider the following examples of the steps involved in preparing fish.

No Transitions

Catch the fish. Clean the fish. Filet the fish. Cook the fish. Eat the fish. Catch another fish.

Inconsistent Transitions

First, catch the fish. Secondly, clean the fish. When you've done that, filet the fish. Next, cook the fish. Fifth, eat the fish. After all is said and done, catch another fish.

Consistent Transitions

First, catch the fish. Second, clean the fish. Third, filet the fish. Fourth, cook the fish. Fifth, eat the fish. Finally, catch another fish.

Transitions frequently appear as words and phrases, such as those used in the previous example. Transitional sentences, such as the following, often link one paragraph to the next.

> The results of the tests revealed a surprising trend.

> Incredibly, the outcome was far better than we could have hoped.

Transitional paragraphs, such as the following example, call attention to a major shift in focus within a document.

> In the next section, we explore the reasons behind this surprising development. We focus first on the event itself. Then we consider the reasons underlying the event. Our goal is to call attention to the unique set of relationships that made this development possible.

Section headings and subheadings can also act as transitions by signaling to the reader, through formatting that differs from body text, that a new section is beginning. You can read more about formatting headings and subheadings later in this chapter.

As you create transitions, pay attention to the order in which you introduce new information and ideas in your document. In general, it is best to begin a sentence with a reference to information and ideas that have already been presented and to introduce new information and ideas at the end of the sentence.

Common transitions and their functions are presented below.

To Help Readers Follow a Sequence	To Compare
furthermore	similarly
in addition	in the same manner
moreover	like
next	as in
first/second/third	

To Elaborate or Provide Examples	To Contrast
for example	however
for instance	on the other hand
such as	nevertheless
in fact	nonetheless
indeed	despite
to illustrate	although/though

To Signal a Concession	To Introduce a Conclusion
I admit that	as a result
of course	as a consequence
granted	because of
	therefore
	thus
	for this reason

How Can I Draft My Introduction?

All readers expect documents to include some sort of introduction. Whether they are reading a home page on a website or an opening paragraph in a research report, readers want to learn quickly what a document is about. As you begin to draft, consider strategies to frame and introduce your main point. Many writers find that crafting an effective introduction is the most challenging part of drafting. If you run into difficulties, put your introduction aside and come back to it after you've made more progress on the rest of the document. There's no law that says you have to write the introduction first.

Frame Your Introduction

Your introduction provides a framework within which your readers can understand and interpret your main point. By calling attention to a specific situation, by asking a particular question, or by conveying a carefully chosen set of details, you can help your readers view your subject in a particular way. Consider, for example, the differences between two introductions to an essay about buying habits among younger Americans following the Great Recession.

Introduction 1

In the face of a downturn in the economy, frugality was undergoing a revival in America. Young people were cutting up their credit cards, clipping coupons, and sticking to detailed budgets. In effect, they were adopting the very habits they had mocked during the heady days of easy credit and weekend shopping sprees. Secondhand stores and thrift stores like Goodwill and the Salvation Army were drawing record numbers of customers, while once stable retail giants like Circuit City and Sharper

Image had gone out of business (*Wall Street Journal*). In fact, retail sales during the Christmas season were down 2.8% in 2008, the lowest since 1995 (CNNMoney.com). The causes of this sea change in the spending habits of young Americans were complex and varied: high rates of unemployment, fewer jobs for recent graduates, difficulty securing credit, and that elusive factor economists call "consumer confidence."

Introduction 2

The new frugal spending habits of American consumers between the ages of 18 and 34 were endangering the very people who were trying to save money. Plagued with rising unemployment, widespread hiring freezes, and difficulty securing credit, young Americans naturally turned to their spending habits as one area they could control. They cut down on how much money they spent in restaurants, bars, and retail stores and on entertainment. As a result, usually robust Christmas sales were down an alarming 2.8% in 2008, the lowest since 1995 (CNNMoney.com). Even once stable retail giants like Circuit City and Sharper Image went out of business (*Wall Street Journal*). Although the desire to hold on to their money was logical, all this coupon clipping, budgeting, and thrift-store shopping threatened the key to economic recovery, what economists call "consumer confidence." It was clear that, if younger Americans hadn't loosened their grip on their wallets and injected some much-needed cash into the system, we would have faced far more dire economic consequences in the years that followed.

The first introduction frames the subject as an explanation of the causes of changing habits of consumption. The second introduction frames the subject as a warning that these changing habits might have caused more harm than good. Even though each introduction draws on the same basic information, and even though both do a good job of introducing the essay, they focus attention on different aspects of the subject.

You can frame your discussion by calling attention to

- the agent: a person, an organization, or a thing that is acting in a particular way
- the action: what is being done by the actor
- the goal: what the actor wants to achieve by carrying out the action
- the result: the outcome of the action

Agent
Action
Goal
Result

Introduction 2

The new frugal spending habits of American consumers between the ages of 18 and 34 were endangering the very people who were trying to save money. Plagued with rising unemployment, widespread hiring freezes, and difficulty securing credit, young Americans naturally turned to their spending habits as one area they could control.

They cut down on how much money they spent in restaurants, bars, and retail stores and on entertainment. As a result, usually robust Christmas sales were down an alarming 2.8% in 2008, the lowest since 1995 (CNNMoney.com). Even once stable retail giants like Circuit City and Sharper Image went out of business (*Wall Street Journal*). Although the desire to hold on to their money was logical, all this coupon clipping, budgeting, and thrift-store shopping threatened the key to economic recovery, what economists call "consumer confidence." It was clear that, if younger Americans hadn't loosened their grip on their wallets and injected some much-needed cash into the system, we would have faced far more dire economic consequences in the years that followed.

Select an Introductory Strategy

The ability to frame your readers' understanding of a subject is a powerful tool. By directing their attention to one aspect of a subject, rather than to others, you can influence their beliefs and, potentially, their willingness to take action.

Your introduction offers probably the best opportunity to grab your readers' attention and shape their response to your ideas. You can introduce your document using one of several strategies.

STATE THE TOPIC

Tell your readers what your subject is, what conversation you are focusing on, and what your document will tell them about it. In the following example, Eileen Ferrer and her colleagues announce the topic of their scholarly journal article in a straightforward manner (see p. 290).

> The goal and purpose of this study was to examine the role of music as a potentially stress-alleviating therapy among college students.

ESTABLISH THE CONTEXT

In some cases, you'll want to give your readers background information about your subject or an overview of the conversation that has been taking place about it. Notice, for example, how Anu Partanen sets up her argumentative essay (see p. 399).

> Everyone agrees the United States needs to improve its education system dramatically, but how? One of the hottest trends in education reform lately is looking at the stunning success of the West's reigning education superpower, Finland. Trouble is, when it comes to the lessons that Finnish schools have to offer, most of the discussion seems to be missing the point.

The small Nordic country of Finland used to be known — if it was known for anything at all — as the home of Nokia, the mobile phone giant. But lately Finland has been attracting attention on global surveys of quality of life — *Newsweek* ranked it number one last year — and Finland's national education system has been receiving particular praise, because in recent years Finnish students have been turning in some of the highest test scores in the world.

STATE YOUR THESIS

If your essay urges readers to accept an argument, an evaluation, a solution, or an interpretation, use your introduction to get right to your main point. In his analytical blog post, Scott Barry Kaufman begins by challenging a widespread belief about creativity (see p. 243).

It's a great myth that creative geniuses consistently produce great works. They don't. In fact, systematic analyses of the career trajectories of people labeled geniuses show that their output tends to be highly uneven, with a few good ideas mixed in with many more false starts. While consistency may be the key to expertise, the secret to creative greatness appears to be doing things differently — even when that means failing.

DEFINE A PROBLEM

If your purpose is to propose a solution to a problem, you might begin your document by defining the problem. The students at one university use this strategy to introduce their essay proposing more bike lanes around campus:

Surprisingly, despite the large number of students who bike to classes and work, Main Campus is severely lacking in bike lanes. We have noted with alarm the increase in motor vehicle accidents involving bikers along Stanhope Street, Broadway, and Central Street. This proposal calls for painted bike lanes, increased signage, and focused marketing efforts to ensure the safety of everyone on campus, regardless of their choice of transportation.

MAKE A SURPRISING STATEMENT

Grab your readers' attention by telling them something they don't already know. It's even better if the information is shocking, unusual, or strange. Consider, for example, how Salvatore Scibona opens his literacy narrative (see p. 137).

I did my best to flunk out of high school. I failed English literature, American literature, Spanish, precalculus, chemistry, physics. Once, in a fit of melancholic vanity, I burned my report card in the sink of the KFC where I worked scraping carbonized grease from the pressure cookers. I loved that job the way a dog loves a carcass in a ditch. I came home stinking of it. It was a prudent first career in that I wanted with certainty only one thing, to get out of Ohio, and the Colonel might hire me anywhere in the world. The starting wage was $3.85 an hour. I was saving for the future.

ASK A QUESTION

Asking a question invites your readers to become participants in the conversation. At the end of his introduction, featured writer Dwight Haynes asks a question and invites his readers to take an interest in his evaluation of programs that aim to prevent binge drinking (see p. 333).

> Over the past few decades, alcohol consumption among college students has received a great deal of attention. Despite humorous portrayals of college parties and the drunken antics depicted in movies and on television, serious concerns have been raised about health, safety, and academic issues associated with heavy drinking on campus. Most alarming, excessive levels of drinking are thought to cause between 1,400 and 1,700 student deaths each year (Jaschik, 2009). Also significant are the physical harm and violent behavior that tend to arise from heavy drinking: 500,000 students each year sustain injuries as a result of alcohol use, and another 600,000 per year report being victims of alcohol-fueled assaults, including rape (Wechsler et al., 2003). Heavy drinking has been blamed for a host of other problems as well, including vandalism, alcohol poisoning, and academic failure. Rather than waiting until after students suffer the consequences of alcohol abuse to intervene, colleges have found that preventative programs can teach better habits and help students avoid the problems caused by underage or irresponsible drinking. What kinds of approaches are colleges using to reduce student drinking, and how well do they work?

TELL A STORY

Everyone loves a story, assuming that it's told well and has a point. You can use a story to introduce a subject to your readers, as featured writer Caitlin Guariglia does for her reflective essay about a trip to Italy (see p. 162).

> Crash! The sound of metal hitting a concrete wall is my first vivid memory of Rome. Our tour bus could not get any farther down the tiny road because cars were parked along both sides. This, our bus driver told us, was illegal. He did not tell us, exactly; he grumbled it as he stepped out of the bus. He stood there with his hands on his hips, pondering the situation. Soon, people in the cars behind us started wandering

up to stand next to the bus driver and ponder along with him. That, or they honked a great deal.

PROVIDE A HISTORICAL ACCOUNT

Historical accounts can help your readers understand the origins of a situation and how the situation has changed over time. One writer compares the days of Henry Ford with the drivers of today to introduce her informative essay about moving toward a hydrogen economy.

> In the early twentieth century, the products of Henry Ford's assembly lines introduced Americans to the joys of the open road. Large, powerful automobiles quickly became a symbol of wealth and success. With record-high temperatures and rising tides, Americans today are being forced to take a good, long look at their choices. The SUVs, trucks, and minivans popular until recently are largely viewed as symbols of excess and environmental irresponsibility, and many consumers now prefer fuel-efficient or hybrid vehicles, like the successful Toyota Prius. In fact, some drivers have become so determined to escape their pricey dependence on fossil fuels that they've begun to seek out alternative energy sources.

LEAD WITH A QUOTATION

A quotation allows your readers to learn about the subject from someone who knows it well or has been affected by it. Featured writer James Hardjadinata prefaces his problem-solving essay with a familiar expression (see p. 385).

> As the famous aphorism goes, a dog is "man's best friend." It might not surprise anyone, then, that nearly 40% of US households own dogs, for a total population of about 72 million dogs (ASPCA). Many pet owners, however, are clueless about the origins of their beloved companions. Sadly, a surprisingly large number of dogs are likely to have started their lives in puppy mills.

DRAW A CONTRAST

Drawing a contrast asks your readers to make a comparison. Don Kusler, for example, begins his counterpoint opinion column "We Need to Continue to Invest in Solar" by acknowledging that, while renewable energy is not perfect, it does offer significant benefits (see p. 413).

> There is no such thing as a perfect energy source. Unless you're watching a sci-fi Hollywood movie. That being said, while solar and other renewable energies are not perfect, when compared to traditional energy sources they are safe, clean, inexhaustible, naturally abundant and the best way forward.

PROVIDE A MAP

The most direct way of signaling the organization of your document is to provide a map, or preview, of your supporting points in your introduction.

> This report will evaluate three approaches to treating attention deficit disorder in elementary school students: stimulant medications, training in organizational and time management skills, and a gluten-free diet.

How Can I Draft My Conclusion?

Your conclusion provides an opportunity to reinforce your message. It offers one last chance to achieve your purposes as a writer and to share your final thoughts about the subject with your readers.

Reinforce Your Points

At a minimum, your conclusion should sum up the major reasons you've offered to support your thesis statement. You might also want to restate your thesis statement (in different words) to reinforce your main point. If you didn't include an overt thesis statement in your introduction, consider stating your main point in your conclusion. Ending with a clear indication of what you want someone to think, believe, understand, or do as a result of reading your document gives you one final opportunity to influence your readers.

In his opinion column, Don Kusler summarizes his argument in favor of solar energy (see p. 414).

> We need to continue to invest in solar and other renewable resources so we can create a future for our children where energy will be naturally abundant, without the wars that we have witnessed for centuries fighting over the earth's declining natural resources.

Select a Concluding Strategy

Conclusions that summarize a document, like the one above, are common — and sometimes effective, especially when the writer has presented complex concepts. But a conclusion can do much more than simply restate your points. It can also give your readers an incentive to continue thinking about what they've read, to take action about the subject, or to read more about it.

As you draft, think about what you want to accomplish. You can choose from a range of strategies to write an effective conclusion.

OFFER ADDITIONAL ANALYSIS

Extend your discussion of a subject by supplying additional insights. In his evaluative essay, featured writer Dwight Haynes summarizes and reflects on the results of his evaluation of programs to reduce binge drinking (see p. 333).

> While social norms marketing appears to offer a strong combination of positive outcomes and ease of implementation, the environmental approach is more effective overall. Despite being more complicated and demanding more school and community resources, it delivers stronger results by involving students' entire college community. The environmental approach has a much greater scope than that of the social norms marketing approach and is suitable for schools of all sizes and types. Therefore, it has the potential to affect not only students who drink heavily because they think that's the normal thing to do but also students who either are unaware of the dangers of using alcohol or will moderate their drinking only in the face of severe consequences for not doing so. Given appropriate resources, a program based on the environmental approach to curb heavy drinking is likely to be the best choice.

SPECULATE ABOUT THE FUTURE

Reflect on what might happen next. Featured writer Ellen Page speculates about the future in her informative essay on controlling the spread of malaria (see p. 213).

> Compounded by poor healthcare systems in many of the countries faced with malaria, the overall health effects of the disease can be severe. For countries with high rates of malaria and little funding available for expensive control strategies, DDT may continue to be the answer.

CLOSE WITH A QUOTATION

Select a quotation or paraphrase that does one of the following:

- offers deeper insight into the points you've made in your document
- points to the future of the subject
- suggests a solution to a problem
- illustrates what you would like to see happen
- makes a further observation about the subject
- presents a personalized viewpoint from someone who has experienced the subject you are portraying

Journalist Carly Lewis concludes her analytical article about publicizing the names of rapists (see p. 227) with a quotation from a victim whose story she had discussed earlier.

> Late last month, the creator of the Toronto Tumblr emailed to say she was no longer in pursuit of a legally sound way to keep the list of names online. "I can't believe how hard it is to speak up about abusers," she says.
>
> "To me, the problem clearly indicates a serious barrier in the way in which we deal with sexual assault," says Downard, of rape lists. "An act like this, if it is emblematic of a dysfunction in our society, it's just the canary in the coal mine."

CLOSE WITH A STORY

Tell a story about the subject you've discussed in your document. The story might suggest a potential solution to the problem, offer hope about a desired outcome, illustrate what might happen if a desired outcome isn't realized, or simply paint a picture of the issue. For instance, author Peter C. Baker concludes his analytical article (see p. 232) with a story that captures the essence of "nerd culture."

> At the reconvened MAGFest panel, it was clear that people were speaking the same language, reveling in both the debate and the shared obsessions. Chu stayed on stage for two hours more, then announced that he wanted a drink and invited anyone who wanted to keep talking upstairs to a hotel suite. A dozen nerds skipped the video-game hall, the board- and card-game rooms, and the live-action roleplay zone and instead squeezed into an elevator together and headed up to keep debating, college-style, nerd culture's glory and excesses, its past and future. It felt optimistic, passionate, welcoming, and, sure, a little awkward: Chu's ideals made manifest. There was music playing from tiny laptop speakers, and someone had set up a disco ball. The crowd stayed for hours, nerding into the night.

CLOSE WITH A QUESTION

Questions provide an effective means of inviting readers to consider the implications of the ideas explored in an essay. Reflecting on her childhood as an upper-class African American growing up in the Chicago suburbs in the 1950s, Margo Jefferson contrasts herself and her sister with another pair of African American girls, the daughters of their family's cleaning woman, Mrs. Blake. Jefferson closes the first chapter of her memoir with a compelling question about the impact of the wealthier girls' hand-me-down clothing (see p. 143).

> [The daughters] had the same initials we did. Mildred and Diane. Margo and Denise. Mother brought us to the front door to exchange hellos with them. Sometimes Mrs. Blake left carrying one or two bags of neatly folded clothes. Did Mildred and Diane enjoy unfolding, surveying, and fitting themselves into our used ensembles and separates?

CALL YOUR READERS TO ACTION

Make a recommendation or urge your readers to do something specific. For example, you might ask them to participate in solving a problem by donating time, money, or effort to a project. Or you might ask them to write to someone, such as a politician or corporate executive, about an issue. Calls to action ask readers not just to accept what you've written but to do something about it, as featured student writer James Hardjadinata does in his problem-solving essay on puppy mills (see p. 391).

> By harnessing the power of social media, the general public, not just animal rights groups, can collectively advocate for laws and government attention, creating a future without puppy mills.

LINK TO YOUR INTRODUCTION

This technique is sometimes called a "bookends" approach because it positions your introduction and conclusion as related ends of your document. The basic idea is to turn your conclusion into an extension of your introduction.

- If your introduction uses a quotation, end with a related quotation or respond to the quotation.
- If your introduction uses a story, extend that story or retell it with a different ending.
- If your introduction asks a question, answer the question, restate the question, or ask a new question.
- If your introduction defines a problem, provide a solution to the problem, restate the problem, or suggest that readers move on to a new problem.

How Can I Help Readers Follow My Argument?

As you draft your document, think about how your readers will follow your line of argument. Surprises can be pleasant, but few readers will be able — or willing — to follow a complex argument without at least a general sense of where you plan to lead them. Clue your readers in right from the start and provide useful guidance throughout your document about its overall organization. A well-organized document will provide an introduction that states or suggests your purpose, gives enough organizational cues to help your readers follow your argument, makes them want to keep reading, and does so as concisely as possible.

Let Readers Know Where Your Document Is Taking Them

You can use several strategies to give your readers a sense of where your document is going to take them. The most direct strategy, and one that's common in most genres of academic writing, is to provide a "map" — a preview of your main point and supporting points. You can also take advantage of commonly used organizing patterns, such as pro/con or cause/effect, that readers will understand easily.

GIVE READERS A MAP

Think of maps as promises to your readers that help establish their expectations and convey your purpose for writing. If you are working on an informative document, you might promise to explain the details of a complex issue to your readers. If you define a problem in your introduction, that definition serves as a promise to present a solution by the end of your document. If you begin with a surprising argument, you are promising to back it up with reasons and evidence that will intrigue your readers. As you draft and revise your document, keep your eyes open for unfulfilled promises.

BUILD ON READERS' EXPERIENCES

Like you, your readers probably have read widely and have become familiar with some of the more commonly used organizing patterns, such as pro/con, cause/effect, or comparison/contrast. Let their experiences work to your advantage. Try to provide what readers are likely to expect where they are most likely to expect it. However, your content doesn't need to be exactly what they expect. Instead, focus on their expectations about structure and organization. If you've presented the pro side of an argument, for instance, you can be fairly confident that your readers will expect to read the con side before long.

When you anticipate and meet expectations, you'll increase readers' confidence in you. Moreover, you won't need to keep announcing what's coming next or circling around to explain why you said what you just said — they'll already know.

Keep Related Ideas Together

Structure your document logically, with related ideas presented in a sequence that readers will be able to follow. For example, if a particular idea needs to be explained so that readers can understand the rest of your argument, start with that idea. Presenting ideas in a logical order is critical, largely because readers find it challenging to rethink the order of entire sections and paragraphs so that they can follow your argument. Readers count on writers to organize clearly in the first place.

Presenting ideas in a logical order can be tricky because, while writing is linear, the relationships among ideas may not be. As you think about how to organize a complex set of ideas, think again about readers' expectations. Ask what idea your readers are likely to expect to learn about next. Or set their expectations with a map at the beginning of a section.

Your readers will also expect you to provide enough information about an idea for them to understand it. When you introduce a new idea, ask yourself how much your readers will know about it. If it's likely to be unfamiliar to them, you'll need to help them understand it, but you'll want to provide that information in a way that doesn't detract from your argument. Handled badly, explaining complicated background information just when your readers are expecting you to launch into your new idea can make your document seem unorganized. You can solve this problem by signaling to your readers why you're providing background information before moving on to your next major point.

Keep the Flow of Your Document Moving Forward

You're pursuing a particular purpose — for example, to inform your readers about an emerging style of music, to evaluate a travel destination, or to argue against new local regulations. So far, you've met expectations and even built them up, so that your readers are coming along with you gladly. Don't frustrate them now. Keep moving forward.

If you're relating something chronological, use a chronological organizing pattern (see p. 536). If you've provided a map early in your document, you can simply refer back to it. You don't have to say anything as obvious as "The third point to be made is . . ." Instead, connect one point to the next with transition words (see p. 555) or a transitional sentence. If you've kept readers clued in about what you're doing, you won't need to keep telling them. They're already expecting you to do as you said.

You can also use your readers' expectations to show them how you're moving forward. If, for instance, you're developing a pro/con argument, readers will expect you to make a claim, present evidence to support the claim, present evidence against it, and so on. Simply by following this standard sequence, you'll maintain your readers' momentum.

Be wary of cramming material in somewhere just because you can't think of a better place to put it. This can stop your readers from moving forward. If you think you might be doing this, ask whether your readers will need to know the information to understand your main point. If the answer is "no," consider leaving it out. If it's necessary but seems to be slowing down your readers, study your outline to determine whether it might fit better somewhere else.

Say Things Just Once

Writers frustrate their readers when they repeat themselves. Sometimes writers do this because they think the idea or information is important and they want to emphasize it. Unfortunately, readers are more likely to view the repetition as a waste of their time rather than as a helpful reinforcement of a key idea.

As you write, watch out for ideas that seem a little too familiar. That feeling of familiarity probably means that you're repeating yourself. When you find a familiar passage, check your outline, decide on a logical place to make the point, and make it there definitively. Then either get rid of the repetitive passage or change it so that it refers to your definitive discussion of the point.

You can refer to another part of your composition with words and phrases such as the following:

Again,	As we'll see,
As I will explain,	Here, too, it's worth keeping in mind . . .
As previously noted,	You'll recall that . . .

Some of these phrases — such as *I will explain* and *As we'll see* — work best when you're in the middle of making a point and want to introduce the new point later in your document. Keep in mind, however, that readers prefer to get information as soon as it's relevant. They don't like to wait. It's best to refer to ideas and information that you've already addressed, using phrases such as *You'll recall that* or *As previously noted.*

How Can I Design My Document?

Many writers think of designing a document as something that comes at the end of the writing process, after drafting, revising, and editing are complete. In fact, design can be a powerful tool during the planning and drafting stages. By considering design as you plan and work on your draft, you can create a document whose appearance helps you achieve your purpose, address your readers effectively, and take advantage of the context in which it will be read.

Understand Design Principles

Before you begin formatting text or inserting illustrations, consider how the design principles of *balance, emphasis, placement, repetition,* and *consistency* can help you accomplish your goals as a writer.

Balance is the vertical and horizontal alignment of elements on your pages (see the example on p. 571). Symmetrical designs create a sense of rest and stability and lead readers' eyes to focus on a particular part of a document. In contrast, asymmetrical — or unbalanced — designs suggest movement and guide readers' eyes across the page.

Emphasis is the placement and formatting of elements, such as headings and sub-headings, so that they catch your readers' attention. You can emphasize an element in a document by using a color or font that distinguishes it from other elements; by inserting a border around it and adding a shaded background; or by using an illustration, such as a photograph, drawing, or graph.

Placement is the location of elements on your pages. Placing elements next to or near each other suggests that they are related. An illustration, for example, is usually placed near the passage in which it is mentioned.

Repetition is the use of elements, such as headers and footers, navigation menus, and page numbers, throughout the pages in your document. As readers move from page to page, they tend to expect navigation elements, such as page numbers, to appear in the same place. In addition, repeated elements, such as a logo or Web navigation menu, help establish a sense of identity across the pages in your document.

Consistency is the extent to which you format and place text and illustrations in the same way throughout your document. Treating each design element — such

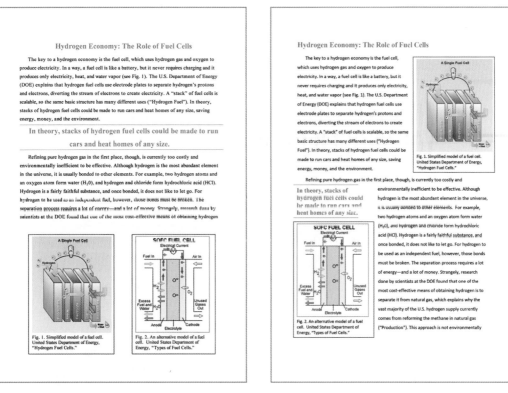

▲ Symmetrical (left) and asymmetrical (right) layouts

as illustrations, headings, and footnotes — consistently will help readers recognize the role it plays in your document and, by extension, will help them locate the information they seek. A consistent design can also convey a sense of competence and professionalism to your readers, increasing their confidence in the quality and credibility of your document.

Keep two other principles in mind: simplicity and moderation. An overly complex design can obscure important ideas and information. Using design elements moderately to create a simple yet effective design is the best approach.

Design for a Purpose

A well-designed document presents your information, ideas, and arguments in a manner that helps you accomplish your purposes.

WIRED   Zika Isn't the Mosquito-Borne Virus You Should Fear   SUBSCRIBE

| BUSINESS | CULTURE | DESIGN | GEAR | SCIENCE | SECURITY | TRANSPORTATION |

SHARE

f   SHARE 984

  TWEET

P   PIN 8

  COMMENT 2

  EMAIL

LIZZIE WADE   SCIENCE   03.17.16   7:00 AM

ZIKA ISN'T THE MOSQUITO-BORNE VIRUS YOU SHOULD FEAR

A man fumigates the Nueva Esperanza graveyard in the outskirts of Lima, Peru on January 15, 2016, to prevent the spread of the chikunguya and zika viruses.   ERNESTO BENAVIDES/AFP/GETTY IMAGES

IT WAS ON her fifth day in the hospital in Bandung, Indonesia that Stevie Bergman finally lost it. She had checked in with a fever and a headache so severe that she wasn't able to walk or eat; a friend half-carried her through the doors of the emergency room. The diagnosis: dengue, a mosquito-borne virus that is a scourge of tropical areas around the world. Over the next few days, she got weaker and weaker as her platelet count fell and her temperature climbed above 104°F. She didn't have enough energy to spend any of it worrying, or even thinking about what was happening to her.

▲ **Using images to create an emotional impact**

You might use design to achieve any of the following goals:

- **Setting a tone.** One of the most powerful tools writers have for accomplishing their purpose is establishing an emotional context for their readers. You can set a tone by using a particular color scheme, such as bright, cheerful hues, or by selecting photographs or drawings with a strong emotional impact.

- **Helping readers understand a point.** Design your document so that your main and supporting points are clear and easy to understand. Headings or pull quotes can call your readers' attention to central ideas and information. To introduce a main point, you might use a contrasting font or color to signal its importance. To highlight a definition or an example, you might enclose it inside a border or place the passage in a pull quote. You can also help readers understand a point by using illustrations.

- **Convincing readers to accept a point.** The key to convincing readers is providing them with appropriate, relevant evidence. Drawing on the principles of emphasis and placement, you can use illustrations, marginal glosses, pull quotes, and bulleted lists to highlight that evidence.

- **Clarifying complex concepts.** Sometimes a picture really is worth a thousand words. Rather than attempting to explain a complex concept using text alone, add an illustration. A well-chosen, well-placed photograph, flowchart, diagram, or table can define a complex concept such as photosynthesis in far less space, and in many cases far more effectively, than a long passage of text can. Bulleted and numbered lists can do the same.

Design for Your Readers

A well-designed document helps readers understand its organization, locate information and ideas, and recognize the function of its different parts. It is also easy on your readers' eyes: readers working with a well-designed document will not have to strain to read the text or discern illustrations. Use document design to do the following.

Help readers understand the organization of a document Use headings and subheadings to signal the content of each part of the document. Keep in mind the design principles of emphasis and consistency: format your headings in a consistent manner that helps them stand out from other parts of the document.

Help readers locate information and ideas Many longer print documents use tables of contents and indexes to help readers find key points. Websites and multimodal essays (see Chapter 19) typically provide a mix of menus and navigation headers and footers to help readers move around the site. You can distinguish these navigation aids from the surrounding text by using bordered or shaded boxes or contrasting fonts or colors.

Help readers recognize the function of parts of a document If you include passages that differ from the main text of your document, such as sidebars and "For More Information" sections, help readers understand their function by designing them to stand out visually. Using emphasis, you might design a sidebar with a shaded or colored box or format a list of related readings or Web links in a contrasting font or color.

> Use of a contrasting font and color helps readers understand the document's organization.

Jenna Alberter
Professor Garcia
AR414
27 April 2013

Images of Women in Seventeenth-Century Dutch Art and Literature

Artists and their artwork do not exist in a vacuum. The images artists create help shape and in turn are shaped by the society and culture in which they are created. The artists and artworks in the Dutch Baroque period are no exception. In this seventeenth-century society of merchants and workers, people of all classes purchased art to display in their homes. As a result, artists in the period catered to the wishes of the people, producing art that depicted the everyday world (Kleiner and Tansey 864). It is too simplistic, however, to assume that this relationship was unidirectional. Dutch Baroque genre paintings did not simply reflect the reality surrounding them; they also helped to shape that reality. For instance, members of seventeenth-century Dutch society had very specific ideas regarding the roles of women. These ideas, which permeated every level of society, are represented in the literature and visual art of the period (Franits, Paragons 17).

The Concept of Domesticity

During the seventeenth century, the concept of domesticity appears to have been very important in all levels of Dutch society. Although hundreds of surviving paintings reflect this theme. Such paintings depict members of every class and occupation, and according to Wayne Franits, a specialist in seventeenth-century Dutch art, they served the dual purpose of both entertaining and instructing the viewer. They invite the viewer to inspect and enjoy their vivid details, but also to contemplate the values and ideals they represent (Franits, "Domesticity" 13).

Images of domesticity in the visual arts grew immensely in popularity around the middle of the seventeenth century. Although there is no definitive explanation for this rise in popularity, there is a long history in Dutch art and literature of focusing on domestic themes. In the early sixteenth century, Protestant reformers and humanists wrote books and treatises on domestic issues. Their main focus was the roles and responsibilities of members of the family, especially the women.

Alberter 2

This type of literature continued to be produced, and flourished, in the first half of the seventeenth century (Franits, "Domesticity" 13). Perhaps the most well-known and influential work of literature of this type is Jacob Cats's book Houwelyck, or Marriage. Published in 1625, this was a comprehensive reference book for women of all ages, but especially young women, regarding matters of marriage and family. Although many other similar books were being published in the Netherlands and England during this period, Cats's work was perhaps the most extensive; it even contained an alphabetical index for quick reference (Franits, Paragons 5).

Cat's How to Guide: Houwelyck

Houwelyck, which by mid-century had sold over 50,000 copies, making it a best-seller for its time, contained instruction for women on the proper behavior for the six stages of life: Maiden, Sweetheart, Bride, Housewife, Mother, and Widow. It is particularly telling that these stages of life were defined in reference to the roles of men. Although Cats's book specifically addressed women, it had implications for men as well (Westermann 119). According to Cats, by laying out the roles and duties of the woman, his book "encompasses also the masculine counter-duties" (qtd. in Westermann 119).

The illustration on the title page of the first edition of Cats's work shows what was considered the ideal role for a woman at this time. Created by Adriaen van de Venne, Stages of Life (Fig. 1) depicts several figural groups arranged on a hill. It shows life as a large hill, with marriage as its pinnacle, and then heading down toward widowhood and death (Westermann 120). This depiction seems to reflect the expectations society held for its women—that a woman's goal in life should be to provide a man with a good, proper wife and, once that duty has been fulfilled, to wait dutifully for death.

Images of young women are numerous in the visual art of this period. Gerard Dou's Portrait of a Young Woman (Fig. 2) exemplifies this type of work. This painting demonstrates that portraiture was highly influenced by contemporary ideals of feminine virtue. The young woman's pose is passive, self-contained, and somewhat rigid, communicating her dignity, humility, and modesty, which were all considered very important in a young girl. She holds a songbook in her lap, which not only indicated her skill in the arts but was also considered a symbol of docility. Near her rest

▲ **Headings and subheadings in an essay**

Design to Address Genre Conventions

Genres are characterized not only by distinctive writing styles, types of evidence, and organizing patterns but also by distinctive types of design. An article in a magazine such as *Time* or *Rolling Stone*, for example, is characterized by the use of columns, headings and subheadings, pull quotes, and illustrations, while an academic essay is characterized by wide margins, double-spaced lines, and comparatively restrained use of color and illustrations. Your readers will expect your document to be similar in design to other examples of that genre. This doesn't mean that you can't depart from those conventions should the need arise, but it does mean that you should take readers' expectations into account as you design your document.

Use Design Elements Effectively

Become familiar with the range of design elements at your disposal. Then you can decide which of these options to use as you design your document. These elements include fonts, line spacing, and alignment; page layout strategies; color, shading, borders, and rules; illustrations; and navigation tools.

USE FONTS, LINE SPACING, AND ALIGNMENT

Font, line spacing, and alignment choices are the most common design decisions that writers make. They are also among the most important, since poor choices can make a document difficult to read. The examples on pages 576–577 provide an overview of the key features of fonts as well as the uses of fonts, line spacing, and alignment.

Style: the format of the font, such as regular body text, *italics*, **bold**, and ***bold italics***.

Effect: changes made to a particular font, such as underline, ~~strikethrough~~, ALL CAPS, SMALL CAPS, superscript[33], and subscript[34].

Typeface: the design of a particular font, such as Times New Roman or Calibri.

Aa Bb Cc

Times New Roman (serif)

Helvetica (sans serif, bold italic)

Courier (fixed-width serif)

Size: Font size is typically measured in points, with 72 points per inch. Body text is usually 10-point or 12-point.

▲ Font basics

Category: *Serif* fonts have small brush strokes or lines at the end of each stroke, are considered easier to read, and are often used for body text. *Sans-serif* fonts lack serifs and are often used for headings and subheadings. Other categories include *decorative* (Limehouse Roman, **Mambo Bold**) and *symbol* (Wingding: ).

Width: Letters in fixed-width fonts, such as Courier, have the same width; these fonts are useful for displaying columns of numbers. Letters in variable-width fonts, such as Times New Roman and Helvetica, have different widths; these fonts are better suited to body text and headings.

Line spacing refers to the amount of space between lines of text. Larger line spacing appears easier to read, so you'll often find increased line spacing in introductory paragraphs, executive summaries (which provide an overview of a longer document), and sidebars (see p. 577).

When text is crammed together vertically, it is difficult to read and to add comments. Keep this in mind if you are creating a document such as an essay on which someone else might write comments.

Alignment refers to the horizontal arrangement of text and illustrations (such as photos and drawings). You can select four types of alignment.

- **Left alignment** has a straight left margin and a "ragged" right margin; it is typically the easiest to read.
- **Right alignment** has a straight right margin and a ragged left margin.
- **Centered alignment** is seldom used for body text but can make headings stand out.
- **Justified alignment** has straight alignment on both the left and right margins. It adds a polished look and can be effective in documents that use columns — but it also produces irregular word spacing and hyphenation, which can slow the reading process.

Fonts are a complete set of type of a particular size and typeface. As you choose fonts, consider the following:

- **Select fonts that are easy to read.** For body text, avoid decorative fonts and italics.
- **Select fonts that complement each other.** A serif body font, such as Times New Roman or Garamond, works well with a sans-serif heading font, such as Arial, Helvetica, or Calibri.
- **Exercise restraint.** Generally, use no more than four different fonts in a document.

FOOD FOR THOUGHT

Metabolize This

If you believe recent claims that you can exercise away junk food, think again.

BY JULIA LURIE

At elementary schools nationwide, a health curriculum called Energy Balance 101 has taught 28 million kids a seemingly simple concept: In order to stay fit, all we need to do is balance the food we eat with exercise. Calories in, calories out.

Sensible enough, right? But there's something odd about the curriculum: Not once does it suggest ditching junk food—in fact, the lesson plan explicitly says, "There are no good foods or bad foods!"

Energy Balance 101's approach isn't surprising when you consider the source. The group behind it is the Healthy Weight Commitment Foundation, a coalition co-founded and bankrolled by food corporations like PepsiCo, Coca-Cola, and Hershey's. In addition to schools, the group, which claims its funders do not influence its curricula, has also developed similar programs for a wide variety of organizations, including the Girl Scouts and the National Head Start Association. And Energy Balance 101 isn't the only exercise campaign supported by junk-food companies. Earlier this year, Coca-Cola came under scrutiny after the *New York Times* revealed that the company had provided another $1.5 million in seed funding to start the Global Energy Balance Network, a think tank devoted to promoting research dedicated to the concept that all calories are created equal. McDonald's has marketed energy balance for years; in 2005, with the rollout of a new jingle ("It's what I eat and what I do…I'm lovin' it"), then-CEO Jim Skinner said, "One of the best things we can do is communicate the importance of energy balance in an engaging and simple way." The most recent corporate social responsibility report of Yum! Brands, the parent of Taco Bell, Pizza Hut, and KFC, reads, "We believe that all of our food can be part of a balanced lifestyle if eaten in moderation and balanced with exercise."

Yet study after study shows that not all calories are created equal, because our bodies metabolize them differently. Take sugar. Virtually every cell in the body contains enzymes that can turn glucose–the sugar in starches like bread and potatoes–into energy. But only the liver has the proteins necessary to do the same for fructose–the stuff that makes table sugar and high-fructose corn syrup so sweet. When the liver is forced to metabolize lots of fructose at once, much of it is converted to fat, leaving us hungry. "It's like what the IRS does to your paycheck: gone before you had the chance to burn it," says Robert Lustig, a pediatric neuroendocrinologist at the University of California-San Francisco. Plus, sugar doesn't trigger the hormone that tells us we're full, so we tend to overeat when we have sweet foods and drinks. Over time, Lustig says, that process of overwhelming the liver drives illnesses from diabetes to heart disease. A 2013 study by Lustig and his colleagues examined data on food availability and diabetes prevalence across the world, and found that while eating an extra 150 calories per day wasn't associated with an increase in diabetes, eating an extra 150 calories of *sugar* per day was correlated with an elevenfold increase in diabetes rates. A similar concept applies to fats. Unsaturated fats–the kind present in olive oil, fish, and avocados–reduce the risk of heart disease, while saturated fats–like those in burgers and fries–do the opposite.

Of course, that fact is exactly what junk-food companies gloss over in programs like Energy Balance 101. "By focusing on calories," Lustig says, "they're basically saying…it's your fault. It's a great way to absolve themselves of culpability." ■

BY FOCUSING ON CALORIES, COMPANIES ARE BASICALLY SAYING, "IT'S YOUR FAULT."

Minutes of Jogging Needed to Work Off...

Starbucks grande hot chocolate — Child (60 lbs.) 95 / Adult (180 lbs.) 72

Kraft Macaroni & Cheese (1 cup) 85 / 32

DiGiorno Pizza (1/4 pie) 114

Ben and Jerry's Half Baked (1 cup) 129

5 KFC chicken tenders 150

Pizza Hut Pepperoni Lovers Pizza (2 slices) 181 / 69

Taco Bell Fiesta Taco Salad 181 / 61

McDonald's Chicken McNuggets Value Meal 240

0   50   100   150   200   250

Source: USDA

For weekly bites, sign up for *Food for Thought* at motherjones.com/newsletters.

BEN VOLDMAN

Article by Julia Lurie, reprint courtesy of *Mother Jones*, November/December 2009. Illustration: © Ben Voldman

▲ Using fonts, line spacing, and alignment

Pull quotes (see p. 576) highlight a passage of text — frequently a quotation — through the use of borders, white space, distinctive fonts, and contrasting colors.

Numbered and bulleted lists (not shown) display brief passages of related information using numbers or symbols (usually round "bullets"). The surrounding white space draws the eye to the list, highlighting the information for your readers, while the brief content in each entry can make concepts or processes easier to understand.

Sidebars are brief discussions of information related to, but not a central part of, your document. Sidebars simplify the task of integrating related or supporting information into the body of the article by setting that information off in a clearly defined area.

White space — literally, empty space — frames and separates elements on a page.

Columns generally appear in newspaper and magazine articles — and, to a growing extent, in articles published on the Web. Essays, on the other hand, are typically formatted in a single column. Columns can improve the readability of a document by limiting the eyes' physical movement across the page and by framing other elements.

Margins are the white space between the edge of the page or screen (top, bottom, right, and left) and the text or graphics in your document.

Headings and subheadings identify sections and subsections, serve as transitions, and allow readers to locate information more easily.

Marginal glosses are brief notes in a margin or in a space following an article that explain or expand on text in the body of the document.

▲ Using page layout elements

Headers, footers, and page numbers (not shown) appear at the top or bottom of the page, set apart from the main text. They help readers find their way through a document; they provide information, such as the title of the document, its publication date, and its author; and they frame a page visually.

Captions describe or explain an illustration, such as a photograph or chart.

USE PAGE LAYOUT ELEMENTS

Page layout is the placement of text, illustrations, and other objects on a page or screen. Successful page layout draws on a number of design elements, including white space, margins, columns, headers and footers, page numbers, headings, lists, captions, marginal glosses and pull quotes, and sidebars. The examples on pages 576–577 illustrate these design elements.

USE COLOR, SHADING, BORDERS, AND RULES

Color, shading, borders, and rules (horizontal or vertical lines) can make your document more attractive, call attention to important information, help readers understand the organization of your document, clarify the function of specific passages of text, and signal transitions between sections. Exercise restraint when working with these design elements. Avoid using more than three colors on a page, unless you are using a photograph or work of art. Be cautious, as well, about using multiple styles of rules or borders in a document.

USE ILLUSTRATIONS

Illustrations — charts, graphs, tables, photographs and other images, animations, audio clips, and video clips — can expand on or demonstrate points made in the text of your document. They can also reduce the amount of text needed to make a point, help readers better understand your points, and increase the visual appeal of your document.

Photographs and other images Photographs and other images, such as drawings, paintings, and sketches, are frequently used to set a mood, emphasize a point, or demonstrate a point more fully than is possible with text alone.

Charts and graphs Charts and graphs represent information visually. They are used to make a point more succinctly than is possible with text alone or to present complex information in a compact and more accessible form. They frequently rely on numerical information.

Tables Like charts and graphs, tables can present complex information, both textual and numerical, in a compact form.

Other digital illustrations Digital publications allow you to include a wider range of illustrations, including audio, video, and animations, which bring sound and movement to your document.

Signal the organization of a document. In a longer print document, headers, footers, headings, and subheadings might be formatted with a particular color to help readers recognize which section they are reading. On a website, pages in each section could share the same background or heading color.

Be consistent. Use the same colors for top-level headings throughout your document, another color for lower-level headings, and so on. Use the same borders and shading for sidebars. Use rules consistently in pull quotes, headers, and footers. Don't mix and match.

Signal the function of text. A colored or shaded background, as well as colored type, can be used to differentiate captions and pull quotes from body text. Rules can also separate columns of text on a page or screen.

Call attention to important information. Color, borders, and shading can subtly yet clearly emphasize an illustration, such as a table or chart, or an important passage of text, by distinguishing it from the surrounding body text.

THE WELL-BEING BALANCING ACT

Pleasure and purpose work together

EVEN THE MOST ardent strivers will agree that a life of purpose that is devoid of pleasures is, frankly, no fun. Happy people know that allowing yourself to enjoy easy momentary indulgences that are personally rewarding—taking a long, leisurely bath, vegging out with your daughter's copy of *The Hunger Games*, or occasionally skipping your Saturday workout in favor of catching the soccer match on TV—is a crucial aspect of living a satisfying life. Still, if you're primarily focused on activities that feel good in the moment, you may miss out on the benefits of developing a clear purpose. Purpose is what drives us to take risks and make changes—even in the face of hardship and when sacrificing short-term happiness.

Working to uncover how happy people balance pleasure and purpose, Colorado State's Steger and his colleagues have shown that the act of trying to comprehend and navigate our world generally causes us to deviate from happiness. After all, this mission is fraught with tension, uncertainty, complexity, short bursts of intrigue and excitement, and conflicts between the desire to feel good and the desire to make progress toward what we care about most. Yet overall, people who are the happiest tend to be superior at sacrificing short-term pleasures when there is a good opportunity to make progress toward what they aspire to become in life.

If you want to envision a happy person's stance, imagine one foot rooted in the present with mindful appreciation of what one has—and the other foot reaching toward the future for yet-to-be-uncovered sources of meaning. Indeed,

research by neuroscientist Richard Davidson of the University of Wisconsin at Madison has revealed that making advances toward achievement of our goals not only causes us to feel more engaged, it actually helps us tolerate any negative feelings that arise during the journey.

Nobody would pretend that finding purpose is easy or that it can be done in a simple exercise, but thinking about which activities you found most rewarding and meaningful in the past week, what you're good at and often recognized for, what experiences you'd be unwilling to give up, and which ones you crave more time for can help. Also, notice whether your answers reflect something you feel that you ought to say as opposed to what you truly love. For example, being a parent doesn't necessarily mean that spending time with your children is the most energizing, meaningful part of your life—and it's important to accept that. Lying to yourself is one of the biggest barriers to creating purpose. The happiest people have a knack for being honest about what does and does not energize them—and in addition to building in time for sensory pleasures each day, they are able to integrate the activities they most care about into a life of purpose and satisfaction. **PT**

TODD B. KASHDAN is a psychologist at George Mason University and the author of *Mindfulness, Acceptance, and Positive Psychology*. **ROBERT BISWAS-DIENER** is the author of *The Courage Quotient*. Together they are coauthoring a book on a new approach to well-being in the business world.

HAPPINESS BY THE NUMBERS

.62
Distance from home, in miles, at which point people's tweets begin declining in expressed happiness (about the distance expected for a short work commute).

40
The percentage of our capacity for happiness that is within our power to change, according to University of California, Riverside researcher Sonja Lyubomirsky.

85
Number of residents out of every 100 who report feeling positive emotions in Panama and Paraguay, the most positive countries in the world.

20
The percentage of the U.S. population wealthy enough that their feelings of happiness are not affected by fluctuations in Americans' income equality.

Sources: The University of Vermont, *The How of Happiness*, Gallup, *Psychological Science*

THERAPISTS: *Interested in receiving Continuing Ed credit for reading this article? Visit* **NBCC.org**

July/August 2013 **Psychology Today** 59

▲ **Using color, shading, borders, and rules**

Psychology Today © Copyright 2013 www.psychologytoday.com

As you work with illustrations, keep the following guidelines in mind:

- **Use an illustration for a purpose.** Illustrations are best used when they serve a clear function in your document. Avoid including illustrations simply because you think they might make your document "look better."

- **Place illustrations near the text they illustrate.** In general, place illustrations as close as possible to the point where they are mentioned in the text. If they are not explicitly mentioned (as is often the case with photographs), place them at a point in the document where they are most relevant to the information and ideas being discussed.

- **Include a title or caption that identifies or explains the illustration.** The documentation system you are using, such as MLA or APA, will usually offer advice on the placement and format of titles and captions. In general, documentation systems suggest that you distinguish between tables and figures (which are all other illustrations), number tables and figures in the order in which they appear in the document, and use compound numbering of tables and figures in longer documents (for example, the second table in Chapter 5 would be labeled "Table 5.2"). Consult the documentation system you are using for specific guidelines on illustrations.

USE NAVIGATION TOOLS

Longer documents — and in particular digital documents such as multimodal essays, websites, and blogs — often include navigation tools that allow readers to move quickly from one part of the document to another.

- **Next and Previous buttons or links** allow readers to move from one part of an essay to another.

- **Internal links** help readers move from one page to a related page.

- **External links** help readers open related documents.

- **Tables of contents** allow readers of longer multimodal essays to move directly to a particular part of the essay.

- **Essay maps** help readers visualize the essay as a set of concepts, sections, or pages. You can click on part of the map to navigate to a particular point within the essay.

- **Menus** can appear on each page, listing major sections within the essay.

- **Headers and footers** provide information about the document, helping readers recognize which part of the essay they are reading and providing access to links to, for example, a works cited list and an "About This Essay" page.

What Should I Consider as I Design an Academic Essay?

Some writers might be surprised to see the terms *design* and *academic essay* used in the same sentence. They're aware, of course, that they should use wide margins, readable fonts, and double-spaced lines, and they generally understand that they should do this to help readers — typically an instructor — read and respond to their work. Beyond these elements, however, they think of design as having little or no role in their essays.

They're wrong. Thoughtful design can help you achieve your goals, address your readers' expectations, and adapt to the context in which your essay will be written and read.

Consider How Design Can Help You Achieve Your Goals

Traditionally, essay assignments have focused on the written expression of ideas and arguments. As a result, writers have tended to use images sparingly, if at all, and to make limited use of design elements such as color, shading, borders, and rules in their academic essays. Writers have also tended to avoid the use of tables and charts, perhaps thinking that these kinds of design elements would be more appropriate for genres such as reports and professional articles.

Yet these design elements can help you present complex information and ideas more clearly, distinguish between items considered in an evaluation, illustrate the aspects of a particular problem, or frame your argument by calling readers' attention to particular information and ideas. As you draft your essay, consider how the wide range of design elements discussed on pages 570–580 might help you accomplish your goals as a writer. As you consider your options, keep in mind your instructor's preferences regarding the use of these elements. If you are uncertain about your instructor's preferences, ask for guidance.

Consider Reader Expectations

Readers approach an essay with a set of writing and design conventions in mind. They expect you to make a main point, to support your point with reasons and evidence, and to identify the sources you've drawn on in your essay. They also expect you to follow generally accepted design conventions, such as the guidelines provided by documentation systems such as MLA and APA (see Chapters 23 and 24). Your assignment will frequently provide guidance on how to format an academic essay. You can also consult your instructor if you have any questions.

As you design your essay, consider how you can build on readers' expectations to accomplish your goals as a writer. You can use design elements such as fonts, color, shading, borders, and rules to help readers anticipate and more easily follow the organization of your essay. You can use tables, charts, and figures to let your readers view, understand, and analyze the information you include in your essay. If you are distributing your essay in digital form, you can link to related information, such as video clips, audio clips, animations, and data sets, or you can embed these materials directly in your essay. You can read more about how these design elements can help you on pages 570–580.

Consider Your Context

The context in which your essay is written and read can affect your design decisions in important ways. Think carefully about the resources you can use to write and design your essay. Do you own a computer or tablet? Do you have access to computers at your college or university? Do you have access to color printers? What kind of software programs or Web-based resources can you use, and how well do you know them? If you are working on a deadline, you might have limited time to learn how to use a new software program or an e-Portfolio tool. Perhaps the time required to use these resources would be better spent on collecting additional sources or revising and editing your draft.

Think equally carefully about how you will submit your essay. Will you deliver your essay to an instructor in printed form, send it as an e-mail attachment, or submit it through a course management system? Will it be included in a print or digital portfolio along with your other work? Will it be available on a blog or Web page?

Finally, consider how and where your essay will be read. Will it be read in print in a quiet office or perhaps on a bus or train during a commute? Will it be "required reading" — that is, will it get the careful attention an instructor provides during grading? Or is it something that can be put aside in favor of something else, as might happen if it were being read by a visitor to a website or blog?

Good document design can help you adapt to the contexts in which your essay will be written and read. You can read more about using design elements to adapt to particular contexts in Chapter 20.

View an Essay

The following pages are from an essay written by college freshman Gaele Lopez for his composition class. They reflect his awareness of his instructor's expectations about line spacing, margins, documentation system, page numbers, and a title page.

For another sample essay formatted in MLA style, see page 162. For a sample essay formatted in APA style, see page 213.

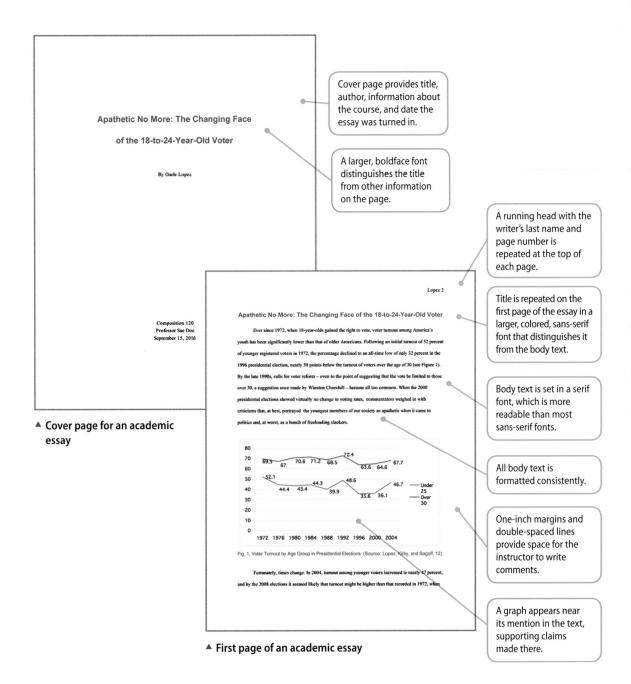

Cover page provides title, author, information about the course, and date the essay was turned in.

A larger, boldface font distinguishes the title from other information on the page.

A running head with the writer's last name and page number is repeated at the top of each page.

Title is repeated on the first page of the essay in a larger, colored, sans-serif font that distinguishes it from the body text.

Body text is set in a serif font, which is more readable than most sans-serif fonts.

All body text is formatted consistently.

One-inch margins and double-spaced lines provide space for the instructor to write comments.

A graph appears near its mention in the text, supporting claims made there.

▲ Cover page for an academic essay

▲ First page of an academic essay

Lopez 3

anger and frustration over the Vietnam war resulted in the largest turnout to date among younger voters. In the 2008 primaries, turnouts among younger voters doubled, tripled, and in some case quadrupled the turnouts recorded in any previous primary (Pew Charitable Trust, par. 2). Analysts – even some of those who had suggested raising the voting age – quickly began to investigate why younger voters were turning out in such unprecedented numbers, what impact their votes would have on the upcoming presidential election, and what this change in behavior would have on future elections.

Factors Contributing to the Change in Voting Behaviors

Why the sudden change? Or is it as sudden as it seems? Analysts Mark Hugo Lopez, Emily Kirby, and Jared Sagoff, writing after the 2004 presidential elections, pointed to "the confluence of extensive voter outreach efforts, a close election, and high levels of interest in the 2004 campaign" as factors that drove turnout among younger voters to "levels not seen since 1992" (1). They cautioned, however, that it was unclear whether the 2004 results were indicators of a significant change or simply an aberration.

It would appear, based on patterns seen in the 2006 mid-term elections and in the 2008 presidential primaries, that there really is evidence of a change. In its report on record turnout in the 2008 primaries and caucuses, the Pew Charitable Trust notes,

The research showed that college students are deeply concerned about issues, involved personally as volunteers and ready to consider voting. But they want political leaders to be positive, to address real problems and to call on all Americans to be constructively involved (par. 5).

As we look toward the fall 2008 elections, it seems clear that young voters will not only play an important role in the election, but might in fact play the deciding role. Voters such as Reid Vincent,

> A heading, formatted in blue and using a sans-serif font that differs from the serif body font, calls attention to a shift in the writer's ideas.

> A block quotation is set off by indenting the text on both sides. Quotation marks are not needed for block quotations.

▲ **Interior page of an academic essay**

Work Cited

Casper, Lynne M., and Loretta E. Bass. "United States Census Bureau Population Reports: Voting and Registration in the Election of November 1996." *US Census Bureau*, Jul. 1998, www.census.gov/prod/3/98pubs/p20-504.pdf.

Lopez, Mark Hugo, et al. "Fact Sheet: The Youth Vote 2004." *CIRCLE: The Center for Information and Research on Civic Learning and Engagement*, Tufts University, July 2005, www.civicyouth.org/PopUps/FactSheets/FS_Youth _Voting_72-04.pdf.

"Record Youth Turnout for '08 Presidential Primaries and Caucuses." *Pew Charitable Trusts*, 13 June 2008, www.pewtrusts.org/en/about/news-room/press -releases/2008/06/13/record-youth-voter-turnout-for-08-presidential -primaries-caucuses.

Vincent, Reid. Personal interview, 7 Sept. 2012.

"Why Young People Don't Vote." *The Economist*, 29 Oct. 2014, www.economist.com /blogs/economist-explains/2014/10/economist-explains-24.

> Reference page is titled "Works Cited" per MLA style.

> MLA format is used to cite sources. Entries are double-spaced with a hanging indent and alphabetized by author.

▲ **Works cited page of an academic essay**

✔ Reflect on how design can help you accomplish your purpose and carry out your role as a writer.

✔ Consider how design can help you address reader expectations.

✔ Think about how the context in which you write your essay will affect your design decisions.

✔ Think about how the context in which your essay will be read will affect your design decisions.

✔ Be aware of the design conventions associated with academic essays, including the following:

- Cover page or essay header, depending on your instructor's preferences or the formatting requirements of the documentation style you are following

- Readable body font (example: 12-point Times New Roman)

- Double-spaced lines

- Wide margins, at least one inch

- Consistent use of the documentation system you are following

- Headers and footers in a readable font distinct from the body font

- If used, headings and subheadings formatted in fonts and colors that distinguish them from the body text and show the relative importance of heading levels

- If used, illustrations labeled and placed either within the text near relevant passages or in an appendix, according to your instructor's preferences

Checklist for Designing Academic Essays

In Summary: Drafting and Designing

* Use your outline to begin drafting your document (p. 549).

* Write clearly and effectively (p. 552).

* Draft your introduction (p. 557).

* Draft your conclusion (p. 563).

* Help readers follow your argument (p. 566).

* Design your document (p. 570).

* Design an academic essay (p. 581).

Working with Genres

You might have the opportunity to decide which genre you'll use to contribute to a conversation. Or you might be asked to adapt the contents of an academic essay for presentation in another genre, such as a brochure or website. As you consider your choices, you'll find you can use a wide array of documents to reach your readers. This chapter discusses how to draft and design some of the most important print and digital genres.

How Can I Choose the Right Genre?

Experienced writers base their choice of genre on three primary factors: their purpose and role, the expectations of their readers, and the context in which their document will be written and read. One of these factors will probably be more important than the others. For example, if your readers are unlikely to treat your document seriously unless it is presented in a particular genre, such as a scientific journal article, then you would be foolish to choose another genre. To select an appropriate genre, analyze your assignment, reflect on your writing situation, and consider the resources you can draw on as you compose your document.

Analyze Your Assignment

If you are writing in response to an assignment for a class, determine whether your assignment restricts your choice of genre. If your assignment contains a statement such as *write an essay* or *create a website*, then you'll know that your instructor has a specific genre in mind.

If you find no mention of a particular genre, you should look for statements that can help you choose an appropriate genre.

- **Look for statements about your readers.** Your assignment might provide information about the characteristics of your readers, such as their ages, their educational backgrounds, and their interests. You might be asked, for example, to address the members of a particular academic discipline. If so, identify genres that are commonly used in that discipline.

- **Look for statements about your purpose and role.** Most assignments offer guidance on what you should attempt to accomplish. Words such as *inform* and *report*, for example, suggest that your purpose is to write an informative document. In contrast, words such as *convince* and *persuade* indicate that you should write an argumentative document. Although you'll find that some genres, such as essays, articles, and blog posts, can be used to accomplish both purposes, some are better suited to one purpose than to another. Opinion columns, for example, are typically used to advocate an argumentative position, while reports are used primarily to inform.

- **Look for statements about your context.** If your assignment indicates the format in which your document should be submitted, use that information to help determine which genres might be appropriate. If you are expected to submit a printed document, for example, you'll be more likely to choose an essay, a report, or an article than a website, a blog post, or a multimodal essay.

Look as well for any statements that indicate where your document might be read, such as references to particular types of publications (newspapers, magazines, websites, and so on).

- **Look for statements about limitations.** Many assignments provide information about word limits or page length. You'll also find guidance about due dates, deadlines for rough drafts or annotated bibliographies or outlines, and the type of documentation system you should use. Use this information to choose your genre. Length limitations are particularly useful, since many genres would simply be too long for an assignment that asked for a document of no more than 500 words. Similarly, some documents, such as a multimodal essay, would be difficult to complete in a short period of time.

You can read more about analyzing an assignment on page 37.

Reflect on Your Purpose, Role, Readers, and Context

If you are not given a detailed assignment, use your understanding of your writing situation to choose your genre.

- Spend time thinking about your purpose and role, and then ask yourself which genres might best help you accomplish your goals. If you are writing an article about a complex problem, for example, you'll want to read widely about the problem's origins and effects. You'll also want to find out as much as you can about how the problem has been defined, what solutions have been offered, and which solutions have been tried so far. As you learn more about the problem, you're likely to become interested in a particular solution and to want to advocate for that solution in your article. Whether you move into the role of advocate will depend on the nature of the publication.

- Reflect on the knowledge, interests, purposes, and backgrounds of your readers, and then ask what this might tell you about appropriate genres. Try to understand what your readers are likely to expect from you and what they might find familiar and easy to read. A well-written scientific report, for example, might be less effective than an informative essay or article simply because your readers might be unfamiliar with the scientific-report genre.

- Reflect on the context in which your document will be read. If you know that your readers have easy access to computers, tablets, or smartphones, you'll have more options than if you know that they can read documents only in print form.

Consider Your Writing Resources

In addition to your assignment and your writing situation, think about the tools you can use to write and design your document. In some cases, you might lack the tools necessary to create a particular genre, such as a multimodal essay or a website. If you don't have the right software or a computer or tablet powerful enough to run that software, it's probably best to choose another genre. Similarly, lack of access to a color printer might work against creating a colorful brochure or flyer.

Your choice of genre might also be influenced — in a more positive way — by what you know how to do. If you have experience using desktop publishing programs such as Microsoft Publisher or Adobe InDesign, you'll have far more options for creating a polished print or digital document. Similarly, you can create a website if you know how to use a Web editing program such as Adobe Dreamweaver or are familiar with online website creation tools such as Google Sites.

As you consider your writing resources, keep in mind the wide range of documents that can be created using word-processing and presentation tools such as Word, Pages, Keynote, and PowerPoint. These programs include templates that you can use to create a variety of genres.

How Can I Write an Article?

Articles appear in a variety of publications, including newspapers, magazines, scholarly and professional journals, and websites. Articles rely heavily on information obtained from sources such as books, websites, government reports, interviews, surveys, and observation. Writers of articles should consider several factors as they plan, draft, design, revise, and edit an article: the audience addressed by their target publication, the subjects typically written about in the publication, the style and tone used elsewhere in the publication, and the overall design of the publication.

Analyze Your Target Publication

Analyzing a publication involves asking questions about its readers, the subjects its articles address, its writing conventions, and its design. To locate a print publication, visit your library's periodicals room (see p. 492) or consult a reference librarian. You can also search for information about the publication on the Web (see p. 484) or in databases (see p. 481). To locate information about a digital publication, such as *Slate*, visit its website, conduct database searches, or consult a reference librarian.

Readers   Examine the publication as a whole to learn what you can about its readers.

- Can you find a letters-to-the-editor or comments section? If so, reading the letters and any responses from the editors and other readers might give you insights into who reads the publication and why they read it.

- If the publication contains advertisements, do they tell you anything about the readers? Who advertises in the publication? What products or services do they offer, or what issues or problems do they address?

- What can you learn about the readers from the range of subjects or issues addressed in articles and other parts of the publication?

- Can you find any information about the publisher? Can you tell whether it is a commercial enterprise, a government agency, a nonprofit organization, a scholarly or professional organization, or an individual? Does the publication have a mission statement? Does the publication describe its purpose or goals, the audience it hopes to reach, or its origins?

Subjects   Look at recently published articles in the publication. You can often find them in tables of contents, article indexes, and digital archives. Depending on the publication, you might also be able to search a full-text database (see p. 482) or search the Web for archived articles.

- What issues and subjects do the articles address?

- How long are the articles? Which are the shortest? Which are the longest? Where do they fall on average?

- What do you think is the purpose of the publication? Is its goal to inform, to advocate, to address problems? Or does it address a range of purposes?

Writing Conventions   Study the articles in the publication to learn about its writing conventions.

- How would you characterize the style and tone of the articles? Is the tone generally formal, informal, or somewhere in between? Are contractions (*can't, won't, isn't*) used? Are individuals identified by their full names and titles ("Dr. Shaun Beaty")?

- How are sources identified? Do the articles use an in-text citation system, such as MLA or APA (see Chapters 23 and 24)? Do they use footnotes or endnotes? Do the articles link directly to the source? Do they informally identify the source?

- What do the authors of articles seem to assume about their readers? Do they use specialized language (or jargon)? Do they expect you to know a great deal about the subject? Do you think the authors expect you to be an expert in the field to understand their articles?

Design   To gain an understanding of your readers' expectations about the design of your article, scan articles in the publication, read a few carefully, and take notes.

- Would you characterize the articles as heavy on text? Or are images, tables, charts, figures, and other illustrations used liberally? If the article is published in a digital format, does it include audio or video clips? Does it include other digital illustrations, such as animations or apps that a reader could work with?

- How is color used in the article, if at all? Does the article make use of borders, rules, and shading?

- Does the article use headings and subheadings? If so, how are they formatted? What kinds of fonts are used? Is there much variety in the fonts?

- How is the article laid out? Does it use columns? Sidebars? Block quotes?

Even the most narrowly focused publication is likely to display quite a bit of variety. Understanding your potential readers and the subjects they seem to care about, however, can help you compose an article that is well suited to your target publication.

Develop and Organize Your Argument

Your line of argument should reflect your understanding of the issues and subjects addressed in your target publication and the needs, interests, and knowledge of its readers. As in other types of documents, you should develop a main point, select reasons to accept it, and choose evidence to support your reasons (see Chapter 16). Then you should choose an organizing pattern that is consistent with your purpose and role and create a map or an outline of your argument (see Chapter 17).

Your choice of organizing pattern will vary according to your role and purpose as well as the expectations of your readers. In general, you'll find that the chronology and description patterns are often used in informative articles, while the strengths/weaknesses and costs/benefits patterns are well suited to articles that focus on analysis, evaluation, and argument. You can read more about organizing patterns on pages 536–537.

Collect and Work with Sources

The sources you choose to provide evidence in your article should reflect your understanding of the types of sources typically found in other articles in the publication. Some publications, particularly those focused on news and current events, depend heavily on field research — primarily interviews, observation, and correspondence (see Chapter 14) — and personal experience. Others, such as professional and scholarly journals, rely primarily on published work and, in some cases, original research. For a successful article, make sure that your sources are consistent with those you've identified during your publication analysis.

Draft, Design, and Review Your Article

The process of writing, designing, revising, and editing an article is similar to that used for academic essays (see Chapter 18). You'll find some differences in the areas of word choice, design, and source documentation. Your choice of language should be consistent with that of the other articles in the publication. In particular, pay attention to the level of formality (including the use of contractions and slang), the use of specialized terminology (jargon), and references to the work of other authors. Review your publication analysis to determine how you should address these issues.

The design of your article should also build on what you learned through your publication analysis. It is generally not necessary to design your article so that it mimics the layout used in the publication; the publication's editors and design staff will handle that. It can be helpful, however, to draft your article with particular design elements in mind. By placing images, tables, charts, and figures in your draft, you can gain a sense of how the article will appear to readers. By creating sidebars or setting up pull quotes (see p. 577), you can determine which points will be highlighted for your readers. Similarly, you can format your headings and subheadings in ways that mirror how they are formatted in the publication and use colors to set a particular mood or to highlight key information. Using design as a composing element can help you view your draft as your readers will, allowing you to anticipate how they are likely to understand and respond to your article.

As you revise and edit, be sure to ask for feedback from people you trust. Ask them to put themselves in the role of a reader of your target publication. If they are unfamiliar with the publication, share the results of your publication analysis with them. Depending on your purpose and role, you might choose one of the peer-review activities in the chapters in Part Two. You can also review the advice for effective peer review in Chapter 5.

View an Article

The articles that follow were published in the *DePaulia*, the student newspaper at DePaul University. Paired with photos, the articles make use of font formatting and visual elements to set a mood, call attention to key points, and convey information.

For more examples of articles, see pages 183, 287, and 345.

✔ Consider your writing situation and in particular your purpose and role.

✔ Analyze your target publication, focusing on its readers, the subjects and issues addressed in the publication, typical writing conventions, and typical design conventions.

✔ Develop and organize your argument.

✔ Collect information to support your argument.

✔ Draft, design, and review your article, keeping in mind the results of your publication analysis.

Checklist for Writing Articles

Images in the masthead call attention to articles elsewhere in the newspaper.

The masthead (title) at the top of the front page contrasts with the text and the headlines for individual articles.

Bylines are set in a bold font to differentiate them from main body text.

Captioned photos add visual interest and information.

Newspaper article is formatted in columns.

SPIRITED AWAY

Blue Demon Week is met with lukewarm enthusiasm **News, page 6**

LINCOLN LAND

Abe's lasting legacy in Chicago **Focus, page 14**

The DePaulia

Pinnacle award winner, No. 1 College Weekly Newspaper

Volume #100 | Issue #13 | Feb. 1, 2016 | depauliaonline.com

One-third of DePaul students low income

By MARIAH WOELFEL
Multimedia Editor

On the 17th floor of 55 E. Jackson Blvd., in a corner office enclosed by windows that look out onto the Chicago skyline, Division of Enrollment Management and Marketing Vice President David Kalsbeek keeps his head down, working to develop strategies to improve academic profiles of students, increase socioeconomic diversity and increase student retention rates.

On the ground, DePaul senior Abdus Saleem works not only to finish his degree, but to pay for it. His school day starts at 6 a.m., ends at 10:30 p.m., with a commute, class, homework, an hour at the gym and online job searches in between, Twitter if he's not too tired. The rest of his week is dedicated to working 40 hours at an IT company where he hopes to be hired after graduation.

This heavy workload is a tradeoff Saleem has accepted to avoid the burden of student debt. Instead of taking on loans, Saleem relies on federal and state grants — money that doesn't need to be paid back — to offset the rising costs of a college degree.

He's not alone. Saleem is part of 34 percent of DePaul's student body that is eligible for and receives the federal Pell Grant, and is therefore considered by the Department of Education to be low-income.

When compared to other private, four-year research institutions, this 34 percent is somewhat high. Out of 101 universities in that same category, with the No.1 university enrolling 70.8 percent low-income students, DePaul holds its spot at number 20.

But when Pell Grants were instituted in 1965 to help low-income students pay for college, the average cost of four-year university tuition, room and board was around $2,000.

Today, tuition skyrockets past $30,000 at private universities, and even with federal and state grants and scholarships, United States college tuition still far exceeds that of universities abroad, and that which students, specifically low-income students, can afford.

And when there is a balance still owed after Pell Grants and other scholarship awards go through, many DePaul students have to make tough decisions about how they will earn or borrow the money they still owe.

While Saleem found a way to balance a full-time job in order to pay

See PELL GRANTS, page 9

CLOSE QUARTERS

REVAN LOWE-WATKINS | THE DEPAULIA

Taylor Truskowski sits in the floor of her dorm in Clifton-Fullerton, which is meant for two but currently houses three people.

Students face overcrowding in dorms

By REVAN LOWE-WATKINS
Contributing Writer

Freshman Jolie Mills came to DePaul from Michigan excited for the experience of living away from home. Like many first-year students, Mills looked forward to having a roommate and was eager to move into Clifton-Fullerton.

Hoping for a spacious room, Mills was soon notified she would be one of three roommates living in a space originally meant for two. She didn't anticipate the tight living conditions.

"We always knew there was going to be a third person in the room, but we didn't necessarily ask to be in a three-person room," Mills said. "It was hard to get situated at first, because it's a smaller room, with more people and more stuff."

Like Mills, many other students are placed in housing that isn't designed for the number of residents who are actually living in it. According to a 2015 Housing Occupancy Report, many of DePaul's dorms on the Lincoln Park and Loop campuses are over capacity.

The Clifton-Fullerton Hall by design can hold up to 333 residents. The report shows that the residential hall is holding 378 students at the moment. This brings Clifton-Fullerton in at a 114 percent occupancy rate, with 45 expanded spaces (number of occupied spaces over capacity), which add beds and appliances to the dorm rooms.

"I wouldn't really suggest like putting three people in a room that's the size of a double," Mills said. "They say it's bigger, but it's only a little bigger."

When Mills and her roommates first arrived at their room, there was barely any space for their belongings. "The room was a mess when we first got here," Mills said. The three roommates ended up having to rearrange the entire room to create as much space as they could. Even with the rearrangements, they still struggled with space creating enough space.

Mills and one of her roommates share a bunk bed a few steps away from the entrance door. Mills sleeps on the bottom

See DORMS, page 8

A BARK TO ACTION: DePaul dog group promotes advocacy

By KIRSTEN ONSGARD
Digital Managing Editor

It started as a joke: Wouldn't it be funny to create a Facebook group for DePaul students, devoted to posting pictures of dogs?

But by word of mouth and a love of dogs, DePaul Dogspotting blew up to the point where it came full circle for some of its original members.

"It got way past just us — there's a ton of people I don't know in the group," said freshman Pedro Escobar, one of the admins and original members of the group. "I had people come up to me and tell me, 'hey, do you know about this DePaul Dogspotting page? It's so cool, you should join.'"

DePaul Dogspotting now boasts nearly 700 dog lovers, who pore over photos of their favorite local pets. And the once tongue-in-cheek notion has spun off into its own animal rights student group, Animal Advocates of DePaul.

The group was founded one day on a whim, when freshmen Simon Handmaker and Emily Dunn invited a few of their friends — like Escobar, who shared a discover class with Handmaker — to join and become admins. But then, it

See DOGS, page 19

Photo courtesy of NATHALY SHAMMO

Lola, a popular dog, on DePaul Dogspotting, a Facebook group.

▲ **Front page of a student newspaper**

The DePaulia/depauliaonline.com

How Can I Create a Multimodal Essay?

As it has become easier to integrate images, audio, video, and other forms of media into essays, a new genre has emerged: the multimodal essay. Multimodal essays are characterized by their essayistic form and their use of multiple types of media. As essays, they present information in a linear sequence, one idea after another. As multimodal documents, they combine text with images, animation, sound, and/or video to establish a line of argument and support the writer's points.

Multimodal essays began appearing several years ago, most often on websites such as CNN.com and *Salon*, but also in blogs whose writers wanted to make use of images, video, and audio. More recently, publications that have focused traditionally on print have begun developing sophisticated multimodal essays. Increasingly, writing instructors are assigning multimodal essays, sometimes as original documents that incorporate images and media and sometimes as extensions of more traditional print-based academic essays.

To create a multimodal essay, build on your understanding of how to compose an academic essay, and then use digital composing tools to accomplish your writing goals and address your readers' expectations.

Build on Your Experiences Writing Academic Essays

The processes writers typically use to compose a multimodal essay are similar to those used to compose academic essays. You need to do the following:

- **Choose a written conversation** by reading widely and looking for a match with your interests, knowledge, and experiences.
- **Listen in on the conversation** by locating sources — including multimodal sources as well as those that are primarily textual — and reading them critically.
- **Reflect on the conversation** by taking notes and evaluating the information, ideas, and arguments you encounter.
- **Decide on your role** and choose a main point.
- **Reflect on your writing situation** by considering your purpose, your readers' expectations and interests, and the contexts in which your essay is likely to be read.
- **Support your main point** with reasons and evidence.
- **Organize your argument.**
- **Draft, revise, and edit your document** with your purpose, readers, and context in mind.

You can read more about the processes involved in choosing, listening in on, and reflecting on a written conversation in Part One. You can read more about the processes associated with particular roles — observing, reporting, analyzing, evaluating, problem solving, and advocating — in the relevant chapters in Part Two.

Develop and Organize Your Argument

As with most documents, you'll need to spend time choosing a main point, selecting reasons to accept your main point, choosing appropriate evidence, and making decisions about organization. With the exception of issues related to digital media, these decisions are nearly identical to those you'll face as you work on various types of academic essays. You can read more about the composing strategies associated with particular writing roles in Part Two.

Collect and Work with Sources

Multimodal essays, by definition, rely on sources such as images, animations, video clips, audio clips, and data files. Like academic essays, they also draw on information, ideas, and arguments from written sources and field research. As you work on your multimodal essay, your first concern should be identifying sources that can be used to support your main point and illustrate the positions and approaches taken by other writers. Then consider how you can use nontextual sources to bring your essay to life.

CHOOSE AMONG MEDIA SOURCES

As you consider the sources you might include in your essay, give some thought to the effect each type of source will have on your ability to achieve your writing goals, address the expectations of your readers, and adapt to the context in which your document will be read. Think about the differences, for example, between presenting a written transcript of an interview, linking to an audio clip of the interview, and embedding a video clip of the interview into your essay. Each has its advantages. A written transcript can be skimmed, while readers will need to spend more time opening and listening to an audio or video clip. In contrast, the audio and video clips would allow the reader to pick up on the speaker's tone of voice or facial expressions, neither of which can be conveyed clearly through a transcript. Similarly, consider the trade-offs between presenting a concise, well-designed table and embedding a spreadsheet containing raw data that a reader could open and work with. Better yet, think about the advantages of including the table and the spreadsheet — you'll not only allow your readers to view your conclusions as you've presented them in the table but also give them a chance to work with the data and come to their own conclusions.

PLACE AND STAGE MEDIA SOURCES

Consider how your sources will appeal to your readers and how your readers might interact with them. If your readers are actively engaged with your essay — navigating its contents, viewing images and other illustrations, following links to related sources, and so on — they are more likely to find themselves intrigued with and influenced by your line of argument.

Focus on where you'll place each media source and how you'll call attention to it. In most cases, you'll want to introduce the source before the reader encounters it in the text. In this sense, placing media sources follows the general guidelines for placing illustrations, found on page 580. You should refer to the source in the body of the text, position the source near where it is mentioned, and provide some sort of caption or figure title to help readers see the connection between it and its mention in the text.

Focus as well on how you'll call attention to a media source — that is, how you'll stage it. If a media source is a critical part of your essay, you'll want to ensure that your readers pay attention to it. A video source might be placed so that it takes up the complete width of the page, and a detailed caption or figure title might provide information that would lead the reader to view or listen to it. If the source provides only modest support, however, then you need not call your readers' attention to it. A photograph of a speaker, for example, might do little more than allow readers to connect a face to a name. In this case, the photo might simply be set off in the margin of the document or aligned along the right side of a paragraph.

IMPORT OR LINK TO MEDIA SOURCES

Multimodal essays can include complete files downloaded from media sources, as would be the case if you placed a photograph in your essay, or they can link to media sources, as you might do if you wanted your readers to play a YouTube video. When you import a file into your essay, the file is literally saved within your essay. In contrast, when you link to a file, as you might do if you used the "embed code" that YouTube provides for its videos, the link sends your readers to a source on a website or some other sort of network location.

Your decisions about importing a file versus linking to it will depend on factors such as design, the length of time you want your essay to be available, concerns about file size, the software you will use to create your essay, and copyright restrictions (see p. 518).

Consider the following factors as you decide whether to import or link to a media source.

- **Design.** Importing sources gives you the highest degree of control over the appearance and behavior of the media source, while linking allows you to minimize the file size of your essay and often allows you to ensure that all media elements will play properly when they are opened.

- **Availability.** If your essay will continue to be available to readers for a lengthy period of time, as might be the case if you are publishing it on a website or in a blog, you need to ensure that your media sources will be available even if they disappear from the site where you found them. In this case, importing the media source would be the best choice. In contrast, if your essay will be available only for a short time, as might be the case with a class assignment, your sources will probably be available long enough for your essay to be read and reviewed. In this case, linking would be a reasonable option.

- **File size.** If you import a video file, your essay might become so large that it would be impossible to send as an e-mail attachment or upload to a course management system. In contrast, if you link to your media sources, the overall size of your essay will be quite small, making it easy to distribute.

- **Software.** Your choice of composing tools (see the next section) can also affect whether you link to or import your media sources. Some software programs, including most word-processing programs and multimedia presentation tools, can import a wide range of sources, from images to audio to video to data files. In contrast, Web editing programs, such as Adobe Dreamweaver, allow only linking. Although you can certainly save your media files on a website, they will be separate from your essay, and you will need to ensure that they can be viewed with a Web browser.

- **Context.** If you know that your readers are likely to be reading your essay on a smartphone rather than on a computer or tablet with a larger screen and faster connection, you might choose an audio clip or an image rather than a video clip because it will open more quickly. Similarly, if you are uploading your essay to a course management system, you might have to work within particular file size limitations. Or, rather than importing the video into your essay, you might upload it to YouTube and include a link to it in the essay.

Choose Composing Tools

The composing tool you'll use to create your multimodal essay will affect not only *what* you can do in terms of composing, designing, and distributing your essay but also *how you think about* the essay itself. The capabilities of a particular software program allow you to envision particular types of documents. For example, if you decide to use a multimedia presentation program such as Keynote or PowerPoint, you'll most likely think of your essay as a series of pages that readers will move through in a linear manner, rather than jumping around as they might on a website. The same will be true if you choose a word-processing program, such as Word or Google Docs. In contrast, if you choose a graphics program such as Adobe Photoshop or a multimedia presentation program such as Prezi, the idea of distinct pages might not be a consideration. In this sense, as rhetorician Kenneth Burke has written, a way of seeing is a way of not seeing. The features of a particular composing tool will direct your attention to some possibilities even as they obscure others.

Keep Burke's observation in mind as you consider the wide range of software programs that can be used to create a multimodal essay:

- word-processing programs, such as Apple Pages, Google Docs, Microsoft Word, or OpenOffice Writer
- multimedia presentation programs, such as Apple Keynote, Google Slides, Microsoft PowerPoint, or OpenOffice Impress
- Web development tools, such as Adobe Dreamweaver or Google Sites
- publishing tools, such as Adobe InDesign or Microsoft Publisher
- graphics programs, such as Adobe Illustrator or Photoshop, Corel Draw or PhotoPaint, or OpenOffice Draw

As you choose your composing and design tools, consider how their distinctive features will help you accomplish your goals as a writer. A word-processing program might be a better choice than a multimedia presentation program if, for example, you plan to rely more heavily on text than on images and video. In contrast, a multimedia presentation program offers more options for including multimedia elements than do most word-processing or Web development programs.

TECH TIP: COMPOSE YOUR ESSAY WITH A MULTIMEDIA PRESENTATION PROGRAM

Microsoft PowerPoint and other multimedia presentation programs, such as Apple Keynote, Google Slides, Microsoft Sway, or OpenOffice Impress, offer a set of tools that are well suited to integrating multimedia sources with text. The Insert ribbon in PowerPoint, for example, allows you to add images, audio, video, and other media sources along with tables, text boxes, and links. To get started, create a new presentation, and then click on the Insert menu in the command ribbon.

▲ **PowerPoint Insert ribbon**

Using a multimedia presentation program to create a multimedia essay invites you to think of the essay not as a set of bulleted slides, but as a group of pages that can be filled with various types of media. If you look at each page as a blank canvas, you can design an essay with pages like those you might find in a magazine or on the Web.

Develop a Consistent Design

If your multimodal essay uses pages, ensure that they are designed in a way that helps your readers view each page as part of a larger essay. If you've watched a PowerPoint presentation, you've probably seen this idea in action. Even though each page might have radically different content — a bulleted list of information on one page, a video on another, and an image on yet another — they use the same color scheme, headers and footers, fonts, and background colors.

Regardless of the composing tool you choose, ensure a sense of continuity across your essay by using a consistent color scheme and font scheme, using background images consistently (or not at all), and placing recurring information, such as page

▲ Text, a video, and images are used on a multimedia presentation slide.

numbers and navigation tools (see p. 580), in the same place on each page. You can view how this is accomplished in the example multimodal essay below.

View a Multimodal Essay

The following examples are drawn from a multimodal essay written by five first-year seminar honors students at Columbia College Chicago: Jack Dorst, Sarah Lemcke, Lia Miller, Joe Erwin, and Izzy Ruta. The students developed their essay using WordPress, a free website development program that requires no knowledge of coding. Note their use of text, illustrations, color, headings and subheadings, and menus to clearly convey their argument about what we can do to reduce food waste.

A consistent look and feel (p. 600) is provided through the use of a common color scheme, font scheme, page layout, and page background image.

The pages are designed in an attractive, uncrowded manner, similar to a magazine ad.

A menu appears in the same location on each page.

Checklist for Creating Multimodal Essays

✔ Use your experiences writing academic essays as a foundation for your work on a multimodal essay.

✔ Reflect on your purpose and role, the expectations of your readers, and the context in which your essay will be written and read.

✔ Develop and organize your line of argument by choosing a main point, reasons, and supporting evidence. Consider your role as you plan, and consult other sections of this book that focus on composing processes related to that role.

✔ Choose your composing tools, keeping in mind their appropriateness for your writing situation and their tendency to drive design decisions in particular directions.

✔ Develop an appropriate and consistent design for your document, paying particular attention to the following:

- Consistent use of fonts, colors, shading, borders, and rules

- Larger fonts for headings and subheadings (such as 16-point Times New Roman or Verdana)

- Readable body font designed for on-screen reading (such as 11-point Calibri or Georgia)

- Placement of titles, text, and illustrations, with illustrations labeled and located near relevant text passages

- If used, transitions between pages (dissolves, page flips) that are quick and not distracting

- If used, background images and sounds that are chosen to enhance rather than obscure the elements on each page

✔ Create navigation tools such as Next and Previous buttons, links, menus, and tables of contents (see p. 580).

How Can I Create a Website?

A few years ago, the number of documents available on the Web grew larger than those available in print. Not surprisingly, writing courses have begun to pay more attention to how to write and design websites. Websites can engage readers in ways that print documents cannot — they can link directly to related sites, allow visitors to access video and audio files, and support communication among the site's readers and writers. This wealth of organization, navigation, and design options, however, carries significant planning, composing, and design challenges, such as keeping your readers focused on your website instead of inducing them to follow links to other sites.

Plan Your Site

The most important concerns to pay attention to during planning include content — the words, images, and other elements you'll include on each page — and the links and other navigation tools your readers will use to find their way to related pages elsewhere on the website.

CREATE CONTENT

Web pages can include textual information, images, audio, video, animations, linked files, and applications, among other types of material. As you consider your purpose and role, think about what you want your readers to know, do, or believe after they've visited your site. Your decisions about the content and how to create it should reflect your understanding of your writing situation.

CHOOSE NAVIGATION TOOLS

Your choice of navigational tools (see p. 580) will depend on the size and complexity of your site. To help readers navigate a website, developers typically create menus that appear on each page, and they often provide page headers, page footers, site maps, tables of contents, and search tools. They also consider how extensively to rely on internal links and links to external websites.

Design Your Site

Over the past decade, the appearance of websites has grown similar to that of magazines, with a heavy use of images and other illustrations. Writers typically design websites with many of the same considerations they apply to the pages in a magazine, choosing a consistent color scheme, formatting headings and subheadings consistently across pages, and using borders, shading, and rules in a manner similar to that of many print publications. Writers of websites, however, must also address the placement and appearance of navigation menus and digital illustrations, such as audio and video clips, animations, embedded applications, and downloadable files.

Keep the following principles in mind as you design your site:

- **Simple is better.** Less is more. Don't try to cram too much on a single page.

- **Place the most important information at the top of each page.** Readers often jump to another website if they don't easily find what they're looking for.

- **Avoid overuse of graphics.** Large images can increase the time it takes for a browser to open a Web page. More important, research suggests that readers of Web pages are drawn to textual information as opposed to graphical information — a behavior that is strikingly different from readers' typical behavior with print documents. Perhaps because so many websites use images largely as decoration rather than as sources of information (for example, news photographs, diagrams, and charts), readers typically look first at text on a Web page.

As you begin to design your website, browse the Web for sites that attempt to accomplish a purpose similar to your own. Evaluate their page designs, making note of features and layouts that you might want to use.

Create Your Site

Web developers create websites using a variety of software tools. The easiest and most straightforward options are free online tools such as Google Sites (sites .google.com), Wix (wix.com), and WordPress (wordpress.com). You can also use word-processing programs, such as Microsoft Word, which allow you to save documents in the HTML format used by Web pages. If you know HTML and CSS — the coding language and style definition specifications used to create websites — you can also create your site with tools ranging from simple text-editing programs such as Notepad to specialized Web editing programs such as Dreamweaver.

⬈ TECH TIP: CREATE A WEBSITE WITH A WORD-PROCESSING PROGRAM

Word-processing programs offer a number of advantages to people new to website development. These programs are often familiar, inexpensive, and relatively easy to use. They allow you to place and format images, video, and audio clips. They are particularly good at formatting text. And saving a document as a Web page can be done easily using the Save As command. Word-processing programs have a number of disadvantages — they're designed primarily to edit print documents and are not nearly as easy to use as free Web tools such as Google Sites — but they work quite well for simple websites and individual pages.

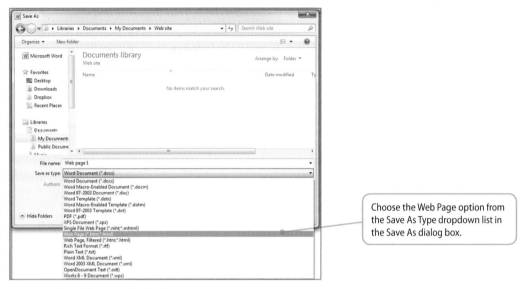

Choose the Web Page option from the Save As Type dropdown list in the Save As dialog box.

▲ Microsoft Word Save As dialog box

To create an attractive, functional website using a program such as Microsoft Word, you need to know only a small number of features and commands. The following commands can be found in the Insert ribbon in Microsoft Word:

- **Insert Hyperlink.** Links allow you to move from one Web page to another or to move to a location on the current page.

- **Insert Pictures.** You can place a picture within or alongside a passage of text. You can also use pictures as a page banner.

- **Insert Table.** You can use tables to display information, act as a container for menu items, or control the layout of your page. You can add more columns or rows as you edit the table.

- **Insert Text Box.** Text boxes are like sidebars (see p. 577). They can be placed within other passages of text or along the sides of a Web page.

▲ Microsoft Word Insert toolbar

To view your website, open the folder containing your page files and double-click on the site main page. It should open in your default Web browser, such as Chrome, Edge, Firefox, Opera, or Safari. To make changes to a page, edit the file in your word-processing program or Web editing program, save it, and then click on the Reload or Refresh button in your browser.

Put Your Site Online

If you've created your website using a tool such as Google Sites, your site is already online. If you've used Dreamweaver or a word-processing program, you will need to upload your page files and any associated media files. You will find guidance, usually in the form of help pages, from the website provider that is hosting your site.

Once your website is online, test it. Make sure that your pages open and display properly, that links work, and that media elements open properly on different computers and devices. If you are satisfied with the results of your work, share the URL with the people you want to view your site. In a few days, you'll also find that it will be available through search sites such as Google and Bing.

View Web Pages

The following figures show pages from a website that Quinn Jackson created for future writing teachers. The site was created at wix.com, which offers free websites and an easy-to-use set of authoring tools.

A navigation bar provides links to major sections.

The heading identifies the issue addressed by the site.

The site is highly visual, with easy-to-find links to its main sections.

A footer provides contact information, links to an e-mail list, and links to social-networking sites.

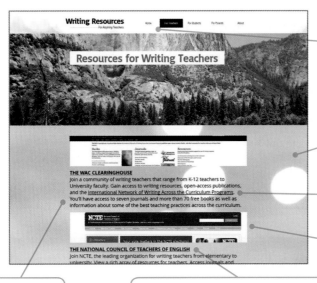

A link to the home page is provided on all other pages.

The background color remains the same, creating a consistent design.

Hyperlinks to other websites are underlined.

A photograph illustrates a key point in the text.

The body text is set in paragraphs in a readable sans-serif font.

A heading is set in boldface and uppercase font to distinguish it from the body text.

Checklist for Developing Websites

✔ Reflect on your writing situation, paying particular attention to your purpose and role as well as your readers' expectations.

✔ Plan your site. Focus on its content and navigation tools.

✔ Design your site. Focus on ensuring that your design is consistent with the design of the site on which it will appear and on the appearance and placement of elements on the page. Pay attention to the following:

- A readable body font designed for on-screen reading (such as 11-point Verdana or Georgia)

- Headings and subheadings formatted in fonts and colors that distinguish them from body text and show the relative importance of levels of headings

- Labels, captions, and pop-up flags (titles) used to help readers understand links and images

- Information presented in brief, readable chunks, using bulleted and numbered lists whenever possible

- Color used to set a mood, highlight information, and help readers understand the function of text and illustrations on the site

- Illustrations placed near the passages that refer to them

- Images kept as small (in kilobytes) as possible, while being clear and easy to see

✔ Create your site. Choose a Web development tool such as Google Sites, a dedicated Web editing program such as Dreamweaver, or a word-processing program.

✔ Put your site online.

✔ Test your site.

✔ Distribute the site's URL.

In Summary: Working with Genres

* **Choose the right genre (p. 587)**
* **Write articles (p. 589).**
* **Create multimodal essays (p. 595).**
* **Create a website (p. 603).**

Presenting Your Work

 Writers are frequently asked to share their work with others. A presentation might accompany a formal written document, such as a report or a proposal, or it might take the place of a written document. Traditionally, presentations have included an oral component — anything from a casual talk to a formal address. Today, however, writers can present their work in the form of a recorded talk, a set of multimedia slides, or a print or digital portfolio. In this chapter, you'll find discussions of strategies for presenting your work in face-to-face and online settings.

How Can I Make an Oral Presentation?

Writers frequently make presentations, lead discussions, or share their thoughts through speaking rather than writing. The ability to present your ideas orally is an important skill that you'll use not only in your courses but also throughout your professional and personal life.

Making an effective oral presentation involves much more than simply taking what you've written and reading it aloud. When you share your ideas in person, you connect with your audience through your words, your physical appearance, and your tone of voice. You rely on gestures and other forms of nonverbal communication, as well as your ability to maintain eye contact. That said, it's not simply how you say something. The success of your presentation depends on your audience's ability to follow your line of argument. Remember that most people find it easier to read (and reread) something than to hear it explained a single time. Listening to the presentation of complex information, ideas, and arguments can be challenging. Be sure, as you plan and deliver your presentation, to focus on helping your readers follow your points and establishing yourself as credible.

Consider Your Purpose, Role, and Audience

When you make an oral presentation, your most important goals are engaging your audience and keeping them interested in your ideas. As you plan your presentation, ask what you want to accomplish, what your audience expects to hear, and how you can balance your purpose with their needs and interests. The answers to these questions will shape everything in your speech from language choices to visual aids.

Narrow Your Scope

How much does your audience know about your topic? With their knowledge and expertise in mind, focus on a few key points and decide how much detail you'll need to provide to help them follow your line of argument. If you have already drafted a written document, use it as the basis for your presentation, but don't try to cover every point and every piece of supporting evidence included there.

Draw on your thesis statement (see p. 529), reasons and evidence (see p. 533), and conclusions to create a brief overview of your presentation that you can use in your introductory remarks. This "preview statement" will help your audience understand your line of argument and the organization of your presentation right from the start.

Create a Bare-Bones Outline

Once you've developed a focus for your presentation and determined its main point and general organization, you can create an outline (see p. 542). It's a good idea to begin with a basic outline that includes the following:

- an opening line that captures the attention of your audience

- a statement of your main point — typically in the form of a thesis statement

- a sentence establishing your credibility and purpose so that your audience can see that you care about and understand the issue, either through personal experience or through research, and that they can trust what you have to say

- two to four key points

- evidence to support your key points

- transition statements to guide your audience through your talk

- a conclusion that reinforces your audience's understanding of the main ideas they should take away from your talk

- a closing line or an invitation to ask questions that makes it clear to your audience that you have finished your presentation

Think about Language

Through your choice of words, metaphors, imagery, and turns of speech, you'll engage your listeners in your argument and ideas. Keep your purpose and role in mind as you decide how to address your audience. For example, if you are attempting to solve a problem, your goal might be to engage your audience personally with the problem. You might talk about how the problem affects "us" and ask them to consider what "we" should do to address it.

As you consider your language choices, bear in mind that spoken language is usually more casual than written language. If you adopt the formal tone of your academic research essay, you might sound stiff and unnatural. Remember as well the power of repetition in speeches and other oral presentations. You'll help your audience follow your line of argument by stating important points more than once and in different ways. Finally, consider the role of emotional appeals in your presentation (see p. 437). To connect personally with your audience and to engage your audience with your issue, explore the use of vivid descriptions, anecdotes, and humor. Don't rely too heavily on emotional appeals, however. To maintain your credibility, you'll want to balance pathos with logic by presenting sound reasoning and support for your argument (see p. 438).

Prepare Speaker's Notes

Although many speakers write their presentations word for word, this strategy usually does not produce outstanding results. It's better to create notes to prompt yourself as you present your points. Using notes, instead of a word-for-word speech, will force you to speak directly to your listeners, rather than read from a script. Many seasoned speakers use note cards for their speaker's notes, as they are easy to hold in one hand and are not as distracting as fluttering paper. As you prepare your notes, make sure that the text is large and easy to read so that you can view your next point with a quick glance. Your speaker's notes should include the following information:

- your opening line, written out in full, to get you started in case your mind goes blank because of nervousness

- your preview statement

- any statements that you need to give word for word, such as carefully worded statements about a controversial point or clear descriptions of a complex concept

- your supporting points and reminders of important evidence, including direct quotes, statistics, and names of important people

- transition sentences from one part of the presentation to the next

- memory prompts for any parts of your presentation that you've found yourself forgetting as you practice

- reminders to use a visual aid, such as a chart

Engage with Your Audience

When you give an oral presentation, *how* you say something is almost as important in getting your message across as *what* you say. The following techniques will help you polish your delivery.

- **Maintain eye contact with your audience.** Eye contact communicates that you know your topic and that you care about making sure the audience understands your arguments.

- **Vary the pitch of your voice.** Speaking in a monotone is the fastest way to put your audience to sleep. When you mention a startling statistic, raise your pitch. To demonstrate weight and importance, go to a lower register in your voice. Practice using vocal variety to make sure that it sounds natural.

- **Speak loudly.** You might feel as though you're yelling, but the audience will let you know (by looking surprised) if you are too loud. Speakers rarely are.

- **Articulate every word clearly.** Consonants are often dropped in casual conversation, so try to make them clearer than you would in normal speaking.

- **Slow down.** Most presenters speak too quickly. Slow down your normal rate of speaking to give the audience time to process your words. As you practice, note where you tend to speed up, and add a comment (such as "Slow down!") to your speaker's notes.

View Speaker's Notes

The following speaker's notes are from an oral presentation on the use of steroids by adolescent girls involved in sports.

1. Intro

Barry Bonds, A-Rod, Marion Jones, Lance Armstrong — what do all of these big names have in common? *(pause, wait for audience response)*

- All accused of using performance-enhancing drugs
- Used to seeing athletes break records, find out later about steroid use
- Happening for younger athletes — including young women

> Include nonverbal cues in your note cards as a reminder to interact with your audience.

> Use short phrases to cue your thoughts.

2. Establish credibility & preview
   - My background as an athlete
   - Explain why I care about the topic

SLOW DOWN!

Preview:
(1) First, I am going to talk about the positive impact that competitive athletics can have on young women.
(2) Then, I'll go over some of the negative consequences of competitive athletics on these young women, including steroid use.
(3) Finally, I want to talk about what parents and coaches can do to help create a positive athletic experience for these young women.

> Use brief reminders about nonverbal communication. Format your nonverbal cues in a different color so you don't accidentally speak them out loud.

> Write your preview statement word for word in your notes.

3. Positive impact of competitive athletics on young women

> Include your source citations. Refer to your sources to establish your credibility.

- President's Council on Physical Fitness and Exercise — ways sports impact young athletes

For the body:

- Less risk of heart disease and certain cancers as adults
- Improves:

> Use internal transition cues to provide time for you to switch to your next note card as your audience thinks about the point.

  - Immune system
  - Posture
  - Strength
  - Flexibility
  - Endurance

Internal transition: Also improves mental health

Checklist for Preparing and Delivering Oral Presentations

✔ Determine the presentation's purpose.

✔ Narrow your presentation's scope to between two and four key points.

✔ Write a preview statement.

✔ Choose supporting evidence for your key points.

✔ Create a bare-bones outline of your presentation.

✔ Prepare speaker's notes that you can read easily and quickly.

✔ Consider how the size and physical arrangement of the room will affect your ability to interact with your audience.

✔ Practice your presentation, and ask for feedback from your practice audience.

✔ Arrive early to ensure adequate time for setup.

✔ During the presentation, observe and respond to your audience.

✔ Vary the pitch of your voice, speak loudly, and clearly articulate your words.

How Can I Create a Multimedia Presentation?

As a student, you've probably seen more than a few multimedia presentations. You've probably also become far too familiar with how easily these kinds of presentations can go badly. If so, you're not alone. Search the Web for phrases such as *death by PowerPoint* and *PowerPoint boredom*, and you'll find thousands of pages that discuss — often quite humorously — efforts to ban the use of programs such as PowerPoint and Keynote.

Fortunately, PowerPoint boredom is a curable condition. Whether you are speaking in front of a group, presenting a recorded talk online, or simply sharing a set of slides, you can create multimedia presentations that engage your audience and might even bring them around to your point of view. With care and planning, you can use multimedia presentation tools to illustrate points using more than spoken words alone, allowing your audience to follow your argument more easily and better understand complex ideas.

Plan Your Presentation

A strong multimedia presentation can accompany an oral presentation in front of a group of listeners, or it can function independently. In this sense, context — and in particular the setting in which your presentation is delivered and any time limits you might have to work within — has important implications for how you pursue your writing goals.

Once you understand the context for your presentation, consider how it will shape your efforts to achieve your purpose, adopt your role, and meet the expectations of your audience. If it supplements an oral presentation, the multimedia portion should highlight your points without stealing the show. Your slides should complement rather than compete with what you have to say. You've probably seen more than your fair share of presentations in which speakers have read their slides aloud and offered little or nothing beyond the words on the slide. It is far more effective to use your slides to expand on or illustrate — not simply repeat — what you are saying out loud.

If the multimedia presentation serves as your only point of contact with your audience — that is, if it will be viewed on a computer, tablet, or smartphone — it needs to stand on its own. Make sure your slides convey your key points clearly and concisely in writing, since your audience will not be able to ask questions of you. Put yourself in the place of someone who will be encountering your ideas for the first time. Ask yourself what you'd find confusing, surprising, or interesting. Better yet, ask some friends to read a draft of your presentation. Observe their reactions to each slide, and ask them how you might improve the presentation.

Choose Your Sources

The distinguishing feature of a multimedia presentation is the wide array of sources you can use to engage with your audience. The sources you choose should support your points or allow you to distinguish your ideas from those advanced by others.

As you might do with a multimodal essay (see p. 595), consider how the differences among various types of sources — such as images, audio clips, video clips, tables, and charts — can help you achieve your purpose. An image projected on a screen while you talk is more likely to complement your words than will a video clip, particularly one that has a sound track. On the other hand, a video clip can convey far more information. If you are developing a presentation that will be viewed on a computer, tablet, or smartphone, the video clip might be more effective in getting your points across to your audience. In both cases, make sure your sources will work within the time limits you face. A video clip might be compelling and highly persuasive, but if it is too long, it will crowd out other points you want to make.

As you decide which sources to include in your presentation, keep in mind the needs, interests, knowledge, experiences, and backgrounds of your audience. Choose sources carefully. Images and video clips that one audience might view without a great deal of concern could be offensive to another. If your subject matter requires exposing your audience to disturbing images or explicit language, as might happen if you are addressing issues such as gun violence or censorship, warn your audience. If you are uncertain about the potential impact of a source, consult your instructor, a librarian, or a friend or classmate who might be similar to the audience you are trying to reach.

Choose Composing Tools

The program you choose to create your multimedia presentation will have a strong effect on its organization and design. Conventional multimedia presentation programs, such as Apple Keynote, Google Slides, Microsoft PowerPoint, Microsoft Sway, and OpenOffice Impress, organize presentations as a collection of slides ordered in a linear sequence from a cover slide to a closing slide. If you don't specify a particular layout, these programs use default slides consisting of a heading and a

bulleted list. In contrast, a multimedia presentation program such as Prezi (prezi
.com) allows you to create "zooming" presentations that can be useful for creative
purposes such as digital storytelling, while Capzles (capzles.com) arranges slides
along a timeline, which works well when your points have a chronological or
sequential structure.

Your choice of composing tool will affect not only how you conceptualize your
presentation but also the kinds of multimedia sources you can include and how they
will appear. Conventional programs such as PowerPoint offer the greatest flexibility
in the types of sources that can be included in a presentation. They also offer a wide
range of tools for linking to sites and various types of media on the Web. If you
decide to use a less conventional program, however, you need to consider not only
that program's capabilities, which might surprise and intrigue your audience, but
also its limitations in handling various types of sources.

Look for program features that can help you during a presentation. The "presenter
view" tools in conventional presentation programs allow you to see information that
is not projected on the screen, such as notes on the current slide and small images of
upcoming slides. These tools can remind you of important ideas that are related to
but not displayed on the slide and can help you keep track of where you are in your
presentation. Essentially, they serve the same function as the speaker's notes you
might use during an oral presentation (see p. 612).

▲ **Presenter view in PowerPoint**

Develop a Consistent Design

Over the past two decades, audiences in settings ranging from business meetings to lecture halls seem to have been subjected to more poorly designed multimedia presentations than there are drops of water in the ocean. Perhaps you, too, have been at some of these presentations. If so, you'll be aware of the benefits of the following design guidelines:

- Choose a color scheme that reflects the purpose and tone of your line of argument. Use bright colors, for example, for a lighthearted topic. Use neutral colors for a serious presentation.

- Be consistent in your choice of fonts, colors, and page layout.

- Use readable fonts, such as 44-point Corbel for headings and 28-point Calibri for body text. Avoid elaborate script fonts, which are often unreadable from a distance, or overly playful fonts like Curlz, which can come across as unprofessional.

- Keep text to a minimum: some general rules include six words per bullet point, six bullet points per slide, and no more than six slides of all text in a row.

- To enhance the readability of slides, use either a light background with dark text or a dark background with light text, and use a minimum of text effects (such as shadows or flashing text).

- Use audio, video, and animation with moderation. Generally, clips should run no longer than one minute each.

- Avoid the use of slow or overly complex transitions between slides.

- Avoid the use of distracting sound effects on slides or during slide transitions.

Organize Your Presentation

The organizing pattern (see p. 536) you select for your presentation should help you achieve your purpose and meet the expectations of your readers. It should also be consistent with your line of argument. If you are giving a presentation to an audience, as opposed to creating a presentation that will be viewed in digital form, you should consider other factors as well. A live audience can't refer back to what you've already presented if they get confused or forget something you said earlier. As a result, you might find it useful to summarize key ideas or information at various points in the presentation, to forecast what you'll be talking about in the next part of your presentation, to be open to questions from the audience, and even to ask for questions at particular points.

You can learn more about organizing patterns and strategies for organizing your presentation in Chapter 17.

Make Your Presentation

If you are making a presentation to an audience, you can draw on the same set of techniques used in effective oral presentations, including observing and responding to your audience, maintaining eye contact, varying the pitch of your voice, speaking loudly enough to be heard clearly, using gestures, and slowing down so that your audience can follow your argument (see p. 612). In addition, make sure that you are facing your audience and that you can advance your slides easily — either by using a slide clicker, which is similar to a computer mouse, or by standing close enough to your computer or tablet to advance the slides manually. In case your equipment fails — for instance, if a laptop loses power or an LCD display fails to work properly — be sure that you have a backup plan. You could bring printouts of your presentation, for example, or create a handout summarizing your points.

If your presentation will be viewed in digital format, make sure that you've removed any notes that you don't want your audience to see; check that the format in which you've saved the file can be read on a wide range of computers, tablets, and smartphones; and choose a means of distributing the file. You can distribute a file by placing it on a website, uploading it to a blog or social-networking site, attaching it to an e-mail message, sharing it through a service such as Dropbox, or saving it on a flash drive and giving it to people you want to view it.

View a Presentation

The following figures show slides from a multimedia presentation designed by Quinn Jackson, a first-year student who had worked on a writing project that focused on how to prepare future teachers to teach writing.

Title is formatted in a clear, eye-catching font.

PREPARING THE NEXT GENERATION OF WRITING TEACHERS

Quinn Jackson
English 402 – Teaching Writing

The name of the presenter is clearly identified.

Fonts are large and easy to read.

ASSIGNMENT DESIGN

- Stage and Explain Major Assignments
  - Focus on the Assignment's Purpose
  - Discuss the Assignment's Rhetorical Situation
  - Discuss Key Intermediate Assignments and Their Sequence
  - Identify Due Dates
  - Identify Resources
- Learn From Experienced Teachers
  - Bring in Other Voices
  - Talk about Writing About Writing

Karen Jackson, On Rhetorical Context

A video clip provides visual interest and an expert's voice to support the presentation.

FEEDBACK ON WRITING

- Determine Your Goals for the Assignment
- Choose Your Feedback Methods
- Define the Role of Peer Feedback
  - Develop Rubrics for Peer Feedback
  - Choose the Review Method
  - Establish Ground Rules
- Create a Schedule
  - Make Sure You Can Give Feedback in a Timely Manner

The speaker uses the slides to support her presentation rather than to take its place.

PEER REVIEW ACTIVITIES

- Share Your Goals for Each Activity
  - Global Concerns?
  - Supporting an Argument?
  - Clarity and Style?
- Develop Clear Guidelines
  - Guiding Questions
  - Role as Development Editor
  - Review of Comments by Teacher
- Provide Clear Feedback
  - To Writers
  - To Reviewers

A multi-level bulleted list conveys a strategy for developing peer review activities.

An illustration supports a key point.

Checklist for Creating Multimedia Presentations

✔ Create an outline of your presentation, focusing on the line of argument you want to present to your audience.

✔ Identify points that would benefit from nontextual sources such as audio, video, or images.

✔ Collect and work with sources that will illustrate or support those points.

✔ Choose a multimedia presentation program that is consistent with your context, purpose, role, and audience.

✔ Follow effective design principles regarding color scheme, fonts, and page layout, paying particular attention to the following:

- Consistent use of fonts, colors, shading, borders, and rules

- Readable fonts for headings and subheadings

- A readable body font designed for viewing on a screen

- If used, transitions between pages (dissolves, page flips) that are quick and not distracting

- If used, background images and sounds are chosen to enhance rather than to obscure the elements on each page

✔ Use multimedia elements in moderation to advance your line of argument, pointing out important information and illustrations on slides.

✔ To ensure that your slides are readable and well designed, preview your presentation on a screen similar in size to the one you will be using during your talk.

✔ Face your audience as you make your presentation.

✔ Create a backup plan in case your equipment fails. Consider using slide printouts or a handout as a backup.

✔ If you are distributing your presentation in digital format, ensure that it displays properly on computers, tablets, and smartphones.

How Can I Work on a Group Presentation?

Group presentations have become common not only in writing and writing-intensive classes but also in business, nonprofit, and government settings. The extent of collaboration can vary widely: each member of the group might be assigned to work on a different section of the presentation, or the whole group might work together — online, on the phone, or in person — to plan, design, draft, polish, revise, and edit the entire presentation. To prepare to work collaboratively on a group presentation, become familiar with the purposes, processes, and potential pitfalls of working with a team. Learning how to work together while you are a student can help you succeed on projects long after you've completed your degree.

Working Together: Learn from Past Experiences with Group Work

Most writers can look back at a group project and find something they didn't like about the experience. They might have been in a group dominated by an ineffective leader. They might have had to do far more than their fair share on a project. At the last minute, they might have been left in the lurch by someone who failed to deliver a critical part of the project. Whatever the reason, some writers prefer to work alone. Yet group work can be productive and satisfying, and most experienced writers can point to a wide range of situations in which working with other writers significantly improved their work on a writing project.

To get ready to work with other writers, reflect on your experiences with group work. Then, working with the members of your group, develop a set of guidelines that would improve the quality of group work. To carry out this activity, follow these steps:

1. Individually, spend five minutes brainstorming (see p. 41) or freewriting (see p. 42) about your experiences with collaborative work. List both positive and negative experiences.

2. As a group, discuss your experiences. Each person should note the advantages and disadvantages of collaborative work.

3. As a group, identify the most significant challenges to working together effectively.

4. As a group, create a list of guidelines that would address these challenges.

Once you've completed the activity, share your guidelines with other groups in the class. As a class, create a list of guidelines for collaborative work in your course.

Understand the Purposes of Working in a Group

Asking a group to work together reflects belief in the value of collaboration. In corporate settings, for example, working together might be a means not only of ensuring that a project succeeds but also of building a sense of togetherness and commitment among team members. In an academic setting, a group project allows students to carry out a project that a single student would find difficult to produce alone, helps them learn more about a subject, and familiarizes them with the collaborative processes they might encounter in their professional lives. In this sense, collaborating on a project might be as important as — or even more important than — making a presentation or producing a document.

Understand Potential Problems and Develop Solutions

Recognizing potential pitfalls can increase the likelihood that a collaborative project will succeed. Common problems encountered during group work range from individual concerns about participating in a group to behaviors that undermine the group's effectiveness. If you want to collaborate successfully, be aware of these problems and learn how to avoid them.

- **Some people prefer to work alone,** and they make those feelings all too clear, often to the point of insulting their classmates. Remind such people of the reasons the group is working together and the danger their attitude poses to the long-term success of the project.

- **Some people worry about losing a sense of individual worth.** Assure them that their contributions not only are important but also will be recognized as such — if not formally, then by other members of the group.

- **Some individuals will try to dominate a group,** perhaps believing that the project will fail unless they take control. Make sure at the outset of the project that everyone's ideas are heard and respected, and explain that developing a plan for the project is not a process of arguing for the superiority of a particular set of ideas so much as it is the synthesis of useful ideas.

- **Some members will find it difficult to schedule or attend group meetings.** Ensure that meeting times and locations accommodate everyone's needs. If you can't do so, have the group discuss the problem with the instructor.

- **Some members of a group will use meeting time unproductively** — at least in the eyes of other members of the group. This can cause problems, particularly when it is difficult to find time to meet or if meeting time is limited. To address this issue, be sure the group establishes and sticks to an agenda for each meeting.

- **Some group members will want to work only on what they feel capable of doing well.** In nonacademic settings, where a strong emphasis is often placed on the effectiveness of the final document, this is usually not a problem. In academic settings, however, where the goals of most collaborative projects include learning new skills and acquiring new knowledge, it is important that all members of a group take on new challenges.

- **Some members of a group won't contribute as much as others — and some won't contribute at all.** In collaborative projects for a class, you'll find that some members refuse to participate. Perhaps they assume that they can't make much of a contribution, or perhaps they're trying to save time by not participating. Regardless of their intentions, their lack of participation causes hurt feelings and might affect the overall quality of the project. Discuss as a group how you will address unequal participation.

- **Some members of a group will resent the extra time required to coordinate work on a project.** Remind these people of the reasons for working together and the benefits of doing so.

- **As the group works on a project, disagreements will arise.** As you develop ground rules for working together, consider how you'll address disagreements. Strategies include voting, discussing until consensus emerges, and seeking guidance from an instructor or a supervisor.

Working Together: Establish Ground Rules for a Group Project

In your writer's notebook, develop a set of ground rules for your group by responding to the following prompts. Share your responses with the members of your group, and agree on a formal set of rules.

1. Meetings will be held [at location or on Skype, Google Hangouts, etc.] on [dates and times].

2. Discussions will be [moderated by the same person at each meeting, moderated by a different person at each meeting, unmoderated], and notes will be taken by [the same person at each meeting, a different person at each meeting].

3. When disagreements arise, they will be resolved by _____.

4. The following members of the group will take the lead on the following activities: [list names and activities].

5. To ensure equitable contributions by each group member, we will _____.

6. Group members who do not contribute equitably will face the following consequences: [list consequences].

7. Group members who drop out of the project will face the following consequences: [list consequences].

Establish Ground Rules

Use your discussion of potential difficulties to establish ground rules for working together. These can include guidelines for selecting meeting times and locations, conducting discussions, resolving disputes, determining individual contributions to the project, ensuring equitable contributions from group members, and defining the consequences for inadequate participation. Ground rules can take various forms, ranging from an informal agreement among group members to a detailed statement signed by each member.

Create a Plan

An effective plan will define the overall goals of the project, identify key steps and deadlines for the completion of each step, establish who is responsible for specific activities, and suggest strategies for carrying out those activities.

Working Together: Create a Plan for a Group Project

In your writer's notebook, develop a plan to complete your project. Then share your plan with the members of your group, and develop a group plan.

1. The overall goal of this project is
   _____.

2. This project will require completing the following steps: [Fill out this information for each step.]

Step:

_____

Deadline:

_____

Ideas for completing the step:

_____

Responsible group member:

_____

How Can I Develop a Portfolio?

Portfolios are collections of documents, reflections on the development of those documents, and related materials such as sources, notes, outlines, and brainstorming. Portfolios are sometimes created to showcase a writer's work, as might happen when you are seeking a job or wish to share your work with friends and family. They may also be created in response to class assignments and institutional assessment plans. Some colleges and universities, for example, ask students to create portfolios so that they can measure the overall writing ability of their students.

Portfolios are typically, but not always, distributed via the Web. Some writers use programs such as PowerPoint or Dreamweaver to create digital portfolios (commonly called e-Portfolios) that can be presented on a flash drive or some other form of offline storage. Still others use free Web tools such as Google Sites (sites.google .com) and Wix (wix.com) to create websites to present their e-Portfolios.

Most of these tools allow you to add documents, develop a table of contents, and choose a design template. Some tools, such as Google Sites and Wix, allow you to make a wide range of design choices, such as choosing color and font schemes, designing custom page banners, and editing the HTML code on individual pages. As you create an e-Portfolio, you should consider a number of issues that affect design, including your purpose for sharing your work and the expectations of your readers.

Select Your Materials

Your choice of materials will depend on your purpose, your readers' expectations, and the context in which your portfolio will be read. If you are responding to an assignment for a writing course, pay particular attention to the specific requirements of the assignment. Some instructors, for example, will want you to include not only the final draft of an assignment but also your rough drafts, outlines, notes, sources, and any feedback you've received from classmates. Your instructor might also ask you to include a reflective statement that looks back over your work and writing process. This reflection often takes the form of a letter or brief essay (see p. 629). In an e-Portfolio, you could also share your reflections through video or audio clips. If you are highlighting your writing skills for a potential employer, you might want to show only your best work — or you might want to show two or three drafts that indicate how you revised and improved a draft over time.

A writing portfolio typically includes some or all of the following materials:

- your contact information (e-mail address, phone number, and/or mailing address)
- an introduction to the portfolio that addresses its purpose and contents
- a reflection on the documents in the portfolio, on your growth as a writer, and on your goals as a writer
- final drafts of documents
- rough drafts of documents, often with comments from instructors or other writers
- sources used in a particular writing project, along with any notes or source evaluations
- planning notes, freewriting and other forms of idea generation, and maps or outlines
- your comments on the work of other writers
- grades and comments from instructors

Organize and Design Your Portfolio

If you are submitting work for an assessment portfolio that your institution has required you to complete, you might have few options when it comes to organization and design. You'll simply be following a template. If you are working on a class project, you might have more freedom, but you'll certainly want to review the assignment carefully for guidance about organization and design.

As you organize and design your portfolio, think about how your readers will work with it. You should choose a single organizing pattern, such as chronology or definition (see Chapter 17), that allows you to accomplish your goals and that your readers will find reasonable. If you are creating a print portfolio, you might use a table of contents to help readers see how your portfolio is organized. You might also attach colored tabs to pages to help readers find the start of each document. If you are creating an e-Portfolio, think about providing navigation tools, such as tables of contents and menus, and about using hyperlinks to help readers move from one part of the e-Portfolio to another. (See p. 605 to learn more about hyperlinks.)

Keep the design principles of simplicity and consistency in mind (see p. 570). You should also develop a consistent look and feel for your portfolio, focusing in particular on issues such as color and font scheme, page layout, and navigation tools. Your design decisions should help your readers work easily and quickly with the materials you've included in your portfolio. In general, simple, uncluttered designs that use readable fonts, consistent colors, and consistently placed navigation tools will allow your readers to view your portfolio without distraction.

It is likely, of course, that the individual documents in your portfolio will have their own distinctive designs. Readers will expect this, and if the design of these documents is essential to their effect, you should not redesign them. However, if you are working with a set of essays in which your design decisions are less important than what you've written, you might consider reformatting them so that they follow the design you've chosen for the portfolio as a whole.

Introduce and Reflect on Your Work

Your introduction should provide a framework within which your readers can understand your work. By focusing on particular issues, such as your desire to address the needs of your audience or your ability to use sources effectively, you can direct your readers' attention to areas in which you demonstrate strengths as a writer. Similarly, your introduction can direct your readers' attention to areas in which you hope to improve, allowing them to offer feedback and advice that might help you become a stronger writer.

Reflections are often included with a portfolio, in particular in portfolios that are assigned in a writing class. If you are working on a class portfolio, be sure to review your portfolio assignment for guidance on reflection. Generally, it is useful to set aside time to write about changes in your composing processes and your growth as a writer. Your reflections can help you decide how you might share your development as a writer with your readers. This might include discussion of areas in which you are strong and areas in which you could improve. In your reflections, draw on evidence from your portfolio materials. As in other types of writing, providing evidence to support your conclusions will increase the effectiveness of your reflections.

View a Reflective Statement from a Portfolio

The following reflective statement was created by a first-year writing student who developed a portfolio that highlighted his best work over the course of two semesters of writing classes.

The introduction frames the reflection by looking to the writer's expectations at the beginning of the course.

The writer mentions the course goals.

A reflection on how the student's writing has changed during the course.

A reflection on how the student has learned to pay attention to his writing situation.

James Hardjadinata

Professor Lynda Haas

Writing 39C

1 June 2015

Portfolio Reflection

From the first day of class, I recognized that 39C was not going to be a standard writing course. Even with 39B I realized that, amidst all the rumors and scare gossip surrounding the course, it was going to be demanding in preparing students for upper division scholarly writing. Although I have always been told that I was proficient in writing, I skipped a quarter to take this class due to sheer apprehension that I could not fully meet its objectives: exploring and writing scholarly pieces using credible research and articulating strong arguments through various mediums. Before 39C my essays were more or less lackadaisical and written on the spot without much planning, using sources that were given to me, simply dumping whatever came to mind on the paper, and still achieving good grades. Entering 39C, I realized this would have to change.

As the end of the quarter draws near, I see just how right I was in these uneasy assumptions; through the various pieces of writing I have written throughout the course, my approach to writing has developed more awareness and analysis of the arguments and ideas I seek to include. Now having written the review of the literature on a topic and the advocacy essay — essays where we had to find credible, appropriate sources instead of having them spoon-fed to be used as with other classes — I realize the benefit of preplanning and structuring essays, and of being fully aware of the context and medium I am writing in. Overall, amidst the minor syntactical and formatting errors which I learned about and fixed throughout the quarter, I can say I am now much more aware of my writing process. It is no longer simply a game of word and sentence improvisation as it was before. It is now an intricate development of conscious rhetorical decisions, a recursive sequence of expanding what is being written in order to better foster persuasive arguments across various mediums and audiences.

The cornerstones of 39C, the Historical Conversations Project and the Advocacy Project, were pivotal essays that required me to dig deep in structuring the arguments I wanted to make. Gathering a large number of sources, I learned how to look for evidence to support an argument, and how to weigh the information from several different sources to develop a cohesive stance. That is, instead of having some given number of sources laid out for me as in other courses, writing these essays required starting from scratch and finding our own sources which were both pertinent to our arguments and sufficient for a scholarly audience and medium. Writing the historical Conversation Project and the Advocacy Project meant having to understand the information they presented firsthand. For me, that meant essentially annotating every single one of them, as one of our Connect assignments suggested, to even begin considering how I might want to draw from each of them for my essays. As seen throughout these artifacts, it is through engaging these sources and summarizing them that I began to develop ideas on how to structure my argument in the essays.

▲ **A reflective letter from a digital portfolio**

✔ Reflect on your writing situation, paying particular attention to the purposes of the portfolio, your readers' expectations, and the context in which your portfolio will be read.

✔ Select materials for your portfolio.

✔ Choose a tool to compose and publish your portfolio.

✔ Choose an organizing pattern for your portfolio.

✔ Develop a simple, consistent design for your portfolio. Pay particular attention to

- Font scheme

- Color scheme

- Page layout

- Navigation tools

✔ Create an introduction that calls attention to particular aspects of your portfolio.

✔ Reflect on the materials presented in your portfolio, calling attention to key issues and offering evidence to support your conclusions.

Checklist
for
Developing
Portfolios

In Summary: Presenting Your Work

✱ Make oral presentations (p. 610).

✱ Create multimedia presentations (p. 615).

✱ Work on group presentations (p. 623).

✱ Develop a portfolio (p. 627).

21 Using Sources Effectively

Using evidence from sources can strengthen your document and show how knowledgeable you've become about the conversation you're joining. In this chapter, you'll learn how to integrate sources into your document and how to work with numerical information, images, audio, and video.

Much of the information in this chapter is based on MLA style, which is commonly used in the humanities. See Chapter 24 for guidelines on APA style, which is used in many social sciences.

How Can I Use Sources to Accomplish My Purposes as a Writer?

Your sources can help you introduce ideas, contrast the ideas of other authors with your own, provide evidence for your points, align yourself with an authority, define concepts, illustrate processes, clarify statements, set a mood, provide examples, and qualify or amplify a point. You can present information from sources in several ways:

- as a quotation, paraphrase, or summary
- as numerical information
- as illustrations such as images, audio, video, and animations

As you draft your document, consider how your use of sources might lead your readers to view your issue in terms that are most favorable to your purposes. By selecting source information carefully, you can make your points more directly than you could in your own words. Calling opponents of a proposal "inflexible" and "pig-headed," for example, might signal your biases too strongly. Quoting someone who uses those terms, however, allows you to get the point across without undermining an otherwise even and balanced tone.

The following are some of the most effective ways to use information, ideas, and arguments from sources as you contribute to a written conversation about a subject.

Introduce a Point

You can use a quotation, paraphrase, or summary to introduce a point to your readers.

Quotation Used to Introduce a Point

"When I came around the corner, a black bear was standing in the middle of the trail," said Joan Gibson, an avid hiker. "We stared at each other for a moment, wondering who would make the first move. Then the bear looked off to the right and shambled up the mountain. I guess I wasn't worth the trouble." Joan Gibson's story, like those of most hikers who encounter bears in the woods, ends happily. But the growing encroachment of humans on rural areas once left largely to wildlife is causing difficulties not only for people who enjoy spending time in the wide-open spaces but also for the animals that make those spaces their home.

Paraphrase Used to Introduce a Point

A *New York Times* article recently reported that human-bear encounters in Yosemite National Park, which had been on the decline during most of the last decade, have more than doubled in the past year (Spiegel A4). Although no humans have been injured and only one incident resulted in a decision to destroy a bear, park officials point to the uptick in encounters as a warning sign that . . .

Your choice of a quotation or paraphrase will frame the point you want to make, calling your readers' attention to a specific aspect of an idea or argument and laying the groundwork for a response. Think about how the following quotation leads readers to view a public debate about education reform as a battle between reformers and an entrenched teachers union.

> Phrases such as "balked at even the most reasonable proposals" and "their obstructionist behaviors" place the blame for the problem on the teachers union.

"The teachers union has balked at even the most reasonable proposals for school reform," said Mary Sweeney, press secretary for Save Our Schools, which has sponsored a referendum on the November ballot calling for funding for their voucher plan. "We believe the November election will send a wake-up call about the need to rethink their obstructionist behaviors."

If Sweeney and supporters of Referendum D are successful, the educational landscape in . . .

In contrast, note how the following quotation frames the debate as a question of how best to spend scarce education funds.

> Phrases such as "funding of public education in real dollars has declined" and "further erode that funding" call attention to the financial challenges faced by schools.

"In the past decade, state and local funding of public education in real dollars has declined by 7.2 percent," said Jeffrey Allister, state chair of the governor's Special Commission on Education Reform. "Referendum D, if passed, would further erode that funding by shifting state dollars to private schools." As the state considers the merits of Referendum D, which would institute a statewide voucher program, opponents of the measure have . . .

Contrast Ideas

When you want to indicate that disagreement exists on a subject, you can use source information to illustrate the nature and intensity of the disagreement. The following example uses partial quotations (see p. 640) to highlight differences in proposed solutions to a problem.

Solutions to the state's higher education funding shortfall range from traditional approaches, such as raising taxes, to more radical solutions, among them privatizing state colleges and universities. Advocates of increased taxes, such as Page Richards of the Higher Education Coalition, argue that declines in state funding of higher education "must be reversed immediately or we will find ourselves in a situation where we are closing rural community colleges and only the wealthiest among us will have access to the best education" (A4). Those in favor of privatizing higher education suggest, however, that free-market approaches will ultimately bring about "a fairer situation in which the poor, many of whom have no interest in higher education, are no longer asked to subsidize higher and higher faculty salaries and larger football stadiums" (Pieters 23).

Base your choices about how to contrast ideas on the clarity and length of your sources and on the effects you hope to achieve. If you want to express complex ideas as concisely as possible, you might use paraphrase and summary. If you want to convey the emotional qualities of an author's position on a subject, use quotations.

Provide Evidence

Documents that consist of a series of unsupported assertions amount to little more than a request for the reader's trust. Even when the writer is eminently trustworthy, most readers find such documents easy to dismiss. In contrast, providing evidence to support your assertions increases the likelihood that your readers will accept your main point. Note the differences between the following passages.

Unsupported Assertion

Given a choice between two products of comparable quality, reputation, and cost, American consumers are far more likely to purchase goods that use environmentally friendly packaging. Encouraging the use of such packaging is a good idea for America.

> No evidence is provided to support the writer's assertion.

Supported Assertion

Given a choice between two products of comparable quality, reputation, and cost, American consumers are far more likely to purchase goods that use environmentally friendly packaging. A recent study by the High Plains Research Institute found that the shelf life of several biodegradable plastics not only exceeded the shelf life of the products they were used to package but also cost less to produce (Chen and Lohann 33). In addition, a study by the Consumer Products Institute found that, when made aware

> Summaries of the results of two studies provide evidence for the assertion made in the first sentence.

that products were packaged in environmentally friendly materials, consumers were more likely to buy those products (271).

Similarly, visual sources can lend support to an assertion. An assertion about the unintended consequences of military action, for example, might be accompanied by a photograph of a war-torn street or a wounded child.

Align Yourself with an Authority

Aligning yourself with an authority — such as a subject-matter expert, a scientist, a politician, or a religious figure — allows you to borrow someone else's credibility and status. Start by making an assertion and follow it with supporting information from a source, such as a quotation, paraphrase, or summary.

> New developments in computers and robotics promise to bring about significant changes in both the workplace and daily life. "We are nearing the point where computers and robots will be able to see, move, and interact naturally, unlocking many new applications and empowering people even more," said Bill Gates, co-founder and former chairman of Microsoft Corporation (2015, para. 3).

Define a Concept, Illustrate a Process, or Clarify a Statement

Writers commonly turn to information from sources when that information is clearer and more concise than what they might write themselves. For example, to define a concept, you might quote or paraphrase a dictionary or an encyclopedia. To help readers understand a complex process, such as the steps involved in cellular respiration, you might use an illustration.

Writers also use information from sources to clarify their statements. A writer might explain a point by providing examples from sources or by using quotations or paraphrases to back up an assertion.

> Studies have found connections between weight loss and coffee intake. This doesn't mean that drinking a couple of cups of coffee each day leads to weight loss. However, three recent studies reported that individuals who increased their coffee intake from fewer than three cups to more than eight cups of coffee per day experienced weight losses of up to 7% over a two-month period (Chang; Johnson and Salazar; Neiman). "It may be that increased caffeine intake led to a higher metabolic level, which in

turn led to weight loss," noted John Chang, a senior researcher at the Centers for Disease Control. "Or it might be that drinking so much coffee depressed participants' appetites" (232).

Set a Mood

You can also choose quotations and illustrations with an eye toward establishing an overall mood for your readers. The emotional impact of images of a celebration at a sporting event, an expression of grief at a funeral, or a calming mountain vista can lead your readers to react in specific ways to your document. Similarly, a striking quote, such as "The screams of pain coming out of that room will stay with me as long as I live," can evoke a particular mood in your readers.

Provide an Example

It's often better to show with an example than to tell with a general description. Examples provide concrete evidence in your document. Featured writer Caitlin Guariglia uses an example from a well-known film to illustrate a point in her essay about her family's relationship with food.

> And the obsession with eating! My grandmother feeds us constantly. My dad and I always laugh at that scene in *Goodfellas* where the mobsters show up at two in the morning after killing someone, and one mobster's mother whips up a full pasta meal for them. We know that my grandmother would do the same thing: "Are you hungry? Here, sit, eat!" Grandma holds interventions over pasta. If she is unhappy with something someone in the family is doing, she invites everyone over for pasta, and we hash it out together.

Amplify or Qualify a Point

You can use amplification to expand the scope of a point. In his argumentative essay, featured writer James Hardjadinata uses information from a source to broaden his discussion of the dangers of puppy mills.

> Several other states have adopted laws that cap the number of puppies living in any one location, a moderate solution that at the very least remediates the mistreatment of animals in these facilities due to overcrowding (Widner 235).

Qualifications, in contrast, allow you to narrow the scope of a statement, reducing the possibility that your readers might misunderstand your meaning.

James Hardjadinata makes it clear that the existing law does not require sufficient inspections of puppy mill breeders.

> Unfortunately, the AWA is poorly defined and difficult to enforce. First, as a federal law designed to regulate interstate transactions, it requires inspections of animal dealers — breeders who sell to pet stores or other outlets — only. Puppy mills who sell directly to the public circumvent these inspections (Burger 263).

How Can I Integrate Sources into My Draft?

You can integrate information, ideas, and arguments from sources into your draft by quoting, paraphrasing, summarizing, presenting numerical information, and using illustrations. As you do so, be sure to distinguish your ideas and information from those found in your sources.

Identify Your Sources

You should identify the sources of information in your document for several reasons. First, doing so fulfills your obligation to document your sources. Second, it allows you (and your readers) to recognize the boundaries between your ideas and those borrowed from sources. Third, it can help you strengthen your document by calling attention to the qualifications or experiences of the person whose ideas you are incorporating.

USE ATTRIBUTIONS AND IN-TEXT CITATIONS

Whenever you quote, paraphrase, or summarize, distinguish between your ideas and the information you obtained from your sources by using attributions — brief comments such as "according to" or "as the author points out" — to alert your readers that the point is not your own.

Writers who use the MLA or APA documentation system also provide citations — or acknowledgments of source information — within the text of their documents to indicate where borrowed material ends. These citations, in turn, refer readers to a list of works cited or a list of references at the end of the document.

Note the following examples, which use attributions and in-text citations.

MLA Style

Pamela Coke argues, "Education reform is the best solution for fixing our public schools" (22).

"Education reform is the best solution for fixing our public schools" (Coke 22).

APA Style

Pamela Coke (2008) has argued, "Education reform is the best solution for fixing our public schools" (p. 22).

"Education reform is the best solution for fixing our public schools" (Coke, 2008, p. 22).

> Attributions identify the author of the quotations.

> MLA-style in-text citations include the author's name and exact page reference.

> APA-style in-text citations include the author's name, publication date, and exact page reference.

When you acknowledge material you've borrowed from sources, try to vary the wording of your attributions. Be aware, however, that the verbs in attributions can convey important shades of meaning. For example, saying that someone "alleged" something is quite different from saying that someone "confirmed" something. The form your attributions take will depend on your use of citation style. MLA recommends present tense ("the author points out"), while APA recommends past tense ("the author pointed out") or present perfect tense ("the author has explained").

Some Common Attributions

according to	claims	expresses	reports
acknowledges	comments	inquires	says
affirms	confirms	interprets	states
alleges	declares	muses	suggests
asks	denies	notes	thinks
asserts	describes	observes	wonders
assumes	disputes	points out	writes
believes	emphasizes	remarks	

You can learn more about in-text citations in Chapter 23 (MLA style) and Chapter 24 (APA style).

PROVIDE A CONTEXT

Skilled writers know the importance of providing a context for the source information they include in their documents. It's not enough to simply put text within two quotation marks and move on. Such "orphan quotations" — quotations dropped into a paragraph without any introduction — are confusing. Worse, paraphrases and summaries inserted without context can easily be mistaken for plagiarism.

To provide a clear context for your source information, establish why the quotation, paraphrase, or summary is reliable by identifying the source's credentials. In addition, indicate how it relates to your main idea and what it contributes to the point you are making. If you don't, readers will wonder why it's there.

> Description of the findings

> Attribution identifies the source as experts.

> The writer follows APA style; parenthetical citation identifies the page number where the quotation was found.

However, Wechsler et al. (2003) analyzed trends at schools using social norms marketing and revealed that the campaigns did not necessarily decrease student drinking; in some cases, schools even reported higher alcohol consumption, according to seven criteria that measured whether students drank, how much, and how often. The team from the Harvard School of Public Health's College Alcohol Study suggested that because social norms marketing was first developed at a small school that wasn't very diverse, it might not be as suitable for schools with many different kinds of people. As the researchers explained, "Individual student's drinking behaviors align more closely to the drinking behaviors of their immediate social group rather than to the overall student population at a given school" (p. 492).

Quote Strategically

A well-chosen quotation can have a powerful impact on your readers' perception of your main point and on the overall quality of your document. Quotations can also add a sense of immediacy by bringing in the voice of someone who has been affected by a subject or can lend a sense of authority to your document by conveying the words of an expert. Quotations can range in form from brief partial quotations to extended block quotations. As you integrate quotations, you might need to modify them to suit your purpose and to fit the flow of your sentences. When you do, be careful to punctuate them properly.

USE PARTIAL, COMPLETE, OR BLOCK QUOTATIONS

Quotations can be parts of sentences (partial), whole sentences (complete), or long passages (block). When you choose one type of quotation over another, consider the length and complexity of the passage as well as the obligation to convey ideas and information fairly.

Partial quotations can be a single word, a phrase, or most of a sentence. They are often used to convey a well-turned phrase or to complete a sentence using important words from a source, as in the following example.

Weitzman (2004) notes that by changing the "contextual forces," such as the availability of alcohol, that encourage students to drink, this approach more strongly emphasizes policies that directly put a stop to excessive drinking — unlike the social norms marketing approach, which relies on influencing individual behavior (p. 187).

> Quotation marks indicate the borrowed phrase.

> Source information, including the page number containing the quotation, is clearly identified.

Complete quotations are typically one or more full sentences and are most often used when the meaning of the passage cannot be conveyed adequately by a few well-chosen words, as in the following example.

> I smiled when I read Elizabeth Gilbert's memoir *Eat, Pray, Love*. Gilbert writes, "The Neapolitan women in particular are such a gang of tough-voiced, loud-mouthed, generous, nosy dames, all bossy and annoyed and right up in your face just trying to friggin' *help* you for chrissake, you dope — *why they gotta do everything around here?*" (78).

Block quotations are extended quotations (usually more than four typed lines) that are set off in a block from the rest of the text. In general, use a colon to introduce the quotation, indent the entire quotation one inch from the left margin, and include source information according to the documentation system you are using (such as MLA or APA). Since the blocked text indicates that you are quoting directly, you do not need to include quotation marks.

> Instead of cutting education funding, states should provide more money for schools, especially now when jobs are scarce and even trained workers are eager to return to school. Patrick Callan, president of the National Center for Public Policy and Higher Education, observes:
>
> > When the economy is good, and state universities are somewhat better funded, we raise tuition as little as possible. When the economy is bad, we raise tuition and sock it to families, when people can least afford it. That's exactly the opposite of what we need. (qtd. in Lewin)

> Parenthetical citation indicates that this material was quoted in another source. In block quotations, the citation information is placed after the period.

MODIFY QUOTATIONS APPROPRIATELY

You can modify quotations to fit your draft. It is acceptable, for example, to delete unnecessary words or to change the tense of a word in a partial quotation so that it fits your sentence. Keep in mind, however, that writers have an obligation to quote sources accurately and fairly. You should indicate when you have added or deleted words, and you should not modify quotations in a way that distorts their meaning. The most useful strategies for modifying quotations include using an ellipsis mark

(. . .) to indicate deleted words, using brackets ([ ]) to clarify meaning, and using "sic" to note errors in a source.

Modify a direct quotation using an ellipsis mark When only part of a passage relates to your writing project, you might want to quote only that part in your document. To indicate that you have changed a quotation by deleting words, use three spaced periods, called an ellipsis mark (. . .). If you don't, your readers will assume that the quotation you are presenting is identical to the text found in the source.

Original Passage

> Under Congressional Republicans, however, funding to encourage community and national service through the Corporation has dropped in both nominal and real dollars. This year, the Republican FY 2007 Labor–Health and Human Services–Education appropriations ("LHHS") bill cuts these efforts $77 million (9 percent) below FY 2006 and $112.5 million (12 percent) below FY 2004, when the Corporation's funding was at its peak. In real terms, support for these volunteer programs will have been slashed 20 percent in the last four years. The result has been cuts in participation in all three national service programs.

> Source: U.S. House of Representatives, Committee on Appropriations — Democratic Staff. *House Republicans Slash National Service.* September 12, 2006, p. 2.

Quotation Modified Correctly Using Ellipsis Marks

Three periods indicate that material was deleted from within a sentence.

Four periods indicate the deletion of one or more full sentences.

> "Under Congressional Republicans . . . , funding to encourage community and national service through the Corporation has dropped in both nominal and real dollars. . . . In real terms, support for these volunteer programs will have been slashed 20 percent in the last four years. The result has been cuts in participation in all three national service programs" (U.S. House of Representatives, Committee on Appropriations — Democratic Staff 2).

Modify a direct quotation using brackets To modify a direct quotation by changing or adding words, use brackets ([ ]). If you don't, readers will assume that the quotation you are presenting is identical to the text found in the source.

The following example shows the use of brackets to change the tense of a verb in a partial quotation.

Original Quotation

> "They treated us like family and refused to accept a tip."

Modified Quotation

It's a place where the staff treats you "like family and refuse[s] to accept a tip," said travel writer Melissa Ancomi.

> Brackets indicate that the tense of a word has been changed.

Modify quotations using "sic" If a passage you are quoting contains a misspelled word or an incorrect fact, use the word "sic" in brackets to indicate that the error occurred in the original passage. If you don't, your readers might think that the mistake is yours.

Quotation Modified Correctly Using "Sic"

"George W. Brush's [sic] interest in faith-based initiatives strongly shaped his national service agenda" (Vincent 221).

PUNCTUATE QUOTATIONS CORRECTLY

Use the following rules for punctuating quotations:

- Use double quotation marks (" ") around partial or complete quotations. Do not use quotation marks for block quotations.

- Use single quotation marks (' ') to indicate quoted material within a quotation.

  "The hotel manager told the guests to 'make yourselves at home.'"

- Place commas and periods inside quotation marks.

- Place question marks and exclamation points outside quotation marks if the punctuation pertains to the entire sentence rather than the quotation. In the following example, the original quotation is not a question, so the question mark should be placed after the quotation mark.

  But what can be gained from following the committee's recommendation that the state should "avoid, without exceptions, any proposed tax hike"?

- Place question marks and exclamation points inside quotation marks if the punctuation pertains to the quotation itself.

  Dawn Smith asked a critical question: "Do college students understand the importance of avoiding running up the debt on their credit cards?"

- Place colons and semicolons outside quotation marks.

  Many college students consider themselves "free at last"; all too often, however, they find that freedom has its costs.

- When citation information is provided after a partial or complete quotation, place the punctuation mark (comma, period, semicolon, colon, or question mark) after the parenthetical citation.

  > "Preliminary reports have been consistent," Yates notes. "Without immediate changes to current practices, we will deplete known oil supplies by mid-century" (335).

- At the end of a block quotation, place the final punctuation before the parenthetical citation (see p. 641).

- Use three spaced periods (an ellipsis mark) to indicate an omission within a sentence.

  > According to critic Joe Robinson, Americans are overworked: "Ask Americans how things are really going and you'll hear stories of . . . fifty- and sixty-hour weeks with no letup in sight" (467).

- Place a period before the ellipsis mark to indicate an omission at the end of a sentence.

  > The most recent information indicates, says Chen, that "we can expect a significant increase in costs by the end of the decade. . . . Those costs, however, should ramp up slowly" (35).

Checklist for Quoting

- ✔ Identify the source of the quotation.
- ✔ Punctuate the quotation appropriately.
- ✔ Use ellipsis marks, brackets, and "sic" as necessary.
- ✔ Check each quotation against the source to be sure you aren't introducing errors or misrepresenting the source.
- ✔ Use transitions and attributions to integrate the quotation effectively into your draft.
- ✔ Ensure that the source is cited in your works cited or references list.

Paraphrase Information, Ideas, and Arguments

A paraphrase is a restatement, in your own words, of a passage from a source. Paraphrases can be used to illustrate or support a point you make in your document or to illustrate another author's argument about a subject. Writers choose to paraphrase rather than quote when a paraphrase would present the point more clearly or concisely than would a quotation from a source. Writers also choose to use paraphrases to add variety to a document — particularly when a large number of quotations have already been used — or when they find that the original passage would alter the tone or style of their document. For example, a writer of an article about a band that was purposefully pushing the boundaries of contemporary music might want to note that an important music reviewer had written, "I found this 'concert' to be a complete waste of my time." If the writer had already quoted more compelling statements from several other reviewers, however, the writer might use a paraphrase to indicate that the reviewer had found little in the band's most recent concert to recommend their music.

ENSURE THE ACCURACY AND FAIRNESS OF EACH PARAPHRASE

Your notes are likely to include a number of paraphrases of information, ideas, and arguments from your sources. Before you integrate a paraphrase into your document, make sure that it is an accurate and fair representation of the source. Reread the source, and double-check your paraphrase against it. Then revise the paraphrase as necessary so that it fits the context and tone of your document. Be sure that you have conveyed the meaning of the passage but that the wording and sentence structure differ from those in the original passage. (See pp. 82–83 for more on paraphrasing.)

INTEGRATE EACH PARAPHRASE INTO YOUR DOCUMENT

Use author attributions and transitions to help readers distinguish your ideas, information, and arguments from those drawn from your sources. Be sure to cite the source in the text and in your works cited list or references list (see Chapters 23 and 24).

In the following example, note how one writer lets readers know where his statement ends and where the support for his statement, in the form of a paraphrase, begins.

> As digital music and video gained popularity, inventors assumed that the same rules would apply to the new hardware and software they developed for digital files. Instead, the DMCA let music, computer, gaming, and other companies restrict technology and research that could have been used to get around their restrictions — including research that would have helped address computer security (Electronic Frontier Foundation).

The writer's idea

Source of paraphrase (in this case, a Web document) is cited per MLA style.

<table>
<tr>
<td>

Checklist
for
Paraphrasing

</td>
<td>

✔ Identify the source of the paraphrased material.

✔ Compare the original passage with your paraphrase. Make sure that you have conveyed the meaning of the passage but that the wording and sentence structure differ from those in the original passage.

✔ Use transitions and attributions to integrate the paraphrase smoothly into your draft.

✔ Ensure that the source is cited in your works cited or references list.

</td>
</tr>
</table>

Summarize Sources

A summary is a concise statement, written in your own words, of the information, ideas, and arguments found in a source. When you integrate a summary into your draft, review the source to make sure your summary is an accurate and fair representation. In addition, be sure to identify the source and include a citation.

You can summarize an entire source, parts of a particular source, or a group of sources to support your ideas.

SUMMARIZE AN ENTIRE SOURCE

Writers frequently summarize an entire work. In some cases, the summary might occupy one or more paragraphs or be integrated into a discussion contained in one or more paragraphs. In other cases, the summary might be as brief as a single sentence.

In an analytical essay about the health risks faced by overweight athletes, a student writer offers a brief, "nutshell" summary of another source.

> The entire source is summarized; because it is a summary, not a direct quotation, page numbers are not necessary.

In an editorial in the medical journal *Neurosurgery*, three sports-medicine specialists noted that after a 1994 federal law exempted dietary supplements from regulation by the Food and Drug Administration, heat-related injuries among football players began to rise (Bailes, Cantu, & Day, 2002).

SUMMARIZE SPECIFIC INFORMATION AND IDEAS FROM A SOURCE

You can also use summaries to convey key information or ideas from a source. In the following example, the writer of an essay summarizes a section of a book about college admissions. His summary is highlighted.

Bill Paul, author of *Getting In: Inside the College Admissions Process*, a book that tells the stories of several students applying to an elite Ivy League institution, shares three suggestions for students who want to get into a college. Paul bases these suggestions on his discussions with Fred Hargadon, a former dean of admissions at Princeton. Hargadon suggested that the best way students can enhance their chances for acceptance into the college of their choice is to read widely, learn to speak a second language, and engage in activities that interest and excite them and that also help them develop their confidence and creativity (235-49).

> Summary is introduced with the author of the book, title, and specific source of the ideas.

> Per MLA style, exact pages are cited.

SUMMARIZE A GROUP OF SOURCES

In addition to summarizing a single source, writers often summarize groups of sources. Such collective summaries (often introduced by phrases such as "Numerous authors argue . . ." or "The research in this area seems to indicate that . . .") allow you to establish a point briefly and with authority. They are particularly effective at the beginning of a document, when you are establishing the nature of the conversation you are joining, and can serve as a transitional device when you move from one major section of the document to another.

When you summarize a group of sources, separate the citations with a semicolon. MLA guidelines require including author and page information, as in the following example.

> Several critics argue that the Hemingway code hero is not always male (Graulich 217; Sherman 78; Watters 33).

In APA style, the author and the date of publication must be included.

> The benefits of early detection of breast cancer have been well documented (Page, 2016; Richards, 2013; Vincent, 2012).

✔ Identify the source of the quotation.

✔ Ensure that you have summarized the source in your own words. Make sure that you do not merely string together a series of close paraphrases of key passages.

✔ Use transitions and attributions to integrate the summary smoothly into your draft.

✔ Ensure that the source is cited in your works cited or references list.

Checklist for Summarizing

Present Numerical Information

If it suits your subject, you might use numerical information, such as statistics, in your document. You can present this information within sentences. Or you might use tables, charts, or graphs, as featured writer Ellen Page did in her informative essay about the use of DDT in preventing malaria.

If you use tables, charts, or graphs, you still need to accurately and fairly present the numerical information in your document and clearly identify the source of the data, just as you would for textual information. For more information about using tables, charts, and graphs, see page 578.

Use Images, Audio, and Video

Including images in your print document or adding images, audio, or video files to your electronic document can enhance its effectiveness. Use caution, however, when taking images and audio or video files from other sources. Simply copying a photograph or an audio or video file into your document might be a form of plagiarism.

One student writer carefully documented the source of the image she used in her informative essay. Because she was writing an academic essay — rather than a document intended for publication and wide distribution — she did not seek permission to use it. (In contrast, the publisher of this book sought and received permission to publish that image.)

If you are creating an electronic document, such as a Web page or a multimedia presentation, use the following guidelines to integrating digital illustrations:

- Make a link between your document and a document that contains an image, a sound clip, or a video clip — rather than copying the image and placing it in your document.

- If it isn't possible or appropriate to create a link to another document, contact the owner of the image, sound clip, or video clip for permission to use it.

- If you cannot contact the owner, review the fair-use guidelines discussed on page 518 for guidance about using the material.

As you would for any sources you cite in your document, make sure you fairly present images, audio, or video and identify the author or creator.

Only by investing in educating their citizens during hard economic times will states see the benefits of having educated workers and business owners — and higher-earning taxpayers — in the state during better times. For this reason, higher education should be a top priority in even trimmed-down state budgets so that students and their families won't face drastic increases in tuition.

At the same time, students still ultimately bear the responsibility for finding the best path to an affordable college education. Students and their families are a necessary part of the solution. They should be willing to apply to a variety of schools, including those they can afford more easily without financial aid. Many students and their families are now considering less expensive routes to a college degree, such as enrolling in public universities or community colleges in their home states (Saleh). Out of eighty-seven college freshmen surveyed at Colorado State University, 80% were likely to recommend community college to a sibling or friend concerned about tuition costs (Tillson). When asked about the benefits of attending community college, students responded that they saw it as "easier to afford" and appreciated that it "makes it easier to work and attend school at the same time" (see Fig. 1). The survey shows that students today are giving community colleges serious thought as an alternative to a four-year university.

> A parenthetical reference to the figure is provided.

> The figure is located immediately below where it is mentioned in the text.

> The figure summarizes key findings from a survey.

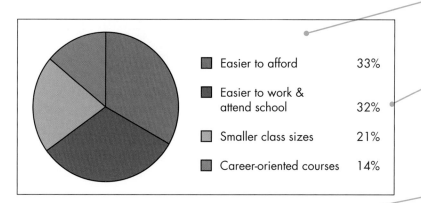

■	Easier to afford	33%
■	Easier to work & attend school	32%
□	Smaller class sizes	21%
■	Career-oriented courses	14%

Fig.1: The perceived benefits of choosing a community college. Based on survey data from Tillson.

> A caption provides information about the source of the data.

▲ **A chart presenting information in an essay**

the most promising alternatives in development is hydrogen — an abundant fuel that is environmentally safe, is far more versatile than gasoline or diesel, can be used to create electricity and fuel internal combustion engines, and produces no waste. Because of these attributes, some experts have argued that a hydrogen economy — an energy system that uses only a hydrogen-oxygen reaction to create energy and electricity — could solve many fuel-related problems, from global warming to America's dependence on foreign oil (Crabtree, Dresselhause, and Buchanan 39). At first glance, hydrogen appears to be the perfect choice. However, three barriers stand in the way of widespread hydrogen usage: as a fuel, it is expensive to produce, difficult to store, and complicated to distribute.

The figure is located next to where it is referred to in the text.

The key to a hydrogen economy is the fuel cell, which uses hydrogen gas and oxygen to produce electricity. In a way, a fuel cell is like a battery, but it never requires charging and it produces only electricity, heat, and water vapor (see Fig. 1).

A parenthetical reference to the figure is provided.

The U.S. Department of Energy (DOE) explains that hydrogen fuel cells use electrode plates to separate hydrogen's protons and electrons, diverting the stream of electrons to create electricity. A "stack" of fuel cells is scalable, so the same basic structure has many different uses ("Hydrogen Fuel"). In theory, stacks of hydrogen fuel

Text is "wrapped" around the figure and caption (see Chapter 18).

The figure illustrates a complex process that would be too difficult to describe using text alone.

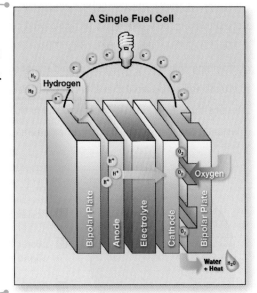

Fig.1: Simplified model of a fuel cell. United States Department of Energy, "Hydrogen Fuel Cells."

A caption provides information about the source of the figure.

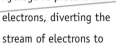
▲ An image providing an overview of a complex process

How Can I Ensure I've Avoided Plagiarism?

Because plagiarized material will often differ in style, tone, and word choice from the rest of your document, your readers are likely to notice these differences and wonder whether you've plagiarized the material — or, if not, why you've written a document that has so many stylistic inconsistencies. If your readers react negatively, it's unlikely that your document will be successful.

You can avoid plagiarism by quoting, paraphrasing, and summarizing accurately and appropriately; distinguishing between your ideas and ideas in your sources; and identifying sources in your document.

Quote, Paraphrase, and Summarize Accurately and Appropriately

Unintentional plagiarism usually occurs when a writer takes poor notes and then uses the information from those notes in a document. As you draft, do the following:

- Look for notes that differ from your usual style of writing. More often than not, if a note doesn't sound like your own writing, it isn't.

- Place quotation marks around any direct quotations, use ellipsis marks and brackets appropriately (see pp. 642–643), and identify the source and the page or paragraph number of the quotation.

- Make sure that paraphrases differ significantly in word choice and sentence structure from the passage being paraphrased, and identify the source and page or paragraph number from which you took the paraphrase.

- Make sure that summaries are not just a series of passages or close paraphrases copied from the source.

Distinguish between Your Ideas and Ideas in Your Sources

Failing to distinguish between your ideas and ideas drawn from your sources can lead readers to think other writers' ideas are yours. Examine how the following writer might have failed to distinguish his ideas from those of Joel Levine and Lawrence May, authors of a source he used in his essay.

Failing to Credit Ideas to a Source

According to Joel Levine and Lawrence May, authors of *Getting In*, entrance exams are an extremely important part of a student's college application and carry a great deal of weight. In fact, a college entrance examination is one of the two most significant factors in getting into college. The other, unsurprisingly, is high school grades.

Because the second and third sentences fail to identify Levine and May as the source of the information about the second important factor affecting admissions decisions — high school grades — the passage implies that the writer is the source of that information.

As it turns out, the writer actually included the necessary attribution in his essay.

Giving Credit to the Source

> The attribution "they claim" credits the source of the information to Levine and May.

According to Joel Levine and Lawrence May, authors of *Getting In*, entrance exams are an extremely important part of a student's college application and carry a great deal of weight. In fact, they claim that a college entrance examination is "one of the two most significant factors" in getting into college (the other, unsurprisingly, is high school grades).

> Quotation marks are used to indicate a partial quotation.

You can use attributions to distinguish between your ideas and those obtained from your sources. As you draft your document, use the name of an author or the title of the source you're drawing from each time you introduce ideas from a source.

Examples of Attribution

According to Scott McPherson . . .

Jill Bedard writes . . .

Tom Huckin reports . . .

Kate Kiefer observes . . .

Bob Phelps suggests . . .

In the words of William Hochman . . .

As Shirley Guitron tells it . . .

Shaun Beaty indicates . . .

Jessica Richards calls our attention to . . .

Check for Unattributed Sources in Your Document

Writers sometimes neglect to identify the sources from which they have drawn their information. You should include a complete citation for each source you refer to in your document. The citation should appear in the text of the document (as an in-text citation, footnote, or endnote) or in a works cited list, references list, or bibliography.

The following examples use MLA style for citing sources; more detailed information about the sources appears in a list of works cited at the end of the document. In the first example, the writer uses a combination of attribution and parenthetical information; in the second example, the writer provides only a parenthetical citation.

> Gavin Miller argues, "We must explore emerging energy technologies before we reach a peak oil crisis" (322).

MLA-style in-text citations include the author's name and exact page reference.

> Some critics argue that "we must explore emerging energy technologies before we reach a peak oil crisis" (Miller 322).

How Should I Document My Sources?

In addition to citing your sources within the text of your document, you should provide complete publication information for each source you've used. Fully documenting your sources can help you achieve your purposes as a writer, such as establishing your authority and persuading your readers. Documenting your sources also helps you avoid plagiarism, gives credit to others who have written about a subject, and creates a record of their work that your readers can follow and build on.

Choose a Documentation System

The documentation systems most commonly used in academic disciplines are the following:

- **MLA.** This style, developed by the Modern Language Association, is used primarily in the humanities — English, philosophy, linguistics, world languages, and so on. See Chapter 23.
- **APA.** Developed by the American Psychological Association, this style is used mainly in the social sciences — psychology, sociology, anthropology, political science, economics, education, and so on. See Chapter 24.

- *Chicago.* Developed by the University of Chicago Press, this style is used primarily in history, journalism, and the humanities.

- **CSE.** This style, developed by the Council of Science Editors (formerly the Council of Biology Editors), is used mainly in the physical and life sciences — chemistry, geology, biology, botany, and so on — and in mathematics.

Your choice of documentation system will be guided by the discipline or field within which you are writing and by any documentation requirements associated with your writing project. If your project has been assigned to you, ask the person who assigned it or someone who has written a similar document which documentation system you should use. If you are working on a project for a writing class, your instructor will usually tell you which documentation system to follow.

Your choice of documentation system will also be guided by the genre you have chosen for your document. For example, while academic essays and articles appearing in scholarly journals typically use a documentation system such as MLA or APA, newspaper and magazine articles often do not; instead, they identify sources in the main text of the document rather than in a works cited or references list. If you write a digital document that cites other online sources, you might simply link to those sources.

Provide In-Text References and Publication Information

The specific format of your in-text citations will depend on the documentation system you are following. If you use MLA or APA style, you will refer to sources in the text of your document using a combination of attributions and parenthetical information and will include a list of sources at the end of your document. The works cited list (MLA) or references list (APA) includes the following key publication information about each source:

- author(s) and/or editor(s)

- title

- publication date

- publisher (for books)

- periodical name, volume, issue, and page numbers (for articles)

- URL and access date (for online publications)

Each documentation system creates an association between in-text citations and the works cited or references list. See Chapters 23 and 24 for documentation models.

In Summary: Using Sources Effectively

* Use sources to support your points (p. 633).

* Indicate the boundaries between source material and your own ideas (p. 638).

* Modify direct quotations carefully (p. 641).

* Use paraphrases to present ideas more clearly or concisely than is possible through direct quotation (p. 644).

* Revise paraphrases to fit your tone and style (p. 645).

* Summarize entire sources, parts of sources, or groups of sources (p. 646).

* Integrate numerical information appropriately (p. 648).

* Integrate images, audio, and video responsibly (p. 648).

* Check for unintentional plagiarism (p. 651).

* Document your sources (p. 653).

 # Revising and Editing

When writers revise and edit, they evaluate the effectiveness of their drafts and work to improve them. Although the two processes are related, they focus on different aspects of a document. Revising involves assessing how well a document responds to a specific writing situation, presents a main point and reasons to accept that point, and uses evidence. Editing includes evaluating and improving the expression — at the sentence and word levels — of the information, ideas, and arguments in the document.

What Should I Focus on When I Revise?

Revising involves rethinking and re-envisioning what you've written. It focuses on such big-picture issues as whether the document you've drafted is appropriate for your writing situation; whether your thesis statement is sound and well supported; whether you've properly integrated sources into your document; whether you've organized and presented your information, ideas, and arguments clearly and effectively; and whether you've made appropriate decisions about genre and design.

Consider Your Writing Situation

As you revise, ask whether your document helps you achieve your purposes. If your assignment directed you to inform readers about a particular subject, for instance, consider whether you've provided appropriate information, whether you've offered enough information, and whether that information is presented clearly. If your purpose is to convince or persuade your readers, ask whether you have chosen appropriate reasons and evidence and presented your argument as effectively as you can. You'll find revision suggestions for specific types of assignments in Chapters 6 through 11.

In addition, review your readers' needs, interests, backgrounds, and knowledge of the subject. During revision, imagine how your readers will react to your document by asking questions such as these:

- Will my readers trust what I have to say? How can I establish my credibility?

- Will my readers have other ideas about how to address this subject? How can I convince them that my ideas are worth considering?

- Will my readers find my evidence appropriate and accurate? Is my selection of evidence consistent with their values, beliefs, and experiences?

Finally, identify your requirements, limitations, and opportunities (see p. 39). Ask yourself whether you've met the specific requirements of the assignment, such as length and number of sources. Evaluate your efforts to work around limitations, such as lack of access to information. Think about whether you've taken full advantage of your opportunities and any new ones that have come your way.

Consider Your Argument and Ideas

As you revise, ask how well you are conveying your argument and ideas to your readers. First, check the clarity of your thesis statement. Is it phrased in a way that is compatible with the needs and interests of your readers? Second, ask whether your reasons will help your readers understand and accept your thesis statement. As you make this assessment, keep in mind your primary role as a writer — such as advocate, reporter, or interpreter.

- **Writing to reflect.** Have you created a dominant impression of your subject or indicated the significance of your observations for readers? (See Chapter 6.)

- **Writing to inform.** Is the level of detail you've provided consistent with your readers' knowledge of the subject? Have you clearly defined any key concepts and ideas? (See Chapter 7.)

- **Writing to interpret or analyze.** Are your analyses clear and accurate? Have you provided appropriate and sufficient background information to help your readers follow your reasoning? (See Chapter 8.)

- **Writing to evaluate.** Have you clearly described the subject, defined your evaluative criteria, and provided a clear rationale for your judgments? (See Chapter 9.)

- **Writing to solve problems.** Have you clearly defined the problem, considered alternative solutions, and discussed your proposed solution? (See Chapter 10.)

- **Writing to convince or persuade.** Have you made a clear overall point, provided reasons, and presented evidence to support your reasons? (See Chapter 11.)

Consider Your Use, Integration, and Documentation of Sources

Think about how you've used source information in your document. Review the amount of evidence you've provided for your points and the appropriateness of that evidence for your purpose and readers. If you are arguing about an issue, determine whether you've identified and addressed reasonable opposing viewpoints.

As you do so, determine whether you've presented information, ideas, and arguments from your sources accurately and fairly. Be sure that quotations are accurate and appropriately documented. Ensure that paraphrases and summaries represent the source reasonably and fairly. Although fairness can be difficult to judge, ask whether you've achieved it. For example, writing that an author "ridiculed" a particular idea might enhance the impact of a passage. If the author was only raising questions about the idea, however, using that term would be unfair to your source, your readers, and to the idea itself.

Ask yourself, as well, how effectively you've introduced the work of other authors. Begin by considering your use of attributions in terms of your purpose and role.

By characterizing the contributions particular sources are making to the overall conversation, you can frame their arguments — and yours — in a way that helps you achieve your goals. You can also show how particular sources approach your issue, helping your readers better understand how your contribution advances the conversation.

Then consider the relationship you are trying to establish with your readers. Readers appreciate clear identification of the source of a quotation, paraphrase, or summary. (For more information about quoting, paraphrasing, and summarizing, see Chapter 21.) Readers also appreciate some variety in how evidence from sources is introduced. To make your writing stand out, vary the words and phrases that identify the sources of the information, ideas, and arguments you use in your document.

Common Attributions	More Specific Attributions
The author wrote . . .	The author expressed the opinion that . . .
The author said . . .	The author denied this, noting . . .
The author stated . . .	In response, the author observed that . . .

It's also important to review your works cited or references list for completeness and accuracy. Remember that lack of proper documentation can reduce your document's effectiveness and diminish your credibility. You can learn more about integrating sources in Chapter 21. For guidelines on documenting your sources, see Chapters 23 and 24.

Consider the Structure and Organization of Your Document

Your readers should be able to locate information and ideas easily. As you read your introduction, ask whether it clearly and concisely conveys your main point and whether it helps your readers anticipate the structure and organization of your document. Reflect on the appropriateness of your organizing pattern (see p. 536) for your purpose and readers. If you've used headings and subheadings, evaluate their effectiveness.

Make sure your document is easy to read. Check for effective paragraphing and paragraph structure (see p. 550). If you have several small paragraphs, you might combine paragraphs with similar ideas. If you have a number of long paragraphs, break them up and add transitions. Finally, ask whether your conclusion leaves your readers with something to think about. The most effective conclusions typically provide more than just a summary of your argument.

Consider Genre and Design

Consider both the genre — or type — of document that you are writing and your use of design principles and elements (see Chapter 18). If your assignment gave you a choice of genre, ask whether the genre you've selected is appropriate, given your purpose and readers. For example, would it be more effective to reach your readers via an informative website, an opinion column, or a brochure? Would it be more effective to publish your document as a blog entry or as a letter to the editor of a magazine or newspaper? Regardless of the type of document you're writing, make sure that you've followed the conventions associated with it, such as level of formality, accepted sources of evidence, and organization.

Take a careful look, as well, at how you've designed your document (see Chapter 18). Does it resemble what your readers will expect? For example, if you're writing an academic essay, have you double-spaced your lines, used a readable font, and set wide margins? If you're creating a website, have you made it easy for your readers to find their way around? Have you consistently formatted your headings and subheadings? Have you used design principles and elements to achieve your purpose and consider your readers?

What Strategies Can I Use to Revise?

You can draw on several strategies for reviewing and improving your document. As you use them, keep track of your ideas for revision by writing comments on sticky notes or in the margins of print documents, by using the Comment tool in word-processing documents, or by creating a to-do list in your writer's notebook.

Save Multiple Drafts

You might not be happy with every revision you make. To avoid wishing that you hadn't made extensive revisions to a draft of your document, save a new copy of your draft before every major revising session. You can add a number to your drafts' file names, such as Draft1.doc, Draft2.doc, and so on; add the date, such as Draft-April6.doc and Draft-April10.doc; or use some other naming system that works for you. What's important is that you save multiple versions of your drafts in case you don't like the changes you've made.

Highlight Your Main Point, Reasons, and Evidence

As you revise, make sure that your main point (usually expressed as a thesis statement), reasons, and evidence are fully developed. An effective way to do this is to identify and examine each element in your draft, both individually and as a group of related points. If you are working with a printed document, use a highlighter, colored pens or pencils, or sticky notes. If you are working on a digital document, use a highlighting tool to mark the text. You might use different colors to highlight your main point, reasons, and evidence. If you are focusing solely on the evidence in your document, use different colors to highlight evidence from different sources (to help you check whether you are relying too heavily on a single source) or to differentiate the types of evidence you are using (such as quotations, paraphrases, summaries, and numerical data).

When you have finished highlighting your draft, review it to determine whether your reasons support your main points as effectively as you had hoped and whether the evidence you've provided to support your reasons is sufficient and varied. If you have relied too heavily on a particular source, for example, your readers might wonder why they shouldn't simply read that source and ignore your document. If you've provided too little evidence, they'll question the basis for your conclusions.

Challenge Your Assumptions

It's easy to accept ideas and arguments that you've worked so hard to develop. But what would a reader with fresh eyes think? Challenge your main point, reasons, and evidence by using one of the following strategies. Keep track of your challenges by using the Comment tool in your word-processing program.

PUT YOURSELF IN THE PLACE OF YOUR READERS

As you read, pretend that you are one of your readers. Try to imagine a single reader — or, if you're ambitious, a group of readers. Ask questions they might ask. Imagine concerns they might bring to their reading of your document. A reader interested in solving a problem might ask, for example, whether a proposed solution is cost-effective, is more appropriate than alternative solutions, or has unacceptable side effects. As you revise, take these questions and concerns into account.

PLAY DEVIL'S ADVOCATE

A devil's advocate raises reasonable objections to ideas and arguments. As you review your document, identify your key claims, and then pose reasonable objections to them. Make note of these potential objections, and take them into account as you revise.

PLAY THE "SO WHAT?" GAME

As you read your document, ask why readers would care about what you are saying. By asking "So what?" questions, you can gain a better understanding of what your readers are likely to care about and how they might respond to your arguments and ideas. Make note of your responses to these questions, and consider them as you revise.

Scan, Outline, and Map Your Document

Use the following strategies to review the structure, organization, and design of your document:

- **Scan headings and subheadings.** If you have used headings and subheadings, they can help you track the overall flow of your ideas. Ask whether the organization they reveal is appropriate for your writing situation and your role as a writer.

- **Scan the first sentence of each paragraph.** A quick reading of the first sentence of each paragraph can reveal points at which your ideas shift. As you note these shifts, think about whether they are appropriate and effective.

- **Outline your document.** Create a topical or sentence outline of your document (see p. 545) to assess its structure and organization. This strategy, sometimes called a reverse outline, helps you identify the sequence of your points and the amount of space you've devoted to each aspect of your document. If you are viewing your document in a word-processing program, use the Styles tool to assign levels to headings in your document; then view it in Outline view.

- **Map your document.** On paper or in a graphics program, draw a map of your document. Like an outline, a map can help you identify the organization of your points and the amount of evidence you've used to support them. As you review the organization and structure of your document, reflect on whether it is appropriate given your purpose, readers, argument, and available information.

Ask for Feedback

After spending long hours on a project, you might find it difficult to identify problems that your readers could have with your draft. You might read the same paragraph eight times and still fail to notice that the evidence you are using to support a point actually contradicts it. Or you might not notice that your document's organization could confuse your readers. You can ask for feedback on your draft from a friend, relative, colleague, or writing center tutor. It's generally a good idea to ask for help from someone who will be frank as well as supportive. You should also be specific about the kinds of comments you're looking for. Hearing "it's just fine" from a reviewer will not help you revise. You can learn more about engaging in a peer review in Chapter 5.

Checklist for Revision

✔ Review your writing situation. Does your document help you achieve your purposes? Does it address your readers' needs, interests, knowledge, and backgrounds? Is it well adapted to the context in which it will be read?

✔ Consider your writing assignment. Does your document address the writing assignment's requirements? Does it effectively work around limitations and take advantage of opportunities?

✔ Evaluate the presentation of your ideas. Does your document provide a clear and appropriate thesis statement? Do your reasons and evidence support your thesis statement, and are they consistent with your primary role as a writer?

✔ Assess your use, integration, and documentation of sources. Have you offered adequate support for your points, considered reasonable opposing viewpoints, integrated and acknowledged your sources, and distinguished between your work and that of other writers? Have you used variety in your introduction and attribution of sources? Have you documented your sources appropriately?

✔ Examine the structure and organization of your document. Is the introduction clear and concise, does it convey your main point, and does it help your readers anticipate the structure of your document? Is the organization of the document easy to follow? Are paragraphs easy to read? Are transitions effective? Does the conclusion provide more than just a summary of the document?

✔ Evaluate genre and design. Does the genre you've chosen help you accomplish your purpose? Have you followed the style and design conventions associated with the type of document you've created?

What Should I Focus on When I Edit?

Editing involves assessing the effectiveness, accuracy, and appropriateness of the words and sentences in a document. Before you begin to edit, remember that editing focuses on your document's words and sentences, not on its overall structure or ideas. If you're uncertain about whether you've organized your document as effectively as possible or whether you've provided enough support for your argument, deal with those issues first. In the same way that you wouldn't start painting a house until you've finished building the walls, hold off on editing until you're confident that you've finished revising.

Focus on Accuracy

You risk damaging your credibility if you provide inaccurate information in your document. To reduce this risk, do the following:

- **Check your facts and figures.** Your readers might think that you're deliberately misleading them if you fail to provide accurate information. As you edit, return to your original sources or your notes to check any facts and figures.

- **Check every quotation.** Return to your original sources or consult your notes to ensure that you have quoted each source exactly. Make sure that you have noted any changes to a quotation with ellipsis marks or brackets and that those changes haven't altered the original meaning of the passage (see pp. 642–643). Be sure to cite each source both in the text and in a works cited or references list (see Chapters 23 and 24).

- **Check the spelling of every name.** Don't rely on electronic spelling checkers, which provide the correct spelling for only the most common or prominent names.

Focus on Economy

Editing for economy involves reducing the number of words needed to express an idea or convey information. Often you can achieve greater economy in your writing by removing unnecessary modifiers, removing unnecessary introductory phrases such as *there are* and *it is*, and eliminating stock phrases (see pp. 552–553). Editing for economy generally makes it easier for your readers to understand your meaning, but you should use care; your readers still need to understand the point you are trying to make (see Chapter 18).

Focus on Consistency

Editing your document for consistency helps you present information and ideas in a uniform way. Use the following techniques to edit for consistency:

- **Treat concepts consistently.** Review your document for consistent treatment of concepts, information, ideas, definitions, and anecdotes.

- **Use numbers consistently.** Check the documentation system you are using for its guidelines on the treatment of numbers. You might find, for instance, that you should spell out the numbers zero through nine and use Arabic numerals for numbers larger than nine.

- **Treat your sources consistently.** Avoid referring to some sources using first names and to others using honorifics, such as *Dr., Mr.,* or *Ms.* Also check that you have cited your sources appropriately for the documentation style you are using, such as MLA or APA (see Chapters 23 and 24). Review each reference for consistent presentation of names, page numbers, and publication dates.

- **Format your document consistently.** Avoid any inconsistencies in your use of fonts, headings, and subheadings and in your placement and captioning of images, tables, charts, and other illustrations (see Chapter 18).

Focus on Style

Your readers will judge you — and what you have to say — not only on what you say but also on how you say it. Edit for matters of style by choosing the right words, using active and passive voice appropriately, adopting a consistent point of view, rewriting complex sentences, varying your sentence length and structure, providing transitions, and avoiding sexist language.

Focus on Spelling, Grammar, and Punctuation

Poor spelling doesn't necessarily affect your ability to get your point across — in most cases, readers will understand even the most atrociously spelled document — but it does affect what your readers think of you. If you ignore spelling errors in your document, you'll erode their confidence in your ability to present ideas or make an argument. The same goes for grammar and punctuation. If your sentences have subject-verb agreement problems or don't use the appropriate punctuation, readers might not trust that you have presented your facts correctly. As you put the finishing touches on your document, keep a dictionary and good grammar handbook close by.

What Strategies Can I Use to Edit?

Thorough editing involves making several passes through your document to ensure that you've addressed accuracy, economy, consistency, style, spelling, grammar, and punctuation. The following tips can make that process both easier and more productive.

Read Carefully

As you've worked on your document, you've become quite familiar with it. As a result, it can be easy to read what you *meant* to write instead of what you actually wrote. The following strategies can help you read with fresh eyes:

- **Set your document aside before you edit.** If time permits, allow a day or two to pass before you begin editing your document. Taking time off between revising and editing can help you see your document more clearly.

- **Pause between sentences for a quick check.** Avoid getting caught up in the flow of your document by stopping after you read each sentence. Slowing down can help you identify problems with your text.

- **Read aloud.** Reading your document aloud can help you find problems that might not be apparent when it's read silently.

- **Read in reverse order.** To check for problems with individual sentences, start at the end of your document and read the last sentence first, and then work backward through the document. To check for problems at the word level, read each word starting with the last one in the document. Disrupting the normal flow of your document can alert you to problems that might not stand out when you read it normally.

Mark and Search Your Document

Use the following marking and searching strategies to edit for accuracy, economy, consistency, and style:

- **Mark your document.** As you read, use a highlighter pen or the highlighting tool in your word-processing program to mark errors or information that should be double-checked. Consider using different colors to highlight specific types of problems, such as sexist language or inconsistent use of formal titles.

- **Use the Find and Replace tools.** Use your word-processing program to edit concepts, names, numbers, and titles for consistency and accuracy. Once you've identified a word or phrase that you'd like to check or change, you can search for it throughout your document. If you are referring to sources using a parenthetical citation style, such as MLA or APA, use the Find tool to search for an opening parenthesis. If you discover that you've consistently misspelled a word or name, use the Replace tool to correct it throughout your document.

- **Use the Split Window tool.** Some word-processing programs allow you to split your window so that you can view different parts of your document at the same time. Use this tool to ensure that you are referring to a concept in the same way throughout your document or to check for consistent use of fonts, headings, subheadings, illustrations, and tables.

Use Spelling, Grammar, and Style Tools with Caution

Most word-processing programs provide tools to check spelling, grammar, punctuation, and style. Used with an awareness of their limitations, these tools can significantly reduce the effort required to edit a document.

Spelling checkers have two primary limitations. First, they can't identify words that are spelled correctly but misused — such as *to/two/too*, *their/they're/there*, and *advice/advise*. Second, spelling checkers are ineffective when they run into a word they don't recognize, such as proper names, technical and scientific terms, and unusual words. To compound this problem, spelling checkers often suggest replacement words. If you accept suggestions uncritically, you might end up with a document full of incorrect words and misspelled names.

The main limitation of grammar, punctuation, and style checkers is inaccurate advice. Although much of the advice they offer is sound, a significant proportion is not. If you are confident about your knowledge of grammar, punctuation, and style, you can use the grammar- and style-checking tools in your word-processing program to identify potential problem areas in your document. These tools can point out problems you might have overlooked, such as a subject-verb agreement problem that occurred when you revised a sentence. However, if you don't have a strong knowledge of grammar, punctuation, and style, you can easily be misled by inaccurate advice.

If you have any doubts about advice from your word-processing program's spelling checker, consult an up-to-date dictionary. If you have concerns about the suggestions you receive from the grammar-, punctuation-, and style-checking tools, consult a good grammar handbook.

Ask for Feedback

One of the biggest challenges writers face is reading a draft of their own work as a reader rather than as the writer. Because you know what you're trying to say, you'll find it easy to understand your draft. And because you've read your document so many times, you're likely to overlook errors in spelling, punctuation, and grammar. After you've edited your document, ask a friend, relative, or classmate to proofread it and to make note of any problems.

Checklist for Editing

✔ Ensure that your document is accurate. Check facts and figures, quotations, and the spelling of names.

✔ Edit for economy. Strive to express your ideas and argument concisely yet clearly.

✔ Ensure that your document is consistent. Use concepts, numbers, and source information consistently. Check your document for consistent use of formatting and design.

✔ Improve your style. Strive for economy, use appropriate words, check your verbs, rewrite overly complex sentences, vary sentence length and structure, and remove sexist language.

✔ Check for correct spelling, grammar, and punctuation. Use your word-processing program's spelling, grammar, punctuation, and style tools cautiously; consult a grammar handbook and a dictionary; and ask someone to proofread your draft.

In Summary: Revising and Editing

* Focus on the big picture when you revise by keeping your writing situation, argument, sources, organization, genre, and design in mind (p. 657).

* Revise more effectively by saving multiple drafts; highlighting; challenging your assumptions; scanning, outlining, and mapping your document; and asking for feedback (p. 660).

* Focus on accuracy, economy, consistency, style, spelling, grammar, and punctuation when you edit (p. 664).

* Take advantage of editing strategies (p. 666).

PART FIVE

Documenting Sources

23 Using MLA Style

Modern Language Association (MLA) style, used primarily in the humanities, emphasizes the authors of a source and the pages on which information is located in the source. Writers who use the MLA documentation system cite, or formally acknowledge, source information within their text using parentheses, and they provide a list of sources in a works cited list at the end of their document.

The following student essays are formatted and documented in MLA style:

- Caitlin Guariglia, *Mi Famiglia*, page 162

- Mackenzie Owens, *Deadly Force: A Conservative Political Writer Takes on a Quickly Evolving Issue*, page 275

- James Hardjadinata, *The Truth about Puppy Mills: Exposing a Heartrending Industry*, page 385

- Elisabeth Layne, *Trigger Warnings on College Campuses*, page 444

For more information about MLA style, consult the *MLA Handbook*, Eighth Edition. Information about the *MLA Handbook* can also be found at www.mla.org.

Using MLA Style

672

How Do I Cite Sources within the Text of My Document?

MLA style uses parentheses for in-text citations to acknowledge the use of another author's words, facts, and ideas. When you refer to a source within your text, provide the author's last name and specific page number(s) — if the source is paginated. Your reader can then go to the works cited list at the end of your document to find a full citation.

1. Basic format for a source named in your text Most often, you will want to name the author of a source within your sentence rather than in a parenthetical citation. By doing so, you create a context for the material (words, facts, or ideas) that you are including, and you indicate where the information from the author begins. When you are using a direct quotation, paraphrase, or summary from a source and have named the author in your sentence, place only the page number in parentheses after the borrowed material. The period follows the closing parenthesis.

> According to Tattersall, when early humans emerged from the dense forests to the adjacent woodlands, their mobility and diet were forced to change dramatically (45).

When you are using a block (or extended) quotation, the parenthetical citation comes after the final punctuation and a single space (see p. 641).

If you continue to refer to a single source for several sentences in a row within one paragraph — and without intervening references to another source — you may place your reference at the end of the paragraph. However, be sure to include all relevant page numbers.

2. Basic format for a source not named in your text If you have not mentioned the author in your sentence, you must place the author's name and the page number in parentheses after the quotation, paraphrase, or summary. Again, the period follows the closing parenthesis.

> It would have been impossible for early humans to digest red meat, as their stomachs lacked the necessary acids to break down the muscle and tissue before delivery to the intestines (Tattersall 46).

3. Entire source If you are referring to an entire source rather than to a specific page or pages, you do not need a parenthetical citation.

> Author Jhumpa Lahiri adapted the title for her book of stories *Unaccustomed Earth* from a line in the first chapter of Nathaniel Hawthorne's *The Scarlet Letter*.

4. Corporate, group, or government author Cite the corporation, group, or government agency as you would an individual author. You may use abbreviations for the source in subsequent references if you add the abbreviation in parentheses at the first mention of the name.

> The Social Security Administration (SSA) estimates that a twenty-year-old has a three in ten chance of becoming disabled before he or she reaches retirement age (4). If a worker does become disabled, SSA assigns a representative to review the case individually (7).

5. Unknown author If you are citing a source that has no known author, such as the book *A Woman in Berlin*, use a brief version of the title in the parenthetical citation.

> The narrator pays particular attention to the culture of rape in Berlin during World War II, calling it a "collective experience" and claiming that German women comforted one another by speaking openly about it—something they never would have considered during peacetime (*Woman* 147).

6. Two or more works by the same author For references to authors with more than one work in your works cited list, insert a short version of the title between the author and the page number, separating the author and the title with a comma.

> (Sacks, *Hallucinations* 77)

> (Sacks, *Mind's Eye* 123)

7. Two or more authors with the same last name Include the first initial and last name in the parenthetical citation.

> (F. McCourt 27)

> (M. McCourt 55)

8. Two authors Include the last name of each author in your citation.

> In the year following Hurricane Katrina, journalist and activist Jane Wholey brought together a group of twenty New Orleans middle schoolers in an effort to reimagine their school system's food environment from the ground up (Gottlieb and Joshi 2).

9. Three or more authors Use only the last name of the first author and the abbreviation "et al." (Latin for "and others"). There is no comma between the author's name and "et al."

> (Johnson et al. 17)

10. Literary work Along with the page number(s), give other identifying information, such as a chapter, scene, or line number, that will help readers find the passage.

> One prominent motif introduced at the opening of *Beloved* is bestiality, exemplified in Sethe's being described as "down on all fours" at the first appearance of her dead daughter's ghost (Morrison 27; ch. 1).

11. Work in an edited collection or anthology Cite the author of the work, not the editor of the collection or anthology. (See also item 28 on p. 681.)

> In his satirical essay "A Presidential Candidate," Mark Twain outlines his plan to thwart the opposition, insisting that "if you know the worst about a candidate, to begin with, every attempt to spring things on him will be checkmated" (3).

12. Sacred text Give the name of the edition you are using, along with the chapter and verse (or their equivalent).

> It is still very sage advice to "withhold not good from them to whom it is due, when it is in the power of thine hand to do it" (*King James Bible*, Prov. 2.27).

> The Qur'an points to the bee and its natural ability to produce honey as proof of God's existence ("The Bees" 16.68).

13. Two or more works cited together Use a semicolon to separate entries.

> Byron Bancroft Johnson founded the American League in 1901 by raiding the National League for its best players, offering them competitive salaries to jump leagues (Appel 3; Stout and Johnson 8).

14. Source quoted in another source Ideally, you should track down the original source of the quotation. If you must use a quotation cited by another author, use the abbreviation "qtd. in" (for "quoted in") when you cite the source.

> When Henry Ford introduced the Model T, he insisted on making it a practical and affordable family car, maintaining that "no man making a good salary will be unable to own one — and enjoy with his family the blessing of hours of pleasure in God's great open spaces" (qtd. in Booth 9).

15. Source without page numbers Give a section, paragraph, or screen number, if numbered, in the parenthetical citation.

> First-time American mothers and fathers both have aged an average of three to four years since 1970 (Shulevitz, par. 4).

If no numbers are available, list only the author's name in parentheses.

> It is adults, not children, who present the greatest challenge in gift giving, as adults tend to long for intangibles — like love or career success — that are harder to pin down (Rothman).

How Do I Prepare the List of Works Cited?

MLA-style research documents include a reference list titled "Works Cited," which begins on a new page at the end of the document. If you wish to acknowledge sources that you read but did not cite in your text, you may include them in a second list titled "Works Consulted." In longer documents, the list of works cited may be given at the end of each chapter or section. In digital documents that use links, such as a website, the list of works cited is often a separate page to which other pages are linked. To see works cited lists in MLA style, see pages 166, 392, and 449.

The list is alphabetized by author. If the author's name is unknown, alphabetize the entry using the title of the source. If you cite more than one work by the same author, alphabetize the group under the author's last name, with each entry listed alphabetically by title (see item 21 on p. 678).

All entries in the list are double-spaced, with no extra space between entries. Entries are formatted with a hanging indent: the first line of an entry is flush with the left margin, and subsequent lines are indented one-half inch. Unless otherwise noted, use commas to separate items within each entry. Titles of longer works, such as books, journals, or websites, are italicized. Titles of short works, such as articles or chapters, are enclosed in quotation marks. MLA generally indicates the "container" of the source — the larger object, if any, in which the source can be found. Some sources may have multiple levels of containers, such as a periodical article that is accessed via a database. Occasionally, sources may be identified by a descriptive label (editorial, map, letter, photograph, and so on).

Since sources today can often be found in both print and digital form — for instance, you can easily access a *New Yorker* article in the print magazine or on the magazine's website — the source types that follow include model citations for both media. The section on digital sources (see p. 691) features source types that are native to digital formats, such as blogs or social media platforms.

Books

16. One author List the author's last name first, followed by a comma and the first name. Italicize the book title and subtitle, if any. List the publisher (abbreviating University Press as UP), then insert a comma and the publication year. End with a period.

> Bowker, Gordon. *James Joyce: A New Biography*. Farrar, Straus and Giroux, 2012.

Cite an online book as you would a print book, providing the website and DOI (digital object identifier, a unique number assigned to specific content). If a DOI is not available, provide a stable URL.

> Piketty, Thomas. *Capital in the Twenty-First Century*. Translated by Arthur Goldhammer, Harvard UP, 2014. *Google Books*, books.google.com/books?isbn=0674369556/.

Cite an e-Book as you would a print book, then provide the name of the e-reader.

> Doerr, Anthony. *All the Light We Cannot See*. Scribner, 2014. Nook.

17. Two authors List both authors in the same order as on the title page, last name first for only the first author listed. Use a comma to separate authors' names.

> Stiglitz, Joseph E., and Bruce C. Greenwald. *Creating a Learning Society: A New Approach to Growth, Development, and Social Progress*. Columbia UP, 2015.

18. Three or more authors Provide the first author's name (last name first), followed by a comma, and then the abbreviation "et al." (Latin for "and others").

> Cunningham, Stewart, et al. *Media Economics*. Palgrave Macmillan, 2015.

19. Corporate or group author Write out the full name of the corporation or group, and cite the name as you would an author. This name is often also the name of the publisher.

> Human Rights Watch. *World Report of 2015: Events of 2014*. Seven Stories Press, 2015.

20. Unknown author When no author is listed on the title or copyright page, begin the entry with the title of the work. Alphabetize the entry by the first word of the title other than *A*, *An*, or *The*.

> *The Kingfisher History Encyclopedia*. Macmillan, 2012.

21. Two or more books by the same author Use the author's name in the first entry. Thereafter, use three hyphens followed by a period in place of the author's name. List the entries alphabetically by title.

> García, Cristina. *Dreams of Significant Girls*. Simon and Schuster, 2011.
>
> ---. *The Lady Matador's Hotel*. Scribner, 2010.

22. Editor Use the descriptive label "editor" or "editors" after the editors' names.

> Horner, Avril, and Anne Rowe, editors. *Living on Paper: Letters from Iris Murdoch*. Princeton UP, 2016.

23. Author with an editor or a translator Start with the author's name, then give the title. Include the label "Edited by" or "Translated by" and the name of the editor or translator, first name first.

> Ferrante, Elena. *The Story of the Lost Child*. Translated by Ann Goldstein, Europa Editions, 2015.

24. Graphic narrative or illustrated work List the primary author/illustrator in the first position. If the author is also the illustrator, simply list him or her in the first position.

> Gaiman, Neil. *The Sandman: Overture*. Illustrated by J. H. Williams III, DC Comics, 2015.

> Kerascoët, illustrator. *Beautiful Darkness*. By Fabien Vehlmann, Drawn and Quarterly, 2014.

> Smith, Lane. *Abe Lincoln's Dream*. Roaring Brook Press, 2012.

25. Edition other than the first Include the number of the edition and the abbreviation "ed." (meaning "edition") after the title.

> Eagleton, Terry. *Literary Theory: An Introduction*. 3rd ed., U of Minnesota P, 2008.

> Nadakavukaren, Anne. *Our Global Environment: A Health Perspective*. 7th ed., Waveland Press, 2011. *Google Books,* books.google.com/books?id=NXkbAAAAQBAJ&dq/.

26. Republished book Indicate the original date of publication after the title. Include any information relevant to republication, such as a new introduction. For online books, give the website and URL.

> Trilling, Lionel. *The Liberal Imagination*. 1950. Introduction by Louis Menand, New York Review of Books, 2008.

> Langer, Judith A., and Arthur N. Applebee. *How Writing Shapes Thinking: A Study of Teaching and Learning*. 1987. WAC Clearinghouse, 2011. *WAC Clearinghouse,* wac.colostate.edu/books/langer_applebee/.

27. Multivolume work End with the total number of volumes and the abbreviation "vols."

> Stark, Freya. *Letters*. Edited by Lucy Moorehead, Compton Press, 1974-82. 8 vols.

If you have used only one of the volumes in your document, include the volume number after the title. List the total number of volumes after the publication information.

> Stark, Freya. *Letters*. Edited by Lucy Moorehead, vol. 5, Compton Press, 1978. 8 vols.

How do I cite books using MLA style?

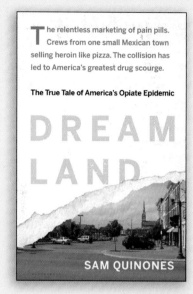

The relentless marketing of pain pills. Crews from one small Mexican town selling heroin like pizza. The collision has led to America's greatest drug scourge.

The True Tale of America's Opiate Epidemic

DREAM LAND

SAM QUINONES

When citing a book, use the information from the title page and the copyright page (on the reverse side of the title page), not from the book's cover or a library catalog. Consult pages 677–681 for additional models for citing books.

© Sam Quinones, 2015, *Dreamland*, Bloomsbury Publishing, Inc.

┌── A ──┐ ┌────────────── B ──────────────┐
Quinones, Sam. *Dreamland: The True Tale of America's Opiate Epidemic.*
┌── C ──┐ ┌ D ┐
Bloomsbury, 2015.

A **The author.** Give the last name first, followed by a comma, the first name, and the middle initial (if given). Omit titles such as "MD," "PhD," or "Sir"; include suffixes after the name and a comma (O'Driscoll, Gerald P., Jr.). End with a period.

B **The title.** Give the full title; include the subtitle (if any), preceded by a colon. Italicize the title and subtitle, capitalizing all major words. End with a period.

C **The publisher.** Provide the full name of the publisher, but abbreviate "University Press" as "UP" (for example, abbreviate "Oxford University Press" as "Oxford UP.") Do not include the words "Publisher" or "Inc." Follow with a comma.

D **The year of publication.** If more than one copyright date is given, use the most recent one. End with a period.

28. Work in an edited collection or anthology Give the author, then the title in quotation marks. Follow with the title of the collection in italics, the label "edited by," and the names of the editor(s) (first name first), the publication information, and the inclusive page numbers for the selection or chapter.

> Sayrafiezadeh, Saïd. "Paranoia." *New American Stories*, edited by Ben Marcus, Vintage Books, 2015, pp. 3-29.

If you are using multiple selections from the same anthology, include the anthology itself in your list of works cited and cross-reference it in the citations for individual works.

> Eisenberg, Deborah. "Some Other, Better Otto." Marcus, pp. 94-136.

> Marcus, Ben, editor. *New American Stories*. Vintage Books, 2015.

> Sayrafiezadeh, Saïd. "Paranoia." Marcus, pp. 3-29.

29. Foreword, introduction, preface, or afterword Begin with the author of the part you are citing and the name of that part. Add the title of the work; "by" or "edited by" and the work's author or editor (first name first); and publication information. Then give the inclusive page numbers for the part.

> Dunham, Lena. Foreword. *The Liars' Club*, by Mary Karr, Penguin Classics, 2015, pp. xi-xiii.

If the part has a title, include the title in quotation marks directly after the author.

> Sullivan, John Jeremiah. "The Ill-Defined Plot." Introduction. *The Best American Essays 2014*, edited by Sullivan, Houghton Mifflin Harcourt, 2014, pp. xvii-xxvi.

30. Sacred text Include the title of the version as it appears on the title page. If the title does not identify the version, place that information directly after the title.

> *The Oxford Annotated Bible with the Apocrypha*. Edited by Herbert G. May and Bruce M. Metzger, Revised Standard Version, Oxford UP, 1965.

31. Dissertation or thesis Cite as you would a book, but include an appropriate label such as "Dissertation" or "Thesis" after the title. Add the school and the year.

> Kidd, Celeste. *Rational Approaches to Learning and Development*. Dissertation, U of Rochester, 2013.

How do I cite articles from periodicals using MLA style?

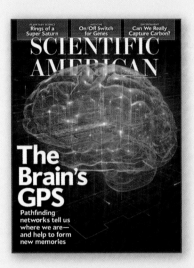

Periodicals include journals, magazines, and newspapers. This tutorial gives an example of a citation for a print magazine article. Models for citing articles from journals and newspapers are on pages 683 and 685.

If you need to cite a periodical article you accessed online, follow the guidelines on page 684.

```
        ┌──── A ────┐ ┌──────── B ────────┐ ┌──── C ────┐ ┌─ D ─┐
Kenworthy, Matthew. "Rings of a Super Saturn." Scientific American, Jan. 2016,
        ┌─ E ─┐
        pp. 34-41.
```

A The author. Give the last name first, followed by a comma, the first name, and the middle initial (if given). Omit titles such as "MD," "PhD," or "Sir"; include suffixes after the name and a comma (O'Driscoll, Gerald P., Jr.). End with a period.

B The article title. Give the full title; include the subtitle (if any), preceded by a colon. Enclose the title and subtitle in quotation marks, and capitalize all major words. Place a period inside the closing quotation mark.

C The periodical title. Italicize the periodical title, including the article "The"; capitalize all major words.

D The date of publication. For journals, give volume number, issue number, and the season and year of publication. For monthly magazines, give the month and year. For weekly magazines and newspapers, give the day, month, and year, in that order. Abbreviate the names of all months except May, June, and July.

E Inclusive page number(s). For numbers 100 and above, give only the last two digits and any other preceding digits if different from the first number (22-28, 402-10, 1437-45, 592-603). Include section letters for newspapers, if relevant. End with a period.

Sources in Journals, Magazines, and Newspapers

32. Article in a journal Enclose the article title in quotation marks. After the journal title, list the volume number, issue number, season and year of publication, and inclusive page numbers.

> Matchie, Thomas. "Law versus Love in *The Round House*." *Midwest Quarterly*, vol. 56,
>   no. 4, Summer 2015, pp. 353-64.

For an electronic journal, provide the print information, if given, and end with the URL.

> Amao, Olumuyiwa Babatunde, and Ufo Okeke-Uzodike. "Nigeria, Afrocentrism, and
>   Conflict Resolution: After Five Decades — How Far, How Well?" *African Studies*
>   *Quarterly*, vol. 15, no. 4, Sept. 2015, pp. 1-23, asq.africa.ufl.edu/files/Volume-15
>   -Issue-4-OLUMUYIWA-BABATUNDE-AMAO.pdf/.

If the article is assigned a DOI (digital object identifier, a unique number assigned to specific content), cite the source as you would a print article, then give the DOI. For an article from a database, cite the database name before the DOI.

> Coles, Kimberly Anne. "The Matter of Belief in John Donne's Holy Sonnets."
>   *Renaissance Quarterly*, vol. 68, no. 3, Fall 2015, pp. 899-931. *JSTOR*,
>   doi:10.1086/683855/.

33. Article in a monthly or bimonthly magazine After the author's name and title of the article, list the title of the magazine, the date (use abbreviations for all months except May, June, and July), and inclusive page numbers.

> Bryan, Christy. "Ivory Worship." *National Geographic*, Oct. 2012, pp. 28-61.

34. Article in a weekly or biweekly magazine Give the exact date of publication, inverted.

> Grossman, Lev. "A Star Is Born." *Time*, 2 Nov. 2015, pp. 30-39.

Cite online articles the same as you would a print article, and then give the URL.

> Leonard, Andrew. "The Surveillance State High School." *Salon*, 27 Nov. 2012,
>   www.salon.com/2012/11/27/the_surveillance_state_high_school/.

How do I cite articles from databases using MLA style?

Libraries subscribe to services such as LexisNexis, ProQuest, InfoTrac, and EBSCOhost that provide access to databases of digital texts. The databases provide publication information, abstracts, and the complete text of documents in a specific subject area, discipline, or profession. (See also Chapter 13.)

Kumanyika, Chenjerai. "Policing and the 'War on Black Bodies.'" *College Literature* 43:1 (2016), 252. © 2016 Johns Hopkins University Press and West Chester University. Reproduced with permission of Johns Hopkins University Press.

A ———————— B ——————————————— C ————

Kumanyika, Chenjerai. "Policing and the 'War on Black Bodies.'" *College Literature,*

D ———— E ———— F —— G ———— H ————

vol. 43, no. 1, Winter 2016, pp. 252+. *Academic OneFile,* go.galegroup.com/.

A **The author.** Give the last name first, followed by a comma, the first name, and the middle initial (if given). Omit titles such as "MD," "PhD," or "Sir"; include suffixes after the name and a comma (O'Driscoll, Gerald P., Jr.). End with a period.

B **The article title.** Give the full title; include the subtitle (if any), preceded by a colon. Enclose the full title in quotation marks, and capitalize all major words. Place a period inside the closing quotation mark.

C **The periodical title.** Italicize the periodical title, including the article "The." Capitalize all major words.

D **The volume number and issue number if appropriate.** Use the abbreviations "vol." and "no." to indicate the volume number and issue number.

E **The date of publication.** For journals, give the season and year of publication. For monthly magazines, give the month and year. For weekly magazines and newspapers, give the day, month, and year, in that order. Abbreviate the names of all months except May, June, and July.

F **Inclusive page number(s).** Include section letters for newspapers, if relevant.

G **The name of the database.** Italicize the name of the database, followed by a comma.

H **The DOI or URL.** Many sources from databases include a stable identifier called a permalink or a DOI (digital object identifier). Include the DOI in your works cited entry. If a source does not have a permalink or a DOI, include a URL.

35. Article in a newspaper If the newspaper is not a national newspaper (such as the *Wall Street Journal*, *Christian Science Monitor*, or *Chronicle of Higher Education*) or if the city of publication is not part of its name, add the city in square brackets after the name of the newspaper: "[Salem]." List the date in inverted order, followed by the page numbers (use the section letter before the page number if the newspaper uses letters to designate sections). If the article does not appear on consecutive pages, write only the first page number and a plus sign (+), with no space between.

> Sherry, Allison. "Volunteers' Personal Touch Turns High-Tech Data into Votes." *The Denver Post*, 30 Oct. 2012, pp. 1A+.

For newspaper articles found online, cite as you would a print article and give the URL.

> Humphrey, Tom. "Politics Outweigh School Vouchers." *Knoxville News Sentinel*, 24 Jan. 2016, www.knoxnews.com/opinion/columnists/tom-humphrey/tom -humphrey-politics-outweigh-arguments-about-school-vouchers-29c77b33-9963 -0ef8-e053-0100007fcba4-366300461.html/.

36. Unsigned article Begin with the title of the article.

> "Zika Virus." *World Health Organization*, 6 Sept. 2016, www.who.int/mediacentre/ factsheets/zik/en/.

37. Editorial Include the word "Editorial" after the page number or URL.

> "City's Blight Fight Making Difference." *The Columbus Dispatch*, 17 Nov. 2015, www.dispatch.com/content/stories/editorials/2015/11/17/1-citys-blight -fight-making-difference.html/. Editorial.

38. Letter to the editor Include the word "Letter" after the page number or URL.

> Adrouny, Salpi. "Our Shockingly Low Local Voter Turnout." *AJC.com*, 8 Nov. 2015, www.ajc.com/news/news/opinion/readers-write-nov-8/npHrS/. Letter.

39. Review Start with the author and title of the review, then the words "Review of" followed by the title of the work under review. Insert a comma and the word "by" or "editor" (for an edited book) or "director" (for a play or film) and the name of the author or director. Continue with publication information for the review. Use this citation format for all reviews, including books, films, and video games.

> Walton, James. "Noble, Embattled Souls." Review of *The Bone Clocks* and *Slade House*, by David Mitchell. *The New York Review of Books*, 3 Dec. 2015, pp. 55-58.

Cite online reviews as you would a print review, then give the URL.

> Savage, Phil. "*Fallout 4* Review." Review of *Fallout 4*, by Bethesda Game Studios. *PC Gamer*, Future Publishing, 8 Nov. 2015, www.pcgamer.com/fallout-4-review/.

40. Published interview Begin with the person interviewed. If the published interview has a title, give it in quotation marks. If not, write the word "Interview." If an interviewer is identified and relevant to your project, give that name next. Then supply the publication information.

> Weddington, Sarah. "Sarah Weddington: Still Arguing for *Roe*." Interview by Michele Kort. *Ms.*, Winter 2013, pp. 32-35.

Cite an online interview as you would a print interview, then give the URL.

> Jaffrey, Madhur. "Madhur Jaffrey on How Indian Cuisine Won Western Taste Buds." Interview by Shadrach Kabango. *Q*, CBC Radio, 29 Oct. 2015, www.cbc .ca/1.3292918/.

Reference Works

41. Entry in a dictionary or an encyclopedia (including a wiki) Unless the entry is signed, begin your citation with the title of the entry in quotation marks, followed by a period. Give the title of the reference work (beginning with the first word other than *A*, *An*, or *The*), italicized, and the edition (if available) and year of publication. If there is no date of publication, include your date of access.

> "Ball's in Your Court, The." *The American Heritage Dictionary of Idioms*. 2nd ed., Houghton Mifflin Harcourt, 2013.

Cite an online entry as you would a print entry, then give the URL.

"House Music." *Wikipedia*, 16 Nov. 2015, en.wikipedia.org/wiki/House_music.

42. Map or chart Generally, treat a map or chart as you would a book without authors, listing its title and publication information. For a map in an atlas or other volume, give the map title (in quotation marks), followed by publication information for the atlas and page numbers for the map. If the creator of the map or chart is listed, use his or her name as you would an author's name.

"Greenland." *Atlas of the World*. 19th ed., Oxford UP, 2012, p. 154.

For a map or chart found online, cite as you would a print source, then give the URL.

"Map of Sudan." *Global Citizen*, Citizens for Global Solutions, 2011, globalsolutions
.org/blog/bashir#.VthzNMfi_FI/.

43. Government publication In most cases, cite the government agency as the author. If there is a named author, editor, or compiler, provide that name after the title.

Canada, Minister of Aboriginal Affairs and Northern Development. *2015-16 Report on Plans
and Priorities*. Minister of Public Works and Government Services Canada, 2015.

United States, Department of Agriculture. *Eligibility Manual for School Meals:
Determining and Verifying Eligibility. National School Lunch Program*. Food and
Nutrition Service, July 2015, www.fns.usda.gov/sites/default/files/cn/SP40
_CACFP18_SFSP20-2015a1.pdf/.

44. Brochure or pamphlet Format the entry as you would for a book (see p. 677).

The Legendary Sleepy Hollow Cemetery. Friends of Sleepy Hollow Cemetery, 2008.

Field Sources

45. Personal interview Place the name of the person interviewed first, words to indicate how the interview was conducted ("Personal interview," "Telephone interview," or "E-mail interview"), and the date. (Note that MLA style is to hyphenate *e-mail*.)

Akufo, Dautey. Personal interview, 11 Apr. 2016.

46. Unpublished letter If the letter was written to you, give the writer's name, the words "Letter to the author" (no quotation marks), and the date the letter was written.

> Primak, Shoshana. Letter to the author, 6 May 2016.

If the letter was written to someone else, give that name rather than "the author."

47. Lecture or public address Give the speaker's name and the title of the lecture (if there is one). If the lecture was part of a meeting or convention, identify that event. Conclude with the event information, including venue, city, and date. End with the appropriate label ("Lecture," "Panel discussion," "Reading").

> Smith, Anna Deavere. "On the Road: A Search for American Character." National Endowment for the Humanities. John F. Kennedy Center for the Performing Arts, Washington, 6 Apr. 2015. Address.

For lectures and public addresses found on the Web, provide the URL after the date. End with the appropriate label ("Lecture," "Panel discussion," "Reading").

> Khosla, Raj. "Precision Agriculture and Global Food Security." *US Department of State: Diplomacy in Action*, 26 Mar. 2013, www.state.gov/e/stas/series/212172.htm/. Address.

Media Sources

48. Film or video Generally begin with the title of the film or recording. If you want to emphasize an individual's role, such as the director or actor, list that name first. Always supply the name of the director (followed by a comma and the label "director"), the distributor, and the year of original release. You may also insert other relevant information, such as the names of the performers or screenplay writers, before the distributor.

> *Birdman or (The Unexpected Virtue of Ignorance)*. Directed by Alejandro González Iñárritu, performances by Michael Keaton, Emma Stone, Zach Galifianakis, Edward Norton, and Naomi Watts, Fox Searchlight, 2014.

> Damon, Matt. *The Martian*. Directed by Ridley Scott, Twentieth Century Fox, 2015.

For videos found on the Web, give the URL after the publication information.

> Fletcher, Antoine. "The Ancient Art of the Atlatl." *Russell Cave National Monument*,
> narrated by Brenton Bellomy, National Park Service, 12 Feb. 2014, www.nps.gov/
> media/video/view.htm?id=C92C0D0A-1DD8-B71C-07CBC6E8970CD73F/.

49. Television or radio program Begin with the title of the episode in quotation marks. Then give the title of the program, italicized, and relevant information about the program, such as the writer, director, performers, or narrator. Then provide the episode number (if any), the network, and the date of broadcast. If the material you're citing is an interview, include the word "Interview" and, if relevant, the name of the interviewer.

> "Federal Role in Support of Autism." *Washington Journal*, narrated by Robb Harleston,
> C-SPAN, 1 Dec. 2012.

> "The Key to Zen for Tony Bennett: 'Life Is a Gift.'" *Talk of the Nation*, narrated by Neal
> Conan, NPR, 20 Nov. 2012.

If you accessed the program on the Web, include the URL after the date of publication.

> "Take a Giant Step." *Prairie Home Companion*, narrated by Garrison Keillor, American Public
> Media, 27 Feb. 2016, prairiehome.publicradio.org/listen/full/?name=phc/2016/02/
> 27/phc_20160227_128/.

50. Sound recording or audio clip Begin with the name of the person whose work you want to highlight: the composer, the conductor, or the performer. Next list the title, followed by the names of other artists (composer, conductor, performers). The recording information includes the manufacturer and the date.

> Bizet, Georges. *Carmen*. Performances by Jennifer Larmore, Thomas Moser, Angela
> Gheorghiu, and Samuel Ramey, Bavarian State Orchestra and Chorus, conducted by
> Giuseppe Sinopoli, Warner, 1996.

If you wish to cite a particular track on the recording, give its performer and title (in quotation marks), and then proceed with the information about the recording. For live recordings, include the date of the performance between the title and the recording information. For recordings found online, include the URL after the publication date.

> Adele. "Hello." *25*. XL, 2015.

For audio clips accessed on the Web, add the URL after the publication information.

> Goldbarth, Albert. "Fourteen Pages." *The Poetry Foundation*, 15 Apr. 2016, www
> .poetryfoundation.org/features/audio/detail/89129/.

51. Work of art, photograph, or other image Give the name of the artist; the title of the work (italicized); the date of composition; the name of the collection, museum, or owner; and the city. If you are citing artwork published in a book, add the publication information for the book. If you are citing a photograph, add the label "Photograph" after the city.

> Bradford, Mark. *Let's Walk to the Middle of the Ocean*. 2015, Museum of Modern Art,
> New York.

> Feinstein, Harold. *Hangin' Out, Sharing a Public Bench, NYC*. 1948, Panopticon Gallery,
> Boston. Photograph.

For online visuals, including charts or graphs, include the website (italicized), and the URL.

> Hura, Sohrab. *Old Man Lighting a Fire*. 2015, *Magnum Photos*, www.magnumphotos
> .com/C.aspx?VP3=SearchResult&ALID=2K1HRG681B/.

> *Brazilian Waxing and Waning: The Economy*. The Economist, 1 Dec. 2015, www
> .economist.com/blogs/graphicdetail/2015/12/economic-backgrounder/.

52. Advertisement Provide the name of the product, service, or organization being advertised, followed by the usual publication information. End with the word "Advertisement." For advertisements found online, include the URL before "Advertisement."

> AT&T. *National Geographic*, Dec. 2015, p. 14. Advertisement.

> Toyota. *The Root*. Slate Group, 28 Nov. 2015, www.theroot.com/. Advertisement.

53. Cartoon Treat a cartoon like an article in a newspaper or magazine. Give the cartoonist's name, the title of the cartoon if there is one (in quotation marks), the publication information for the source, and the word "Cartoon."

> Zyglis, Adam. "City of Light." *Buffalo News*, 8 Nov. 2015, adamzyglis.buffalonews
> .com/2015/11/08/city-of-light/. Cartoon.

54. Live performance Generally, begin with the title of the performance. Then give the author and director; the major performers; and the theater, city, and date.

> *The Draft*. By Peter Snoad, directed by Diego Arciniegas, Hibernian Hall, Boston,
>   10 Sept. 2015.

Digital Sources

55. Short work from a website Provide the name of the author; the title of the work in quotation marks; the title of the website, italicized; the date of publication in reverse order, and the URL.

> Enzinna, Wes. "Syria's Unknown Revolution." *Pulitzer Center on Crisis Reporting*, 24 Nov.
>   2015, pulitzercenter.org/projects/middle-east-syria-enzinna-war-rojava/.

If there is no author given, begin the citation with the title of the work and proceed with the rest of the publication information. If the title of the website does not indicate the sponsoring organization, list the sponsor before the URL. If there is no date of publication, give the date of access after the URL.

> "Social and Historical Context: Vitality." *Arapesh Grammar and Digital Language Archive*
>   *Project*, Institute for Advanced Technology in the Humanities, www.arapesh.org/
>   socio_historical_context_vitality.php/. Accessed 22 Mar. 2016.

56. Academic course or department website For a course page, give the name of the instructor, the course title, the institution in italics, year, and the URL. For a department page, give the department name, a description such as "Department home page," the institution in italics, the date of the last update, and the URL.

> Masiello, Regina. ENG 101: Expository Writing. *Rutgers School of Arts and Sciences*,
>   2016, wp.rutgers.edu/courses/55-355101/.

> Film Studies. Department home page. *Wayne State University, College of Liberal Arts and*
>   *Sciences*, 2016, clas.wayne.edu/FilmStudies/.

57. Message posted to a newsgroup, electronic mailing list, or online discussion forum Cite the name of the person who posted the message and the title (from the subject line, in quotation marks); if the posting has no title, add the

How do I cite works from websites using MLA style?

You will likely need to scan the website to find some of the citation information you need. For some sites, all the details may not be available; find as many as you can. If you cannot find a publication date, provide the date you accessed the website. Remember that the citation information you provide should allow readers to retrace your steps to locate the sources. Consult pages 691–694 for additional models for citing Web sources.

The Chronicle of Higher Education, via The YGS Group

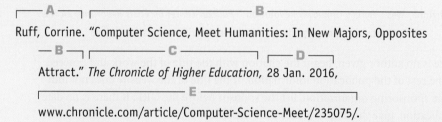

Ruff, Corrine. "Computer Science, Meet Humanities: In New Majors, Opposites Attract." *The Chronicle of Higher Education,* 28 Jan. 2016, www.chronicle.com/article/Computer-Science-Meet/235075/.

A   **The author of the work.** Give the last name first, followed by a comma, the first name, and the middle initial (if given). Omit titles such as "MD," "PhD," or "Sir"; include suffixes after the name and a comma (O'Driscoll, Gerald P., Jr.). Insert a period. If no author is given, begin with the title.

B   **The title of the work.** Give the full title; include the subtitle (if any), preceded by a colon. Enclose the title and subtitle in quotation marks, and capitalize all major words. Place a period inside the closing quotation mark.

C   **The title of the website.** Give the title of the entire site, italicized. If there is no clear title and it is a personal home page, use "Home page" without italicizing it. If the sponsoring organization is different from the website title, list that information next. Follow with a comma.

D   **The date of publication or most recent update.** Use the day-month-year format; abbreviate all months except May, June, and July. End with a comma. (If no publication date is given, provide the date of access at the end of the entry. After the URL, insert the word "Accessed" and the date you accessed the work.)

E   **The URL.** Give the URL for the article, and end with a period.

phrase "Online posting." Then add the name of the website (italicized), the sponsor or publisher, the date of the message, and the URL.

> Robin, Griffith. "Write for the Reading Teacher." *Developing Digital Literacies*, NCTE, 23
>   Oct. 2015, ncte.connectedcommunity.org/communities/community-home/
>   digestviewer/viewthread?GroupId=1693&MID=24520&tab=digestviewer
>   &CommunityKey=628d2ad6-8277-4042-a376-2b370ddceabf/.

58. Blog To cite an entry or a comment on a blog, give the author of the entry or comment (if available), the title of the entry or comment in quotation marks, the title of the blog (italicized), the sponsor or publisher, the date the material was posted, and the URL.

> Cimons, Marlene. "Why Cities Could Be the Key to Solving the Climate Crisis."
>   *Thinkprogress.org*, Center for American Progress Action Fund, 10 Dec. 2015,
>   thinkprogress.org/climate/2015/12/10/3730938/cities-key-to-climate-crisis/.

59. E-mail message Start with the sender of the message. Then give the subject line in quotation marks, followed by a period. Identify the recipient of the message and provide the date of the message.

> Thornbrugh, Caitlin. "Coates Lecture." Received by Rita Anderson, 20 Oct. 2015.

60. Facebook post or comment Follow the general format for citing a short work on a website.

> Bedford English. "Stacey Cochran explores Reflective Writing in the Classroom and
>   as a Writer." *Facebook*, 15 Feb. 2016, www.facebook.com/BedfordEnglish/
>   posts/10153415001259607/.

61. Twitter post (tweet) Provide the entire tweet in place of the title, and include the time after the date.

> Curiosity Rover. "Can you see me waving? How to spot #Mars in the night sky: https://
>   youtu.be/hv8hVvJlcJQ." *Twitter*, 5 Nov. 2015, 11:00 a.m., twitter.com/marscuriosity/
>   status/672859022911889408/.

62. Computer software, app, or video game Cite computer software as you would a book.

Words with Friends. Version 5.84. Zynga, 2013.

63. Other online sources For other online sources, adapt the guidelines to the medium. Include as much information as necessary for your readers to easily find your source. The example below is for a podcast. Because no publication date is given, the citation ends with the access date instead.

Tanner, Laura. "Virtual Reality in 9/11 Fiction." *Literature Lab*, Department of English, Brandeis U, www.brandeis.edu/departments/english/literaturelab/tanner.html/. Accessed 14 Feb. 2016.

24 Using APA Style

 American Psychological Association (APA) style, used primarily
in the social sciences and in some of the natural sciences,
emphasizes the author(s) and publication date of a source.
Writers who use the APA documentation system cite, or
formally acknowledge, information within their text using
parentheses and provide a list of sources, called a references
list, at the end of their document.

To see student essays formatted and documented in APA style,
use one of the following examples in Part Two:

- Ellen Page, *To Spray or Not to Spray: DDT Use for Indoor
Residual Spraying*, page 213

- Dwight Haynes, *Making Better Choices: Two Approaches to
Reducing College Drinking*, page 333

For more information about APA style, consult the *Publication
Manual of the American Psychological Association*, Sixth Edition.
Information about this publication can be found on the APA
website at www.apa.org.

Using APA Style

How Do I Cite Sources within the Text of My Document?

APA uses an author-date form of in-text citation to acknowledge the use of another writer's words, facts, or ideas. When you are summarizing or paraphrasing, provide the author's last name and the year of publication either in the sentence or in parentheses at the end of the sentence. You may include a page or chapter reference if it would help readers find the original material in a longer work. When you are quoting, the citation in parentheses must include the page(s) or paragraph(s) (for sources that do not have pages) in which the quotation can be found.

Although APA requires page or paragraph numbers only for direct quotations, your instructor might prefer that you include a page or paragraph number with every source you cite in your document. If you're not certain of the requirements for your project, ask your instructor for guidance.

1. Basic format for a source named in your text Place the publication year in parentheses directly after the author's last name. Include the page number (with "p." for "page") in parentheses after a direct quotation.

> Jennings (2012) pointed out that humans are poor students of probability, meaning that we're prone to "develop paranoid nightmare-inducing phobias about the unlikeliest things (plane crashes, strangers kidnapping our kids) while ignoring far more pressing risks (heart disease, car accidents)" (p. xiv).

> According to Jennings (2012), humans have a tendency to fear the most unlikely phenomena, while brushing off more apparent dangers.

Note that APA style requires using the past tense or present perfect tense to introduce the material you are citing: *Jennings argued* or *Jennings has argued.*

2. Basic format for a source not named in your text Insert a parenthetical note that gives the author's last name and the year of the publication, separated by a comma. For a quotation, include the page or paragraph number of the source.

> Psychoneuroimmunology, a new field of medicine, "studies the ways that the psyche — the mind and its content of emotions — profoundly interacts with the body's nervous

system and how both of them, in turn, form an essential link with our immune defenses" (Mate, 2011, p. 5).

Psychoneuroimmunology is a new field of medicine that examines the link between human emotion and physiology and how that unity affects health and immunity over the course of a life (Mate, 2011).

3. Two authors List the last names of both authors in every mention in the text. If you mention the authors' names in a sentence, use the word "and" to separate the last names, as shown in the first example. If you place the authors' names in the parenthetical citation, use an ampersand (&) to separate the last names, as shown in the second example.

Tannenbaum and Marks (2012) indicated that "many of [MTV's] most important founders came from radio backgrounds, which freed them from abiding by the existing rules of the television industry" (p. 14).

MTV was largely founded by individuals with radio expertise, which allowed the network to operate outside the constraints of the television industry (Tannenbaum & Marks, 2012).

4. Three, four, or five authors In parentheses, name all the authors the first time you cite the source, using an ampersand (&) before the last author's name. In subsequent references to the source, use the last name of the first author followed by the abbreviation "et al." (Latin for "and others").

Those who suffer from body dysmorphic disorder (BDD) are preoccupied with one or more areas of the body they feel are imperfect or deformed (Wilhelm, Phillips, & Steketee, 2013). As a result, they tend to engage in compulsive rituals to improve or conceal the perceived flaw (Wilhelm et al., 2013).

5. Six or more authors In all references to the source, give the first author's last name followed by "et al."

While their study suggests that female Operation Enduring Freedom and Operation Iraqi Freedom soldiers are just as resilient to combat-related stress as are male soldiers, Vogt et al. (2011) submitted that further research is needed to evaluate gender differences in the long-term effects of stress postdeployment.

6. Corporate, group, or government author In general, cite the full name of the corporation, group, or government agency the first time it is mentioned in your text. If you add an abbreviation for the name in square brackets the first time you cite the source, you can use the abbreviation in subsequent citations.

> A new international treaty has been signed to help combat the illicit trade of tobacco products (World Health Organization [WHO], 2013). This protocol not only will establish a global tracing system to reduce and eliminate illicit tobacco trade but also will play an important role in protecting people around the world from a serious health risk (WHO, 2013).

7. Unknown author Sources with unknown authors are listed by title in the list of references (see item 18 on p. 702). In your in-text citation, shorten the title as much as possible without introducing confusion. Add quotation marks to article titles, and italicize book titles.

> While life expectancy in general has improved for those living in developed countries, the improvement has been far more drastic for men — a phenomenon that is closing the gender gap in longevity ("Catching Up," 2013).

8. Two or more works by the same author in the same year After organizing the works alphabetically by title, insert a lowercase letter after the publication year ("2013a" or "2013b").

> Garfield (2016b) noted that our evolution as a society is consistently reflected in how we map our world: from the origins of triangulation and the fixing of longitude to aerial photography and, now, GPS and satellite navigation.

9. Two or more authors with the same last name Use the authors' initials in each citation.

> While both R. Cohen (2012) and L. Cohen (2012) have presented stark and sincere biographies free of bias, L. Cohen has introduced a new concept to the genre by chronicling three worthy subjects at once.

10. Two or more works cited together List the sources in alphabetical order, and separate them with semicolons. If you are referring to two or more sources by the same author, order those sources chronologically and separate them with commas; give the author's last name only once ("Gharib, 2010, 2012").

Rather than encourage exploration into more difficult and inaccessible energy stores, our new awareness of the finite nature of the earth's resources should incite a change in lifestyle that no longer strains the limits of our environment (Dietz & O'Neill, 2013; Klare, 2012).

11. Source cited in another source   Ideally, you should track down the original source of the information. If you cannot find the original, mention its author and indicate where it was cited.

Slater posited that the rise in online dating services has led to a decrease in commitment, as this technology fosters the notion that one can always find a more compatible mate (as cited in Weissmann, 2013).

12. Source with no page numbers   Many visual documents, such as brochures, and digital sources, such as websites and full-text articles from databases, lack page numbers. If the source has numbered paragraphs, indicate the paragraph number using the abbreviation "para." If the paragraphs are not numbered, include the section heading and indicate which paragraph in that section contains the cited material.

Doig (2012) examined the rise in tactical urbanism, a kind of city planning newly employed by big government to take small bits of unusable public space and re-create them as parks, gardens, and other areas designed for public use (para. 3).

13. E-mail, letters, and other personal communication   Give the first initial(s) and last name of the person with whom you corresponded, the words "personal communication," and the date. Don't include personal communication in your references list.

(C. Soto, personal communication, May 13, 2016)

14. Website   For an entire website, give the URL in parentheses in your text, and don't include it in your references list. To cite a quotation from a website, give the paragraph number or section heading and include the source in your references list.

The Library of Congress (http://loc.gov) offers extensive online collections of manuscripts, correspondence, sound recordings, photographs, prints, and audiovisual materials spanning decades of American history.

The Environmental Protection Agency (2016) combats climate change by evaluating policy options that "range from comprehensive market-based legislation to targeted regulations to reduce emissions and improve the efficiency of vehicles, power plants and large industrial sources" (para. 2).

How Do I Prepare the References List?

The references list contains publication information for all sources that you have cited within your document, with two exceptions. Entire websites and personal communication, such as e-mail messages, letters, and interviews, are cited only in the text of the document.

Begin the list on a new page at the end of the document, and center the title "References" at the top. Organize the list alphabetically by author (if the source is an organization, alphabetize it by the name of the organization; if the source has no known author, alphabetize it by title). All the entries should be double-spaced with no extra space between entries. Entries are formatted with a hanging indent: the first line is flush with the left margin, and subsequent lines are indented one-half inch. Only the initial word and proper nouns (names of people, organizations, cities, states, and so on) in a source title and subtitle are capitalized.

In longer documents, a references list may be given at the end of each chapter or section. In digital documents that use links, such as websites, the references list is often a separate page to which other pages are linked.

For examples of references lists in APA style, see pages 219 and 338.

Books

15. One author List the author's last name followed by a comma and the first initial. Insert the date in parentheses and italicize the title. Follow with the place of publication and the publisher, separated by a colon.

> Orenstein, P. (2016). *Girls and sex: Navigating the complicated new landscape.* New York, NY: HarperCollins.

Cite the online version only if a print version is not available or is hard to find. Insert "n.d." if no publication date is given.

> Robinson, K. (n.d.). *Beyond the wilderness*. Retrieved from http://onlineoriginals.com /showitem.asp?itemID=113

If you consulted an e-reader, list the format in square brackets. The URL stands in place of information about the publisher. If you accessed the online version from a paid site, such as Amazon.com, use the phrase "Available from" rather than "Retrieved from."

> Inoue, A. B. (2015). *Antiracist writing assessment ecologies: Teaching and assessing writing for a socially just future* [ePub]. Retrieved from http://wac.colostate.edu /books/inoue/ecologies.epub

16. Two or more authors   List the authors in the same order that the title page does, each with last name first. Use commas to separate authors and use an ampersand (&) before the final author's name. List every author up to and including seven; for a work with eight or more authors, give the first six names followed by three ellipsis dots and the last author's name. (Do not use an ampersand in such cases.)

> Watkins, D., & Brook, Y. (2016). *Equal is unfair: America's misguided fight against income inequality*. New York, NY: St. Martin's Press.

> Grant, A., & Sandberg, S. (2016). *Originals: How non-conformists move the world* [Kindle]. Available from http://amazon.com

17. Corporate or group author   Write out the full name of a corporate or group author. If the corporation is also the publisher, use "Author" for the publisher's name.

> Linguistic Society of America. (2016). *Annual report: The state of linguistics in higher education*. Washington, DC: Author.

18. Unknown author   When no author is listed on the title or copyright page, begin the entry with the title of the work. Alphabetize the entry by the first significant word of the title (not including *A*, *An*, or *The*).

> *The book of Aquarius: Alchemy and the philosopher's stone*. (2011). Charleston, SC: Forgotten Books.

19. Two or more books by the same author(s) Give the author's name in each entry and list the titles in chronological order.

> Duhigg, C. (2012). *The power of habit: Why we do what we do in life and business.* New York, NY: Random House.

> Duhigg, C. (2016). *Smarter, faster, better: The secrets of being productive in life and business.* New York, NY: Random House.

20. Translated book List the author first, followed by the year of publication, the title, and the translator (in parentheses, identified by the abbreviation "Trans."). Place the original date of the work's publication at the end of the entry.

> Mauriac, F. (2015). *What I believe* (W. Fowlie, Trans.). London, England: Forgotten Books. (Original work published 1963).

21. Edition other than the first Note the edition ("2nd ed.," "Rev. ed.") after the title.

> Spatt, B. (2016). *Writing from sources* (9th ed.). Boston, MA: Bedford/St. Martin's.

22. Author with an editor Include the editor's name and the abbreviation "Ed." in parentheses after the title.

> Newport, M. T. (2011). *Alzheimer's disease: What if there was a cure?* (P. Hirsch, Ed.). Laguna Beach, CA: Basic Health Publications.

23. Work in an edited collection or anthology, including a foreword, introduction, preface, or afterword Begin with the author, publication date, and title of the selection (not italicized). Follow with the word "In," the names of the editors (initials first), the abbreviation "Ed." or "Eds." in parentheses, the title of the anthology or collection (italicized), inclusive page numbers for the selection (in parentheses, with the abbreviation "pp."), and the place and publisher.

> Sargeant, S. (2016). Psychology and models of health. In A. Tom & P. Greasley (Eds.), *Psychology for nursing* (pp. 21-34). London, England: Polity Press.

> Joli, F. (2016). Foreword. In J. Arena, *Legends of disco: Forty stars discuss their careers* (pp. 1-2). Jefferson, NC: McFarland.

How do I cite books using APA style?

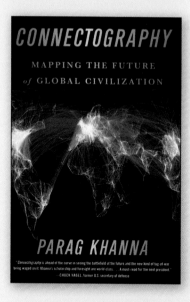

Penguin Random House, LLC.

When citing a book, use the information from the title page and the copyright page, not from the book's cover or a library catalog. Consult pages 701–705 for additional models for citing books.

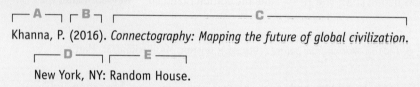

Khanna, P. (2016). *Connectography: Mapping the future of global civilization.*
New York, NY: Random House.

A **The author.** Give the last name first, followed by a comma and initials for first name and, if any, middle name. Separate initials with a space (Leakey, R. E.). Separate the names of multiple authors with commas; use an ampersand (&) before the final author's name.

B **The year of publication.** Put the most recent copyright year in parentheses, and end with a period (outside the closing parenthesis).

C **The title and, if any, the subtitle.** Give the full title; include the subtitle (if any), preceded by a colon. Italicize the title and subtitle, capitalizing only the first word of the title, the first word of the subtitle, and any proper nouns or proper adjectives. End with a period.

D **The place of publication.** If more than one city is given, use the first one listed. Use an abbreviation for U.S. states and territories; spell out city and country names for locations outside the United States (Cambridge, England). For Canadian cities, also include the province. Insert a colon.

E **The publisher.** Give the publisher's name. Omit words such as "Inc." and "Co." Include and do not abbreviate such terms as "University," "Books," and "Press." End with a period.

24. Sacred text Treat as you would a book (see items 15–18 on pp. 701–702).

> *Holy Bible: King James version.* (2011). New York, NY: American Bible Society.

25. Dissertation or thesis Give the author, date, and title before identifying the type of work (doctoral dissertation or master's thesis). End with the name of the database and the identifying number, or the URL.

> West, R. (2012). *Hostility toward the unattractive: Challenging current "sexual harassment" law* (Doctoral dissertation). Available from ProQuest Dissertations and Theses. (AAI 3545458)

26. Two or more sources by the same author in the same year List the works alphabetically, and include lowercase letters (*a*, *b*, and so on) after the dates.

> Roach, M. (2013a). *Gulp: Adventures on the alimentary canal.* New York, NY: W. W. Norton.

> Roach, M. (2013b). *My planet: Finding humor in the oddest places.* White Plains, NY: Reader's Digest.

Sources in Journals, Magazines, and Newspapers

27. Article in a journal Most journals continue page numbers throughout an entire annual volume, beginning again at page 1 only in the first volume of the next year. After the author and publication year, provide the article title, the journal title, the volume number (italicized), and the inclusive page numbers.

> Thonus, T. (2016). Time to say goodbye: Writing center consultation closings. *Linguistics and Education, 33*, 40-55.

If every issue of the journal begins at page 1, include the issue number in parentheses, not italicized, directly after the volume number.

> Garicano, L., & Rayo, L. (2016). Why organizations fail: Models and cases. *Journal of Economic Literature, 54*(1), 137-192.

Many online journal articles now have DOIs (digital object identifiers), unique numbers assigned to specific content. If an article has a DOI, list it at the end of the entry; you do not need to list the database you used to access the article or the date you accessed the database.

> Logan, J. R. (2016, March 29). As long as there are neighborhoods. *City & Community,*
> *159*(1), 23-28. doi:10.1111/cico.12149

If no DOI is available for an article accessed on the Web or in a database, give the URL for the journal's home page instead.

> West, M. R. (2016). Schools of choice. *Education Next 16*(2). Retrieved from http://
> educationnext.org/

28. Article in a magazine Give the publication date as year and month for monthly magazines; year, month, and date for weekly or biweekly magazines. Place the issue number, if any, in parentheses directly after the volume number. Include all page numbers. For articles accessed on the Web, end with the URL of the magazine's home page.

> Fecht, S. (2012, December). Reef in a box. *Popular Science, 281*(6), 16.

> Galea, S. (2016, April 5). Your healthy lifestyle won't necessarily make you healthier.
> *Wired*. Retrieved from http://www.wired.com/

29. Article in a newspaper Give the publication date as year, month, and date. Next give the article title followed by the name of the newspaper (italicized). Include all page numbers, preceded by "p." or "pp."

> Levenson, M. (2016, April 11). School closings bring pain, and not always savings.
> *Boston Globe*, p. A1.

30. Unsigned article Begin with the article title, and alphabetize in the references list by the first word in the title other than *A, An,* or *The.* Use "p." or "pp." before page numbers.

> RNA-only genes: The origin of species? (2012, April 28). *The Economist, 388*(8592), p. 40.

31. Editorial Include the word "Editorial" in square brackets after the title.

> Affirm gays' right to marriage [Editorial]. (2012, December 14). *The Dallas Morning*
> *News*, p. B12.

32. Letter to the editor Include the words "Letter to the editor" in square brackets after the title of the letter or, if the letter is untitled, in place of the title.

> Gonzalez Hernandez, L. (2012, November 23). Stores should close on holidays [Letter to the editor]. *Newsday*, p. A24.

33. Review After the title of the review, include the words "Review of the book . . ." or "Review of the film . . ." and so on in square brackets, followed by the title of the work reviewed. If the reviewed work is a book, include the author's name after a comma; if it's a film or other media, include the year of release. If the review is untitled, give the bracketed information in place of the title.

> Lane, A. (2014, December 15). Swinging seventies [Review of the film *Inherent Vice*, 2014]. *The New Yorker*, p. 76.

> Green, J. (2016, March 10). Theater review: Michelle Williams and Jeff Daniels in a superb *Blackbird* [Review of the play *Blackbird*, 2016]. Retrieved from http://www.vulture.com/

Reference Works

34. Entry in a dictionary or an encyclopedia (including a wiki) Begin your citation with the name of the author or, if the entry is unsigned, the title of the entry. Proceed with the date, the entry title (if not already given), the title of the reference work, the edition number, and the pages. If the contents of the reference work are arranged alphabetically, omit the volume and page numbers. If the entry was found online, provide the DOI or URL. Because the material on a wiki is likely to change, include a retrieval date as well.

> Ray, S., & Schwarz, H. (2016). Globalization. In *Encyclopedia of post-colonial studies*. Malden, MA: Wiley-Blackwell.

> House music. (2015). *Wikipedia*. Retrieved November 16, 2015, from en.wikipedia .org/wiki/House_music

35. Government publication Give the name of the department, office, agency, or committee that issued the report as the author. If the document has a report or special file number, place that in parentheses after the title. If the publication was found online, provide the DOI or URL.

> United States Congress. (2015). *Economic indicators, October 2015*. Washington, DC: Government Printing Office.

How do I cite articles from print periodicals using APA style?

Periodicals include journals, magazines, and newspapers. This page gives an example of a citation for an article in a magazine. Models for citing articles from journals and newspapers are on pages 705–706. To cite a periodical article you accessed online, see page. 710.

Discover Magazine, Kalmbach Publishing Co. © 2015.

McCommons, J. (2015, July/August). A dream of flight. *Discover, 36*(6), 24-29.

A   **The author.** Give the last name first, followed by a comma and initials for first and middle names. Separate the names of multiple authors with commas; use an ampersand (&) before the final author's name.

B   **The year of publication.** Put the year and the month, separated by a comma, inside parentheses. For weekly magazines and newspapers, include the day (2012, April 13). End with a period.

C   **The article title.** Give the full title; include the subtitle (if any), preceded by a colon. Do not underline, italicize, or put the title in quotation marks. Capitalize only the first word of the title, the first word of the subtitle, and any proper nouns or proper adjectives. End with a period (unless the article title ends with a question mark).

D   **The periodical title.** Italicize the periodical title, and capitalize all major words. Insert a comma.

E   **The volume and issue number, if relevant.** For magazines and journals with volume numbers, include the volume number, italicized. For magazines and for journals that start each issue with page 1, include the issue number in parentheses, not italicized. Insert a comma.

F   **Inclusive page number(s).** Give all the numbers in full (248-254, not 248-54). For newspapers, include the abbreviation "p." or "pp." for page and section letters, if relevant (p. B12). End with a period.

36. Brochure or pamphlet Format the entry as you would a book (see items 15–18 on pp. 701–702); insert "n.d." if there is no publication date.

> UNESCO. (n.d.). *The world heritage brochure*. Paris: Author Press.

Field Sources

37. Personal interview Treat unpublished interviews as personal communications, and include them in your text only (see item 13 on p. 700). Do not cite personal interviews in your references list.

38. Unpublished survey data Give the title of the survey first, followed by the date the survey was distributed, and the words "Unpublished raw data."

> *The University of Iowa graduation exit survey*. (2012, April 22). Unpublished raw data.

39. Unpublished letter Treat unpublished letters as personal communications, and include them in your text only (see item 13 on p. 700). Do not cite unpublished letters in your references list.

40. Lecture or public address Provide the name of the speaker, followed by the full date of the presentation and the title of the speech if there is one. End the entry with a brief description of the event and its location.

> Wolin, P. (2016, May 3*). Descendants of light: American photographers of Jewish ancestry*. 92nd Street Y, New York, NY.

Media Sources

41. Film or video recording List the director and producer (if available), the date of release, the title, the medium in square brackets ("Motion picture," "DVD," or "Blu-ray disc"), the country where the film was made, and the studio or distributor.

> Nichols, J. (Director). (2016). *Loving* [Motion picture]. United States: Focus Features.

42. Television or radio program List the director, writer, producer, host, or reporter (if available); the broadcast date; the title, followed by "Television" or "Radio" and "broadcast" or "series episode" in square brackets; the name of the series; and the city and name of the broadcaster.

> Bee, S. (Host). (2016, February 15). Episode 2 [Television series episode]. In *Full Frontal with Samantha Bee*. Atlanta, GA: TBS.

How do I cite online periodical articles using APA style?

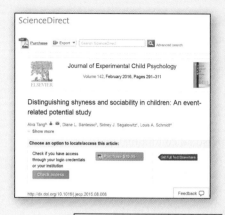

Many periodical articles can be accessed online, either through a journal or magazine's website or through a database. Provide the print publication information, then the Web information. (See also Chapter 13.)

This image was published in *Journal of Experimental Child Psychology*, vol. 142, Alva Tang, Diane L. Santesso, Sidney J. Segalowitz, Louis A. Schmidt, Distinguishing shyness and sociability in children: An event-related potential study, © Elsevier 2016.

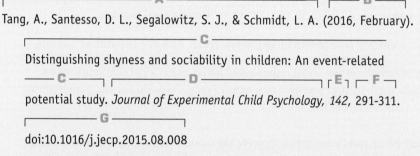

A
B
Tang, A., Santesso, D. L., Segalowitz, S. J., & Schmidt, L. A. (2016, February).

C
Distinguishing shyness and sociability in children: An event-related

C
D
E
F
potential study. *Journal of Experimental Child Psychology, 142,* 291-311.

G
doi:10.1016/j.jecp.2015.08.008

A **The author.** Give the last name first, followed by a comma and initials. Separate the names of multiple authors with commas; use an ampersand (&) before the final author's name.

B **The date of publication.** Put the year and the month, separated by a comma, inside parentheses. For weekly magazines and newspapers, include the day (2012, April 13). End with a period.

C **The article title.** Give the full title; include the subtitle (if any), preceded by a colon. Do not underline, italicize, or put the title or subtitle in quotes. Capitalize only the first word of the title, the first word of the subtitle, and any proper nouns or proper adjectives. End with a period.

D **The periodical title.** Italicize the periodical title, and capitalize all major words. Insert a comma.

E **The volume number and issue number.** For magazines and journals, include the volume number, italicized. For magazines and for journals that start each issue with page 1, include the issue number in parentheses, not italicized. Insert a comma.

F **Inclusive page number(s).** Give all the numbers in full (317-327, not 317-27). For newspapers, include the abbreviation "p." or "pp." for page numbers and, if relevant, section letters (p. B12).

G **The DOI or URL.** If the article has a DOI (a unique digital object identifier), provide it, preceded by "doi:" without a space after the colon. If there is no DOI, include the words "Retrieved from" and the URL of the journal or magazine home page.

43. Sound recording List the author of the song; the date; the song title, followed by "On" and the recording title in italics; the medium in square brackets; and the production data. If the song was recorded by an artist other than the author, add "Recorded by" plus the artist's name in square brackets after the song title and the recording year in parentheses after the production data.

> Clapton, E. (2016). Catch the blues. On *I still do* [CD]. Encinitas, CA: Bushbranch/
>   Surfdog Records.

Digital Sources

44. Web document For a stand-alone Web source such as a report, or a section within a larger website, cite as much of the following information as possible: author, publication date, document title, and URL. If the content is likely to be changed or updated, include your retrieval date.

> Matz, M. (2016, March 24). *Five reasons to protect the Cherokee National Forest.*
>   Retrieved from http://www.pewtrusts.org/

45. E-mail message or real-time communication Because e-mail messages and real-time communications, such as text messages, are difficult or impossible for your readers to retrieve, APA does not recommend including them in your references list. You should treat them as personal communication and cite them parenthetically in your text (see item 13 on p. 700).

46. Message posted to a newsgroup, electronic mailing list, or online discussion forum List the author, posting date, and the title of the post or message subject line. Include a description of the message or post in square brackets. End with the URL where the archived message can be retrieved. Include the name of the group, list, or forum if it's not part of the URL.

> Nelms, J. (2016, January 14). Re: Evaluating writing faculty [Online discussion list
>   post]. Retrieved from https://lists.asu.edu/cgi-bin/wa?A1=ind1601&L=WPA-L#50

47. Blog To cite an entry on a blog, give the author (or screen name, if available), the date the material was posted, and the title of the entry. Include the description "Blog post" or "Blog comment" in square brackets and provide the URL.

> Wade, L. (2016, March 10). Does your vote affect public policy? [Blog post]. Retrieved
>   from https://thesocietypages.org/socimages/2016/03/10/does-your-vote-affect
>   -public-policy/

How do I cite works from websites using APA style?

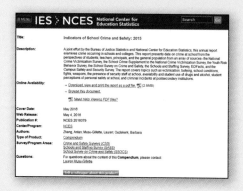

You will likely need to scan the website to find some of the citation information you need. For some sites, all the details may not be available; find as many as you can. Remember that the citation information you provide should allow readers to retrace your steps to locate the sources. Consult pages 711–713 for additional models for citing Web sources.

National Center for Education Statistics

Zhang, A., Musu-Gillette, L., & Oudekerk, B. (2016, May 4). *Indicators of school crime and safety: 2015*. Retrieved from http://nces.ed.gov/pubsearch /pubsinfo.asp?pubid=2016079

A   **The author of the work.** Give the last name first, followed by a comma and initials. Separate the names of multiple authors with commas; use an ampersand (&) before the final author's name. If the source has no author, list the title first and follow it with the date.

B   **The date of publication.** Put the year in parentheses and include the month and day, if available. If there is no date, use "n.d." in parentheses. End with a period (outside the closing parenthesis).

C   **The title of the work.** Give the full title, italicized; include the subtitle (if any), preceded by a colon. Capitalize only the first word of the title, the first word of the subtitle, and any proper nouns or proper adjectives.

D   **Retrieval information.** Include a retrieval date if the material is likely to be changed or updated, or if it lacks a set publication date. (Because this report has a set publication date, the retrieval date is not necessary.) End with the URL.

48. Facebook post Start with the author's name exactly as it appears and the date of the post. Give the first few words of the post in place of the title, and include the label "Facebook post" in square brackets. Include the retrieval date and the URL. If the Facebook page is private and will not be accessible to readers, cite it as you would cite personal communication within the body of your text, not in the reference list.

> Macmillan Learning. (2016, April 28). College readiness and remediation go hand in
>   hand [Facebook post]. Retrieved from https://www.facebook.com/MacmillanLearn/

49. Twitter post Use the author's real name, if possible, followed by the screen name in brackets. Include the entire tweet in place of the title, followed by the label "Tweet" in square brackets. End with the URL.

> Applebaum, Y. (2016, March 29). I can say as a historian, with a fair amount of
>   confidence, that scholars will certainly mine social media in the future —
>   they already are [Tweet]. Retrieved from https://twitter.com/YAppelbaum
>   /status/714822912172285952

50. Podcast Give the name of the producer, the date of the podcast, and the title. Include a description in square brackets and the URL.

> Blumberg, A. (Host). (2015, November 15). The Secret Formula. *StartUp*
>   [Audio podcast]. Retrieved from https://gimletmedia.com/episode
>   /16-the-secret-formula/

51. Online video Give the name of the creator, the date it was posted, and the title. Include a description in square brackets and the URL.

> Neistat, C. (2012, November 3). Staten Island hurricane destruction [Video file].
>   Retrieved from https://www.youtube.com/watch?feature=player_embedded&
>   v=Wr9594oKZNQ#

52. Computer software or game Sometimes a person is named as having rights to the software or game: in that case, list that person as the author, followed by the date in parentheses. Identify the source in square brackets as "Computer software" or "Computer game." End with the place of publication and the publisher, or list the URL if the software is available online. If the creator is not known, begin with the name of the software or game, followed by the label in square brackets and the date in parentheses. End with the location and publisher or URL. If you're referring to a specific version that isn't included in the name, put this information last.

> Rosetta Stone Spanish (Latin America) Level 1 [Computer software]. (2010) Arlington, VA: Rosetta Stone.

Other Sources

53. General advice about other sources For citing other types of sources, APA suggests that you use as a guide a source type listed in its manual that most closely resembles the type of source you want to cite.

Acknowledgments

Index

in MLA style, 691–94
search terms and strategies for, 474–77
websites, 91, 93–94
wikis, 94
Ellipses
with quotations, 641–42, 644
to show omission, 642, 644
E-mail
in APA style, 700, 711
bibliographic information about, 468
collaboration via, 109, 110
evaluating lists, 91
in MLA style, 693
source management and, 465
thank-you notes via, 502
Emotional appeals
in analytical writing, 270
in argumentative writing, 437, 438–39
in oral presentation, 611
Emotional impact, of images, 572
Emphasis, in design, 570
Encyclopedias
entry, in APA style, 707
entry, in MLA style, 686–87
print, 461, 495
Endnotes, 311–13
E-portfolio, 627, 628
Essay maps, 580
Essays
analytical, 280–82
argumentative, 399–404
as assignment, 38
informative, 175–80
problem-solving, 345–49
reflective, 117–23
Ethics, in research, 516–20
Evaluating, sentence starters for, 48
Evaluation
conducting, 321–23
fairness of, 323, 328, 331
of solution to problem, 393–94
of sources, 201, 202–3
of websites, 91, 93–94, 202

Evaluative writing
defined, 284–85
design in, 329
drafting of, 323–30
evidence in, 284–85, 322–23, 324, 326–27
genres in, 315, 329
Haynes, Dwight, "Making Better Choices: Two Approaches to Reducing College Drinking" (student essay), 333–38
media reviews, 301–3, 317
process of, 315–31
product reviews, 315, 317, 339
progress reports, 303–14, 340–41
project ideas for, 339–41
reviewing and improving, 330–32
scholarly articles, 287–94
subjects for, 320
thesis statement for, 325
types of documents in, 286–315
Web-based articles, 294–300
Evaluators, 11, 285, 286, 316
Events, analyzing, 281
field research on, 511
public, 167, 511
Events, sequence of, 220–21
Evidence. *See also* Supporting points
in analytical writing, 259, 269
in argumentative writing, 428–30, 442
clustering of, 539, 540
and context, in evaluative writing, 284–85
in evaluative writing, 284–85, 322–23, 324, 326–27
feedback on, 102–3
genre and, 534
grouping, 539
in informative writing, 205–8
labeling, 538
mapping, 539, 541
in problem-solving writing, 378–79
qualitative *vs.* quantitative, 322–23
reasons supported with, 269–70, 428–30, 533–34, 661

in revision process, 331
on source reliability, 201
to support main point, 68–69, 635–36
to support thesis statement, 533–34
use of, 89
Examples, transition words for, 556
Executive summary, 305–6
Experience. *See* Personal experience
Explanation, sentence starters for, 47
Expressivists, 31

Facebook, 5, 6, 8, 423
post, in APA style, 713
post, in MLA style, 693
Fact checking, 664
Fairness
in evaluative writing, 323, 328, 331
in paraphrasing, 645
in problem solving, 368
in use of evidence, 89
Fair use provision, 518, 648
Fallacies, in arguments, 432–34
False analogies, 433–34
Family, feedback from, 102, 110
Fast fashion, film about, 419
Favorites, saving electronic, 466–67
Feedback, 58–62
from classmates, 8, 102–3
on draft, 104–9
in editing, 667–68
about fairness in judgment, 328
from friends and family, 102, 110
on informal outline, 103
from instructors, 28, 110–11
in peer review, 103–7, 109
in revision process, 662–63
on thesis statement, 102–3
Ferrer, Eileen, et al., "Playing Music to Relieve Stress in a College Classroom Environment," 287–94
Field research, 101, 497–512. *See also* Interviews; Observations; Surveys
bibliographic information about, 468
enlisting help for, 511
evaluating, 94–95
methods of, 461, 498–99

Parenthetical citation, 521–22, 644
Partanen, Anu, "What Americans Keep Ignoring about Finland's School Success," 399–404, 559–60
Partial quotations, 640–41
Participant observer, as writer's point of view, 156–57
Passive voice, 554
Peer review, 92. *See also* Group(s)
  of analytical essay, 274
  of argumentative essay, 443
  context in, 105
  of evaluative essay, 332
  feedback in, 103–7, 109
  guidelines for, 105–9
  to improve document, 104
  of informative essay, 212
  for major project, 104
  plagiarism and, 513–14
  of problem-solving essay, 384
  of reflective writing, 161
  technological tools for, 105
Performance, evaluating, 339
Periodical articles. *See also* Magazine articles
  in APA style, 705–7, 708
  in MLA style, 682, 683
  online, in APA style, 710
Periodical databases, 492, 494
Periodicals, in library, 51, 492
Period (punctuation)
  with ellipses, 644
  with quotation marks, 643, 644
Permission
  to observe, 504–5
  to record interviews, 502
  sample request for, 519
  for using a source, 518–20
Personal communication, in APA style, 700
Personal connections, in ownership of project, 33
Personal experience
  in analytic writing, 257
  in argumentative writing, 427
  building on, 567

  in reflective writing, 117–18, 147, 151, 167
Personal interview. *See also* Interviews
  in MLA style, 687
Persuading
  documents for, 404–19
  use of term, 397
Persuasive writing. *See also* Argumentative writing
  advertisements as, 404–10
Photo essays, as reflective writing, 123–36, 169–70
Photographs, 66. *See also* Visual elements
  in article design, 594
  captions for, 57, 63, 594
  digital tools for, 465–66
  in document design, 578
  in MLA style, 690
  in multimodal essay, 597
  in persuasive advertising, 404–10
Phrases
  avoiding repetition in, 569
  for electronic searches, 474–77
  removing unnecessary, 553
Physical context, 17, 266
Placement, in design, 570
Plagiarism, 513–24
  avoiding, 520–23, 651–53
  excuses for intentional, 522–23
  in group projects, 515–16
  research ethics, 516–20
  response to accusation of, 523–24
  unintentional, 514–15, 521, 524, 651
Play, reflective writing on, 167–68
"Playing Music to Relieve Stress in a College Classroom Environment" (Ferrer et al.), 287–94
Plot, in story, 155
Plot summary, 75–76
Podcast, in APA style, 713
Poem
  analysis of, 283
  reflection on, 167–68
Point/counterpoint editorials, 410–14

Point of view
  counterarguments and, 439
  in reflective writing, 117–18, 156–57
  in story, 155
"Point: Solar Power Presents Significant Environmental Problems" (Kreutzer), 411–12
Portfolio development, 627–31
  organization and design, 628–29
  publishing tools for, 627
Position, on issue, 528–29. *See also* Thesis statement
Possibility, exploring, 48, 424
Post hoc fallacies (*post hoc, ergo propter hoc* fallacies), 434
PowerPoint presentation, 24, 67, 615, 617, 620–21
  multimodal essay, 599–600
Prediction, sentence starters for, 47
Preface
  in APA style, 703
  in MLA style, 681
Principles, appeals to, 437
Print resources, 91, 461
  indexes to, 494–95
  in libraries, 491–96
  locating sources in, 461, 491
  managing, 462
  publication date on, 90
  reference works in APA style, 707
  reference works in MLA style, 686–87
  skimming, 57
Problem/solution
  in group presentation, 624–25
  as organizing pattern, 537
Problem solvers, 11, 343–44
Problem-solving writing
  advice writing, 361–64
  defined, 343–44
  defining a problem, 368, 369–70, 375–76, 381, 383
  developing a solution, 340, 369, 370, 372–75
  drafting of, 375–84
  essays and articles, 345–49

Inside LaunchPad for *Joining the Conversation*

 **LaunchPad**
macmillan learning

Where Students Learn

launchpadworks.com

Genre Talk

The new Genre Talk feature that appears throughout Part Two includes additional examples of distinctive genres, annotated to highlight their design features. An accompanying quiz helps students assess how well they understand key concepts of genre and design.

> **Chapter 6:** Reflective Writing
>
> **Chapter 7:** Informative Writing
>
> **Chapter 8:** Analytical Writing
>
> **Chapter 9:** Evaluative Writing
>
> **Chapter 10:** Problem-Solving Writing
>
> **Chapter 11:** Argumentative Writing

Reading Comprehension Quizzes

In **LaunchPad**, every reading selection in Part Two is accompanied by an automatically graded reading comprehension quiz.

LearningCurve

LearningCurve is an adaptive quizzing engine with activities on topics such as critical reading; thesis statements; using evidence; organizational patterns; evaluating, integrating, and acknowledging sources in MLA and APA style; grammar, style, and punctuation; and more.

Exercise Central

Customizable research exercises are available in Exercise Central, a searchable quiz bank.